Studies in the Legal History of the South

EDITED BY PAUL FINKELMAN AND KERMIT L. HALL

This series explores the ways in which law has affected the development of the southern United States and in turn the ways the history of the South has affected the development of American law. Volumes in the series focus on a specific aspect of the law, such as slave law or civil rights legislation, or on a broader topic of historical significance to the development of the legal system in the region, such as issues of constitutional history and of law and society, comparative analyses with other legal systems, and biographical studies of influential southern jurists and lawyers.

The Rise of
Judicial Management in
the U.S. District Court,
Southern District of Texas,
1955–2000

STEVEN HARMON WILSON

The Rise of Judicial Management in the U.S. District Court, Southern District of Texas, 1955–2000

The University of Georgia Press
Athens & London

Athens, Georgia 30602

Designed by Walton Harris
Set in 10/13 Minion by Bookcomp, Inc.
Printed and bound by Maple-Vail

The paper in this book meets the guidelines for permanence and durability of the Committee on Production Guidelines for Book Longevity of the Council on Library Resources.

Printed in the United States of America

06 05 04 03 02 C 5 4 3 2 1

Library of Congress Cataloging-in-Publication Data

Wilson, Steven Harmon, 1964–
The rise of judicial management in the U.S. District Court, Southern District of Texas, 1955–2000 / Steven Harmon Wilson.
p. cm. — (Studies in the legal history of the South)
Includes bibliographical references and index.
ISBN 0-8203-2363-2 (hardcover : alk. paper)
1. United States, District Court (Texas : Southern District)—History. 2. Justice, Administration of—Texas—History. 3. Complex litigation—Texas—History. 4. Court administration—Texas—History.
I. Title. II. Series.
KF8755.T48 W55 2002
347.73'53—dc21 2002004201

British Library Cataloging-in-Publication Data available

Dedicated, with much love and affection,
To my friend, collaborator, and finally, at long last, wife,
Dr. Cheryl Ann Matherly

Contents

Acknowledgments

I WISH TO ACKNOWLEDGE MY GRATITUDE to all of the sitting, senior, and retired judges of the U.S. District Court, Southern District of Texas, who granted me lengthy interviews and allowed me access to personal papers. I am also indebted to the Southern District's clerk, Michael Milby, and his staff for allowing me on several occasions to disrupt their office while I examined their administrative files. Barbara Rust and her efficient staff at the National Archives and Records Administration's Southwest Regional facility in Fort Worth, Texas, have also earned many thanks. The indispensability of their preservation work—and their ability to locate on demand the many trial and appellate court case files that I examined for this book—is shown by the frequent appearance of the Fort Worth archive in the notes of nearly every chapter. An archive of another sort has been made available to me and many other grateful historians through the efforts of Larry Turk, the owner of ¼ Price Books—his "headquarters for thinkers"—in Houston, Texas.

I also wish to thank my colleagues at Rice University—professors and fellow students alike, in both the sciences and in the humanities. I am especially grateful for the assistance over many years of Dr. Harold Hyman and Ms. Ferne Hyman. Because their dedication to students has been in the best tradition of Rice's residential college system and its associates program, Harold and Ferne were my close friends long before they were my mentors. By ably filling both roles and by frequently opening their home to host Harold's ongoing graduate seminar in legal history, they made a genuine pleasure out of fulfilling Harold's admonition to "work, work, work."

Finally, I want to thank my parents, family, and friends for seeing me through the long process of researching, writing, and editing this book. I am particularly indebted to Tim Harvey and Steve Reeves, who provided me with unvarnished criticism as well as unconditional friendship during our weekly political seminar known as Burger Night. Most important, I must note that Cheryl Matherly has earned my gratitude and recognition here by her exemplary service in both her personal and professional roles. This book could not have been completed without Cheryl's generous contributions of time, energy, patience, and insight—and I have dedicated it to her, with much love and affection.

Abbreviations

ACLU	American Civil Liberties Union
AGIF	American G.I. Forum
AISD	Austin Independent School District
ARMAS	Advocating Rights for Mexican American Students
AUSA	assistant U.S. attorney
BHCA	Bank Holding Company Act
BNDD	Bureau of Narcotics and Dangerous Drugs
CCISD	Corpus Christi Independent School District
CISD	[Driscoll] Consolidated Independent School District
CJRA	Civil Justice Reform Act
CRA	Civil Rights Act
DEA	Drug Enforcement Agency
DIBB	Deposit Insurance Bridge Bank
DOHSA	Death on the High Seas Act
DPD	Dallas Police Department
DTPA	Texas Deceptive Trade Practices Act
EEOC	Equal Employment Opportunity Commission
FBI	Federal Bureau of Investigation
FBN	Federal Bureau of Narcotics
FDIC	Federal Deposit Insurance Corporation
FELA	Federal Employees' Liability Act
FIRREA	Financial Institutions Reform, Recovery, and Enforcement Act
FISA	Financial Institutions Supervisory Act
FLSA	Fair Labor Standards Act
FM	farm-to-market
FTCA	Federal Tort Claims Act
HEW	Department of Health, Education, and Welfare
HIDTA	High Intensity Drug Trafficking Areas
HISD	Houston Independent School District
HPD	Houston Police Department

IA	internal affairs
INA	Immigration and Naturalization Act
INS	U.S. Immigration and Naturalization Service
IRCA	Immigration Reform and Control Act
ISD	Independent School District
IWA	Independent Workers' Association
KKK	Ku Klux Klan
LADS	Legal Aid and Defender Society
LDF	Legal Defense Fund
LHWCA	Longshoremen's and Harbor Workers' Compensation Act
LULAC	League of United Latin-American Citizens
MAEC	Mexican American Education Council
MALDEF	Mexican American Legal Defense and Education Fund
MAYO	Mexican American Youth Organization
MLA	Migratory Labor Act
NAACP	National Association for the Advancement of Colored People
NCC	National Credit Corporation
NFWA	National Farm Workers Association
OCC	Office of the Comptroller of the Currency
OCR	Office of Civil Rights
OCSLA	Outer Continental Shelf Lands Act
OEO	Office of Economic Opportunity
PASSO	Political Association of Spanish Speaking Organizations
PCA	Packaging Corporation of America
PHS	Public Health Service
RFC	Reconstruction Finance Corporation
SDS	Students for a Democratic Society
SFI	Southwest Forest Industries
SMU	Southern Methodist University
TAB	Texas American Bancshares
TDC	Texas Department of Corrections
TRO	temporary restraining order
TSU	Texas Southern University
UFWOC	United Farm Workers Organizing Committee
UH	University of Houston
UT	University of Texas
VISTA	Volunteers in Service to America
WISD	Westheimer Independent School District

The Rise of Judicial Management in the U.S. District Court, Southern District of Texas, 1955–2000

Introduction

THE SOUTHERN DISTRICT OF TEXAS embraces more than 44,100 square miles, approximately one-fifth of the real estate in Texas. Its edge is delineated on the southwest by 250 miles of the Rio Grande, the river that marks the border between the United States and Mexico. In its nearly 400-mile sweep to the northeast from the Rio Grande, the district encompasses a ribbon of Texas that ranges in width from 100 to 200 miles. The ranches and farms of the Lower Rio Grande Valley lie within the southern part of this territory. The hill country of central Texas begins on the western edge. The mostly rural region known as the Piney Woods is on the northern rim. The district's eastern rim, which includes all but 50 miles of the Texas coastline, boasts several ports that service the busy commercial lanes of the Gulf of Mexico.[1]

Judges of U.S. District Court for the Southern District of Texas have statutory jurisdiction to preside in trials involving federal criminal, civil, and administrative matters, in cases and controversies involving the U.S. Constitution, federal questions, diversity of citizenship, and the rules of equity, and, finally, in suits brought under admiralty and maritime law.[2] These grants of jurisdiction, especially the last, were important sources of the court's business throughout its history. Four of seven divisions, Houston, Galveston, Corpus Christi, and Brownsville, are deep-water ports on the gulf. The last of these also sits at the mouth of the Rio Grande, where it shares a responsibility to be a forum of federal judicial business on the border with Laredo and McAllen. Victoria, the last division, is centrally located, and, not coincidentally, it is the only one of the seven courts that usually boasts a current docket.[3]

Southeast Texas, like much of the South, saw unprecedented commercial development, industrial expansion, and population growth during the post–World War II era.[4] In addition to economic and demographic shifts, moreover, Texas, like many other and not only southern states, experienced dramatic social and political transformations during this period.[5] This book examines the role that was played in these developments by the federal trial judges, staffers, lawyers, plaintiffs, and defendants who participated in the history of the Southern District of Texas. This book also describes the effect that regional, national, and international changes in the latter decades of the twentieth century had on the personnel, policies, and procedures of the Southern District.

The varied jurisdiction of the federal trial courts justifies declarations by several political scientists that federal district judges are the "gatekeepers" or the "workhorses" of the federal judiciary.[6] Social scientists have studied these important courts for decades, whether examining changing workloads, focusing on policy-making aspects of judging, or even comparing the behavior of federal trial judges to that of their local, state, or foreign counterparts.[7] But, until relatively recently, federal district courts have not been well investigated by historians, especially in comparison to the historical focus on developments in the U.S. Supreme Court. Some histories have examined shifts in doctrine at the highest level of the federal judiciary; traced the origins, progress, and legacies of landmark cases; and narrated the careers of influential justices, judges, and lawyers. Historical studies of the federal judiciary are available, but few examine in detail the specific authority, duty, and behavior of district judges.[8] As Kermit Hall and Eric Rise noted, in one of the exceptions to the general neglect, "legal historians have paid scant attention to the nation's [lower] federal courts . . . for the most part federal judges have toiled in historical obscurity."[9]

This book seeks further to redress both forms of scholarly imbalance—that existing between historical and social scientific analysis, and that created by historians' tendency to focus on the higher rather than lower courts and judges—by presenting a history of a single representative federal district court during a period of great change.[10] I tell the story through an examination of court documents, especially case files and published opinions, but also including administrative memoranda. I rely on judicial biography, augmented where possible by oral history interviews. The lower court histories that have emerged in the past few years, such as Hall's and Rise's, have been useful guides to this work. Because my history focuses on the rather recent past, however, this book is by necessity interdisciplinary, in that I also rely heavily on the published work of legal and social science academics who may be but often are not historians. As a result, this book occupies the interstices between legal histories and empirical studies of judicial process and criminal justice.[11]

The present book is also something of a continuation of, and I hope a complement to, one of the other outstanding exceptions to the historians' neglect of lower federal courts, Charles Zelden's history of the Southern District of Texas from its 1902 creation through 1960, *Justice Lies in the District.*[12] Zelden showed that, during the boom years of the first half of the twentieth century, private law issues dominated the Southern District's dockets, because businessmen, in Texas as elsewhere, have relied on federal courts to create a stable legal environment that minimized uncertainty in property and contract questions.[13] The federal district judges in southeast Texas mediated private disputes between individuals or businesses in a wide array of lawsuits concerned with contracts, mergers, antitrust, intellectual property, bankruptcy, admiralty, torts, insurance, and many other commercial matters. The federal district judges who presided in the Southern District were from elite circles of Texas politics and business, and, according to Zelden, they "consistently applied a private agenda in setting their priorities and in making their judicial decisions." At the top of that agenda, he noted, the judges of the Southern District put "the promotion of Southeast Texas' economic, social, and political development through private means."[14]

The Southern District judges' attention to regional commerce and private law led them to delay resolution of disputes involving the rights and duties owing between governments and citizens, or so-called public law. Zelden found that if private law and public law imperatives clashed, the Southern District court "subordinated the public to the private, most often by minimizing its duties as the enforcement arm of the federal government to the benefit of private development."[15] He noted, however, that near the end of the period he studied, the judges in the Southern District began to grapple with long-deferred public law controversies. The courts' priorities did not change abruptly, but judges could no longer focus on private lawsuits to the exclusion of public law issues. The latter, especially in the form of civil rights litigation, began to appear on dockets in numbers too great to ignore.[16]

This book takes up where Zelden's left off, at a time in the middle of the twentieth century when social, political, and legal tensions too long deferred burst forth in the streets, legislative chambers, and courthouses of the nation. In part, the history of the Southern District of Texas demonstrates that the independence federal district judges might have enjoyed in the past, in terms of a certain freedom to set their own courts' agendas, has since disappeared. The loss of judicial autonomy has been celebrated by some and lamented by others, especially judges themselves, but it occurred for concrete reasons. The first was the changing nature of cases filed, which has been in part the result of Americans' rising expectations that the federal government in general and the judiciary in particular would provide higher levels of service and social justice. Another reason for transformations in the court's business was that the mandates that the district judges received from higher levels of all three branches of the federal government changed, often in response to demands by constituents.

The rising expectations can be measured, although crudely, by the rising volume of litigation. Rising caseloads in both state and federal courts have led some observers of the American courts to decry a "litigation explosion" and to bemoan our "litigious society."[17] The legal scholar Lawrence Friedman has expressed his doubt that the high level of litigation is a sign of a troubled society. He has argued instead that Americans have a developing sense of "total justice," which he then defined as "a general expectation of justice, and a general expectation of recompense for injury and loss." Friedman accepted that, as a consequence of these higher expectations, there has been "a tremendous increase in certain uses of legal process." He suggested, however, that the "courts have not expanded their work quantitatively as much as their work has altered in a more qualitative sense."[18]

Mandates from higher levels of the federal government have had a powerful impact on federal court business. Article III of the U.S. Constitution protects judicial independence by providing that judges, "both of the supreme and inferior Courts, shall hold their Offices during good Behaviour, and shall, at stated Times, receive for their Services a Compensation, which shall not be diminished during their Continuance in Office."[19] Although it was granted formal independence of politics by these provisions, the federal judiciary has always been subject to the power of Congress to fix its size, budget, and jurisdiction. Congress also added to or subtracted from court business during the period under study by enacting, amending, or repealing federal civil and criminal laws. Periodic transitions in presidential administrations, moreover, changed the priorities of federal regulatory and criminal law enforcement, which were manifested in levels of litigation as well as in the patterns of prosecution. Finally, the U.S. Supreme Court issued decisions—especially controversial opinions regarding civil rights, civil liberties, due process in criminal investigations and trials, and the boundaries of federalism—that have drastically altered the role of the lower federal judiciary in American life.[20]

The Southern District of Texas was itself changed by this transformation of its role. The court's perennially high caseload, for example, resulted in part from new public law cases, but also from increased population, more complex business, and, especially after 1960, new or amended federal laws. The rising demand led the Congress periodically to increase the number of Southern District judges. Until 1938 just one federal district judge was charged with administering federal justice in the entire Southern District of Texas. Congress had authorized only four judgeships by 1960. By 2000 the Southern District boasted nineteen seats, making it one of the largest federal district benches in the nation.[21] This book describes some of the reasons for and the results of this increase in the number of judges, discusses individual judges' backgrounds and behavior, and focuses on the judges' responses to the internal and external legal, social, and political shifts that affected the Southern District court. Yet I also discuss the increase in the number of court-supporting personnel, especially clerical staff, necessary to attend to the business of the court. For example, the first judge in the Southern District, U.S. District

Judge Waller T. Burns, had the support of the clerk of court, Christopher Dart, who recorded judgments, maintained files, and acted as the court's administrative officer. A century later, there is still just one clerk of court, Michael Milby, but he oversees two hundred deputy clerks and many other clerical staffers.[22]

Legal scholar and federal appellate judge Richard Posner has discussed the increasing power delegated by judges to their law clerks, who directly assist the judges in preparing opinions. Judge Posner accepts that this delegation has been rendered necessary by rising caseloads, but he sees it as another symptom of a "crisis" in the courts.[23] In the present book, however, I spend little time discussing law clerks and focus instead on the variety of court officers and judicial adjuncts that Congress has authorized in recent decades to assist federal judges as they dispose of the large number of cases on civil and criminal dockets. In 1968, for example, the Congress established the office of U.S. magistrate; magistrates were granted the authority to arraign defendants, record pleas, and schedule felony trials to be conducted by a judge. A federal district judge can also assign a magistrate to preside over pretrial conferences, to conduct discovery hearings, and to submit findings of fact and recommendations to the court. Congress has steadily increased magistrates' authority to render decisions in cases. The judges retained responsibility to accept or reject decisions on appeal, but magistrates increasingly have acted as "gatekeepers" of a sort by sifting the facts and sharpening legal issues that may only later come before a federal district judge. There are now more than a dozen magistrates in the Southern District.[24]

Congress has authorized other varieties of adjuncts as well. For most of the last century, for example, bankruptcy cases were filed as part of federal district courts' civil dockets.[25] In 1978, however, the Congress created bankruptcy judges with the authority to hear cases in lieu of a federal district judge. After a period of transition, the federal bankruptcy courts were in operation by 1984. There are currently six bankruptcy judges authorized in the Southern District.[26] Like the magistrates, however, the bankruptcy judges are subordinate officers in that their rulings are subject to appeal to a district judge.[27] Federal trial judges also have the authority, under the Federal Rules of Civil Procedure, to appoint for limited purposes temporary adjuncts known as special masters.[28]

Federal district judges rely on their law clerks, staffers, and adjuncts to help them to do their job better.[29] But what is the judges' job? One of the major organizing themes of this book is the stated goal of the Federal Rules of Civil Procedure. The first rule directs federal district judges to use their authority "to secure the just, speedy, and inexpensive determination of every action."[30] Judge Posner put it another way: federal trial judges seek to "dispos[e] of cases by trial or settlement with fairness and with the optimum blend of prompt decision and rightness of result." Efficient administration serves judges' self-interest, of course, by keeping dockets more current. According to Posner, however, trial judges "also have the responsibility of demonstrating the quality of federal justice to ordinary citizens—parties, witnesses and jurors."[31]

The growing reliance on supporting personnel to accomplish these basic goals is another topic of study where legal scholars and social scientists have outpaced legal historians.[32] In his history of the federal courts, Erwin Surrency suggested that "[t]he gradual growth in supporting staff for judges has impacted the administration of justice in many ways which have not been documented either in decisions or other sources." Unfortunately, Surrency only outlines the administrative impact he mentions.[33] I attempt to fill in at least some of these administrative details in this history of the Southern District of Texas.

In what follows I attempt to demonstrate, through a narrative that is generally organized along chronological and topical lines, that the rise in both criminal and civil caseloads in the Southern District of Texas, and the changing nature of the judicial service sought by politicians or plaintiffs, led to the multiplication of supporting personnel, which in turn forced the federal district judges to become by necessity managers—of their growing courts, burgeoning dockets, and proliferating personnel—as well as to continue acting as the umpires of legal disputes. This is a history rather than a systematic, longitudinal treatment of developments. The story I relate, however, is in line with much of the empirical work that has been published on the judiciary.[34]

I consider several varieties of judicial management in this book. The first is docket management, through which judges sought to maintain orderly and efficient case flow. A second variety of judicial management is case management, efforts by federal district judges to shepherd complex litigation, such as antitrust cases, through the courts. In recent decades judges proposed procedural reforms to facilitate the disposition of the large numbers of cases that continually crowd both criminal and civil court dockets. Both docket and case management concern the attempts to rationalize the flow of cases through the litigation process.[35] Both of these manifestations of judicial management aim broadly to provide the plaintiffs and defendants in federal trials a "just, speedy, and inexpensive" disposition of their case. The quest for administrative efficiency in the courts, moreover, has embraced both civil and criminal dockets.[36] A third variety of federal judicial management that emerged during the latter half of the twentieth century aimed to employ judicial power outside the courtroom, in the service of broad social reform. This has been the most controversial mode of judicial management, and it bears elaboration below.

Professor Abram Chayes examined, in an influential *Harvard Law Review* article in 1976, the role that federal judges played in the what he named "public law litigation." In what Chayes called the "traditional model" of adjudication, lawsuits involve "private disputes about private rights." The judge was merely "a neutral umpire, charged with little or no responsibility for the factual aspects of the case or for shaping and organizing the litigation for trial." In public law litigation "the object . . . is the vindication of constitutional or statutory policies." In Chayes's conception, moreover, public law litigation is defined not only by its object, but by the role played by the trial judge, who is the "dominant figure in organizing and guiding the case." The judge was both "the creator and manager of complex forms of ongoing relief, which have widespread effects on persons not before the court and require the judge's continuing involvement in administration and implementation."[37]

Law professor Owen Fiss later called this extensive judicial intervention for remedial goals "structural reform." According to Fiss, federal district judges seek to attain this goal through the extensive use of equitable instruments, especially injunctions.[38] The structural injunction, he wrote, "initiat[es] a relationship between a court and a social institution." It was a judicial "declaration that henceforth the court will direct or manage the reconstruction" of an institution, to bring it into compliance with constitutional standards.[39] The equitable tools that the federal district judges used to reform constitutionally flawed institutions were not identical to the "managerial" tools the judges employed to manage crowded dockets and complex cases, but the tools clearly were related to one another.[40]

One of the best examples of public law litigation, of course, was the court-ordered desegregation of public schools. During the 1930s the U.S. Supreme Court began striking down state-supported segregated schools, initially taking aim at law schools and other graduate programs. These cases laid the groundwork for the 1954 landmark *Brown v. Board of Education,*[41] in which Chief Justice Earl Warren wrote for the unanimous court that state-mandated and race-based public school segregation denied African American students the equal protection of the laws, because "[s]eparate educational facilities [were] inherently unequal."[42] With this decision, the Warren Court altered the basic allocations of power in American government in ways that subsequent courts have found difficult, if not impossible, to reverse. *Brown,* in particular, emerged as the central, intellectually formative case for a new generation of lawyers and professors and shaped their basic approach to law. The court encouraged high expectations in post-*Brown* decisions. After directing southern school administrators to desegregate with "all deliberate speed," the justices charged federal district judges with the responsibility for divining the local details.[43]

The 1954 opinion, usually known as *Brown I,* did not herald the swift dismantling of segregation in schools or in any other public institution. Rather than signaling the end of "separate but equal," which the court had sanctioned in the 1896 opinion *Plessy v. Ferguson*,[44] *Brown I* actually marked the beginning of a new stage in African Americans' long civil rights struggle. Political and legal equality required the enactment of new legislation and, of course, follow-on litigation to enforce the judicial decisions. Significant social change came only with boycotts, marches, and martyrdom.[45] Nevertheless, *Brown I* removed the key constitutional underpinning from state-supported segregation—which existed across the nation but was most notorious in the southern regime of "Jim Crow"—and put the Supreme Court on record as at least supporting an ideal of legal equality over the ideology of racial separation. African Americans could justifiably celebrate the decision as a major turning point in their history.[46]

Scholars, too, have long understood *Brown I* to be a turning point, if only by virtue of its impact on American race relations. Alpheus T. Mason had concluded by 1962, for example, that in condemning segregation the court initiated "the greatest social revolution" of the generation.[47] James Patterson reminds readers of his recent reexamination of *Brown v. Board of Education* that, from the moment that Chief Justice Earl Warren read the unanimous ruling aloud, many contested its legitimacy. But early criticism contributed less to the case's "troubled legacy," as Patterson describes it, than the fact that, nearly fifty years after *Brown* was decided, scholars continue to debate not only the legitimacy, but also the social, political, educational, and legal meaning of this still controversial "civil rights milestone."[48]

The litigation to enforce the *Brown* mandates obliged federal district judges to assume quasi-administrative responsibility for entire school systems, and, in many cases, federal courts retained oversight for decades, as cases passed from the first generation of judges to the next and the next. The combined effect of many individual post-*Brown* remedial suits demonstrated, as Chayes perceived, that the justices had committed the federal courts to lead "an enterprise of profound social reconstruction."[49]

The duty to implement *Brown* and subsequent decisions related to public law litigation kept the federal judiciary under intense and extended scrutiny for decades. Southern judges, especially, found themselves in a quandary that justified their tenure.[50] After nomination by the president and confirmation by the U.S. Senate, federal judges exercise authority without fear of retaliation. But the benefits of "judicial independence" served only to forestall professional sanctions. John R. Brown, a Houston lawyer who was appointed to the U.S. Court of Appeals for the Fifth Circuit in 1955, just as the school desegregation crisis commenced, explained in 1959 that tenure only "insulates judges from anxiety over worldly cares for body and home and family." But tenure could not, Brown said, "protect them from the unconscious urge for the approbation of their fellow-man, and fellow-man most often means those of like interests and backgrounds, business and professional experience and predilections, and even prejudices."[51]

Southern federal district judges had a duty to enforce the High Court's ruling, with which some of them disagreed, and which was unpopular with the majority of the public. The judges might fall into disrepute (at least on the national scene) within the legal profession, or risk reversal by higher courts, if their decisions seemed to obstruct the process of desegregation. But the judges faced the scorn of neighbors and erstwhile friends—and potentially much worse than scorn in areas where resistance to federal court authority turned violent—if they seemed too enthusiastically to implement the *Brown* decision.[52]

The southern federal judiciary's professional and personal predicament inspired the title of J. W. Peltason's early study of the role that judges played, and, at the time of its publication, continued to play, in school desegregation. Peltason called his now-classic 1961 book *Fifty-eight Lonely Men.*[53] What follows presents evidence that appears to contradict that title, because it shows that, once the *Brown* decisions were issued, the judges of the Southern District of Texas were *rarely* left alone. They were also subjected to much criticism, as Peltason argued with regard to all federal judges in the post-*Brown* South.[54]

In political, procedural, and administrative context, *Brown* is an important milestone in the history of the Southern District, and other federal district courts, not because it revolutionized the civil rights laws, but because it changed the course of civil rights litigation. In the wake of *Brown,* judges took up the task of managing the transition to desegregation. The National Association for the Advancement of Colored People's strategy, joining of the plaintiffs and filing suit in class-actions, was not original,[55] but the success of *Brown* seems to have inspired many imitators. In public law cases suits filed in the Southern District of Texas, for example, the judges stepped out of their traditional neutral stance to broker and to supervise settlements. The lawsuits aimed variously at ending unconstitutional racial distinctions in housing, employment, and voting rights, and also extended rights of criminal defendants, prison inmates, mental patients, and other disenfranchised groups.[56] By the 1970s the scholarly examination of court-ordered "structural" reform was well underway, and Chayes's seminal 1976 article "The Role of the Judge in Public Law Litigation" was a part of this discourse.[57]

Certainly, that subject did and does deserve scholarly attention, and it receives that attention in several chapters of this book. Two public school desegregation cases discussed in the first chapter of this history—the first phase of a lengthy suit in Houston and the entirety of the shorter case outside Corpus Christi—illustrate how and why federal judicial oversight of institutional reform emerged and became the dominant feature of civil rights lawsuit. But the procedural and substantive contrasts between the cases demonstrate that the new species of public law litigation did not immediately supplant even other civil rights strategies. As this book will attempt to illustrate through varied examples of judicial activities in the

Southern District of Texas, moreover, public law did not immediately supplant other concerns.[58]

Nor did new issues need to displace the old. As Chayes noted in his article on the subject, "it would be mistaken to suppose that [public law] is confined to [school desegregation, employment discrimination, and prisoners' rights cases]. . . . Antitrust, securities fraud and other aspects of the conduct of corporate business, bankruptcy, and reorganizations, union governance, consumer fraud, housing discrimination, electoral reapportionment, environmental management—cases in all these fields display in varying degrees the features of public law litigation."[59] Accordingly, many of these fields receive attention in this book.

CHAPTER ONE

The Varieties of Public School Desegregation

"IN THE LONG RUN," U.S. District Judge James V. Allred Jr. cautioned the plaintiffs in his Corpus Christi courtroom in 1957, "I don't know whether you are going to be able to accomplish a great deal by lawsuits or not."[1] Allred offered this observation during one of the earliest school desegregation suits to be filed in the Southern District of Texas after the U.S. Supreme Court announced the landmark 1954 decision *Brown v. Board of Education*, usually known as *Brown I*,[2] and its 1955 follow-up, *Brown II*.[3] The judge was not seeking to discourage the parents who had sued the Driscoll Consolidated Independent School District (CISD), a rural system thirty miles west of the gulf port city of Corpus Christi. He had already indicated his willingness to enjoin the segregation that was practiced in the Driscoll school systems. Yet he doubted the Supreme Court's wisdom in relying on federal district judges like himself to enforce by court order the far-reaching social reconstruction that would be required to implement *Brown*.[4]

Allred was not a conservative who simply resented the court's "activism" in declaring that state-supported racial segregation in public schools denied African American students equal protection of the laws. The judge was a longtime liberal Democrat who had enjoyed a distinguished career in state politics before his appointment to the federal bench. He was born in Bowie, Texas, on 29 March 1899 and attended Bowie Commercial College before transferring to the Rice Institute in Houston. He served as a yeoman second class in the U.S. Navy during World War I. After the war Allred studied law at Cumberland University, in Lebanon, Tennessee, where he earned the LL.B. in 1921. He practiced law in Wichita Falls, entered politics, and served as the city's district attorney from 1923 to 1925. He built support within the Democratic Party and was elected state attorney general in 1931 and then governor of Texas in 1935, in the midst of the Great Depression. Allred had been an unwavering supporter of the New Deal at a time when conservative Democrats resisted the federal government's program of economic recovery.[5]

President Franklin D. Roosevelt appointed the steadfast New Dealer to the newly created second seat in the Southern District in 1938. The judge resigned in 1942, however, to run in the Democratic primary for the U.S. Senate. Allred lost against W. Lee "Pappy" O'Daniel. The next year, the newly elected Senator O'Daniel invoked senatorial "courtesy" and objected to the president's proposal to nominate Allred to an open position on the U.S. Court of Appeals for the Fifth Circuit.[6] Roosevelt yielded to the custom that reserved to senators the right to use judgeships in their own states to reward their own political supporters—or to use them to buy off rivals.[7] Allred resumed private legal practice in Texas. He was offered a rare second opportunity to gain a lifetime sinecure on the federal district court in 1949, when President Harry Truman nominated Allred to another new seat. The appointment received the full support of U.S. Senator Lyndon B. Johnson, who had succeeded O'Daniel. Although in later years Johnson was among the leaders of the conservative wing of the Texas Democratic Party, he had been Allred's ally (albeit also a sometimes rival) during the New Deal.[8]

Allred recognized the government's potential power to foster change. But, as he and other survivors of 1930s political battles could recall, the New Deal had to be defended *against* judges, not implemented *by* them. He now wondered aloud to the Driscoll parents "whether the courts should undertake the monumental job of trying to determine the justice [or the] injustice of the treatment of particular students."[9] He seems to have intended these comments to be general observations on the role of the judiciary, rather than specific findings on the case before him. The parents in Driscoll were not asking the judge to undertake a "monumental job" at all, because the Driscoll CISD enrolled around three hundred students. Allred invested a minimum of time and energy while presiding over the brief case: he listened to witness testimony, considered the lawyers' arguments, and found in favor of the plaintiff parents. The judge then issued an injunction that directed the trustees of the Driscoll CISD to desegregate their classrooms in short order. Allred's pessimism—which indicated both his skepticism about using litigation to reform public institutions and his concern for the expanding role of the federal courts in the post-*Brown* era—were just spoken obiter dicta, a form of judicial aside.

The judge's comments readily applied, however, to the public school desegregation litigation that U.S. District Judge Ben C. Connally, Allred's colleague on the bench in the Southern District of Texas, presided over around the same time. Although not a former officeholder as was Allred, Connally gained substantial political connections through his family. He was born 28 December 1909, in Marlin, Texas, but spent much of his youth in Washington, D.C., after his father was elected to Congress in 1914.[10] Connally returned to Texas to attend college. He was a top performer at the University of Texas (UT) at Austin, both as an undergraduate and as a law student. He received the LL.B. at the UT law school in 1933, and the next year earned his master of laws at Harvard University. Connally practiced law in Houston until 1942, when he joined the U.S. Army Air Forces to serve during World War II and reached the rank of lieutenant colonel. He resumed his legal career in 1945 with a partnership at one of Houston's top firms, Butler, Binion, Rice, and Cook. In 1949, also at the suggestion of Senator Johnson, President Truman appointed Senator Connally's thirty-nine-year-old son to another new seat—which made a total of four judgeships—in the Southern District.[11]

Houston was the largest city in the South by the 1950s, and the Houston Independent School District (HISD), which enrolled some 170,000 students in 173 schools, was the largest segregated school system in the United States. The Houston plaintiffs called upon Judge Connally to formulate, and over the course of the subsequent fifteen years periodically to reformulate, detailed court orders that proved difficult to implement.[12] The HISD case remained on the docket for almost thirty years and required the attention of several of Connally's successors. The enormous growth and demographic shifts that Houston, and HISD, experienced during those three decades contributed greatly to the complexity of the desegregation problem and the judges' difficulties in resolving it.[13]

This chapter examines the challenges faced by these federal district judges in the Southern District of Texas in the first ten years after *Brown*. During that decade race relations emerged as a dominant domestic policy issue in America, and the federal courts, especially in the South, were at the forefront of the very public controversy. The attention to administrative detail demanded by desegregation cases came to blend the district judge's traditional responsibilities to manage both trials and the court's docket with new duties to oversee a racial realignment of school systems. The judge's task in school desegregation cases, as Allred noted, was often a "monumental job" that placed unprecedented demands upon judges' time, energy, and patience. Connally and the subsequent generation of Southern District judges, although not Allred in the Driscoll CISD case, grappled fully with this "monumental job." The judges had first to solve institutional problems—affecting the institutions outside as well as inside the courtroom—that arose during the decades-long project to reform and restructure public organizations through the form of legal action that the scholar Abram Chayes later called "public law litigation."[14]

The aims of the plaintiffs in the two school desegregation lawsuits examined in this chapter contributed to their different dispositions by their respective trial judges. Both of the suits were class actions filed by parents seeking judicial intervention to bring about compliance with the Fourteenth Amendment. The suits possessed fundamental differences, however, quite apart from the disparate size and complexity of the defendant school systems. The first major distinction is that only one of the two cases actually involved a claim based on the *Brown* decision. In

Houston, African American parents sued precisely because the 1954 decision had made available a new constitutional foundation upon which to build the legal claims. In Driscoll, however, Mexican American parents based their claims upon judicial rulings that were unrelated to, and in fact predated, the Supreme Court's desegregation opinion. Hence, they argued that *Brown* was not a significant case.

Another distinction between these two cases—and the critical difference that explains the disparate reliance on *Brown*—was the race of the plaintiff parents. In the Driscoll CISD case, Mexican Americans did not sue the trustees of the Driscoll CISD because the latter had continued race-based segregation even after *Brown* condemned it as unconstitutional. In Texas, as in most southern states, there were only two racial categories, "colored" and "white," and the relevant statutes defined the "colored" race strictly to include "all persons of mixed blood descended from Negro ancestry."[15] By this definition Mexican-descended persons were legally white. Despite having a claim to "whiteness" and its privileges, however, many Mexican Americans in Texas, as in other southwestern states, faced discrimination by an Anglo majority.[16]

African Americans faced de jure discrimination that was supported by statutes and pre-*Brown* court decisions, while the Mexican-Texans faced de facto discrimination that was unsupported by the state's constitution and laws. What specifically troubled the parents in the Driscoll lawsuit was that the Anglo administrators misappropriated legal provisions allowing segregation and used them to separate Anglo- and Mexican-descended students, almost as if the latter were "colored."[17]

The Driscoll CISD, like many rural districts in Texas, served families that were dependent on agriculture, and many of the Mexican Americans in that category were migrant farm workers. The Driscoll administrators placed all of their children, even the students who spoke and understood *only* English, in classrooms that had been designated for the Spanish speakers. The plaintiff parents' lawyers (who were usually also Mexican Americans) claimed that, because the segregation of Anglos from Mexicans had never been sanctioned by Texas statute or state constitution, the Driscoll CISD's policies denied the students the due process rights guaranteed by the Fourteenth Amendment.[18]

It was significant that the emphasis was on due process rights rather than on the equal protection rights at the heart of *Brown*. Neither the litigants nor Judge Allred asserted that the Supreme Court's ruling in support of claims by African Americans in a race-based suit could apply directly to the legal attack upon the Driscoll CISD's heritage-based discrimination against Mexican Americans. It was not obvious that it would be either necessary or desirable to adapt the *Brown* rationale to the Mexican Americans' particular legal stance. The question whether *Brown* did or could apply to Mexican Americans remained open for nearly fifteen years.

A PALPABLE SHAM AND SUBTERFUGE

African Americans did accomplish a great deal through lawsuits. In addition to its constitutional significance, *Brown* stands as a monument to persistence in litigation. American blacks entered the twentieth century at a very low point, socially and constitutionally. The U.S. Supreme Court upheld the principle of statutory segregation in the 1896 decision *Plessy v. Ferguson,* in which a majority of the justices declared that enforced separation of the races was acceptable as long as elements of the separate public spheres were equal.[19] African Americans refused to accept the *Plessy* doctrine's legitimacy, and several generations of black leaders argued, both in courts of law and in the court of public opinion, that the practical reality of social, political, and economic segregation of the races was incommensurable with the theory of legal equality the court had announced in 1896.[20] The dissenters included W. E. B. Du Bois, who in 1903's *The Souls of Black Folk,* famously wrote that "[t]he problem of the twentieth century is the problem of the color line."[21] Among the solutions to this seemingly intractable problem was determined litigation.

The National Association for the Advancement of Colored People (NAACP) led the fight after Du Bois and others founded the organization in 1909. The association eventually incorporated a separate litigation arm, the Legal Defense Fund (LDF), usually known simply as the "Inc. Fund." Inc. Fund attorneys challenged racial segregation in a wide variety of contexts such as schools, stores, and voting booths, generally arguing in court that "separate but equal" was fundamentally at odds with the equal protection clause of the Fourteenth Amendment. They slowly but surely chipped away at the edifice of "Jim Crow."[22]

The *Plessy* decision merely ratified the status quo in many southern states, where Jim Crow already operated under the rules of "separate but equal." When the Texas legislature created a new system of "public free schools" in 1893, for example, it enacted a statute that satisfied the state constitutional requirement that schools for "white and colored children" must be separate but also "impartial."[23] The Inc. Fund lawyers, led in the post–World War II years by Thurgood Marshall, first attempted to undermine *Plessy*-style segregation by demanding that state governments live up to their commitments and actually spend the money necessary to make black and white facilities equal. Spendthrift legislators usually balked and gave Marshall's team the legal basis for lawsuits.[24]

The Inc. Fund's legal strategy climaxed when Heman Sweatt, an African American mail carrier from Houston, sued to gain the right to attend the segregated school of law at UT. The U.S. Supreme Court ruled in 1950's *Sweatt v. Painter* that the law school that Texas legislators hastily established for blacks in Houston, in direct response to Sweatt's lawsuit, was not and could never be the equal of the UT law school. The court declared that, apart from obviously unequal resources the legislature had allocated between the two schools, UT enjoyed many "intangible" advantages as the premier graduate legal institution in the state. The reputation of UT's faculty and the daily interaction of its students, the justices agreed, rendered the white law school in Austin inherently superior to the black school in Houston.[25]

The ruling in *Sweatt* proved to be a significant prelude to *Brown,* but it made its point only about the reality of segregated graduate education. That further litigation would be necessary was shown by the Inc. Fund's loss, around the same time that it won *Sweatt* in the Supreme Court, in a high school desegregation suit in the Southern District of Texas. In April 1948 Julius Brown filed a federal suit in Houston, on behalf of "all other persons of Negro blood and African descent," to desegregate the La Grange Independent School District (ISD), because the black and white schools were unequal. Brown claimed in particular that the La Grange ISD trustees deprived African American students of equal protection because his oldest daughter, Vivian, could not take chemistry. That subject was not offered at the black high school.[26]

U.S. District Judge Thomas Kennerly ruled in March 1950 that the black and white schools in La Grange were substantially equal, and he refused therefore to issue an injunction to desegregate the district. Brown appealed Kennerly's decision, in the apparent hope that *Sweatt* had set a new standard. The Fifth Circuit's response to this appeal demonstrated that, even after the landmark ruling on graduate education, Inc. Fund lawyers had miles to go before they overturned school segregation at all levels.[27]

In January 1951 the chief judge of the Fifth Circuit, Joseph C. Hutcheson Jr., wrote the opinion for a three-judge appellate panel. Hutcheson, the son of a former Confederate officer who had migrated from Virginia to Texas after the Civil War, was born in 1879 and educated at Bethel Military Academy and the University of Virginia. The future judge returned to Texas around the turn of the century and embarked on a dual career in law and politics. Hutcheson was Houston's mayor in 1918, when President Woodrow Wilson appointed him to what was then the single judgeship in the Southern District of Texas. Judge Kennerly had succeeded Hutcheson when the latter was elevated to the Fifth Circuit court in 1931.[28]

The appellate judges were not satisfied merely to affirm Kennerly in their opinion *Brown v. Board of Trustees of La Grange.* Hutcheson instead remanded with an order that Kennerly dismiss the complaint. Hutcheson characterized Brown's goal in filing the suit as an attempt to get a federal judge to "supervise and control by injunction the general conduct of a political subdivision of the State." The judge noted that Brown's claim "has for its purpose not the mere according of a specific right that has been denied," which had been Sweatt's central goal, "but the establishment of a sort of general government by injunction over the school district in respect to its schools and school system."[29]

Judge Hutcheson's assessment of the implications of Brown's case was apt. Sweatt had filed and won a fairly traditional suit in equity (albeit one that served the NAACP's larger goals), which required a court to issue a single decree. But the logical end that Hutcheson saw in Brown's claim against La Grange ISD—federal judicial supervision over a state institution as elemental as the school system—would have set the federal courts on a dangerous new tack that the chief of the Fifth Circuit refused to countenance without direction from the Supreme Court. *Sweatt* was not explicit enough to convince the appellate court to authorize an injunction that would "requir[e] detailed and continuous supervision over the conduct of a political subdivision," because, Hutcheson wrote, such an order "is not congenial to equitable principles and practices and will not usually be granted."[30]

The Inc. Fund lawyers finally achieved their longstanding goal when Chief Justice Earl Warren spoke for the unanimous court to declare that "[s]eparate educational facilities are inherently unequal."[31] In the estimation of the legal scholar Derrick Bell, *Brown* "triggered a revolution in civil rights law," because it increased African Americans' "leverage" in the court. That leverage would prove necessary because *Brown I* also raised blacks' expectations that federal judges would begin to enforce their rights.[32] As such, the milestone decision marked only the beginning of a new phase of desegregation litigation rather than the end of that struggle.[33]

Warren, in *Brown I,* set out the basic rationale for the court's decision but declined to broach the more contentious question regarding remedial actions that would be required to restore the rights that were violated by segregation. The justices requested additional arguments on that issue and invited interested parties to suggest the language to be included in the court's order that would instruct state and local officials in their responsibilities for desegregating their school systems.[34]

Texas had not been a defendant in *Brown I,* but the state's attorneys accepted the Supreme Court's invitation to participate in the discussions that would lead to *Brown II.* They argued, on the basis of the maps they brought to illustrate the uneven distribution of the black population in Texas, that the justices should allow individual federal judges to tailor court orders that accounted for such local variations in segregation. The Inc. Fund's Marshall scoffed, "I am sure that the state of Texas does not . . . administer their own constitution in varying [ways] in various sections of the country."[35]

The Inc. Fund attorneys insisted that federal constitutional rights should not be applied piecemeal. They argued that, because the court had already decreed segregation to be unconstitutional, they could and should instruct administrators to desegregate their schools right away, or perhaps, in a formula that Chief Justice Warren reportedly favored, "as soon as practicable." Lawyers for the school districts maintained that it would be better if the court neither specified the remedy nor set out the timetable. They argued that, because the extent of school segregation varied from state to state, and even within certain states, it would be more practical if the court's remedial order left the task of planning and implementing desegregation to knowledgeable and experienced local school administrators.[36]

The justices announced in *Brown II* that a version of the latter argument prevailed. The local authorities would, the court declared, have "primary responsibility for elucidating, assessing, and solving" problems of administration that could be expected to delay desegregation, although, the court added, officials should seek to achieve that ultimate goal with "all deliberate speed." The justices anticipated reluctance or opposition, even to this vague order, but noted that "it should go without saying that the vitality of these constitutional principles cannot be allowed to yield simply because of disagreement with them."[37]

The court did not leave the enforcement of these landmark school decisions completely to the uncertain consciences of local, usually elected, boards. In addition to directing administrators to desegregate with "all deliberate speed," the justices charged the nation's federal district judges with monitoring the progress of desegregation. The decision directed judges to use "equitable principles" and to "take into account the public interest" when rendering judgments in cases. Above all, however, the justices commanded the district judges to bring about "systematic and effective" compliance with the desegregation mandate. The court concluded with the fateful statement that the federal district courts would retain jurisdiction over the school cases until desegregation was substantially completed.[38]

Although *Brown II* was vague with regard to the timing and even to the preferred manner of desegregation, the court made two things perfectly clear. First, because southern opposition could be both predicted as well as expected to continue for some time, it was obvious that most African Americans would not gain the full benefits of the NAACP's court victory unless and until they filed and prevailed in many more lawsuits. Second, and also due to the foreseeable southern recalcitrance, it was plain that the federal judges, rather than school administrators, actually held "primary responsibility for elucidating, assessing, and solving" problems. The heaviest burden of implementing desegregation, moreover, fell disproportionately on federal judges who lived in the South.[39]

The ambiguous directives in *Brown II* initially seemed to be adequate to accomplish the Supreme Court's goals. Some officials, especially in western states where there were comparatively few black students to accommodate, did move speedily to desegregate. The board of trustees of Big Spring ISD, in Howard County, Texas, for example, soon voted to end segregation in the first through sixth grades. But some Big Spring residents sought to enjoin that action in the state district court, arguing that the board had violated the state constitutional and statute laws that controlled the disbursement of public funds.[40] According to the relevant state law, a public school that allowed integration of the races stood to lose its state funding.[41] The Big Spring plaintiff parents only succeeded in inadvertently accelerating the judicial repudiation of Jim Crow. The state district judge who heard the complaint read *Brown* broadly as voiding state provisions—whether constitutional or statutory—that mandated racial segregation. He denied the request for an injunction, and the Texas Supreme Court affirmed that decision in October 1955.[42]

By the end of the next school year, approximately 145 of the 714 Texas school districts had implemented limited desegregation plans. Most of them were in the western and south central areas of the state, however, and 90 percent of Texas's blacks lived in northern and eastern counties. One in six students in Dallas, and one of five in Houston, was African American. Trustees in those two urban districts were faced with the prospect of desegregating much larger and more diverse populations of students.[43] But Judge Allred's brand of liberalism was rare in Texas politics by the 1950s, and if blacks ever entertained hopes that Jim Crow schools could be swiftly dismantled in the South, those hopes collapsed under the weight of that region's building "massive resistance."[44]

The *Brown* decisions inspired dedicated segregationists to form "white citizens' councils" and to organize protests against compliance with the Supreme Court decisions, and therefore lower federal court injunctions. They received rhetorical support from Texas Governor Allan Shivers, who led the conservative wing of the state Democratic Party, and even supported the Republican candidate, Dwight D. Eisenhower, in his two successful presidential campaigns against the liberal Democrat Adlai Stevenson.[45] Shivers fortified resistance to *Brown* when he noted that "[n]either the Texas nor the United States Supreme Court has said that schools must desegregate immediately . . . no school district should feel compelled to take hasty or unnecessary action."[46]

In 1956 African Americans constituted 20 percent of the student population of 1,500 in Mansfield, Texas, a town south of the Dallas–Fort Worth urban center. The students were segregated into two elementary schools, but there was only one high school. Before *Brown* Mansfield High enrolled white students only, and the African American students had to provide their own transportation to attend a black high school twenty miles north in Fort Worth. When black parents sued to end the practice, U.S. District Judge Joe Estes, of the Northern District of Texas, accepted the school board's proposal to implement *Brown* by purchasing a school bus to take black students to Fort Worth. The African American plaintiffs appealed Estes' ruling to the Fifth Circuit. A three-judge panel, including two Texans, Chief Circuit Judge Hutcheson and Circuit Judge John R. Brown, and Circuit Judge Richard T. Rives of Alabama, heard the appeal and reversed Estes' ruling. Hutcheson wrote the opinion. As was indicated by his strong statement in the *La Grange* case, Hutcheson was a conservative who disliked judicial activism. Yet, although still publicly critical of the *Brown* decision, the chief judge did oversee the expansions in judicial authority that were required to enforce the court's school desegregation mandate.

He had received in *Brown* the guidance he had missed in the *La Grange* case.[47] When Hutcheson remanded the case, he noted that there were no barriers to desegregation in Mansfield except the "difficulty arising out of the local climate of opinion."[48]

Estes took the hint and ordered Mansfield High to admit all qualified students regardless of race. Segregationists threatened violence if the school officials tried to implement that order. Governor Shivers dispatched Texas Rangers, ostensibly to keep the peace, authorized the transfer of any student whose admission to Mansfield would create problems, and, finally, declared that he hoped that the Supreme Court would attend to the "effect of its desegregation decision on a typical law-abiding Texas community."[49] At that point the African American students decided to resume their bus trips to Fort Worth. The outcome of the Mansfield affair discouraged black litigants and emboldened white segregationists.[50]

In Houston a few political leaders possessed sufficient influence and independence to implement reforms without waiting to be prodded by the courts. Roy Hofheinz, a millionaire real estate developer who served as Houston's mayor from 1953 to 1956, ordered the desegregation of restrooms, water fountains, and waiting areas in the city's new airport; directed the removal of "whites only" and "colored" signs from restrooms at city hall; and arranged the integration of the municipal golf course. Only the last of these executive actions was a response to a federal court order. Mayor Hofheinz broke the initial resistance to this step by reminding the members of the city council that it would be very expensive for the city to build a separate-but-equal "colored" golf course.[51]

Pocketbook issues clearly resonated in Houston. It was an ambitious city where bottom-line business interests might trump race bias. During the African American students' movement of 1960, for example, Houston's political and business leaders conspired to keep news of "sit-ins" and other civil rights protests out of the media spotlight. This was possible, at least temporarily, because Houston's newspapers, television stations, and radio stations were owned by a relatively small number of influential individuals or families. The owners of businesses facing protests concluded that racial strife might damage the city's self-promoted progressive image and hence harm its economic prospects. As a result of their agreements with local black community leaders, who were similarly business-minded, most of Houston's major downtown businesses were desegregated during an orchestrated media "blackout."[52]

The HISD board of trustees initially explored the possibility of quickly and quietly desegregating Houston's dual school system. In June 1955 the HISD trustees established a twenty-five-person commission, which included ten African American members, to study the school district's options. After deliberating for two months, the biracial commission recommended that the board allow immediate integration of the HISD administration and undertake preparations for complete integration of the schools by September 1956.[53] This early response does not indicate that Houston was a color-blind city. Segregationists objected when HISD eliminated the race designations in a directory of school teachers in 1955, and the district resumed printing the designations the next year.[54]

The board of trustees had not responded to the commission's proposals by January 1956, when its president, Verna Rogers, asked the public for patience.[55] But black Houstonians were already dissatisfied with delay. The local chapter of the NAACP prepared to force the desegregation issue in the courts. George T. Nelson, a Houston barber and longtime NAACP volunteer, persuaded Mary Alice Benjamin to attempt to enroll her eight-year-old daughter, Delores Ross, in the all-white Sherman Elementary. Benjamin lived only two blocks from Sherman but nearly a dozen blocks from the all black Crawford Elementary. Nelson tried to prepare Ross for the jeers that were to be expected from the white students, and he invited two of the little girl's school-age male cousins to come along the first morning, for protection as well as companionship. He also notified news reporters of the plan. As Nelson expected, a hostile crowd awaited the group on Monday morning, offering verbal abuse but constituting no real physical threat. The administrators of the Sherman School did not allow Ross to register.[56]

The publicity forced the HISD board to discuss desegregation in its next scheduled hearing, on 27 February. Hattie Mae White, an African American teacher, delivered a speech before the board that, according to one white Houstonian who watched the televised proceedings, was "lucid and compelling." White had impressed, said this witness, because "she had the facts—statistics on Negro teachers' heavier student loads, the lack of libraries and kindergartens in many Negro schools, and many other inequalities—and she delivered them beautifully. . . . [f]or many whites in Houston it was their first glimpse of an educated, intelligent, attractive Negro."[57] But White's eloquence alone could not overcome HISD's inertia. In March the HISD board claimed that "severe overcrowding" prevented earlier desegregation and justified postponing further action.[58]

The board next tied school desegregation to voters' approval of a $30 million bond issue to be used for the construction of new facilities. The proposed expansion, or so proponents of the bonds argued, would "largely resolv[e]" the desegregation question. The initiative would also delay facing up to the controversy. Simply arranging the bond election would consume several months, and, if the voters actually approved the board's plan, the contracting and construction would take several years to complete. Ballots served supporters of continued segregation in other ways. Segregationists had revived the notion that a state legislature could overturn a federal law or even a court ruling that the legislators deemed unconstitutional. In the 1956 Harris County Democratic primary, voters endorsed by four to one a ballot proposition in support of such "interposition" to end federal court-ordered desegregation.[59]

At the opening of the school term in September, officials at Sherman once again refused to register Delores Ross. Another black mother, Marion Williams, sought to register her fourteen-year-old daughter, Beneva, at an all-white junior high school and was also turned away.[60] The two women joined forces to file a federal suit on 26 December 1956, on behalf of their daughters as well as all other African American schoolchildren in Houston. The complaint sought an injunction to force HISD to comply with *Brown*.[61] Three weeks later, in mid-January 1957, HISD's board reacted to the suit by appointing yet another study panel.[62]

Judge Connally appeared to accept that it was his duty to enforce *Brown*, but he was never enthusiastic about desegregation. Fifth Circuit Judge John Brown recalled of his fellow Houstonian that, "in his heart, Connally always felt that *Brown v. Board of Education* was wrong—that it made bad law."[63] Despite his evident reservations about the wisdom of the Supreme Court's decisions, however, Connally was not a friend of strict segregationists. He demonstrated his ambivalence in December 1955, when he ordered the desegregation of the cafeteria in the Harris County courthouse. The judge gave the managers ninety days to comply.[64] Ninety days satisfied no one, but to Connally it seemed to be a fair compromise between the extremes of desegregation "now" and desegregation "never."

Connally seems to have viewed judge-mediated delays in these emotionally charged cases as something of a cooling-off period. The first thing that he sought to accomplish in the HISD case, for example, was to persuade the plaintiffs to withdraw their motion for an injunction until he convened a formal hearing. He sought to avoid publicity—and therefore to minimize demagoguery on both sides—by arranging informal, closed-chambers conferences in the interim. During these off-the-record meetings, Connally reportedly expected the litigants to speak relatively freely.[65] These "pretrial" meetings were authorized by the Federal Rules of Civil Procedure and increasingly encouraged during the 1950s by court reformers who began to promote discretionary procedures as a way to improve the efficiency of trial judges.[66] As indicated by his reliance on pretrial meetings, Connally was an apt pupil. The emergence of public law litigation, of which the desegregation suits were only the most prominent example, demanded that judges become aggressive managers of cases, rather than merely referees of controversies. The skillful use of pretrial procedures was a key attribute of "managerial" judging.[67]

The judge's efforts to subsume the political and emotional dimensions of desegregation by relying on measured and moderate procedures also marked Connally as an adherent, whether by study or by natural temperament, of the "legal process" scholarship that emerged during the 1950s.[68] Process scholars argued that judges could reach legitimate conclusions—in the sense that case outcomes were independent of the judge's ideology or personal concerns—only through an objective application of well-formulated rules.[69]

The judge finally convened an open-court hearing in May 1957, and over several days he heard testimony from black parents and white HISD board members. The board's new president, Dallas Dyer, admitted that her staff had yet to develop a plan to desegregate. She declared, however, that the board had considered "many plans to mitigate [desegregation's] impact." Connally sought to broker a compromise and reportedly suggested, during another in-chambers conference, that it was high time for the board to present a plan that the plaintiffs' lawyer "could sell to his people." Connally waited four months for the HISD's lawyers to respond to his gentle suggestion. He then issued a firmer, although still not yet final, order in November 1957, that formally voided Texas's segregation laws. Connally then entered a decree, with no terminal date, that directed the HISD board to develop a suitable plan to comply with *Brown*. Connally warned that "delay will be warranted only if the board immediately comes to grips with its problems." He suggested as well that "[a] court of equity will not countenance inordinate delay or evasion where the enjoyment of a constitutional right is involved, though its recognition and enforcement be difficult and unpopular."[70] Connally clearly hoped that persuasion would prevail, but the HISD board did not respond to this order until June 1960.[71]

Hattie Mae White, the teacher who had distinguished herself as a public speaker during the televised meetings, was elected to the HISD board in November 1958. She was the first black person to be elected to public office in Houston since Reconstruction.[72] Soon after her election, she discovered a burning cross in her yard. As a board member, White soon learned that there was a legal strategy behind HISD's delay. When she attended a meeting in Houston of the National Association of School Boards, White heard an attorney advise the assembled administrators to "[k]eep them in the courts . . . because eventually their money will run out and we have the taxpayers' money, and that supports . . . suits on our side."[73]

The NAACP was apparently included among the "them" to be kept in court. The national office provided guidance and encouragement to would-be litigants, but lawyers usually acted on their own when they organized local suits. Weldon Berry, a young black lawyer who was just beginning a practice in Houston, managed the plaintiffs' lawsuit against HISD after Connally's initial hearing. When it appeared that his suit had stalled, NAACP leaders did urge Berry to produce quicker results and offered several suggestions, but they exercised no authority over him or his case.[74] Nevertheless, in Houston, as elsewhere in the South, school attorneys began to complain that the troublesome desegregation cases were "trumped up" by the NAACP.[75] The Texas attorney general, John Ben Shepperd, lobbied for legislation to constrain the national organization's activities in Texas. He investigated and eventually filed charges of barratry, that is, soliciting clients, against the civil rights group. These charges did not amount to much in the courts, but the necessity of defending against the attack depleted NAACP funds and diverted energy from desegregation projects.[76]

After it became clear that the HISD board was not responding in a timely fashion to Connally's November 1957 order simply to begin planning, the plaintiffs asked Connally to order desegregation in HISD to begin by September 1959.[77] Instead, the judge ordered the board to report its progress in August 1959. Henry Peterson, the board's latest president, finally admitted to the judge that it was "not politically wise for us to desegregate until we are forced to by a court deadline." He claimed that, even if ordered to begin, the board would need "eight to ten years to prepare for desegregation." Dyer, the board's former president, said that the public would consider swifter action to be "a traitorous act."[78]

Soon after that rather candid hearing, the board submitted to the judge a hundred-thousand-word report that purported to provide ample support for the board's central claim that, because of vast problems with housing, academics, and finances, HISD could never desegregate by 1959. The board's data-driven argument for delay worked: Judge Connally once again instructed the HISD board simply to file a plan with him by 1 June 1960. But if the board missed that deadline, the judge warned, he would be obliged to "grant the relief which the plaintiffs have sought" and immediately to order desegregation.[79]

In June 1960 the desegregation issue appeared once more on the Democratic primary ballot. Critics of the latest referendum noted that it was superfluous, since the district was already under a court order to plan desegregation. But supporters of the ballot measure argued that the election results would help the board to make some hard decisions. HISD board member Stone Wells declared, for example, that the neighborhoods that supported desegregation in the referendum would be desegregated first.[80] Connally publicly rebuked Wells for such provocative statements. In a letter he sent to Joe H. Reynolds, HISD's attorney, which he also released to the press, the judge wrote, "Your clients must recognize that this is not a popularity contest, but is the performance of a duty which the law imposes." Connally added that he still expected the HISD board to propose a plan shortly.[81]

As the deadline approached, the board proposed to initiate "voluntary" integration during the 1961 term—allowing parents to choose to enroll their children in either a segregated or a desegregated school. The plan designated one elementary school, one junior high school, and one high school for the integration. The board based this "salt-and-pepper" strategy on a plan Dallas schools developed at the specific direction of a federal judge. The result would be three varieties of schools: white, black, and integrated. Connally rejected the "salt-and-pepper" plan, because, he said, it did not comply with his previous orders, or constitute "a good faith attempt at compliance." He complained, in fact, that the HISD proposal was "a palpable sham and subterfuge designed only to accomplish further evasion and delay."[82]

Connally had presided over the suit to dismantle Houston's segregated school system for three years. The HISD board had taken advantage of his indulgence and frustrated his attempts to arrange an orderly and mostly voluntary transition from a segregated dual to unitary school system. The judge resolved, therefore, to devise his own plan. Connally ordered that the HISD board would commence desegregation in September 1960, beginning with the first grade. The rest of the HISD schools would thereafter desegregate at the rate of one additional grade per year.[83]

The judge's "grade-a-year" or "stair-step" plan was similar to those proposed or accepted by many judges elsewhere across the South. Under Connally's plan, desegregation begun in 1960 would be completed by 1972. But even his "deliberate," and extremely slow, solution to the conundrum of desegregation was too rapid for the HISD board. HISD attorneys applied for a stay of the judgment on 26 August, with less than a month remaining until Connally's plan would take effect. A Fifth Circuit judicial panel refused to stay the order.[84] The board sought relief from the U.S. Supreme Court, but Associate Justice Hugo Black, who oversaw the Fifth Circuit, also refused to countermand Connally's grade-a-year order.[85]

Justice Black's denial finally had exhausted the HISD board's appeals. HISD lost its dubious distinction as the nation's largest segregated school system on 8 September 1960, when six-year-old Tyronne Day became the first black student to enroll at Kashmere Gardens, a formerly all-white elementary school. Within a short time, approximately one dozen African American first graders were attending formerly all-white HISD schools.[86]

With the first phase of the Houston litigation at an end and desegregation underway, although at a trickle, attorneys from both sides of the divide publicly praised the judge's handling of the case. Joe Reynolds, the HISD's lawyer, noted that Connally "stood between Houston and disaster." Connally himself observed that, if he had much to do with the success of desegregation in Houston, it was because he kept negotiations behind the closed doors of his chambers.[87] Later commentators concluded that "desegregation of the Houston public school system was a responsibility recognized and shouldered by local school administrators, community groups and the federal district court."[88]

But praise and self-congratulations were not universal at the time. In his 1961 study of court-ordered school desegregation in the South, J. W. Peltason concluded that Connally had simply not accomplished much. Peltason disparaged the initial rulings, because in them Connally did "no more than tell the board it should desegregate with all deliberate speed." The result of the judicial indulgence, Peltason wrote, was that "[f]or two years the Houston School Board—one of the few large city boards which has more defiantly resisted desegregation than even the state legislatures or the governors—did nothing."[89] Peltason's contemporaneous assessment seems a valid description of the total lack of progress that prevailed in Houston until the summer of 1960. Moreover, because the HISD board did not then fulfill its responsibilities under the stair-step plan, Connally was soon obliged to abandon it, and to accelerate desegregation.[90]

Judge Connally appeared satisfied that he had prevailed over HISD's recalcitrant segregationists. He noted in 1962, after the first and second grades had been at least nominally desegregated, that "the transition has been accomplished thus far in an orderly manner, with no disruptions of the school curriculum, and with a minimum of friction and discontent." He suggested, with obvious satisfaction, that Houston "may well take pride" in the fact that desegregation had occurred without the public violence that had attended similar court-ordered actions in other southern cities.[91] It became clear, as he discussed developments in Houston, that the judge favored order over justice. He would allow desegregation to proceed at a snail's pace if that promised continued peace and quiet. The uncomfortable fact remained, however, that he offered these optimistic remarks in response to renewed complaints.[92]

When African American parents regarded the success of school desegregation in Houston, they were not as content as was Connally. Although it was true that the HISD board formally rescinded its rules specifically requiring segregation, administrative policies remained in place that prevented large numbers of black students from exercising their rights to attend formerly all-white schools. Administrators at Allen Elementary, for example, had not allowed an African American child, Sheila Smith, to enter the first grade in September 1961. Her father, Norman E. Smith, had tried to enroll Sheila at Allen on 14 September, for the term that started on 7 September, and the school officials claimed that their three first-grade classes were already full. They advised Smith that he should enroll Sheila in another school. The school they named in Smith's neighborhood hired only black faculty and enrolled only black students. Smith added his daughter's name to the growing list of active plaintiffs in the still open HISD litigation.[93]

Connally, as directed by *Brown II,* kept jurisdiction in the case, and he convened hearings to assess the new complaints. The Allen school officials admitted that "it was not unusual to admit scholastics thereafter for late registration" and noted that they might have enrolled Sheila if there had been space. James Hippard, Smith's counsel, did not dispute their contentions that the Allen rosters had already reached their limit of thirty-six children per class. He also did not dispute that, both before and after 14 September, the school had refused to enroll white children whose presence would exceed the limit in Allen's classes. Hippard argued nonetheless that, because it was within the principal's authority to permit classes to become oversized on a temporary basis, Sheila should have been enrolled provisionally, until transfers or other adjustments reduced the total number of students.[94]

Connally noted the mitigating factors in the administrators' favor. He believed that the Allen Elementary officials had acted properly and within their discretion, and he found no evidence of racial discrimination in Smith's case. He declared the complaint to be moot, moreover, because the term had ended by the time he heard the complaint. The judge suggested to Smith that Sheila could attend Allen Elementary during second grade. He said that "if the plaintiff makes timely application for enrollment, the question presented here will not arise again."[95]

The judge also had to hear from several other new plaintiffs who had joined the revived *Ross* case. One HISD policy under attack in this second wave of complaints was a so-called "brother-sister rule," which required all school-age children of the same family to attend the same school. A seven-year-old boy could not transfer to a desegregated school, for example, while his eight-year-old sister attended a still-segregated school. Black parents argued that a brother-sister rule prevented many African American first and second graders from enjoying the benefits of the 1960 court-ordered stair-step plan. Connally reminded the plaintiffs that the brother-sister rule had been in effect for "some 40 to 50 years" and was common to many districts. The rule had been promulgated both to maintain family coherence and to enhance administrative efficiency. He decided that the rule was rational and noted, "While it is true that application of the rule will perhaps prevent certain colored scholastics from attending the school of their choice, it does not necessarily follow that the rule thereby becomes invalid. Under the same circumstances, the rule also prevents white children from attending the school of their choice."[96] Since both white and black children were equally deprived of a choice, the judge concluded that the brother-sister rule was a "valid administrative measure." Connally found no evidence that the policy had been promulgated or was being enforced simply to discriminate against African American children.[97]

A second disputed HISD policy, known as the "transfer rule," required students to obtain written permission from the principals of both the old and the new school before transferring. As with the brother-sister rule, Connally found no evidence that HISD had discriminated in its enforcement of this long-standing policy. The judge noted that, despite enforcement of these rules, HISD had agreed to enroll twelve of nineteen "colored" children who sought to be admitted to formerly all-white schools during the 1960–61 school year. During the second year of the stair-step schedule, he noted, HISD had accepted thirty-three of fifty applicants.[98]

These were not numbers to be celebrated. They indicate that by 1962, when HISD enrolled about 190,000 students and African Americans constituted approximately one-third of the city's overall population, forty-five black children were attending desegregated schools in Houston. Yet, Connally declared that the numbers were "hardly indicative of any concerted scheme systematically to exclude the Negro applicant." The judge charged that in these latest complaints "the colored plaintiffs do not seek the same treatment as is afforded white students, to which they are entitled." Instead, he wrote, they were seeking "a different, and superior, treatment, by reason of their race [and the] law does not grant them this." Connally appeared satisfied that the HISD officials were acting in good faith and enforcing administrative regulations in a color-blind fashion. He therefore both denied a plaintiff's request to declare the board in contempt for evading the 1960 order and declined to enjoin HISD's rules.[99]

The plaintiff parents appealed Judge Connally's decision regarding the brother-sister rule. Circuit Judge Brown wrote the opinion for the three-judge panel, which included Circuit Judges Elbert Tuttle and Hutcheson. Brown first reviewed the history of the Houston school desegregation case and of HISD administrative policies. He noted that Connally seemed to be considering merely whether a brother-sister policy violated the letter of his order, rather than its spirit. That is, he had not considered whether the policy was "a discriminatory practice which should be forbidden in the light of existing conditions without regard to whether they were, or were not, within the compass of the 1960 order." Judge Brown declared that even though the order "prescribes a plan in specific detail, this is not the end of the matter." He said that "of necessity" the federal district court retained "continuing jurisdiction over the cause." This implied that the judge "must make such adaptations from time to time as the existing developing situation reasonably requires to give final and effectual voice to the constitutional rights of Negro children."[100]

Although he did not dispute that Connally's ruling was "one of pure logic," Judge Brown wrote that "logic alone is insufficient to overcome the practical effect" of the brother-sister rule on African American families. The rule "perpetuates a segregated system," Brown stated, "despite the plain purpose of the stair-step plan to ameliorate it."[101] Brown accepted that the Supreme Court's order that school desegregation should be concluded at "all deliberate speed" rather than immediately, was sensible in light of administrative concerns. But he noted that Connally's stair-step plan would not eliminate segregation in the Houston elementary schools until 1966. That fact brought "into sharp focus the question whether an administrative practice such as this rule could be deemed reasonable," because some black children would be denied the benefits of the *Brown* decision on a "purely accidental basis," namely, family composition. Judge Brown thought that the brother-sister rule could actually "bring about the rankest sort of discrimination as between Negro children living side by side in the same neighborhood," because it worked against African American children with older siblings.[102]

The Fifth Circuit judges agreed with Judge Connally that the school officials had not intentionally disobeyed the 1960 order by enforcing the brother-sister rule. But because that rule created more problems than it averted, in terms of discrimination, Brown thought that the rule must be rescinded. In December 1962 the Fifth Circuit panel reversed Connally on the brother-sister rule. They remanded the case for "further and not inconsistent action."[103]

Judge Hutcheson, the other Houstonian on the appellate panel, wrote a separate concurring opinion, in which he declared that he "prefer[red] to reach [the conclusion] by a slightly different and certainly shorter road." His thinking had advanced significantly in the decade since he had rejected, in the 1951 La Grange case, the principle of continual judicial oversight of school districts. Hutcheson now noted that the brother-sister rule simply had not been among the issues raised by the earliest litigants in school desegregation litigation. As a consequence, the federal circuit and district courts had approved schemes like the stair-step plans without ever considering the probable effect of such an apparently incidental rule. It was now clear, however, that a brother-sister rule fostered discrimination in many school districts. Hutcheson declared that the unforeseen emergence of this unfortunate twist "had the effect . . . of setting aside . . . our mandate." The point of judicial monitoring for compliance with an earlier court order was that it allowed a judge to make appropriate adjustments. In school desegregation, judicial management was a hands-on job.[104]

A CASE THAT DOES NOT RAISE THE PROBLEMS IN THE NEGRO CASES

Mexican Americans, who have been a large and recognizable minority group within the United States since at least the 1840s, did not become claimants in judicially managed civil rights suits until the end of the 1960s, when the trend to organize public law litigation was well underway. The plaintiffs in the Driscoll CISD suit did not seek to appropriate either constitutional principles or procedural lessons from the two *Brown* decisions. The Mexican Americans' lawyers in the Driscoll case, in fact, consistently and specifically denied that they sought to have Judge Allred consider their claims in light of *Brown*. They could call upon earlier, and apparently more suitable, judicial precedents to be their tie to the Fourteenth Amendment.

By the 1950s a host of federal and state judges across the Southwest had ruled in numerous cases that, for the purposes of racial classification, including the rules that defined Jim Crow, persons of Mexican descent were not "colored." By virtue of their Spanish heritage, in fact, they belonged to one of the so-called "other white" races—that is, white but not Anglo-Saxon. Mexican Americans in Texas and elsewhere sought to maintain white status because, although de jure racial segregation of public schools was condemned in *Brown,* the binary racial classifications survived in a variety of public spheres.[105] What follows examines how this "other white" strategy operated during the Jim Crow era. A later chapter will show how these claims became counterproductive as Jim Crow waned.

Mexican Americans' claims to whiteness emerged gradually as a logical response to many judicial rulings in cases concerned with naturalization, education, grand jury service, and other issues. A major milestone was established in 1897 when a federal trial judge upheld the right of Mexicans to be naturalized. Ricardo Rodriguez, a thirty-seven-year-old native of Mexico, petitioned to become a U.S. citizen after living in San Antonio for a decade. A federal attorney contested Rodriguez's eligibility, on the grounds that he was "not a white person, not an African, nor of African descent."[106]

U.S. District Judge Thomas Maxey, who presided in the Western District of Texas, took the government's objection to Rodriguez's petition to be an invitation to embark on taxonomical speculation. Maxey noted that "as to color, [Rodriguez] may be classed with the copper-colored or red men. He has dark eyes, straight black hair, and high cheek bones." But, because Rodriguez "knows nothing of the Aztecs or Toltecs," the judge concluded that "[h]e is not an Indian." Maxey conceded, moreover, that if "the strict scientific classification of the anthropologist should be adopted, [he] would probably not be classed as white." But, the judge noted, the 1836 constitution of the Texas Republic, the 1848 Treaty of Guadalupe-Hidalgo, and other agreements[107] either "affirmatively confer[red] the rights of citizenship upon Mexicans, or tacitly recognize[d] in them the right of individual naturalization." He concluded that the varied stipulations in these documents covered "all Mexicans, without discrimination as to color." The petitioner Rodriguez, therefore, was "embraced within the spirit and intent of our laws upon naturalization." Despite his statement that Rodriguez looked like a "copper-colored or red man," the judge accepted Rodriguez's claim that he was neither Indian, Spanish, nor African, but a "pure blooded Mexican." That is, of European stock and "white."[108]

Judge Maxey's decision in the last years of the nineteenth century that Mexicans were not excludable from citizenship merely on racial grounds complicated Mexicans' place in twentieth-century U.S. immigration and naturalization law. Nativists mixed eugenics theories with anthropological observations to create immigration restrictions that linked cultural attributes directly to national origin. The 1924 Immigration and Naturalization Act (INA) categorized all immigrant groups according to the notion that whiteness was an indication of desirability and eligibility, while other-than-white, as the sign of alien values or permanently foreign character, was indicative of undesirability and legal excludability.[109]

Secretary of Labor James Davis—who was the government's top bureaucrat on immigration, because new immigrants were expected to work—in 1929 advised

Congressman Albert Johnson, a member of the House immigration committee and a coauthor of the 1924 INA, that a precedent of mass and automatic naturalization in the nineteenth century made it difficult to apply the twentieth-century rules of exclusion to Mexican nationals. Davis recognized that enforcement of a race-based immigration policy was impeded by the vagaries of self-identification. He told the congressman that "the Mexican people are of such a mixed stock" and "individuals have such a limited knowledge of their racial composition that it would be impossible for the most learned and experienced ethnologist or anthropologist to classify or determine their racial origin. Thus, making an effort to exclude them from admission or citizenship because of their racial status is practically impossible."[110]

As a result, Mexican-descended individuals were given the benefit of the doubt with regard to legal whiteness. Mae Ngai notes that, nevertheless, "by the late 1920s, a Mexican 'race problem' had emerged in the Southwest, impelled by contradictions wrought by the burgeoning of commercial agriculture, an all-time high in Mexican immigration, and the formation of a migratory, landless agricultural proletariat and of segregated communities."[111]

Because immigration policy was implicated in the Southwest's agricultural economy, Congress was reluctant to impose quotas on Mexican immigration or to exclude Mexicans altogether on racial grounds. Yet, civil servants did develop categories of difference that were often simultaneously national, geographical, and racial. The Census Bureau enumerated Mexicans as a separate race in 1930, although under the imprecise definition of persons born in Mexico or with parents born in Mexico, who were "not definitely white, Negro, Indian, Chinese, or Japanese."[112] The Mexican government protested the U.S. government's creation of this separate racial classification. To lessen international tensions the 1940 census classified persons of Mexican descent as "white" if they were not "definitely Indian or of other non-white race."[113]

The inclusion of Mexican-descended peoples in the white race had practical consequences under a Jim Crow regime. Texans, like most other white southerners, enacted statutes that were silent regarding the varieties of non-African descent. By the same token, the law was also silent regarding the definition of "white."[114] Texans nevertheless found a way to create a system of "Mexican schools."[115] The legislature enacted a statute in 1905 that provided that "it shall be the duty of every teacher in the public free schools . . . to use the English language exclusively, and to conduct all recitations and school exercises exclusively in the English language."[116] Anglo schoolteachers believed, or else pretended to believe, that Mexican-descended students (whose ethnic heritage often was identifiable on class rosters only by Spanish surnames) all lacked English proficiency. The language provisions resulted in classes that contained few students with Spanish surnames.[117]

Other discriminatory practices in Texas were sanctioned by long-standing customs even when they were not mandated by statute. Mexican Americans endured this discrimination at the hands of the Anglo American majority in Texas because, even among the "white" races, society privileged pale over dark skin, skilled over nonskilled (especially migrant) work, and native-born persons over recent immigrants. Presumptively "white" Mexican Americans faced Jim Crow–style segregation in public accommodations, housing, and recreation facilities. As a result, Mexican American Texans had long-standing grievances against the Anglo majority.[118]

A variety of Mexican American civic groups emerged in the twentieth century, and some organized specifically to resist the rising wave of nativism that led to the 1924 INA. Mexican American businessmen in Corpus Christi established the League of United Latin-American Citizens (LULAC) in 1929. They sought to end the prevailing discriminatory practices, but also hoped to integrate their community into the social mainstream of the United States, that is, to "Americanize." LULAC's constitution called for members to become loyal American citizens and to indicate assimilation by learning English.[119] Hector P. Garcia, a physician and veteran of World War II, founded the American G.I. Forum (AGIF) in 1948, also in Corpus Christi, in order better to protect the interests of fellow Mexican American veterans.[120]

When AGIF's and LULAC's demonstrations of civic patriotism failed to lower the barriers to equality with Anglos—that is, when Mexican Americans were denied privileges of "white" citizenship under Jim Crow—these Mexican American organizations resorted to litigation. Unlike African American organizations like the NAACP, which also sought to vindicate rights in the courts, the Mexican American groups did not deny the basic legitimacy of Jim Crow. Mexican Americans merely demanded that courts enforce the rights they deserved through their "white" status. Mexican Americans did not challenge segregation on the grounds that it denied the equal protection guaranteed by the Fourteenth Amendment. Rather, they stressed that, in creating segregation for the "other white" race, Texas authorities denied Mexican Americans due process, a right also guaranteed by the Fourteenth Amendment, which led to the loss of equal protection. Mexican Americans used process-based "other white" arguments in a long line of state and federal suits.[121]

In 1930, when approximately 90 percent of the public schools in south Texas were segregated according to the "Anglo" or "Mexican" enrollment,[122] the newly founded LULAC sponsored the first suit to challenge the segregation of Mexican Americans.[123] Del Rio, a border town on the Rio Grande, established an elementary school exclusively for Mexican-descended children, although no statute authorized the Del Rio ISD to do so. LULAC-funded attorneys sought a state court injunction to end the separation. The superintendent of the Del Rio ISD justified the segregation by noting that many of the Mexican American children were from migrant families that worked well into the school term. Because the district's Anglo children, most but not all of whom were not the children of migratory workers, would have several months' advantage in class, the Mexican American students would suffer from low esteem if they were measured against the Anglos. The Mexican American students' lower English language skills, the superintendent claimed, would result in still further damage to their morale. He said that the segregation was not at all biased, but offered "fair opportunity" to all of the children in the Del Rio district. The practice of segregation, he concluded, benefited all students by meeting each group's "peculiar needs."[124]

The superintendent admitted during cross-examination that the few Anglo migrant students who entered school late each term were not segregated, but the state court nonetheless refused to enjoin the Del Rio ISD. The LULAC lawyers appealed, and, in *Del Rio ISD v. Salvatierra,* the Texas Court of Civil Appeals ruled that public school officials could not "arbitrarily" segregate their Mexican-descended students. As practiced by Del Rio ISD, the court said, the segregation was unacceptable because the rules were "arbitrary [and] applied indiscriminately to all Mexican pupils . . . without apparent regard to their individual aptitudes . . . while relieving children of *other white races* from the operation of the rule."[125]

The judges rejected LULAC's request for an injunction, however, because, as they wrote, "to the extent that the plan adopted is applied in good faith . . . with no intent . . . to discriminate," the plan was not unlawful or violative of the Constitution.[126]

Because the Del Rio segregation was motivated by a "benign" distinction, namely the "fact" that Mexicans were linguistically and culturally incompatible with Anglos, Mexican American scholar George A. Martinez has concluded that this 1930 victory "dealt a serious blow to the struggle."[127] Notwithstanding the *Salvatierra* decision, schools across the Southwest continued to apply the criteria for separation indiscriminately.[128]

When Mexican Americans in California filed the next important suit in 1946, this time in a California federal court,[129] linguistic segregation of Mexican American children was rooted even more deeply in southwestern states.[130] Like Del Rio ISD in Texas, the Westminster, California, school district maintained segregated classrooms for its Mexican-descended children. A federal district judge held that the Westminster schools had violated the plaintiffs' rights under the Fourteenth Amendment. In a startling precursor to the *Brown* decision's condemnation of "separate but equal," the judge ruled that the equal protection requirements were not met merely by providing "separate schools [with] the same technical facilities." Because "[a] paramount requisite in the American system of public education is social equality," the judge stated, all classes "must be open to all children by unified school association regardless of lineage."[131] He suggested that "commingling of the entire student body" was appropriate in the aftermath of the recently concluded war—in which America had repudiated Nazi racism and fascism—and because "commingling . . . instills and develops a common cultural attitude among the school children which is imperative for the perpetuation of American institutions and ideals."[132]

The U.S. Court of Appeals for the Ninth Circuit, on the state's appeal, upheld the district judge's decision for the plaintiff Mexican Americans in *Westminster School District v. Mendez.* The circuit judges were decidedly less critical than the district judge of the doctrine of "separate but equal," however, and less concerned with the benefits of "commingling." Instead, the appellate judges reasoned that because California's statutes (like Texas's Jim Crow laws) did not expressly mention Mexican Americans, educational separation denied the children due process as well as equal protection. The Ninth Circuit ruled against the district, therefore, only because administrators had acted beyond statutory authority.[133] The appellate judges wrote that they were "aware of no authority justifying any segregation fiat by an administrative or executive decree as every case cited to us is based upon a legislative act."[134]

But the Ninth Circuit echoed the 1930 Del Rio case by noting that the language deficiencies in Mexican children "may justify differentiation by public school authorities in the exercise of their reasonable discretion as to the pedagogical methods of instruction . . . and foreign language handicaps may . . . require separate treatment in separate classrooms."[135] The Ninth Circuit judges once again suggested that Mexican American children could be segregated even at whim, if the state constitution and its legislature merely authorized it. In such a case the California situation would be the same as the system that the Supreme Court upheld in *Plessy.* Nevertheless, after winning in *Mendez,* Mexican American advocates developed litigation strategies that relied even more heavily on the alleged advantages derived from their "white" status.[136]

Texas was in the Fifth Circuit, and so Texas laws were not directly affected by the ruling. The Ninth Circuit Court's dicta, however, inspired Texas Attorney General Price Daniel to issue an advisory opinion that forbade automatic segregation of Mexican-descended pupils. He continued to justify separate classes for "linguistically deficient" students.[137] Daniels's advisory opinion became an issue in the next suit Mexican Americans filed in Texas.

U.S. District Judge Ben C. Rice of the Western District of Texas decided in 1948's *Delgado v. Bastrop ISD*[138] that linguistic segregation in the Bastrop school district, located between Austin and Houston, violated the Fourteenth Amendment because, as it was implemented, the system was "arbitrary and discriminatory." Judge Rice did not criticize language segregation. But he declared that the Bastrop district could segregate any individual student only after school authorities had determined students' proficiency in English through "scientifically standardized" examinations. Rice declared that all Bastrop students, Anglo Americans as well as Mexican Americans, should be examined for language proficiency.[139]

The state superintendent of public instruction subsequently announced to all school officials that he was "glad to be able to tell you that arrangements have been made for the official tests to be used to comply" with Judge Rice's decision.[140] Under these arrangements the "Inter-American Test in Oral English" was to be administered to "[a]ll pupils in the white school, irrespective of their language ability." Students in the same grade were to be given the same test at the same time, and "[t]here must be no discrimination at any time in the testing program." The state superintendent specified, for example, that even the children of migrant workers entering school four months behind the rest of the grade were to be tested with all of the students who entered at that time. This would preserve the objective basis of comparison, the official wrote, since "[t]he tests are 'scientifically standardized' as required by the court decision."[141]

The superintendent was not, however, directing all district schools to administer exams. Tests should be conducted, he wrote, "only in those schools desiring to divide first year children unable to follow instructions in English, from the children who are able to follow such instructions."[142] After describing the plan to comply with the federal court order, the state's chief school officer wrote that he trusted that superintendents, principals, and teachers "will move forward courageously and harmoniously, without prejudice, and without bitterness, as we strive to work out for ourselves a more practical democracy."[143] School districts either ignored the mandate, or established standards that made it extremely easy for schools to prevent any Mexican Americans from sharing public classrooms with Anglo Americans.[144]

The life and career of James DeAnda illustrated why Mexican American claims of whiteness seemed sensible during the Jim Crow era. His parents were among the thousands of Mexican nationals who immigrated to Texas early in the twentieth century to escape the social, political, and economic chaos of the Mexican Revolution. DeAnda was born in Houston in 1925 and so grew up as his own "other white" status was being established by the courts. He earned a B.A. from Texas A&M University in 1948, and enrolled at UT law school in Austin. His choice was unremarkable, because Mexican-descended students had been attending UT for years. DeAnda graduated in 1950, the year that the Supreme Court ordered the UT law school desegregated.[145]

Although many Mexican Americans in Texas, then as now, were mired in poverty, middle-class Mexican Americans like DeAnda could attend the best state institutions of higher education that Texas offered and could enter careers in business and the professions with relative ease. DeAnda's immediate postgraduate experience, however, illustrated the ambiguous social status Mexican Americans had achieved in Texas, where they were neither separate from nor quite equal with the Anglo majority. DeAnda discovered that, after his graduation from UT law school, none of the established firms in Houston would hire him. He saw several promising leads vanish soon after he disclosed that his parents had been born in Mexico.[146]

DeAnda found work in Houston with John J. Herrera, a self-employed general practitioner, that is, a lawyer who both accepted criminal defense work and represented clients in civil cases. Herrera also lent his support to litigation efforts that aimed to promote Mexican Americans' social progress. Sometimes these goals overlapped, and Herrera was soon able to introduce DeAnda to the peculiarities of making claims under the Fourteenth Amendment in cases that involved Mexican Americans. A recurring obstacle to their efforts was the difficulty of demonstrating to an individual judge's satisfaction that, for Mexican Americans in Texas, the practical results of their "otherness" often trumped the formal status of their "whiteness." The lawyers had to accomplish this tricky business in court without actually undermining the general appeal to the privileges that attached to whiteness. The result was a balancing act, a careful straddling of the Jim Crow color line, and, ultimately, a self-defeating constitutional argument.

In 1951 Herrera and DeAnda defended a client in his murder trial in Fort Bend County, adjacent to Houston's Harris County. Aniceto Sanchez was convicted and received a ten-year sentence. The attorneys appealed on the grounds that there were no Mexican American grand jury commissioners or grand jurors in the county. Herrera and DeAnda sought to demonstrate that this was the result of "a systematic, continual, and uninterrupted practice in Fort Bend County of discriminating against the Mexican Americans as a race, and people of Mexican extraction and ancestry as a class." To indict, try, and convict Sanchez under those circumstances had been, they argued, "a violation of the due process clause."[147]

Herrera and DeAnda filed what Judge Beauchamp of the Court of Criminal Appeals of Texas noted was "quite an exhaustive brief" in the case. In it they described pronouncements, including judicial rulings from other jurisdictions, that had "either intentionally or loosely, refer[red] to Mexican people as a different race." But the appellate judges stood firm on the distinction between de jure and de facto discrimination. Beauchamp spoke for the court on 21 November 1951, to declare that the "Mexican people" "are not a separate race but are white people of Spanish descent, as has often been said by this court. We find no ground for discussing the question further." The appellate court upheld the conviction.[148]

DeAnda and Herrera soon had an opportunity to sharpen this argument and try it again with a new client. Pete Hernandez was a migrant cotton picker who in 1952 was convicted of murder in the district court of Jackson County, Texas, and sentenced to life in prison. Herrera and DeAnda obtained financial support for their subsequent appeal from both LULAC and AGIF, and sought legal assistance from two more experienced attorneys from San Antonio, Carlos C. Cadeña and Gustavo C. "Gus" Garcia. The defense team argued during their appeal that, like Sanchez before him and a host of Mexican American criminal defendants in countless cases, Hernandez had been discriminated against because Mexican-descended individuals were deliberately and systematically excluded from both the grand jury that returned his indictment and from the petit jury that tried his case.[149]

To support their contention that the exclusion of Mexican Americans from the juries must have been deliberate, Cadeña and Garcia obtained a stipulation from the state and county attorneys that there were males of "Mexican or Latin American" descent in Jackson County who were eligible to serve as members of either a commission or a jury. The state and county attorneys also agreed to stipulate that, at least during the previous twenty-five years, no one with a Spanish surname had served on a jury commission, grand jury, or petit jury in Jackson County.[150]

Cadeña and Garcia added slightly to Herrera's and DeAnda's arguments by claiming that the logical result of a denial of due process was denial of equal protection. When they presented the case before the Texas Court of Criminal Appeals, Cadeña and Garcia sought to appropriate a "rule of exclusion" that the U.S. Supreme Court had announced in 1935's *Norris v. Alabama.* Alabama's state supreme court had let stand the conviction of Clarence Norris—one of the nine black "Scottsboro Boys" who had been convicted of the rape of two white women—despite the exclusion of African Americans from both the grand and petit juries. The U.S. Supreme Court had reversed, ruling that when the state acted, whether by the legislature, courts, or executive, to exclude from jury service "all persons of the African race, solely because of their race or color," if the same were both available and qualified to serve, then the state had denied "a person of the African race" the equal protection of the laws, contrary to the Fourteenth Amendment.[151] Cadeña and Garcia sought to persuade the Texas court to apply this reasoning to Mexican Americans. The failure to do that, they said, would be tantamount to extending "special benefits" to blacks.[152]

The Texas judges refused to extend that ruling concerning race-based jury discrimination to Hernandez's case involving allegations of heritage-based discrimination. A previous Texas Court of Criminal Appeals, the present judges reminded Cadeña and Garcia, had written in a similar case in the early 1940s that "[i]n the absence of a holding by the Supreme Court of the United States that nationality and race bear the same relation, within the meaning of the [equal protection clause of the Fourteenth Amendment], we shall continue to hold that . . . in the absence of proof showing express discrimination by administrators of the law, a jury so selected in accordance [with the statute] is valid."[153]

The appellate judges in Hernandez's case quoted that 1944 opinion to support their declaration that the equal protection clause of the Fourteenth Amendment contemplated only two classes: the white race and the Negro race. The court noted that "no member of the Mexican nationality challenges that statement." It appeared to the appellate judges that Cadeña and Garcia sought merely to have the state courts recognize Mexicans to be a "special class" within the white race that was entitled to enjoy the "special privilege" of a trial by juries that included Mexican Americans.[154]

With LULAC and AGIF still paying their fees and with Herrera and DeAnda listed "of counsel," Cadeña and Garcia took Hernandez's murder conviction to the U.S. Supreme Court.[155] In their arguments before the High Court, Cadeña and Garcia continued the attempt to demonstrate that Anglos in Texas actually considered Mexicans to be a separate, subordinate group, "distinct from 'whites.'" This resulted in biases in action, despite the laws on the books. The attorneys quoted "responsible officials and citizens" who admitted that Anglo Texans distinguished "white" from "Mexican." Cadeña and Garcia referred to the *Delgado* case, noting that "until recently" children of Mexican descent were required to attend a segregated school for the first four grades. They explained to the justices how Mexican Americans could be eliminated from juries. They showed that county commissioners selected potential jurors from a list of property taxpayers. Although many Mexican Americans were included on tax rolls as "citizens, householders, or freeholders," those persons' names never made it into the jury selection pool. This showed that qualified Mexican Americans must have been excluded solely on the basis of their Spanish surnames.[156]

Attorneys arguing the case for the State of Texas continued to deny that the mere reliance on a list of names might facilitate systematic discrimination. They once more stated that "there are only two classes—white and Negro—within the contemplation of the Fourteenth Amendment." But the justices were convinced by Cadeña's and Garcia's evidence that, "just as persons of a different race are distinguished by color, these Spanish names provide ready identification of the members of this class." The court announced its decision in *Hernandez v. Texas* on 3 May 1954, exactly two weeks before the justices announced their decision in *Brown I.*[157]

Chief Justice Warren spoke for the unanimous court to reverse Pete Hernandez's conviction, because the "systematic exclusion of persons of Mexican descent" from the jury pool at all levels had deprived him of due process and equal protection of the laws. The justices condemned this as obvious discrimination of "ancestry or national origin."[158] Warren noted that "[t]hroughout our history differences in race and color have defined easily identifiable groups which have at times required the aid of the courts in securing equal treatment under the laws." Moreover, the chief stated, because the "community prejudices are not static . . . from time to time other differences from the community norm may define other groups which need the same protection." Whenever the existence of "a distinct class" was demonstrated and it could be shown that laws "as written and applied, single out that class for different treatment not based on some reasonable classification," the court concluded, then "the guarantees of the Constitution have been violated."[159]

Although the cases are not explicitly linked, the Supreme Court's reliance on the equal protection clause in both *Hernandez* and *Brown* invites association. It is worth noting, however, that in *Hernandez* both the Texas and the Mexican American lawyers argued that Mexican Americans were in fact legally white. The successful conclusion of *Hernandez* on that basis seemed to justify continued reliance on the "other white" strategy. *Hernandez* committed Mexican Americans to defending their whiteness through future litigation, led them to discount the utility of *Brown,* and kept them too long on what proved to be an unfruitful constitutional trajectory.[160]

The growing line of "other white" victories that included *Hernandez, Mendez,* and *Delgado* had very limited effect in terms of ending discrimination. This was illustrated when DeAnda found it necessary to represent the plaintiff parents in the Driscoll CISD suit, which became the first post-*Brown* Mexican American school desegregation case to be decided by a federal court. Since 1949, when Judge Rice ruled for the plaintiffs in *Delgado,* the Driscoll district's restrooms, cafeterias, buses, and playgrounds had been desegregated, at least with respect to Anglo and Mexican descent. The Mexican Americans in the first and second grades, however, were still being taught in classrooms that contained no Anglo students. Mexican American students made up three-quarters of the enrollment in these grades, although actual attendance fluctuated with the seasonal demands of migrant farm work. Teachers, despite the ruling in *Delgado,* had continued to assess English aptitude without exams, and apparently they believed that none of their Mexican American students spoke or understood English.[161]

The district rules required that Mexican American students spend four years in the segregated first-grade classes before they were promoted to the segregated second-grade classes. This meant, in theory, that when Mexican American students did enroll in the third grade, they shared a classroom with Anglo children who were roughly three years younger. The result in practice—and Mexican American lawyers argued that this was intended—was that Mexican American students, many of whom were children of migrant workers, did not reach the third grade until the age when many dropped out to join their families in the fields. A threat by LULAC in 1955 to challenge this rule in court convinced the Driscoll administrators "experimentally" to reduce "linguistic" segregation in the first grade from four to three years.[162]

DeAnda had moved from Houston to Corpus Christi at the suggestion of AGIF founder Hector Garcia and became involved in the case in September 1955. The parents of nine-year-old Linda Perez enrolled her in the Driscoll school, and she was promptly placed in the "Mexican" class. DeAnda accompanied the Perez family to the school the next day. He informed the administrators that Linda's parents had taught their daughter to speak English, and, in fact, deliberately spoke no Spanish at home. DeAnda demanded that the school superintendent shift her to the English-speaking class.[163] The superintendent complied, but DeAnda discovered more English speakers in the Mexican classes. He also learned that Linda Perez was the only Mexican American allowed into an English-speaking first-grade classroom in the dozen years that the serving superintendent had been in charge of the district. DeAnda contacted more parents, sought assistance from Gus Garcia and AGIF, and, in November, filed suit on the parents' behalf in Corpus Christi.[164]

DeAnda claimed in his formal complaint that Driscoll CISD officials acted "under color of custom, common design, usage or practice," to deprive children "of Mexican descent" of privileges and immunities guaranteed under the Fourteenth Amendment, and of civil rights secured by existing laws of the United States.[165] The result, DeAnda argued, was that Mexican American students in Driscoll were deprived of "educational, health, psychological and recreational benefits provided . . . for other school children." He sued "in equity and at law" and asked that the federal court enjoin the Driscoll schools from continuing the segregation.[166]

Judge Allred commenced pretrial hearings in late February 1956. Allan Davis, of the Corpus Christi firm Boone, Davis, Cox, and Hale, answered DeAnda's complaint for the Driscoll CISD.[167] Davis denied that the school district discriminated on the basis of ancestry. He contended that the separation of the children who could not speak English was a long-accepted necessity.[168] Allred ordered DeAnda to file a clear and more concise statement of the plaintiffs' claims by 26 March, and instructed Davis to file the defendants' reply by 23 April.[169]

DeAnda stated in more detail the basic claim contained in his original complaint, that the Driscoll CISD had maintained classes consisting solely of children of Hispanic descent in the first and second grade, and required a majority of these children to spend three years in the first grade before promotion to the second grade. This practice, DeAnda argued, was implemented without due process and denied the children equal protection of the law.[170]

In his more concise reply, Davis reminded the judge of the Texas statutes that required schools to instruct in English and insisted that the school maintained the segregation for no other reason than that Mexican American students lacked English. Davis criticized the Mexican American parents in the district who, he claimed, failed to teach their children to speak English before enrolling them in the school, refused to use English in the home, and did not require that, during school breaks, their children "associate only with those who speak English."[171] Davis charged, moreover, that the lawsuit was groundless, politically motivated, and had "resulted solely from the insistence of certain G.I. Forum organizations."[172]

DeAnda referred to the *Brown* decision in his pretrial memorandum, but only to dismiss its relevance. He stated that, according to earlier judicial rulings, if "Mexicans, being members of the Caucasian or Caucasoid race," were segregated in separate buildings or classes without first being tested, they were being denied due process and hence equal protection of the laws. This had been settled law, he noted, "even before" the Supreme Court ruled in *Brown* that the "segregation of children based on race pursuant to statutory or State constitutional authority violated the [Fourteenth] Amendment." DeAnda instead relied on *Hernandez*, noting that the court "held untenable the argument of the State of Texas that discrimination *within* the white race did not violate the equal protection clause." With *Hernandez* available, *Brown* was not necessary, DeAnda argued, because "the instant cases do not raise the problems present in the Negro cases. There is present in these cases no question of segregation because of race."[173]

DeAnda so carefully distinguished between these landmarks for two reasons. First, *Brown* was about racial segregation, which he considered inapplicable to the Mexican American complaint, while *Hernandez* specifically referred to national origin. Second, *Brown* was concerned only with statutory segregation, while *Hernandez* overturned discriminatory practices that had not been authorized by statute. Because he was not now contending that segregation in the Driscoll CISD was race-based or that Texas law had authorized the type of segregation that was practiced in the Driscoll CISD, *Brown* was not a useful precedent. This was a well-measured strategy. DeAnda risked losing the case altogether if he relied too heavily on *Brown* and the judge decided that the major differences between that case and the present case overrode the minor resemblance. Yet, after arguing for these legal distinctions, DeAnda indicated that he would gladly accept support from *Brown* if Allred chose to view that case as a favorable precedent. He concluded his brief by stating that "cases which have dealt with segregation of Mexican school children control here even without the reinforcement given them by the Supreme Court's segregation decisions." DeAnda would cite *Brown* when it suited him, and only for general support.[174]

DeAnda's limited strategy fit his modest goals. On the first day of the proceedings, Allred asked whether DeAnda was asking for an injunction to end segregation involving language proficiency. DeAnda answered no, because he agreed that there were good reasons for the school to keep Spanish-speaking children segregated until they could speak and understand English. He objected only to the automatic and extended segregation of Mexican American children on the excuse that, because they were Mexican American or belonged to migrant families, they could not be as proficient with English as Anglo students, who were automatically placed in English-speaking classes.[175] Davis retorted that language segregation was necessary for the education of both classes of students.[176]

DeAnda called several trustees and teachers of the Driscoll CISD to testify to the district's system of segregation. None of the witnesses disputed that, without exception, Mexican-descended students were segregated for three years in the first grade.[177] The sole dispute for the judge to resolve was whether Driscoll CISD's rules were reasonable or arbitrary and therefore discriminatory. DeAnda mainly relied on the testimony of two varieties of expert witnesses: social scientists and the schoolchildren themselves. George I. Sanchez, a professor of Latin American education at UT, had studied the effects of language segregation on children, and he frequently served as a consultant and as an expert witness in Mexican American segregation litigation. Sanchez testified in Allred's court that, because extended segregation prevented the social interaction and conversation necessary for learning a language, the best way to address language disparities was to group the children together. Driscoll CISD's segregation during the early grades, he declared, actually reduced the Mexican American students' future ability to learn.[178]

Davis did not wish to allow Allred to consider Sanchez to be an objective witness, or to take as authoritative Sanchez's books, which DeAnda had offered as plaintiffs' exhibits. During cross-examination, Davis elicited Sanchez's admission that his testimony did not mesh with opinions he had expressed in some of his earlier work. Sanchez protested that his thinking had changed, as had the opinions of other experts, although, at the same time, he had to admit that his previous analyses remained sound on many points.[179] Davis entered into evidence a diverse array of opinions from other authorities, whom even Sanchez admitted on the stand were worthy of consideration, that flatly contradicted Sanchez's opinions.[180]

The so-called expert authority, Davis argued, did not yield a consensus sufficient to justify overruling a local administrator's judgments.[181] To stress the point, Davis called as his own "experts" the Driscoll officials, who denied that the segregation harmed the children.[182] Davis would later argue, in his concluding brief, that Sanchez was not an unbiased scholar who had changed his opinion when he was confronted with new data. Rather, he was "an advocate, a crusader, and a zealot." Sanchez's monographs were briefs, Davis suggested, and the professor's views "should be given no more weight than the argument of an attorney in the case."[183]

DeAnda's second group of plaintiffs' "experts," although less sophisticated, were more difficult for Davis to attack on cross-examination. They were first graders of Mexican descent who were enrolled in Driscoll CISD. DeAnda invited the judge to ask the children questions about their school, friends, and families. A child occasionally misapprehended a question, or stumbled in an answer. The judge asked one boy, for example, "What is your oldest brother's name?" The boy answered "I don't have just one."[184] Davis argued that the blunders indicated that the children did "not have the understanding of English and facility of use which the average English-speaking child would have."[185] But their performance proved to Allred's satisfaction that the claims of the Driscoll officials were preposterous. The judge noted that "these children appeared to be as bright as Anglo children of the same age . . . their mistakes were no more than those that might have been made by any other child under the excitement or other emotions of a first appearance in court."[186]

Allred invited the parties to submit final briefs in lieu of their closing statements. Before bringing the court proceedings to an end, however, Allred gave what he called "some indication of my thinking at the present time." He recognized that there might be reasons for maintaining separate classes for beginners, he said, although he added that Sanchez's opinion to the contrary was "entitled to a great deal of weight."[187] But, despite the fact that holding back the non-English speakers "for the first year, or a portion of the year" could be justified, Allred declared that "I think any treatment of these students as a class beyond that is unreasonable and discriminatory, any treatment that does not take into consideration the ability of the individual student."[188]

Allred also had a warning for DeAnda. "Considerable progress has been made, you say, as a result of lawsuits." But the judge admitted doubts. "I don't know," Allred said, "I don't want to dictate to a school the method they should follow. I don't think I have the right to do that."[189] Allred therefore revealed sympathy for the plaintiffs, but also announced his reluctance to dictate an end to all forms of separation. Just in case the administrators had not recognized his inclinations, however, Allred added: "[T]his method is unreasonably discriminatory and violative of a particular plaintiff's or particular group of plaintiff's rights. I know that any treatment of these people, on the basis that they are of Latin extraction, as a group, or treating an individual that way because he happens to come from that group, is, on its face, discriminatory and based on an unreasonable basis. It can't stand."[190] "[Y]ou can file briefs on it," the judge concluded; "I am just telling you what I am thinking off hand. It is not final. You can direct your arguments to those points if you want to."[191]

After both of the legal teams had requested and received extensions, Allred had the briefs in hand by mid-December.[192] In his final brief, as in his original complaint, DeAnda did not seek to end language segregation. He sought an order from the judge that would require the Driscoll trustees to end the present system of classroom assignment, to maintain no segregated classrooms after the first grade, to segregate children only after proper testing, and to move any student to the

English-speaking class as soon as he or she demonstrated sufficient understanding of that language.[193]

DeAnda was inspired to invoke *Brown* only once more, in reply to Davis's closing brief. Davis argued in his brief that the judge ought to allow the administrators to follow their own "good faith" judgment about what would be best for the children. Davis referred as well to the children's testimony that they were happy with the present arrangement. Davis suggested that the happy students would only become more aware of their language deficiencies if they were placed in a class with native English speakers.[194]

DeAnda suggested in his response that Davis "cannot conjure a more emphatic method of emphasizing or creating differences than by the policy of segregation" at Driscoll CISD. DeAnda suggested that his limited plan was "more than justified under the evidence . . . and actually benign, in light of the holding in *Brown*."[195] In this riposte, DeAnda used *Brown* only as a negative example, not as a model for judicial action. DeAnda concluded on a more positive note, however, by stressing that the Supreme Court in *Brown* had declared separate education facilities "inherently unequal."[196]

Allred condemned the Driscoll CISD's practices on 11 January 1957. Because it was clear that the district had violated existing rules, and therefore the plaintiffs were seeking only to bring compliance, Allred limited his memorandum opinion to a restatement of earlier "other white" rulings. He referred, for example, to the ruling in *Delgado* that said that segregation of Mexican Americans was permissible if it was not arbitrary. Language handicaps might justify segregation, Allred agreed, but only after an examination. He found that the Driscoll segregation criterion was "not a line drawn in good faith." It was "unreasonable race discrimination against all Mexican children as a group." The judge concluded, "If scientific or good faith tests were given the *result* might not weigh so heavily," but, "when considered along with the other facts and circumstances, . . . it compels the conclusion that the grouping is purposeful, intentional and unreasonably discriminatory."[197] Allred issued his injunction on 15 March and ordered that a new system of assigning students was to begin in Driscoll by the next academic year. He noted that this would give "school authorities ample time to formulate a program accordingly without undue interference with its current work."[198]

This case had not presented Allred with a "monumental job." The Mexican Americans' complaint against the Driscoll CISD and the judicial remedy they sought and obtained were limited. Once in court, it proved elementary for DeAnda to demonstrate to the judge's satisfaction that the administrators had acted contrary to Texas statutes and the U.S. Constitution. Yet, because his ruling did not condemn outright the school's use of language segregation, some scholars of Mexican American civil rights have criticized the judge in the Driscoll CISD case. George A. Martinez, for example, has complained that Allred relied on stale reasoning and outmoded precedents in order to sustain segregation in the face of "clear evidence that school officials used the linguistic rationale as a pretext for segregating Mexican Americans from Anglos." Martinez argues that the judge could, and should, have relied on *Brown* to prohibit altogether the segregation of Mexican Americans.[199] That criticism is untenable in light of the record. In reiterating the arguments of earlier decisions, Allred relied not merely on precedent but on the very reasoning DeAnda advanced during the proceedings. Judges ordinarily do not give more than is asked.

The record indicates, moreover, that DeAnda did not think at that time that *Brown* offered anything fresh for Mexican Americans. His arguments might appear in hindsight to have been out of step with the revolution in rights that *Brown* sparked.[200] DeAnda's and others' inclinations to seek "due process" rights rather than "equal protection" seemed sound, if winning in court is the sole criterion for success. Sound or not, however, the end result of the victory was disappointing. The investment in time, money, and legal talent brought the enrollment in "white" classrooms of a few dozen first-grade Mexican American children of the Driscoll CISD. The limited benefits did not justify the expense of the litigation, and, in fact, this was among the last public school desegregation suits Mexican Americans filed for a decade.[201]

In the late 1950s Mexican American rights advocates all but abandoned organized litigation and instead sought to gain greater political influence. Mexican American leaders demonstrated their importance to the Democratic Party during a massive "Viva Kennedy" get-out-the-vote project that delivered crucial support to Senator John F. Kennedy during his hard-fought and ultimately successful 1960 presidential campaign against Vice President Richard M. Nixon.[202]

The success of the "Viva Kennedy" effort left President-elect Kennedy indebted to Mexican Americans. He had the opportunity to pay the debt in short order. Judge Allred had died in July 1959, leaving one of the Southern District's four judgeships vacant. Because both U.S. senators from Texas were Democrats, the custom of senatorial courtesy did not oblige President Eisenhower to seek their approval before nominating Allred's successor. He considered nominating the Houston lawyer T. Everton Kennerly, a former Republican candidate for the Senate and the son of Judge Kennerly, who had retired in 1954. Eisenhower apparently was not fully behind the younger Kennerly's appointment, however, and, as a result, the Republicans squabbled among themselves over the chance to nominate various friends and political supporters. The vacant judgeship languished through the 1960 election cycle, and Eisenhower missed that opportunity to appoint a Republican. Kennedy soon announced his intention to appoint a Mexican American to Allred's seat.[203]

Lyndon Johnson, who when Allred died was the senior senator from Texas and also the majority leader in the Senate, publicly endorsed Kennerly, but Johnson had been in no hurry to see the job filled. Johnson was an old hand at the giving or withholding of patronage. As Senate majority leader he reportedly had blocked more than a dozen unrelated judicial nominations until Eisenhower appointed Johnson's friend Joe J. Fisher to a vacant federal district judgeship in the Eastern District of Texas. Johnson gambled that, if he delayed Kennerly's appointment long enough, he would be able to fill the vacancy with a candidate of his own choosing. He and the other Democrats in the Senate no doubt were delighted when Republicans helped derail the search for Allred's successor. Johnson had hoped to lead the Democrats into the White House after 1960, but his disappointment in settling for the second spot on the ticket did not diminish his ambitions for his own friends and supporters.[204]

The junior senator from Texas, Ralph W. Yarborough, was a leader of the Democratic Party's liberal wing, and therefore he was Johnson's great rival. Yarborough had been in his office only one year, but he became Texas's senior senator in January 1961, at the moment Johnson was inaugurated as vice president. Yarborough maintained that, under the long-standing tradition, it was his prerogative to name Allred's successor. At the suggestion of the liberal Democratic Mexican American leaders, including Garcia of AGIF, Yarborough suggested that state district judge Ezequiel D. Salinas of Laredo, Texas, be appointed to fill Allred's seat. Mexican Americans also suggested DeAnda as an alternative to Salinas. At thirty-five years old, however, DeAnda probably was too young to be considered a serious candidate for the federal judiciary.[205]

Vice President Johnson, although no longer eligible for the courtesy ordinarily due to a senator, refused to give up seniority in Texas political matters to his rival Yarborough. He pressed Kennedy to appoint Reynaldo Guerra Garza of Brownsville, Texas. Garza was born in Brownsville on 7 July 1915. He graduated from Brownsville Junior College in 1935 and earned his B.A. two years later at UT in Austin. He remained in Austin to attend UT law school and received the LL.B. in 1939. Garza was a self-employed lawyer in Brownsville until 1942, when he entered the U.S. Army Air Forces. He returned home to reenter solo practice in 1945 and then formed a small legal partnership in 1950. Garza became active in Democratic politics, and served as a commissioner of Brownsville and as a trustee of the local school board.[206]

Garza was an old friend and loyal supporter of the newly elected vice president. Garza met Johnson in the late 1930s, during one of Johnson's early campaigns for office. Garza continued to support Johnson for successively higher offices. He had worked hard to deliver votes to his friend in a "Viva Johnson" campaign during the Democratic primary in 1959 but had joined "Viva Kennedy" once Johnson was on that ticket in 1960. This long-lived loyalty motivated Johnson to press very hard for Garza's candidacy. In April 1961, nearly two years after Allred's death but less than three months after Kennedy's inauguration, Garza assumed Allred's seat. He became the first Mexican American federal judge in American history.[207]

President Kennedy's appointment of Garza provoked rather than pleased some Mexican American leaders in Texas, and it exacerbated the ideological rifts in the Democratic Party. Although it pleased the Mexican American community in principle finally to have one of their own on the federal bench in south Texas, Garza's appointment was not a cause for celebration among liberal Mexican Americans. Judge Garza was a living reminder to them of Johnson's continued sway over politics in Texas.[208] Another Johnson ally, Henry B. Gonzalez of San Antonio, won election to the U.S. House of Representatives in 1961. Yet progress in politics continued for Mexican Americans as a community. The Political Association of Spanish Speaking Organizations (PASSO), which was founded around 1960, led the campaign in 1962 that resulted in the brief Mexican American domination of the municipal government in Crystal City, Texas.[209]

For Mexican Americans, however, especially the veteran civil rights activists, it was necessary but never sufficient that some Mexican Americans gain influential elected or appointed positions. It was more important that the occupants of influential positions use them to fight the social discriminations, economic hardships, and inferior education that many Mexican Americans continued to endure in Texas because of their ethnic, if not racial, heritage. These historic disabilities were not lifted merely by the personal and professional rise of conservative political elites like Judge Garza and Congressman Gonzalez. Despite some significant political successes, therefore, Mexican American dissatisfaction simmered. Liberal activists wondered when, if ever, it would boil over.[210]

Allred's pessimism in 1957 seemed justified. Mexican Americans repeatedly won their points in court but did not in the long run "accomplish a great deal by lawsuits." In fact, Mexican Americans accomplished little in the federal district courts, and achieved only slightly more through politics, until they changed course and abandoned their "white" status. The stubborn embrace of whiteness in the decade after *Brown* prevented all Mexican Americans, whether conservative or liberal, from grappling with the real distinctions between de jure segregation of African Americans that the Supreme Court had condemned in *Brown* and de facto segregation of Mexican Americans that continued to occur in Texas public institutions.[211]

When Mexican Americans resumed desegregation litigation in the late 1960s, DeAnda stood in the vanguard, as one of the first Mexican American attorneys to repudiate whiteness in court and to adapt the equal protection rationale of the *Brown* decisions to fit Mexican Americans' circumstances. This shift from "other white" to *Brown* was controversial, and it was contested by Anglos as well as by Mexican Americans. It will be examined in a later chapter.[212]

NOT BY JUDGES ALONE

In the years after *Brown*, southern school desegregation proceeded in fits and starts, but mostly stops, until the slow pace of court-ordered reform itself became an issue in the larger civil rights struggle.[213] Federal district judges grew frustrated as southerners' open defiance receded but was replaced by stalling tactics and tokenism. The monumental task, as Allred called it in 1957, of "trying to determine the justice [or the] injustice of the treatment of particular students," was, according to the scholar J. Harvie Wilkinson, more difficult than it might have been. He noted that, between 1955 and 1968, the Supreme Court "abandoned the field." During those critical years the court's "pronouncements were few," and its "leadership was almost non-existent."[214]

During the 1960s initiatives from the political branches, and additional rulings by the federal appellate courts, expanded the type and number of personnel available to offer support to the federal district judges in superintending reform. In 1964 the Congress passed a landmark Civil Rights Act (CRA) that banned discrimination in employment and public accommodations.[215] The CRA mandated that the Department of Health, Education, and Welfare (HEW) and other federal agencies take affirmative steps to attack discrimination. Under Title VI of the 1964 CRA, administrators at HEW could either share or withhold housing or other grants to states. As the level of federal assistance offered to the states increased in ensuing years, any threat to cut off funds to states that countenanced discrimination in schools became significant. State authorities faced the choice either of abandoning segregated schools or losing federal funds.[216]

The HEW also established guidelines for assessing the progress of desegregation, and the agency's examiners assisted federal district judges in developing schedules for school districts' compliance with the guidelines. Some federal district judges resisted this intervention of an executive department in judicial business. But the Fifth Circuit judges declared in a 1965 decision, *Singleton v. Jackson* (usually known as *Singleton I*), that district judges should give "great weight" to HEW-developed guidelines.[217] In *Singleton II*, however, decided the next year, the Fifth Circuit appellate judges made it clear that HEW guidelines were minimum standards, not final goals. The appellate court declared that the federal district judges should not "abdicate" their responsibilities by ordering only that school districts comply with the guidelines.[218]

District judges sitting in the South fortunately received this guidance, and occasionally much-needed stiffening of resolve, from the "unlikely heroes" of the Fifth Circuit court of appeals.[219] Yet, the Fifth Circuit's resolve threatened to fail as *Brown I*'s tenth anniversary came and went. A Fifth Circuit panel declared in 1966 that "[a] national effort, bringing together Congress, the executive, and the judiciary may be able to make meaningful the right of Negro children to equal educational opportunities." Unfortunately, the judges admitted, "[t]he courts acting alone have failed."[220] Peltason had all but predicted judicial failure five years earlier, although he had not necessarily blamed the lower court judges. In *Fifty-eight Lonely Men,* he maintained that the president, Congress, and Supreme Court had abdicated their own responsibilities for implementing *Brown.* Peltason concluded that the desegregation project could succeed in the South, but not if the country relied on "judges alone."[221]

These worries, that the courts simply were not up to the task of delivering desegregation with more deliberate speed, echo the pessimism Allred expressed in the Driscoll case. The lawsuits in Houston and Driscoll indicate, however, that implementing lasting reforms required the long-term commitment of judges and attorneys to manage the life cycle of the litigation. The Houston case was a wholly different form of lawsuit from the suit filed in Driscoll. Allred and Connally solicited suggestions from counsel, conducted pretrial hearings, and sought to balance the legitimate interests of the parties. But no one expected Allred to establish an ongoing relationship with the Driscoll CISD that required him periodically to check up on its progress. By contrast, the Houston plaintiffs expected Connally to maintain a continuing presence in the affairs of HISD. They aimed to transform the district, and the case therefore became a classic example of public law litigation.

An unfortunate truth, of course, is that neither victory in the limited traditional suit in equity against Driscoll CISD nor in the expansive structural reform suit against HISD satisfied the plaintiffs. In the former a limited aim brought a limited result. In the latter ambitious aims brought painfully slow results. The recalcitrance of the school districts may have frustrated some federal judges and liberal court watchers, but the slow pace of court-ordered desegregation disappointed the African American parents most of all. Despite the delays and diversions, however, momentum seemed to build after 1960. As African Americans marched for equality in schools, voting, housing, and other areas, their desires for desegregation were transformed into demands for actual integration. Although African Americans remained disappointed with the slow pace of change in the schools, they gained political and judicial support for related goals.[222]

Efforts in desegregation moved other aggrieved individuals, as well as disfranchised groups, to appropriate not only the style and rhetoric of the African American freedom struggle, but also its legal focus. Most of them eventually found it necessary to seek judicial intervention against their own perceived oppressors. As new plaintiffs filed suit with new complaints, moreover, they deepened the legacies of *Brown I* and *Brown II.* Among the results was the continually expanding role of federal district judges in managing public law litigation.[223]

CHAPTER TWO

Legislation, Litigation, and Judicial Economy

AMONG THE METHODS FOR JUDICIAL SELECTION, Benjamin Franklin declared during the Constitutional Convention of 1787, was "the Scottish practice," under which the "nomination proceeded from the Lawyers, who always selected the ablest of the profession in order to get rid of him, and share his practice among themselves."[1] The vice president's motives were distinguishable from the venality that Franklin had suggested 172 years earlier, but Lyndon B. Johnson clearly had taken a personal as well as a professional interest in the choice of U.S. District Judge James Allred's successor in the Southern District of Texas. Reynaldo G. Garza offered his patron little in terms of reciprocal financial reward or continued political service. Garza had been named to the federal district cour simply for demonstrating early political savvy and showing long-lived personal loyalty to Johnson. The judicial appointment was not a matter of what Johnson's friend could do for him. It was what Johnson could do for his friend.[2]

Garza's personal ties to Johnson had put him in the running for the federal bench in ways that his political and professional pedigree could not, because his stature in Texas was, like his ethnicity, a significant departure from the norm for a judge in the Southern District. Garza's brother judges had all been born in small towns, but each had eventually established ties in Houston, the largest city in the Southern District of Texas. Like several of the other judges, Garza had attended the University of Texas (UT) law school in Austin, and he had become a prominent lawyer with political connections. Unlike the others, however, he had returned to his hometown, apparently very far from the levers of power and influence. As a result of that decision, which was perhaps linked with his ethnic identity, Garza's legal and political career paled next to those of the late Judge James Allred, who had been governor of Texas, and Judge Ben Connally, who was a senator's son.

Allen Burroughs Hannay, by contrast with Garza, was a small-town boy who had seemed destined by birth for the federal bar and bench. Hannay, the son of a U.S. attorney, was born in Hempstead, Texas, on 14 February 1892. He attended

Texas A&M University and then the UT law school, where he earned his LL.B. in 1913. Hannay was a judge in Waller County from 1915 until 1917, when he resigned the bench to enlist in the U.S. Army during World War I. He trained pilots during the war. Hannay, it seems, was a man of many talents. In addition to practicing law, serving as a judge, and training pilots, he played baseball professionally, for the old Houston Buffs. Hannay resumed his state judicial career in 1930 and was judge of the 113th District Court for a dozen years. President Franklin D. Roosevelt appointed Hannay to replace Judge Allred in the Southern District in 1942.[3] By reason of his long service, Hannay was the chief judge of the Southern District when Garza joined the court in 1961.[4]

The Southern District's fourth judge, Joe McDonald Ingraham, was born in Pawnee County, Oklahoma, on 5 July 1903. He earned his LL.B at the National University Law School (now George Washington University) in Washington, D.C. Ingraham entered solo practice in his native Oklahoma, although only for a few months in the winter of 1927 and 1928. He moved steadily up the legal career ladder the farther south he traveled. Ingraham worked as an attorney with a small Fort Worth firm for seven years and then migrated to Houston, where he practiced solo for six months before landing at Baker, Botts. He specialized in oil and gas law for that prestigious firm from 1935 until 1942. Like Judge Connally, Ingraham served in the U.S. Army Air Forces and reached the rank of lieutenant colonel during World War II. He returned to Houston in 1946 and spent one more year at Baker, Botts before reentering solo legal practice. Ingraham became a leader in the Harris County Republican Party and gained his position on the federal bench in 1954, when President Dwight D. Eisenhower appointed him to fill the vacancy left by Judge Kennerly upon his retirement.[5]

Judge Ingraham was the first Republican ever to serve on the Southern District court since its 1902 founding. That Democratic senators abetted an almost two-year lapse between Allred's death and Garza's confirmation indicated how willing they were to let court efficiency suffer, as long as they could deny Eisenhower the privilege of giving another "plum" to a Republican in Majority Leader Johnson's home state.[6] Partisanship has attended debates over the character of the federal courts since the emergence of parties at the turn of the eighteenth century,[7] but political contests over the creation and allocation of federal judgeships assumed even greater ideological dimensions in the years after the *Brown* decisions. With the advent of court-ordered public school desegregation in the mid-1950s, patronage and ideological aspects of judicial appointments were more entwined than ever.[8]

Congressional Democrats limited the Republican president's opportunities to appoint federal judges by vigorously asserting their constitutional responsibility to advise and consent to the appointments. Conservative senators screened nominees to judicial vacancies, seeking to lower the risk that liberal activists would reach the federal bench. The result was that, of the two dozen or so district judges President Eisenhower managed to appoint in the South, most were ambivalent on, and some were openly hostile to, public school desegregation. Congressional conservatives worried needlessly with regard to racial issues, because the president was lukewarm on *Brown.* Rather than linking his appointments to policy, Eisenhower used judgeships, in traditional fashion, to spread patronage among party loyalists. Conserving patronage, of course, gave Democratic leaders reason enough to delay confirmations.[9]

More significantly, Congress refused to create federal judgeships during President Eisenhower's last six years in office, that is, after 1954. The legislative branch is responsible for the jurisdiction, budget, and size of the formally "independent" federal judiciary. Opponents of Earl Warren's activism regarded the chief justice's calls for enlarging the judiciary to be politically suspect.[10] But congressional leaders ignored pleas to expand the federal bench whether entreaties to do so came from the president, individual legislators of both parties, or the judiciary itself, speaking through representatives of the Judicial Conference.[11]

The Democratic leadership rebuffed all petitions to create judgeships while a Republican occupied the White House. The irony was that concerted neglect of the judiciary—whether because of the fears of judicial activism regarding civil rights, or else through simple partisan competition—diminished the ability of the sitting judges to fulfill their responsibilities that had nothing to do with desegregation or other civil rights issue.[12] Congress constrained growth of the bench during Eisenhower's administration, moreover, despite evidence that the growth of federal court business increased the threat of congested dockets. The Southern District of Texas, like other federal courts, began to see rising caseloads in the late 1950s. Figure 1 shows the caseload in the Southern District from 1950 to 1960.

Executive and legislative priorities directly affected the court's business. The total numbers of both civil and criminal case filings fluctuated in direct response to specific actions by the "political" branches of the government. Increased prosecutions for immigration violations in the Southwest, which were related to the government's concerns with the state of labor relations during the Korean conflict, account for high numbers in the early part of the decade. The prosecutions dropped off sharply during the second half of the decade, after the Eisenhower administration initiated "Operation Wetback," a quasi-military campaign that involved mass arrests and deportations of undocumented workers.[13]

The civil statistics reflect the results of a legislative effort to ease docket pressures in the courts. Congress adjusted federal jurisdiction in 1958, by raising the requirement for standing in district courts from controversies that involved a minimum of three thousand dollars to cases that involved at least ten thousand dollars.[14] Civil case filings, exclusive of bankruptcies, declined as a result of the legislation. The

FIGURE 1. The Caseload in the Southern District, 1950–1960

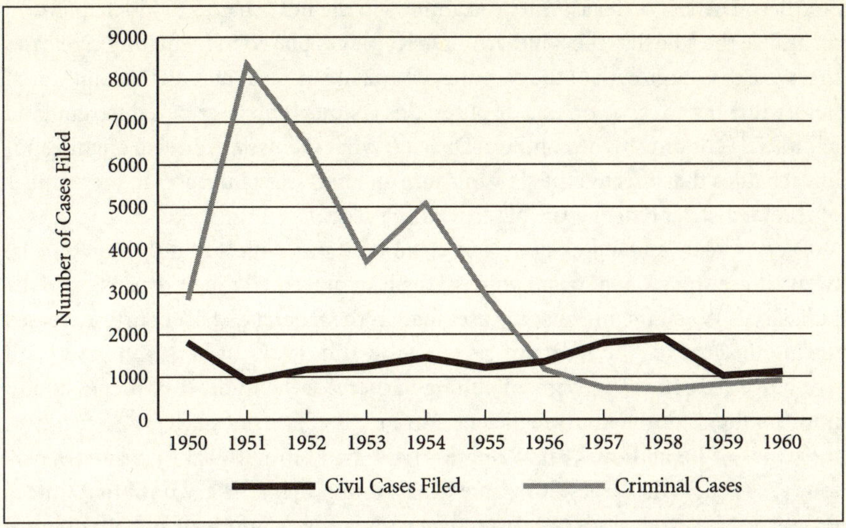

Source: *Federal Court Management Statistics* (Washington, D.C.: Administrative Office of the United States Courts, 2000).

effect was temporary and in fact lasted only a few years in the Southern District of Texas.[15] While they awaited the appointment of Allred's successor, the three surviving judges tried to keep the court's docket current. By the end of September 1961, only 170 civil cases filed before January 1959 remained pending. Although Judges Hannay, Connally, and Ingraham kept pace, they could have ill afforded to remain shorthanded much longer.[16]

The ebb and flow of cases filed in the Southern District clearly was sensitive to shifts in political priorities. But the rising number of cases in both civil and criminal categories was also driven by the tremendous economic boom that Texas experienced after World War II. The discovery of new oil and gas reserves contributed to prosperity and attracted new industries and people to Texas, but petrochemical refineries along the coast were only one element to the state's economy. The Gulf of Mexico was a major conduit for international commerce and a reservoir of regional employment. Texas ports were channels for a wide variety of goods. In addition to oil refining and related industries, for example, an enormous volume of agricultural products was harvested in and then shipped from south Texas's Lower Rio Grande Valley. Judges played a role in the region's economic health by presiding over the maritime and mainland insurance, labor contract, and tort disputes that were perennial contributors to the caseload.[17]

Criminal cases, and the judicial response to the rise in prosecutions in the Southern District of Texas, will be examined in the next chapter. This chapter will scrutinize the role that the Southern District judges played in mediating civil cases that were the outgrowth of the commercial activity in Texas and on the Gulf Coast. Before turning to those private disputes, this chapter will describe a different kind of judicial economy in the Southern District. What follows introduces ongoing political battles that affected the slow but sure and necessary increases in the number of federal district judges available to hear the cases.

Federal economic regulations and criminal statutes increased throughout the twentieth century, but partisan political rivalries prevented timely expansion of the judiciary.[18] When the number of cases filed in the federal district courts increased during the 1920s,[19] the resultant rise in costs and delays of litigation gave birth to a judge-led reform movement aiming to increase the number of judges and to improve their administrative efficiency. In 1922 the levers of power were firmly in the hands of Republicans, and Congress passed an omnibus act to create twenty-four judgeships, the largest one-time expansion in the judiciary until that time.[20] Proportionate expansions have waited on comparable alignments of both political branches. President Roosevelt was able to remake the federal courts, despite his failure to expand and "pack" the U.S. Supreme Court, because Congress added judgeships during all but four years of his lengthy presidency.[21]

President Truman enjoyed a similar opportunity, but only after suffering under a briefly divided government. After their victories in the 1946 midterm elections raised the Republicans' expectations that they would regain control of the White House in 1948, Republicans in the Senate sought to preserve patronage for themselves and so refused to act on many of Truman's judicial nominations. When Truman retained the presidency and Democrats regained control of the Congress, Senate Democrats confirmed the Truman nominees. In 1949 they also created a record twenty-seven judgeships. These included two judgeships in the Southern District of Texas, one permanent position that went to Connally and one temporary position that went to former Judge Allred.[22]

As a result of both the long service of Roosevelt and the expansion under Truman, approximately four of every five sitting federal judges were Democrats by January 1953, when Eisenhower assumed the presidency with Republican majorities in both houses of Congress.[23] The new Republican Congress passed legislation in 1954 that increased the number of federal district judgeships from 218 to 245.[24] The 1954 law did not add any new judges to the bench in the Southern District of Texas, although Congress made Allred's temporary seat permanent. Judge Ingraham later assumed Kennerly's existing position on the court.[25] Republican mastery of Congress and control of federal judicial patronage proved short-lived.

Democrats regained control of Congress in November 1954, and they held it during the rest of the Eisenhower presidency. During his second term Eisenhower pleaded vainly with Congress to create more judgeships. Despite resistance at the top, some Democrats did attempt to work with the Republicans. They supported expanding the judiciary in order to relieve court congestion. These bipartisan efforts failed. In 1956 a House bill sought to create twenty-one judgeships and a Senate bill to create thirty-five, but neither bill passed. The administration asked Congress in 1958 to create between forty-five and fifty judgeships. The Judicial Conference repeated that request in 1959.[26]

The Democrats therefore denied Republicans the opportunity to put judges into new positions. By filling vacancies during his first six years in office, however, Eisenhower nearly restored parity to the federal courts.[27] He reportedly was confident enough in that position to authorize his attorney general in August 1959 to inform the Democrats that he would fill judgeships on a "50–50 basis" if Congress enacted the recommendations of the Judicial Conference. A subcommittee of the House Judiciary Committee held hearings on proposed judgeships in February 1960. Its chairman asked Deputy Attorney General Lawrence Walsh whether the president would nominate "true" Democrats or Democrats "across party lines." Walsh assured the congressman that "everyone would be satisfied with the appointments." In March the subcommittee recommended the creation of forty-five judgeships. The bill never made it to a vote. Senator Everett Dirksen of Illinois, the Republican minority leader, later implied from the Senate floor that the reason the Democrats refused to act was "ostensibly because we might have been getting just a little closer to the 1960 elections."[28]

The Democratic delaying tactics had denied Republicans the opportunity to name dozens of judges to brand new positions. By the end of the decade, however, these tactics were becoming much harder to defend. The lawmakers had to increase the size of the judiciary in order to accommodate the rise in cases. According to the best available data from the Judicial Conference, the federal district courts faced a 71,992-case backlog in 1961. In his last message to Congress, on 16 January 1961, less than one week before leaving office, Eisenhower repeated his support for the Judicial Conference's recommendation for the creation of fifty judgeships.[29]

After their party had recaptured the White House, Democratic leaders moved rapidly to address the problem of court congestion.[30] In January 1961, just a few weeks before Kennedy's inauguration, members of the new Eighty-seventh Congress began introducing the legislation necessary to add dozens of new judges.[31] The Republicans could not oppose judgeship bills without opening themselves to charges of hypocrisy, and they conceded the debate. By forcing the Democratic leadership to defend years of inaction, however, Republicans were able to charge the majority party with that hypocrisy. When the Senate resumed debate on 3 March, Dirksen noted that his fellow senators were suddenly "writing in judgeships rather briskly" and "plucking plums from this very juicy plum tree." He regarded the swift addition of judgeships taking place during the floor debate and noted that not only had Eisenhower given Democrats assurances that he would appoint a balanced bench, he had given them proof. After filling the vacancies created by deaths or retirements, Eisenhower left office after eight years with 35 Republicans, 29 Democrats, and 4 vacant seats on the federal circuit courts. There were 119 Republican and 125 Democratic judges, and 2 vacancies on the federal district courts. Senator Dirksen hoped, he said, that the Democrats would be equally balanced, so that at least some of the plums being plucked would "carry a modest Republican tag."[32]

Although Republicans continued to tweak the Democrats in these minor ways, few in Congress questioned that the judges were needed. The most interesting objection was from Senator Richard B. Russell, a conservative Democrat from Georgia, who declared that he would vote against any judgeship bill "as a protest against the wanton abuses and excesses inflicted upon our constitutional system by the Federal judiciary under the direction and dictation of the present Supreme Court." Russell condemned *Brown* at length and proclaimed his support for "state's rights."[33]

The Senate passed its omnibus judgeship bill on a voice vote and transferred it to the conference committees for consolidation with the House version of the bill. The respective chairmen of the Judiciary Committees formally reported their agreement to a joint conference committee on 4 May.[34] This flurry of legislative activity enabled President Kennedy to sign the Omnibus Judgeship Act of 1961 on 19 May, only four months after entering office. The act created seventy-three federal district and circuit judgeships. This included four new district judgeships in Texas, two in the Northern and one each in the Western and Southern Districts.[35]

The Republicans in Congress called upon Kennedy to appoint a "balanced bench" by choosing qualified men from both parties. The senate did not act upon the suggestion,[36] and neither did President Kennedy. By the time he filled the vacancies, which grew slightly during his administration because of deaths and retirements, eighty additional Democrats had taken their seats on the federal bench. Kennedy did, however, appoint eleven Republicans.[37] Kennedy sought to maintain a more important "balance" by appointing judges from both sides of the Democratic divide in Texas. By the early 1960s, according to J. W. Peltason, no successful nominee to a federal district judgeship in the South could provoke the strong opposition of the local, invariably conservative, social, legal, and political elite. This tended, he said, to "rule out lawyers who [had] represented trade unions, publicly advocated civil rights, or otherwise conspicuously participated in liberal causes."[38] Garza was Johnson's man and fit the criteria Peltason described. But the bitter struggle for mastery in Texas between Vice President Johnson and Senator Ralph Yarborough allowed the moderate Kennedy to split the patronage between the factions. The fifth judgeship in the Southern District went to a friend of Senator Yarborough.[39]

James Latane Noel Jr. was born 28 October 1909, in Pilot Point, in Denton County in north Texas. Noel earned the B.S. in civil engineering and commerce in 1932 from Southern Methodist University (SMU) in Dallas. He served as the assistant budget officer of Dallas County from 1935 to 1937, while attending the SMU law school. Noel passed the bar examination and received his license to practice law before he completed his legal coursework, which enabled him to work as a Dallas County assistant district attorney during his last year in law school. Noel earned the LL.B. in 1938 and became an assistant attorney general of Texas. He was responsible for the state's legal business in and around Dallas and Fort Worth. He joined the U.S. Navy during World War II and was assigned to be a legal officer in Hawaii. He reached the rank of lieutenant commander during the war. After his discharge, Noel returned to the attorney general's office and became chief of the oil and gas division. In 1946 he took his experience to Houston and joined Butler, Binion, Rice, and Cook. Noel established his own firm seven years later. He became active in the local and state bar associations, SMU alumni clubs, and the Democratic Party. U.S. Representative Sam Rayburn of Texas, who was Speaker of the House during the 1950s, put Noel's name forward in 1956 to serve a two-year term on the U.S. Commission on Government Security.[40]

Kennedy named Noel, at Yarborough's urging, to the fifth judgeship in the Southern District. On 16 March 1962, during the second session of the Eighty-seventh Congress, the Senate confirmed the recess appointment.[41] Senator Yarborough commented after the vote, "This is a most historical occasion," because "it is the first time in the history of the United States that the nominations of four U.S. district judges in my home State of Texas have been sent to the Senate by one President, and it is the first time that four such nominations have been confirmed by the Senate in 1 day."[42]

Yarborough then described the personal qualities of each of the new judges and introduced their biographical sketches into the *Congressional Record.* The senator claimed to know Noel very well, through their shared years of public service. They met in 1938, Yarborough said, when Noel was an assistant attorney general in Dallas and Yarborough was a state district judge in Austin. Noel "tried many cases in that court," Yarborough remembered, claiming, "I learned then of his outstanding ability."[43]

THE HUMANE AND LIBERAL CHARACTER OF ADMIRALTY LAW

Maritime litigation was a staple of judicial business in the Southern District of Texas.[44] One-third of the 1,111 civil cases that were filed in the district in 1960 were on admiralty dockets. That year, in fact, the Southern District ranked as the nation's fourth busiest admiralty forum, according to the total number of maritime cases filed. It was the third busiest court, if the work is measured by maritime cases per judge.[45] Many of these cases were filed in admiralty, however, merely because they involved disputes regarding ships, ship's cargo, ship's owners, or ship's insurers. If cargo arrived damaged, if a ship collided with the dock or with another ship, or if a maritime worker suffered a debilitating injury or death on the job, then the resultant legal dispute over fault or damages became a matter for an admiralty judge.[46]

A large proportion of admiralty cases filed every year were worker compensation or personal injury suits initiated by maritime workers. Except for the fact that the plaintiffs, or "libellants," as the plaintiffs are known in admiralty cases, are sailors, longshoremen, or harbor workers, these sorts of suits are almost indistinguishable from other personal injury cases.[47] The relief available under the statutory and judge-made rules of admiralty turned on the distinction, drawn by a particular federal district judge in a specific case, between a claimant who could be classed as a "seaman" and the variety of maritime workers who lacked that status.[48] As with complaints regarding the federal judiciary's role in school desegregation, moreover, conservatives within the specialist's arcane world of admiralty law criticized judges who granted seamen's benefits to injured workers who were not seamen. An example of convergence of criticisms of judicial activism came from the authors of the leading admiralty text of the 1950s. They were moved to comment that "the perils of the sea, which mariners suffer and shipowners insure against, have met their match in the perils of judicial review."[49]

Judges in the Southern District of Texas occasionally did extend seamen's remedies further than some conservative critics would have endorsed. Some granted to land-based personal injury plaintiffs judicial relief which either ancient marine customs or relatively recent Congresses had conferred exclusively on the "true" or "blue water" seamen who were crew members of ocean-going ships. In deciding the seaman's injury cases, the judges blurred the line between law, equity, and admiralty. This harmonized with a long-standing rule of the federal judiciary that "it better becomes the humane and liberal character of proceedings in admiralty to give than to withhold the remedy."[50] But, if the judges in the Southern District made decisions in admiralty cases with a preference for "humane and liberal" results, they usually did so well within the statutory and customary distinctions.[51]

Carl O. Bue, one of Houston's most respected admiralty lawyers, wrote in 1966 that the explosive increase in seaman's personal injury litigation since World War II had "outstripped any other aspect of the maritime law." The field of maritime personal injury law was undergoing constant rapid change, Bue said, like the "volcano that continues in eruption." This had the unfortunate result, he announced, that "no charts can be reliable, even until the next term of the court."[52] Bue agreed explicitly with the admiralty textbook authors just mentioned, who had concluded that "a revolution has taken place" in rules governing maritime workers' remedies. Although the authors noted that by the late 1950s "the main outlines of the new law [were] reasonably clear," they predicted that "the lower courts will be occupied for a generation in filling in the details."[53] Bue lamented that until the details were known, proctors such as himself could not assume that federal district judges would observe the various substantive and procedural differences that had historically developed and formally still existed between admiralty and equity.[54]

As he regarded the increase in personal injury suits, moreover, the conservative Bue was troubled that dramatic growth was accompanied by "a noticeable increase in emphasis upon equitable considerations in the admiralty decisions, with less reliance being placed upon the application of stare decisis and the letter of the law." The intrusion of equity into admiralty paralleled "the trend of the law in various nonmaritime areas."[55] Specifically, he had noticed an increase in admiralty suits filed in personam, against individuals, rather than brought in rem, which were liens against property such as ships. Bue recognized that admiralty's absorption of equity was incomplete. He noted, for example, that federal district courts still refused to issue injunctions, which was an equitable remedy, except in a few cases, such as limitation of liability proceedings. At the time Bue was writing, admiralty was still isolated, procedurally, from the other domains of federal jurisdiction. That isolation was ended in 1966, however, when Congress formally merged admiralty procedures with the revised federal rules of civil procedure. Bue worried that, after unification, "admiralty actions will have access to all equitable remedies including injunctive relief."[56]

Bue and other conservative lawyers who specialized in admiralty law considered these innovations to be misguided and unnecessary, because maritime law already encompassed a variety of flexible and charitable remedies that were based on customary law but sustained by modern statutes. Judges had long regarded seamen as "poor and friendless" individuals, for example, who became the "wards" of admiralty courts whenever they sustained injury. As U.S. Supreme Court Associate Justice Joseph Story once observed when on circuit duty in the nineteenth century, these customary guarantees of judicial protections for seamen served "the great public policy of preserving this important class of citizens for the commercial service and maritime defense of the nation" by encouraging individuals to "engage in perilous voyages with more promptitude, and at lower wages."[57]

Under maritime law, an injured seaman was entitled to receive "maintenance and cure" from his employer, and if it was denied, he could seek relief from a federal judge to gain it.[58] This tradition preceded by centuries the development of a workmen's compensation remedy for land workers. In the early twentieth century, however, the U.S. Congress as well as state legislatures sought to improve economic conditions and workplace safety for industrial workers. As a result, maritime workers' benefits lagged in comparison with those of mainland workers.[59] Industrial workers might win damages, while seamen's relief for work-related injuries was limited to his contracted wages and the old "maintenance and cure." Under general maritime law, moreover, a sailor was entitled to an indemnity for his future lost wages only if his injury was due to the vessel's unseaworthiness, not if another crew member was at fault.[60]

Congress had repealed a similar "fellow-servant" rule for railroad employees engaged in interstate commerce and authorized monetary damage awards for employers' negligence, with the Federal Employees' Liability Act (FELA) of 1908.[61] To bring parity between the nation's seamen and its industrial workers, Congress increased the former's benefits through the La Follette Seaman's Welfare Act of 1915, which regulated a seaman's wages, treatment, and working conditions. Its Section 20 abolished a fellow-servant (or perhaps, a "fellow-sailor") rule for injuries occurring aboard ships.[62] But the U.S. Supreme Court subsequently overturned Section 20, ruling that a seaman's claims were satisfied by maintenance and cure.[63]

Congress revisited the issue in 1920. Section 33 of the Jones Act abolished contributory negligence under the fellow-sailor doctrine, and allowed recovery of damages for injury or death that resulted from the negligence of a ship's owner, master, or crew members. The act further provided that "[a]ny seaman who shall suffer personal injury in the course of his employment may, at his election, maintain an action for damages at law with the right of trial by jury." Finally, it applied to an injured seaman "all statutes of the United States modifying or extending the common-law right or remedy in cases of personal injury to railway employees."[64] The Jones Act incorporated standards of negligence established under FELA. It was not immediately clear, however, what this change actually meant for seamen. The federal district judges subsequently had to adapt "a statute transplanted from the switchyard to navigable waters" to account for "the essential differences in conditions and circumstances of employment."[65] Although the Jones Act allowed wrongful death suits for negligence, for example, it did not allow such recovery for unseaworthiness. And the Jones Act did not define "seaman."[66]

Due to these and other perceived deficiencies, the Congress passed the Longshoremen's and Harbor Workers' Compensation Act (LHWCA) in 1927. The seamen's unions had lobbied successfully to maintain merchant mariners in a separate category from stevedores and, at the same time, denied to the members of a ship's crew the right to sue under the LHWCA. The statute limited relief for injuries suffered by longshoremen and harbor workers to fixed compensation benefits, in contrast to maintenance and cure, which continued during the time of disability.[67]

Despite the LHWCA's statutory distinctions, longshoremen and harbor workers remained "seamen" for some purposes, under the general maritime law.[68]

One result of this legislative attention has been that maritime personal injury litigation became, as one admiralty lawyer put it, "one of the most dynamic, complex and rapidly changing areas of the law," where "both the courts and the Congress have sought to fashion new remedies to meet the social, economic and human needs resulting from ever-expanding maritime operations."[69] But another result of the multiplication of the customary and statutory protections afforded seamen and other maritime workers is that in lawsuits injured workers seek to be defined in the terms that will maximize their potential relief under federal admiralty jurisdiction. As a consequence of these exercises in self-definition, Fifth Circuit Judge John R. Brown, who practiced admiralty law before his appointment to the federal appellate court, noted that this case added "a further wrinkle" to "the never ceasing riddle" for the federal courts. That riddle was sorting a working seaman's legitimate claim for relief from that of "the ambiguous amphibious worker." The issue, with "its tri-cornered intramural controversy between state-federal compensation and the ubiquitous possibility of a pseudo-seaman's claim," according to Circuit Judge Brown, was complicated by "the mutations in the vast body of law as it passed through the phases of maritime but local, the twilight zone, the first-come-first-served theory and as some might characterize the most recent development, the doctrine of the last chance."[70]

The vagaries of seaworthiness and negligence as legal categories were at the heart of many seamen's personal injury lawsuits. The legal distinctions between seagoing and land-based maritime work further complicated the judge's task. One Southern District case involved longshoremen who were loading wheat in the hold of a ship when they were overcome by fumes of a chemical insecticide. The case required the judge to decide questions of negligence on the part of the owner of the grain elevator and also to rule on the seaworthiness of the ship.[71] In another case the issue was whether the libellant was working as a seaman or an offshore drilling employee at the time he sustained an injury.[72] Another suit involved a seaman who had injured his wrist when a ship's door closed on his arm. The case raised the question, could a swinging door make the ship unseaworthy?[73] The absence of a jury in many of these cases empowered the federal judges with the sort of discretion they exercised while presiding over, for example, a civil rights plaintiff's motion for an equitable injunction.[74]

Judges in admiralty cases often took an active interest in the results and granted relief based on their sense of what was "fair." They often displayed a marked preference for libellants. This harmonized with a long-standing attitude of the judiciary, that admiralty ought to be "humane and liberal." The quest for "humane and liberal" outcomes sometimes led judges to stretch the definition of *seamen.* One admiralty lawyer complained that judges applied the rules unevenly, and in the absence of proper Supreme Court guidance, he noted, "federal appellate courts have created their own inconsistent definitions of the term [seaman]."[75]

Judge Connally encountered difficult questions of legal definition and distinction in one maritime case he heard, yet he demonstrated no tendency to bend customary or statutory rules of admiralty in favor of equity. The case arose from an accident aboard the SS *Grelmarion,* which was berthed in Galveston, Texas, to receive a cargo of wheat from a pier-side grain elevator owned and operated by the city. The grain was poured directly from the elevator's spout into the ship's storage bins, and longshoremen then "trimmed" the resulting piles of wheat, that is, they used shovels to move the pile of grain from the center of the bin to the corners. Late on 14 March 1957, when bin number 2 was about three-quarters full, the elevator operator released a last "shot" of grain, which filled the bin to the hatch opening. This hatch was the only passage for entering or exiting the storage bin, and the only source of ventilation. The grain in this last shot had been treated with a chemical insecticide, and noxious fumes were concentrated in the closely confined area. The longshoremen became disoriented, dizzy, and hysterical, effects apparently brought on by the fumes. But with the assistance of deck personnel, they dug themselves out. Eight were disabled for extended periods but received medical treatment and compensation payments of between five hundred and fifteen hundred dollars under the LHWCA.[76]

The afflicted longshoremen sought additional damages for the injuries, however, and filed suit in admiralty in the Southern District. They charged the city of Galveston with negligence and the ship owners with maintaining an unseaworthy vessel. Under the maritime law "negligence" connoted a breach of the duty imposed upon a "reasonably prudent" shipowner to use due care in selecting and keeping in order "reasonably suitable" equipment. The doctrine of "seaworthiness" imposed an absolute duty to ensure that the ship and equipment were "reasonably suitable" for their intended purposes.[77] Connally agreed that improperly treated grain had been the source of the fumes that brought on the longshoremen's difficulties, but the judge ruled that neither of the "respondents," as the defendants in admiralty proceedings were known, knew or else reasonably should have known that the grain had been improperly treated. Moreover, the judge found that the *Grelmarion*'s cargo spaces were of "customary design and construction," although they lacked a "forced" ventilation system.[78] Connally ruled that there was no negligence and that the vessel was not unseaworthy, and on 24 March 1959 he ruled in favor of the city and the shipowner.[79] The longshoremen appealed. Judges from the Fifth Circuit affirmed Connally's judgment.[80]

The U.S. Supreme Court granted certiorari, because the complaint involved "a seemingly significant question of admiralty law."[81] On 11 June 1962 Justice Stewart, for five members of the court, affirmed Connally's major findings that neither Galveston nor the owner were negligent, and that even if unventilated the *Grelmarion* was seaworthy.[82] Justice Douglas, joined by two fellow justices, dissented on the ground that because the ship lacked a ventilation system it became temporarily unseaworthy while fumigated grain was being loaded.[83] More "seemingly significant" is the conclusion, as Connally and the circuit judges had ruled and the justices accepted without comment, that longshoremen belonged to the class of maritime workers owed the duty of seaworthiness.[84]

Connally faced similar questions of legal distinction and statutory definition in a case arising from the injury of Clarence D. Tipton, who worked as an oil-drilling roughneck. Tipton plied his trade for the Socony Mobil Oil Company on a fixed, offshore platform in the Gulf of Mexico, but occasionally worked aboard the barge that tended the platform. He was injured while performing these secondary duties. Tipton accepted compensation benefits, approximately fourteen hundred dollars, under the LHWCA, as it applied through the Outer Continental Shelf Lands Act (OCSLA).[85] Tipton sued under the Jones Act, and he elected to have his case heard before a jury.

The principal issue for the jury was whether Tipton when injured was a seaman or an offshore drilling employee. At the trial Connally admitted evidence, over the objection of Tipton's attorneys, that he had already accepted compensation under the OCSLA, which had extended the longshoremen's compensation regime to offshore workers. The OCSLA, as did the LHWCA, explicitly denied longshoremen's benefits to a "member of a crew of any vessel."[86] Connally exercised his right to comment on the evidence when charging the jury. He declared that he thought it a fact that Tipton was undeniably a member of the drilling platform's team, but not a member of the barge's crew. The jury, concerned during its deliberations with the potential effect of its decision on Tipton's future legal remedies, asked Connally whether a finding that Tipton was not a seaman left him with an option of further compensation under the OCSLA. The judge sent a handwritten note instructing jurors that they should be concerned only with the question before them, whether Tipton was or was not a seaman at the time of the accident. The jury rejected Tipton's claim of seaman's status and denied him relief under the Jones Act.[87]

On Tipton's appeal the Fifth Circuit affirmed the result. Circuit Judge Hutcheson, for a two-judge majority, held that Judge Connally erred in admitting evidence of earlier LHWCA compensation benefits but ruled that it was a harmless error, since the jury decided against Tipton and had not reached the issue of damages.[88] Circuit Judge Brown, the only judge on the appellate panel who had practiced in admiralty before his appointment to the judiciary, dissented. He agreed with the majority that Connally had acted within his authority when commenting on the evidence of Tipton's employment status. However, the admission of LHWCA evidence was prejudicial. Brown thought that the case should have been reversed and remanded to Connally for a new trial.[89]

On Tipton's further appeal, eight members of the Supreme Court agreed with Judge Brown, that admitting the LHWCA evidence was not a harmless error. The justices declared in a per curiam opinion that the only relevant aspect of the fact that Tipton had accepted compensation was that it indicated what he had considered to be his own legal status. Connally should have framed a more cautionary charge to the jury indicating that the evidence was "not dispositive of the ultimate fact of whether he was a seaman."[90] Once the judge admitted the LHWCA evidence into the case, however, it had a prominent place during the proceedings, which led the jury "to place undue emphasis on the availability of compensation benefits." The justices vacated the jury's judgment on 21 October 1963 and remanded the case to the District Court.[91]

The cases Connally heard regarding maritime workers who were not seamen in the strict sense were modern variations on the ancient theme. A 1963 maritime personal injury case Judge Noel decided in the district's Galveston Division illuminated admiralty doctrines in practice when there were very few modern twists.[92] Burl Haire was a utility mess-man, that is, an assistant in the ship's galley. On 29 August 1961 he signed ship's articles for duty aboard the SS *Steel Seafarer,* a ship that was owned by the Isthmian Lines company, for a general mercantile voyage.[93] The voyage was general in the sense that, under the articles, the *Steel Seafarer* would leave Houston, potentially stop in one or more U.S. ports, visit one or more Mediterranean, Persian Gulf, or Indian Ocean ports, and, perhaps, call at "other ports and places in any part of the world as the Master may direct." The ship would come to a "final port of discharge in the Continental United States."[94]

The ship initially steamed to Galveston to load cargo and provisions for the long voyage. On the morning of 1 September, Haire reported to the ship's officers that he had injured his left wrist during the previous night, when a heavy door of the ship's vegetable "reefer" closed on his arm as he was coming out of the compartment.[95] Haire signed off the ship, went ashore, and made his way to the U.S. Public Health Service (PHS) Hospital at Galveston, where doctors diagnosed several fractures.[96] The doctors admitted Haire to the hospital, where he remained until 16 September. He was then released as an outpatient with a cast on his wrist. The doctors certified that he had reached his "maximum recovery" on 3 October, and Haire received no further treatment.[97]

The *Steel Seafarer* left Galveston on 3 September. The master of the ship noted in his official log that Haire failed to report for duty, and he left a voucher for $28.45 with the company agent, to pay Haire for the three days' wages he had earned on the voyage through Galveston. In the next port of call at New Orleans, the master registered that Haire "failed to join" the ship for the continuing journey.[98] On 18 September Haire went to the office of the Isthmian Lines agent in Galveston and requested his wages. Before paying him the $28.45 (less $3.06 for Social Security and withholding tax), the agent required Haire to sign a "certificate of mutual release" before the shipping commissioner. This was a standard practice, but Haire, under advice from counsel, notified the commissioner that he was signing the form "under protest."[99] Haire sought his full wages, payable through the end of the voyage under the terms of the articles, which he considered due to him because he had been injured *after* the voyage commenced. In addition, he sought damages through a personal injury suit he filed under general maritime law in the Southern District. He based his claim on the *Steel Seafarer*'s unseaworthiness rather than under the Jones Act.[100]

Judge Noel determined that because Haire was the only witness to his own injury, there was insufficient evidence to declare that the Isthmian Lines was liable for negligence in that the company had created unseaworthy conditions aboard the *Steel Seafarer.*[101] Because Haire had unquestionably been injured aboard the ship, however, Noel ruled that he was due the wages promised under the articles he signed.[102] Haire had signed on at the rate of $284.52 per month, and Noel therefore declared that Isthmian Lines owed him $1,166.63 (for wages excluding the money already paid, board and maintenance, and potential overtime). In addition, since the standard maintenance and cure was then $8.00 per day, the judge held that Haire deserved $144.00 for his maintenance between 16 September and 3 October. Judge Noel also awarded 6 percent interest on the total $1,303.63, which he calculated from the date of the judgment until Isthmian Lines actually paid. Finally, Isthmian Lines was to pay Haire's court costs.[103]

Once the facts were established to Judge Noel's satisfaction, his decision had required little more than a multiplication table. Later, Noel regarded the conditions for maintenance and cure in a much more complicated case, but, once more, the amount of relief followed logically after he had sorted out the facts.[104] On 10 April 1964 Charles Pyles Jr., after having been pronounced fit for duty by his doctor, signed articles for a voyage on the SS *Maryland Trader.* During a cleaning operation on 16 July, Pyles had injured his back as he attempted singlehandedly to lift a Butterworth machine, a cleaning unit that employed two rotating nozzles to inject high-pressure steam and hot water into a ship's storage tanks. The second mate treated him the next morning, but Pyles did no further work during the remainder of the voyage, which terminated 28 July at Portland, Oregon. Pyles returned to Texas and entered Galveston's PHS hospital on 31 July. He remained there until 4 August. The staff certified that for another fourteen days Pyles would be "not fit for duty." After those two weeks, he would be "fit for duty." On 20 August Pyles sued American Trading, the owner of the *Maryland Trader*, for damages.[105] Pyles then resumed work and served on several vessels over the next few months. On 16 September, for example, a doctor for the ship *Aimee Lykes* found him fit for duty, and Pyles was hired the same day. He injured his back on 29 October and received maintenance payments from the *Aimee Lykes* from 30 November until 18 December.[106]

According to the jury that decided the case against the *Maryland Trader* on 17 June 1965, Pyles's back injury was entirely his own fault. But the same jury found that he had not yet reached maximum cure. The jury, therefore, essentially overturned the PHS doctor's diagnosis of Pyles's fitness. On the basis of this finding Pyles filed a motion asking for additional maintenance and cure, for a total of 305 days, as well as attorney's fees.[107] American Trader's lawyers opposed the motion on the grounds that Pyles did not qualify for maintenance and cure while employed, and that the maintenance obligation transferred to the last vessel which he served. Finally, American Trader asserted that the case was not a proper one for allowing attorney's fees.[108]

Judge Noel noted the Supreme Court's recent statement that "[m]aintenance and cure is designed to provide a seaman with food and lodging when he becomes sick or injured in the ship's service; and it extends during the period when he is incapacitated to do a seaman's work and continues until he reaches maximum medical recovery."[109] Therefore, according to Noel, the fact that Pyles returned to regular employment did not bar his entitlement to maintenance and cure: the jury had just declared that he was actually "not fit" at the time. His right to recovery, moreover, was undiminished by periods of work between the certification as "fit" and the date of the jury verdict that he remained "unfit."[110] And as for the responsibility transferring to his last vessel, the *Aimee Lykes*, the judge noted that the case cited by American Trader involved asthma, a chronic condition, and as precedent was limited to cases involving that sort of recurring condition.[111]

Judge Noel ordered Pyles to return all money received as maintenance and cure from the owners of the *Aimee Lykes*. Noel decreed that American Trader would be liable for 305 days at $8 per day, or $2,440. However, the judge found that American Trader acted in good faith when it trusted the PHS prediction that Pyles was fit for duty. Because attorney's fees were allowed as damages only in cases of bad faith or when a company had acted callously or unreasonably, the company was not liable for fees.[112]

Judge Garza decided a pair of cases in summer 1963 that were far more complicated than these claims before Noel. Each was brought in the District's Brownsville Division by the widow of a shrimp boat captain who had operated in the Gulf of Mexico. The cases illustrate the discretion federal district judges enjoyed in Jones

Act cases. Although they shared surface resemblances to each other, the circumstances specific to each captain's death tinted Garza's decision. In the first case Susana Ramirez Moore, the common-law widow of Lindy Adams Moore, who had been master of a gulf shrimper, brought suit in rem against his boat, the *Fram,* and sued in personam its owner, Wilhelm Seafoods, Incorporated.[113] Moore also filed suit under the Death on the High Seas Act (DOHSA), which Congress had passed in 1920 as a companion to the Jones Act. The DOHSA authorized a deceased person's spouse or a representative of the estate to file an action for a wrongful death occurring more than one marine league (6,075 yards, slightly less than three and one-half miles) from the coast of any state.[114]

Lindy Moore drowned approximately twelve miles off the coast of Mexico on the early morning of 7 February 1962. The toilet facilities (or "head") on the *Fram* were not working, and Moore had slipped overboard while sitting on the shrimp boat's rail to relieve himself. The other two crew members immediately stopped the boat, located him with a searchlight, and cast rescue lines in his direction, but Moore drowned before they were able to reach him. The *Fram* had life jackets on board, but the boat had recently been painted, and these items of safety equipment had been moved to the front part of the boat, where they were apparently inaccessible. There was also a rescue ring on board, but at the time of Moore's accident, there was no line attached to it.[115] The attorneys for Wilhelm Foods claimed that, according to the legal doctrine of comparative negligence supported by the Jones Act, Moore had contributed to his own death, and the judge should reduce the company's liability for the accident.[116] Moore had contributed in three ways, they argued. First, he had been drinking on board, against the orders of his employers. Next, as master, he was the person responsible for seeing that the life-saving apparatus was available. Finally, he should not have been sitting on the rail: as an experienced shrimper, he must have known it was slick.[117]

Although a seaman could forfeit his rights to relief through his own gross misconduct, insubordination, and disobedience to orders, which were actions that "even simple men of the calling" ought to recognize as wrong, a seaman could not be contributorily negligent merely by *being* a simpleton.[118] With this customary indulgence in mind, Judge Garza rejected each of the company's points in turn. Instead, on 23 April 1963 Garza ruled that the *Fram* had been rendered unseaworthy by the unavailability of life jackets and a secured ring, and Wilhelm Foods had been negligent in allowing these conditions to exist uncorrected.[119]

Garza discussed the possibility that the inoperative toilet was a proximate cause of the accident, but he dismissed that issue as irrelevant after evidence presented during trial showed that many shrimping crews were accustomed to relieving themselves over the side even when the head was functional. Under the rules of admiralty law, Judge Garza took into consideration Moore's life expectancy, the ages of his surviving family members, especially any children, as well as pain and suffering, when he calculated a monetary damage award. Moore was twenty-eight years old when he drowned. He was survived by two children by Susana, a daughter aged four and a baby son who was born after he had died, and two sons by a previous marriage, aged seven and eight. Moore had also cared for his fifty-four-year-old mother. Under the circumstances, Garza awarded the Moore family a total of $12,500.00, to be divided as follows: Moore's two older sons would receive $1,000.00 each, his mother $500.00, the two youngest children $3,000.00 each, and Susana $4,000.00. In addition, Garza ordered Wilhelm Foods to reimburse Susana $1035.95 for funeral costs, because such expenses were traditionally a part of a seaman's "maintenance and cure."[120]

A shrimp boat captain also died in the second case, but the facts of the second incident were more complex. Three boats, and three captains, were involved: John F. Farmer of the *Fluffy D,* Calvin J. Hebert of the *Arlene,* and Dennis Touchet of the *June.*[121] They were ten miles off the coast of Mexico on 31 May 1962. The shrimpers pulled alongside one another, so that the *Fluffy D* and *Arlene* could off-load their catch into the *June.*[122] After the transfer Captain Touchet invited Hebert and Farmer to his galley for drinks. Although drinking on board was against the rules of the boat's proprietor, the captains consumed two bottles of liquor and some beer in short order. Touchet sent one of his crew to another boat to fetch more liquor. Afterwards, the "talking, laughing, and horse-playing" continued, until Farmer, in reply to a remark from Touchet, referred to his host as a "coon ass," a derogatory name primarily reserved for Cajuns, that is, Louisianans of French descent. In what apparently began as a playful scuffle, Farmer hit Touchet's shoulder and Touchet responded by punching Farmer in the face. As Farmer's nose and mouth began to bleed, he opened his pocket knife, and reportedly asked, "So you want to see blood spill?"[123]

Touchet retreated by jumping to the deck of the *Fluffy D.* Hebert and one of Touchet's crew members tried unsuccessfully to restrain Farmer, and he wounded both of them in the struggle. In addition to his knife, Farmer armed himself with a chain, and he began to swing it as he searched the boat for Touchet. Hebert armed himself with a twelve- to fourteen-inch butcher knife and once more attempted to restrain Farmer. As he confronted Farmer, Farmer made a threatening move toward him. Hebert plunged his knife into Farmer's back and killed him.[124]

Farmer's widow, Mary, sued under both the Jones Act and the DOHSA. Judge Garza found that Captain Touchet had been negligent in several instances. He had encouraged heavy drinking on his boat, had incited Farmer to fight, and had abandoned his boat in a crisis. These factors rendered the *June* unseaworthy. Garza held that Touchet's actions were a proximate cause for Farmer's death. Therefore,

Touchet's employer, the J. R. Hardee Shrimp Company, was liable for damages. The judge also considered that Farmer had contributed to his own death by drinking and "joining in an affray." Garza declared him to be 50 percent responsible for the tragedy. Farmer had been forty-seven years old. The judge calculated that he might have lived another twenty-six years, with fifteen or sixteen of those years as a shrimp boat captain. His wife was forty-five, his daughter was sixteen, and his son was nine years old. Because Farmer was one-half responsible for their loss, Garza awarded seventeen thousand dollars in damages to his survivors.[125]

In the years since the Jones Act's enactment, the federal courts had consistently ruled that negligence provisions were to be read "liberally."[126] Judge Garza followed this practice in these shrimp boat cases. Although he demonstrated the range of maritime remedies available under the Jones Act, Garza did not regard it as the source of unlimited largesse. He was constrained by the Jones Act's provisions. But the act was flexible enough to allow him to rule equitably. Garza considered the circumstances and actions leading to the suit and assessed the economic state of survivors before granting remedies. He measured out the relief carefully, however, because equity meant fairness, not charity.[127] In the case of Farmer's death by stabbing, Garza took into account the needs of his widow and family but was compelled to reduce their award because their provider so clearly shared the blame for the loss.[128]

The Southern District judges enjoyed a great deal of flexibility when granting relief under admiralty laws. But the variety of remedies could not match the variety of accidents. In 1965, for example, Garza heard the case of another seaman's widow who sued the shipping company that had employed her husband. She claimed its negligence caused his fatal heart attack.[129] John Fair worked as an oiler, that is, he was responsible for maintaining various machines in the engine room. He served aboard the cargo vessel MS *Trans Gulf*, from 31 May through 11 June, and then from 26 July through 28 July 1964. On those two occasions, the *Trans Gulf* was discharging bauxite, the primary ore used in aluminum manufacture, at the pier the Reynolds Metals Company maintained near Corpus Christi. Hot air was discharged via a skylight at the top of the *Trans Gulf*'s engine room, but four forced-draft blowers provided most of the ventilation. All ships' engine rooms are hot, but that of the *Trans Gulf* was especially oppressive when the ship was in port discharging bauxite, because, according to a promotional brochure provided by the owners, the vessel had been equipped for "a new and unusual shipping service." They meant that the *Trans Gulf* employed cranes, hoppers, and a conveyor system that encircled the ship. Bauxite was an extremely dusty cargo, however, and the system created a larger quantity of dust than the previous manner of loading. If this dust entered the engine room, it could damage the machinery. To avoid this, the ship's officers closed the engine room hatches and the skylight, and shut down at least three of the four ventilators. Under these conditions the temperature in the engine room was generally above one hundred degrees.[130]

On 11 June Fair experienced chest pains and reported to the captain, who released him from duty and recorded the circumstances in his log: "Reason for separation—medical relief—had a mild stroke about the heart just before the vessel sailed." Fair had requested no assistance and went ashore to the PHS hospital in Corpus Christi. He was treated there and declared fit for duty on 26 July.[131] Fair returned to the *Trans Gulf*, which had undertaken another voyage in the meantime but had returned to Corpus Christi to discharge a new load of bauxite. Fair worked in the engine room until 28 July, when he once again suffered chest pains. These were diagnosed (the record is unclear by whom) as angina pectoris. An engineering officer and a seaman's union patrolman helped Fair negotiate the ship's stairways to his quarters. Later, he met the captain and told him he would have to leave the ship again. As before, Fair made his way to the captain's cabin to be formally signed off from the ship, and once more he went to the hospital without assistance. Fair was treated but suffered a heart attack and died on 15 December.[132]

Fair's widow sued the owner of the *Trans Gulf* under the Jones Act.[133] Although Fair's heart condition had probably deteriorated during a very long period of time, Judge Garza held that there was an obvious causal connection between the working conditions aboard the *Trans Gulf* and Fair's heart attack. The widow testified that various activities unconnected with his employment also caused Fair to experience chest pains, but Garza found that this did not negate the connection between the *final* heart attack and the exertion of climbing so many stairs and working in an oppressively hot and poorly ventilated area of the engine room. The judge ruled that conditions were unsafe as a result of the shipowner's negligence in not providing proper ventilation. He declared that the "great efficiency provided by the equipment aboard this vessel in discharging a cargo, was not matched by a ventilating system sufficient to maintain minimal conditions for working safely within the engine room."[134] Before the 11 June incident, Garza noted, Fair's heart condition might have been unknown, but after Fair's first episode, the ship's master should have been aware of the health risk created by the working conditions in the engine room. In addition, Garza found that the shipowner was negligent because, in the interim between attacks, no one had attempted to solve the ventilation problem. Finally, the company's employees had simply allowed Fair, a sick man, to climb stairs, leave the ship, and make his way to the hospital without assistance.[135]

Judge Garza heard evidence regarding Fair's lifetime earning potential based on recent earnings as well as his probable life and work expectancy as a person forty-six years old, with his existing heart condition. From this information, the judge calculated the earnings that Fair would have contributed to his wife had he lived.

Garza decided that the pecuniary loss to the widow, including earnings attributable to the shipowner's negligence, was $18,000. He added funeral expenses of $1,737.[136]

DISTINCTIONS SO NICE AS TO BE ARBITRARY

The Southern District judges did not transgress boundaries that Congress had set for seamen. As they concurrently managed a changing economy and technological transformations in the maritime professions, the federal district judges and Congress retained the ancient custom of reserving special legal remedies for seamen. The Jones Act and the seaworthiness doctrine afford seamen redress not available to mainland plaintiffs. The guardian-ward relationship of judges to seamen, however, did not result in large awards in personal injury cases. The legal remedies made the injured seaman whole, perhaps, but they did not make him rich.[137]

An interesting counterpoint to the seamen's claims arose in cases that involved land-based workers in the district, that is, disputes concerning employees in construction, manufacturing, and agriculture. These sorts of cases will now receive attention. The cases show close parallels to the judicial role in admiralty, namely, distinguishing workers who were covered by laws granting relief from workers not covered. When deciding to grant or withhold remedies, Southern District judges took into account social and economic considerations. Equitable considerations, if not substantive rules of equity, therefore played an important role in land-based labor law.

In most admiralty and maritime personal injury suits, even in those that featured complex, sometimes even bizarre situations, the obligation for the presiding federal district judge was to distinguish between members of the classes covered by various compensation schemes and the individuals who were not covered. After making that initial determination, the judge's remaining task was comparatively simple. The judge had to decide the level of relief due to an injured seaman according to statutory formulas and judicial precedents. The judge often estimated the relief by resorting to rules of thumb, or, in cases where a seaman's death had resulted, by considering the needs of his survivors. These activities had parallels in more mundane cases of labor law that came before the Southern District judges, including suits filed under federal statutes such as FELA, or even under states' worker's compensation laws, if a plaintiff's claims qualified under the federal district court's diversity jurisdiction.[138]

These kinds of cases were judges' and lawyers' mainstays in the Southern District of Texas. For example, James DeAnda, the plaintiffs' attorney in the 1957 Driscoll school desegregation lawsuit, could not have made a career by participating solely in occasional civil rights litigation. Instead, he represented clients involved in more homely disputes, including injured industrial workers suing employers under Texas's workmen's compensation laws.[139] In addition to compensation for workplace injuries, under the federal Fair Labor Standards Act (FLSA) of 1938, many employees who were "engaged in commerce or in the production of goods for commerce," specifically interstate commerce, were guaranteed a minimum wage, a standard forty-hour work week, and overtime pay.[140]

In some of their private law decisions, federal district judges sought to affect positive change in economic relationships. In other decisions they sought to prevent certain undesirable economic effects. As was true with public law litigation aiming at desegregation, the equitable effect in private law was uneven. The judges were reluctant to intervene in labor disputes in the Lower Rio Grande Valley. Instead, judges tended to respect the divisions between workers that Congress established in labor statutes. Since many laborers in the valley were Mexican-descended, their economic predicament resembled the segregated conditions experienced by the Mexican-descended schoolchildren in south Texas. Judges either accepted the fact that a large number of individuals would remain outside the "covered" class, or else they ignored the fact that employers frequently violated laws regulating conditions, hours, wages, and benefits even when the employees were formally covered. Unlike the schoolchildren, however, adult workers had few private advocates who were willing to sue on their behalf. They depended on the federal Department of Labor to monitor the region, and to file suit to bring employers into compliance with applicable law. The difficulty for agricultural workers, however, was that few federal statutes applied to them.

The FLSA authorized the U.S. Department of Labor to investigate workers' claims and to file suit on their behalf against employers, but the department lacked authority administratively to determine judgment. Congress assigned responsibility for ascertaining the validity of workers' claims to the federal district judges. They could enjoin an employer's failure to pay wages "found by the court to be due to employees under this Act."[141] This directive required a judge to decide whether a specific employee's work was covered by FLSA, which in practice demanded that a judge also determine the boundaries of "interstate commerce," "goods," and "production." The distinctions the judges made according to FLSA were analogous to those they made under the Jones Act regarding "seamen," "negligence," and "unseaworthy." And, as in maritime cases, disputes concerning wages properly due to construction, manufacturing, and agriculture workers demonstrated that small differences in the basis of litigation had large consequences on its outcome. Unfortunately, as Supreme Court Justice Felix Frankfurter observed in 1949, "Both in the employments which the Fair Labor Standards Act covers and in the exemptions it makes Congress has cast upon the courts the duty of making distinctions that often are bound to be so nice as to be arbitrary in relation to each other."[142]

Judge Allred contemplated the scope of FLSA, shortly before he died, in a case that pitted the Labor Department against one of Texas's largest construction firms. In 1958 the Lower Nueces River Water Supply District, which provided water to Corpus Christi, contracted the H. B. Zachry Company to build a large dam approximately fifteen hundred feet downstream from an existing dam. The project would increase the reservoir's total capacity by an order of magnitude and leave the old dam intact but submerged. Because Corpus Christi's local industries consumed approximately half of the water provided by the existing system, and the Supply District expected industrial concerns to continue to use a substantial percentage after Zachry completed the $6 million project, federal inspectors from the Labor Department's Wage and Hour Division concluded that FLSA applied to the dam builders. They reasoned that the water was a "good" produced "for commerce" because facilities that consumed a significant volume of the water engaged in interstate commerce. Zachry had considered the dam project to be local construction and had not been paying its employees the one dollar per hour mandated under the most recent provisions of FLSA. The inspectors sought an injunction to restrain what they charged was Zachry's ongoing violation.[143]

At a pretrial hearing Judge Allred indicated that he tended to accept the labor inspectors' interpretations but denied their motion for a preliminary injunction. He subsequently concluded that Congress had "intended to narrow the scope of coverage" through a 1949 amendment of the 1938 FLSA statute, when it changed the definition of "production of goods," from "employed in producing, manufacturing, mining, handling, transporting, or in any other manner working on such goods, or in *any process* or occupation *necessary* to the production," to the sharper terms "employed in producing, manufacturing, mining, handling, transporting, or in any other manner working on such goods, or in *any closely related process or occupation directly essential* to the production."[144] Notwithstanding this recent statutory limitation, the judge agreed with the federal government's contention that the Zachry Company's workers were engaged in activities that were "closely related" and "directly essential" to the production of goods for commerce. Therefore, he concluded that their construction of the new dam remained within the coverage of FLSA. Allred enjoined the company's wage structure that applied specifically and narrowly to the dam project.[145]

The Zachry Company appealed Allred's ruling. Because the government sought a much broader injunction that would apply not only to the dam construction but to all of Zachry's activities, the Labor Department also appealed the decision. On 5 January 1959, a three-judge panel from the Fifth Circuit unanimously reversed Allred's ruling. For the panel, Circuit Judge Elbert Tuttle wrote that the 1949 substitution of the words "directly essential" for the word "necessary," and the addition of the requirement that covered employment had to be "closely related" to production, had narrowed the statutory definition of "production of goods" more than Allred believed. In light of the FLSA's latest, restricted definition, the appellate judges held that the construction of the dam did not qualify as production of goods for interstate commerce, whatever use to which the water might eventually be put.[146]

The secretary of labor appealed the ruling. On 4 April 1960 Justice Frankfurter, for five members of the U.S. Supreme Court, affirmed the Fifth Circuit's decision, in *Mitchell v. H. B. Zachry Co.* In passing FLSA, Frankfurter said, Congress had attempted to balance its concern for the well-being of all of the nation's workers with a competing desire to avoid displacing the states' power to regulate local activities. The majority justices ruled that the construction's remoteness from production, and the lack of the dam customers' dedication either exclusively or primarily to production, combined to indicate that the activities of the Zachry Company's employees were not "closely related" or "directly essential" to the production of goods for interstate commerce.[147]

By contemporary measures the *Zachry* majority did not hold a narrow view of interstate commerce. Only four years earlier, for example, the justices had rejected a similar distinction between construction and production, to rule that FLSA applied to the builders of a new canal lock on the gulf's Intracoastal Waterway. In that earlier case, however, the court declared that when federal district judges considered the boundaries of interstate commerce in FLSA wage and hour cases, they must rely on "practical considerations" rather than "technical conceptions."[148]

Justice William O. Douglas, joined by three justices, including Chief Justice Earl Warren, dissented. They thought the activities of Zachry's builders clearly met the FLSA's "closely related" and "directly essential" measures of production of goods. The dam would not only supply water to local industries that produced goods in Corpus Christi, but it would also serve the needs of the local railroads, trucking firms, and airlines that would carry products into interstate commerce. With regard to the majority's narrowing of the categories of employment covered by FLSA to exclude such necessary construction, Douglas wrote, "I regret that today we give up territory that Congress has fairly claimed, that we take a backward step from the measures Congress designed to protect the lowest paid and weakest group of wage earners in the Nation."[149] Douglas and the other dissenters declared that through its "retreat" the majority was inviting future "hostile constructions that will undermine the broad base which Congress gave the Act." If the law was to be narrowed, Douglas wrote, then congressional intent ought to be clearer than it had been through the 1949 amendment, because Congress was "far better suited than [the court] to mark the farthest areas which the liberal policies of the Act were designed to cover."[150]

Soon after the *Zachry* decision, the U.S. Court of Appeals for the Eighth Circuit followed its reasoning to declare that construction work on a series of dams was outside the boundaries of FLSA coverage, notwithstanding that the dams crossed the White River Basin in Missouri and Arkansas and that the entire project was supervised by the U.S. Army Corps of Engineers. Circuit Judge Harry A. Blackmun, for a three-judge panel, observed that the decision "may be one of the 'hostile constructions' anticipated" by the *Zachry* dissenters, but the judges concluded nonetheless that the work in question was "essentially collateral and local."[151]

Despite the fact that *Zachry* allowed some narrowing of FLSA, subsequent Fifth Circuit decisions indicated that Douglas's dire predictions were exaggerated. For example, the Labor Department sought an injunction against the P. & L. Equipment Company, a Houston construction firm that paid its night watchman, a man named Taylor, less than the FLSA minimum wage. The government argued that Taylor was involved in interstate commerce because he guarded a portion of a Houston street under construction which, when completed, would pass under a railroad bridge. Moreover, the street would lead into, but not be designated a segment of, a U.S. highway. Finally, the street would be used, on occasion, by trucks carrying the U.S. mail. These factors did not persuade Judge Connally, who concluded that Taylor's work on a city street was an isolated and local activity. In December 1962 Fifth Circuit Chief Judge Hutcheson, for a two-to-one plurality of a three-judge panel, declared that "the case [was] a simple one," that the Labor Department had "the right of it on the facts and the law," and that Connally had erred. The Fifth Circuit panel reversed his decision in a very brief opinion. The third judge wrote a much longer dissenting opinion, which like Connally's decision relied heavily on the *Zachry* rationale.[152]

Other Southern District judges also leaned on the *Zachry* precedent during the 1960s, and also faced reversal by the Fifth Circuit. For example, Judge Garza dismissed the Labor Department's wage claims against a shoe retailer doing business in several states, since the administrative and clerical employees in question merely handled paperwork regarding sales at four stores in Texas. The circuit reversed Garza, on the grounds that the employees worked with financial records that they later mailed to the home office in Saint Louis. These actions, the unanimous three-judge panel concluded, drew the office workers into interstate commerce. When they reversed Garza's decision in August 1967, the circuit judges noted that, even at that late date, the federal courts had developed "no dependable touchstone or acceptable standard for ascertaining whether an employee is engaged in commerce." In place of hard and fast rules for deciding FLSA disputes, the appellate panel stated, the "enforcement of the Act and its application to particular fact situations require the courts to utilize an empirical process of drawing lines from case to case."[153]

Garza thereafter followed the Fifth Circuit's lead. The next year, he ruled in favor of the Labor Department's request to enjoin a small loan company in Brownsville, because it received funds from and mailed reports to another company in Nashville,

Tennessee. When he issued the injunction, he referred explicitly to the Fifth Circuit's reversal of his earlier decision regarding shoe stores.[154] The loan company appealed. In a one-paragraph per curiam opinion, the Fifth Circuit judges declared that they agreed "in all material respects" with Garza's opinion.[155]

These and many similar FLSA decisions throughout the decade did not "undermine the broad base" of the act, as Douglas had warned. Instead, many federal judges strove to distinguish the facts that led to the Supreme Court's *Zachry* decision from the facts in many subsequent cases. This necessitated a swift about-face by the Fifth Circuit judges, because *Zachry* had affirmed their own 1959 ruling. But after narrowing FLSA in *Zachry*, a majority of Fifth Circuit judges subsequently committed themselves to draw the circle of interstate commerce around as many workers as possible. The Southern District judges fell in line. They did not yield territory "fairly claimed" by Congress, as Douglas had feared, and they had not abandoned "the lowest paid and weakest group of wage earners in the Nation." But, judicial constructions that almost invariably distinguished *Zachry* from new cases confounded FLSA's provisions and blurred its critical distinctions.[156]

Agriculture further compounded the problem of distinctions under FLSA, especially for the Southern District judges. Thousands of farm and ranch hands in the Lower Rio Grande Valley of south Texas cultivated diverse vegetables and citrus fruits, and tended cotton, grain, and livestock. During the 1960s the fertile fields in Cameron, Hidalgo, Starr, Zapata, and Webb Counties, which adjoined the U.S.-Mexico border, yielded more than $25 million worth of citrus fruit and $50 million worth of vegetables every year. The valley farmers shipped approximately 65 percent of these crops to other states by rail or truck, or to foreign countries through the ports in Brownsville and Corpus Christi.[157] These crops clearly entered interstate and international commerce, and many farm workers followed the jobs from state to state. Yet, Congress exempted agricultural workers from FLSA wages and hours provisions.[158]

But the act's exemptions were as open to judicial interpretation as its inclusions. For example, Judge Garza ruled in 1964 that a crop dusting pilot and the person who waved a flag to guide the pilot to the proper field to be dusted were agricultural workers and therefore were not covered by FLSA. But the mechanic who repaired and maintained the airplane *was* engaged in commerce, not in agriculture, and was covered. The Fifth Circuit affirmed this distinction.[159]

The differences between agricultural work and employment covered by FLSA were also at issue in the complaint the Labor Department filed against J. L. Beck, where circumstances were more convoluted than in the crop-dusting case. Beck was president, principal owner, and manager of two manufacturing businesses in Beeville, Texas, the Fortuna Broom Company and the South Texas Broom Corn Company. Beck had several full-time, year-round employees but hired extra workers each summer, when area farmers harvested their broom corn and brought it to Beck's firms for processing. During this busy season Beck hired minors as well as adults, and all worked long hours. A substantial percentage of the broom corn the two companies handled and processed, and most of the brooms and mops they produced, were shipped and sold outside Texas.[160] Beck did not keep accurate records of his seasonal employees, their employment periods, the number of hours each worked per day or week, or, in many instances, the wages he paid them. FLSA regulations required all this information. Moreover, Beck often paid summer employees in cash; yet his corporations kept no consistent records of the payments.

Beck's bookkeeping habits confounded government inspectors. They could not establish which employees worked for Beck personally at any particular time or for which company they worked. The inspectors had no doubts that Beck paid the majority of his employees less than the minimum wage and never paid them for overtime work. Also, Beck had violated the child labor prohibitions of FLSA. The Labor Department filed a formal request for an injunction from Judge Garza, seeking both to force Beck to pay back wages and overtime compensation, and to forbid future violations.[161]

At the trial Beck's defense attorneys argued that, although the Labor Department had free access to the books and records of both companies and to Beck's personal financial records, the government could not provide Garza with the documentation necessary to determine the wages or overtime pay Beck allegedly owed to his employees. But Garza noted that an investigator had compiled adequate information from the incomplete records and made a transcription that Garza ruled to be "accurate and worthy of belief." Also, several of Beck's full-time employees at Fortuna and South Texas had kept their own records, on calendars or other personal papers, which showed their work patterns. Garza, impatient with Beck's argument that sloppy bookkeeping ought to exempt him from making good on his obligations to his employees, declared that "[t]o allow the Defendants here to shirk their duties under the Act because of their failure to keep proper records, would be placing a premium on their failure to conform with their statutory duty."[162]

Beck's lawyers offered another, only slightly more substantial, defense against his having to pay back wages to at least a few employees. Most of Beck's workers had processed the broom corn after farmers harvested it from the fields. Therefore, the defense attorneys argued, those workers had handled agricultural commodities bound for the market and were exempt from the FLSA's minimum wage and overtime pay provisions. Furthermore, Beck occasionally sent his broom company employees to perform tasks on farms he owned near Beeville. Beck's attorneys claimed that those employees were also exempt from the FLSA's provisions. Garza gave little credence to these contentions. Of the latter excuse, the judge observed that "[w]hile it is true that some of these employees did work for a few hours or a day or two on the farms belonging to Mr. Beck," the employees primarily worked at his manufacturing concerns and so were subject to the FLSA.[163]

Judge Garza concluded that over the course of three years, Beck withheld the minimum wage and associated overtime pay from many employees who qualified for FLSA coverage. All had worked for Beck for different amounts of time, and received different pay for their hours worked, ranging from $50.00 to $70.00 per week for the adults and between $.30 and $.50 per hour for the minors. Garza estimated how many hours each employee had worked over the years. At the applicable statutory rates, which for work accomplished before 3 September 1963 was $1.15 per hour and $1.25 per hour thereafter, Garza calculated that Beck owed back wages that ranged from $120.90 due to one teenager to $3,367.67 due to one adult employee. In round numbers Garza reckoned that Beck owed a total of approximately $14,000.00 in back wages. The judge ordered Beck to pay each individual worker the amount owed and enjoined him from violating FLSA in the future.[164] Beck appealed, but the Fifth Circuit upheld Garza's ruling.[165]

Unlike Beck's marginally agricultural corn-broom makers, many south Texans were unquestionably employed in agriculture. For them the most important labor statute, at least until the mid-1960s, was not FLSA but the federal Migratory Labor Act (MLA). It regulated wages, benefits, and other employment relations between American growers and Mexican nationals who came to the United States to work in agriculture.[166] The MLA established the regulatory framework for the Mexican Labor Program, customarily known as the bracero system (the term translates roughly as "strong arms," from the Spanish *brazo*), which had provided U.S. employers with contracted "guest workers" since the 1940s. Under the MLA, the Congress authorized the secretary of labor to allow a specified number of Mexicans to establish temporary legal residence in the United States, to work on farms and ranches according to standard contracts. The United States negotiated the initial bracero agreement with the Mexican government during World War II, to replace the large number of Americans serving in the armed forces. Promoters of the idea argued that unless Mexicans were admitted to pick crops, the fruit and vegetables necessary to feed troops would rot in the fields. After the war ended, the two governments renewed the program.[167] The first bracero program lasted from August 1942 to December 1947; a second version was in effect from February 1948 to 1951, to supply labor during a wage dispute; and a third incarnation arose in 1951, to supply farm labor during the Korean conflict. The lawmakers reauthorized the program until 1965.[168]

The MLA authorized the Department of Labor to provide prospective bracero workers with transportation to and from Mexican recruitment centers, to establish "reception centers" in the United States for the workers, and to feed and house them until they were hired. The federal government helped bracero workers secure the "Standard Work Contract," which provided for transportation to and from job sites. A "standard" contract also provided that "employers shall pay the Mexican worker not less than the prevailing wage rate paid to domestic workers for similar work at the time the work is performed and in the manner paid within the area of employment, or at the rate specified in the work contract, whichever is higher," and empowered the secretary of labor to determine the "prevailing wage rate." The secretary could also forbid the braceros to accept employment if the wages offered were "insufficient to cover the Mexican worker's normal living needs." These provisions for extensive Labor Department supervision of employment benefits served several disparate purposes. First, the oversight would fulfill the U.S. government's obligation to prevent American employers from exploiting their Mexican workers. Next, it allowed the department to increase the labor supply during the peak harvesting seasons. Finally, the regulations enabled the government to monitor the braceros' effects on the wages and working conditions of domestic workers, that is, those who were U.S. citizens rather than "guests." The labor secretary's obligation to maintain parity between domestic workers' wages and braceros' wages was implicit in the MLA's requirement that "Mexican workers shall not be employed . . . in any jobs for which domestic workers can be reasonably obtained or where [the employment of bracero workers] . . . would adversely affect the wages and working conditions of domestic agricultural workers."[169] In addition, the statute empowered the secretary to curtail the supply of bracero workers unless Labor Department officials had certified that "able, willing, and qualified" domestic workers were not available in numbers sufficient to satisfy employers' labor needs, that the employment of bracero workers would not adversely affect domestic wages, and that the employers had made reasonable efforts to attract and hire domestic workers.[170]

The MLA did not authorize the labor secretary to enforce a minimum wage for agricultural workers in contradiction to exemptions in FLSA. However, through manipulations of the estimated "prevailing wage," the terms of the "standard" contract, and the number of authorized bracero workers, government officials could indirectly regulate farm wages. The resultant wages, especially piecework rates for crops harvested by the bushel or crate, were invariably below the FLSA minimum wage. Even so, the "prevailing wage" was often higher than the wage employers wanted to pay, and farm and ranch owners in the valley frequently supplemented the labor force with undocumented workers. Unlike legal and regulated braceros, these illegal employees did not work under federal government oversight, except for encounters with the officers of the U.S. Border Patrol, the uniformed service of the Immigration and Naturalization Service (INS).[171] From the employers' point of view, the potential for run-ins with the INS added at least one benefit. Undocumented workers were unlikely to complain about low wages and poor conditions when they could be threatened with arrest and deportation.[172] But farm and ranch owners who supplemented the authorized braceros with undocumented workers did not fear arrest. The Immigration and Nationality Act of 1952 (the McCarran-Walter Act), provided that employers were not to be charged with the crime of "harboring" illegal immigrants. This immunity from prosecution was contained in the so-called "Texas Proviso," named for its major proponents, U.S. Senator Lyndon B. Johnson and House Speaker Sam Rayburn.[173]

As a result of the FLSA's agricultural exemptions, the long life of the bracero program, and the constant presence of illegal but tolerated undocumented workers, the labor market in the valley operated in management's favor. Individual employers did not always approve of specific Labor Department decisions, and in some instances they drew the federal judiciary into disagreements. In 1960 numerous growers asked U.S. District Judge Joe M. Ingraham to enjoin the Labor Department's determinations that they were no longer eligible to employ bracero workers because they allegedly had violated the record-keeping provisions of the MLA. In the first case Ingraham found for the plaintiffs and issued the injunction. The Fifth Circuit court reversed the ruling, however, on the grounds that the growers had not named the secretary of labor as a defendant, when he was an indispensable party to the suit.[174]

For varied reasons, the expiration of the bracero program did not immediately improve conditions for domestic farm workers. First, Congress did not repeal the FLSA's agricultural exemption. Second, U.S. workers still faced potential competition from Mexican laborers because private individuals, rather than the government, could legally recruit and hire resident aliens with INS "green cards" if the Labor Department declared a shortage of domestic workers. Third, undocumented immigration from Mexico increased dramatically soon after the bracero program expired.[175] Fourth, national unions were slow to capitalize on the program's demise. Rather than organizing the agricultural workers, they studied the issue.[176]

Factors dooming most attempts to organize the valley's farm workers included extensive reliance on piece rates for harvesting crops, the seasonal nature of migrant agricultural work, and the ready availability of laborers, domestic, legal, and illegal, hirable through independent brokers known as "crew leaders."[177] Although Texas historically is an antiunion state, vigorous local unions of industrial or maritime workers existed.[178]

But Congress amended FLSA on 23 September 1966.[179] Effective 1 February 1967, agricultural workers were covered under the minimum wage provisions of FLSA. However, the nation's agricultural employees were still a special class under the amended law. The minimum wage for farm workers lagged behind the minimum established for other employees. Agricultural workers were still exempt from overtime provisions of the act. Approximately three-quarters of the farm workers were still not covered by the FLSA's provisions. As usual, the actual boundaries of the exemptions and the variations in practice became subject to judicial interpretation.[180]

The FLSA case the Labor Department filed in 1969 against Barr Ewing, who operated a large farm in Hidalgo County, traced the transitions in the agricultural exemptions. From 1967 to 1969, Ewing contracted to level land for other farmers in the Lower Rio Grande Valley. He leased his tractors, trailers, and drivers to the Progresso Co-op Gin, to haul cottonseed to producers of cottonseed oil. Federal inspectors concluded that while administering his several businesses, Ewing had violated the wage, overtime, and record-keeping requirements of FLSA. The Labor Department sued to restrain Ewing from continuing these alleged violations. Ewing admitted his failure to comply with the FLSA's provisions. Garza's task was simply to determine whether Ewing should have complied. Specifically, he had to decide whether Ewing's personal secretary, his truck drivers, and the mechanics and mechanics' helpers who repaired and maintained his leveling equipment were producing goods for commerce, as the government argued. If so, Ewing was to comply with the FLSA's various provisions. If his employees were subject to the agricultural exemption, as Ewing maintained, FLSA was not relevant.[181]

Wayne Jackel, assistant manager of the Valley Co-Op Oil Mill, testified that all of the cottonseed the mill purchased was commingled before processing, and that between 25 and 50 percent of the cottonseed oil the mill manufactured was shipped outside Texas. Ewing's attorneys argued that there was no evidence that the cottonseed hauled by Ewing's drivers, approximately 2,650 tons during 1968 and 1969, had been processed into cottonseed oil that was later shipped to another state. Garza ruled that the government was not required to trace the source of the cottonseed and cottonseed oil subsequently shipped in interstate commerce. Proof of commingling, in this case proved through testimony, was sufficient. The judge concluded that a "substantial amount" of the cottonseed hauled by Ewing's drivers was rendered into oil, which was eventually shipped outside Texas. Moreover, whether or not a driver was an employee of an interstate manufacturer, it was a well-settled judicial rule that any driver who hauled goods used in the manufacture of goods for interstate commerce was engaged in the production of goods for interstate commerce. Garza ruled that each of Ewing's three regular drivers were covered by FLSA.[182]

Garza then considered Ewing's leveling business. Periodic leveling allowed area farmers to irrigate their fields better and therefore to increase crop production. After 1 February 1967, that is, since the agricultural exemption had been amended, Ewing had entered into approximately one hundred leveling contracts. His employees had leveled approximately twenty-six hundred acres of farmland, most of which produced citrus fruits, vegetables, grain, or cotton. No one testified that the crops raised on any of this acreage had been shipped outside Texas, but in a decision similar to the one he made regarding the commingling of cottonseed, Garza ruled that the government was not required to prove that specific crops were grown on a specific leveled acre. It was sufficient for Garza to note the large volume of leveled land, the diverse farming operations of the region, and the fact that a "substantial amount" of the produce grown in the valley was shipped outside Texas. Logically, the judge assumed that some of the land produced some of the interstate fruit and vegetables.[183]

Questions regarding the remaining scope of the amended agricultural exemption existed in the distinctions Garza made between Ewing's mechanics, who maintained the earth-moving equipment necessary for leveling, and employees who actually operated the leveling equipment. The government conceded that the operators were not covered by FLSA. But the mechanics, the Labor Department argued, were covered. The essential difference was that the mechanics performed a job that facilitated the production of goods, and they performed it away from the field. The equipment operators, however, were engaged in the purely agricultural task of moving dirt. Judge Garza agreed with the government's rationale and noted that there was "no difference" between the mechanics and mechanics' helpers in this case and the mechanic in the 1964 crop-dusting case. Even under the 1966 amendments, employment requiring contact with cropland, that is, work done "on the farm," was still subject to an agricultural exemption.[184]

Moreover, the work done "on the farm" still had to be actual farm work to be exempt from FLSA. Ewing maintained an office at his farm and employed a secretary there to perform general office work consisting of answering the telephone in connection with his business, including land leveling jobs, and the preparation of payrolls for all employees, including the mechanics. This secretarial work took place on the farm, but it was not purely agricultural, in the way driving a tractor was purely agricultural. Rather, the secretary's job was involved with all aspects of Ewing's business, which Garza had already ruled had various connections to interstate commerce. On 27 January 1971 he declared that Ewing had violated the wage, hour, and record provisions of FLSA and issued the injunction the government sought.[185]

The outcome of labor relations cases inevitably turned on the crucial distinctions judges made between interstate and local commerce, as well as on the similarly key divisions of covered and exempted employment. Garza's sorting of Ewing's business concerns demonstrated that legal differentiation remained a fundamental judicial duty after Congress enacted the 1966 amendments to FLSA. Congress eliminated a statutory distinction, which eased the task of judging labor cases. The FLSA finally covered all but the most basic agricultural tasks, such as picking and planting; that is, to quote Justice Douglas, the law protected all but the nation's "lowest paid and weakest group of wage earners." However, the practical effect of the amendment was to shift, but not to eliminate, the line separating covered and exempted categories. Whether the disputes involved maritime, manufacturing, or agricultural employment, the judges' task remained, as Justice Frankfurter observed, a matter of identifying distinctions "so nice as to be arbitrary."[186]

JUST, SPEEDY, AND INEXPENSIVE

Congress frequently received recommendations to expand the judiciary from local, state, and national bar associations, legal scholars, individual courts, and various judicial councils, but before the 1960s the federal judiciary itself had no systematic method for lobbying Congress for the creation of judgeships. The members of the Judicial Conference reviewed at each meeting the materials collected by the Committee on Judicial Statistics and the Committee on Court Administration. The conference approved, denied, or amended any recommendations for judgeships to be forwarded to the Congress every session. The recommendations accumulated during the Eisenhower years, only to be cleaned out through an omnibus act in the first weeks of the Kennedy administration. The Judicial Conference wanted to avoid, if possible, the recurrence of that cycle of events. In September 1964 the conference resolved that it would conduct its own surveys of judgeship needs and make its own recommendations approximately every four years. Congress began periodically to approve unprecedented increases in the judiciary.[187]

Rather than agreeing merely to increase the number of judges endlessly, however, the Congress encouraged the federal judiciary to discover ways to improve judicial efficiency. This approach had many supporters within the legal profession and the judiciary as well. One of the prominent administrative reformers was Warren E. Burger, a judge on the Court of Appeals for the D.C. Circuit. Burger addressed the southern regional meeting of the American Bar Association, in Atlanta, in February 1958 and discussed "The Courts on Trial" (a somewhat disingenuous title, given the criticism of the federal courts in the South at the time). Burger's talk would have been more accurately billed as "The Tribulations of Trial Courts." The future chief justice focused on the "grave and long-standing problem of delays in the administration of justice."[188] In order to reduce the delays caused by caseload congestion, Burger called on leaders of the federal judiciary, specifically chief judges of the circuits, to perfect the "management machinery" they commanded through their judicial councils.[189] Administrators must be their own worst critics, study the problems of the district courts in their circuits, communicate among themselves, sponsor judges' conferences, and, Burger said, "be managers, not just spectators, of how the courts are run."[190]

Rather than simply expanding the number of inefficient judges, these reformers argued that better administration, for example, through the skilled use of pretrial procedures, would enable the judges already sitting to seize control of clogged dockets. They would be better able to facilitate the disposition of protracted cases and finally would secure the goal the federal judiciary enshrined in the first rule of civil procedure: "the just, speedy, and inexpensive determination of every action."[191]

Some suggestions for reform were mutually agreeable to both the judicial and legislative branches of government. Congress created a new government organization in 1967, for example, the Federal Judicial Center, which was to be specifically dedicated to the study of court administration.[192] Individual federal judges probably found other legislative innovations less helpful, as when the Congress abolished terms of court, effective 1 January 1964.[193] This meant that the district courts were to remain in "continuous session" for "the purpose of transacting jurisdictional business, on all business days throughout the year." It is difficult to imagine how this particular reform could have improved efficiency in the Southern District of Texas, where the trials in the six court divisions—Houston, Galveston, Victoria, Corpus Christi, Brownsville, and Laredo—were conducted by only five judges.[194]

Ben Connally became chief judge of the Southern District of Texas on 14 February 1962, the day Judge Hannay turned seventy years old and was required by statute to relinquish that position.[195] As chief judge, Connally gained no new authority or power to wield over his judicial colleagues, except that which arose incidentally from his role as the head of the still small but growing court bureaucracy. In addition to trying the civil and criminal cases on his dockets in Houston, Victoria, and Laredo, and managing his own law clerks, secretary, and court reporter, Connally began to oversee the work of probation officers, bankruptcy judges, U.S. commissioners, and, by decade's end, federal magistrates. To fulfill these new duties, Judge Connally worked closely with the Southern District's clerk of court, V. Bailey Thomas.[196]

The judge had already shown his interest in improving the court's administration. Connally led a lobbying effort in the late 1950s, for example, that succeeded in persuading Congress to limit options to remove land-based workmen's compensation cases from the state courts to the federal courts. According to the data Connally compiled to support the lobbying, the workmen's compensation cases filed during the three years prior to the congressional action had accounted for between one-third and one-half of the civil caseload in all four of the Texas federal district courts.[197] Just after he became the chief judge, Connally completed his three-year elective term (1959–62) as the Fifth Circuit's district judge representative to the Judicial Conference. He had served or was then still serving on several other committees for the conference, including those concerned with supporting personnel

(1950–56) and court administration (1955–75). He was later chair of the conference's subcommittee on judicial improvements (1971–75). He was also a charter member of the Metropolitan Chief Judges Conference.[198]

As chief judge, Connally was responsible for implementing many of the administrative changes that congressional and judicial reformers contrived during the 1960s. In addition to worrying generally about administration, Connally also became the Southern District judge who had to worry specifically about the caseloads that were once again on the rise. He received the memorandum, for example, from the Fifth Circuit's chief judge, Elbert P. Tuttle, in September 1964, that shared the results of a study undertaken by the Judicial Conference's Committee on Judicial Statistics. The committee had counted civil actions that had been filed in federal district courts before 1 July 1961 that were still pending on 30 June 1964. The review showed that there were 135 of these three-year-old cases on the dockets in the Southern District of Texas. Of these, 111 were on the Houston dockets, and only one (a land dispute) was in the Victoria Division. Tuttle was just passing along the information to the district courts in his circuit, not complaining. He wrote in his cover letter that "[this] is sent, not with the idea that any specific steps are to be taken, but as a reminder that may enable you to give such attention to these cases as you find possible under the circumstances."[199]

Among the circumstances to which Chief Judge Tuttle referred was that, even with the significant increase in the judiciary that had been authorized by the 1961 Omnibus Judgeship Act, there was a caseload crisis. Chief Justice Warren, in an address he delivered at the annual meeting of the American Law Institute, on 20 May 1964, noted that there were various explanations for the failure of the 1961 act to solve the caseload problem. One was that the nomination and confirmation process took so long that many of the new positions had gone unfilled for several years. Another factor was that it had become the habit of the Congress to let problems of congestion build until they were at the crisis point. Throwing support behind administrative reformers, the chief justice said that the expectation that more and more judges were the solution was misguided. Warren stated that "we will never solve our basic problems merely by adding additional judges."[200] By the middle of the decade, however, even the usual proponents of administrative reform agreed with the Judicial Conference that it was also necessary for Congress once more to expand the judiciary.[201]

Vice President Johnson had hoped to have the fifth judgeship in the Southern District of Texas go to another of his supporters, a Houston attorney named John V. Singleton Jr., but the position went to Yarborough's man, James Noel. Despite the defeat, Johnson presided at Judge Noel's swearing-in ceremony at the Music Hall in Houston. That gesture did not mend any fences with the Yarborough camp.

Johnson and Yarborough continued to contest federal appointments. But, through the mediation of President Kennedy, who ultimately was responsible for distributing their patronage, the two Texans were able to strike a balance of power. Johnson suggested to his friend Singleton that he could be the U.S. attorney. Singleton declined, however, and Kennedy appointed Woodrow B. Seals, another Yarborough supporter, to be the Southern District's top federal prosecutor. The careers of the two Houston lawyers, Johnson's protégé Singleton and Yarborough's protégé Seals, remained entwined over the next several years, until their respective patrons had more "plums" to offer them.[202]

Singleton was born in Kaufman, Texas, on 20 March 1918. He attended UT both as an undergraduate, earning a B.A. in 1940, and as a law student. Singleton's long friendship with Lyndon Johnson began at UT in 1941, when, at the suggestion of his friend and fellow student John Connally (who was unrelated to Ben Connally), he volunteered to work on Congressman Johnson's unsuccessful first campaign for the U.S. Senate. Like Judge Noel, Singleton was admitted to the Texas Bar before he graduated. Singleton then took a commission in the U.S. Navy rather than a position in a law firm. He graduated from the Judge Advocate School, worked as a lawyer during World War II, and reached the rank of lieutenant commander. In 1946, after four years in uniform, and four months of postwar work in the Veterans Administration and the Price Administration, Singleton began to practice private law. He became an associate of the Houston firm Fulbright, Crooker, Freeman, and Bates, which later became the firm Fulbright, Jaworski. Singleton and two other Fulbright associates formed their own partnership, Bates, Riggs, and Singleton, in 1953. Three years later, he established a two-lawyer practice, Bell & Singleton, which lasted five years. Finally, he was a partner in Barrow, Bland, Rehmet, and Singleton after 1961.[203] Singleton was once a vice president of the Houston Bar Association and occasionally served as an editor of its publications. But he made his mark in Democratic Party politics. Singleton was a delegate-at-large to the 1956 Democratic convention, and in 1960 he cochaired the Harris County "Johnson for President" Committee.[204]

Woodrow Bradley Seals was born 24 December 1917, in Bogalusa, Washington Parish, Louisiana. Seals entered the Pearl River Junior College in Poplarville, Mississippi, in 1938, and received a junior college certificate in June 1941. He enlisted in the U.S. Army Air Forces in October, was a pilot in Europe during World War II, and attained the rank of major. After his discharge in 1946, Seals enrolled in the UT law school, where he earned his LL.B. in 1949. Seals entered solo practice in Houston and served on a number of advisory committees in the local and state bar associations. He chaired the Houston Bar Association's Committee on Criminal Law and Procedure, chaired a state bar special committee that inquired into revising the Texas Code of Criminal Procedure and was the president of the Houston Criminal Defense Lawyers Association. He was active in the liberal wing of the Democratic Party and became a friend of Senator Yarborough. Seals was also a campaign manager for Kennedy's 1960 campaign and in that role he arranged a pivotal meeting between the candidate and the Houston Ministerial Association that allowed the Catholic Kennedy to address, and to defuse, the issue of the separation of church and state. Memory of that success no doubt predisposed the new president to appointing Seals the U.S. attorney for the Southern District. Once in that position, Seals established his liberal credentials by appointing the District's first African American Assistant U.S. Attorney (AUSA).[205]

Seals's and Singleton's level of personal investment in the feud between Johnson and Yarborough, and the level of pettiness the feud could attain, was revealed during Kennedy's final fund-raising tour of Texas. Singleton was by then a trusted political fixer—the "Texas Contact Man at Demo Headquarters"—for Johnson as well as John Connally, who had been elected governor. Connally asked Singleton to make the arrangements for Kennedy's arrival and departure from Houston on 21 November 1963. Among Singleton's tasks was to organize the receiving line for the president and the first lady. He asked Lyndall Wortham, the wife of the Houston insurance magnate Gus Wortham, to present Jacqueline Kennedy with a bouquet of yellow roses. Just minutes before the president's plane landed, however, Opal Yarborough, the senator's wife, arrived unexpectedly. Singleton did not make a place for her in the receiving line. U.S. Attorney Seals refused to take his own place in the line because Opal Yarborough was excluded. Singleton snatched the roses from Mrs. Wortham and allowed Mrs. Yarborough the honor of presenting them to the first lady. Another crisis developed as the motorcade prepared to leave the airport. The Connallys, naturally, were riding with the Kennedys. Singleton had arranged for the Yarboroughs to ride with the Johnsons. But the senator refused to ride with the vice president. A few moments of confusion followed, until Singleton arranged for the Yarboroughs to ride with Houston's congressman, Albert Thomas, who was to be honored at that evening's fund-raising dinner. The near–blood feud between Johnson and Yarborough took on tragic overtones the next day in Dallas, where President Kennedy was assassinated.[206]

Singleton was a delegate-at-large at the 1964 Democratic Party convention, when Johnson secured the party's nomination for the presidency. He became a regional coordinator for the Johnson-Humphrey campaign, with responsibility for organizing the election effort in eight states.[207] Johnson was reelected, and, with the Republicans dispirited and in disarray after the campaign, it seemed a foregone conclusion that an omnibus judgeship bill would be passed by the Eighty-ninth Congress. Even so, it was not until February 1966 that a member introduced a House resolution that opened the bidding. A Senate bill was in the works a few weeks later.[208] One Republican member of the House voiced the hope, no doubt shared by many of his party colleagues, "that this bill will not be merely considered as a political grab bag, another case of dipping into the patronage pork barrel to reward the party faithful." But the Republicans already knew what sort of balance to expect from the president. Of the thirty-five federal judges Johnson had appointed during his first two years in office, only one was a Republican.[209]

President Johnson signed the new Omnibus Judgeship Act on 18 March 1966. The legislation created some four dozen judgeships, including three federal district judgeships in Texas. The Western District gained a fourth judgeship. The Southern District gained two, for a grand total of seven.[210] Johnson, finally able to reward his old friend, appointed Singleton to the sixth judgeship in the Southern District. He then elevated U.S. Attorney Seals into the seventh seat. The Senate confirmed the appointments of Singleton and Seals on the same day, 22 July 1966.[211] When he signed their individual commissions, however, the president dated Seals's letter one day later than Singleton's. Johnson therefore ensured that his ally would always be senior to his rival's supporter.[212]

Margaret Mayer, a reporter for the *Dallas Times Herald,* noted correctly that the choices of Singleton and Seals simply continued the "50–50 division of Texas patronage" that began when Johnson became vice president.[213] This sort of intraparty horse trading was not limited to Texas, however, and it led to something approaching an ideologically "balanced" (although certainly not a bipartisan) bench. Johnson appointed a total of 125 federal district judges, 41 circuit judges, and 2 justices of the Supreme Court. Johnson's judicial legacy, moreover, despite his reputation for conservatism relative to Yarborough, was a bench that was loaded with supporters of the liberal goals of the "Great Society."[214]

Among the incidental powers that proceeded from the chief judge's responsibility to collaborate with the clerk's office in the management of the court's business was the authority to assign cases to a particular judge. Chief Judge Hannay initially gave the Houston Independent School District (HISD) desegregation case to Ingraham, for example, who was the most recently appointed judge at the time, the sole Republican, and a native of Oklahoma rather than Texas. Any, all, or none of these details may have been significant factors in Hannay's choice, but scheduling conflicts on Ingraham's docket reportedly led Hannay to shift the controversial desegregation case to Judge Connally.[215]

Most civil actions filed in the federal district courts were more prosaic than bedeviled, however, and the chief judge was able simply to establish the criteria for the clerk to use in assigning incoming cases to the various judges' dockets. Connally made these work assignments annually. For 1963, in addition to his districtwide duties as chief, Connally instructed the clerk to assign him 17 percent of the civil cases filed in Houston, all of Houston's criminal cases in June and July, all proceedings in Laredo and Victoria, and, finally, all matters involving missing or deceased seamen. Judge Hannay, by contrast, would have all of the Houston criminal cases during January, February, March, and December, and 33 percent of Houston's civil cases. Judge Ingraham would take up the criminal docket from August through November, and would also have 33 percent of the Houston civil docket. In addition, Ingraham would have the responsibility for naturalization proceedings in Houston. Judge Noel was assigned all cases in Galveston, Houston criminal cases in April and May, and the remaining 17 percent of Houston's civil cases. The clerk's criterion for assigning cases to Judge Garza's docket was simple: Garza heard all cases and proceedings in Brownsville and Corpus Christi.[216]

The judges' work assignments were subject to changes because of judicial recusals and emergencies, and, of course, the cases could be traded among the judges by "mutual consent." Work assignments for the next several years were made on exactly the same basis. In 1966 Connally changed his memorandum order to the clerk only to shift the months scheduled for criminal docket duties and to give Judge Hannay the responsibility for vetting admissions to membership in the Southern District's bar in Houston.[217] By applying these criteria, with necessary adjustments and negotiated changes, Clerk of Court Thomas assigned the Houston civil caseloads to the judges as indicated in Table 1 (Connally's and Noel's cases in court divisions other than Houston are not represented).

In August 1966, a few weeks after Judges Singleton and Seals were confirmed by the Senate, Connally wrote a memorandum to the Houston-based judges, requesting that each of them set aside some of their pending, although nearly ready-for-trial, civil cases. These would be distributed between the two new judges. Connally was donating 40 of 131 pending cases. Judge Noel gave up 60 cases from his backlog of 163, probably with few regrets. Judges Ingraham and Hannay each trimmed his civil docket by 150 cases, no doubt with even less regret, since each carried a backlog of approximately 500 cases. Judge Garza corresponded separately with the chief judge to discuss the 144 cases pending in Corpus Christi. Garza retained the admiralty and criminal dockets there, and gave up approximately 100 civil actions. Connally directed the clerk to give all cases that involved the United States to Singleton, since Seals had just finished five years as the government's top lawyer in the Southern District. After the docket trading was completed, Connally hoped, Singleton and Seals would begin their careers as federal trial judges with civil dockets of around 200 cases.[218]

The 1967 judicial work assignments obviously would require the clerk to perform more complicated mathematical calculations. Perhaps for that reason, or perhaps because he was excited at the prospect of a lighter caseload, Connally issued the annual order to establish the new criteria one month early, in November 1966. The chief judge, in addition to duties in Laredo and Victoria, would receive just 5 percent of the Houston civil cases and would retain the criminal docket there during one month of the year. Judge Seals would be responsible for all proceed-

TABLE 1. Civil Caseloads of Houston-Based Judges

JUDGE	1963	1964	1965	THREE-YEAR TOTAL
Connally	140	182	184	506
Hannay	294	256	331	881
Ingraham	287	289	389	965
Noel	149	151	187	487

Source: Chief Judge Ben C. Connally, Judicial Work Assignments, 25 November 1966, clerk's files of Chief Judge Connally, folder 2, Office of the Clerk of the Court, U.S. District Court, Southern District of Texas.

ings in Corpus Christi, take the Houston criminal cases for one month, and be assigned 11 percent of the Houston civil cases. Judge Noel kept his full responsibility for Galveston, had Houston criminal cases for one month, and would receive 12 percent of the civil cases in Houston. Judge Singleton would take 26 percent of the civil caseload in Houston and would hold the criminal docket there during three months. Judges Hannay and Ingraham would take the Houston criminal cases for three months each, and each would be assigned 23 percent of the incoming civil cases. Judge Garza retained full responsibility for the Brownsville court, and would take on Corpus Christi cases in which Seals was disqualified.[219]

These percentages were the clerk's guidelines, and, as noted, the judges could negotiate and adjust their caseloads by mutual consent. At a meeting on 10 January 1967, the Houston-based judges noted that it was necessary to "equalize" the civil docket. The judges agreed to make the following changes: Judge Hannay would surrender another 76 cases; Judge Ingraham, 55; and Judge Noel, 18. Judge Singleton assumed 111 of the cases, and Judge Seals assumed 38, with the assignment made by random selection or by lot, "to the end that any particularly difficult or troublesome cases may be assigned in that fashion." After this adjustment Ingraham, Hannay, Noel, and Seals would have a backlog of 278 cases, and Singleton would have a backlog of 279 cases.[220] Judge Singleton had the impression that, because his docket had been cobbled together from old cases that the other Southern District judges had not wanted to try, he spent his first months as a federal district judge hearing nothing but admiralty suits.[221]

TO ASSIST JUDGES TO THE MAXIMUM EXTENT POSSIBLE

Circuit Judge John R. Brown, who became the Fifth Circuit's chief judge in 1967, wrote to the chief judges of the districts in September 1969, to share the results of the latest review by the Administrative Office of the U.S. Courts. That organization had compiled a list of civil actions that had been filed in the federal district courts before 1 July 1966 that were pending as of 30 June 1969. Like Chief Judge Tuttle before him, Chief Judge Brown was not suggesting that anything specific could be done to correct the backlog. He was merely suggesting that, perhaps, the matter needed attention. He concluded by noting that the Judicial Council of the Fifth Circuit had a "statutory responsibility" for the administration of justice in the circuit and "a special one to assist District Judges to the maximum extent possible."[222]

The statistics on three-year cases indicated that, by the end of the 1960s, the Southern District judges were not much in need of assistance. They were, in general, keeping pace with the cases. The report listed not just the court divisions but named the judges whose docket contained three-year-old cases. Chief Judge Connally had five in this category, but three of these were very old land disputes (one from 1955, two from the 1940s). Judge Singleton had disposed of all but two of his three-year-old cases. Judge Garza had responsibility for twelve; Judge Noel, eleven; and Judge Seals, fourteen. Judge Ingraham had thirty-four of the three-year-old cases on the docket, but twenty-eight of these listed the Kinnear Weed Corporation as the plaintiff and were therefore connected to the long-lived patent dispute that company had filed in 1953. Only Judge Hannay seemed to be falling behind the pace, but only by contrast with the rest of the judges. He had forty-four of these cases on his docket, all but one filed in the mid-1960s. That one, *Glasscock v. Stewart Farm Co.*, was an equity case that had been filed in 1922. The statistics indicate that there were some cases that just would not be closed. The judges were keeping up with the rest.[223]

The seven federal district judges worked to reduce docket congestion, but the number of new cases in the Southern District still continued to rise faster than the number of judges there. Both civil and criminal filings fluctuated from year to year, but the general trend was clear. Figure 2 shows the number of civil and criminal cases filed in the Southern District each year during the 1960s.

Chief Judge Connally found the rise in criminal filings at the end of the decade especially troubling. After considering the issue and consulting the other Houston-based judges, he wrote to Clerk of Court Bailey Thomas in December 1968, informing him that the system of passing the Houston criminal docket from judge to judge every month or so was no longer satisfactory. Connally instructed Thomas that, effective 1 January 1969, he should assign criminal cases "on a random basis in precisely the same fashion (although not in the same ratio) as are the civil cases." This would entail the clerk office's preparation of cards bearing the concealed names of the Houston judges "thoroughly commingled." When a criminal case was filed, a deputy clerk would draw a card and assign the case to that judge's docket. The percentages for the criminal assignments, the Chief Judge decided, would be

FIGURE 2. The Caseload in the Southern District, 1961–1970

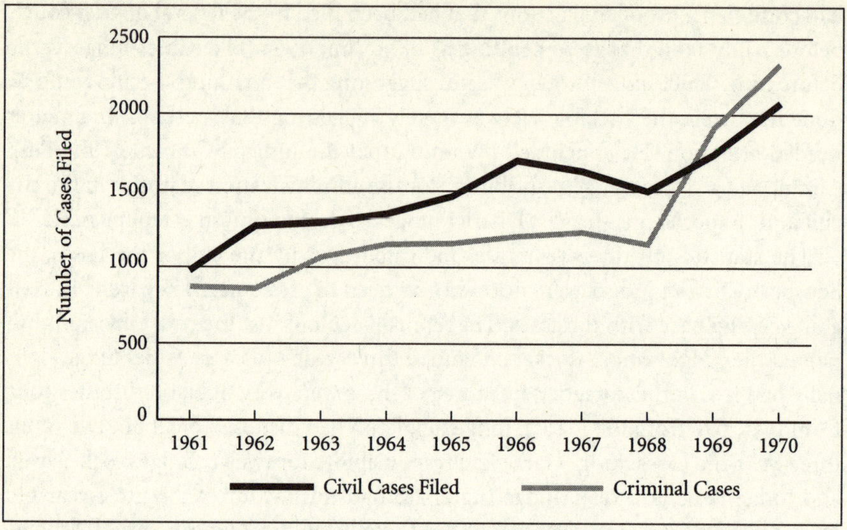

Source: *Federal Court Management Statistics* (Washington, D.C.: Administrative Office of the United States Courts, 2000).

25 each for Judges Singleton, Ingraham, and Hannay, and 8 ⅓ each for himself, Judge Noel, and Judge Seals, because they also had criminal dockets in other divisions. Judge Garza was not affected by the change in procedures.[224]

The chief judge's order went into effect just before the sharp rise in criminal cases, from 1,153 in 1968 to 1,913 in 1969 and 2,326 in 1970, that is reflected in Figure 2. His prescience can be explained by his long experience with the trends in criminal prosecutions in the Southern District of Texas. Judge Connally in the Laredo Division and Judge Garza in the Brownsville Division tried by far the largest number of criminal cases filed in the Southern District. The judges' experience with these cases in the 1960s, and the changing character of the cases, will be explored in the next chapter.

CHAPTER THREE

The Rules and Exceptions of Border Justice

WHEN JUDGE REYNALDO GARZA REPLACED the late Judge Allred in the Southern District of Texas, he became one of only four federal district judges responsible for trying federal civil and criminal cases in the six court divisions.[1] Judge Garza principally held court in Brownsville, his hometown on the U.S.-Mexican border, but he periodically trekked north 150 miles, to preside over cases in Corpus Christi. Similarly, Judge Ben Connally shuttled between his home in Houston and the border court at Laredo, with stops at the courthouse in Victoria in between. Judge James Noel tried cases both in Houston and Galveston. The number of court divisions exceeded the number of judges until 1966, when Judges Woodrow Seals and John Singleton joined the court. Seals thereafter shared some of the caseload in Corpus Christi, but Singleton primarily held court in Houston. As chief judge after 1962, Connally might have assigned one or more of the new judges to Laredo. Instead, he retained his responsibility for that border court. Perhaps the chief enjoyed the variety, because the typical cases in the border divisions were quite different from those that filled the dockets farther north. It is also likely that Judge Connally kept the duty because that allowed him to hunt on the weekends he was in south Texas.[2]

Brownsville, Laredo, and numerous smaller points of entry on the border were major conduits for U.S. trade with Mexico. Private commercial controversies, including admiralty and labor cases, did appear in the border courts. Because the Laredo and Brownsville court divisions served the mostly agricultural Lower Rio Grande Valley, however, the number of private disputes arising in the two border divisions was negligible compared to the large number of civil suits docketed in the commercial, industrial, and maritime boomtowns like Houston, Corpus Christi, and Galveston. That did not mean that the border courts were judicial backwaters. They were in fact the Southern District's laboratories of *criminal* case management. The valley did not share equally in the benefits of the state's growth, but south Texas always was at the center of a booming illicit economy.[3]

The U.S. attorney's office prosecuted more of the Southern District's criminal cases in either Laredo or Brownsville than in any of the much larger divisions in Houston, Galveston, and Corpus Christi.[4] In 1964, for example, when the government prosecuted 1,150 cases in the Southern District, it filed 255 of those in Laredo (22.2 percent of the total). The same year, by contrast, the government filed only 41 criminal cases in Corpus Christi (3.5 percent). In 1965 the government filed 280 criminal cases, out of the annual total of 1,156, in Laredo (24.2 percent). Since federal attorneys prosecuted a comparable number of cases every year in Brownsville, the border divisions collectively processed nearly half of the district's criminal cases. When the number of prosecutions rose in subsequent years, the disproportion in the criminal caseloads grew as well, until, by the end of the decade, the border divisions accounted for almost 90 percent of the Southern District's total criminal caseload. Of the 1,913 criminal cases they filed in 1969, federal prosecutors brought 819 in Laredo (42.8 percent), and 858 in Brownsville (44.85 percent).[5]

The U.S. attorney's office in the Southern District of Texas prosecuted the variety of federal crimes that might also occur in other judicial districts,[6] and, as a result, Garza and Connally tried border defendants under various federal statutes covering, for example, vehicle theft[7] or securities fraud.[8] But Texas always attracted would-be immigrants and smugglers, who were not deterred by the often slow and shallow Rio Grande, which separated the state from Mexico. Trials for alleged violations of federal immigration or customs laws consistently dominated dockets. Prosecutions of these categories of crime, moreover, rose to unprecedented levels during the 1960s. The demand for cheap, unskilled labor usually outstripped the number of workers available through government-sponsored plans like the bracero program. The ready availability of work, even difficult, dangerous, and low-paid work, ensured that undocumented aliens regularly attempted to cross the border from Mexico. The sustained effort to arrest and to prosecute these immigrants is a relatively recent development. And after Congress halted the flow of the braceros, undocumented entry into the United States dramatically increased.[9]

The problem of prosecuting undocumented immigration was compounded by the fact that, during these same years, there was also a remarkable increase in the American appetite for exotic, and illicit, intoxicants. Traffickers supplied much of the demand from Mexico. Marijuana became a major cash crop in Mexico, and, along with a rising tide of other narcotics, it often entered the United States through southwestern border states like Texas.[10] Prosecutions for narcotics violations flooded the Southern District's border divisions in the 1960s, much as bootleg liquor cases had swamped the same courts in the 1920s, during the Prohibition era.[11]

As a result of these two developments, the judges were generally preoccupied, while in the border divisions, with trying three major classes of defendants, each charged with a form of smuggling. Individuals in the first class had been indicted on immigration violations after their arrest by officers of the U.S. Border Patrol, the uniformed service of the Immigration and Naturalization Service (INS).[12] Defendants in the second class had been indicted for smuggling narcotics, in amounts varying from a single marijuana cigarette up to hundreds of pounds of the same substance. These individuals were usually detected at a border checkpoint by inspectors of the U.S. Customs Service.[13] Smuggling cases in these two categories dominated the dockets in Laredo and Brownsville in the 1960s. The legal questions and trial management issues particular to these two classes are the subject of the first half of this chapter. Defendants of the third class were alleged drug smugglers who had been arrested, usually well north of the border, by Border Patrol officers. Their arrests raised legal and constitutional questions, regarding criminal procedure and the authority of law enforcement officers operating near the border, that were more difficult for the judges to answer in the 1970s than they were in the 1960s. For that reason, these defendants will be discussed in the second half of this chapter.

Criminal trials typically are short and straightforward. Yet, by reason of quantity if not complexity of the cases, Judges Garza and Connally encountered challenges in Brownsville and Laredo that could present as daunting a problem of administration as the burgeoning civil dockets in their other court assignments. The judicial role in the management of federal criminal cases was different from the part judges played in managing civil cases. This was because the judges' role in criminal trials was, for reasons to be discussed, necessarily secondary to the part played by a prosecutor. Despite this fact, the methods prosecutors developed to clear the criminal dockets in the Southern District's border divisions were complementary with the methods judges used in civil litigation.

Judges act as "gatekeepers" of the federal courts during pretrial proceedings in civil cases, whenever they rule on various points of law, fact, or procedure.[14] They assume a more subdued role in criminal cases, since prosecutors perform the primary gatekeeping function in the administration of criminal justice. Judges exercise great authority during the course of a criminal trial, but the prosecutors are first to determine whether the government is to pursue the case in the first place. Similarly, the government attorneys influence the character of the docket by deciding what charges to file against a defendant. Among other factors, prosecutors weigh the risk that the defendant will be acquitted on one specific charge against the likelihood that the government will win conviction on that charge. Before seeking an indictment from a grand jury, prosecutors first have to conclude that the crime alleged is serious enough to merit the expense of a trial.[15]

The U.S. attorney's office employs techniques that can be regarded as a "criminalized" version of the pretrial conference familiar from civil cases. As often as possible, in order to avoid the delay and expense of a full-blown trial, prosecutors bargain with defendants. To induce a defendant to "settle" a criminal case before trial, a prosecutor might file a multicharge indictment but offer to dismiss the most serious charge or charges if the defendant agrees to plead guilty to the less serious offenses. A prosecutor may agree to recommend a light sentence or probation in return for the guilty plea but, of course, cannot promise probation or a specific sentence. Sentencing remains a judicial prerogative, and federal criminal procedure prohibits the judge from participating in negotiations. The rules direct judges, moreover, to question the defendant in order to make an independent determination that a plea of guilty is voluntary, in the sense that it is not the result of force, threats, or promises for a particular sentence. A judge is bound to quash a deal, for example, if the defendant has pled guilty but continues to proclaim innocence.[16]

Plea bargains are not unique to the border. Prosecutors and judges, as well as defense attorneys, engage in similar exercises in most courts. The plea bargaining in the border divisions of the Southern District, however, took on a uniquely ceremonial quality in the 1960s, partly because of the large number of similarly situated defendants, the predominance of the classes of cases described above, and the participation of only two like-minded judges in two like courts. The result of the plea-bargaining process on the border, moreover, resembled an assembly line. This appearance was reinforced by the scheduling of similar trials in consecutive order, a result that apparently required the clerk of the court to collaborate at some level with prosecutors during the pretrial management of the dockets. Whatever the mechanics of the process, the effect was that cases arising from indictment on the same or related criminal statutes came up for trial—or, more often, for arraignment, guilty plea, and sentencing—on the same day, in succession. Connally and Garza rarely upset the necessary plea negotiations.[17] For a plea-bargaining system to have one of its important intended effects, that is, for the system to reduce the burden of trying routine cases, the judges had to play their assigned roles.[18]

An overwhelming number of border defendants, especially if they had been charged with immigration and narcotics violations, agreed to plead guilty. And in the overwhelming number of their cases, the prosecutor typically dismissed any remaining counts, and Judges Connally and Garza suspended the associated prison sentence in order to set conditions for probation. The judges consistently rewarded cooperative defendants with light sentences and imposed a heavy sentence when a defendant in a routine case (at least, routine from the judge's perspective) sought a full trial. Frequent judicial rebuffs of the prosecution's tactics, whether manifested as rejection of guilty pleas, imposition of heavy sentences in return for guilty pleas, or imposition of light sentences after conducting a trial, risked reducing the efficacy of this tool of court administration. Knowledgeable defense attorneys would lose confidence in the plea bargain and advise their clients to decline any proposed deals.[19]

Judges Connally and Garza were particularly reliant on the success of plea agreements. The viability of the court system itself was the larger issue at stake in the smooth operation of plea bargains and other management mechanisms in the Southern District's Laredo and Brownsville Divisions. The judges were, therefore, especially concerned when defendants bucked the system, for the court's administrative machinery would grind to a halt if the prosecutors attempted to try more than a small percentage of these routine border cases.[20]

The rules of criminal procedure that were particular to the border divisions of the Southern District seemed to be principles of management based on a fair exchange: judicial leniency for a defendant's accommodation. Defendants seemed to know, if only from jailhouse gossip, how the system operated and what was expected of them. The defendants, like the judges and prosecutors, had to play their assigned roles. The experience of one exceptional drug defendant, Dr. Timothy Leary, proved this rule. Leary was arrested in Laredo on a marijuana smuggling charge in late 1965, and he refused to plead guilty. Instead, in his 1966 trial he mounted a vigorous defense. Unlike most defendants, he commanded substantial sympathy and resources that enabled him to challenge the federal criminal justice system on more equal footing. Leary's experience illustrated in spectacular fashion the risks narcotics defendants on the border took when they resisted being "managed" by the judge and prosecutor. Leary was able to disrupt the management machinery by 1970, but, in the long run, he gained little relief for himself or any other drug defendants, including those who agreed to plea bargains. The spectacle of Leary's legal exertions, however, did much to establish his abiding image as the 1960s' most celebrated and notorious proselytizer of the psychedelic.[21]

PROSECUTING THE UNDOCUMENTED AND DOCUMENTING THE PROSECUTED

The assembly line characteristics of the court's disposition of routinely plea-bargained undocumented alien cases was enhanced by the routine practice of docketing together cases based on indictments brought under the same criminal statutes, a docketing procedure that required the clerk of the court to participate in pretrial management in collaboration with the prosecutors. The administrative benefit of this filing system was that a judge could call consecutively numbered cases for trial, or more often for arraignment where the defendants would all enter guilty pleas, and could then could dispose of a large number in swift succession.[22]

Assistant U.S. Attorney (AUSA) Thomas Morrill sought indictments on 19 April 1965, for example, against more than two dozen undocumented aliens who had been apprehended within the previous month on the border.[23] Morrill confronted fewer of these defendants than he might have faced, however, because officers of the Border Patrol routinely performed a gatekeeping function of their own. The officers processed many of the violators but allowed most of the Mexican nationals they apprehended to depart from the U.S. "voluntarily."[24] Morrill sorted the remaining cohorts according to the applicable immigration statutes and indicted them in that order. On 17 May, when Judge Connally arraigned the defendants in his Laredo courtroom, he maintained the order.[25]

According to long-standing doctrine, undocumented alien defendants were among the "persons" protected under the Fourteenth Amendment, and they enjoy the same legal rights in court as U.S. citizens, including the right to have a defense attorney provided at public expense, the right to a jury trial, and the right to appeal an unfavorable judgment to a higher court.[26] But the first defendant in the queue on 17 May, Benito Soto Cano, a thirty-four-year-old Mexican national, waived counsel and pled guilty to the charge of falsely representing himself to be a U.S. citizen. The judge sentenced him to ninety days but suspended the sentence for five years on the condition that Cano attempted no illegal return to the United States.[27] This interaction established a pattern only rarely disrupted. Cano was followed by seven defendants who were charged with the identical crime. All mimicked Cano's waiver and guilty plea; all received the same judgment.

The remaining defendants in this "docket run" likewise waived counsel and pled guilty, whatever the specific violation charged. A few received the judge's individual attention, however, usually because that defendant was a repeat offender. For example, members of a second cohort of defendants were charged with unlawful reentry.[28] The first in this line, fifty-two-year-old Antonio Medina Delgado, waived counsel, pled guilty, and received a sentence of eighteen months, suspended for five years.[29] Then Andres Juarez Gallegos, twenty-seven years old, also pled guilty. The judge gave the younger man, as well as each of the next thirteen defendants indicted on this same charge, ninety days. As with the previous cohort, Judge Connally suspended the sentences for five years, conditioned on no illegal return. Whatever the judge's motive (which he did not record) for giving Delgado a longer sentence, he gave every defendant the same conditions for probation.[30] The next three defendants, beginning with the thirty-six-year-old Homero Delgado Salazar, pled guilty to impersonating another person for the purpose of evading immigration laws, which implied that when challenged by the Border Patrol, the defendants presented a forged or altered "Non-Resident Alien Mexican Border Crossing Card."[31] Again, Connally imposed ninety days, which he suspended for five years on condition of no illegal return.[32]

This "run" of consecutively filed, indicted, and arraigned cases concluded with Connally's judgment of two defendants charged with more serious violations. Tomas Rojas Leal, twenty-five, waived counsel and pled guilty to a single count of alien smuggling, that is, "unlawfully importing, landing, and transporting aliens" in the United States.[33] Leal had been indicted on four counts, an indication that he had been guiding four others when the Border Patrol arrested him, but the government dismissed three of these counts after Leal pled guilty to one. Connally sentenced Leal to thirteen months, but, again, he suspended the penalty for five years.[34] Finally, Socorro Castillo De Leyna, forty-two, pled guilty to violating probation.[35] The judge sentenced De Leyna to two years, to be served consecutively with a recent sentence that Connally himself, ironically, had suspended. After betraying the judge's trust by accepting his probation but then returning to the United States, De Leyna now faced several years in federal prison before probable deportation.[36]

Undocumented alien cases do not make the best examples of plea-bargaining procedures. It is unlikely that the prosecutors actually "negotiated" with the defendants, or that the defendants adequately understood their rights. Nevertheless, the proceedings in the Laredo court on 17 May 1965 illuminate the "assembly line" docket management that had emerged in the Southern District. Garza and Connally had apparently inherited the system. Well before they sat on the border, previous Southern District judges faced similar institutional pressures and used comparable techniques to dispose of routine cases. This administrative machinery worked smoothly by the mid-1960s. The rate of immigration violations rose steadily throughout the decade, but the district's staff kept pace.

In complex cases the docket sheet was a chronological record of motions, hearings, and judgments in a trial. In simpler cases, however, such as these alien proceedings, a few handwritten lines or typed phrases, on an otherwise blank form, make up the complete written record. In 1965 a clerk usually typed a standard note to indicate that on a certain date a particular defendant waived the right to counsel, pled guilty to a specified charge, and received a short sentence that was then immediately suspended. Frequently, the typist left a blank for the sentence to be filled in by the judge upon final disposition. The consecutively numbered runs of cases were longer than ever by 1969. In that year the docket sheets began to bear, rather than typed notes, an inked block that indicated the standard round of waivers, pleas, and sentence. There were still blank lines on the page to be filled in by hand, but the change indicated that the Southern District's processing practices had advanced to the point (or else had grown so routine) that Judges Connally and Garza literally rubber-stamped the pleas.

The delay between indictments and arraignments had also contracted by then, until, in many instances, key events apparently (and officially) occurred simultaneously, or at least on the same day. On 4 August 1969, for example, Judge Connally arraigned more than three dozen undocumented alien defendants whom, according to the court's records, the prosecutor also had indicted on 4 August. The first cohort was the largest. The judge arraigned twenty-four defendants charged with unlawful entry. Each waived counsel, pled guilty, and received a ninety-day sentence that Connally suspended for five years on the condition that the defendant must agree not to return illegally.[37] Next, the judge arraigned four defendants, who pled guilty to unlawful reentry into the United States. These four received the same sentence as the preceding two dozen first-time entrants.[38] Six defendants followed to plead guilty to falsely claiming U.S. citizenship. The judge sentenced all six to ten months but suspended that sentence for five years conditioned on no illegal return.[39] Connally assessed the same sentence and conditions on the next five defendants, who all pled guilty to false "personation."[40]

The next day, Connally arraigned another large group of undocumented aliens whom the prosecutor had indicted that day. The process repeated the pattern of earlier docket calls. When variations arose they, as usual, went unexplained. Belen Medina Flores, one of the defendants charged with unlawful entry on 5 August, did not waive counsel. Connally appointed attorney Mancisco Flores to represent the defendant. But the outcome was the same as with any of the unrepresented aliens: the judge declared a ninety-day sentence and suspended it for five years, in exchange for Flores's guilty plea.[41] In another variation, AUSA Ron Blask indicted Manuel Dario Monreal De La Cruz, the last alien Connally arraigned on 5 August, on the charge of transporting aliens into the U.S. Trafficking was a more serious matter than unlawful entry and its variants, and the judge typically treated those offenders more harshly. De La Cruz, perhaps realizing this, retained a defense attorney but nonetheless pled guilty. Connally sentenced him to three years. The judge ordered De La Cruz to serve just six months of the sentence, however; he suspended the balance for five years, on the condition of no return, legal or not.[42]

The Southern District administrators could not sustain the swift, same-day turnarounds of indictment and arraignment but continued to schedule consecutive days to process undocumented alien cases. Connally arraigned a large group of alien defendants, a docket call of forty-four, on 23 September, for example. They had been indicted three weeks earlier, on 30 August.[43] But on the same day the judge arraigned twenty-four aliens who had been indicted on 12 September.[44] The next day, Judge Connally arraigned relatively few aliens, but those he did arraign were repeat offenders who had earned special wrath by violating the conditions Connally had established for leniency. The judge afforded them more attention than was usually possible. In these instances, at least, Connally refrained from passing judgment by his rubber stamp. This was both a literal and a figurative change. The docket sheets in these case files seem to mark the first appearance of a customized new form, with the violation preprinted.

Despite this small measure of individualism, the cases were indicted together on 22 September, presumably to facilitate Judge Connally's disposition of them in efficient, consecutive order. Each defendant waived counsel and pled guilty to unlawful reentry to the U.S. Mario Sepulveda Davila, the first in line, had gotten a suspended sentence for unlawful entry in the spring of 1967 but was reapprehended on the U.S. side of the border in August 1969. Judge Connally sentenced him to nine months to be served.[45] Luis Maldonado Flores, the next defendant in line, had been arrested in February 1969, processed and repatriated, then rearrested in August. Despite this recidivism the judge sentenced Flores to the standard ninety days suspended, conditioned on five years with no illegal return. Connally did not record his reasons for extending Flores but not Davila a second chance at a suspended sentence.[46] It is clear, however, why Jose Roberto Martinez Garcia received nine months to be served. He was arrested on 14 August, processed by the court and repatriated to Mexico, but rearrested in the U.S. less than one week later, on 20 August.[47] Connally gave the remaining defendants sentences between ninety days suspended (the lightest),[48] and two years to be served (the heaviest).[49] The thin case records do not explain the judicial rationale.

These cases suggest the potential effects—on individual alien defendants—of closer inspection and due deliberation by the judge. Increased judicial attention resulted in individual sentences. But it is not obvious whether that outcome indicated that there was any greater justice in the sentencing. Assembly line arraignment in undocumented alien cases, despite the absence of consideration of the individual defendants' circumstances, guilt, or innocence, provided for a measure of judicial impartiality. The result of the pragmatic numerical filing scheme was a near-automated courtroom. The courtroom procedures were dehumanizing in their rubber-stamped efficiency. Nonetheless, they ensured judicial evenhandedness, in that most of the same charges yielded the same sentences. It was fortunate for the defendants that Judge Connally generally favored repatriation over incarceration.

In Brownsville, and occasionally in Corpus Christi, where he tried some overflow alien and drug cases, Judge Garza followed the example set by Judge Connally and presided over a ritual that amounted to a collective trial. Approximately once every month, and more frequently late in the decade, the local prosecutors indicted dozens of undocumented persons who, when brought into the federal court, waived counsel, pled guilty, and then received suspended sentences in consecutive order. Whatever their failings as due process, Garza maintained that these routine docket calls responded reasonably to conditions on the border. It was a foregone conclusion that the alien defendants would have to be repatriated to Mexico, and the collective proceedings reduced the INS detainees' misery by limiting the length of their confinement to the time they had served awaiting arraignment. Furthermore, as indicated by the name Judge Garza gave the process—"jail delivery days"—the practice benefited the federal court system by clearing cells as well as dockets. The docket calls freed physical space and judicial attention for more serious matters. Among the serious matters to be addressed was the large number of narcotics trials.[50]

The routine disposition of narcotics cases provides the best examples of systematic plea bargaining in the Southern District's border divisions. Most drug defendants in Laredo and Brownsville had been arrested after being searched at the border by inspectors of the U.S. Customs Service. They were particularly motivated to plead guilty, because they had even less hope of prevailing in a trial than undocumented aliens. Congress had authorized customs inspectors to combat the importation of untaxed or prohibited merchandise by searching "any vehicle, beast, or person" that the agent suspects is carrying items subject to duty or exclusion, or "any trunk or envelope" which the agent "may have a reasonable cause to suspect" contains such illicit merchandise.[51]

A U.S. Customs agent has the authority to conduct peremptory warrantless searches while entertaining a "mere suspicion" that contraband is being smuggled. This is a routine exception—the so-called "border search" exception—to the Fourth Amendment to the U.S. Constitution.[52] The "touchstone" of a search authorized under the Fourth Amendment, according to the U.S. Supreme Court, is the reasonableness of the search.[53] Federal courts have held that a warrantless search by customs officers stationed at the border is inherently reasonable, because the U.S. possesses a sovereign's power to restrict or regulate imports. Federal courts supported this exception as long as it was subject to statutory limitation. The judiciary usually endorsed the border search exception only if the warrantless search had been conducted by actual U.S. Customs agents, on the physical border, at a designated point of entry.[54]

The first federal Congress established a version of the exception when the Atlantic seaboard was still the main border of consequence to the United States. In July 1789, two months before the same legislators would propose adding the warrant requirement to the Constitution and two years before the ratification of the Fourth Amendment, Congress passed a statute empowering "specially appointed" collectors to search any vessel for "goods, wares or merchandise subject to duty." The act did not require that customs collectors first obtain warrants to search a ship.[55] The 1789 act did, however, restrict the exercise of this power to the agents at ports of entry. Collectors whose responsibilities took them away from the entry ports did not carry border search authority with them, and they could not delegate that authority to any other law officers. The Congress declared that even a customs officer must obtain a warrant before searching "any particular dwelling-house, store, building, or other place." The officer, moreover, could search such places only during the day.[56]

Federal judges, in order to foster effective law enforcement, occasionally admitted other "reasonable" exceptions to the Fourth Amendment. This was an uneven process, however, and it was not until the early twentieth century that the federal courts actually defined a "reasonable" search as a search accompanied by a warrant. This process apparently culminated in 1914, when the U.S. Supreme Court declared, in *Weeks v. United States,* that federal district judges must "exclude" from trial evidence that had been obtained without a valid warrant and probable cause. Although it was a milestone of Fourth Amendment law, *Weeks* initially had a limited impact on the evolution of the rights of defendants. Until the Prohibition era, federal law enforcement agencies were quite small compared to the state and even some local police organizations. Hence, there were comparatively few federal relative to state defendants.[57]

The rules announced in *Weeks,* moreover, did not pertain to border searches. Ironically, the border search exception's future prominence was presaged when Congress passed the Harrison Narcotic Drug Act, the first major federal legislation intended to combat international drug trafficking, in the same year the Supreme Court announced *Weeks.* The act regulated manufacture, import, and possession of opium and its derivatives. The Congress did not give Customs primary responsibility for enforcing the Harrison Act. The duty did go to another organization within the Treasury, however, a new narcotics division of the Bureau of Internal Revenue.[58] Lawmakers later folded that division into yet another Treasury office, the Prohibition Bureau, which was created by the National Prohibition Act of 1919. This statute, known as the Volstead Act, implemented the recently ratified Eighteenth Amendment's prohibition, within the United States or its territories, of the "manufacture, sale, or transportation of intoxicating liquors."[59]

A key clause of the Volstead Act gave Prohibition agents the authority to conduct warrantless searches of vehicles traveling on roads that were "known" arteries for liquor traffic. Defendants charged with bootlegging challenged this grant of authority. In a 1925 opinion, *Carroll v. United States,* the U.S. Supreme Court reiterated its longstanding doctrine that the Fourth Amendment "does not denounce all searches or seizures, but only such as are unreasonable." The justices accepted the government's argument that it was "not practicable" to require its prohibition agents to obtain a warrant to search each car or truck they stopped on the road, "because the vehicle can be quickly moved out of the locality or jurisdiction in which the warrant must be sought." The court also wrote, however, that "[i]t would be intolerable and unreasonable if a prohibition agent were authorized to stop every automobile on the chance of finding liquor, and thus subject all persons lawfully using the highways to the inconvenience and indignity of such a search."[60]

The Supreme Court therefore affirmed a core principle of the border search doctrine—which was that customs inspectors required operational flexibility in order to perform legitimate duties—but it also stretched the traditional narrow boundaries of the border exception to include at least some of the activities of prohibition agents. Prohibition officers were similar to customs agents, in that they were both a species of Treasury officer, but they were concerned less with the importation than with the transportation and possession within the United States of a particular species of illicit goods. Moreover, they often fulfilled their mission at some distance removed from the border.[61]

In 1930, again at the direction of Congress, the treasury secretary transferred responsibility for narcotics law enforcement to yet another new entity within the Treasury Department, called the Federal Bureau of Narcotics (FBN). The first commissioner of the FBN, Harry J. Anslinger, served in that position until 1962, and he became the nation's greatest advocate for maintaining the narcotics prohibitions after liquor prohibition ended in 1933.[62] Anslinger lobbied in the 1930s, for example, to persuade Congress to outlaw marijuana and to place responsibility for enforcement within his bureau. He and his allies succeeded, and, at the same time, spread two persistent but spurious beliefs among lawmakers and the public. The first was that marijuana's narcotic effect, and hence its potential dangers as an "assassin of youth," was on par with opiates such as heroin that were already under the FBN's authority. Second, Anslinger identified the use of the drug with the decadent character of Mexicans, an already despised minority.[63]

The evolution of narcotics law enforcement authority within, and without, the Treasury Department would have a great impact on the Southern District's border courts in the 1970s. In the 1960s, however, customs searches still provided most of the defendants. Under protection of the border search exception, customs agents discovered all manner of contraband, including illicit narcotics, during the routine searches they conducted at checkpoints on the border. Most often, the inspectors found marijuana, in quantities ranging from a single cigarette one careless twenty-two-year-old American tourist carried back from Mexico in April 1965 to the dozens of one-kilogram "bricks," totaling 938 pounds, that one person drove across the border into the United States in November 1969.[64]

Similarly fruitful searches and seizures required federal prosecutors in Laredo and Brownsville to seek hundreds of new drug indictments each year. The vast majority of defendants eventually agreed to plead guilty, no doubt on the advice of their attorneys, who usually realized they had no viable defense strategy to offer. To keep abreast of the narcotics cases multiplying on the Southern District's docket, and to facilitate plea bargains, the federal prosecutors developed a basic template that could be applied, with minor adaptations, to the majority of circumstances, regardless of the quantity of drugs involved. This was a three-part indictment, consisting of the following charges: first, importing marijuana;[65] second, transporting marijuana;[66] and third, failing to pay federal transfer taxes on that marijuana.[67] The first two charges described violations of the narcotics statutes and carried mandatory prison sentences. The possible penalty for either of these crimes was five to twenty years in federal prison, and a fine of as much as twenty thousand dollars. A judge could not suspend the sentence or grant probation upon conviction of either of these charges.[68] The penalty for failure to pay tax on marijuana was two to ten years and a possible twenty-thousand-dollar fine. A judge could grant probation, however, for a conviction under the third charge, which was a violation of the internal revenue code rather than a narcotics crime. This so-called "tax count" became the federal prosecutor's bargaining chip.[69]

Under this three-part indictment, a defendant appeared for arraignment to plead guilty on the tax count; the presiding judge imposed a short sentence, suspended it, and granted probation; and the prosecutor then moved to dismiss the two narcotics charges. An occasional variation in the model appeared, relating to the youth or prior criminal record of the defendant, but the disposition of the overwhelming majority of marijuana cases—three counts but two dismissals, in return for one guilty plea—was nearly automatic.

The prosecutors relied on a similar arrangement even if the drug in question was heroin rather than marijuana. The model for a heroin-related indictment also included three charges: unlawful importation of heroin, conspiracy to transport or to facilitate transport and concealment of heroin, and unlawfully purchasing heroin "not in or from the original stamped package." The possible penalties for these three heroin violations were identical to those imposed for the corresponding marijuana violations. In heroin prosecutions, however, the unlawful purchase charge was the bargaining chip equivalent to the "tax count" for marijuana. Otherwise, the plea-bargaining system for heroin was the same as that used in the Southern District marijuana prosecutions.[70]

Southern District prosecutors adapted the consecutive-cases model from immigration cases to narcotics-smuggling prosecutions. There were days in the border divisions when the court processed large numbers of consecutively numbered narcotics indictments. Yet drug cases were more complex than the immigration cases, and more varied. The general pattern might be disrupted, for example, by a defendant who refused to plead guilty to the tax count, or by a defendant who agreed to plead guilty only after unsuccessfully filing a motion to suppress the evidence. The judges in the border courts almost inevitably denied such motions, because the border search exception was in full force in most cases.

The willingness to seek and grant probation in these cases indicates that, at least during the 1960s, both the prosecutors and the judges in the Southern District considered marijuana and other drug smuggling to be a relatively minor, routine offense. For that reason, they regarded the mounting of a vigorous defense, including a call for a trial by jury, to be a serious waste of the court's time.[71] Defendants took a risk by resisting plea bargains, because expressions of a hostile attitude frequently resulted in a longer-than-usual sentence if and (often) when a defendant sought to be rearraigned to plead guilty to the tax count. The judges ordinarily suspended even these longer sentences.[72]

Judge Connally supported a very broad interpretation of the customs inspectors' power to search. The judge's attitude is shown in the early 1960s prosecution of Gilbert Rodriguez Jr. The case only indirectly concerned drugs or other contraband but directly illuminated the scope of the border search exception. In January 1956 Connally had convicted Rodriguez in the district's Houston Division for "unlawfully acquiring marijuana."[73] After his term in prison, Rodriguez returned in 1959 to Houston. The customs agents there doubted that confinement had rehabilitated Rodriguez, and they predicted that he would travel to Mexico for marijuana. In June 1959 the agents distributed a description of Rodriguez's car and alerted customs personnel in Laredo. On 25 July Rodriguez did visit Mexico, but the inspectors on duty at the border did not recognize him. When Rodriguez returned from Mexico on 1 August, he still attracted no attention. After the casual customs inspection most tourists experienced upon their return to the United States, Rodriguez received a copy of his customs declaration form and continued his trip.[74] A federal statute required persons previously convicted for narcotics violations to register with the customs inspectors when either exiting or entering the country, but Rodriguez did not do so.[75] During a similar trip five weeks later, Rodriguez registered as required, but inspectors allowed him to proceed without further scrutiny. Only after he left Laredo for Houston did the inspectors realize that Rodriguez was an individual the Houston office had identified as a suspicious traveler. The Laredo inspectors alerted their colleagues at a highway checkpoint twenty miles north of the border, where agents detained Rodriguez and returned him to the Laredo border station. Inspectors searched the vehicle but failed to discover narcotics. They found instead Rodriguez's copy of the declaration from his earlier trip. When a customs agent called a clerk on the telephone to determine if the suspect had registered in July, Rodriguez volunteered that he had not. At that point the agents arrested Rodriguez and charged him with two counts of violating the registration statute: one count for exiting the country without registering and one for entering.[76]

Rodriguez faced Judge Connally, this time in Laredo, on 1 April 1960. Rodriguez did not dispute the charges. But his defense attorney asserted that the case rested entirely on evidence from a "confession" Rodriguez offered regarding his failure to register. The attorney asked the judge to suppress the admission.[77] Connally denied the motion because the admission had been "voluntary in every respect [and had been] forthcoming from the defendant without his having been questioned, and before the officers had considered the defendant to be under arrest."[78] Rodriguez's lawyer also moved to suppress the registration form itself, arguing that customs agents lacked probable cause to initiate the warrantless search of a vehicle that had been stopped twenty miles north of the border. Connally declared that the standard of probable cause was relaxed at or near the border. He noted that no authority had restricted Customs' power to search to the immediate proximity of the border. The judge doubted, he announced, that federal laws of search and seizure were intended to render a suspect immune from interrogation and examination by customs agents after "momentarily escap[ing] detection and pass[ing] safely through" the checkpoint at the physical border. The judge ruled that the information the customs supervisors transmitted in June 1959 gave the inspectors probable cause to detain Rodriguez, that is, once they recognized him. Connally declared that this suspicion was adequate reason to heighten scrutiny, particularly in south Texas, where "it is common knowledge (at least to those of us who through duty or choice have considerable familiarity with the narcotic traffic) that the Mexican border immediately opposite the city of Laredo, Texas, is a prolific source of illegal narcotics, and that large quantities are smuggled through that port daily."[79] The judge declared the defendant guilty. Rodriguez appealed, but the Fifth Circuit Court of Appeals affirmed the conviction.[80]

Judge Connally's rationale for approving the sloppy customs enforcement in Rodriguez's case typified the prevailing judicial attitude about the extended boundaries in border searches. Judges would consistently defend the actions of customs agents, and this "exception" became the rule. Some narcotics defendants who were arrested after warrantless searches continued to question the customs inspector's power to conduct them and attempted to undermine the force of the exception by moving to suppress the evidence. Judges rarely consented to these motions. The vitality of the exception for customs searches at the border and the judges' perception of its necessity forestalled any realistic reliance, for example, on the due process protections that the U.S. Supreme Court advanced during the celebrated "criminal procedure revolution" of the 1960s.[81]

A heroin-smuggling case from 1965 further illustrated the level of judicial deference in the Southern District to the principle of border searches. Late on 18 November 1965, fifteen miles south of Falcon Heights, a small Texas community on the Rio Grande, an off-duty customs agent named Galanos observed a slow-moving car on U.S. Highway 83. The slow driver made a U-turn, proceeded a short distance, completed another U-turn, then left the highway. He took a road that led to a shallow section of the Rio Grande directly across the border from Nueva Ciudad Guerro, a Mexican town customs officials considered a haven of narcotics dealers. Galanos waited on the highway. After fifteen minutes had passed, the car reappeared and resumed its progress along U.S. 83. Galanos followed for seventy miles, to Laredo, where he observed the occupants register at a motel.[82]

While shadowing the suspicious vehicle, Galanos radioed for assistance. On-duty customs agents learned that the car was registered to Robert Brett of Houston, who, as authorities in Houston confirmed by telephone, was either a user or a dealer of narcotics. They also learned that Brett had been convicted on a narcotics charge. The customs agents, suspecting that Brett had visited south Texas either to acquire or to arrange a purchase of narcotics, maintained surveillance until Brett's party emerged from the motel the next afternoon. Because the suspects seemed to be preparing for departure, the agents converged and identified themselves. They confirmed Brett's identity and learned that he was traveling with his wife, their infant child, and his mother, Mary Garcia Cruz. The agents advised Brett of his Fifth Amendment rights against self-incrimination but also informed him that they "knew what he was up to." Finally, they warned Brett that they planned to make a thorough search for contraband. Brett replied that he "had what the officers were seeking" but then asked if he could speak with his mother before he cooperated any further. When mother and son had conversed briefly in Spanish, Cruz told the agents that she desired to visit a bathroom. The officers agreed, but warned her that they would turn off the water, to make it impossible to flush the toilet. Faced with that prospect, Cruz suddenly declared that she was concealing drugs on her body. She revealed a fifty-gram package of heroin. The Southern District prosecutors charged both Brett and Cruz under the standard three-count narcotics indictment.[83]

In May 1966 Judge Connally conducted Brett and Cruz's trial in Laredo. Charles Tucker, the defendants' Houston attorney, moved to suppress the heroin, the federal government's only physical evidence. Tucker argued that the defendants had been under arrest from the moment the agents identified themselves and threatened to conduct a search. This occurred before they could know that Cruz was carrying heroin. The arrest, therefore, preceded establishment of probable cause. The defense attorney also noted that the agents arrested Brett and Cruz without a warrant and that they had not attempted to obtain a warrant during the many hours they sat and watched the motel room. To Tucker, this fact indicated the agents knew that they had no "probable cause" to justify a warrant, and therefore Judge Connally must suppress the heroin evidence. The defendants' acquittals or convictions hung on whether the judge accepted this interpretation, because Brett and Cruz had waived their right to a jury trial. If Connally agreed that the agents' actions before seizing the heroin rendered that evidence inadmissible, then the defendants would be acquitted.[84]

On 31 May 1966 Judge Connally announced that he could not accept Tucker's argument. Instead, he noted that the "highest authority" sustained the "well-recognized principle" that a law enforcement officer may temporarily detain citizens and question them without actually placing them under arrest. Any incriminating evidence that came to the officer's attention while he was performing this duty might become the basis for a valid arrest. The detention and questioning "took no more than a few minutes," during which the officers' conduct was "unexceptional." The officers used no force to restrain the defendants. Connally concluded that Brett and Cruz were not under arrest until the agents formally arrested them. This occurred after Cruz produced the heroin. Therefore, Judge Connally denied the defense motion to suppress the heroin and convicted Brett and Cruz.[85]

Judge Connally suggested that his reasoning in this case could be generalized to apply to most brief encounters between citizens and law enforcement personnel. But his opinion went much further, in order to reaffirm in the broadest possible terms that, under the border search doctrine, a customs officer had specific authority to detain and search a vehicle and its occupants at or near the border. Connally noted that the authority to conduct warrantless searches had been "extended to its constitutional limits by statute."[86] The power to search, and hence the validity of subsequent seizures, was in no way contingent on the customs agent's authority to make arrests supported by probable cause. Rather, the judge said, searches and seizures were justified merely by the "reasonable cause" the officer has for a belief that the contents of a vehicle offended the law.[87]

The judge believed that the facts supported the "inescapable conclusion" that Galanos, an experienced customs officer who was "knowledgeable in the ways of the violator," could know to a "moral certainty" that the defendants' curious behavior meant they had traveled to the border area to purchase narcotics. Connally heaped praise on Galanos, who, the judge said, "showed ingenuity and dedication . . . [and] brought about the seizure of a large commercial quantity of heroin, and did so without prejudice to the constitutional rights of these defendants."[88]

The experiences of Brett, Cruz, and Rodriguez suggest why most of the narcotics defendants in the border divisions never went to trial. It makes an interesting contrast, especially after Judge Connally's sharp words to these defendants, to examine the leniency he showed to defendants who demonstrated the proper attitude and accepted the plea-bargained arrangements of the prosecutor's three-part indictment. These cases are legion, and so similar that what follows attempts only to show the general outline of the criminal case management in the Southern District.

One of the variants on the three-part marijuana indictment was the occasional addition, or substitution, of a conspiracy count. On 3 November 1965, for example, Hector Gonzales Isquierdo and Josephine Ann Bucey were charged (under a criminal information filed directly by the prosecutor, that is, without the grand jury) with conspiracy to obtain fifty pounds of marijuana without paying the federal transfer tax.[89] The case record suggests, however, that they were actually involved in plans to smuggle approximately two hundred pounds of marijuana. Isquierdo and Bucey faced Judge Garza in his Corpus Christi courtroom, where they both pleaded guilty. Garza sentenced them both to ten years. He ordered that they serve six months only, with the balance of the sentence to be suspended, and that they spend five years on probation. Isquierdo seems to have taken the opportunity to avoid further trouble, and his probation ended early. By contrast, the judge revoked Bucey's probation in August 1969, after her husband, who was allegedly involved in the 1965 conspiracy, was sentenced to three years in federal prison for smuggling fifty pounds of marijuana. The case lacked the tax count, and the defendants were arraigned in Corpus Christi, but the disposition of this case nevertheless is typical of the Southern District's plea-bargained narcotics cases. It was also only the forty-fifth, and last, criminal case on the Corpus Christi docket in 1965.[90]

By the end of the same year, 277 criminal cases had been filed in the Laredo Division.[91] One of the last of these cases involved the thirty-five-year-old Zach Clark Hayes Jr. The cases began as a typical border criminal case, but Hayes's actions showed another possible variant within the process. While walking across the border, apparently as a tourist, Hayes had been caught carrying one-half pound of marijuana by customs inspectors. He was charged under a three-part indictment and faced arraignment before Judge Connally on 13 December 1965. His lawyer during that court proceeding was to have been Robert O'Conor, who, like many Laredo lawyers, was often in the federal courthouse representing one or more drug defendants. O'Conor lost his client when Hayes skipped bond. Hayes returned to court and answered the charges in August 1970, claiming to have been battling psychiatric problems during the intervening years. At that time Judge Connally allowed Hayes to plead guilty to the tax count, and, on the government's motion, he dismissed the remaining two counts. Hayes's penalty, even after five years as a fugitive, was a three-year sentence, suspended for five years' supervised probation. In addition, the judge fined him $250, to be garnished from Hayes's wages in $50 installments.[92]

Zach Hayes had bucked the system but returned, respectful and chastened, to face his punishment. As a result, he did not receive much punishment. That was nothing like the experience of Timothy Leary. As he later reportedly expressed it, Leary was "probably the first person ever caught trying to smuggle pot *into* Mexico."[93] Leary had already achieved some celebrity prior to 1965, through a combination of unquestioned professional achievement and unorthodox personal philosophy. In 1950 he had helped establish the Kaiser Psychiatric Clinic in Oakland, California, where over eight years he conducted important research into mental illness, wrote influential monographs, published more than a dozen well-received articles, and developed a series of widely disseminated diagnostic tests used to assess and treat mental patients. On the strength of his record at the Kaiser, Leary was offered in 1959 an appointment to the psychology faculty at Harvard University. But in 1960, while vacationing in Mexico, Leary consumed a handful of so-called sacred mushrooms, which contained the hallucinogenic compound psilocybin. He had, he later testified, the "most intense religious experience" of his life.[94]

Upon his return to Harvard, Leary formed a religious research group. He experimented with a variety of "psychedelic" drugs, both naturally occurring and synthetic, including psilocybin and LSD.[95] Leary became more prolific than ever. He wrote five books in five years and published thirty-eight articles regarding the religious and scientific use of drugs for expanding human perception. His work was respected and even fashionable during the early 1960s, and Leary delighted in the simultaneous attention of scholars, journalists, and celebrities. But Leary's academically sanctioned articulations ceased after Harvard abruptly fired him in 1963.[96]

The dismissal diminished Leary's scientific credibility but removed any remaining constraints on subject matter and experimental method. Thereafter, he traveled widely in search of religious, scientific, and pharmacological enlightenment, notably in Mexico and India, or else retreated to his new headquarters on a borrowed estate in upstate Millbrook, New York. He founded the Castalia Foundation and initiated wide-ranging research on drug-induced consciousness expansion. Leary studied Hinduism in India, participated in religious rituals in which marijuana was used as a sacrament, and in 1964 became a member of the Brahmakrishna sect.[97]

Leary continued to grant interviews to popular magazines, entertained celebrity visitors, and no doubt launched a thousand trips during his Millbrook idyll, but he steadily drifted toward the fringes, rather than gravitating to the center, of an emerging counterculture. Even for an individual with Leary's prodigious capacity for self-promotion, it is unlikely that he would have attained lasting fame from either his early diagnostic texts or the mystical works he produced after leaving Harvard.[98]

At this critical juncture Leary leased a new station wagon in the name of the Castalia Foundation and drove south from New York. He intended to spend the holidays on the Yucatan Peninsula and planned to stay in Mexico for six weeks to write a new book. In the early evening of 22 December 1965, he drove his traveling companions, including a girlfriend, his eighteen-year-old daughter, Susan, and his sixteen-year old son, Jack, across the international bridge spanning the Rio Grande between Laredo and its sister city, Nuevo Laredo, Mexico. A Mexican immigration official informed the group that their entry papers were not in order. It was too late to amend the documents that day, so the official instructed the would-be tourists to return the next morning. Leary turned around and drove back to the U.S. side of the river, where the customs inspectors conducted a routine border search.

Leary arrived at the customs station on the U.S. side of the border just before seven o'clock in the evening. He argued that, because he did not actually enter

Mexico, he naturally had nothing to declare. But because Leary had crossed the border, for whatever duration, the inspector was entitled to undertake a border search, and he asked Leary and his passengers to get out of the car.[99] The officer noticed what appeared to him to be "vegetable matter" and seeds in the vehicle, which he took to be ounces of marijuana residue.[100] A more thorough search revealed traces of marijuana scattered on the floor and in the glove compartment.[101] Other inspectors then conducted personal searches of the group. A female officer found three partially smoked marijuana cigarettes in a small silver box that Susan Leary had concealed in her underwear. She refused to make any statement when the officer asked who owned the silver box.[102]

Leary was not as wise as his teenage daughter. The container belonged to his girlfriend, who had panicked and passed it to the younger woman as the station wagon approached the customs port and a search seemed more and more likely.[103] When the customs officers told Leary that his daughter had been compromised, he foolishly, albeit perhaps gallantly, took responsibility for the marijuana by claiming the box was his property.[104] Furthermore, he "took the whole thing as a joke," an inspector later testified, and wondered aloud why customs officials were concerned with "such a small amount" of marijuana.[105] He compounded the situation, but revealed a key component of his future legal strategy, when he informed the officers who questioned him that "he knew more about narcotics and marijuana than either one of [them]."[106] This was probably true, but the inspectors certainly knew much more than Leary about narcotics and marijuana laws. They arrested Leary and the rest of his party. The Laredo incident revived Leary's career as a celebrity radical.[107]

The U.S. attorney, Woodrow Seals, soon to become the federal district judge, authorized his assistants to indict Leary and his daughter under the three-part model. By the standards of the Laredo Division, where prosecutors occasionally saw marijuana seizures cases involving several hundred pounds, Leary's case was a paltry bust. Despite his already notorious penchant for drugs, this was his first narcotics offense. It was possible that Leary could have gotten the routine bargain. Susan Leary, probably on the advice of counsel, actually did plead guilty to the tax count when she was arraigned on 21 February. Two days later, however, no doubt on the advice of her father, she withdrew the guilty plea and entered a new plea of not guilty on all counts. Part of the routine was for a defendant to act contrite. Leary found that unacceptable and also entered a plea of not guilty to all counts.[108]

Judge Connally presided during Leary's three-day criminal trial in Laredo. During the first day, on 9 March 1966, customs agents testified to the details of the seizure, and AUSA Ronald Blask soon rested the government's case. After some preliminary witnesses, Leary took the stand in his own defense. He began a multipronged attack on America's marijuana prohibition. Leary continued his testimony the next day. His central claim was that, under the First Amendment of the U.S. Constitution, he had a right both "as a scientist and as an initiated Hindu to use marijuana as a research tool and a sacrament."[109] One curious development during the trial was that Connally, whom Leary would later refer to as a notoriously tough "old tiger,"[110] let the witness wander rather far afield from the legal questions. The judge let Leary, for example, testify to the depth of his religious feeling. Leary stressed the necessity of employing drugs, and particularly marijuana, in order to achieve spiritual ends. Blask objected repeatedly, and Connally consistently overruled the objections. The judge was careful to see that the prosecutor did not ridicule Leary's religious views. Eventually, Connally did prod Leary's defense attorney to move his questioning along to the actual arrest.[111]

The judge was less indulgent, however, regarding legal points that had little to do with Leary's religious beliefs. When the defense attorney asked his client, for example, whether he had "a constitutional right to transport this marijuana," Blask objected and Connally sustained him. Susan Leary's defense counsel asked the judge for a clarification of the ruling. Judge Connally answered, "I simply am not interested in what this gentleman considered his constitutional rights to be."[112]

Although she was often lost in the proceedings, Susan Leary was in fact facing trial concurrently with her father. She waived trial by jury, however, and instead faced Connally's own judgment. Although it was too late at that point for her to change her plea, the judge ruled almost as if she had taken the standard plea deal. He declared that Susan Leary was guilty on the tax count, but not guilty on the two narcotics counts. Connally suspended imposition of sentence and placed the young woman on unsupervised probation while she was a minor.[113] Her father, by contrast, had gambled by trusting his luck with the jury. He lost when the jurors, unmoved by his passion and conviction, quickly voted to convict him. Judge Connally sentenced Leary to thirty years in prison.[114]

Leary appealed and remained free on bond.[115] Over the next few years he sustained his rhetorical attacks on marijuana and other drug laws. His publicity and fundraising efforts while he was seeking to overturn his conviction ensured that an otherwise very routine and trivial marijuana arrest grew into an infamous confrontation. Leary spoke at political rallies and on campuses, appeared on television and on film, starred in an off-Broadway show, and had his name written into at least two popular songs. In the summer of 1967, while he was still pursuing his appeal, Leary famously advised America's youth to "turn on, tune in, drop out."[116]

BORDER JUSTICE VERSUS THE COUNTERCULTURE

By the time Leary embarked on his crusade, it had become clear to the Southern District judges that the already heavy criminal caseload in the border divisions was on the rise. The judges decided in January 1967 to "equalize" their civil dockets to approximately 278 cases apiece. Both of the judges with duties on the border, however, were allowed to carry about one-half of the district's average, with Garza having 142 civil cases and Connally 138. The reason given for assigning them this (only comparatively) lighter civil docket was "the increased criminal cases which both handled."[117] Perhaps Connally's experience with Leary had awakened the judge to the coming crisis, but no other federal organization was as well prepared as the Southern District for the emergence during the 1960s of a new drug-celebrating counterculture.[118]

The Treasury Department's FBN had retained its responsibility for enforcing federal narcotics laws relative to heroin, cocaine, and marijuana into the 1960s, but the law enforcement bureaucracy had in general become fragmented and inefficient. The Department of Health, Education, and Welfare (HEW), for example, through its Bureau of Drug Abuse Control,[119] had gained responsibility in the mid-1960s for seeking ways to curb the abuse of the increasingly popular "psychedelic" drugs. President Lyndon Johnson called the government's combination of law enforcement and drug regulations "a crazy quilt of inconsistent approaches and widely disparate criminal sanctions." In special messages to Congress on 7 February 1968, Johnson announced a new get-tough approach. He recommended more effective statutes, proposed hiring more agents, and called on the Congress to create "a new and powerful" federal law enforcement organization dedicated to fighting the scourge of drugs.[120] Congress responded by abolishing the FBN and establishing in its place the Bureau of Narcotics and Dangerous Drugs (BNDD) within the Justice Department.[121]

Richard Nixon filled his presidential campaign speeches in 1968 with a rhetoric of law and order, playing on public fears of violent crime, dangerous drugs, and allegedly impotent law enforcement.[122] After his electoral victory and inauguration in January 1969, Nixon demonstrated unmatched antagonism to drugs. He was unsatisfied with the reformed laws he inherited from Johnson, and by July he proposed a new comprehensive narcotics statute.[123]

As Congress deliberated on Nixon's legislative suggestions, his own Special Presidential Task Force Relating to Narcotics, Marijuana, and Dangerous Drugs launched an ambitious publicity stunt named Operation Intercept. It began on 21 September 1969 with the announcement that customs inspectors would search every vehicle crossing the southwest border from Mexico. Intercept was unprecedented, because the task force directed customs officers to inspect every vehicle and container rather than the selected few. Unlike later, quieter, and more notorious activities undertaken by Nixon's special assistants, however, this stop-and-search campaign was both well publicized and completely lawful.[124] It was simply the maximum application of the "border search" doctrine. The White House canceled the operation three weeks later, but until then, the round-the-clock inspections interfered with legitimate trade, annoyed tourists, and alienated erstwhile "good neighbors."[125]

Operation Intercept's architects deliberately created this "world-class traffic jam," and courted the political backlash, to "bend Mexico to [America's] will." And the acknowledged "exercise in international extortion" largely succeeded.[126] The Mexican government protested, but within three weeks it had agreed that, if the United States lifted the quasi-embargo, Mexico would attempt to eradicate domestic marijuana and opium crops, and would begin to cooperate more fully with U.S. efforts to curb narcotics traffic across the border they shared.[127] On 10 October the Nixon administration replaced Intercept with "a less economically severe plan," dubbed Operation Cooperation. Nixon nonetheless defended the "shock treatment" on the grounds that "Operation Intercept was . . . believed necessary and it did accomplish a great deal."[128]

Domestic critics complained that the crackdown had cost American taxpayers $30 million but had not yielded larger caches of narcotics.[129] BNDD Director John E. Ingersoll countered with the claim that one of the benefits of Intercept was that the flow of narcotics from Mexico, especially marijuana, was "substantially curtailed." He noted that one of the effects of the shortage was that "in most places where it is available, at least the Mexican form, the prices have doubled and in some cases tripled." The dearth of Mexican-grown marijuana proved short-lived, however, and the federal government's subsequent interdiction only sustained the price hike.[130]

The predictable result of Operation Intercept in the Southern District of Texas was a surge in the workload of the judges and prosecutors. The effect began immediately. On 22 September 1969, for example, the prosecutors opened a case against John H. Bright and Bradford James Wirt, who were caught at the border with forty-one pounds of marijuana. They were charged in Laredo with a standard three-part indictment plus a conspiracy charge. Judge Connally arraigned the pair on 24 September. Bright pleaded guilty to the tax count and was sentenced to three years but saw all other charges dismissed. Wirt pleaded not guilty to all charges and asked for a jury trial. At his trial, which began the next week, Wirt moved to suppress the evidence and dismiss the tax count. When the judge denied the motions, Wirt asked to be rearraigned, and he pleaded guilty to the tax count. The prosecutor dismissed the remaining charges, but Connally sentenced Wirt to serve seven years in federal prison. The lesson in Laredo that was constantly reinforced was: do not try the federal district judge's patience or waste his time with procedural maneuvers or defense motions.[131]

Lewis C. Walters, Joseph Love Kennedy, and Pedro Negron were also arrested on 22 September and arraigned two days later. They were charged under the standard three-part indictment after being arrested with only three ounces of marijuana. The court appointed Robert O'Conor to represent Walters and appointed another local attorney, Roger Roha, to represent Kennedy and Negron. Walters pleaded guilty to the tax count, saw the other charges dismissed, and received a two-year sentence, suspended for three years of supervised probation. He was also fined $250 to be paid at $50 per month. Curiously, however, the government dismissed the cases against Kennedy and Negron, who had pleaded not guilty on all counts. It is not clear what had worked in their favor, whether the prosecutor realized that the two were innocent after all or was simply too overwhelmed by the pressure of cases after Operation Intercept to care about a three-ounce bust.[132]

The daily press of cases abated after Intercept became Cooperation, but there were plenty of leftovers from Intercept in the months that followed. One marijuana case that could not be dismissed as paltry was a 938-pound seizure that led in November 1969 to the indictment of Maximiliano Galaviz. The government did not offer Galaviz a deal on the tax count. His defense attorneys, including the Laredo lawyer George P. Kazen (who was the nephew of Abe Kazen, a prominent liberal Democratic congressman from Texas), apparently advised him nonetheless to plead guilty to transporting the marijuana. He did so, and the associated charge for unlawful importation was dismissed. Galaviz received the maximum sentence, twenty years to be served. Connally received contrite letters from the prisoner, however, and reduced that sentence to seven years.[133]

One last case in this cohort bears examination, because of what it reveals of Judge Connally's concerns with the changes he was seeing around him during the late 1960s. Robert L. Hunter and Robert Eugene Powell apparently were caught during Intercept but were not arraigned until 25 November, when their case was number 820 for the year on the Laredo criminal docket. They were charged with the unlawful purchase of two grams of heroin, which was for heroin the equivalent of the "tax count" for marijuana. George Kazen and his brother, Philip Kazen, represented the two young men (the Kazens paid five hundred dollars each to bail out their clients). Powell and Hunter pleaded guilty. Powell received a five-year sentence that the judge suspended in lieu of the same number of years of strict supervision, during which Powell was to have no association with drugs or drug users. Hunter received the same sentence, with the additional "conditions of the probation being that the defendant not associate with anyone whom he has reason to believe deals in or is associated with narcotics, amphetamines or any other type of drugs, that he continue his education for at least two years more and that he not play in any type of rock and roll band."[134]

The publicity that accompanied Leary's legal difficulties thrust him into the national spotlight and kept him onstage for years. Leary actively encouraged and ably exploited the fanfare as he attempted to persuade the dubious federal judiciary to confirm his asserted right to "alter his own consciousness."[135] On 19 May 1969, four years after his fateful encounter in Laredo, the U.S. Supreme Court accepted Leary's latest legal argument, this based on the Fifth Amendment, that the marijuana tax statute tended to *require* individuals to incriminate themselves by *acquiring* the forms necessary to pay the marijuana tax. The justices therefore called the "tax count" into question, which, of course, called into question all of the plea bargains based on its existence.[136]

Leary reaped few lasting benefits from his Supreme Court victory. The justices remanded his case to the Southern District court in Laredo. He was subsequently tried once more before Connally, convicted for transport, and sentenced to ten years. Leary then continued the crusade,[137] although during this phase he filed his appeals from his cell. Unable to face this situation for long, Leary escaped from prison with the assistance of the radical domestic terrorist group the Weathermen, also known as the Weather Underground.[138] Leary was recaptured after several years on the run. He resumed his appeal but finally lost.[139] When he was finally free of legal entanglements in the late 1970s, Leary had served a total of forty-two months on the twelve-year-old marijuana arrest.[140]

These actions cemented his place in the popular memory of the era. For proponents of the counterculture, Leary was a martyred saint. For that movement's detractors, he was the archvillain.[141] Leary declared, in the autobiography he published in 1983, that he began his crusade because, as he sat in the Laredo jail the night of his arrest, he knew he had "to fight this case in the courts of the land, to mobilize legal teams, to devise courtroom tactics, to file appeals, motions, briefs, depositions, to speak in defense of the right of American citizens to manage their own bodies and brains."[142] Although the result of his case cannot be listed among the greatest landmarks of the procedural rights revolution of the sixties,[143] Leary played a major role in the history of criminal case management in the Southern District of Texas.

Leary's attempt to persuade the federal judge to affirm his constitutional right to an altered consciousness was probably doomed from the beginning. The effect of his battle against the marijuana laws, however, which finally focused on the tax statute, brought that example of institutional plea bargaining to an end. The first shudders came in 1969, when a wave of drug defendants who had already plea bargained to receive lighter sentences but were nonetheless sentenced to prison, filed civil litigation to apply the Fifth Amendment retrospectively to their admissions. In each case Connally decided that the guilty plea had waived all defenses, including the privilege against self-incrimination.[144] Defendants coming before Connally for sentencing, apparently believing that the Supreme Court's decision would free them altogether, sought to be rearraigned so that their tax pleas could be voided.

The judge rejected these attempts to break the plea bargains. The surge of appeals thereafter subsided.[145]

During the year after Leary's case overturned the tax count, the federal prosecutors and defense attorneys briefly revived the standard plea bargaining, through the use of formal waivers. The defendant could plead guilty to the tax count only if they signed a statement to the effect that they understood that in pleading guilty they were relinquishing rights to appeal—under the Supreme Court decision in *Leary v. United States*—on the grounds that they had been asked to incriminate themselves. This waiver system creaked along until 1970, when the U.S. Congress repealed the marijuana tax act and passed a new narcotics law that did not leave prosecutors with the same discretion on indictments, or judges the discretion in sentencing. The final result was that plea bargains for probation, once standard, became extremely rare. Marijuana defendants, under the new laws, had little reason to accept the prosecutor's offer. More took their chances on a jury trial than before. The habit of treating a drug case as a relatively minor matter ended. It was an ironic legacy for the self-styled "High Priest of LSD."[146]

NOTHING TO DO BUT TRY A WETBACK NOW AND THEN

The annual prosecutions in the Southern District of Texas rose 66 percent over the five years from 1964 to 1969. Judge Connally's criminal caseload in Laredo, however, more than tripled during that time. Because of their assignments on the border, Judges Garza and Connally were the Southern District's chief arbiters of federal criminal justice throughout the 1960s. This period saw the federal government's mounting concern with the rise in violent crime, especially in urban areas. There were widespread public (and presidential) demands for "law and order." But the surge in federal prosecutions in the Southern District's border divisions was not the result of more aggressive law enforcement. The higher number of prosecutions was an accurate reflection of the increase in the number of crimes being committed on the border. In general, however, the criminal activities on the border were nonviolent.[147]

By 1970 the three most frequently prosecuted federal crimes nationwide were, from first to third, interstate automobile theft,[148] illegal immigration,[149] and narcotics violations.[150] For a time in the early 1970s, it seemed possible that an old consensus, namely, that prohibition and prosecution was the solution to the problems of drug abuse, was dissolving. For example, the National Commission on Reform of Federal Criminal Laws, a body that Congress created in 1966, finally recommended in 1970, "over the objections of a substantial body of opinion," that the government begin to treat marijuana possession as a minor offense meriting a fine but no imprisonment. President Nixon's "Commission on Marihuana and

Drug Abuse" also recommended at that time that possession of marijuana in the home be decriminalized. The president publicly opposed such "legalization," as he did any recommendation that appeared to soften his administration's hard line on drugs.[151]

By the time these commissions' experts had made their report, the tougher statute Nixon had been seeking since 1969 was on the books, as the Comprehensive Drug Abuse Prevention and Control Act of 1970.[152] Among other changes, this law repealed previous narcotics statutes and replaced them with the Controlled Substances Act.[153] This prohibited the manufacture, distribution, and possession of a lengthy catalogue of chemical compounds and various natural extracts. The 1970 statute reclassified a variety of substances that previously had been lumped into a general class of "narcotics and dangerous drugs." These were separated into five new categories, or schedules, with the penalties for violations assessed according to a calculus of estimated potential for abuse versus extant medically accepted uses.[154]

The 1970 act, significantly, also authorized federal prosecutors to distinguish an alleged consumer's possession of a small amount of a prohibited substance from an alleged supplier's possession of an amount large enough to indicate the "intent to distribute."[155] This statutory innovation acknowledged that smuggling had emerged on a larger scale by the 1970s. The market shift to high-volume traffic was due in part to the U.S. government's continuing efforts to maintain pressure on the southwestern border and other points of entry. It encouraged smugglers to bring larger and more profitable loads across the border. Leary recalled, for example, that in the early days "[m]ost of the pot traffic was conducted by amateurs and semi-pros," by "kids, who would pool their money and head for Mexico, and smuggle back a few kilos for personal use back home, or for sale to cover expenses." Marijuana was "too bulky and too cheap to interest the organized criminals much." Perhaps the marijuana dealers of the 1960s did resemble the freelancers that some chroniclers of the drug culture described,[156] but, if so, they were put out of business during the 1970s, when the risks and the rewards of trafficking increased. The prices that Americans were willing to pay began to attract the attention of professional criminals. As a result, the business of drug smuggling on the southwestern border, including traffic in both marijuana and heroin, was soon dominated by violent gangsters.[157]

These troubling developments were ongoing as President Nixon made a whirlwind reelection campaign tour through south Texas on, coincidentally, Operation Intercept's third anniversary. As he inspected the customs facility in Laredo on 22 September 1972, he revived the law-and-order rhetoric he perfected during his 1968 campaign and denounced judges who allegedly were obstructing the war on drugs.[158] The nation's prosecutors, he claimed, were becoming frustrated because any progress against drugs was being thwarted by "lenient" judges who would convict a heroin dealer but then "would let him out, [so] he went right back to what he had been doing before."[159] He praised Laredo inspectors for their efforts, however, noting that "others farther up the chain of our criminal justice system must do their part." "[W]e simply cannot tolerate a weak link anywhere in that chain," the president declared, "and this is why I am distressed by some indications that some judges may now have become such a weak link." He promised to "do whatever is necessary to halt this dangerous, permissive trend."[160]

The Warren court had long been a favorite target for Nixon, who disdained the court as much for its liberal criminal procedure decisions as for its stance on race relations. As president he had begun to shape the U.S. Supreme Court "in his own image" in 1969, by appointing Circuit Judge Warren Burger to replace Earl Warren as chief justice.[161] Nixon then elevated Judge Joe Ingraham, still the only Republican on the Southern District bench, to a vacancy on the Fifth Circuit Court of Appeals.[162] Ingraham's appointment gave the president an opportunity to name a judge to the Southern District of Texas who, presumably, met his own law-and-order criteria. Rather than choose a tough prosecutor or a state judge with a known record, however, Nixon appointed Carl Olaf Bue Jr., a distinguished admiralty attorney from Houston.

Bue had been born in Chicago on 27 March 1922. He attended the University of Chicago for two years and earned the A.A. in 1942. Like many young men (and future judges) of his generation, Bue interrupted his career to serve in the military during World War II. He had been a cadet in the reserves since 1939 and so joined the U.S. Army. He was commissioned as a captain in the Department of the Adjutant General. While stationed in Italy during 1944 and 1945, Bue studied at the University of Rome. He completed a fourth year of college at Elmhurst College in Illinois. He then attended Northwestern University from 1948 to 1951 and earned a Ph.B.[163]

Bue followed a friend's advice about the opportunity to gain a good legal education for a bargain price in Texas, and he went on to earn his LL.B. at University of Texas (UT) at Austin in 1954. Bue joined a Houston admiralty firm, Royston, Rayzor, and Cook, where he was a protégé of a senior partner, John R. Brown, until the latter took his seat on the Fifth Circuit. Bue was made a partner at the firm after four years. He practiced in maritime law, lectured on the subject at Houston's South Texas School of Law, and published articles in professional journals and law reviews.[164] Although Bue was later described as the closest thing Houston had to a "world-class" jurist, before his appointment to the Southern District he was relatively unknown outside admiralty and maritime circles.[165]

Bue was nominated in August 1970 to the Southern District seat vacated by Ingraham and confirmed by the Senate in October. On 6 November 1970 Chief Judge Connally presided over the investiture ceremony in Houston. Connally invited each one of the sitting judges to offer congratulations to their new colleague. Judge Garza observed that he already knew Bue to be a fine trial lawyer and expected that he would make a fine federal trial judge. Garza added further that he would welcome Judge Bue's company in Brownsville, "anytime you feel that you have done your job [in Houston]." As Garza was resuming his seat, Connally rose again, to suggest to the audience of lawyers, judges, and local worthies that a trip to the border would be a waste of the brilliant Bue's time. In Brownsville, Connally declared, Garza had "nothing to do but try a wetback now and then."[166]

This dubious remark, apparently, was Chief Judge Connally's attempt at gallows humor. By the 1970s, indeed, the problem of criminal case management at the border was growing more complex than ever. What follows examines this development.

A ONE-HUNDRED-MILE STRIP OF CITIZENRY WITHIN THE DECONSTITUTIONALIZED ZONE

After the Twenty-first Amendment ended the nation's thirteen-year experiment with liquor prohibition, the Supreme Court seemed to resume its slow progress toward a broad reading of the Fourth Amendment. The justices noted by 1958, for example, that judicial exemptions to the amendment's provisions ought to be "jealously and carefully drawn."[167] Then, during the 1960s under Chief Justice Earl Warren, the court presided over the celebrated "criminal procedure revolution" that became the rhetorical target of so many conservatives, including President Nixon. The revolution commenced in 1961 with the landmark Fourth Amendment decision *Mapp v. Ohio.* In *Mapp* the justices ruled that the exclusionary rule that had been used in federal courts for more than forty years must also apply in state criminal trials.[168] With this and subsequent decisions, judicial suppression of evidence became the recognized remedy for Fourth Amendment violations.[169]

The border search exception persisted, very nearly intact, throughout the Warren Court years. A Fifth Circuit panel observed in a 1963 case, for example, that a customs agent's authority to conduct warrantless searches at a border was "nearly unfettered."[170] But federal judges did forge "fetters" if they concluded that the practices of individual customs agents were constitutionally wanting. In 1965's *Marsh v. United States,* for example, the Fifth Circuit reversed the conviction of a narcotics defendant whose car was searched by a Texas state constable sixty-three miles north of the U.S.-Mexico border. Although the appellate judges scrutinized the circumstances of the case through the new lens of *Mapp* and related decisions, they did not need to refer to that ruling to overturn Marsh's conviction. Instead, the Fifth Circuit judges reaffirmed the border search's historic limitations. The constable had stopped and searched the car because a customs agent called to warn him to be "on the lookout" for a certain vehicle. The appellate court ruled that a customs agent's description was insufficient to create the probable cause the constable needed in order to search the vehicle.[171]

Judicial interpretation then grew to meet the nation's changing demands. For example, federal judges began to speak of an "elastic border," which they would define "by dynamic parameters dependent upon the facts of each case, instead of by a static, linear front." In other words, judges thought it more reasonable to allow "extended" border searches to be conducted in a "border area," rather than limiting border searches to a physical barrier that corresponded to a line drawn on the map.[172] The Fifth Circuit judges had not yet considered whether Congress possessed the power to delegate border search authority to noncustoms law-enforcement personnel. But federal judges had ample opportunity to examine that issue during the 1970s, after the Congress designated Border Patrol officers to be surrogate customs agents.[173]

As the mobile enforcement branch of the INS, the Border Patrol is the arm of the Justice Department specifically charged with detecting and preventing the entry of undocumented persons into the U.S. Federal statutes authorized its officers to question persons to verify citizenship or residency status, to detain their vehicle in order to check the immigration status of the occupants, and to inspect compartments or containers large enough actually to conceal a person. If, moreover, an individual's encounter with the Border Patrol occurs "within a reasonable distance from any external boundary of the United States"—usually one hundred miles from the geographic border—officers are empowered to detain, to question, and to inspect without a search warrant or probable cause that a crime has been or might be committed.[174]

An increase in illicit traffic in the 1960s provoked the federal government to increase border enforcement in the 1970s. In south Texas, smugglers sought to satisfy both farmers' seasonal need for cheap labor and Americans' constant appetite for illegal drugs—such as heroin and especially marijuana. Congress expanded the scope of the border search exception in 1971 to authorize the Border Patrol to exercise much broader law enforcement powers than the law previously allowed. The statute authorized INS personnel to "act" as treasury agents—as customs inspectors—during routine searches for undocumented aliens. This was the first of several so-called cross-designations that committed the Border Patrol to fight two wars, one against aliens and the other against drugs, on a single front. This obscured the division of duties between the Treasury Department's customs inspectors, who searched for goods, and the Justice Department's Border Patrol officers, who chased people. Border patrolmen might "change hats" in midstream during an immigration check in order to search for narcotics. A dramatic increase in the number of drug arrests by the Border Patrol soon flooded the federal trial courts in south Texas. Accused narcotics smugglers often had means (unlike undocumented aliens) to question the Border Patrol's authority during a trial, and if that proved unsuccessful, many convicted traffickers appealed. The federal trial and appellate judges began to disagree about the boundaries of the border search exception. Did the exception reach beyond the ports of entry? If so, how far did it extend? Could officers other than customs agents actually search vehicles and persons without warrants? If so, how far from the border did the exception reach? The federal judiciary, in sum, strained to construct "reasonable" boundaries for the emerging War on Drugs.

In a sense the cross-designation was a minor extension of responsibility: some Border Patrol officers were already deputized to act as "Customs Patrol Inspectors."[175] The 1971 statute, however, seemed to draft *all* Border Patrol officers into the war on drugs, by mandating that they perform a role as acting customs agents.[176] After their designation as the proxies of customs agents, Border Patrol officers began to sniff out more drug violators—literally so, in cases involving large-volume marijuana smuggling—during the brief immigration inspections conducted during routine stops somewhat removed from the physical border. The Supreme Court subsequently reversed several convictions on the grounds that the particular details of some stops violated the Fourth Amendment.[177]

The justices apparently accepted cross-designating the Border Patrol as reasonable, but they left open troubling questions for the lower federal judiciary to answer. How far could the Congress expand the previously narrow doctrine of the border search? Did the cross-designation vest the "acting" agents with full authority to make border searches on suspicion alone? In sum, judges hearing cases from the border area had to decide how far to "stretch" the Fourth Amendment in order to serve the serious national ends of federal narcotics law enforcement policy.

The remainder of this chapter will examine a representative sampling of these Border Patrol drug cases and controversies, and will analyze in particular the legal thought of Judge Garza. As a native of the border city of Brownsville, and as the first Mexican American federal judge, Garza declared a belief that Border Patrol checkpoints constituted a virtual "second river" for smugglers to cross. Garza stated at various times that the Fifth Circuit judges and the justices of the Supreme Court who wanted to narrow the Border Patrol's authority simply did not understand the realities of his home region. Garza therefore employed his broad judicial discretion to interpret law and language in order to instruct—and to verge on obstructing—these higher courts.

Judge Garza favored an expansive, flexible extension of the border search exception to the Border Patrol. The Supreme Court's and also the Fifth Circuit's early opinions in Border Patrol cases frequently ran afoul of his sense of reasonableness. The decisions by appellate judges above him had the potential to force lower federal judges to set free defendants who had been arrested, in some cases, with hundreds of pounds of marijuana. Garza refused lightly to accept that outcome for his hard-pressed jurisdiction. He grappled most often with the judges of the Fifth Circuit. He wrote trial opinions in which he carefully distinguished details of the cases before him from the similar cases treated in previous appellate decisions.[178] Garza was bound by appellate rulings. But, blessed with tenure, he risked reversal rather than discipline by attempting to hold the line where he thought it best to draw one.[179]

Among the pivotal issues in this controversy was the legal status of immigration checkpoints in the Border Patrol's theater of operations in south Texas, the Lower Rio Grande Valley. The roughly triangular area is outlined by three main highways. Highway 83 follows the Rio Grande from Brownsville to Laredo. Highway 77 also originates in Brownsville but heads north through Kingsville and to the outskirts of Corpus Christi. Texas 44 travels west from Corpus Christi and intersects Highway 83 north of Laredo.

The Border Patrol maintained at least twenty permanent checkpoints in Texas, as well as many others the agency considered temporary because its officers periodically shifted operations along a stretch of highway. In addition, Border Patrol officers monitored key intersections in the web of county and farm-to-market (FM) roads that crisscrossed the region. Garza's colleague in the district's border divisions, Chief Judge Connally, noted in 1974 that it was the Border Patrol's mission—"with its limited manpower"—to monitor these highways.[180] The Border Patrol relied on roving patrols and traffic checkpoints to accomplish its mission. It was increasingly the duty of the federal judges in the border area to evaluate procedures at patrols and checkpoints.

The distinction between temporary, permanent, and "fixed"—a category between temporary and permanent—mattered a great deal to the resolution of particular cases. By the time an individual judge issued an opinion regarding one checkpoint, however, the Border Patrol might have responded to a previous ruling from the same or a different judge, and changed either that checkpoint's location or its rules of operation. With the increasing Border Patrol involvement in drug arrests, the number of challenges increased. The timing of one arrest, trial, and appeal, moreover, overlapped with other drug trials. This situation made precedents moving targets in federal courtrooms from south Texas in the Fifth Circuit to southern California in the Ninth Circuit. The appellate and trial judges across the greater Southwest attempted to sort out the key points in dozens of opinions.[181] Judges of the Fifth Circuit, to assist themselves in deciding one case in 1975, compiled a list of the "so-called Texas border search cases" that they had reviewed during the previous five years. There were fifty-three cases on the list.[182]

This painstaking case-by-case jurisprudence was unavoidable, because no general rules for deciding the border checkpoint cases existed until the judges created them. For that reason, judicial opinions constituted elements in an extended conversation—or else a long argument—between robed colleagues. Garza's contribution to this dialogue was his imagined "second river" in south Texas—which he argued was as important to immigration and narcotics law enforcement as the Rio Grande, the first river. By charting this "second river," Garza sought to maintain the Border Patrol's effectiveness in the valley. He did not want its mission there to be eroded by what he criticized as impractical constraints imposed by distant appellate judges. Garza risked weakening constraints legitimately imposed on law enforcement by the Fourth Amendment to the Constitution.

The 1971 cross-designation did not indicate the federal government's intentional shift of focus in the war on drugs. It is significant in this respect that Congress designated Border Patrol officers as *uncompensated* "acting Customs Patrol officers."[183] The Congress therefore added personnel at no extra cost, because the Border Patrol officers were already serving in the border region, and they were paid, trained, and equipped with previously allocated funds. The patrol's strength in the Southwest, approximately fourteen hundred officers, remained fairly constant during the 1970s. Although INS budgets grew in these years, they grew less rapidly than the budgets for traditional narcotics enforcement. For example, the INS budget for fiscal year 1971 was $121.3 million, for 1972, $127.8 million, and for 1973, $137.5 million. During fiscal year 1974 the president's requested budget for the INS was $139.7 million, but the allocation for overall narcotics control, across all agencies involved, was around $785 million. Moreover, the 1974 increase was not for more personnel but for modernizing INS vehicles and communications, and also for the installation of an electronic sensor system along the Mexican border. One contemporary analyst suggested that Nixon's comparative lack of interest in immigration enforcement was shown when he appointed Romana Banuelos to be U.S. treasurer, even after it was discovered that a food-processing plant she owned had been a "flagrant employer of illegal aliens." The same analyst blamed Nixon for the INS's relatively low budget priority. He noted that the president "may have been influenced in the apportionment of funds by his high preoccupation with drugs."[184]

Federal judges in the Fifth Circuit considered the Border Patrol's changed status during a case arising from an arrest at an immigration checkpoint approximately eight miles north of Laredo on Interstate Highway 35. The Border Patrol considered this a "permanent" checkpoint, because it was well marked with signs declaring "slow," "stop ahead," and "stop" and featured a line of cones to direct the flow of traffic. On 27 January 1971 the two officers on duty from midnight to 8 A.M. were determined to stop and inspect every vehicle that passed during their shift. They stopped Richard McDaniel and Herman Canada and verified that they were both U.S. citizens by checking driver's licenses and vehicle registration. One of the officers, Gordon Aker, a ten-year veteran of the Border Patrol, later testified that he became suspicious of the pair because "[t]heir reactions were a bit abnormal to what the average person would be." McDaniel, the driver, appeared to be nervous although "very cooperative," which contrasted greatly with the attitude of his passenger, Canada, who "acted almost frozen."[185] Aker asked McDaniel to open his car's trunk. McDaniel complied. Aker wondered about the trunk's contents—four bulging burlap sacks that were poorly wrapped in Guadalajara newspapers—and McDaniel told the officer that the sacks contained alfalfa. Aker, skeptical, opened a sack and decided that the substance inside looked and smelled like marijuana. Aker arrested the pair, led them to a nearby holding van, and advised them of their rights.[186]

Federal prosecutors indicted McDaniel and Canada for concealing marijuana, transporting it, and for failure to declare and to pay the transfer tax on 181 pounds of marijuana.[187] Judge Connally, during pretrial hearings in Laredo, considered a motion by McDaniel's defense attorneys to suppress the evidence as the product of an unconstitutional search. Connally denied the motion. One month later he presided over McDaniel's one-day trial, during which Aker testified that McDaniel was "nervous" but "a little bit too glib [and] too cooperative." Aker also confirmed that he searched the car as his predetermined routine. Donald Scoggins, one of McDaniel's attorneys, suggested during cross-examination of Aker that his initial suspicion of McDaniel and Canada was related to the way they looked. Specifically, he asked the officer whether the two defendants were "what has been previously referred to as hippie types?" Aker testified that, on the contrary, "[t]hey were both blond, fair complected, very personable-looking young men." They wore their hair "somewhat" long, Aker said, but "not in [the] extreme."[188] If Scoggins hoped to elicit sympathy for his clients by implying that the officer had acted out of prejudice rather than according to a plan, the effort fell flat. The jury, after briefly deliberating, convicted the fair-haired, personable-looking young man who had been caught with 181 pounds of marijuana. Connally sentenced McDaniel to five years in federal prison.[189]

McDaniel's lawyers appealed, but on 11 May 1972 the Fifth Circuit affirmed Connally's denial of the motion to suppress. Fifth Circuit Judge Irving Goldberg delivered the opinion of the unanimous three-judge panel. He acknowledged the novel aspects of the case, noting, for example, that Congress had only recently assigned the Border Patrol to enforce the nation's customs laws. Because of that fact, McDaniel's prosecution had been "allegedly" brought under the "aegis of the 'border search' doctrine."[190]

The judges agreed that it belonged under that aegis. Goldberg declared that, although McDaniel's "unusual hour of travel" did not in itself establish probable cause, the timing of the trip might "properly arouse a 'reasonable suspicion.'" Also, the checkpoint was "reasonably situated" on a highway which led from Laredo to several major cities. The judges concluded that the sum of the circumstances justified the Border Patrol's "reasonable stretch" of the Fourth Amendment.[191] Goldberg declared that "proximity to the frontier does not automatically place a hundred-mile strip of citizenry within a deconstitutionalized zone, with its attendant de-escalation of Fourth Amendment requirements."[192] But in this case the patrol's actions had not crossed "that sometimes uncertain but always potent constitutional line which encircles the Government's relationships to its individual citizens."[193]

Goldberg's opinion in *McDaniel* gave federal district judges the language and reasoning they needed to decide later Border Patrol cases. The most significant phrase in *McDaniel* proved to be Goldberg's declaration that Border Patrol officers "wear two hats, one as an immigration officer and the other as a customs officer."[194] Although, during an immigration stop, Border Patrol officers could not search areas too small to conceal a person, Goldberg wrote that it was the " well-settled principle of law in this Circuit" that Border Patrol officers could search even a small compartment if a "reasonable suspicion" justified "donning their customs hats."[195] Goldberg's "two-hat" rule signaled the Fifth Circuit's acceptance of the Border Patrol's expanded role in the war on drugs. Judges in other jurisdictions, especially in the Ninth Circuit, also incorporated the analogy into justifications for admitting drug evidence collected by the Border Patrol.

The Fifth Circuit would not, however, merely rubber-stamp district judges' decisions. The appellate judges overruled, for example, Judge Connally's decision to admit as evidence 643 pounds of marijuana that narcotics officers had discovered in a white camper truck owned by Mary Storm, a single mother camping near Hebbronville with her two-year-old daughter. Connally denied a pretrial motion to suppress the evidence. At the July 1972 trial the agents testified that they searched Storm's truck only after they had received a "disturbing" tip about a vehicle matching its description. Storm testified that the male friend who accompanied her had borrowed the camper for one day, but she claimed to have had no prior knowledge of the 643 cellophane-wrapped bricks of marijuana that he apparently stashed in her truck. Connally, exercising his authority to ask his own questions during trials, was overtly skeptical and implicitly criticized Storm's morals and judgment for traveling with her child in those circumstances. The jury found Storm guilty.[196]

On 22 June 1973 the Fifth Circuit overturned Storm's conviction. In an opinion that drew heavily on the 1965 *Marsh* ruling involving the "tipped-off" constable,[197] Fifth Circuit Chief Judge John R. Brown wrote that the marijuana was "the fruits—or, more precisely, the weeds—of an unlawful search."[198] The perimeters of a "border search" and the looser standards of suspicion it implied could not be infinitely extended or stretched. Brown noted that, as far back as the *Carroll* decision, there were limits beyond which the federal courts would not allow narcotics agents to go, despite the social dangers of drug use. The search in *Marsh* was not declared invalid because it had been conducted by a state rather than a federal officer, Brown noted, but because the record did not contain facts sufficient for the constable to have even a reasonable suspicion that the car contained contraband or had crossed the border. In Storm's case government agents could not justify the search without observation of facts that supported a reasonable suspicion. The officers who stopped the camper were not engaged in a border search, and they should have established probable cause and obtained a warrant before undertaking the search. Brown's opinion put trial judges on notice that, even in cases that involved narcotics, they were expected to guard the boundaries set out by the Constitution just as conscientiously as customs officers monitored the borders of the nation. As Judge Brown wrote, "[A] badge and a hat are not impregnable talismans merely because of the elasticity of our Nation's perimeter."[199]

By repeated invocations of the *McDaniel* opinion, however, Judge Brown made clear that the panel's reversal in *Storm* was "in no way a denigration" of legitimate powers to conduct warrantless searches under existing border search doctrine. In this instance, he wrote, the government was simply misguided in its attempt "to bring the search [of the camper] within the broad and liberal ambit of the term 'border search' [and] to envelop the actions of the arresting officers . . . with the extensive panoply of statutorily-created, judicially-recognized powers to search without a warrant."[200]

With its 1973 decision in *Almeida-Sanchez v. United States,* the Supreme Court implicitly rejected the notion that the border was "elastic." The justices declared that the border exception articulated in 1925, in *Carroll,* "[did] not declare a field day for the police in searching automobiles."[201] Although the justices agreed with district and circuit judges that Congress could authorize the Border Patrol to search for either aliens or drugs, or both, because the United States had a right to protect itself from illegal importations, the court majority concluded that "no Act of Congress can authorize a violation of the Constitution."[202]

In a concurring opinion Justice Powell summarized the majority ruling by noting that "one who merely travels in regions near the borders of the country can hardly be thought to have submitted to inspections in exchange for a special perquisite."[203] The justices concluded that, in addition to the physical border, the proper constitutional boundary for a border search was the "functional equivalent" of the border. The court offered two examples: either an "established station near the border, at a point marking the confluence of two or more roads that extend from the border" or the "St. Louis airport after a nonstop flight from Mexico City."[204]

Unfortunately, most Border Patrol practices were less stark than these two examples. The Supreme Court therefore with one hand denied the trial judges' power to define the "elastic" border arbitrarily to accommodate the federal government's compelling interests, but with the other hand offered a similarly subjective standard of "functional equivalence." The ruling encouraged appeals by a host of narcotics defendants seeking to establish that their particular arrests occurred beyond the "reasonable" limits on terms such as *function* and *equivalent.*[205]

A panel of Fifth Circuit judges commented nearly fifteen years later that, after announcing this new standard in *Almeida-Sanchez,* the justices had "not otherwise explained the meaning [of the concept] . . . nor has the Court since elaborated its understanding of what types of checkpoints qualify as functionally equivalent to the border. The circuit courts, however, have examined in some detail the notion of functionally equivalent borders."[206] Because the court's decisions left the criteria for establishing the boundaries of the border search exception "largely unexplained," the Fifth and Ninth Circuits employed different approaches and charted different limits.[207]

The Fifth Circuit judges interpreted *Almeida-Sanchez* narrowly, for example, and defended an expansion of the Border Patrol's search activities. Conversely, the judges in the Ninth Circuit interpreted *Almeida-Sanchez* broadly; that is, they treated the decision as a narrowing of the Border Patrol's authority. The Fifth Circuit's rulings in cases such as *McDaniel* and *Marsh,* according to the Ninth Circuit, had created a concept of the border that had only a "tangential relationship to the law emerging from the Ninth and Tenth Circuits."[208] When the Supreme Court reviewed one of the Ninth Circuit decisions, the justices also noted that there was "some ground for confusion about the state of the law in the Fifth Circuit at the time *Almeida-Sanchez* was decided." Early cases seemed to affirm the officers' authority to search for aliens at checkpoints—although *McDaniel* "seemed to hold" that power to search there was qualified by a requirement that the location and operation of the checkpoint be reasonable—but the justices understood a subsequent Fifth Circuit opinion as adopting the Ninth Circuit's distinction between warrantless searches for aliens and searches for contraband.[209] The disparity and confusion meant that the rights of the residents in the Southwest depended more than ever on the discretion of individual judges, who, in addition to deciding what was "reasonable," now also had to grapple with the meaning of "functional equivalent."[210]

Judge Garza soon developed his own response to the Supreme Court's tightening of the elastic border in *Almeida-Sanchez.* On 19 July 1973, just before midnight, Border Patrol officers observed two vehicles, a van and a car, parked together near a levee one-half mile north of the Rio Grande. The driver of the car left and made a U-turn, and the van's driver departed on the feeder road to FM 494. As one officer later testified, this route was suspicious because the residents of the small nearby village of Granjeno were rarely abroad from their homes at that hour; in fact, said the officer, they would "roll up their sidewalks, if they had any." The officers stopped the van north of FM 494's intersection with FM 1016, two miles from the river. As they interviewed the driver, Gary Duane Conner, through his open door, the officers noticed his pants and shoes were muddy. The officers also looked beyond the driver's cab to check for hidden passengers in the cargo space, and saw several large bundles similar to those they had seen containing marijuana. The officers advised Conner of his *Miranda* rights, opened one of the bundles, and found that it was a bag of marijuana. The prosecutors charged Conner with importing and possessing with intent to distribute 675 pounds of marijuana.[211]

In an oral hearing before Judge Garza, on 20 September 1973 in Brownsville, Conner's attorney argued that *Almeida-Sanchez* justified suppression of the evidence: he alleged that the officers had conducted a roving search and had acted without probable cause. After considering the issue for two weeks, Garza announced that the facts of Conner's arrest were "distinguishable" from *Almeida-Sanchez.* The sight of two cars on the levee engaged in what appeared to be a clandestine meeting, he reasoned, gave the officers "more than probable cause" to stop and search the van for smuggled aliens. Moreover, Conner's muddied clothes and his possession of what appeared to be bundles of marijuana also gave the officers "more than probable cause" to search the van. Garza concluded that in the given circumstances—"[t]he proximity to the river, the time of the night, an automobile making U-turns on the river levee"—the Border Patrol had "founded suspicion" upon which to base their initial stop of Conner's van.[212]

The judge warned that, if the actions of the Border Patrol officers in this case could not be allowed, with the result that "only those stopped at the regular points of entry or their equivalent, such as the check points . . . can be stopped and searched"; then, he declared that "we better make up our minds that if we are to protect our vast borders against the entrance of illegal aliens and contraband into this country, we be prepared to spend millions of dollars to assure that those who are prone to violate our immigration and smuggling laws are caught at the river's edge when they land."[213] Garza declared that he "cannot believe that this was the intended holding of *Almeida-Sanchez.*" He denied Conner's motion to suppress the evidence.[214]

In a case he decided in June 1974, Garza transformed the Supreme Court's concept of functional equivalence into a model of the Border Patrol dual mission that he labeled guarding a "second river." The "second river" standard justified Garza's subsequent decisions that allowed almost any search by a patrol officer, but especially searches conducted at checkpoints, to fall within the extended border search criteria of *Almeida-Sanchez.* The judge first employed the phrase to describe the Border Patrol checkpoint on Highway 1017, nine miles northwest of the town of La Gloria, or some forty miles from Rio Grande City, a port of entry on the border boasting fewer than six thousand permanent inhabitants. Garza noted that the La Gloria checkpoint was "in an area and along a route commonly used for the smuggling of aliens and contraband into the interior of the country." [215] He commented that two other checkpoints, at Falfurrias and Sarita, respectively, were located at similarly strategic highway sites, and his reasoning, therefore, also applied to them.[216]

On 13 February 1974 a Border Patrol officer at the La Gloria checkpoint stopped a car that he noticed was riding low. As he spoke to the two occupants, Rodolfo T. Fuentes and his son, the officer detected an odor of marijuana. He asked Fuentes to open the trunk, but Fuentes claimed that he did not have the key. The officer found the key to the trunk hanging on the ring with the ignition key, opened the trunk himself, and discovered 660 pounds of marijuana. In May, Garza conducted a hearing in Brownsville to consider a motion to suppress the evidence. The government called as witnesses both the officer who made the search and his supervisor, the assistant chief of the U.S. Border Patrol station at McAllen. The latter testified that the checkpoint was ordinarily open only during one eight-hour shift per day, but it was a standard procedure during that shift to stop every car for an immigration check. He said that the Border Patrol did not always establish a checkpoint in the same location; however, the officers shifted the operation along the same stretch of Highway 1017.[217] The defense attorney contended that this testimony proved that the La Gloria checkpoint was neither a permanent site nor a "functional equivalent" of a border. According to *Almeida-Sanchez,* he said, the warrantless search of Fuentes's trunk was not sustainable.[218]

Garza declared that the facts showed that the pervasive odor of marijuana had established probable cause for the search.[219] He might have concluded his opinion with that observation. Garza, however, went further than strictly necessary because he believed that *Almeida-Sanchez* had left open a significant question of "what is and what is not an 'established,' 'fixed,' or 'permanent' checkpoint." Garza declared that it was his belief—which he noted was shared by his brother judge Connally—that the Supreme Court had reacted only to the "capricious and whimsical" nature of the search in *Almeida-Sanchez;* that is, the justices had intended to criticize its manner, not its location.[220]

Garza announced that he "simply cannot believe" that the court had "meant to say that the Fourth Amendment rights . . . rise and fall with the presence or absence of 'permanent' electrical outlets, large steel signs and concrete buildings." He said that a movable checkpoint that could be relocated within a strategic section of highway was not arbitrary, especially if it was administered regularly and the officers routinely required all travelers to stop. Realities of illegal immigration and illicit narcotics importation, Garza declared, demanded fluid arrangements such as the Border Patrol had employed at La Gloria. He understood this better than most, he said, by "virtue of handling the Brownsville Division of the Southern District of Texas for over thirteen years and having lived in the Rio Grande Valley all my life." During this extended service, he had become "intimately acquainted with immigration methods and problems peculiar to border areas." He used the balance of his opinion to impart to others "a more complete comprehension" of border realities, knowledge he felt was "necessary to understand why the La Gloria checkpoint and those similarly situated are border equivalents and why searches carried out at such operations are reasonable."[221]

Garza began by enumerating what he understood were the "three types of aliens" that passed through the Rio Grande Valley. The first cohort consisted of noncitizens who were authorized to enter the United States either to travel or to work. Members of the second group had been temporarily admitted—normally for seventy-two hours. Their mobility was restricted by the terms of a border-crossing card that allowed the bearer to travel freely within an area twenty-five miles from the border. The third group of aliens were illegal entrants, "the legendary mojados," as Garza described them, who "literally swim the river, often under the cover of night."[222]

Garza said that a significant number from this category successfully crossed the Rio Grande but were later caught at the Border Patrol's traffic checkpoints. The checkpoints therefore were a "second river" to cross before these would-be immigrants could "vanish into the Latin communities in the north."[223] The judge believed that "because of its strategic location" a checkpoint was the first place a member of this third class of immigrant came under the scrutiny of the INS. Therefore, a traffic checkpoint "serves the same function as the several international bridges that span the Rio Grande."[224]

As Judge Garza interpreted *Almeida-Sanchez,* the La Gloria checkpoint was permanent, strategically located, and nonarbitrary, because it was a barrier to all travelers. These facts were sufficient to define it as a "functional equivalent" of the border. Garza noted that the Fifth Circuit judges had stated that *Almeida-Sanchez* holding was narrow,[225] as had Connally, who was—because of his own long service in a border court—as "widely versed in the subject of alien control in border areas" as Garza himself. Familiarity with the border, Garza said, not merely knowledge of the law, was required for a judge to come to the proper conclusion in a Border Patrol case.[226]

The guiding principle was "reasonableness," he knew, but "in determining reasonableness, the needs of society must be balanced with the rights of individuals vital to our concept of liberty." It was unfortunate but true, Garza complained, that "it does not appear to be widely held knowledge among either the citizenry or the judiciary that the American crossing the river steps into a zone to which are also admitted tens of thousands of aliens daily who, unlike their American counterparts, do not have the same right to travel anywhere in our nation." The only way to catch these violators was to check everyone as they leave the border area. "Viewed in this posture," he concluded, the "checkpoints bear a rational relationship to a legitimate governmental interest." Garza believed that the traffic checkpoints' "very minor intrusion" was balanced by the "all but impossible" task that would be required of the Border Patrol if it had to dispense with it.[227] Unsurprisingly, Garza decided to convict Fuentes. The Fifth Circuit upheld the conviction on Fuentes's appeal, but the appellate judge neither accepted nor repudiated the "second river" theory. They accepted the opinion without filing a written opinion. As a result, the question went unanswered whether the "second river" was a truly viable judicial model for measuring functional equivalency.[228]

Judge Garza therefore was at liberty to return to his model in another 1974 case involving the La Gloria checkpoint.[229] Once again the Border Patrol officer on duty noticed that an automobile was riding low. Enrique Alvarez-Gonzalez, an American citizen, told the officer he was returning home to Kingsville from Zapata. This story raised rather than reduced the officer's suspicion: even if it was a true statement, it meant that Alvarez-Gonzalez had taken an unnecessarily roundabout route. Alvarez-Gonzalez willingly opened the trunk, the officer later testified, as soon as he was asked. The trunk contained 152 pounds of marijuana. Alvarez-Gonzalez was indicted for possession with intent to distribute, and subsequently filed a motion to suppress the marijuana. Like so many others caught in the Border Patrol's net, Alvarez-Gonzalez was willing to bet everything on the question of the marijuana's admissibility. He waived his right to a jury trial and submitted his case to Garza. The judge denied the motion to suppress and found Alvarez-Gonzalez guilty in January 1975. However, Garza offered to delay sentencing until the Supreme Court ruled on several cases then pending that concerned searches at Border Patrol checkpoints. Alvarez-Gonzalez elected to wait.[230]

The Supreme Court decided three cases related to Border Patrol traffic checkpoints on 30 June 1975. Of the three, Garza considered *United States v. Ortiz,*[231] which concerned a search at a fixed checkpoint, to be most relevant to *Alvarez-Gonzalez.*[232] Although functional equivalence was not at issue, in Garza's view that opinion supported his *Fuentes* holding because *Ortiz* did "not cast any doubt upon the Supreme Court's earlier suggestion that a checkpoint may be the functional equivalent of the border." More important was the fact that the court's *Ortiz* opinion did not call into question the "separate and independent ground [Garza] asserted in *Fuentes*" under the theory of the "second river." Hence, Garza now declared the search of Alvarez-Gonzalez's car legal.[233] For the first time Garza explicitly equated his pet theory to a "functional equivalent." Because *Ortiz* neither supported nor undercut Alvarez-Gonzalez's conviction, the judge could declare that the "second river theory remains a viable basis for upholding searches at the La Gloria checkpoint without any reference to the presence or absence of probable cause or reasonable suspicion."[234] Garza noted that his conclusion was "buttressed" by a post-*Ortiz* Fifth Circuit opinion in a separate case the judges announced around this time, in which the appellate court both affirmed his denial of a motion to suppress evidence and declared that the La Gloria site was a permanent checkpoint.[235]

When Alvarez-Gonzalez appealed, however, the Fifth Circuit once again failed either explicitly to adopt or to reject Garza's analogy of a "second river." Rather, the circuit judges noted only that permanence alone did not equal functional equivalence, and Border Patrol officers could conduct searches without probable cause, "only at the border or its functional equivalent."[236] The appellate judges declared that their opinion in *Fuentes* affirmed only the probable cause justification for that particular search, not Garza's holding that the La Gloria site was a functional equivalent.[237] Therefore, to settle La Gloria's status, the Fifth Circuit panel remanded the *Alvarez-Gonzalez* case. They returned it to Garza's court with the instruction that he ponder whether the site exhibited three specific characteristics before making an amended decision. First, the Border Patrol officers must operate the La Gloria site as if it were a permanent traffic checkpoint rather than a roving patrol or a "radically shifting" roadblock. Second, the ratio of the international traffic to the domestic traffic that passed through the checkpoint must indicate a connection to the border. The circuit judges noted, for example, that the presence of a "continuing and significant percentage of domestic traffic" would argue against treating the checkpoint as a "functional equivalent." If the international traffic outstripped the domestic, then all travelers reasonably could be treated as though they had recently crossed the border. Third, the checkpoint must regulate traffic coming from the border. The Fifth Circuit judges summarized the three criteria as "relative permanence, relatively minimal interdiction of domestic traffic, [and] a capability to monitor portions of international traffic not otherwise practically controllable." The appellate judges did not intend their list to be exhaustive; therefore Garza "should feel free on remand to consider whatever else [he] deem[ed] appropriate."[238]

Garza reset the case for trial. He heard testimony that the Border Patrol had once been in the habit of shifting officers along Highway 1017, but in 1973 the service had established the La Gloria checkpoint at a single, fixed location. There were no permanent buildings at La Gloria, and personnel limitations prevented the Border

Patrol from operating the checkpoint continuously, but the existing checkpoint did feature "permanent road signs, a light pole, an electric power drop, telephone lines and a paved apron for secondary inspections."[239]

Garza examined evidence offered by the government regarding traffic patterns and concluded that "the interdiction of domestic traffic at the La Gloria checkpoint is relatively minimal."[240] On the basis of the Fifth Circuit's own criteria, therefore, Garza ruled that the La Gloria checkpoint had been operating as a "functional equivalent" at the time the Border Patrol stopped Alvarez-Gonzalez. The Fifth Circuit affirmed Alvarez-Gonzalez's conviction in October 1977. At the same time the appellate judges added to their three-pronged test by stating that a permanent checkpoint must provide drivers "fair notice" of its existence. Finally, the circuit judges encouraged trial judges to favor findings of equivalence by taking a simple majority of the international traffic to be proof of a connection to the border.[241]

Unfortunately, while affirming Garza's decision, the Fifth Circuit judges mentioned his "second river" theory once, and that mention came in a footnote. Moreover, the appellate judges seem to have misunderstood the theory: the opinion stated that Garza initially had approved of the placement of the La Gloria checkpoint on the grounds that it was a "second river" for temporarily, legally admitted Mexican nationals, that is, the category of aliens who carried border-transit forms. The circuit judges apparently understood that the "second river" formed by the traffic checkpoints prevented these people from traveling beyond their twenty-five-mile limit. The circuit judges felt that La Gloria's alleged status as a "second river" had therefore no bearing on the question in the case, because the purpose of a functional equivalent of the border was to prevent illegal entry, not "overextended" entry of legal aliens. In the footnote to this discussion, however, the judges wrote that a checkpoint's potential function as a "second river" was "a factor deserving attention."[242]

It is not clear whether the Fifth Circuit court would have explicitly approved the "second river" theory if the appellate judges had understood the theory as Garza actually formulated it, that is, that the line of checkpoints acted a secondary barrier to the so-called "legendary mojados." It is likely that the circuit judges would have accepted the formulation on those grounds, because, in the opinion in *Alvarez-Gonzalez,* they accepted that the Border Patrol encountered undocumented aliens in the interior of Texas. The appellate judges wrote, for example, that the various alien smuggling techniques that the Border Patrol encountered had a common element that was "almost invariably to be found in every scheme: a rendezvous on the Texas shore of the Rio Grande, with the aliens being responsible for fording the river on foot and presenting themselves there for departure inland."[243] Therefore, Border Patrol officers at the traffic checkpoints were concerned with people who had already successfully crossed the first river, which Circuit Judge Gee, the author of the majority opinion, wrote was rather "inappropriately named Rio Grande," because "aliens can swim, wade, and in some places walk across it easily."[244]

Circuit Judge Goldberg, who as the author of *McDaniel* wrote the "two hat" analogy as well as the warning that "proximity to the frontier does not automatically place a 100-mile strip of citizenry within a deconstitutionalized zone,"[245] firmly dissented in *Alvarez-Gonzalez.* He feared that the Fifth Circuit had abandoned its principles for the sake of the Border Patrol's convenience. The majority opinion was "inconsistent with the standards we announced in our earlier opinion in this very case"—an earlier opinion that Goldberg had joined, he now wrote, "in the hope that it charted the moderate course adumbrated by the Supreme Court in *Almeida-Sanchez.*"[246] He offered as evidence of inconsistency the fact that the Fifth Circuit recently refused to extend the status of functional equivalence to a checkpoint near the town of Freer, on the grounds, the judges had said, that "the functional equivalency label is one not lightly to be bestowed."[247] Now, Goldberg charged, the circuit judges were assigning that label to "a garden variety permanent checkpoint."[248]

Goldberg said that he was "not insensitive to the law enforcement interests" and admitted that the majority "may well be correct that allowing searches at La Gloria without probable cause would increase the detection of aliens illegally entering the country." However, many aliens might also be discovered if the Border Patrol operated the site "simply as a permanent checkpoint" where officers were "free to stop all cars, to question all occupants, and to search whenever after the questioning there was probable cause under the none-too-stringent standards that have emerged in this context." Goldberg argued that the Supreme Court had established this distinction in procedure to balance competing public and private interests. To maintain that necessary balance, Goldberg believed, Alvarez-Gonzalez's conviction should have been reversed by the Fifth Circuit.[249]

THE ATTENDANT DE-ESCALATION OF FOURTH AMENDMENT REQUIREMENTS

The "functional equivalent" of the border had proved to be an inhospitable environment for cultivating judicial standards in other courts as well. All of the tests or models judges offered were subjective and predicated on a trial judge's discretion. But from Garza's perspective his theory of the "second river" had advantages over both the Supreme Court's examples in *Almeida-Sanchez* and the Fifth Circuit's three-pronged test in *Alvarez-Gonzalez.* For Garza, and for other federal trial judges serving on the border during this early phase of the war on drugs, the analogy of the "second river" could be a concrete expression of the abstract "functional equivalent." A judge could refer to it to justify decisions to prosecutors, defendants, and other federal judges in the circuit.[250]

In December 1974 Judge Connally turned sixty-five years old and entered semi-retirement. He accepted senior judge status, which allowed him to retain his life-tenured judgeship but carry a reduced docket. President Gerald R. Ford appointed the Laredo criminal defense attorney Robert O'Conor Jr. in April 1975 to replace Judge Connally in the Laredo Division of the Southern District.[251]

O'Conor was born on 22 June 1934, in Los Angeles, California, where his Texas-born father worked as a stuntman and extra in Westerns. The family eventually returned to Texas, where O'Conor attended UT as an undergraduate, earning the B.A. in 1956, and as a law student, earning his LL.B. in 1957. He entered private general legal practice in Laredo as soon as he graduated. O'Conor was the first Southern District judge in a generation to have missed service during wartime, but he was a U.S. Army Reserve captain in the Judge Advocate General Corps from 1957 to 1964.[252] O'Conor was not particularly active in local politics. Perhaps, in the aftermath of the Watergate crisis, disgrace and resignation of President Nixon, and accession of President Ford, O'Conor's basic neutrality in partisan matters was a benefit.[253]

Judge O'Conor had defended scores of accused drug defendants in Laredo, but he soon demonstrated that he was not sympathetic to the defense in the Border Patrol cases. Randado, Texas, is thirty-two miles northeast of the border, on Highway 16, and some forty miles north of the border on Highway 649. The presence of these highways close to the river, in a sparsely populated area, attracted undocumented aliens as well as narcotics smugglers. The Border Patrol established a traffic checkpoint one mile east of Randado, near the confluence of the highways, always at the same location. It consisted of a mobile van that the Border Patrol officers on duty used as an office, portable signs and lights, and a portable generator. The patrol did not operate the checkpoint continuously, and when it was not in use the officers dismantled it and "no trace of its whereabouts remain[ed]." The courts later concluded, however, that only inclement weather and "a shortage of personnel prevented its continuous operation." When they had the checkpoint open and operational, however, the Border Patrol officers on duty stopped all traffic.[254]

The Border Patrol stopped John David Wilson at the Randado checkpoint during one week in February 1975, when officers had it open twenty-four hours a day. After completing the typical change of law enforcement hats, the officers on duty discovered that Wilson was in possession of 493 pounds of marijuana. Although Judge O'Conor's review of the circumstances during Wilson's trial in January 1976 predated the Fifth Circuit's final decision in *Alvarez-Gonzalez,* the judge employed both the circuit's "three-prong" test and Garza's "second river" theory to conclude that the checkpoint met the Supreme Court's criteria to be considered the border's "functional equivalent." Having done that, he denied the defense motion to suppress the evidence and easily convicted Wilson of possessing the marijuana with an intent to distribute. The judge assessed a five-year sentence and fined Wilson two thousand dollars. But, taking his cue from Connally's habits in Laredo, with which he was so familiar, O'Conor suspended the sentence and placed Wilson on five years' probation.[255]

Despite the probated sentence, Wilson complained that the search had been unconstitutional, and he appealed the conviction. He argued that the Randado site both lacked permanent structures and was operated sporadically, and therefore did not qualify as a permanent checkpoint. On 8 June 1977, Fifth Circuit Judges Gewin, Gee, and Fay affirmed O'Conor's ruling. The appellate judges did not question either the reasoning or the reliance on the theory of the "second river," but they did not need to address the question. The appellate court simply accepted that the facts had justified Wilson's conviction. The Randado checkpoint thereafter was a judicially accepted as a "functional equivalent" of the border, at which every car could be stopped for a citizenship inquiry without probable cause or reasonable suspicion.[256]

These decisions were not completely at odds with the general trend in the courts. For example, in 1977 Associate Justice Rehnquist wrote for the majority of the Supreme Court that border searches were "reasonable simply by virtue of the fact that they occur at the border."[257] In some other context, such a simple qualifying phrase—"at the border"—might be taken to be the definitive judgment. With regard to border searches, however, the line dividing a reasonable from an unreasonable search was not as bright as a line on a map. Fourth Amendment jurisprudence is typically characterized by judicial regulation of law enforcement activities that inevitably intrude on some civil, criminal, or even human rights. Federal judges are entrusted with the burden of deciding "[w]hen the right of privacy must reasonably yield to the right of search."[258]

The separate but parallel border law enforcement issues that Garza had joined in his "second river" opinions—the flow of drugs and aliens—were unified in the public imagination by the late 1970s. Mexican American community leaders spoke against a growing tendency of Anglo law officers to treat all Mexican Americans living near the border as possible illegal aliens and all aliens as potential drug smugglers—that habit that by the 1990s began to be called profiling. And beyond the problem of unrestrained law enforcement officers, the resident Mexican Americans of south Texas took seriously threats by vigilante groups, including the Ku Klux Klan, to defend the border.[259]

To reassure Mexican Americans, and also to reward them for their support of his election, President Jimmy Carter appointed Leonel I. Castillo, a Houston politician and activist, to become director of the INS.[260] As chief of the INS Castillo was the first Mexican American to run the Border Patrol. He sought to reform the agency from both above and below by establishing new training directives and by hiring more minority officers. Because of his publicly stated sympathies for the plight of undocumented workers from Mexico and his forceful denunciation of the Klan's threats to police the border, Castillo was criticized for being too "soft" on illegal immigration.[261] Carter faced similar criticism for asking Castillo to lead the INS. The president flirted briefly with the idea of decriminalizing possession of some drugs, in particular marijuana.[262]

President Carter's early, very brief support for "dovish" approaches to narcotic and immigration law enforcement ran counter to the prohibitionist goals Congress and many Americans continued to support. The president eventually abandoned efforts seriously to rethink the nation's war on drugs and aliens. That his ideas about reform were ambivalent at best was indicated when Carter offered the cabinet-level post of attorney general—the most influential law enforcement position in the federal government—to the "hawkish" Judge Garza. Garza declined the top job at the Justice Department, but in 1979 he accepted Carter's nomination to an open seat on the Fifth Circuit Court of Appeals.[263]

As revealed through his frequent references to direct experience of the border, Judge Garza's opinions were informed by lifelong residence in Texas. He was never a disinterested party in the twin struggles against drugs and aliens nor a neutral mediator between the federal government's perceived needs and the public's stated rights. Rather, Garza was an unabashed advocate for the Border Patrol. His "second river" idea easily translated into uncritical acceptance of almost any expedient by an officer that interdicted illicit traffic. Unfortunately, Garza's warning that, unless the appellate courts let him and like-minded trial judges extend the Border Patrol's powers in the Southwest, then the federal government must "be prepared to spend millions of dollars" to control the border proved too conservative. The Fifth Circuit judges—over the rare dissenting voice—yielded the point and unleashed the Border Patrol. Over the ensuing two decades, the campaign against traffic in illegal narcotics and alien immigrants cost billions. The trials and appeals that resulted from higher funding for law enforcement added to the already heavy burden on the federal courts.[264]

CHAPTER FOUR

Managing "Our Federalism" in the Southern District

DURING THE LATE 1960S minority claimants' goals expanded, grew diffuse, and became more controversial. Would-be "structural reform" litigants challenged federal district judges to intervene in and to reform the alleged constitutional deprivations in school discipline, criminal prosecutions, and other domains of public governance traditionally considered to be within the sole purview of state officials. Affected federal judges faced hard choices in the 1970s: first, to separate frivolous complaints from legitimate grievances; second, to determine if the latter cases could be remedied by federal judicial intervention; and, third, to decide whether to act on behalf of a meritorious plaintiff or to abstain in a legitimate case in the name of bedrock principles of comity and federalism.[1]

Comity is the courtesy a judge extends to another judge when their jurisdictions overlap or appear to be in conflict. Judicial references to comity usually imply the unwillingness of a federal judge to rule in a case concerning a state law, in the absence of a rule of decision on that issue by the appropriate state court. It is a gesture of respect, of deference in recognition of the obligation of the state courts to enforce the U.S. Constitution; however, comity is not obligatory. Under Chief Justice Earl Warren, the Supreme Court frequently placed perceived denials of due process and/or equal justice above the principle of comity or other features of dual federalism. Various Warren Court decisions concerning Fourteenth Amendment rights bolstered the claims of emergent or newly militant minority groups. After *Brown* one of the most significant of these decisions was 1961's *Monroe v. Pape.*[2]

In *Monroe* the court revitalized the Civil Rights Act (CRA) of 1871, better known as the Ku Klux Klan (KKK) Act, which authorized citizens to file federal civil rights suits against state officials.[3] Between the 1870s and the Great Depression of the 1930s, the court gave wide latitude to states' power to enforce state laws. As result, the KKK Act became moribund. The justices revived the 1871 statute in the 1939 case *Hague v. CIO*, when it affirmed a federal district judge's order enjoining Jersey City, New Jersey, officials from enforcing an ordinance to prevent a labor rally in a public park.[4] But until the court ruled in *Monroe* that a search by Chicago police had been conducted as official harassment, the justices did not resurrect the full potential of the statute. The justices declared that the officers were personally liable to the plaintiffs for damages and, in doing so, rescued this statute from "ninety years of obscurity."[5] Despite its alleged abdication of leadership in enforcing *Brown,* the *Monroe* decision proved the Supreme Court's basic commitment to supporting the struggling civil rights movement. The justices' willingness to protect citizens' exercise of constitutional rights encouraged supporters of civil rights to push harder for fundamental reform in the Jim Crow South. Their political efforts in the early 1960s led to legislative victories and then to further progress through civil rights litigation in the federal courts.[6]

Congress eventually responded to southern abuses by enacting the 1964 CRA. It expanded the federal government's authority to initiate lawsuits or to provide support to litigation private citizens filed to combat racial, ethnic, and in some cases gender discriminations, in schools, accommodations, employment, and housing.[7] Further, lawmakers recodified the KKK Act, and provided that "[e]very person" who, "under any statute, ordinance, regulation, custom, or usage . . . causes to be subjected, any citizen of the United States . . . to the deprivation of any rights, privileges, or immunities secured by the Constitution and laws, shall be liable to the party injured in an action at law, suit in equity, or other proper proceeding for redress"(after recodification, this provision is usually referred to as Section 1983).[8] Thereafter, the number of requests filed in the federal courts for equitable injunctions of state action increased sharply.[9]

When the Supreme Court created exceptions to long-standing abstention doctrines in the 1960s, federal judges were more willing to hear federal civil rights lawsuits. In *Dombrowski v. Pfister*[10] a civil rights worker named Dombrowski sued to enjoin the enforcement of a Louisiana statute prohibiting participation in "subversive" activities, which state prosecutors and state judges interpreted as including organizing civil rights activities. According to comity principles, federal judges were not empowered to interfere in ongoing state prosecutions without evidence of bad faith in the application of the state law or the possibility that the prosecution would cause the defendant "irreparable injury." A federal three-judge panel dismissed the complaint because civil rights workers had failed to demonstrate the necessary conditions for judicial intervention.[11] The Supreme Court reversed the three-judge panel's decision. An irreparable injury had occurred, the court said, when individuals had to forego constitutionally protected activities to avoid arrest or other sanction. The prospect of facing criminal charges for exercising the rights of free speech or association created a "chilling effect upon the exercise of First Amendment rights [which] may derive from the fact of the prosecution, unaffected by the prospects of its success or failure."[12]

The *Dombrowski* and *Monroe* rulings expanded the range of state-initiated actions the justices deemed appropriate for federal intervention.[13] Editors of a leading casebook on the federal courts noted that the decisions loosed "an impressive flood of litigation against state officers in the federal courts," as civil rights activists brought Section 1983 actions at an increasing rate. In 1960, one year before *Monroe,* plaintiffs brought only 280 cases under the provision. By 1971 the number of Section 1983 complaints filed annually had risen to 4609.[14] Reviewing this increase in litigation to enjoin state action, and federal courts' willingness to hear such cases, Philip Kurland declared in 1970 that "[i]n a Court as active as the Warren Court, it was not surprising that the abstention doctrine became moribund."[15]

But in the early 1970s, under Chief Justice Warren Burger, a Nixon appointee, the Supreme Court's opinions revived abstention and restraint. In 1971, in *Younger v. Harris,* the justices announced that federal district judges should abstain from enjoining state laws if a criminal prosecution was under way, unless they found evidence of bad faith or official harassment. Harris had been distributing leaflets suggesting the elimination of private ownership of industry. He was indicted under California's criminal syndicalism law, which proscribed activity advocating an illegal overthrow of the government or private industry.[16]

Harris sought relief from the state's prosecution under the *Dombrowski* doctrine. In the name of restoring comity and shoring up what he referred to as "Our Federalism," Associate Justice Hugo Black, for an eight-to-one majority of the Supreme Court, announced a preference for abstention even concerning alleged state limitations on First Amendment rights of free speech, unless by abstaining a federal judge would be allowing the defendant in a state prosecution to "suffer irreparable damages." Black wrote that it was a "basic doctrine of equity jurisprudence" that equitable relief should be withheld if the parties had "an adequate remedy at law."[17] In dismissing the suit from the federal courts, however, the justices did not consider Harris's statutory right to proceed under Section 1983.[18]

The *Younger* decision contained no new restrictions on a state defendant's right to seek relief in a federal court. Instead, it restated the traditional exceptions to federal equitable power.[19] But *Younger* and related decisions represented the Burger court's effort to reinvigorate principles of comity and federalism by curtailing the permissive resort to federal injunctive relief. Essentially, the justices sought to resolve the legislative-political tensions that had developed during Warren's tenure, to restore a perceived lost balance of national and local governance, and to repair badly frayed federal-state relations.[20]

Further, the decision to leave many emerging civil rights questions to be resolved by state courts indicated the justices' efforts to reduce the federal trial and appellate court workload. That workload rose throughout the 1960s, as federal judges managed desegregation suits and other "public law litigation," as they faced rising criminal caseloads, and, with the introduction of Section 1983 suits, as they decided a variety of novel civil rights and civil liberties issues.[21]

It was in this latter area that old labels of liberal and conservative truly ceased having any utility as a predictor of judicial attitudes. Judges Seals and Singleton, for example, had emerged from opposite sides of the ideological divide within the Democratic Party. Yet, when the rights of free press and free speech were at issue, they were both strikingly liberal. Judge Noel, by contrast, had been, like Seals, a protégé of the liberal Senator Yarborough. But on many of these issues he sat among the conservatives calling for federal judicial restraint and respect for "Our Federalism." This chapter investigates the results of the Southern District judges' grappling with these novel controversies.

VIVA LA RAZA

Many farm workers in Texas were Mexican-descended. But the middle class leaders of the Mexican American political organizations such as the League of United Latin-American Citizens (LULAC) did little more for farm workers than support the end of the bracero program.[22] During the 1960s younger leaders emerged. They exerted an enormous direct influence on Texas labor organizations. Less directly, the new generation of Mexican American leaders inspired a working-class-centered civil rights movement, sparked a revival in litigation by Mexican Americans, and broadened the applications of Section 1983.

César Chávez, the most prominent and charismatic of a new generation of Mexican American leaders, had been criticizing the bracero program since the 1950s. In 1962, before the repeal of the bracero system, Chávez founded in California the National Farm Workers Association (NFWA).[23] The fledgling union gained national attention through its strikes and boycotts, most famously against table grapes. In 1966 Chávez led striking farm workers on a twenty-five-day, three-hundred-mile pilgrimage from California's San Joaquin Valley to Sacramento, the state capital. Shortly, several struck growers recognized the NFWA and agreed to negotiate contracts with the union. In August 1966 Chávez's largely Mexican American membership voted to merge with a Filipino American union. The new union, the United Farm Workers Organizing Committee (UFWOC), affiliated with the AFL-CIO.[24]

Eugene Nelson, one of the NFWA's organizers in California, helped to create the modern farm workers' movement in south Texas. In May 1966 Nelson sought support in Houston for a boycott of products of a struck grape grower, but the parties came to contract terms. With the original purpose of the Texas trip mooted, he organized the valley farm workers. After conferring with interested individuals, including church leaders, Nelson went to Starr County and formed the Independent Workers' Association (IWA). On 1 June, during the peak of the 1966 melon and cantaloupe harvest, IWA members walked off their jobs at eight major farms, declared a strike, which they celebrated as *La Huelga,* and began picketing. The strikers sought a union contract that guaranteed farm wages of $1.25 per hour, equal to the federally established minimum for nonagricultural workers but double the wage that melon pickers usually received.[25]

The growers went to state court and won an injunction against the strikers from Seventy-ninth District Court Judge Woodrow Laughlin. He issued a temporary restraining order (TRO) on 2 June, contending that some IWA strikers were not actually employees of the struck farms and, therefore, lacked standing in any labor disputes at those farms. Since the judge's order prohibited picketing the struck farms, the IWA continued protests at other farms or picketed the packing sheds where fresh produce was prepared for transport by truck or railroad. Judge Laughlin's order kept entrances to struck farms open, but it did not get the ripe melons out of the fields and to market. Growers therefore dispatched "crew leaders" to the border to recruit Mexican "greencarders." On 8 June the IWA's leaders staged a rally at the international bridge at Roma, Texas, where picketers attempted to persuade Mexican workers to refuse employment in Texas. Starr County Deputy Sheriff Raul Peña halted the demonstration and arrested Nelson, ostensibly for violating the judge's order. Peña brought Nelson to Rio Grande City, where County Attorney Randall Nye detained him at the courthouse for four hours but filed no charges.[26]

Also on 8 June the IWA voted to affiliate with Chávez's NFWA. But the next day, Judge Laughlin declared that the strikers were violating Texas's "mass picketing" statute, which required individual protesters to be separated by fifty feet.[27] He issued a temporary injunction against the picketing, effectively ending the strike for the 1966 season. The melons were either already harvested or could be left to rot with little economic loss to the growers. The strike failed. But although Nelson had started very late in the season, with little time to build support, he had attained a key goal, namely, publicity for the NFWA.[28]

Unwilling to lose the union's momentum by disbanding until now-departing migrant workers returned to the valley for the fall harvest, Nelson persuaded the remaining union members and their sympathizers to emulate the NFWA's recent Easter pilgrimage in California. He suggested a four- to five-day march from Rio Grande City to nearby San Juan to visit the local shrine. Begun on 4 July, the event attracted more participants, added new destinations, and gained deeper symbolic meanings with each additional mile. Eventually, the march was transformed from a relatively brief strikers' march into a two-month, four-hundred-mile "people's march" to the state capitol. On the way to Austin, the marchers passed though Corpus Christi, where James DeAnda presided over a rally. Planning to arrive in Austin on Labor Day, 5 September, the participants would call on Governor John

Connally and demand that he summon a special session of the legislature dedicated to enacting a state minimum wage of $1.25. Connally ultimately refused to call a special session.[29]

Although the march had grown so large and diverse that the union's original demand for a contract and a fair wage was obscured, the marchers, many of them Starr County strikers, enabled Nelson to maintain his organization. IWA supporters soon became UFWOC affiliates. The union leaders entered the valley's fall harvest season fully committed to revitalizing the strike.[30]

Officially, the strike had not ended. The UFWOC picketed, demonstrated, and canvassed farm workers' neighborhoods every day, except Sundays, from June 1966 until July 1967. The union's activities provoked further conflicts with growers and associated businesses, and attracted harassment from local authorities. Participants in the strike suffered repeated arrests, prosecutions, and violent confrontations at the hands of law enforcement officers.[31] On 12 October 1966, for example, approximately twenty-five UFWOC members picketed on U.S. Highway 83, adjacent to fields belonging to the Rancho Grande Farms. One organizer used a bullhorn to appeal to laborers still in the field to join *La Huelga.* There was no evidence that these exhortations disrupted work, but they annoyed the Rancho Grande management. At a manager's request, Starr County deputies ordered the picketers to disperse. UFWOC leader Raymond Chandler challenged Deputy Peña's authority to issue this directive. Peña arrested Chandler for disturbing the peace when, according to Peña, he "started talking to me, you know, in very loud and vociferous language."[32]

Other picketers obeyed the order to disperse, and none were arrested. The deputies took Chandler to Rio Grande City and filed the complaint against him at the courthouse. The maximum punishment for the violation alleged was a two-hundred-dollar fine, but the sitting magistrate fixed Chandler's personal bond at five hundred dollars.[33] When his associates came to post the bond for Chandler's release, Peña told them that since they were not lawyers, they had no business in the courthouse and would be jailed if they did not leave. An attorney later returned to secure Chandler's release.[34]

Less than two weeks later, deputies arrested other protesters, including Domingo Arrendondo, the president of Starr County's UFWOC chapter. When the arrestees shouted their rallying cry, *Viva la huelga* ("Long live the strike"), a deputy struck Arrendondo in the face, pointed a gun at his forehead, and warned him not to repeat the union's protest slogan. The courthouse, the deputy declared, was a "respectful place."[35]

Missouri-Pacific Railroad property and businesses were damaged during the strike. Authorities assumed that these were acts of vandalism carried out either by union members or their sympathizers. County Attorney Randall Nye requested assistance from Governor Connally after the UFWOC picketed packing sheds outside Rio Grande City, near Missouri-Pacific tracks, when the green pepper and lettuce crops were ready for harvesting, packing, and shipping. Connally sent Texas Rangers to help local deputies arrest strikers in Starr, Hidalgo, and Cameron Counties.[36]

After consulting with the state attorney general's staffers, Nye charged ten UFWOC leaders with violating the state's secondary picketing statutes.[37] One of the supporters arrested was Reynaldo De La Cruz. While he was in custody, Rangers advised him that they could get work for him for $1.25 per hour, the UFWOC-demanded wage, if he abandoned the strike. They suggested that farm workers could organize a "peaceful" union at a later date. The Rangers warned De La Cruz that they had come to the valley to end the strike and would not leave until they succeeded.[38]

Meanwhile, the UFWOC suffered more of what they claimed were spurious, selective, or harassing incidents of law enforcement by both state and county officials. On 28 December, for example, Deputy Peña filed charges against De La Cruz for impersonating a peace officer. Peña had learned that De La Cruz and Pedro Dimas, another union member, wore badges shaped like shields when directing traffic at the UFWOC headquarters. Deputies and Rangers all wore stars.[39] The day De La Cruz and Dimas were arrested, the union demonstrated at La Casita Farms. One picketer reached through the window of a truck and snatched at the coat of La Casita employee Manuel Balli. Balli shook him off and drove on. This was the most serious physical confrontation initiated by a union member that was reported during the entire strike. Nevertheless, Starr County deputies arrested and filed assault charges against the picketer who grabbed Balli.[40]

Notwithstanding the UFWOC complaints of official harassment and selective enforcement of the laws, the growers convinced Judge Laughlin that the strikers had encouraged vandalism and incited violence. He issued another temporary injunction on 11 July 1967, proscribing further picketing on or near property of La Casita Farms. A panel of judges of the Texas Court of Civil Appeals concluded that Laughlin's findings of fact that the union was responsible for vandalism were unsupported, but nevertheless upheld the injunction.[41]

The union organizers responded to this legal setback by filing a Section 1983 action in the Brownsville Division of the Southern District of Texas. In its complaint, the UFWOC requested that the federal court enjoin the future enforcement of the various state laws that the Starr County prosecutors had invoked to "chill" union members' rights guaranteed by the First and Fourteenth Amendments.[42] In part because the civil docket in the Brownsville division was neglected in favor of the criminal docket, which was perennially choked with immigration and drug cases, and also because lawyers on both sides sought numerous delays, several years lapsed before a federal court examined the case. The decision will be reviewed later in this chapter.[43]

As a result of the delayed federal court action, the union's attempt to organize valley farm workers was delayed until the 1970s. Yet the Starr County strike had immediate consequences, unintended by the UFWOC leaders but eventually appreciated by advocates of Mexican American civil rights. The rumblings from south Texas shook up the established organizations, such as LULAC, which attracted urban professional, middle-class, and liberal Mexican Americans. These groups had abandoned civil rights litigation in favor of politics. Despite notable political wins and patronage gains by some Mexican Americans, most experienced continued discrimination, suffered persistent economic hardship, and received inferior education.

Chávez had not founded a working-class version of the middle-class LULAC.[44] Neither Latin heritage nor American citizenship was a condition for UFWOC membership. And Chávez resisted being labeled an ethnic leader, noting that "[w]e look at workers as workers, not at their nationalities."[45] Nevertheless, most of the union's prospective members, especially in Texas, were Mexican-descended. The heroic image of impoverished but selfless farm workers struggling against corporate growers and defying official repression appealed to many Mexican Americans who came of age during the 1960s, a decade of cultural and political ferment. Civil rights marches were flowering in the South, the Black Power movement was emerging in the North, and antiwar activism was energizing campuses across the nation. But until farm workers in California and Texas marched against unfair wages, dangerous working conditions, and poor treatment, many young Mexican Americans perceived that the struggle towards social, political, and legal equality had stalled. Working-class, barrio-bound youth as well as middle-class, college-bound Mexican Americans counted Chávez among a handful of cultural heroes and role models.[46]

By the mid-1960s continued discrimination against Mexican Americans inspired students at Saint Mary's University in San Antonio, Texas A&I University in Kingsville, and other predominantly Mexican American campuses to reject the liberalism of their parents' generation and to embrace more radical political ideologies. Budding militants rejected aspirations to assimilate with a dominant white culture and identified themselves as "Chicanos," a name that demonstrated pride in their Mexicano heritage. This was a loosely defined movement, but in general the Chicanos were politically progressive, even radical, relative to established spokespersons for the Mexican American community. They eschewed both the goals and tactics of the liberal middle class. Instead of seeking to win elections or promising to exchange votes for patronage, Chicanos celebrated direct action, mass protest, and self-reliance. Despite Chávez's denials of ethnic particularity, these activists romanticized the farm workers' marches as clear demonstrations of Chicanismo.[47]

Tension grew between generations, and the division was widened by the broader issues of the day. For example, after Saint Mary's University students founded the Mexican American Youth Organization (MAYO) in 1967, they used it as a forum to criticize and to protest the Vietnam conflict as evidence of the continued imperialism, violence, and racism they alleged was a major theme in U.S. history. U.S. Representative Henry B. Gonzalez of San Antonio, a longtime friend of President Johnson, responded by denouncing Chicanos' militant rhetoric as "hate." He repeatedly defended Mexican Americans' patriotism on the floor of the House. In 1969 Gonzalez rejected the label "Chicano" and described himself as "an American of Spanish surname and of Mexican descent . . . what is commonly referred to as a Mexican American."[48] Such defense of the status quo led Chicano youth to regard their elders as collaborators in the Anglos' oppression of *la Raza* (the Chicano race). The Chicano activists called them *vendidos* ("sellouts").[49]

These were unfair charges. Although the liberal middle class seemed complacent, the spirit of the decade also animated many members in the older generation. In spring 1966 fifty Mexican American leaders walked out of a conference hosted by the federal Equal Employment Opportunity Commission (EEOC), because the EEOC planners were preoccupied with African Americans and did not place Mexican Americans' concerns on the agenda. The Mexican Americans began to complain that President Johnson took their political support for granted.[50] The early results of the exodus were gratifying for those leaders who worried that by the 1960s Mexican Americans had become the "Minority Nobody Knows."[51] Johnson created the Inter-Agency Committee on Mexican American Affairs, promised a White House conference to study ethnic discrimination in the Southwest, and appointed Mexican Americans to several government panels. For example, the president appointed physician Hector Garcia, the founder of the American G.I. Forum (AGIF), to be the first Mexican American member of the U.S. Commission on Civil Rights.[52]

Unfortunately, Johnson's new exercises in patronage brought few changes in his own priorities. He delayed and ultimately abandoned plans for hosting the White House conference. Instead, he authorized members of his cabinet to meet in El Paso during hearings of the new Inter-Agency Committee. Soon he was distracted by criticisms and protests from other quarters. As a consequence, Mexican Americans' frustrations increased. Leaders like Garcia were impressed by the determination farm workers demonstrated throughout their march and thirteen-month strike. Middle-class leaders also noticed when the farm workers' plight attracted national attention.[53]

Mexican Americans had by then resumed civil rights litigation. In 1967 the San Antonio attorney Pete Tijerina obtained a $2.2 million, multiyear grant from the Ford Foundation. He used it to found the Mexican American Legal Defense and Education Fund (originally abbreviated MALD, now MALDEF). When the Civil Rights Commission held hearings in San Antonio in December 1968, Commissioner Hector Garcia invited Tijerina to describe why he organized MALDEF. Tijerina said that his experience defending Mexican Americans before all-Anglo juries, a decade after the U.S. Supreme Court condemned discriminations in jury selection, convinced him that a legal defense organization was needed.[54] Under "freedom-of-choice" plans for school desegregation, moreover, Mexican Americans were not allowed to transfer their children into Anglo-majority schools, but African American children could transfer into white schools, because, according to existing interpretations of laws, all Mexican American students were already enrolled in "white" schools.[55]

MALDEF lawyers had either filed or were contemplating lawsuits to attack these practices, but Tijerina depicted the great expense of private litigation and called on the U.S. attorney general to fight discrimination against Mexican Americans. He assured the commissioners that he did not intend to compete with black civil rights efforts but sought only to broaden the scope of federal government efforts.[56] As contrasted with federal attorney's recent support of African Americans, Tijerina noted, the federal government had never intervened in a civil rights lawsuit involving Mexican Americans or filed an amicus curiae ("friend of the court") brief to support them.[57] Tijerina did not wait for legal assistance from Washington.[58] But instead of suing to change desegregation rules, MALDEF initially undertook a number of cases that established the organization as an unofficial civil liberties bureau for militant Chicano high school students. The upheavals brought by the black civil rights struggle, the farm workers' movement, and antiwar protests led many Mexican-descended youths to adopt similar goals and direct action tactics to combat the inequities they encountered.[59]

In the late 1960s leaders of MAYO and similar college-based organizations began to encourage high school students to protest substandard facilities, regulations of clothing styles, hair styles, and other personal expressions, and, most often, the Anglo-centered curricula. Beginning in 1968, students in San Antonio, El Paso, Houston, and elsewhere in Texas responded to local school administrators' routine refusals to discuss their Chicano-inspired manifestos for school reform by walking out. The influence of the farm workers' strikes was revealed by the frequent display of the UFWOC's thunderbird flag during student protests.[60] The walkouts seriously disrupted most targeted campuses.[61]

More than any other Chicano organization, MAYO chapters on Texas's college campuses actively advised high school students on the predominantly Mexican American campuses to organize protests. MAYO had only an advisory role in most walkouts until late 1968, when its Pan American University chapter played a key role in precipitating a mass exit of high school students in Hidalgo County's Edcouch-Elsa Independent School Distrcit (ISD). The Pan Am organizers had been instructing pupils regarding Chicano politics and protest tactics for several weeks when, in October, two students were expelled for refusing to comply with district haircut rules. Student activists, accompanied by MAYO advisers, met with the Edcouch-Elsa superintendent to demand that he reinstate the two students. When the superintendent refused, the students resolved to walk out. The school board, consisting of three Anglos and two Mexican Americans, evidently expecting that response, met in early November to develop an official policy regarding the anticipated outbreak of student unrest, then mailed notices to district parents threatening to expel students who engaged in any demonstrations, such as a walkout, or who joined organizations that disrupted schools. The notices blamed "outside agitators" for making necessary the new disciplinary rules.[62]

Students rallied publicly to announce two recommendations and fifteen demands. They included proposals to add Chicano cultural and historical perspectives to the curriculum, and to eliminate the long-standing rule forbidding the speaking of Spanish on school grounds.[63] The board refused to consider the demands, and more than 150 students walked out in mid-November. While students demonstrated across the street, a committee of student leaders met with the principal. He refused to seek an immediate meeting of the board. The contentious students pressed him, and he summarily expelled them. When protests resumed the next day, teachers recorded the name of every student they recognized. The principal had the Hidalgo County sheriff arrest five of the dozens of students who still demonstrated on the second day of the walkout. The charge was loitering on school property.[64]

When the school board next met, four members upheld the mass expulsions but voted to schedule hearings where individual students could petition for readmission. The fifth board member, a Mexican American, abstained. Of seventy-eight students who sought readmission during the first week of hearings, forty-seven were allowed to return to class on probation and the remaining thirty-one were expelled for the rest of the semester. But ninety-four students did not request readmission.[65]

Once arrested or expelled, the Edcouch-Elsa student activists were represented by local attorney Bob Sanchez of McAllen and by MALDEF volunteer lawyers. They sought a TRO from Judge Reynaldo Garza. Sanchez complained that the blanket expulsions deprived students of due process, because they were confirmed *before* individual hearings. Garza agreed, and he ordered the board to admit all ninety-four suspended students pending hearings. The legal team also filed a Section 1983 civil action against the school district, superintendent, board members, and principal on behalf of three of the five students arrested for loitering and two other students. The suit alleged that the school officials' prohibition of demonstrations and their methods of ending the walkout eroded the students' civil rights. The plaintiffs requested fifty thousand dollars in damages.[66]

Garza convened a hearing in Brownsville, where the district superintendent admitted that there were no written criteria for deciding whether a particular student's expulsion was to be permanent. The student's attitude and actions during the walkout were the major factors the panel considered. Incredulous, Garza sought clarification: "In other words, if they kow-towed to you and said you were a nice principal, they got back in?"[67]

On 19 December 1968 Garza ruled that the district's arbitrary expulsion procedure and blanket ban on demonstrations were unconstitutional. He ordered the school district to readmit the students, directed that all traces of the expulsions be expunged from the students' permanent files, and assessed a nominal damage award against the Edcouch-Elsa ISD.[68]

Almost all of the Edcouch-Elsa students returned to class. But beyond obtaining the satisfaction of seeing administrators scolded, they gained little from the walkout. Nevertheless, the students raised the political profile of the MAYO leaders and encouraged larger walkouts in 1969, notably in Kingsville and Crystal City.[69] The MALDEF lawyers dispensed legal advice, which perhaps accounts for the fact that many of the protests after Edcouch-Elsa's, although often tense, ended in negotiated settlements rather than in lawsuits.[70]

One exception to this trend toward settlement concerned the official response to a protest by the seventeen-year-old Lucinda Escalante. The controversy combined the Chicano rights movement in south Texas with a larger student protest of America's involvement in Vietnam, which had begun to build in the district in the late 1960s.[71] Escalante attended high school in La Feria, a border city between Brownsville and McAllen. She distributed leaflets in school corridors to announce a protest rally arranged by the MAYO-influenced La Feria Youth Organization. MAYO had wanted to call attention to the number of Chicanos serving in Vietnam, which was high in proportion to their actual percentage of the U.S. and Texas populations.[72] The principal gave Escalante and two students who had helped her pass out the leaflets a three-day suspension, because they had distributed literature without permission. Escalante pointed out that no announced policy barred passing out leaflets and that other students distributed literature on school grounds, but the principal refused to reconsider.[73]

Escalante then visited La Feria's superintendent to request immediate reinstatement and a "timely" hearing regarding the suspension's legality. She was accompanied by Efrain Fernandez, the MAYO member who had given her the leaflets for distribution, and by Roger Dunwell, who identified himself only as a "civil rights worker" but who had written the letter she presented to the superintendent. In it Escalante suggested that the principal had violated her constitutional right to free speech and had denied her the right without due process. She referred the administrator to the recent U.S. Supreme Court decision in *Tinker v. Des Moines.*[74] In *Tinker* the court had declared that students "do not shed their rights . . . at the schoolhouse door" and reversed the expulsions of three who had protested the war by wearing black armbands to their school.[75]

Escalante had engaged in volunteer activities in the valley, including poverty relief and voter registration, but she was now explicitly identifying her protest with the national struggle for students' rights.[76] The La Feria superintendent refused to discuss her suspension. He denied that Fernandez and Dunwell had the authority to represent Escalante, who was a minor. Escalante later returned with a typed note signed by her father, but the superintendent still refused to intervene, since only one day remained of the suspension.[77]

After the suspension expired, the La Feria school board denied Escalante's written request for a hearing. In December 1969 a Brownsville lawyer named Filemon B. Vela filed a Section 1983 action in Judge Garza's court. He was joined in the suit by MALDEF cocounsel Tijerina and two other volunteer attorneys. The federal complaint, filed one year to the day after Garza enjoined the Edcouch-Elsa board, alleged that Escalante had been deprived of rights of speech and association guaranteed by the First Amendment and equal protection of the laws guaranteed by the Fourteenth Amendment. She had been singled out for punishment, the attorneys argued, because the principal disapproved of the message her leaflet contained, not because of an infraction of his unwritten rule. They also contended that the board's deference to an unwritten rule in denying Escalante a hearing deprived her of due process. The attorneys requested that Judge Garza enjoin this rule, order the removal of any trace of the suspension from Escalante's record, and declare the official's actions unconstitutional.[78] They also requested that he "[a]ward such other relief as is just and proper."[79]

Although the complaint did not employ the term *Chicano,* as did many of the MALDEF-sponsored suits, the district's response to the lawsuit indicates that the authorities believed that the MAYO militants were manipulating Escalante in order to create a political issue that would advance the Chicano cause. Therefore the district's lawyer, Orrin Johnson of Harlingen, seized on every opportunity to discredit MAYO and militant dissent in general. He disputed various points of fact in the complaint but also noted various errors in spelling. Johnson took special exception to the lawyers' use of "Mexican-American citizen" to describe Escalante. He noted that "[a]ccording to her school record, Lucinda is a citizen of the United States and by law is not a hyphenated citizen of the United States." Finally, he claimed, the complaint had not correctly stated the issues in the case. According to Johnson, who posed them as questions, they were:

> (a) must the corridors of the public schools—which belong to everyone—be used as the forum for distribution of unauthorized leaflets which cater to race prejudice and bigotry and which tend to demean or provoke other students purely on the basis of race or national origin?
>
> (b) Does the right of free speech require that one always be allowed to use the corridors of a public school immediately before commencement of classes for leafleting [*sic*] designed to divide and excite the students on the basis of race or national origin and that also tends to disrupt order, discipline and neatness in the school?[80]

Throughout, Johnson focused on the ethnic issues that Escalante allegedly sought to inflame. He explained that La Feria officials were angry that this student had brought "ethnically divisive" and provocative antiwar leaflets to school the day after a patriotic Veterans Day assembly. His argument also relied, however, on a basic procedural question, which was: "(c) May such unauthorized literature be so distributed at school without, first, obtaining the permission of the principal in contravention with the long-standing rules and practices of the school?"[81]

Few of the facts were disputed, and Garza requested that the lawyers summarize their positions on the relevant case law. Vela argued that Supreme Court decisions, including *Board of Education v. Barnette*, the World War II–era "flag salute" case,[82] and *Tinker*, established that unless a student's speech or action "materially disrupted" the education of fellow students, it was protected by the First Amendment. He noted that at La Feria the principal had applied "his" rule regarding announcements inconsistently and had attempted to prevent specific subjects and opinions from being discussed in classrooms. This was the prior restraint that Garza had condemned in the Edcouch-Elsa district, Vela argued, and he must condemn it once again.[83]

Johnson disputed Vela's central argument that, since Escalante's activities were not disruptive, *Tinker* and other precedents applied. To the contrary, Johnson stated, leafleting had caused an "uneasy" feeling to pervade the school for the rest of the day. And he wrote, "If an individual wanted to incite the emotions of the students of La Feria High School just as the day's classes were to begin, she could not have picked a more volatile vehicle than an appeal to ethnic differences with the added force of the impact of the Viet Nam War." But Johnson implied that the impact of Escalante's leafleting on other students' learning environment was the secondary concern. The primary one, he noted, was the maintenance of the La

Feria officials' ability to control the district's schools, free of the fear of students' lawsuits. Johnson appealed to Garza's sense of proportion and his judicial management sensitivities: "If there were a practical question to present to the Court, it would be this: How much time does a Federal Court have to spend on three-day suspensions of seventeen year old students who do not first attempt to work out their complaints about disciplinary actions through the administrative channels of the school?"[84]

Briefs from the attorneys merely restated their contentions: Vela and the MALDEF lawyers claimed Escalante's rights were denied; Johnson argued that she was a pawn in a ploy to disrupt the peace at La Feria High School. On 1 August, Garza sustained the former position. He declared that "[t]here was no evidence that the leaflets disrupted the activities of the school in any manner, and this made the suspension unconstitutional." The judge agreed with the school district that it could regulate the time, place, and manner of distributing literature on its campuses, as long as the rules were "reasonable and non-discriminatory" and content-neutral. Administrators might require that all materials be subjected to review before distribution, but the regulations were permissible only if they did not act as "a cloak for censorship and selective enforcement." The judge withheld the requested injunction against the principal's "so-called unwritten rule," however, and instead urged the La Feria district to develop regulations that met the conditions he outlined. Finally, noting that the three days Escalante had spent under suspension could not be replaced, Garza ordered the school district to expunge its files of any record of the "unconstitutional suspension."[85]

Garza's firm support of the constitutional rights of Mexican American students in these two cases does not indicate that he supported the goals of either Chicano militants or critics of American policies. He did accept the substance of the critiques from both quarters. In the late 1960s Garza had one son in college preparing to apply to law school and another son in the U.S. Army training for possible duty in Vietnam. The judge never denied administrators' duties to keep control in the schools in order to provide an environment suitable for the education of the younger generation. But Garza's rulings in the Edcouch-Elsa and La Feria cases showed that he opposed the arbitrary application of otherwise legitimate administrative authority. The rulings also indicate why liberal Mexican American leaders, who in 1961 had opposed his appointment to the federal district bench in the Southern District of Texas, and even persons associated with the Chicano movement, had lobbied for Garza when President Johnson was considering candidates to appoint to fill the seat left vacant by Associate Justice Tom C. Clark, who resigned from the U.S. Supreme Court in 1967. Clark's seat eventually went to Thurgood Marshall.[86]

MALDEF's early lawsuits helped to reestablish litigation as a tool for vindicating Mexican American civil rights. These efforts indicated that the new organization could contend viably in constitutional disputes.[87] But MALDEF's early victories did not advance claims that Mexican Americans were a group distinct from Anglos. Instead, these cases indicated that in an era of protests, Chicano students in Texas were subject to, and objected to, the same oppressive regulations as Anglo students, as illustrated by the attorneys' strategies in the La Feria case. Vela made few references to the ethnic aspects of Escalante's complaint and instead suggested that, in addition to *Tinker,* Garza should follow the reasoning of his Southern District colleague Judge Seals in a recent decision involving an Anglo high school student's suspension in the district's Houston Division, *Sullivan v. Houston Independent School District* (HISD).[88] But Johnson had repeatedly referred to ethnic politics, especially MAYO's alleged efforts to turn Escalante's case into a Chicano cause célèbre. He argued that Garza should follow *Schwartz v. Galveston Independent School District,* which Judge Noel had recently decided in the District's Galveston Division.[89]

Garza's ruling in *La Feria* followed *Sullivan* rather than *Schwartz,* but if he had taken the opposite course the result would have had the same significance for Chicanos *as* Chicanos, that is, none at all. An examination of the two cases follows.

THE *YOUNGER* GENERATION

Escalante's suit did not represent the struggle for Chicano civil rights. Instead, it was one of many student controversies that the Southern District judges, among others, faced in the late 1960s. Like Escalante, the plaintiffs in the two cases Vela and Johnson cited in their respective briefs had filed Section 1983 claims. The first case, *Sullivan,* concerned the suppression of the students' "underground" newspaper. The second, *Schwartz,* involved the student's haircut. Both suggest the varied claimants who in ever larger numbers were seeking to expand the scope of civil rights laws enacted to advance the rights of African Americans. Both, especially the haircut case, epitomize the essentially local disputes that the U.S. Supreme Court, in *Younger,* ultimately sought to exclude.

The root controversy in the newspaper case was an effort by administrators of Houston's new Sharpstown High School to suppress a student publication, the *Pflashlyte.*[90] During the 1968–69 school term, Sharpstown's first term in operation, seniors Dan Sullivan and Mike Fischer—"B" students with good disciplinary records—complained about the absence of clear regulations governing student dress or conduct. Sullivan, for example, had once violated "school regulations" by wearing a neckerchief, but the principal was unable to cite which rule he had broken. Students' frustrations led to the organization of an after-school rally near the campus, where students and some teachers discussed the concerns. Sharpstown athletic coaches interrupted the rally. They reportedly threw books, ripped notebooks, and accused students of being "Communists and Fascists." Later alleged incidents of harassment by teachers, arbitrary discipline, and administrative hypocrisy added to the students' dissatisfaction.[91]

Sullivan and Fischer learned that they could have a newspaper expressing their criticisms printed at the University of Houston (UH), if an official campus organization sponsored the work. Determining that the Students for a Democratic Society (SDS) would accommodate them, Sullivan and Fischer drafted an introductory issue and attended three SDS meetings at UH, to ensure that the paper would be printed. They did not join SDS because, they later claimed, they disagreed with the organization's radical politics. But when they received copies of the premier issue of their paper, they discovered that "SDS" had been printed at the bottom of each page. They removed the initials by cutting off the bottom portion of each of the 125 sheets. The second issue bore the name *Pflashlyte* on the front, and "Students for a Democratic Society" on the back, the latter banner high enough on the page to prevent its being excised without removing portions of text from the front. The letters SDS were printed in the middle of the reverse side in the third and final issue.[92]

Sullivan and Fischer distributed the first issue on 27 February 1969. The second was ready the next day, and they distributed it as well. Most students apparently did not read or display the *Pflashlyte* on school property. Sharpstown officials discovered copies stacked in a boys' restroom and others stuffed inside sewing machines in the girls' homemaking classroom.[93] The Sharpstown principal and assistant principal called in Sullivan and Fischer separately. Both students admitted that they had printed and distributed the paper. The principals told them that their actions were serious violations of "school regulations," which was compounded by their involvement in a "secret organization" (presumably SDS). However, the principals neither informed the students what disciplinary action, if any, they faced, nor offered them an opportunity to cease printing the *Pflashlyte* in order to mitigate punishment. Instead, several days later, the principal expelled Sullivan and Fischer for the remainder of their senior year.[94]

Represented by Houston attorney Chris Dixie, Sullivan and Fischer filed suit in the Southern District under Section 1983, charging that the expulsions deprived them of free speech and due process. They requested an injunction from Judge Seals that would reinstate them at Sharpstown, and they also sought a declaratory judgment that the rules under which they had been suspended were unconstitutionally vague and overbroad. Finally, they applied for recognition of their lawsuit as a class action.[95]

Joe Reynolds, who had long represented HISD in its school desegregation litigation, also responded to the students' complaint. Arguing that the principal's actions expelling Sullivan and Fischer had been justified because their paper's publication and distribution had resulted in "complete turmoil" at the school, Reynolds contended that the contents of the *Pflashlyte* were "calculated to encourage insubordination to school authority." He asserted that the expulsions were justified by "reports" that two "so-called radical organizations," SDS and a secondary school affiliate, the Student Union for Democratic Schools, were attempting to "infiltrate" Houston high schools.[96] These rumors reflected contemporary mainstream fears, driven by the federal government's own obsession with student radicalism. Federal prosecutors were then subpoenaing major national news magazines for information on SDS activities. Yet SDS had unraveled by 1969.[97]

Neither the unsubstantiated rumors of radical "infiltration" nor the unsupported accusations of "insubordination" convinced Judge Seals that HISD was in imminent danger. After seeing their records and evaluating their behavior in court, the judge concluded that Sullivan and Fischer were "rather typical young American men of high moral character." He entered a TRO that required the school district to reinstate them until he could examine the circumstances that led to their expulsions.[98]

Seals opened a hearing on 9 April 1969. He heard testimony and arguments from the lawyers for five days, then entered his informal "findings of fact." These granted Dixie's motion for a preliminary injunction, which kept Sullivan and Fischer in school. Seals enjoined the Sharpstown authorities from disciplining the students for publishing or distributing any other written materials off school property. As a result of Seals's orders, both Sullivan and Fischer graduated in spring 1969, before the judge's final ruling. The district contended that the graduation mooted the case. Seals disagreed for two reasons. First, the students wanted the district enjoined from maintaining any formal or informal record reflecting the disciplinary action against them. They deserved a final decision. Second, the students sued as a class action, with the designated plaintiff class composed of all HISD secondary students. The issue was not mooted for the rest of the class.[99]

The district claimed that the majority of Houston students did not sympathize with Sullivan and Fischer or share their views or methods; therefore, the mass of students were not "similarly situated" with them.[100] To Seals, HISD's contention "misse[d] the point." All members of the proposed class were subject to the same allegedly unconstitutional application of the regulations. He ruled that it was "irrelevant to speculate how many students might need to invoke the first amendment as protection from official sanctions; the fact that each member is subject to the same specific sort of deprivation of constitutional rights as the representative parties is enough" to maintain the case as a class action.[101]

On 17 November 1969 Seals issued his decision. He noted that in *Tinker* the Supreme Court had "clarified the constitutional principles governing the rights of school pupils to register dissenting opinions at school and the need for maintaining standards of discipline in public schools" and had declared, "In our system, state-operated schools may not be enclaves of totalitarianism. School officials do not possess absolute authority over their students."[102] Seals said *Tinker* "very clearly applies the first amendment in its full force to the high school campus." However, free speech and assembly rights were always "subject to reasonable restrictions as to time, place, manner and duration." The First Amendment did not require, and the *Tinker* decision would not support, the notion that students could read newspapers during a class, or that school officials should tolerate loud speeches or discussions in the corridors during a class period. A reasonable regulation of "place," Seals suggested, might prohibit discussion in the school's library. But, subject to these reasonable limitations, a student had the right to express himself or herself in a nondisruptive manner while on school property. And clearly, the judge said, the school administrators may not enforce rules regarding "time," "place," "manner," or "duration" in a discriminatory fashion.[103]

Seals concluded that there was no question that Sullivan and Fischer were engaged in acts of expression protected by the First Amendment, since "excepting only oral expression . . . the publication of a 'newspaper' is first amendment activity in its purest form." The remaining crucial issue was whether Sullivan and Fischer did "materially and substantially interfere" with operation of Sharpstown High School. Seals concluded that the distribution of the *Pflashlyte* "had no such effect." During 1969 so-called "underground" papers had "sprung up" in high schools all over the United States, many employing harsh language and advocating violence. The *Pflashlyte,* the judge declared, was primarily intended as a forum for the discussion of, and comment upon, legitimate problems affecting students' relations with administrators. Its writer-publishers, Seals noted, were "generally critical of school policy but the criticism [was] on a mature and intelligent level." The introductory issue editorialized that students' poor relationship with administrators could be improved only through the "sincere cooperation of all factions." Further, the writers stated that "[c]onfrontation would result in regression rather than progression." Seals found that these were "not the words of one who is calculating to 'incite insubordination.'" As for HISD's attempt to justify the expulsions by arguing that an organized student movement was attempting to "overthrow" the school system, and that the elimination of these two students and their newspaper was a necessary precaution to prevent further "infiltration," Seals said that he would "resist the temptation to comment" on that contention. Instead, he ruled that Sullivan and Fischer had been disciplined because school officials disliked the contents of the newspaper, and he declared that the Constitution "prohibits such action." All three issues of the *Pflashlyte,* he concluded, were plainly the sort of speech protected by the First Amendment.[104]

Seals's ruling in favor of Sullivan's and Fischer's First Amendment rights did not settle all outstanding issues. The students also contended that the Sharpstown principal's method in expelling them did not meet minimal standards of procedural due process.[105] Judge Seals agreed; parents or guardians, he said, had legal obligations to children of school age and "common sense dictates that they should be included in any disciplinary action . . . which could result in severe punishment." Because parents were not informed that allegations were pending against Sullivan and Fischer prior to the principal's decision to expel them, and the school district afforded them no opportunity to challenge the allegations, Seals decided that due process had been denied.[106]

The final point Sullivan and Fischer raised asked Seals to rule whether "certain regulations" of HISD were unconstitutional under the "void-for-vagueness" doctrine. He declared, "Basic notions of justice and fair play require that no person shall be made to suffer for a breach unless standards of behavior have first been announced, for who is to decide what has been breached?" The district had not been relying on a "clear, specific normative statement," Seals declared, and the rules that led to the expulsions were unconstitutionally vague and overbroad. The class members were entitled to a declaratory judgment to that effect.[107]

Seals considered next what equitable relief would protect the plaintiff class of all HISD secondary students. A regulation's overbreadth coupled with the threat of improper enforcement would "chill" the exercise of First Amendment freedoms and result in immediate and irreparable injury to the students.[108] He ruled that they were entitled to a court order forestalling the future use of the voided rule. Seals issued a permanent injunction against HISD administrators' imposing serious disciplinary sanctions upon any students who wrote, printed, distributed, or "otherwise engaged in the publication of newspapers either on or off of school premises during either school hours or non-school hours unless such activities materially and substantially disrupt the normal operations of the school," and unless administrators acted under "precise and narrowly drawn regulations." Finally, the judge permanently enjoined HISD officials from expelling or suspending any students for "a substantial period of time" without first providing them with minimal standards of procedural due process, including (1) providing the student and the parents or guardian formal written notice of the charges and of the evidence; (2) giving both sides in the dispute opportunity to present witnesses or other evidence in a formal hearing; and (3) imposing sanctions only on the basis of substantial evidence.[109] The school district initially appealed this order but reconsidered and developed a new set of written regulations. After the board adopted these new regulations in Spring 1970, Judge Seals agreed to dismiss the appeal.[110]

Judge Seals was the first federal district judge to apply a due process standard to overturn disciplinary sanctions against secondary school students.[111] He recognized that he was engaged in judicial path breaking. In June 1971, in a follow-up opinion to *Sullivan* in which he referred to "the highly controversial area of student dress and hair style," Seals wrote: "the advocates of judicial interference in this area . . . have been obliged to invoke that ethereal 'right of privacy' which sprang fullblown from the head of *Griswold v. Connecticut,* the 'forgotten ninth amendment,' or, most often, the due process clause."[112] Seals saw no difficulty in accepting such "ethereal" sources of law.

By contrast, Judge Noel's decision in the *Schwartz* "haircut" case, which like *Sullivan* was a suit for injunctive relief of school disciplinary regulations, came to opposite conclusions about high school students' rights.[113] Dress and grooming codes had been commonplace for decades in American secondary schools and at some colleges. But many schools revised the codes during the 1960s. Long hair on men and unorthodox clothing worn by either men or women symbolized political opinions, or at least were so interpreted by many school administrators.

Galveston ISD's regulations on student appearance included rules for hair and clothing. The district superintendent issued a general regulation on dress in March 1967. A specific code at Galveston's Ball High School had been drafted by a committee of students, faculty chosen by students, and Ball's principal and associate principal. The superintendent approved the proposed code on 3 September 1969. The committee had deliberately left the regulation "somewhat vague" to permit students a measure of free expression and to allow flexibility in enforcement. The code provided that "[b]oys must keep their hair clean, combed out of the eyes, and neatly cut." Unlike other contemporary dress codes, the Ball High regulations allowed facial hair, requiring only that "[m]oustaches and sideburns must be kept clean and neatly trimmed." Male students' hair was required to be above the collar, behind the ears, and out of the eyes.[114]

Richard A. Schwartz, a student and the son of liberal state senator A. R. "Babe" Schwartz, had hair that almost reached his shoulders.[115] He was warned by Ball High's associate principal, principal, the district's assistant superintendent, and finally the superintendent, that this did not comply with the regulation. Schwartz refused a haircut and appealed the ruling that he was violating the code to the Galveston ISD school board, which declined to set aside the ruling. The board members threatened Schwartz with suspension unless he complied with the dress code. In response, "Babe" Schwartz contacted David H. Berg, a young Houston attorney who frequently volunteered for cases through the American Civil Liberties Union (ACLU), and asked him to represent his son. On 9 December 1969, Berg filed a Section 1983 action to enjoin the Galveston ISD administrators from enforcing the regulation of students' hair and to force the district to expunge any mention of the threatened suspension from the younger Schwartz's school records. The complaint alleged that by attempting to regulate his hair style, the school officials had violated Schwartz's constitutionally protected rights of privacy, due process, equal protection, and freedom of expression.[116]

Noel heard the case in Galveston and presided over a preliminary hearing on 12 December, where Richard Schwartz testified that he did not wear his hair long to express any idea, opinion, or point of view. Rather, he wore long hair as a matter of personal preference, but with the approval of his parents. At the hearing the Galveston ISD's attorney, Ed Schwab III, countered that the regulations did not violate any right protected by the U.S. Constitution, and that three educational goals justified the dress code. First, the experience of administrators in Galveston and elsewhere showed that without restrictions on dress and hair style, teachers would lose control over their students, control needed for effective teaching. Second, they considered it their responsibility to train students in "the customs and mores pertaining to dress, appearance, taste, and public etiquette considered to be acceptable by the predominant part of our society." The administrators believed that "liberal, but minimum" standards would best fulfill this duty. Third, permitting the students to participate in formulating the dress code was a valuable means of teaching citizenship and the working of the democratic system.

In sum, the actual value of the dress code would be negligible if they allowed exceptions in cases like Richard Schwartz's. Schwab argued that in light of these three educational goals, even if Schwartz's "desire" to wear his hair longer than the code allowed was constitutionally protected, the regulations were nevertheless a "reasonable and permissible" restriction of rights. Finally, Schwab insisted that Schwartz had not exhausted the available state administrative remedies to end the dispute. Schwab moved to dismiss the case.[117]

After reviewing at length the historical background of Section 1983 and then agreeing that Schwartz should have sought state administrative and judicial remedies before filing a federal lawsuit, Noel ruled in favor of the Galveston ISD:

> The manner in which students in public high schools should be educated is a subject for local determination. It is a subject foreign to the competence and expertise of the federal judiciary. Whether or not some measure of conformity is educationally sound, and if so to what degree, is not an appropriate question for resolution by federal judges. Such decisions must be left to the public servants to whom our nation has entrusted its system of public education.[118]

Noel declared that in Texas, the elected state board of education and local boards of trustees, and their appointed professional school administrators, were competent to set their educational policies. Schwartz could seek to influence the policy, including changing the Galveston dress code, through available administrative channels.

And he said that, "as in all such areas of governmental policy," the student plaintiff could seek a remedy at the ballot box or "in this instance through the vote of his parents." This route failing, state courts were available. Finally, Noel declared, "an erroneous decision by a state court on a federal constitutional issue is subject to correction in the Supreme Court of the United States." Without a "convincing showing of severe hardship," students must allow administrative and state judicial forums an opportunity to regulate local boards and officials. "In sum," Noel declared, "I am convinced that students with claims against local school officials in Texas are not entitled to haul them into federal court to review their actions." Because Schwartz had not sought to redress grievances through state channels, the judge dismissed his complaint.[119]

Given Judge Seals's approval of *Tinker* and his strong support for high school students' First and Fourteenth Amendment rights in *Sullivan,* it is little wonder that Johnson, the La Feria school district's lawyer, sought to persuade Garza to rely on Noel's ruling in *Schwartz,* a decision much more favorable to the school board. The decisions in these two suits were not actually in conflict, because neither *Sullivan* nor *Schwartz* denied that school boards enjoyed discretion. But by late 1969 these rulings represented clear alternatives. The U.S. Supreme Court had provided little guidance. In *Tinker* the justices had merely noted that "the problem presented by the present case does not relate to regulation of the length of skirts or the type of clothing, to hair style or deportment. . . . It does not concern aggressive, disruptive action or even group demonstrations. Our problem involves direct, primary First Amendment rights akin to 'pure speech.'"[120]

The justices therefore distinguished political symbolism represented by a black armband from personal expression represented by hair or skirt lengths. But the court's distinction did not settle the question whether the latter were protected. The justices had compared the Des Moines situation to a 1968 Fifth Circuit case, *Ferrell v. Dallas Independent School District,* in which the judges assumed, for the sake of argument, that for student musicians Beatles-style haircuts were a constitutionally protected mode of expression. Notwithstanding, the Fifth Circuit judges ruled that an administrator was justified in prohibiting the style because it had caused "material disruptions." This reasoning was in line with the court's *Tinker* ruling: regulation of protected expression was permissible but must be related to actual disruption rather than fear of potential disruption.[121]

Individual justices occasionally expressed opinions in subsequent decisions, but the whole court never ruled on the hair issue. Because youthful dissent continued in Houston-area schools, and neither *Sullivan* nor *Schwartz* established the bounds of students' civil liberties, high school students continued to sue in federal court.[122] In October 1969, while the *Schwartz* and *Sullivan* cases were still active, the

Bellaire High School principal suspended three students for distributing the *Plain Brown Watermelon,* an antiestablishment newspaper with four pages of stories and cartoons written or drawn by approximately twenty students. The suspended students were told not to return to class until their "attitudes changed." None of the three thought that this change would soon occur. They sought an injunction to overturn the suspensions. David Berg agreed to represent them, and once again he filed a Section 1983 action in the Southern District.[123]

But Judge Joe Ingraham did not consider indefinite suspensions to be as constitutionally suspect or as potentially chilling to speech as had Seals in the *Sullivan* case. Ingraham stated that he "would not be disposed to interfere with the proper exercise of discipline by those in authority." He refused to order Bellaire to readmit the suspended students before he heard arguments.[124] Then the constitutional difference between high school students' speech and their style became blurred. On 17 November, the day Seals issued his *Sullivan* ruling, the Bellaire principal suspended seventeen-year-old Ricky Crawford "until he got a haircut." Crawford claimed that he was being punished because he had testified on behalf of his three classmates who had been suspended over the *Plain Brown Watermelon.* Berg agreed to be Crawford's lawyer as well. Sullivan and Fischer had just prevailed, and Berg amended the students' complaint to claim that, because the *Pflashlyte* suit was a class action, Seals's *Sullivan* ruling applied to all Houston-area high schools. However, during a pretrial in-chambers meeting with Judge Singleton, the school officials denied that Crawford had ever been formally suspended and pointed out that he had already been allowed back into class. Singleton then canceled a scheduled court hearing. But the judge was apparently already convinced that Crawford's hair style was merely the school's cover story for punishing his testimony. Rather than dismiss the case, Singleton announced that he would keep Crawford's case on his docket, so that he could immediately take future action if necessary. Berg told reporters that Singleton had "made it perfectly clear that the minute [Crawford] is harassed, the school will find itself right back here in court."[125]

Federal judges across the country repeatedly wrestled with the issues represented by these Southern District cases, but no single decision definitively established the scope of a high school student's speech and expression rights. Whether the issue was press, speech, or style, Singleton, Garza, and Seals consistently protected the students' civil liberties. In the same sort of secondary students' expression cases, Noel and Ingraham consistently gave school administrators the benefit of the doubt. Because the clerk of the Southern District court assigned cases to judges, rather than plaintiffs or defendants choosing, a high school student plaintiff's chances of prevailing in the district were literally the luck of the draw. This was not the situation if the plaintiffs were college students. In college "hair" cases, the judges, even those who were favorably disposed toward administrators, were normally inclined to rule for the students, because officials bore a greater burden to prove the reasonability of any regulation of college students' rights of expression.

Singleton, for one, decided that the difference of a year or two in age made no difference to the applicability of the First Amendment. When he had announced that he would retain oversight in Crawford's case, Singleton had noted that he had "already ruled" on the question of student hair and grooming regulation, and had added that he did not "intend to change [his] mind until and unless the Fifth Circuit Court of Appeals overrules me."[126] He was referring to a ruling in a college case, but Singleton saw no meaningful difference between college and high school.

In spring 1967 officials at San Jacinto Junior College ("San Jac"), a small campus near Houston, noticed that a "few people called 'hippies' " had enrolled, and they heard that at least one female student "was heard to protest that their odor and appearance was distracting." The San Jac administrators had received a pamphlet issued by the Federal Bureau of Investigation (FBI), which alleged that campus unrest was caused by militants who visited schools to stir up trouble.[127] The FBI advised officials to watch for these troublemakers. When the San Jac officials examined the new students, they discovered that some of the hippies had come from Berkeley. They easily deduced that long hair and a beard were the "badge of hippies." To forestall upheavals, the administrators adopted the rule that "[m]ale students at San Jacinto College are required to wear reasonable hair styles and to have no beards or excessively long sideburns."[128]

The regulation had been in place two years when a journalism student, Carlos Calbillo, grew a beard. In mid-October 1969, after a hearing before the college administration, Calbillo was indefinitely suspended. Represented by David Berg, Calbillo filed a lawsuit under Section 1983.[129] He sought a temporary injunction against the suspension and a permanent injunction of the beard regulation. Calbillo did not claim that he had been denied due process. Instead, he claimed that the enforcement of grooming regulations violated his rights under the Fourteenth Amendment.[130]

Before he met with Singleton, Calbillo admitted to reporters that the grooming issue was "absurd and disgusting. . . . But if people aren't willing to exercise their rights, they will be taken away." Inside the courtroom, the president of San Jac, Thomas Spencer, informed the judge that unless he issued a court order against the school, the regulation and the suspension would remain in force. The judge quickly ordered the school to readmit Calbillo, issued a temporary injunction barring the college from enforcing the ban, and set the date for a second hearing regarding the requested permanent injunction.[131]

At the hearing ten days later, Singleton established that, because Calbillo had been a student in good standing at San Jac at the time of the disciplinary action, there was no question that he had been suspended solely on the strength of the grooming regulation.[132] In light of this fact, Judge Singleton challenged San Jac's attorney, Stanley Baskin, by asking, "Aren't we dealing here with a form of McCarthyism . . . guilt by association or dress?" Baskin responded that he could bring witnesses to testify that they feared bearded students would disrupt the heretofore peaceful San Jac campus. The judge replied, "Unrealized fears do not constitute grounds. . . . I don't want to hear that kind of testimony." But then Academic Dean O. W. Marcom testified that Calbillo originally had come to his attention as a dissident, not because of his beard but because he had written two letters to the school newspaper. Singleton responded: "[I]n other words, [Calbillo] expressed a view contrary to yours . . . do you try to control your students' thought by regulating their hair?"[133] He asked why mustaches were permitted while beards were not, and the officials responded that mustaches were generally worn by all people. At this the judge noted: "Certainly, the democratization of American life has not come to the point where every whim of the majority may be enacted into a mandate for all to follow. If so, then the Bill of Rights is for naught."[134]

Judge Singleton then asked school officials whether they really thought that "beards make hippies." The San Jac administrators admitted that a beard may not be the most accurate indicator of potential troublemakers, but then, in what Singleton later noted was "apparent seriousness," one official testified that the wearing of beards and long hair represented an "attitude of rebellion" with regard to school authority, and to that extent beards and long hair themselves disrupted the school. As proof he testified that he had observed protests on other campuses and noted that "beards were in evidence among leaders of the protest." After listening to this reasoning, Judge Singleton said: "It is interesting to note that none of the reasons given in justification of the rule relate to any disruptions on the San Jacinto Junior College Campus. . . . in fact, this record is completely devoid of evidence that any type of disruption has been occasioned by the wearing of beards." But the officials maintained that the *absence* of campus disruptions was *evidence* of the efficacy of their rule. Singleton once more declared that "[u]nrealized fears cannot justify such an arbitrary classification," and the "only evidence of any adverse campus reaction whatsoever was the testimony of a school official that an unidentified girl had complained of the odor and appearance of several 'hippies.'" Moreover, Calbillo was not a "hippie." Rather, the judge wrote, Calbillo's "appearance in the courtroom was that of a well-groomed, although bearded, student."[135]

Calbillo denied that he was a member of SDS or other any militant group, and he claimed that he did not approve of SDS tactics. Baskin asked Calbillo if he had intended to defy the college regulations when he grew his beard. Calbillo replied that he had intentionally broken the rule and claimed that his reason for doing so was that he "felt it was a violation of my civil rights to be kept from wearing it." When Baskin asked where he had gotten the notion that his rights were being violated, Calbillo answered, "It was taught to me in government class."[136]

At the conclusion of testimony, Singleton decided that, although an educational program required certain rules for the maintenance of an orderly classroom and school officials rightly have discretion in setting rules, officials must ensure that the regulations were reasonable. The judge declared, "It is not for this Court to consider whether such rules and regulations are wise or expedient," but only to decide whether the rules were a reasonable exercise of the administrators' discretion. That is, regulations must be shown to be "essential to maintain discipline on school property." Officials had the burden of showing that the effort to regulate personal appearance was reasonable and that the unregulated exercise of these "forbidden rights" would "materially and substantially" interfere with operations and discipline in the school.[137] Judge Singleton was not persuaded that San Jac had demonstrated this reasonability.

Regarding the other justifications offered for the beard rule, "they can be resolved into the contention that beards and hair styles are a sufficient indicator of potential campus troublemakers. Not only is this contention not supported by the record, it is not supported by logic and common sense."[138] Furthermore, he said:

> In this court's chambers are portraits of six great jurists, starting with Moses and ending with Justice Holmes, one of the great justices of the Supreme Court. . . . Also included among these portraits are those of Justinian, Solon, Coke, and Marshall. All of these men had distinctive hair styles, some had mustaches, and some had mustaches and beards. Many other examples of men who have and do wear distinctive hair styles, sideburns, beards, and mustaches could be given. Certainly, such are not a badge of a troublemaker or a malcontent.[139]

Singleton concluded that the record revealed no reasonable connection between the beard ban and the functioning of San Jac college. It was clear to him that the beard rule was "basically enacted to implement the personal distaste of certain school officials for beards and certain hair styles and for the beliefs and attitudes which they thought these beards and hair styles represented." This was an unreasonable use of power, and the regulations were therefore in violation of the equal protection clause of the Fourteenth Amendment. If San Jac officials continued to deny Calbillo an education through the enforcement of its "sweeping prohibition," the school would "cause him irreparable harm." Consequently, the judge granted Calbillo the injunctive relief he had requested.[140]

Judge Singleton noted the reluctance of federal judges to conclude that "wearing one's hair at a certain length or wearing a beard falls within that category of 'expression' protected by the First Amendment." Curiously, Singleton was just as reluctant to close the issue by directly ruling on the First Amendment implications of the case. Instead, he noted that, because he had reached his decision on the basis of reasonability, it would "not be necessary" to reach the question of hair as free expression. In a footnote, however, he speculated that "[i]f this Court were to accept defendant's position that a beard or a hair style represented an attitude of rebellion or protest, this would be a stronger case for First Amendment protection of a beard as 'symbolic speech' similar to an armband." And although Calbillo had generally invoked his rights under the First Amendment, he actually "never claimed his beard represented any more than a personal preference."[141]

Despite relegating his speculations to a footnote, Singleton supported a broad reading of the First Amendment in matters of speech, press, and expression. His attitude had heartened civil libertarians. In September 1970 James C. Calaway, chair of the local ACLU chapter, announced in an interview that he believed it was only a matter of time before federal judges voided all student grooming rules. He predicted that "within a year, I expect we will have prevailed."[142]

By October 1970 Singleton concluded that there were more important things for school administrators to worry about than hair, dress, and even race. One of the higher worries, said the judge, was the "nitty-gritty" of providing students (presumably students of all races and with a variety of grooming habits) with a good education. Commenting to the press on an unrelated case, Singleton suggested that if the schools concentrated on doing this, "I imagine that many of the problems facing this country would work themselves out."[143]

San Jac administrators apparently disagreed with the judge's suggested priorities. Just before the Calbillo affair began, San Jac hired Lecil Hander as a full-time biology instructor. At the time the school had an "unwritten" policy that faculty were to be clean shaven. Nonetheless, Hander grew a full beard over the summer, after Calbillo's case ended.[144] In December 1970 the San Jac Board of Regents issued the following rule: "Faculty members and all of the male employees of San Jacinto Junior College are required to be clean shaven, wear reasonable hair styles and have no excessively long sideburns." The college notified Hander that he would be expected to comply with the regulation. He refused and received a hearing before the regents, whose members upheld the new rule. Hander kept his beard, the school discharged him and paid the balance of his salary for the year, and Hander sued to have the regulation enjoined.[145]

Except for the fact he was a faculty member, not a student, Hander argued as had Calbillo eighteen months earlier. He asserted that the regulation was enacted to implement the personal tastes of San Jac officials, and was an unreasonable application of administrative authority to manage the college. Hence, he alleged, the regulation violated the equal protection clause of the Fourteenth Amendment. Like Calbillo, Hander did not claim that the wearing of a beard was a protected activity under the First Amendment.[146]

Attorneys for the regents agreed that the wearing of a beard was merely an issue of style, not of maintaining campus order. However, they contended that the grooming regulations were enacted under authority Texas granted to public school officials. Therefore, the lawyers argued, federal courts ought to abstain and let a state court interpret the relevant state law.[147]

Judge Bue presided in the case in Houston. He noted that the Texas legislature had neither delegated authority to regulate personal appearance of faculty members at public junior colleges nor authorized an employee's discharge for violating such grooming regulations. However, Bue held that the state lawmakers had delegated to the San Jac regents the power to manage and control the institution. The question was whether the Regents had exceeded their authority by issuing the beard regulation: "[I]t is well established in Texas that if a rule, order, or regulation promulgated by an agency exceeds the authority conferred by the statute, conflicts with the statute, or has no reasonable relation to the purpose of the statute, then it is not sustainable by the Texas courts."[148]

Before Bue could rule on Hander's case, the U.S. Supreme Court declared that federal district judges should generally avoid intervening in ongoing state prosecutions. For the majority in *Younger v. Harris,* Justice Black affirmed several fundamental principles, among them "a proper respect for state functions, a recognition of the fact that the entire country is made up of a Union of separate state governments, and a continuance of the belief that the National Government will fare best if the States and their institutions are left free to perform their separate functions in their separate ways." These principles, collectively, made up the dual judicial system that Black called, "perhaps for lack of a better and clearer way to describe it," "Our Federalism."[149]

As he considered the beard controversy at San Jac, Judge Bue contemplated the *Younger* decision's effect on the role of federal district judges in settling local controversies. *Younger* had involved a state prosecution, not a civil case involving a local dispute over administrative authority in schools. Nonetheless, in *Younger* Black had strongly affirmed as a principle of federalism and comity that the federal courts should avoid "needless conflict with state administration." Bue then noted "recent pronouncements to the effect that 'hair cases' should be tried in a state court because that is a more proper forum." He said that "a state court decision interpreting these statutes and regulation will foreclose any need for a decision by this Court of a federal question." In view of these issues, Bue declared that "federal courts must acknowledge a sensitivity to the legitimate interests of the state governments." He dismissed the complaint, although he noted that he did so in the "broad spirit of comity without regard to other aspects of this case."[150]

Judge Bue's suggestion that "hair cases" could best be settled in the state courts referred to the Supreme Court's continual refusal to review any of the dozens of federal court rulings, many of them in conflict, on student hair. The court's refusal disappointed many litigants, judges, and even some justices, who had come to rely on federal courts to resolve social controversies.[151] The justices' refusal to review this category of public school complaint reflected the court's efforts to narrow the role of federal district judges in managing the details of state governments' relations with their citizens. Chief Justice Burger led the effort. In his 1970 address to the American Bar Association, entitled "the State of the Federal Judiciary," Burger declared, "We should look more to state courts familiar with local conditions and local problems."[152] Judge Noel foreshadowed judicial retreat in *Schwartz.* Judge Bue then declared it accomplished in *Hander.*

Noel echoed *Schwartz,* with the added support of the *Younger* decision, in a combination dress code student protest suit that emerged from a dispute at a middle school. HISD eighth grader Sabrina Dale Press had been suspended from Jackson Intermediate School for wearing a pantsuit to school and for participating in a demonstration, both of which violated HISD regulations for eighth graders. Press's parents had requested an injunction based on Section 1983. In March 1971 Noel relied heavily on *Younger* to rule that the case presented "an appropriate occasion for a federal district court, in its discretion as a court of equity, to abstain."[153]

Noel noted that his fellow judges' sensitivity to equality, but lack of sensitivity to local conditions, might have resulted in a dress code for students in Alaska identical to that in Texas. Noel criticized the recent school decisions. They relied on what he considered to be overly broad readings of "equal protection of the laws." He ridiculed that approach, referring to Associate Justice Oliver Wendell Holmes's dissent in *Lochner v. New York.*[154] Holmes had noted that the Fourteenth Amendment did not enact Herbert Spencer's theories of social and economic evolution by survival of the fittest. With regard to school discipline, Noel noted that "it might be remarked with aptness that this Amendment does not enact the educational theories of Mr. John Dewey, nor those of any given federal judge."[155]

In 1972 Justice Black, the author of the *Younger* majority opinion, seized the opportunity to apply his conception of "Our Federalism" to a high school student suspended for wearing long hair. In part because of the *Younger* doctrine, the student found no relief in the federal district and circuit courts, and he appealed to the Supreme Court.[156] Black, the presiding justice for the Fifth Circuit, denied the student's motion to suspend the regulations pending the appeal. In doing so Black indicated the Supreme Court majority's new attitude. He declared that "[s]urely few policies can be thought of that States are more capable of deciding than the length of the hair of school boys." He noted that "[t]here can, of course be honest differences of opinion as to whether any government, state or federal, should as a matter of public policy regulate the length of haircuts," but "it would be difficult to prove by reason, logic, or common sense that the federal judiciary is more competent to deal with hair length than are the local school authorities and state legislatures of all our 50 States."[157]

In denying the requested stay, Black concluded, "Perhaps if the courts will leave the States free to perform their own constitutional duties they will at least be able successfully to regulate the length of hair their public school students can wear."[158] Many federal district judges who, like Noel, had welcomed the *Younger* doctrine, also appreciated this further elaboration of the revived spirit of comity, federalism, and restraint.

Younger had not mandated abstention. Rather, the decision reminded federal judges that they had the discretion to abstain from ongoing disputes over state issues and should exercise this discretion generously to avoid being drawn into seemingly trivial local disputes. But federal district judges who were sympathetic to students' complaints, like Singleton and Seals, chose not to abstain in light of *Younger* and continued to decide school discipline and grooming cases rather than defer to authoritarian administrators.

The distinction some courts had drawn between secondary schools and higher education proved to be the defining boundary for deference to state administrators. In October 1972 the Fifth Circuit judges affirmed the decision of a federal district judge from the Eastern District of Texas, who had ruled in favor of a long-haired student who hoped to attend the junior college in Tyler. The appellate judges' opinion upholding the district judge, in *Lansdale v. Tyler Junior College*, echoed Singleton's *Calbillo* decision. That is, the Fifth Circuit judges declared that, in the absence of a legitimate administrative reason for regulating the hair of college students, a policy regarding such was arbitrary by definition and impermissible under the Fourteenth Amendment. The circuit judges were careful to note, however, that they had not therefore overruled their own recent holding regarding the permissibility of hair and dress codes in the high schools. The judges clearly distinguished the college student's rights from the secondary student's rights, and judicial presumptions favored student autonomy in college, but favored high school administrators.[159]

In November 1972 the Fifth Circuit judges vacated Bue's San Jac decision, which Hander had appealed, and remanded it to the Southern District judge. The appellate judges directed Bue to reconsider the case in light of their decision regarding the Tyler Junior College.[160] He did so and ordered the San Jac regents to reinstate Hander and pay him back wages as damages. Moreover, Bue awarded Hander attorney's fees. It was then the San Jac regents' turn to appeal. The Fifth Circuit judges reversed the ruling regarding fees but affirmed the rest of Bue's decision.

Fifth Circuit Chief Judge John R. Brown filed a concurring opinion, in which he expressed relief that the federal courts were "now out of the hair business . . . since by now the public, with growing thousands of entirely responsible adult members of the community wearing all sorts of hair and face trims, has come to its senses and does not see in such variations the seeds of violence and revolution." "Now," Judge Brown concluded, "we can return to the vital matters which overwhelm the Federal Judiciary."[161]

By the early 1970s the federal district judges in the Southern District, with guidance from the appellate courts, settled and turned their attention away from questions of students' rights. But among the "vital matters" overwhelming the federal judiciary were similarly contentious questions regarding the scope of First Amendment protections enjoyed by consenting adults who either produced or consumed adult entertainment. The judges now examined these issues.

CONSENTING ADULTS AND THE FIRST AMENDMENT

In the late 1960s and early 1970s, in addition to mediating disputes between students and administrators, the Southern District judges balanced the traditional prerogatives of state-centered morals enforcement against claims that the Federal Constitution, through the First and Fourteenth Amendments, protected adult citizens' rights to enjoy free and frank discussion and depiction of human sexuality. Because most states criminalized "obscene" expression, and many individuals disputed the definition of obscenity offered at any given moment, the *Younger* decision held the potential, in the view of some scholars, "to effect a radical subordination of federal to state courts as guarantors of federal civil liberties."[162] The Supreme Court had established a legal standard for obscenity in the 1950s, but the court was forced to revisit that standard periodically. Writers, artists, theatrical producers, and film makers continually sought to broaden the range of socially and legally acceptable sexual expression.[163]

Local authorities prosecuted the creators or distributors of allegedly obscene works under state laws, and defendants increasingly challenged these laws in the federal courts. The federal plaintiffs frequently met with success, and as a result sexually explicit books, magazines, films, and stage performances proliferated in the late 1960s. However, rather than leading to fewer criminal prosecutions under state obscenity laws, the increased availability of "hard-core" material sparked renewed local efforts to suppress or censor allegedly obscene literature, pornographic films, and public lewdness. Local prosecutors, including many in Texas, launched an assault on the licentiousness that many conservatives believed had been encouraged by the permissive decisions of the Supreme Court under Chief Justice Earl Warren.[164]

Many of the state criminal defendants subsequently filed federal suits under Section 1983. They sought to enjoin enforcement of state obscenity statutes that they argued infringed on their constitutionally protected expression or conduct. In the midst of this renewed controversy over obscenity, the Supreme Court revived abstention with its *Younger* decision. The *Younger* decision relieved the federal courts of the burden of overseeing many students' expression and hair cases. But it also frustrated federal judges willing and even eager to step in and examine state obscenity prosecutions. They were obliged by the Supreme Court's ideals of comity to abstain while state judges wrestled with this important public issue.

Judge Singleton was particularly frustrated by the strictures *Younger* placed on federal judicial intervention into ongoing state obscenity prosecutions. He and several other judges of the Southern District harbored conflicting thoughts on the issue, and except for *Younger* they might have had the opportunity to shape debate and change laws. Instead, they could merely offer obiter dicta in cases that most often they turned over to the state courts.

When the controversial and especially popular adult film *Deep Throat* reached Texas theaters, state prosecutors overreached their proper constitutional bounds. Singleton seized on the opportunity to rule on the issue, and ultimately he rated that film, constitutionally speaking, for the entire state.[165]

Individuals fought many small legal battles over the local regulation of sexually oriented material before *Deep Throat* forced the question of adult entertainment into the national mainstream. On 9 October 1969 vice squad officers of the Houston Police Department (HPD) entered the Cinne Arts Theatre on Main Street, confiscated that week's featured film, and arrested the theater's manager and projectionist. The local prosecutor charged the men with exhibiting an obscene movie in violation of Texas statute.[166] The defendants admitted that the movie in question "dealt with nudity in a frank and candid manner," but they claimed that it was not legally "obscene." They filed a Section 1983 suit in the Southern District of Texas, claiming that they had been denied due process, because the local authorities did not attempt to determine if the film was obscene before seizing it and had not provided a hearing to assess the film after it was seized.[167] After a preliminary hearing Judge Singleton decided that the complaint raised serious questions regarding the Texas law's constitutionality. He temporarily enjoined further police raids on adult theaters.[168] Mel S. Friedman, the defendants' attorney, asked Singleton to convene a three-judge district court to hear the case. It would have the authority to overturn the state statute.[169]

Before the panel could be convened, Singleton's injunction expired and the raids resumed in Houston and Harris County. The three-judge panel named to consider the constitutionality of the Texas obscenity statute included Southern

District Judges Singleton and Seals and Circuit Judge Ingraham, a recent Nixon appointee to the Fifth Circuit.[170] They announced a decision in mid-November. Judge Seals wrote the majority opinion, in which Ingraham joined. The main issue to settle before considering enjoining a state law, Seals said, was the result of a "collision between the . . . principles of comity on the one hand, and, on the other, the historic decision of the Supreme Court in *Dombrowski v. Pfister* . . . and its confused progeny." He suggested that the Anti-Injunction Act, a federal law that in many instances barred federal judges from intervening in pending state criminal prosecutions,[171] represented comity and federalism. But Seals then noted that *Dombrowski* "carved out a limited exception," because the threat of a criminal prosecution might have a "chilling effect" on "preferred" First Amendment expression.[172]

Seals believed that a recent Fifth Circuit decision, which required that two tests be satisfied before the federal district courts issued an injunction, struck the proper balance between comity and constitutionality. First, plaintiffs must show either that the state employed its legal machinery in "bad faith," that is, with the purpose of inhibiting speech, or that the statute was unconstitutional on its face. Second, the judge must agree that there existed a "probability of irreparable injury" to the plaintiff if an injunction was not forthcoming, such as "a significant chilling effect on speech that cannot be avoided by state court adjudication."[173] The judges assumed, but "without specifically so finding," that the plaintiffs could show probability of irreparable injury. However, the panel considered it unnecessary to discuss this, because the plaintiffs had failed to persuade them that that the police acted in bad faith, or that the state law was unconstitutional on its face. Seals denied the injunction, and scheduled the case to be heard on its merits by a single judge.[174]

Judge Singleton dissented. Not only had the *Dombrowski* criteria been met, he believed, but traditional comity considerations were inapplicable because the state criminal prosecutions had actually " 'begun' only in a technical sense with the filing of an information or indictment, and this is not a case in which trial proceedings are underway."[175] He also insisted that because it was established that ticket takers could not be held accountable for a film's purported obscene content, it was equally inappropriate to arrest projectionists. Finally, he was incensed at the reported claims by officials that they would "continue to arrest and prosecute until they 'shut these places down.' " The judge considered these widely publicized comments to be threats, and that they "would seem harassingly excessive to any good faith prosecution."[176]

State and local authorities also closed live adult entertainment. Sandra Montgomery owned the Seven Veils Theater on Houston's Montrose Boulevard. She had invested three thousand dollars in the business, which included the costs of costume and equipment rentals, licensing fees, building improvements, and at least one announcement in a local newspaper, which advertised the entertainment at the Seven Veils with the slogan "Live on stage the act of love." The first of two scheduled acts on opening night in February 1971 was a drama in which an actor dressed as a gorilla chased Montgomery and tore at her clothing. By curtain time she was totally nude. The second act had less plot, but for that reason it offered more opportunities for improvisation. It required a nude couple, a man and a woman, to simulate various "acts of love," and this included the "vivid" depiction of sexual intercourse on a waterbed. Houston police arrested Montgomery and several employees during the maiden performance of this second act and charged them variously with "vagrancy" and indecent exposure. The city did not close the theater pending the trial, although Montgomery later claimed that several officers warned her that the arrests would resume if the Seven Veils continued to offer the same show. She filed suit in the Southern District to challenge the state and local statutes on the grounds that they were vague and overbroad. Montgomery also sought a TRO against HPD and a temporary injunction against the enforcement of the statutes. Finally, she asked for a three-judge court.[177]

Judge Hannay upheld the arrests. Montgomery had not shown that the police acted in bad faith, and he concluded that she had produced no evidence that her business would suffer "irreparable injury" during the normal disposition of the case in the local courts. Therefore there were no grounds for the "extraordinary equitable relief" of an injunction, or for the appointment of a three-judge court. He dismissed the case with a short explanatory opinion.[178]

Hannay's opinion was most significant in that, in his discussion of the absence of demonstrated cause for enjoining the state and local statutes, he drew on *Younger v. Harris.*[179] Montgomery's complaint was "precisely the type of case to which the Supreme Court was addressing itself," and Hannay declared his support for the principle of comity. It demanded that "federal interference, even to the extent of granting preliminary restraining orders and convening three-judge-courts [*sic*]" become "by far the exception rather than the rule."[180]

Judge Hannay's enthusiasm for *Younger* was not shared by all his Southern District colleagues. In abstaining from the suits brought by two proprietors of bars that featured topless, bottomless, or nude dancers, the three judges on the review panel, Circuit Judge Ingraham and District Judges Singleton and Bue, responded to the implications of the new doctrine in completely different terms. In December 1970 Houston police, joined by state liquor authorities, had raided Roy Hearn's Martinique Lounge. Police arrested several of Hearn's employees and later charged them with violating the state vagrancy and liquor control statutes as well as Houston's city ordinances prohibiting "indecent dancing."[181] Hearn filed a complaint, seeking an injunction and a three-judge panel. He challenged the statutes on the same grounds Montgomery would cite two months later, but because the raids had occurred before the disposition of *Younger*, the judge granted a TRO, which was extended several times until the three-judge court convened to hear the merits of Hearn's case. On 1 January 1971 authorities raided the My-O-My Club, a bar that operated near the Martinique. Its owner also requested a TRO. The three-judge panel, newly convened to hear Hearn's complaint, denied that request but allowed him to join Hearn's suit as a joint plaintiff.[182]

Judge Ingraham wrote the panel's majority opinion. His dismissal of the case prominently cited *Younger*. In his short opinion Ingraham wrote that with the *Younger* decision the Supreme Court "afforded the lower Federal Courts a polestar by which to guide the exercise of their equitable powers" when considering cases in which the "State's criminal legal machinery has been set in operation prior to the plaintiff's seeking redress in Federal Court." The judge noted that in *Younger* the justices "made it abundantly clear that failing proof of bad faith prosecution, harassment or other unusual circumstances," a federal court should, "on the basis of comity and the principles of federalism," abstain from interfering with the state's action.[183] He was confident that the state's legal machinery could decide whether the dancing at the Martinique and the My-O-My was obscene or constitutionally protected expression. Ingraham dismissed Hearn's case in the same terms Hannay used to dismiss Montgomery's.[184]

Judge Singleton offered a very brief, specially concurring opinion noting that he was "reluctantly compelled to follow" the *Younger* decision. If precedents had allowed it, he wrote, he would prefer to "meet the issues raised in the case head-on."[185] Singleton suggested that as a matter of fact, the My-O-My case was not a pending criminal prosecution, and so the panel might have decided to hear it separately; however, because *Younger* compelled dismissal of the joined cases, he agreed with Ingraham's declaration that "no precedential value could be gained by further discussion of the substantive issues involved." Singleton concluded his concurrence with the admission that "I do have strong feelings that the first amendment, and its proscription against censorship, applies to the legal issue of obscenity (if in fact there is any such legal concept)," and he indicated which precedents he would have applied in deciding the case had the Supreme Court not cheated him of the opportunity.[186] The decision to let a state court decide the issue rankled.

Judge Bue also felt that the Supreme Court had cheated him of an opportunity to speak to the obscenity issue. Although he fully agreed with the reasoning and the result described by Ingraham in the main opinion, Bue, like Singleton, wrote a specially concurring opinion. It is clear that, had the panel not dismissed the case, Singleton and Bue would not have agreed on the result. Bue agreed that *Younger* removed the case from his judgment of the "bare legal issues," but he also declared that the dismissal "scarcely comes to grips with the malady which has spread at an ever-increasing rate in recent years—the use and abuse of the First Amendment . . . as a vehicle for the commercial distribution of obscenity in its various forms."[187] His frustration at the denial of an opportunity to examine the facts in Hearn's case, "compelled [him] to write . . . with a somewhat broader sweep, not to render an opinion where none is called for, but to draw together into some cohesive and orderly pattern for assessment the many and varied facets, both legal and philosophical, which have contributed to an endless confusion in this area of the law."[188]

Judge Bue clearly considered the kind of dancing at the two bars to be obscene, and he thought the published record should reflect that; he asserted that the difficulties of the obscenity issue were not "eased by some form of antiseptic resume of the circumstances of the case in order to make for more palatable reading." Whether or not this was "unnecessary" (as Ingraham had claimed) or had any demonstrable "precedential value" (as Singleton had noted), Bue felt impelled to describe the "dancing" observed at the Martinique and My-O-My by "undercover" members of Houston's vice squad. These lurid details warranted recitation in "proper context without regard for the sensitivities of the reader."[189] Bue included facsimiles of advertisements for the clubs. He was annoyed that Hearn had modified his print ads. These had called attention to the Martinique's "BOTTOMLESS Continuous Revue." After the panel placed the TRO on the HPD, Heard had added the words "Now An Additional 10 Days Granted By The Courts."[190]

Perhaps the judge wanted the public to know that, whatever a state court may ultimately decide, he had been on his way to declaring the nightclub dancing to be obscene on any of the several grounds the Supreme Court had fashioned after struggling with the issue.[191] Bue concluded his long essay by stating his own standard. "In large measure," he said, "it is perhaps not inappropriate to state that these issues reduce themselves to a determination of what we as a people want our society to be, since laws lose their viability without the affirmative support of the citizenry."[192] In the end, what mattered was that Bue agreed with his colleagues that *Younger* applied, and that therefore Hearn could no longer make a federal case of his troubles. Although they had unanimously concluded that *Younger* limited their discretion to act, the judges' lack of consensus on the rights of expression reflected the absence of consensus in the nation.[193]

Houston's experience with *Deep Throat* began when the HPD vice squad captain, James Allbright, "read of several other jurisdictions" that had ruled the film to be obscene. Allbright resolved to make a "test case" of the movie in Houston. He later proclaimed his intent "to make a case on every one of the skin flick houses in town." In April 1973 vice squad officers entered the Cinema West Theater and seized its print of *Deep Throat.* Harris County District Attorney Carol Vance indicted the exhibitor, Joseph Spiegel, under Texas criminal obscenity statutes and public nuisance civil laws.[194]

Spiegel filed suit in the Southern District two weeks later. He accused Vance of enforcing the obscenity statute in bad faith and asked Judge Singleton to issue a TRO against the county prosecutor and the vice squad. Spiegel believed that he could show *Deep Throat* to sixty thousand customers in six weeks in his three small Houston theaters, and that thereafter the movie would fill a two-thousand-seat theater indefinitely; he requested that the judge order the movie returned to exhibition until its status as an obscene film was determined in court. At five dollars per admission, this was Spiegel's unprecedented financial opportunity, but Singleton did not believe that losing this revenue would cause "irreparable harm." Therefore he denied Spiegel's motion for a restraining order. However, he approved the application for a three-judge panel.[195]

In the interim prosecutions proceeded in Houston and elsewhere. A Dallas theater owner was also prosecuted for showing *Deep Throat,* and when he filed suit to challenge the obscenity statute in the federal court in the Northern District of Texas, the Fifth Circuit's Chief Judge Brown consolidated the case with Spiegel's suit in the Southern District. Thereafter, prosecutions for alleged obscenity "mushroomed" all over Texas, and as more defendants sought to enjoin the state laws in the federal courts, Brown added the new cases to the list to be examined by the three-judge panel that would hear Spiegel's case.[196]

In mid-August 1973 Singleton held a pretrial conference with attorneys representing the parties in the consolidated cases. These cases involved varied circumstances and disparate challenges to Texas statutes. As a consequence, the final complaint challenged not only the constitutionality of obscenity laws, but also the use of public nuisance and criminal instruments laws that were enacted for purposes other than closing businesses engaged in allegedly obscene commerce.[197]

In November, Spiegel's prosecution in state district court ended in a mistrial when only six of twelve jurors decided that by offering *Deep Throat,* he had conspired to exhibit an obscene film. Assistant District Attorney Mike Hinton filed a misdemeanor charge against Spiegel, for showing an obscene film. Singleton again refused Spiegel's request that he order prosecutors to return the film pending the second trial. The judge also refused to halt the new prosecution until the as yet unappointed three-judge panel ruled on the constitutionality of the relevant portions of the Texas obscenity laws. Judge Singleton justified this lack of action by mentioning the principles of several Supreme Court rulings restricting federal court interference in pending state criminal cases. He was obviously referring to *Younger.*[198]

The Texas statutes were apparently ripe for examination by the federal courts, because in June 1973 the U.S. Supreme Court had decided the quintet of obscenity cases led by *Miller v. California.*[199] In *Miller* the justices offered a new and somewhat improved standard of evaluating obscenity statutes. Under it material could be declared legally obscene if its predominant theme was prurient according to the sensibilities of the average person in the community, if it depicted sexual conduct in a patently offensive manner, or, when taken as a whole, it lacked "serious literary, artistic, political, or scientific value."[200] The Texas legislature responded by repealing the state obscenity statute. It enacted a new statute, effective 1 January 1974, which replaced the term "sexual matters" with the formula "sex, nudity, or excretion" under the portion of the statute defining the formal criteria for declaring material "obscene."[201]

Meanwhile, jurors in Spiegel's misdemeanor trial deadlocked, three to three. District Attorney Vance gave up Harris County's attempt to have *Deep Throat* declared obscene. He announced that thereafter his office would only prosecute "extreme" films depicting pedophilia or bestiality. Presumably, it would be easier to convince a jury that those films were obscene. After Vance issued this policy, Spiegel dropped his suit.[202]

Therefore neither Vance nor Spiegel was involved when hearings for the consolidated cases finally commenced in Houston in November 1974. Of the members of the three-judge panel consisting of Singleton, Judge William Taylor of the Northern District of Texas, and Circuit Judge Ingraham, Singleton emerged as the dominant force, and ultimately he wrote its opinion.

In an effort to simplify the proceedings, Singleton chose three suits that represented the collective issues and presented the fewest jurisdictional complexities.[203] In addition to challenging the constitutionality of the obscenity laws, the attorneys for the federal plaintiffs argued against further enforcement of the state laws on public nuisance and criminal instruments, which were used against owners of adult theaters. The Texas attorney general's office responded that all statutes were enforced according to both the state and federal constitutions, and that the Texas Court of Criminal Appeals was providing clear interpretations of the state laws. Therefore federal judicial intervention was unnecessary.[204]

The first case the panel considered represented the broader issues. King Arts Theater, Inc., operated an enclosed, adults-only theater in San Angelo. In October 1973 the landlord from whom King Arts rented the building notified his tenants that he would soon cancel their lease, because the district attorney for Tom Green County had expressed an opinion that the theater was a public nuisance and had declared his intention to seek an injunction to prohibit future showings of sexually explicit films. King Arts filed a federal lawsuit requesting both a declaratory judgment and injunctive relief. The plaintiffs challenged the constitutionality of the public nuisance statute, which specifically named as nuisances facilities used for commercial obscenity.[205]

Once the Fifth Circuit joined the case to Spiegel's complaint, the San Angelo parties had agreed to maintain the status quo until the larger case was determined. This enabled Singleton to declare that *Younger* did not forestall federal intervention. He noted that the county attorney's decision not "to actively pursue his threatened course of action would certainly lessen the court's considerations of equity, comity, and federalism upon which *Younger* is based."[206] Because King Arts had requested an injunction to prevent the state from utilizing the nuisance statute, Singleton said that one issue remained to be settled before the panel could rule in the case, namely, whether the theater company would suffer irreparable injury without the injunction. The judge established that "traditional prerequisite" to injunctive relief by relying on *Dombrowski,* which warned of the "chilling effect upon the exercise of First Amendment rights [that] may derive from the fact of the prosecution, unaffected by the prospects of its success or failure."[207] The *Younger* decision had narrowed but not eliminated a "chilling effect" standard, and Singleton applied the standard. But he withheld the injunction. The judge noted that the plaintiff was threatened under a civil statute and did not face arrest. Therefore, an irreparable injury from a "chilling effect" would not occur. Singleton confined himself to addressing the question of the declaratory judgment.[208]

The public nuisance statute did not contain a description of obscenity, Judge Singleton noted, and the "logical place" to find the state's definition was in the revised Texas Penal Code. Singleton compared the language in *Miller* to the new obscenity statute and to recent state court decisions regarding obscenity.[209] The *Miller* definitions differed from the new statute in two ways. First, the Texas law retained the phrase "utterly without redeeming social value," which the Supreme Court had described as a virtually impossible standard to define, instead of the new language: "serious literary, artistic, political, or scientific value." Second, the new Texas statute did not specifically define "obscene matters," as the Supreme Court required in *Miller.* Despite these flaws, Singleton concluded that the "cases show that the courts of Texas have adhered rather closely to the ideas of the Supreme Court of what constitutes obscenity." He noted that the court had intended to assist state lawmakers and judges in clarifying their existing statutes, but did not mandate that federal judges overturn laws if they did not match the *Miller* language exactly. Therefore the three-judge panel did not find the statute unconstitutionally "vague, overbroad, or invalid because it fails to give adequate notice." The King Arts plaintiffs, and by implication all twenty consolidated plaintiffs, lost that seemingly critical point.[210]

With regard to the King Arts challenge to the public nuisance statute itself, however, Singleton examined the companion statutes, which Texas had not revised in 1974. These allowed "general reputation" of the premises, and "reliable information" that proscribed behavior occurred on the premises, to be the basis of a state injunction for nuisance abatement.[211] The King Arts plaintiffs accepted that the state could enjoin the showing of a film that had been properly found to be obscene. But they argued that the Texas nuisance statutes represented a "classic" example of prior restraint. Singleton agreed that the King Arts arguments raised a "serious consideration," because "to prove that a motion picture theater has been the scene of the showing of films that are obscene" was "not to prove that every film shown in that theater, in the past, present, or future, was, is, or will be obscene." The statute authorized a state judge to close a theater on the strength of a single incident of "commercially manufacturing, distributing, or exhibiting obscene material." Unless the owner posted bond, the exhibition of *any* movie could constitute contempt of court. If the owner posted bond, films could be shown, but, if at any time the authorities proved that another film was obscene, the bond would be forfeit.[212]

Judge Singleton decided that these regulations were "the essence of censorship," because owners had to think twice about exhibiting any controversial material. By forcing the closure of a theater, or by requiring that a bond be posted to keep the theater open, the state effectively had imposed a prior restraint. Because motion pictures that were not obscene were clearly protected under the First Amendment, the state had the burden of proof in establishing that a specific film was legally obscene. Singleton found that the state made the fatal mistake by allowing the prohibition of future conduct based on a finding of undesirable present conduct. He declared that when potential future conduct may be protected under the First Amendment, the separation of protected expression from unprotected obscenity must be accomplished using sensitive legal and judicial tools, and "not the heavy hand of the public nuisance statute." The three-judge court declared the Texas nuisance statute unconstitutional on its face. Having repudiated the plaintiffs regarding the state's definition of obscenity, the federal panel upheld them on the more practical question that allowed them to continue to operate their businesses.[213]

The second case of the representative trio was a *Deep Throat* case, and it was somewhat more simple for the federal judicial panel to digest. On four occasions in 1974, a San Antonio police officer paid the five-dollar admission to the Fiesta Theatre, and after viewing *Deep Throat* he wrote an official report and also signed a "Motion for Adversary Hearing" and presented it to a magistrate. At the adversarial hearing, the magistrate would determine if probable cause existed to seize the theater's print of the movie and to charge Richard Dexter, the theater's operator, with violating state obscenity laws. The magistrate was responsible for informing Dexter of the complaint, scheduling a hearing, and advising Dexter to contact an attorney.[214]

On each occasion, however, the hearing commenced less than one hour after the notification, usually in the theater itself. They proceeded along similar lines: first, the officer testified regarding the contents of the film; next, the magistrate attended a showing of the film; finally, the magistrate signed a warrant authorizing the officer to arrest Dexter or an employee, to seize the film as "probably obscene," and to impound the projector as a "criminal instrument." After each seizure Dexter obtained a new print of *Deep Throat* and a new projector, and continued to show the movie until the next round of arrests and seizures.[215]

Dexter was charged on two counts. The first was trading in commercial obscenity, a class B misdemeanor. He did not challenge the charge in his federal complaint, and the case was pending in a state court. But Dexter was also charged with unlawful use of a criminal instrument, a class III felony.[216] The criminal instrument statute ordinarily applied to gambling devices, and Dexter challenged its application to a film projector. The state defendants in Dexter's federal complaint, joined under the name of Ted Butler, San Antonio's district attorney, chose not to justify the constitutionality of the criminal instruments statute or its use against Dexter. Instead, the state's attorneys based their defense on the contention that, under the *Younger* rule, the three-judge panel lacked authority to examine the merits of the case.[217]

Although none of the felony charges had yet been heard by a grand jury, the complaints had all been filed, and therefore, the state attorneys argued, the case was "pending." Moreover, they said, Dexter had not charged the police or magistrate with bad faith or harassment, or claimed imminent irreparable injury, the prerequisites for federal intervention under *Younger.* But Judge Singleton saw evidence of bad faith in the repeated seizures of the same film and the new projectors, coupled with the fact that none of the seizures resulted in an indictment or judicial determination that *Deep Throat* was obscene. He found that "[i]t is obvious that San Antonio was engaged in an 'all out' effort to suppress this film." The fourth seizure was the last, he noted, only because Dexter filed the complaint and a federal court had enjoined further action.[218]

To "fully comprehend the innovative tactics San Antonio put into practice," Singleton examined the criminal instruments statute. He determined that it was not a proscription against any item that had lawful uses. Furthermore, because it was essentially a possession rather than a "use" statute, it was not aimed at overt criminal actions. The statute had been aimed at true criminal instruments, made specifically for criminal uses and with the intent to commit crime. An ordinary portable sixteen-millimeter film projector could not reasonably be a criminal instrument, the judge said. District Attorney Butler must have known that he could not obtain a conviction on the charge but rather had calculated that "[s]uch a blatant use of an inappropriate statute, which bootstrapped the misdemeanor offense into a felony[,] was effective in requiring that bail for a felony offense be set, not once but several times."[219]

The San Antonio police's repeated seizures of the same movie without adjudicating its obscene status was gratuitous, Singleton declared; there was "no evidentiary reason why this film should have been seized more than one time." He added, "When viewed objectively, there is no logical reason why this film was seized four times except that the authorities were attempting to harass the theater and its employees and to eliminate the exhibition of this film—prior to any final judicial determination of its obscenity. It is no answer that the authorities were unsuccessful at their chosen task. Resourcefulness in the face of official harassment should not inure to the benefit of the official harassers."[220]

Therefore, when Singleton evaluated the state's interpretation of the *Younger* doctrine, he was convinced that San Antonio not only had acted in bad faith by prosecuting Dexter under an inapplicable criminal instruments statute; it had also engaged in official harassment by seizing the film on multiple occasions. The judicial panel maintained that federal intervention was proper, and the panel enjoined San Antonio from "in future . . . prosecuting any motion picture exhibitor for possession or use of equipment which can be used for any lawful purpose."[221] This decision presaged judicial condemnation of the tools used by authorities in many of the consolidated cases.

The third representative case was the prosecution of the owners of the Ellwest Stereo Theatre in Dallas. The Ellwest featured "peep shows" in private viewing booths, each containing a stool and a coin-operated projector. A Dallas police officer entered the theater in January 1974, with a search warrant, signed by a justice of the peace, that authorized him to seize "property specially designed, made, or adapted for or commonly used in the commission of an offense."[222] The officer seized three films and three projectors; then, using tools he had brought with him, he removed the three coin boxes and their contents. Two days later, the officer returned with a new warrant and seized two more films, two additional projectors, and two stools. On the second visit he also removed the wall separating two viewing booths. In February 1974, the theater owners filed suit for federal injunctive and declaratory relief.[223]

Like earlier defendants, the attorneys for Dallas contended that the federal panel lacked jurisdiction, but they based their argument on the fact that the Ellwest owners had abandoned their claim for injunctive relief. The theater's attorneys had not mentioned an injunction in their pretrial brief. According to Dallas, the panel could not separately hear a claim for declaratory relief.[224]

Once again, Judge Singleton established the federal court's authority to examine the case. Although the plaintiff's brief did not specifically seek to enjoin the police action, the judge said, it "addresses itself fully to the question and all but invites the court to grant injunctive relief." Moreover, Singleton declared, even if the plaintiff had not requested relief, he could find only one opinion, from New York, where judges decided that they lacked jurisdiction to hear a plea for declaratory judgment standing alone. Singleton examined Supreme Court and Fifth Circuit cases, which were ambiguous, and found that these supported the discretion of a judicial panel to decide its own jurisdiction. He declared, "It would appear to this court that

that question is still open and that this court is free to decide the issue, taking into consideration all of the circumstances surrounding the suit." He held that the claim for relief and a declaratory judgment was "properly" before the federal three-judge court.[225]

Singleton examined the Dallas attorneys' second challenge. Although the seized property remained in police custody, the Ellwest proprietors had not been prosecuted for violations of Texas obscenity laws. Therefore, the attorneys maintained, no case or controversy existed for the panel to adjudicate. Singleton dismissed the lack of formal prosecution as irrelevant: the state had acted under a criminal search and seizure statute, and whether or not Texas subsequently prosecuted the case, a controversy existed. Further, the seized property had disseminated material that the court must presume to be protected until it was declared to be obscene. The Ellwest plaintiff's predicament, the judge found, presented a valid and serious constitutional question "which has substantial first and fourteenth amendment overtones worthy of consideration." It remained to be seen only whether or not the plaintiff's claim was "meritorious." Because the Dallas defendants had not claimed shelter from federal intervention under *Younger,* Judge Singleton quickly dispensed with the issue. He declared that there existed "no jurisdictional, equitable, comity, or federal bar to the maintenance of this suit."[226]

Acknowledging the difficulty of establishing what was and was not prior restraint, which he had accomplished in the King Arts case, Singleton summarized the plaintiffs' complaint as the following: under the guise of searching for and seizing as evidence property which is "specially designed, made, or adapted for or commonly used in the commission" of a crime, the Dallas police effectively "shut down" the operations of an adult theater. The judge then summarized the defense: after assuming that the films shown in the Ellwest theater were obscene, and knowing that Texas had laws against the commercial exhibition of obscenity, the Dallas authorities further assumed as an "indisputable fact that the equipment seized is equipment 'commonly used' in the commission of a crime.' " In order to accept the state's argument, one must assume that the films were obscene which, he said, the court could not do. Because films are presumed to be protected by the First Amendment, he reiterated, they must be *judged* obscene under the latest Supreme Court guidelines, which set a theater operator and projectors apart from a gambler and slot machines. Beyond due process, an alleged gambler does not enjoy special constitutional protection. But "no matter how lewd his neighbors and the police and the district attorney's office may think his business to be," Singleton said, an adult theater owner "has an added protection—the protection of the first amendment."[227]

Judge Singleton noted that the prosecutors claimed the projectors, coin boxes, stools, and booth walls the police seized were evidence, but he dismissed the claim, because legitimate proof of obscenity would "seem to rise or fall with the material exhibited," and, in any case, photographs of the booths would suffice in a courtroom. In short, said the judge, this was a "raid accompanied by crowbars and screwdrivers," in which it was apparent that the Dallas Police Department (DPD) abused its authority in order to cause the "maximum amount of disruption of the business." Nonetheless, official abuse did not necessarily render the statute constitutionally flawed. Singleton declared that a good search-and-seizure statute "should be precise enough to guide officials acting in good faith," but the language of this statute, namely, "commonly used in the commission of an offense," was "superfluous and ambiguous."[228] The First Amendment demanded more care and precision. "What disturbs this court," he wrote, was that the term "commonly used" was unconstitutionally "vague and overbroad." The federal panel directed Dallas authorities to cease action against the plaintiffs or any other individuals engaged in "first amendment activities."[229]

On 3 July 1975 the federal three-judge panel released its official conclusions in the cases consolidated under the Vance and Spiegel dispute. Judge Singleton, for the panel, directed that the remaining cases be remanded to the individual federal judges from which they had come and directed them to examine each prosecution for bad faith harassment or special circumstances, to determine whether the cases fit the *Younger* abstention criteria.[230]

After two years of litigation, the public response to the judicial panel's opinion was subdued. District Attorney Vance maintained that although the judicial panel's ruling was "subject to being overturned" on an appeal, the decision would have little impact in Harris County, because, due to the policy he announced in the wake of the two mistrials, "we're not actively prosecuting anyone on obscenity violations." Vance said that he had expended too much time, with too little result, in developing such prosecutions. He claimed that the problem was the Texas penal code and the *Miller* criteria regarding contemporary community standards. Vance noted that in Houston "the community, itself, is divided as to what is an affront to community standards. The liberals are saying that violent movies are really obscene and that explicit sex acts are not. The conservatives are saying that sex acts are obscene and that violence is not. There is no middle ground to all of this."[231] As a result, claimed Vance, it was "next to impossible to get a book off the shelves these days on the grounds of obscenity."[232] Spiegel also maintained that the Houston community had accepted *Deep Throat*. He had been showing the film continuously since his second mistrial had derailed the Harris County prosecutor's policy. He considered himself vindicated. After all, he said, "[i]t is the longest playing movie in the history of the city . . . now in its 74th week."[233]

A REVIEW OF OLDER CASES THROUGH THE *YOUNGER* DOCTRINE

In *Younger* Justice Black declared the Supreme Court majority's support for what he described as a primary goal of Congress "since the beginning of this country's history." "Subject to few exceptions," Black wrote, Congress had "manifested a desire to permit state courts to try state cases free from interference by federal courts."[234] The justices sought to expand the umbrella of "Our Federalism" in many subsequent opinions. The court ultimately foreclosed federal suits aiming to reform civil court and administrative practices, even when the plaintiffs did not seek to enjoin pending state proceedings. With ever rarer exceptions, such as the ongoing public school desegregation cases, state officials were liberated from federal judicial oversight initiated under the Fourteenth Amendment and Section 1983.[235] But the court's decisions during the 1970s did not require federal judges to abdicate its responsibility for protecting constitutional rights. In cases where state prosecutions had been brought in bad faith, or had been filed or threatened merely to harass citizens and to keep them from exercising their civil rights, the federal courts abandoned the "judicially developed policy of self-restraint."[236]

The UFWOC's long-pending Section 1983 suit apparently qualified for federal judicial intervention. The union plaintiffs had alleged that the conduct of Texas Rangers, Starr County deputies, and local officials during the strike had "chill[ed] the willingness of people to exercise their First Amendment rights." According to their complaint government officials conspired to deprive union members and supporters of their rights under the First and Fourteenth Amendments. Under color of law, deputies and Rangers had threatened, harassed, coerced, and physically assaulted the strikers to prevent their exercising the rights of free speech and assembly, and had arrested, detained, and assaulted union members without due process. The UFWOC plaintiffs challenged as unconstitutional Texas statutes that they claimed were enforced against union organizers in a discriminatory and selective fashion. Therefore, they sued to enjoin enforcement of state laws that prohibited unlawful assembly, breach of the peace, and abusive language, and either regulated or proscribed mass picketing, secondary picketing, and boycotting.[237]

Although the union sued in July 1967, when federal courts were relatively open to requests for injunctions against alleged state offenses, Southern District Judges Seals and Garza and Fifth Circuit Chief Judge Brown, the panel that heard their case, did not announce a decision until late June 1972, more than a year after the *Younger* decision. The state challenged the federal judicial panel's authority to examine the case, arguing also that it had become moot when the UFWOC abandoned its efforts to form a union after the state judge enjoined their picketing. The federal panel disagreed. After summarizing the officers' behavior during the strike, Judge

Seals declared that "the conclusion is inescapable." Starr County officials had believed that "maintenance of law and order was inextricably bound to preventing the success of the strike."[238]

As a consequence of that opinion, "[w]hether or not they acted with premeditated intent, the net result was that law enforcement officials took sides in what was essentially a labor-management controversy." Local and state authorities had "exhibited their personal bias and opinions against the strikers and their cause," Seals decided. He added that although "[t]his is not intended as a whitewash of the activities carried on by the union and its sympathizers, . . . the issue that is presented to this court for determination is whether the defendants stepped over the line of neutral law enforcement and entered the controversy on one side or the other. It is the judgment of this Court that such was the case."[239]

Seals declared that the Starr County and state officials' conduct obviously put strike sympathizers in "fear of expressing their protected first amendment rights with regard to free speech and lawful assembly." It was obvious that the UFWOC "abandoned" organizing because of the harassment, not the state judge's injunction, and, Seals declared, that "[t]here can be no requirement that [union members] continue to subject themselves to physical violence and unlawful restrictions upon their liberties . . . in order to preserve" their pending case as a "live controversy." For these reasons, the judicial panel ruled that *Younger* was not a bar to federal court intervention.[240]

The federal panel declared five Texas statutes unconstitutional and enjoined their enforcement, and permanently enjoined the state, county, and local law enforcement officers or other officials from engaging in a variety of unlawful practices that intimidated the farm workers and interfered with their efforts to organize.[241] Texas appealed the ruling. While the appeal was pending, the legislature repealed the criminal statutes that had outlawed unlawful assembly, breach of the peace, and abusive language.[242]

Rulings of a three-judge district court are appealable directly to the U.S. Supreme Court. Chris Dixie, the attorney for high school students Sullivan and Fischer, had represented the UFWOC leaders since their unsuccessful appeal of state judge Laughlin's injunction and would represent the union's position before the Supreme Court. MALDEF did not demonstrate an interest in the farm workers' plight until the case was certified for review by the Supreme Court, more evidence that despite its largely Mexican American membership pool, the union was not necessarily a Mexican American group. In 1973 the justices denied MALDEF's "untimely" request to file an amicus brief on behalf of the UFWOC.[243]

On 20 May 1974 Justice Douglas, for a bare majority of his colleagues, decided that the controversy had not become moot either by the state injunction or by the union's abandonment of their valley efforts. Douglas ruled that, because the union had shown the danger of irreparable injury, the three-judge court's injunction against police misconduct was an appropriate exercise of the panel's equity powers.[244] The justices therefore affirmed the decree granting injunctive relief. However, the court vacated that portion of the district panel's declaratory judgment overturning the Texas statutes and remanded it to the panel for further proceedings. The justices noted that three of the statutes had since been repealed, and the remand was necessary for the panel to establish whether any prosecutions were still pending under any of the laws, including the two statutes that the state had not repealed. Douglas noted that the case would not be governed by *Younger v. Harris* if the UFWOC sought only declaratory relief, or if there were no pending prosecutions.[245]

Chief Justice Burger, joined by Justices White and Rehnquist, concurred in the result of the majority's order to remand the case, but also dissented in part. Burger expressed the view that the majority should have dealt further with the applicability of *Younger.* For example, he suggested that the majority opinion should have reviewed the three-judge panel's conclusion that *Younger* was satisfied. Also, the dissenters concluded that the Supreme Court had no jurisdiction to review on direct appeal an injunction against police misconduct. But assuming such jurisdiction, Burger said, that part of the panel's decision should also have been remanded, since an injunction of police misconduct was not so related to relief against allegedly unconstitutional state laws that it required the attention of a three-judge court. Finally, Burger wrote for the dissenters, the three-judge panel abused its discretion in granting the injunction against police misconduct, because the alleged acts of misconduct were "few and scattered."[246]

Some of the judges in the Southern District of Texas, or in the Fifth Circuit Court of Appeals, might have taken the opportunity to unburden themselves by applying *Younger* to the case. But on remand Seals, Garza, and Brown found no reason to change essential details of their original decision. Perhaps long-haired students and undressed dancers presented problems more suitable for state authorities to settle. But the members of this federal panel regarded their judicial duty to end discriminatory law enforcement and official abuse as more important than the political need to defer to the court's model of "Our Federalism."[247]

The profound cultural, political, and constitutional upheavals of the 1960s extended the significance of the civil rights revolution that had commenced in the 1950s with *Brown,* broadened the judicial protections available under the Fourteenth Amendment, and raised public expectations for additional judicially managed "social reconstructions." The evolution of judicial attitudes in the 1970s had contracted significance, narrowed protections, and lowered expectations.[248] The revival of abstention in the *Younger* opinion was an early indication, in Kurland's estimate, of the "trend away from free and easy access to the federal courts for abstract declarations of constitutional invalidity."[249] And the high court asserted a preference for judicial restraint throughout the decade.

The evolution of standards for federal intervention in state affairs, including the *Younger* doctrine's very slight tightening of discretion, ultimately did not significantly simplify the work of the Southern District judges. The "conventional" civil rights plaintiffs, such as labor organizers, continued to seek protection under Section 1983. But the rash of students facing expulsion for wearing long hair and theater owners facing prosecution under the obscenity statutes confounded judges for only a brief time. Identifying the significant civil rights issues embedded in what seemed to be trivial complaints did consume court time. They were troubling but less so than the familiar problems, such as the desegregation of the public schools, that in the 1970s required more intervention than ever.[250] The next chapter returns to that subject.

CHAPTER FIVE

Judicial Management of Triethnic Integration

NEW FEDERAL CIVIL RIGHTS STATUTES of the 1960s authorized federal oversight of state policies on a scale not seen since the Reconstruction era. The U.S. Supreme Court supported these laws in a series of landmark opinions.[1] Advocates of federal judicial protection of minorities feared that President Nixon's 1969 appointment of Warren Burger to replace Earl Warren as chief justice heralded the cessation of federal intervention in local affairs. But no "constitutional counter-revolution" followed.[2] In the field of public school desegregation, the Burger court could surpass the Warren court's boldness. Under Warren the court waited more than a dozen years to abandon its failed policy of allowing school desegregation to proceed with "all deliberate speed."[3] Finally, in the 1968 decision in *Green v. County School Board of New Kent County,* the justices declared that a school board had the "burden . . . to come forward with a plan that promises realistically to work, and promises realistically to work *now.*"[4]

The *Green* decision forcefully condemned delay, but it nevertheless once again left the formulation of desegregation policy in the hands of local officials who had been subverting *Brown* for years. The court took the next step in the first school desegregation decision in which Burger participated. In October 1969, in a short, sharply worded per curiam opinion in *Alexander v. Holmes County Board of Education,* the justices authorized federal district judges to employ their broad equitable powers to force school boards to begin operating desegregated "unitary" systems "immediately."[5] Despite its subsequent resuscitation of abstention doctrine in 1973's *Younger v. Harris,* the Burger-led court did not intend to slam shut all gates the Warren court had opened.[6]

Although the Supreme Court reinforced the authority of federal district judges to develop remedies, these decisions did not resolve the long-standing desegregation controversy.[7] Various barriers to equal educational opportunity remained in place. They included the routine assignment of students to "neighborhood" schools where segregation had emerged from, and was perpetuated by, segregated residential patterns. Another barrier was the restriction to African Americans of the equitable remedies made available by the original *Brown* decision. Combined, these obstacles kept Mexican Americans in segregated schools. The federal courts did not consider them "identifiable" minorities who were subject to the equal protection clause of the Fourteenth Amendment, a result of the Mexican Americans' long reliance on the so-called "other white" legal strategy. In Texas "Jim Crow" laws, Mexican Americans were members of the "white" race. Mexican Americans had maintained that they were not subject to the same statutory segregation as African Americans. Therefore, the discrimination they experienced in the schools and other public realms denied them due process rather than equal protection. Federal judges had accepted these arguments and had enjoined various forms of segregation.[8]

Mexican Americans maintained their hard-won "white" status as late as mid-1966, when James DeAnda, the longtime legal advisor to the civil rights organization American G.I. Forum (AGIF), resumed school desegregation litigation after nearly a decade's hiatus.[9] In the new suit he sought to enjoin "ability tracking" in the Odem Independent School District (ISD) near Corpus Christi. Officials there assigned students to classes according to past performance, measured aptitude, or a teacher's estimation of student potential. The district had established two separate "tracks," one for the college-bound and another for the "terminal" high school students. Students of Mexican descent dominated the latter category.

In his 1966 complaint DeAnda relied on the precedents he had helped establish in the 1950s. One of these was his own successful 1957 lawsuit to enjoin the linguistic segregation of Mexican American elementary students in the nearby Driscoll Consolidated Independent School District (CISD). DeAnda had argued in that case that the Driscoll CISD officials segregated Mexican Americans on the basis of poorly administered tests purporting to assess English language skills, or without administering any tests at all. He had convinced U.S. District Judge James Allred that this was an arbitrary system that denied the due process guaranteed in the Fourteenth Amendment.[10]

Now, ten years after his victory over the Driscoll CISD, DeAnda faced essentially the same discrimination in different guise at the Odem ISD. He fought this familiar enemy with well-worn weapons. In June 1967, when DeAnda wrote the legal brief in support of his motion for summary judgment, his argument was stalled at the "other white" strategy that Mexican Americans had relied on for decades. He charged that many assignments at Odem ISD were made without testing or else without testing Anglo as well as Mexican American students. When aptitude tests actually were administered, he claimed, principals or teachers who lacked the expertise properly to evaluate the results made track assignments that perpetuated the segregation of Mexican American students. DeAnda once again based his legal argument against segregated conditions on the due process clause.[11]

If he had attempted to base his complaint on an equal protection rationale and had been able to persuade the judge to accept the claim, DeAnda could have sought the expansive court-ordered remedy sanctioned by *Brown*. But in his brief DeAnda only mentioned, without explicitly invoking, *Brown*. As a consequence, when U.S. District Judge Woodrow B. Seals enjoined the Odem ISD ability-tracking system on 28 July 1967, he did so solely on the basis of the due process violation. The judge's holding implied that if Odem ISD administrators chose to commence a regime of proper testing and evaluation, they could resume tracking.[12]

Before Mexican Americans could exploit remedies to race-based segregation that *Brown* made available through the equal protection clause, they had to abandon their "white" status.[13] A variety of employable tools to refashion an ethnic identity became available during the 1960s. The 1964 Civil Rights Act (CRA), for example, had authorized federal officials to withhold funds from states that allowed racial discrimination and also extended similar protections to "national origin" minorities.[14] It authorized the Department of Health, Education, and Welfare (HEW) to issue goals and guidelines for school desegregation.[15] In a key 1965 ruling U.S. Court of Appeals judges for the Fifth Circuit declared that district judges should give "great weight" to such HEW standards.[16]

Despite this Fifth Circuit endorsement, the value of these guidelines for Mexican Americans in Texas was impeded by HEW's Office of Civil Rights (OCR). It investigated allegations of discrimination, but initially collected statistics only about black and white racial categories. HEW examiners began to accumulate evidence of discrimination against Mexican Americans only after Hector P. Garcia, a physician who was the founder of AGIF and the first Mexican American member of the U.S. Civil Rights Commission, rebuked OCR for failing to heed Mexican Americans' complaints.[17]

HEW began publishing in 1967 data on black, white, and "other" groups. The last category included "any racial or national origin group for which separate schools have in the past been maintained or which are recognized as significant 'minority groups' in the community." The examples HEW gave included "Indian American, Oriental, Eskimo, Mexican American, Puerto Rican, Latin, Cuban, etc." Later, HEW published separate statistics on Americans with Spanish surnames and issued a series of "Mexican American studies."[18] Yet this shift to official "other" status was resisted by some Mexican Americans. One student at Texas A&I University, a college in Kingsville, Texas, that was an early hotbed of Chicano activism, wrote a column in the liberal *Texas Observer* magazine in October of 1967 that complained about the Washington bureaucracy's misguided attempt, or perhaps it was a clever ploy, to make "the second largest minority group in the country non-White."[19]

To employ terminology that was by then becoming more relevant to the legal situation, evidence was accumulating that Mexican Americans were a de facto minority in the United States. But changing legislative, administrative, and social positions on the issue did not guarantee that federal district judges would agree to overlook the established "other white" jurisprudence, recognize Mexican Americans as a de jure minority, and grant them equitable relief under *Brown*. Moreover, because most Mexican American segregation in Texas was the result of residential patterns, not illegitimate school tests, the redundant victories under the "other white" due process strategy had little overall impact. When many Chicano students in Texas protested Anglo cultural hegemony by walking out of classes in the late 1960s, for example, two-thirds of them were from Mexican American majority schools. Forty percent were enrolled on campuses where the student body was at least 80 percent Mexican American, and 20 percent attended schools that were at least 95 percent Mexican American.[20]

Before Mexican American civil rights advocates could attack the segregation created by "neighborhood" schools, they had to overcome Mexican Americans' equivocal minority status. DeAnda led the retreat from the strategic ground that he had painstakingly conquered during the 1950s. In a path-breaking lawsuit he led against the Corpus Christi Independent School District (CCISD), DeAnda complained that the CCISD administrators, like those in many Texas school districts, had turned the "other white" strategy to their own illegitimate purposes. In order to delay the court-ordered desegregation of white schools, and also to obscure its slow pace, school district officials frequently assigned African and Mexican Americans to the same neighborhood schools, a practice often facilitated by the close proximity of ghettos to barrios. School administrators maintained that because Mexican Americans were "white," these schools had been desegregated. Federal judges and HEW examiners had accepted this logic.[21]

In his CCISD complaint, although he hedged his bets by referring to the "other white" strategy, DeAnda focused most on the novel contention that the *Brown* rationale should apply to, and condemn, segregation of Mexican Americans.[22] He marshaled much evidence from history, sociology, and demography to demonstrate that despite being "white," Mexican American Texans suffered widespread discrimination at the hands of Anglo Texans. This argument persuaded Judge Seals. He declared that for the purposes of desegregating the public schools in Corpus Christi, Mexican Americans formed an identifiable ethnic minority that deserved but had been denied the equal protection of the laws.[23] Judge Seals's decision delighted Mexican Americans, but it remained to be seen whether he could devise a suitable "triethnic" remedy to desegregate a white, black, and brown student body.[24]

DeAnda sued CCISD at a key moment in the history of the desegregation controversy. Federal district judges were receiving fresh guidance from the Supreme Court from the *Green* and *Alexander* decisions. As a consequence, Seals "managed" the CCISD case differently during two distinct phases of the litigation. During its first two years on the docket, that is, between DeAnda's filing and Seals's decree, the judge held pretrial meetings, conducted evidentiary hearings, and ruled on procedural questions the lawyers raised in various motions. Seals's management responsibilities consisted primarily in facilitating the case's progress toward disposition.[25] Before 1968 many federal judges presiding in desegregation cases limited their participation to formally neutral supervisory activities. Few seemed concerned with the actual content of the plans; hence, the judicial approval for token desegregation under grade-a-year and freedom-of-choice.[26]

In *Green* and *Alexander*, however, the Supreme Court directed federal judges to assume an active role in developing remedies to segregation. These decisions informed Seals's forceful approach to case management during the next phase of the CCISD litigation. After ruling for the plaintiffs, the judge hosted additional consultations with the lawyers, litigants, and witnesses. As a result, Seals became intimately familiar with the district's finances, geography, and infrastructure. This knowledge enabled the judge to wield enormous influence during the year-long effort to formulate a plan to integrate the triethnic student body.[27]

While Seals conferred with the CCISD parties during the remedial phase of the case, the Supreme Court was deliberating whether to support court-ordered busing, which had emerged as the most controversial proposed remedy to residential segregation. In its 1971 *Swann v. Charlotte-Mecklenburg Board of Education* opinion, the justices unanimously approved a federal district judge's order to a school board to initiate busing of students.[28] Thereafter, in the face of enormous resentment in and resistance from affected communities, other district judges sought to achieve racial balance in the schools by redrawing attendance zones, reassigning staff and faculty, and ordering the transportation of students.[29] These expansive decrees led congressmen from northern as well as southern states to propose federal legislation to prohibit busing. The furor over "forced" busing moved Presidents Nixon and Ford both to condemn the revival of judicial activism, although both of the Republican presidents also took credit for the apparently renewed progress toward integration.[30]

A few months after the Supreme Court's *Swann* decision, Seals announced an ambitious integration plan for CCISD. It would require busing fifteen thousand students. His novel triethnic remedy made his busing plan more controversial than most. Judges, some in the Southern District of Texas and others on the Fifth Circuit Court of Appeals, resisted Seals's innovation. By 1971 Southern District of Texas Chief Judge Ben Connally had supervised the National Association for the Advancement of Colored People's (NAACP) school desegregation litigation against the Houston Independent School District (HISD) for fifteen years. He was unwilling to adjust his thinking to grant Mexican Americans in Houston a new legal status that ran against judicial decisions, widespread custom, and what he believed to be common sense.

The judicial doubts encouraged continued opposition from local school boards. Consequently, after *Green, Alexander,* and *Swann,* Mexican Americans endured delays and reversals similar to those that had been frustrating African Americans since *Brown.*

FROM OTHER WHITE TO AN IDENTIFIABLE ETHNIC MINORITY

Advocates of Mexican American civil rights had remained inactive in the courts during the 1960s because lawsuits, even against tiny rural school districts like those in the Driscoll and Odem cases, were costly to undertake.[31] The limited benefits that "due process" victories brought to the Mexican American community did not justify the expense. In October 1967, during the hearings in El Paso of the federal Inter-Agency Committee on Mexican American Affairs, DeAnda described the financial limitations. He testified that the lack of resources prevented the large-scale litigation necessary to fight the segregation of Mexican Americans. He then proposed remedies. First, he noted that the 1964 CRA provided for the judicial award of plaintiffs' attorneys' fees in certain employment discrimination cases. A similar compensation scheme would be appropriate in voting, jury, and school suits.[32] Second, DeAnda challenged the U.S. Department of Justice to fight the discrimination against Mexican Americans.[33]

As noted in chapter 4, San Antonio attorney Pete Tijerina found a different path. In 1967 Tijerina obtained a $2.2 million Ford Foundation grant and used it to found the Mexican American Legal Defense and Education Fund (MALDEF). He modeled the new organization on the NAACP's incorporated litigation arm, the Legal Defense Fund (LDF, or the "Inc. Fund"), and intended to imitate the LDF's strategy of undertaking "planned" litigation.[34] In time, MALDEF supported DeAnda's suit against CCISD as amicus curiae. But the impetus and initial funding for that litigation came from a different and unexpected quarter.

Jose Cisneros was a member of the U.S. Steel Workers union in Corpus Christi. His children attended Mexican American–majority schools in CCISD, and they often complained to him about the dilapidated and dirty conditions of their schools. Cisneros tried to persuade administrators to repair and improve the facilities. He met repeatedly with teachers, principals, and school board members over two years, but Cisneros saw no changes. He discovered, moreover, many inequities in the curriculum and resources available to his children, as compared to the courses and programs offered to students in the Anglo-majority schools. Cisneros informed other parents and community leaders of his findings. At the urging of Civil Rights Commissioner Garcia, who lived in Corpus Christi, HEW studied conditions at CCISD for a year, beginning in September 1967. They found that 83 percent of the Mexican American and African American children attended neighborhood schools that were identifiable as minority schools because they enrolled few if any Anglo students. In late 1968, after the *Green* decision, the HEW examiners advised the CCISD superintendent that the school board should redraw the attendance boundaries to break up the segregated schools. HEW also suggested that the CCISD school board could allow "majority-to-minority" transfers to enable the students who were in the majority at a minority school voluntarily to shift to another school. Such students would be in the minority at the new school, but they would be taught in a desegregated environment.[35]

The CCISD board refused to institute the HEW's suggested improvements or to heed the parents' complaints. Cisneros turned to his union. The leadership of Local 5022 persuaded the national office of the U.S. Steel Workers to approve expenditures. Cisneros and more than two dozen fellow unionists, African Americans as well as Mexican Americans, retained DeAnda to sue CCISD for maintaining a dual school system. In late 1968 he paid the fifteen-dollar filing fee to initiate the litigation.[36] It was the first, and perhaps the only, public school desegregation case to be financed by a labor union.[37]

The suit against the large, urban CCISD was more ambitious than the suits DeAnda had pursued against the Driscoll and Odem school districts. He therefore recruited other reform-minded attorneys to assist him, among them Houston's Chris Dixie. Dixie was representing the plaintiffs in a federal civil rights suit related to their abortive attempt to organize a farm workers' union in south Texas.[38] With this help, DeAnda developed a new legal strategy, gathered documentary evidence, and deposed witnesses. The lawyers had plenty of time to do so. Judge Seals did not begin the pretrial phase until 29 May 1969, when he issued a "Docket Control Order." In it the judge scheduled the first pretrial conference for 24 November, sixteen months after DeAnda had filed the federal civil rights complaint. At a second pretrial conference, in May 1970, Seals denied the CCISD's motion to dismiss the case on summary judgment.[39]

The court hearings commenced in mid-May 1970. A significant portion of the plaintiffs' evidence came from the defendant CCISD's records. From them DeAnda described the percentages of each of the three major ethnic groups, Anglo, Mexican, and African American, that made up the district's student population, and the number, ethnic heritage, and assignment of each teacher in each school. DeAnda illustrated the location of the past and present attendance boundaries, the location, date of construction, and cost of newer schools and the schedule for renovating older schools. Finally, he described the school children that CCISD had bused "in the past and in the present, and who they were, and who they are."[40]

Throughout, DeAnda sought to draw a picture of CCISD as a "dual" school system that segregated its Anglos on a few campuses and placed non-Anglos, blacks and Mexican Americans, on the others. He offered the following breakdown for the 1969–70 school year: 43 percent of the elementary students enrolled in CCISD schools were Anglo and 51 percent were Mexican American; in the junior high schools 48 percent of the students were Anglo and 47 percent were Mexican American; and in the senior high schools 56 percent of the students were Anglo, 39 percent were Mexican American. Furthermore, 15 percent of the total high school enrollment of 9,800 students, 1,300 Mexican Americans and 200 African Americans, attended schools with greater than 90 percent non-Anglo enrollment. And another 16 percent, 1,600 Mexican Americans but fewer than 30 blacks, attended schools with a 70–80 percent non-Anglo student body. Thirty-two percent of the Anglo students attended high schools with a 20–30 percent non-Anglo population (with fewer than 1,000 Mexican Americans enrolled on those campuses). Twenty percent of the Anglo high school population attended schools with a less than 10 percent non-Anglo enrollment.[41] DeAnda argued that if CCISD were integrated, then the percentage of each ethnic group in each school at each grade level would approximate each group's percentage of the total student population. Instead, the enrollment figures showed a substantial ethnic imbalance.[42]

DeAnda made a simple but compelling case with these numbers. In CCISD, Mexican Americans were lumped with the African American minority much more often than they were paired with the Anglo majority. But DeAnda had to prove that this statistical "imbalance" reflected the Mexican Americans' minority status within an Anglo-dominated, segregated system. He called Thomas P. Carter, a professor of education and sociology at the University of Texas (UT) at El Paso, to testify. Carter began by stating that blatant discrimination against the Mexican Americans, such as the formerly common signs that proclaimed "Mexicans and Dogs Not Allowed," were "rapidly disappearing" but that Texas was "moving into a period of very subtle kinds of discrimination."[43] Judge Seals asked Carter whether, in the context of the issues raised in the present lawsuit, Mexican Americans should be considered "an identifiable group." Carter answered that he found that "a very peculiar question," because the U.S. Census Bureau, and the state of Texas, regarded them as a distinct minority. Moreover, Carter declared,

> everyone considers [them] an ethic minority or a cultural minority. In social science, a minority is a group of people who may be a physical majority, but . . . [also] a group of people who are not full participants in the dominant society. In other words, there is discrimination. They don't fill their proportional number of doctors, lawyer, merchant, and chief kind of slot in the society. . . . [P]articularly in Texas, it has been established that many laws were discriminatory against Mexican-Americans. So both from a legal point of view, a Government point

> of view, and a social-science point of view, they are a minority. . . . So, no matter how you cut it, [they] are going to come out as a minority, . . . from social science and from the legal . . . and from the cultural . . . and the racial point of view.[44]

Seals asked Carter whether in his studies he had noted any differences in "Anglo-Saxon culture emanating from Western Europe and England, and the Mexican culture?" Carter replied, "[O]f course, a great body of literature exists that differentiates . . . the Mexicans or the Indian-Spanish tradition of the south of the border, and the Protestant-English tradition." They "represent two identifiably different cultural trends." True, differences were diminishing, but "there have been many studies that will identify cultural characteristics of both groups, or any other number of groups also."[45]

Carter insisted that to overcome patterns of ethnic or racial discrimination and to create equal participation by ethnic or racial groups, children from these groups should attend integrated schools. Integration could play a significant role in fostering equality by stimulating social interaction between the groups. Integrated schools would provide an environment conducive to academic achievement by the disadvantaged group. He emphasized, however, that increased minority achievement would be a secondary effect compared to the broader educational interests to be served by school integration. Among these interests, Carter said, was the facilitation of understanding, acceptance, and equality.[46]

DeAnda needed to connect the enrollment imbalances at CCISD schools to the widespread discrimination against Mexican Americans. He introduced into evidence a map of the locations of various Corpus Christi residential subdivisions that originally had deed restrictions limiting the right of home lot ownership to members of the "white" race. The restricted neighborhoods were clustered along the southern and northern rims of the city. DeAnda demonstrated statistically that very few Mexican Americans lived in the white enclaves. The location of the deed-restricted areas around the edges of downtown left an unrestricted zone in the center where very few Anglos lived, which DeAnda referred to as the "corridor."[47]

In this sharply defined Corpus Christi residential segregation, any scheme of neighborhood schooling would impede integration. DeAnda suggested that the perpetual segregation of Anglo, African, and Mexican American students was such an obvious effect of the neighborhood schools concept that it might have been instituted expressly to defeat efforts to integrate the schools.

This was the crux of DeAnda's case. When the CCISD board drew attendance zones to match well-known segregated residential patterns, its members had acted in their official capacity to perpetuate discrimination against the minority groups. Therefore, DeAnda submitted, they had transmuted de facto segregation into de jure segregation. Since the Supreme Court had condemned de jure discrimination,

Judge Seals had the authority and the duty to apply the equal protection rationale of the *Brown* decision to Mexican Americans.[48]

Over five days of hearings, DeAnda went to great lengths to prove that Mexican Americans were a de jure minority who deserved, but were denied, equal protection of the laws. But at the last moment he resorted to the ancient attorney's practice of arguing in the alternative. DeAnda reminded the judge of Odem and Driscoll, the "other white" due process desegregation victories. Seals took judicial notice of them, and DeAnda prepared to rest the plaintiffs' case.[49]

The district's lead attorney, Richard Hall, did not dispute the statistics DeAnda had offered. He could not argue against the evidence of the unbalanced CCISD enrollments or debate the effects of the "corridor" on the residential patterns in Corpus Christi. Instead, Hall attempted to convince the judge that different interpretations, implications, and conclusions could be drawn from the facts, and that the benefits of neighborhood schooling outweighed the benefits of integration alleged by Carter. Hall called Lawrence D. Haskew, a professor of education and administration at UT in Austin, to testify. Haskew stated that neighborhood schools could eliminate ethnic and racial barriers even when residential segregation caused children to attend segregated schools. The quality of education, not the place where it was offered, was the important consideration. If the education in segregated neighborhood schools gave the students social mobility, motivated students would be able to escape from their disadvantaged environment. Little benefit resulted from transporting students from one area of the city to another, simply to place them in an integrated environment for a mere eight hours each day. Haskew declared that, rather than busing students, "education conducted for people in ghettos is the best route."[50]

Although the *Cisneros v. CCISD* hearings consumed eleven full days in court, Seals had run a tight ship. He had prepared for the efficient examination of the complex and voluminous data in the pretrial phase, and he gave the two legal teams credit for the smooth proceedings: "One great advantage and help to the court was the way and manner all the statistical evidence was worked and catalogued at the beginning of the trial, and which was offered and stipulated to early in the trial, and which was available to the court for study."[51]

The orderly presentation of the case enabled Seals to prepare and deliver his decision quickly. He foreshadowed the content of his ruling by announcing that he had concluded that Cisneros and his fellow steelworkers had properly filed their case as a class action.[52] Although Congress recently had relaxed requirements for filing class actions, by amending the Federal Rules of Civil Procedure in 1966, this judicial finding was a significant victory for the Mexican American and black plaintiffs.[53] Even under liberalized procedural rules, the Supreme Court regarded some groups' labels to be inadequate for class actions. In 1969 the court had rejected as overbroad a proposed plaintiffs' class consisting of "Indo-Hispanos, also called Mexican American and Spanish-American."[54]

Seals then proceeded to examine what he called the "ultimate issues" of the case. He had reduced them to five questions. First, the judge asked, could *Brown* and its progeny cases be applied to Mexican Americans, or was *Brown* to be limited to African Americans? Second, if *Brown* could be applied to Mexican Americans in principle, did it apply to the specific facts in the present lawsuit against the CCISD's allegedly dual school system? Third, with regard to the African American students, was CCISD a dual or unitary school district? Fourth, if CCISD did maintain a dual school system, as defined by the Fifth Circuit cases, was it a de jure or a de facto segregated system? Finally, Seals asked, if CCISD was a dual system, how should he, sitting as a judge in equity, remedy the situation? That is, "under what plans and programs" could he "disestablish a dual school system and establish and maintain a unitary school system?"[55]

On the question of whether *Brown* applied to Mexican Americans, Seals observed that *Brown* condemned segregation, "even though the physical facilities and other tangible factors may be equal," because it deprived children of the guarantees of the Fourteenth Amendment. Although the *Brown* cases had been specifically concerned with the segregation of blacks and whites, "it is clear . . . that these cases are not limited to race and color alone."[56] Seals rejected as "patently unsound" any interpretation of the *Brown* decision, or of the Fourteenth Amendment's equal protection clause, which held that "[a]ny other group which is similarly or perhaps equally, disadvantaged politically and economically, and which has been substantially segregated in public schools," should receive less effective constitutional protection than African Americans.[57]

Seals accepted that the evidence indicated that in CCISD, "no less protection should be fashioned for the district's Mexican Americans than for its Negroes," because Mexican Americans "[had] experienced deprivations and discriminations similar to those suffered" by the blacks in the district.[58] The "proof shows," he declared, that Mexican American students in CCISD "have been segregated and discriminated against in the schools in the manner that *Brown* prohibits" and that because of that segregation and discrimination, they were "certainly entitled to all the protection announced in *Brown*."[59] He realized that this was a novel contention. Seals therefore took great pains to argue against the conventional wisdom that Mexican Americans were "white." Nonetheless, he demonstrated that he was also still grappling with the notion. "It is clear to this court," Seals announced, that

> Mexican-Americans, or Americans with Spanish surnames, or whatever they are called, or whatever they would like to be called, Latin-Americans, or several other new names of identification—and parenthetically the court will take notice that

> this naming for identification phenomena is similar to that experienced in the Negro groups: black, Negro, colored, and now black again, with an occasional insulting epithet that is used less and less by white people in the South, fortunately. Occasionally you hear the word "Mexican" still spoken in a derogatory way in the Southwest—it is clear to this court that these people for whom we have used the word Mexican-Americans to describe their class, group, or segment of our population, are an identifiable ethnic minority in the United States, and especially so in the Southwest, in Texas and in Corpus Christi.[60]

In addition, he said that he had taken judicial notice of "congressional enactments, governmental studies and commissions," and court opinions which seemed either explicitly or implicitly to accept that Mexican Americans endured discrimination.[61] Finally, Seals noted that the myriad Mexican American organizations, "such as LULAC and the G.I. Forum, and now MAYO, were called into being in response to this problem."[62]

Seals found that "the objective manifestations" of ethnic discrimination were "gradually disappearing from our society." Nevertheless, he declared, the "historical pattern of discrimination has contributed to the present substantial segregation of Mexican-Americans in our schools." The result was a segregated dual school system. Then the judge announced that he had concluded that the African American students in CCISD were "also segregated to a degree prohibited by law which causes this to be a dual rather than a unitary school system." Moreover, in a decision "based primarily upon the undisputed statistical evidence," Seals ruled that the segregated conditions also were manifested in the CCISD faculty assignments.[63]

On the question whether CCISD segregation was de facto or de jure, Seals decided that the evidence was mixed. He noted that "some of the segregation was of a *de facto* nature," the result of social and economic factors in Corpus Christi that caused the city's blacks and Mexican Americans to continue to live in the "corridor." But the judge also declared that the segregated dual district in Corpus Christi had "its real roots in the minds of men; that is, the failure of the school system to anticipate and correct the imbalancing that was developing." And it was obvious, he said, that "placing Negroes and Mexican-Americans in the same school does not achieve a unitary system as contemplated by the law." Rather, a unitary school district could be achieved only "by substantial integration of the Negroes and Mexican-Americans with the remaining student population of the district."[64]

In sum, Seals believed that through a host of administrative decisions, the CCISD board had created and perpetuated a dual system. Among the faulty decisions were "drawing boundaries, locating new schools, building new schools and renovating old schools" in the predominantly black and Mexican Americans parts of town. The CCISD board also provided "elastic and flexible subjective" transfer rules that allowed some Anglo children to avoid schools in the "ghetto, or 'corridor'" but had not allowed the Mexican American or black students to transfer into the Anglo schools. He declared that "regardless of all explanations and regardless of expressions of good intentions," these were official decisions that were "calculated to, and did, maintain and promote a dual school system."[65] Therefore, he ruled that "as a matter of fact and law," CCISD was "a *de jure* segregated school system. . . . Wholly so with respect to the district's Mexican-Americans and predominantly so with respect to the district's Negroes." Moreover, Seals ruled,

> the *de jure* nature of the existing patterns of segregation within [CCISD] has as its base state action of a non-statutory variety, that is, the school board's active pursuit of policies that not only do nothing to counteract the effects of the existing patterns of residential segregation in view of viable alternatives of significant integrative value, but, in fact, increase and exacerbate the district's racial and ethnic imbalance. There has been a history of official school board acts which have had such a segregative effect.[66]

In light of a history of "official school board acts," Seals ruled in favor of the plaintiffs and announced that he would grant them injunctive relief against the CCISD's dual school system.[67]

Seals next considered the remedy he would grant. In both the Driscoll and Odem cases, the remedy had been a judicial decree that the practices contested in each case were unlawful and an injunction against continuing them. Those cases concerned at most several hundred students. The CCISD schools enrolled thousands of students in each grade. Complicated administrative maneuvering would be required to disestablish the CCISD dual system and to establish a unitary one. As a starting place, Seals noted that the CCISD's faculty and staff were even more segregated than its student body. He referred to the new test for school integration that the Fifth Circuit had established in *Singleton v. Jackson Municipal Separate School District* (*Singleton III*).[68] In it the appellate judges had mandated that student enrollments and faculty employment in each school must reflect the general population in the school district. Seals declared that CCISD must reassign its minority teachers and staff, and it must hire more minorities, in order to create the so-called *Singleton* ratio in each school.[69]

The greatest obstacle to a satisfactory remedy to the segregation at CCISD was the large number of Mexican American students to be integrated with Anglos. Seals noted that there were "reasonable available methods to effect a unitary system . . . without significant administrative, educational, economic, or transportation costs."[70] But the judge assumed that any remedial plan would involve the busing of students. The question was, busing on what scale, and in combination with what other measures? These questions required further study. Therefore, the plan for dismantling the dual system and erecting the unitary system would be developed in part by a "human relations committee." Seals would appoint its members and would charge them with the responsibility for "investigating, consulting, and advising" the CCISD board, "with respect to all matters tending to promote and to maintain the operation of a unitary school system which will satisfy the law."[71]

The judge invited the plaintiffs and defendants to propose their own plans to achieve "a unitary school system which will be educationally, administratively, and economically reasonable." He suggested few definite remedies at this early stage. However, Seals declared that an acceptable integration plan "shall include" a majority-to-minority transfer rule.[72] The defendants could appeal the ruling, but he would not stay his order pending an appeal. A panel of judges from the Fifth Circuit subsequently denied the CCISD's request to stay Seals's court order. The time for dilatory deliberation had passed. Seals and the appellate judges wanted action.[73]

Seals left to the litigants the nomination of candidates for the human relations committee. But in curiously detailed instructions reflecting Seals's determination to maintain a tight rein over the remedial proceedings, the judge did set forth the process through which the committee's members would be named. The plaintiffs and the defendants would each provide the court with fifteen cards marked with the name, address, and telephone number of a "patron" of CCISD. Cards from each side were to be submitted in three stacks. One stack would include alphabetically arranged names, addresses, and telephone numbers of five African Americans, another set would name five Mexican Americans, and the third five Anglos. Seals's clerk would select two cards from the top of each stack. The resulting panel would boast four white, four black, and four brown members.[74]

The judge and the parties immediately commenced the remedial phase of the litigation. At Seals's direction, in mid-July 1970 both DeAnda and Hall filed their preliminary proposed student reassignment plans. As Seals reviewed them, Corpus Christi was seriously damaged by Hurricane Celia, but even that storm could not deflect the judge's resolve. In early August, soon after the emergency had passed, Seals required the lawyers to schedule a hearing to assess the hurricane's effect on the integration plans. In the interim, he ordered that no repairs were to be initiated except those necessary to prevent further damage, or to render classrooms safe and suitable for students. He further directed that contracts "shall not be let and construction shall not be commenced for extensive and permanent type restoration or expansion . . . without prior submission to the court and approval by the court." Representatives of the CCISD board must attend a meeting in his Houston chambers on 12 August to present him with a "complete, itemized inventory" of the storm damage and to recommend repairs and renovations. Seals ordered the lawyers to meet again separately to discuss the impact of proposed repairs on the creation of a unitary system.[75]

In a telephone conference with Hall and DeAnda one day before Corpus Christi schools were scheduled to open for the new academic year, Seals informed the attorneys that the CCISD's integration plan was unacceptable. Seals ordered the board to submit a new plan at once, because the CCISD opening day was imminent. His demand for an immediate response stemmed from his awareness that administrators of other districts in the process of court-ordered desegregation often sought extensions based on a fear of disrupting students' education during the school term. In most school cases major policy changes came during the summer break. Therefore, Seals also demanded that the board inform him whether the school year ought to be delayed. Finally, the CCISD representatives were to inform Seals whether a unitary system could be implemented after the semester's start. Seals scheduled another Houston meeting to discuss these points, to be held in two days. But the meeting was canceled. The schools opened on schedule, and implementation of integration was delayed, probably for at least nine months.[76]

CCISD submitted a revised unitary plan on 31 August, and Seals scheduled hearings to discuss its merits. The hearings convened on 2 September, in the Southern District's Victoria courthouse, approximately midway between Houston and still-hurricane-damaged Corpus Christi. Busing stayed at the center of the debate. The judge heard testimony from district officials, education experts, the operator of a private bus company, and various interested citizens. On 15 September, one day before the hearings were scheduled to end, DeAnda sought the intervention of the Justice Department and HEW. Seals agreed to consider the motion, although he expressed concern that it was an untimely request.[77] The next day, the judge concluded the hearings. He requested that within ten days the litigants submit briefs to summarize their positions, address factual and legal points, and answer the following questions: Should high school seniors be exempted from any plan? Should HEW be invited to intervene? Should the human relations committee submit its own plan? And should the CCISD plan of 31 August be implemented, and if so, wholly or in part?[78]

The following month, on 16 October, Seals agreed to invite the Justice Department and HEW to intervene in the suit. He had concluded that their expertise in desegregation matters would be useful. The judge ordered CCISD to seek the government's opinion on its integration plans. Thereafter, staff members of the local U.S. attorney's office, as well as representatives of the federal Office of Education, attended hearings and meetings of the human relations committee.[79]

The proponents of early integration by busing received a boost on 20 April 1971, when the Supreme Court decided *Swann v. Charlotte-Mecklenburg Board of Educa-*

tion.[80] This was the court's canonical statement of a federal judge's broad discretion to develop remedial schemes in school desegregation cases. In it the justices ruled that busing was a normal and accepted tool. Chief Justice Burger declared:

> When school authorities present a district court with a "loaded game board," affirmative action in the form of remedial altering of attendance zones is proper to achieve truly nondiscriminatory assignments. . . . [The] remedy . . . may be administratively awkward, inconvenient, and even bizarre in some situations and may impose burdens on some; but all awkwardness and inconvenience cannot be avoided in the interim period when remedial adjustments are being made to eliminate the dual school systems.[81]

Burger rejected "rigid guidelines," including fixed racial quotas, to bring about school integration. Instead, he announced a "reasonableness" standard against which to measure a judge's proposed remedy. As Abram Chayes noted, this was an "elastic standard" by which to define the equitable power of the federal district courts.[82]

Just two days after the Supreme Court ruled in *Swann*, Seals gave the litigants and federal intervenors one week to prepare for a meeting in his chambers. The participants must discuss the impact of the busing decision on their own integration plans.[83] The parties met on 30 April. A few days later, Seals ordered HEW representatives to submit a plan for creating a unitary school system at CCISD, in compliance with *Swann*. HEW submitted the requested plan on 2 June. Seals gave the litigants another week to file objections. Both plaintiffs and defendants registered complaints. The human relations committee encouraged CCISD to propose an alternative plan. The school board declined to submit one.[84] The board objected on financial grounds to any contemplation of busing. It would be expensive and require increased taxes or fees. Rather than develop a plan, the board reargued the benefits of neighborhood schooling. Seals responded to the school board's resurgent defiance by declaring that the status quo was not an option. Citing *Swann*, he reiterated that "insisting that children in a segregated neighborhood attend a school in that neighborhood amounts to government sponsored segregation."[85]

The participants in the CCISD litigation filed their various plans, comments, criticisms, and changes throughout June 1971. The plaintiffs proposed what the judge referred to as the "floating zone" or "transportation island" busing plan. It would be flexible but potentially very expensive to implement. The HEW's experts submitted a proposal to implement a system of "pairing" Anglo and minority schools. It was simple but required busing large numbers of students. Ultimately, even CCISD developed and submitted a plan, a "modified" neighborhood system.[86]

Judge Seals examined the submissions and announced his final judgment on 2 July. He decided to create his own solution, by combining and altering slightly the other plans. In his plan, the judge noted, "it appears that no school at any level will be ethnically identifiable, although one group or another may be in a majority." There would be no schools without "a substantial number of students from the minority ethnic groups, nor is there any school which does not have a substantial number of Anglos." Seals admitted that " '[s]ubstantial' may be a poor word since it cannot be defined with mathematical precision. . . . however, [he was not] seeking mathematical precision, but a system which opens all the schools in the district to attendance by students of *all* groups in significant numbers." He insisted that he had not attempted to achieve a quota or a "certain ratio" of races or ethnicities, either throughout the system or at any school. However, he then suggested that, in a district in which nearly one-half of the student population was Mexican American or black, 20 percent was a reasonable upper and lower threshold. That is, less than 20 percent attendance by Anglo students, or less than 20 percent Mexican American and/or black students at a single school was "probably . . . insignificant."[87]

The judge estimated that under his plan approximately fifteen thousand students at CCISD "might need or qualify" for transportation. He cited the school board's estimate from the Victoria hearings that a plan like his would require CCISD to acquire, operate, and maintain ninety-six buses, at an estimated total cost of $1.718 million.[88] Seals suggested that the city of Corpus Christi had several viable options for financing the busing plan. It could raise taxes or apply for grants from Texas or HEW. The CCISD board might lease rather than purchase buses, vans, or the occasional "Volkswagen bus." The mere fact that CCISD "might not be able to obtain all of the maximum of buses needed should not . . . cause the court to digress from implementing the most practical plan for achieving a unitary system."[89]

Seals implied that he believed his plan constituted the last word on the CCISD integration. He thanked the members of the human relations committee, the attorneys, certain of the district's representatives, and "above all, the citizens of Corpus Christi for the interest, cooperation and patience they have exhibited throughout the course of this case. For many it has been an unsettling and traumatic experience." Seals noted that no one would be satisfied completely with his "court-ordained" plan, but he also maintained that it was "*not* the result of a vendetta against Corpus Christi or of a policy of racism." Rather, the busing plan he proposed was

> the result of the denial of constitutionally guaranteed equal protection to Anglo, Mexican-American, and Negro parents and students. It is the result of a decision by the School Board to defend the status quo and abstain from fashioning a remedy. It is the result of decades of insensitivity to the rights of others and the courts' obligations to secure those rights. . . . The challenge facing Corpus Christi today is to implement this plan even though it may be unpopular, even

though it is appealed. This is the highest test of a free people operating within the framework of a constitution. If we fail, these children will confront the same task tomorrow.[90]

Judge Seals then suggested, as before, that the CCISD board might appeal his ruling. However, also as before, he noted that the judgment would take effect immediately, and he would not stay it pending the expected defendants' appeal. The integration plan, including busing, must begin in the fall 1971 school term. He intended to keep the case on his docket until he was satisfied that a unitary school system had been put into effect in Corpus Christi.[91]

According to the clerk's records, Seals had spent twenty days in trial over the three years of the *Cisneros v. CCISD* proceedings. He had been obliged to live in Corpus Christi seven months of each year. He had made a four-hundred-mile round-trip from Houston each weekend during one busy fourteen-month period, a significant investment of judicial time and energy.[92] With the integration plan in place, Seals embarked on a long vacation. When he returned several weeks later, his holding in the CCISD case was in complete disarray. By then, it was no longer his responsibility.

Notwithstanding Seals's declaration that he would not grant a stay of his order pending an appeal, school-district attorney Hall on 13 July filed a defendants' motion requesting a stay. The next day, he called the judge's office in Houston and learned that Seals was in Jerusalem on vacation. Hall was also told that, because the telephones were unreliable in Israel, Judge Seals was effectively incommunicado until he returned to the United States in late August. This news prompted Hall to call Chief Judge Connally. Connally ordered Bailey Thomas, the clerk of court, to transfer the CCISD case temporarily to Owen D. Cox, the Southern District's new judge in Corpus Christi.

Owen DeVol Cox was born on 20 March 1910, in Joplin, Missouri. He earned his B.A. from the University of Kansas in 1931 and his LL.B. at the University of Kansas School of Law in 1932. He entered private practice in Corpus Christi in 1934 and then entered public service in 1942. Cox spent one year, for example, as the assistant city attorney of Corpus Christi, Texas, and another year as city attorney. He served in the U.S. Army from 1944 to 1945 and then resumed his job as the city attorney. Cox reentered private practice in 1947 and continued to practice law in Corpus Christi until 1970, when President Richard Nixon named him to a new seat in the Southern District of Texas, the eighth permanent position on the court. Cox received his judicial commission on 1 December 1970.[93]

On 16 July Hall told Cox that the board was prepared to reallocate funds to remodel buildings and transfer teachers as Seals had directed. But, Hall argued, if the board spent the money to purchase buses, their appeal of the plan would be mooted. Cox stayed Seals's "final" order for one year, that is, until 1 July 1972. On 27 July Connally assigned the CCISD case to Cox "for further handling."[94] Therefore, when Seals returned from vacation, he was no longer involved in Corpus Christi's integration.[95]

Upon learning of this year-long delay, DeAnda immediately contacted Cox. The new judge refused to remove the stay. But the next day, he issued a supplemental order to clarify the fact that CCISD must continue to prepare to bus the small number of African American students to Anglo schools. The judge's stay therefore applied only to the transfer and transport of Anglo and Mexican American students. This clarification did not satisfy DeAnda. He sought a complete reversal of the stay. On 5 August, on a vote of two to one, a three-judge panel from the Fifth Circuit vacated Cox's partial stay and reinstated Seals's order. Hall then asked for a reconsideration, which the circuit judges denied on 10 August.[96]

The CCISD attorney appealed the panel's action to Associate Justice Hugo Black, who supervised the Fifth Circuit. At this juncture the federal government added its support to the school district's effort: the U.S. solicitor general joined in requesting that Black reinstate the stay. The justice answered on 19 August 1971. After noting that it was "apparent that this case is in an undesirable state of confusion," Black reinstated Cox's stay. His decision meant that Seals's plan would not go into effect until the Fifth Circuit had an opportunity to review the case.[97]

Several days after Black's decision, a delegation from the CCISD human relations committee contacted Cox. The committee suggested that busing the one thousand black children in CCISD, without also implementing the rest of Seals's comprehensive integration plan, would be expensive and yield little benefit. Cox agreed, and, amending his "clarified" order, he broadened the stay explicitly to include African Americans.[98]

With the pressure to begin integration lifted until at least summer 1972, CCISD concentrated on preparing its appeal, which a panel of Fifth Circuit judges agreed to review. The school district expanded its legal team to include David Searls, a partner at Vinson, Elkins, Searls, and Smith, one of Houston's premier firms.[99] But before the panel had a chance to hear the case, the CCISD lawyers complicated the issues by moving for the case to be heard by the full circuit.[100]

DeAnda also recruited more advisers for the appeal. MALDEF and "Inc. Fund" attorneys filed a joint request to submit amicus briefs on behalf of the plaintiffs. The Fifth Circuit judges approved their petition.[101] The two civil rights organizations would be more useful to the plaintiffs' case than the federal intervenors, who had been lukewarm allies so far. Falling in line with the solicitor general's brief for delay when before Justice Black, the Justice Department's appellate brief now asked the circuit judges to remand the case. Although the government suggested the need for immediate relief for blacks, it argued as well that more study was necessary regarding the discrimination against Mexican Americans. The federal lawyers wondered whether Seals had ruled "correctly" on the issue of de jure segregation.[102]

Seals's novel interpretation of Mexican Americans' de jure minority status remained his most controversial finding in the case. DeAnda's cocounsel, Chris Dixie, filed a motion in early September to have the Fifth Circuit judges order the case returned to Seals, in the event that they vacated or remanded the decision. He argued that it was "inconsistent with judicial economy and a severe imposition" to require the plaintiffs to acquaint a new judge with the complexities of the case. The records of the hearings filled eighteen volumes and included 2,783 pages of testimony.

The defendants moved to keep Cox on the case. In support, they cited Seals's complaints regarding his workload and travel burdens and the need for them to travel to Houston to confer in person with Seals. The Fifth Circuit ultimately ruled that Connally had not abused his discretion in reassigning the case. Cox kept it.[103]

On 7 October the Fifth Circuit denied the request that it hear the case en banc. Circuit Judge Griffin Bell dissented. He believed the full circuit court ought to take the opportunity to speak authoritatively on the triethnic case. He noted, "This question is confused by the fetish to give names to legal doctrines—here *de jure–de facto*." Seals was one of the judicial fetishists, Bell suggested. Seals "found some discrimination in a *de facto* school situation (as to Mexican-Americans)," Bell said, and then Seals "leaped across the factual chasm to find *de jure* status." Bell believed that "in the interest of stability in the field of public education," the circuit should meet to hear *Cisneros* and "resolve these questions now."[104]

The denial of an en banc hearing left the responsibility for resolving the triethnic question to Circuit Judges Walter Gewin, Irving Goldberg, and David Dyer. But after the appellate judges heard oral arguments on 16 November, they also declined to settle the issues raised in *Cisneros v. CCISD*. On 10 February 1972 the panel announced that it would delay its ruling. The circuit judges had decided to wait and to let the Supreme Court declare whether a de facto minority like Mexican Americans could suffer de jure discrimination.[105]

FROM DESEGREGATION TO INTEGRATION TO TRIETHNICITY IN HOUSTON

The Fifth Circuit was unable or unwilling to reconcile Seals's and Cox's differing views in the *Cisneros* litigation, and this dallying left the question of Mexican Americans' status open to jurists' individual interpretations. Few federal district judges, statisticians, academicians, or politicians still denied that Mexican Americans were an ethnic "national origin" minority that had been subject to social discrimination and de facto segregation. Judges and other acknowledged experts had for years supervised, studied, or contested public school desegregation, however, as a biracial problem. For them to accept the contention that Mexican Americans were also a de jure minority within the framework of desegregation would take a transformation of the conventional wisdom. At least, many observers from both sides of the battle agreed, the unconventional notion demanded legal or judicial consensus.[106]

Consensus came slowly. In 1960, after much delay and deliberation, Connally had approved a grade-per-year or "stair-step" transfer plan that promised to desegregate all HISD schools by 1972. But in July 1965 Connally entered a court order to accelerate the HISD desegregation schedule to two grades per year, which would meet the higher standards suggested by HEW and the Fifth Circuit. At the same time, the HISD board proposed to adopt a "freedom of choice" plan, which would shift the burden for school desegregation to parents. Under "freedom of choice," which many southern districts adopted after HEW suggested that stair-step plans were failing to desegregate the schools, parents were allowed to choose the school in which to enroll their children. Connally approved the plan. He noted that in *Singleton I,* in addition to accepting HEW guidelines as minimum standards, the Fifth Circuit judges had declared that nondiscriminatory "freedom of choice" plans were acceptable. By 1966 HISD declared all elementary and senior high schools desegregated under freedom of choice. The ninth grade had remained segregated but would be desegregated by September 1967. Therefore, it seemed that the HISD schools would be desegregated five years ahead of Connally's original schedule. Implementation was imperfect, however. Many black parents were not notified that they had any choices.[107]

The HISD administrators had already provided buses to formerly white schools. But the school district had also embarked on a massive construction program that promised to build modern schools in black neighborhoods. This led Onesephor Broussard, his wife, Queen Ethel Young, and other black parents to sue HISD. They asked U.S. District Judge Allen B. Hannay to enjoin HISD from proceeding with construction.[108] The plaintiff parents believed that convenient new schools in African American neighborhoods would entice blacks to exercise their "freedom of choice" just far enough to resegregate themselves and their children. Broussard charged, in fact, that the probable discriminatory effect was the impetus for HISD's commencing the project.[109]

Hannay granted the plaintiffs a hearing and visited some seventeen schools throughout HISD before he ruled. He noted that Houston's black families were overcoming the effects of years of residential segregation. Formerly white neighborhoods were gradually becoming mixed. However, no similar phenomenon was occurring in Houston's black neighborhoods. The judge stated that the "predominantly Negro neighborhood of former times remains predominantly Negro in Houston today." Hannay reminded the parties that families received many benefits from neighborhood schools. He thought that it was probably the case that the black parents, like most parents, would prefer that their children attend neighborhood schools over schools that required a bus ride. Moreover, the parents would choose the nearby modern school if given the choice. But Hannay found "no instance in which the location of the new facility or improvement appears calculated to discriminate racially" against African American students. He ruled that in initiating the construction, the HISD board had acted "in good faith . . . honestly, conscientiously, and with no intention or purpose to maintain or perpetuate segregation." On 13 July 1966 Hannay denied the plaintiffs' request for an injunction.[110]

Broussard and the other plaintiffs appealed Judge Hannay's decision. In the meantime, in June 1967 the U.S. Department of Justice sought to join the *Ross* lawsuit as an intervenor. Since its creation in 1957, the Justice Department's Civil Rights Division had acted as the government's enforcer of civil rights laws. Initially, the division's role in desegregation cases was limited either to ensuring that judicial decrees were followed or to participating in suits as amicus curiae.[111] The government had little independent authority to bring suit until Congress expanded the division's jurisdiction under the 1964 CRA. Thereafter, the division began aggressively to intervene in school litigation.[112] In August 1967 the government asked Connally to complete integration and to order busing of students if necessary. Although Connally granted the government's motion to intervene on 5 September, he was unprepared to order busing.[113]

In May 1968 Judge Connally, sitting temporarily by designation on the Fifth Circuit, found himself in the interesting position of reviewing his colleague Hannay's school desegregation decision. Connally continued to believe that the members of the different races had the right to live separately if they so chose. Speaking for the majority of a three-judge panel, Connally declared that the plaintiff's position was "simply" that

> [n]o new schools should be built or old schools improved, in densely populated colored areas. The child resident in such area, regardless of his wishes, of necessity must be required to attend a school in some other section with a relatively high ratio of colored-to-white students. Considerations of convenience, of traffic hazards, or the wishes of the student and his parents should be disregarded. Such child simply would *have* to attend a high ratio colored-to-white school, *and would be required to do this only because he was a negro.* The Constitution does not require such a result, and we entertain serious doubt that it would permit it.[114]

Judge Connally was exploiting an opportunity to restate his own ruling in 1962's *Ross v. Dyer*, that the law does not grant blacks "a different, and superior, treatment, by reason of their race." The Fifth Circuit judges had reversed that decision.

Now, Connally noted that the plaintiffs wished to restrict, rather than enhance, the options of black children.

Connally reminded the plaintiffs that HISD's "freedom of choice" policy had to be administered fairly for all races, stating that "those negro children who wish to attend a school close to their homes have constitutional rights, too; and they well might assert such rights against a School Board which refused to construct a needed school in their area simply because it would be attended largely by negro students. This would be discrimination with a vengeance, based solely on account of race."[115] He concluded that "in their zeal to press for integration of the races at all levels and in all things . . . many persons, some of good will, completely lose sight of the rights of those who do not desire to be integrated at the moment." Connally, joined by Circuit Judge Rives, believed that the Constitution protected this right to choose, and they affirmed Judge Hannay's decision to allow HISD to build new schools in black neighborhoods.[116]

Fifth Circuit Judge John Minor Wisdom dissented. Wisdom reminded the majority that the circuit had declared that the only legitimate goal of any "freedom of choice" plan was to encourage black parents to act affirmatively on their own behalf to eliminate segregation. Rather than leaving in place patterns of discrimination, school boards were to support this aim by fostering integration. Wisdom also considered it the appellate court's duty to promote integration.[117]

Connally answered Wisdom's dissent in a supplemental opinion. He once more proudly noted that "most of the problems attendant upon desegregation of this largest school district in the south have been solved amicably." He declared that freedom of choice, whatever its supposed affirmative purpose, was peripheral to the case. Before the Fifth Circuit ruled, Houston voters had approved $59 million in school bonds to cover the costs of the construction program. No one had described what would happen to the bonds if the plaintiffs prevailed and the construction ceased, but Connally suggested that Houston voters would be forced to pay interest on money they could not spend. Connally declared that as a judge in a court of equity, Hannay had "acted properly under all the facts and circumstances" in withholding his injunction.[118]

Connally had initially granted, at the HISD school board's request, an exception to the original 1960 stair-step plan. This was the "brother-sister" rule which required that elementary-age children enroll in the elementary school attended by their older siblings. He had repealed this exception after a remand from the Fifth Circuit. After the enactment of the 1964 CRA, Connally sought to follow both the circuit's changing mandates and HEW-developed guidelines. He had ordered the HISD board to accelerate desegregation under a two-grade-per-year plan. In key decisions the Fifth Circuit had also required school districts to merge faculty and staff and desegregate athletics and other extracurricular activities. Connally had ordered HISD to comply with these new requirements. Next, the HISD board had proposed and the judge had accepted a freedom-of-choice plan. Finally, in 1967, the Justice Department had intervened in the *Ross* case. The government suggested that some limited but mandatory busing would be necessary to integrate HISD. Finally, the Supreme Court had raised the bar in the *Green* and *Alexander* decisions.[119]

Judge Connally had already devoted a dozen years to the task of adapting his court decrees to match evolving goals of the litigants, the federal appellate courts, Congress, and the executive branch. He was now disinclined to imitate Seals's leap "across the factual chasm" on the issue of Mexican Americans' place in the HISD desegregation effort.[120]

No one had asked Connally to make this leap during the 1960s. One reason he had not earlier encountered the Mexican American desegregation question was the relative size of the population. There was a large and growing Mexican American community in Houston, but it still ranked well behind the Anglo and African American groups.[121] A more significant reason that he had not considered Mexican Americans as a factor in his 1960s desegregation decisions was that Mexican Americans had not raised the issue. To be sure, Mexican American students in Houston had begun to demand official recognition of and respect for their Chicano heritage. Many joined enthusiastically in the burst of Chicano-inspired walkouts in the late 1960s. But such youth-led protest groups as Advocating Rights for Mexican American Students (ARMAS) complained of the perceived inferior facilities, inadequate offerings and resources, and poor teaching and counseling at the HISD schools with Mexican American majority enrollments.[122] ARMAS and other Mexican American organizations identified and sought to end various discrimination practiced by the Anglos who controlled HISD. Yet neither the Houston students nor their parents had campaigned for the special legal recognition the *Cisneros* plaintiffs were then seeking in Corpus Christi.[123]

The goals of Houston's Mexican Americans evolved with astonishing rapidity. In February 1970 a new student organization, Barrios Unidos, presented the HISD board with a list of thirteen demands. This group's terms were more comprehensive and militant than those expressed several months earlier by ARMAS. Tenth on the Barrios Unidos bill of particulars was the unprecedented provision that "[a] school should not be considered integrated where the majority of students are Mexican American and Negro. The statistical practice of labeling Mexican American students white is misleading and serves as a technique to disguise minimum efforts in meeting federal integration guidelines."[124]

There was no backlash in February 1970 when the HISD school board refused even to acknowledge the Barrios Unidos's catalog of grievances, or when school officials ignored other students' demands. But, in a major turnabout, Mexican Americans reacted with uncommon passion a few months later, when Connally and a panel of Fifth Circuit judges managing the latest phase of the HISD case officially rejected Barrios Unidos's basic thesis.[125]

In 1969 Connally opened what he called "another chapter" in the HISD saga.[126] Since he wrote the first chapter in the 1950s, Houston had become one of the nation's ten largest and fastest growing metropolitan areas.[127] HISD had become the sixth largest school district in the country, and the largest in the South. The district encompassed more than three hundred square miles, with one-half of these miles inside the city limits and the rest in suburban or rural areas. HISD enrolled approximately 240,000 students, of which two-thirds were designated white and one-third black. HEW estimated that 36,000 of the students were "Spanish-surnamed Americans," 15 percent of the total student population. The 9,000 HISD teachers matched the two-to-one white to black racial ratio of the student body. According to standard practice, the HISD board and Judge Connally included the Spanish-surnamed teachers and students in the "white" figures.[128]

The HISD operated the court-approved "freedom-of-choice" plan through the 1969–70 school term. Unsatisfied *Ross* plaintiffs moved for further equitable relief. Judge Connally held several hearings in June and July 1969. HISD enrollment records revealed that after five years under feeedom of choice, one-quarter of the African American students were attending formerly all-white schools. But 95 of the district's 170 elementary schools still enrolled 10 percent or fewer black students. Forty-four elementary schools had student bodies with 10 percent or fewer white students. Nineteen of the 36 junior high schools enrolled 10 percent or fewer blacks, and 11 had student bodies with 10 percent or fewer whites. Finally, 3 of the 24 high school campuses were all black. Four had fewer than five white students. Seven enrolled fewer than fifty white students. There were no all-white high schools, but 6 had fewer than fifty black students. One-half of the high schools were 90 percent white, and 7 were 90 percent black. In all, 77 percent of African American students in the HISD attended schools where the enrollment was greater than 90 percent black.[129] After reviewing this evidence, Connally ruled that it was obvious that freedom of choice had not resulted in the level of integration required by the most recent Supreme Court and the Fifth Circuit decisions. He directed the board to devise and submit a new plan by 1 January 1970.[130]

Before this deadline the HISD Board of Trustees was significantly transformed. In a hard-fought election in November 1969, voters replaced four of seven school board members. Unlike the outgoing members, the incoming majority "favored taking good faith, affirmative steps to carry out HISD's desegregation duties."[131] The new board members assumed office in January 1970. Joe H. Reynolds, the attorney who had represented the school district since the *Ross* litigation began, immediately withdrew from the case. Weldon Berry, who had represented the plaintiffs from the beginning, continued in that role. The HISD's new attorney, W. James Kronzer, requested an extension of several weeks to familiarize himself with the case, which Connally granted. During this interim Kronzer requested that HISD compile detailed "locator" maps listing the residence, race, and grade of each of its nearly quarter-million students.[132]

Connally conducted additional hearings in early 1970 to examine the latest integration plans proposed by the parties. He announced his choice on 30 May. Before ruling, he reviewed the history of the *Ross* case and declared that Houston "has . . . come a long way along the road. Substantial integration has been achieved in many areas . . . and, of almost equal importance, [it] has been achieved without incident or racial confrontation."[133] Continuing in this optimistic vein, the judge stated that with regard to the integration of transportation, services, facilities, athletics, and extracurricular activities, the HISD board had complied with legal requirements. Connally noted that the plaintiffs did not concede these points; however, neither the plaintiffs nor the federal government (in its role as intervenor) had questioned the HISD board's claims regarding facilities, sports, and the rest, or offered evidence to the contrary during the hearings. Moreover, the judge added, "[f]rom my own continuing familiarity with the problem, I am sure that such is the case."[134]

In addition, Connally granted that the HISD's faculty had been integrated, although "not as thoroughly as is now required by law."[135] The requirement to which he referred was the *Singleton* ratio, which for HISD would be two to one, approximately two-thirds white and one-third black. Connally noted that although he had issued his order before *Singleton III,* he had "anticipated that holding to some extent."[136] He directed the board to reassign its principals, teachers, teacher's aides, and "other staff who work directly with children," so that the ratio of the white and black staff and faculty in a school "shall vary no more than 5%, above or below" the prevailing two-to-one ratio, and that the faculty and staff assignments conform to the *Singleton* ratio "at no event later" than the beginning of the September 1970 school term. The judge said he was gratified that the board apparently "recognizes its obligation in this respect and does not contest the issue."[137]

Connally turned to the "only question which remains . . . that of student integration," a question "not easily resolved," because the appellate courts had established "[f]ew meaningful guidelines."[138] In the "great majority of cases," he claimed, appellate judges had not told district judges what was required for integration but "have simply said . . . 'This is not enough.' "[139] Accordingly, Connally set out his own standards for success. He declared that he considered it his judicial duty to adopt a plan for HISD that "will serve realistically . . . to bring about a high degree of overall student integration, . . . to assure that every student, if not receiving his education in an integrated atmosphere today, soon will do so, and . . .

to do this in a manner which is consistent with good education, good administration, and with sound economic practices."[140] With these criteria in mind, Connally examined the proposals.

He was pleased with the HISD's student locator map. With it, the judge declared, "now, for the first time, one may forecast accurately the effect of any new plan of integration which may be invoked."[141] This tool proved indispensable, because Connally had to evaluate seven proposed integration schemes. These were: (1) the plaintiffs' plan, which had been prepared for the Inc. Fund by a Boston computer center; (2) the federal government's plan, known as the Stolee Plan after its architect, Michael J. Stolee, director of the Florida School Desegregation Consulting Center; (3) the so-called Ted-Tac plan, prepared for HISD by the HEW-funded Texas Educational Desegregation Technical Assistance Center of the University of Texas; (4) the existing freedom-of-choice plan, which the outgoing HISD school board had resubmitted in late 1969; (5) the "neighborhood zoning" plan, which the outgoing board also had submitted in 1969; (6) the new HISD board's "equidistant zoning" plan; and (7) the "geographic capacity zoning" plan, which the new board also submitted.[142] Connally quickly dismissed several of these alternatives.

The plaintiffs' plan, to achieve the exact same racial balance in every HISD school, would have required busing thirty-four thousand white and ten thousand black students. The judge noted that the computer-generated plan was silent about how children to be bused should be chosen, "no doubt against the will of many of them." Would HISD draft them, Connally asked, and allow "deferments based on hardships or other valid considerations?" Could the names "be drawn in public from a goldfish bowl?" His more serious concern was whether "provision was to be made for a review procedure, with ultimate appeals to the courts."[143] "This suggestion is not as absurd as it sounds," he noted, given the fact that

> [t]his Court has been called upon in perhaps a dozen instances within the last few months to examine school procedures with respect to the right of a child to attend school with his hair too long; her skirts too short; charged, but not convicted, of possession of marihuana; the distribution of underground newspapers, etc. We well might be called upon to review a procedure, alleged to be discriminatory, which requires some black students to be bussed ten miles to school, while their black neighbors are permitted to attend schools within two blocks of their homes.[144]

In sum, the Inc. Fund's plan might generate as many legal and practical problems as it purported to solve. The judge wanted none of these complications. Moreover, he announced, the "inordinate expense," at least $1 million annually, rendered the plan "completely inappropriate."[145]

Equally summarily, Connally rejected most of the remaining proposals. The Stolee plan combined zoning, pairing, and busing. First, attendance zones would be gerrymandered to reach a high level of integration. Second, a school still racially unbalanced after zoning would be matched to a school with an opposite imbalance, and the pair would exchange their students as necessary. Third, some children would be bused, but only as necessary to eliminate the segregation remaining after zoning and pairing, especially at many elementary schools. Connally criticized the Stolee plan, first, because it had the youngest children carrying the largest burden of busing. This was to be avoided, he said, because "by reason of their tender years any extended travel is undesirable" for children. Also, the plan was an outline rather than a complete proposal. It analyzed only 78 of the 170 HISD elementary schools, and was therefore "too incomplete to be accepted in its present form . . . [when] more attractive proposals [were] available."[146]

The Ted-Tac plan was not one of these "more attractive" proposals. Combining zoning, pairing, and busing, the Ted-Tac plan paralleled the Stolee plan with attendant disadvantages that outweighed the benefits of the slight increase in integration the judge found. In some cases the pairing proposed by the Ted-Tac plan would disrupt the existing grade structure of many affected schools and require HISD to create a new curriculum, and would "require the reassignment of many teachers and almost all students." Finally, the Ted-Tac plan resorted to busing to integrate elementary schools. Connally repeated his concern regarding this recurring feature of integration proposals. "Cross-town busing is objectionable in any event," he said, and "[c]ertainly that is true when applied entirely to children of elementary school age."[147]

Connally exhibited unusual nostalgia for the failed freedom-of-choice plan. He recalled that it "has been administered fairly and completely without discrimination by the defendant District for several years." Under it, he claimed, "any child who was unhappy with his original school assignment could enroll in any school of his choice simply by appearing at the schoolhouse door on the enrollment date. Such a scheme has much to commend it in theory." But since the freedom-of-choice scheme had failed to achieve sufficient integration, "it is condemned by recent authorities . . . [and] cannot be further considered here."[148] None of the active parties endorsed the 1969 "neighborhood zoning" advocated by the late, unlamented HISD board.[149]

Judicious elimination left Connally measuring the present board's proposed "equidistant zoning" plan against the new board's "geographic capacity zoning" plan.[150] The latter was based on a plan approved by the Fifth Circuit in February 1970 for implementation by the school district in Bibb County, Georgia.[151] Under it the district's planners drew an attendance zone around each school in a "nondiscriminatory" manner, with the geographic size of the zone determined by the school's capacity, natural boundaries, and traffic hazards. Once a zone had been drawn for that year, every student within it attended the associated school, unless they made a legitimate majority-to-minority transfer.[152] Connally stated that this plan offered "an attractive solution." It promised to integrate high schools, junior highs, and elementary schools. However, the fact that the school district retained discretion in the drawing of zones to account for hazards and boundaries rendered the plan suspect. Connally declared that no matter how integrated a school was under any plan lacking strict guidelines, "the contention can always be advanced that such lines might have been drawn differently, and with a better result." He was not charging the board with an illicit purpose in proposing the plan. But the judge noted that "whenever a School Board draws its zone lines today in a discretionary fashion, it is subject to being charged with doing so to continue its dual system."[153] For these reasons Connally rejected the plan.

This left the equidistant zoning plan. Patterned after a plan the Fifth Circuit approved, also in February 1970, for the Orange County, Florida, school district,[154] it required the district's planners to draw attendance zone boundaries exactly equidistant between schools. Each student enrolled in the nearest school. If this resulted in student enrollments in excess of school capacity, the geographic area served by that school would be decreased and the area of adjacent attendance zones increased. The new boundary would still parallel the original. Most important, every boundary change would be made to increase the level of integration.[155]

Majority-to-minority transfers were exceptions. A transferring student had two options. Under the first, if a student transferred to the nearest school, he or she gained automatic admission and would receive free transportation between home and school. If the chosen campus was at full capacity, the transferee could "bump" a student of the "opposite" race to a new school. Under the second option, a student who wished to transfer to any campus other than the nearest attended on a "space available" basis and must furnish his own transportation.[156]

Judge Connally concluded that the equidistant zoning plan would "best serve the needs of the student body, and [would] afford as uniformly a fair and nondiscriminatory school assignment plan as well may be devised." This plan, he stated, would create a unitary school system and achieve a high degree of integration, was both "economically and administratively sound," and allowed HISD to make school assignments "as color-blind as it is possible to be"; and no child would be excluded from any school because of his or her race.[157]

In the early stages of the program, as indicated by Table 2, 38 percent of all African American children in the district would attend schools with student bodies in excess of 90 percent black, while 75 percent of the white students would attend schools with student bodies in excess of 90 percent white.

The segregation was a result of Houston's racially identifiable residential patterns.[158] But these children, Connally said, were not permanently to suffer segregated education. Any student could make a majority-to-minority transfer and be

TABLE 2. Predicted Results of the "Equidistant Zoning Plan": Number of Schools with Monoracial Student Bodies

	ALL-BLACK	ALL-WHITE	MORE THAN 90% BLACK	MORE THAN 90% WHITE
High School	0	1	1	10
Junior High School	0	2	3	14
Elementary School	4	51	23	41
TOTAL	4	54	27	65

Source: *Ross v. Eckels*, 434 F.2d 1140 (5th Cir., 1970), 1146.

bused free of charge to the nearest integrated school. He noted that all children, regardless of the level of integration in the school, would receive their education from a faculty integrated according to the *Singleton* ratio.[159] The judge approved the equidistant plan with one stated reservation. He suggested that when the HISD board drew zones, it should allow for impassable objects, such as the Buffalo Bayou, because "a child is not required to swim or to fly to school."[160]

Judge Connally directed the HISD board to prepare to institute equidistant zoning, with the few minor suggested modifications, for the September 1970 school term. He ordered the creation of a biracial committee of local citizens, whose ten members he would appoint. This committee would be responsible periodically to consult with, investigate, and advise the HISD school board, "with respect to all matters tending to promote the operation of a unitary system." And, Connally announced, he would retain jurisdiction of the *Ross* case for "a reasonable time to insure that the system is operated in a constitutional manner."[161]

Only a week after Connally announced his *Ross* decision in Houston, Seals issued his initial ruling in the *Cisneros* case in Corpus Christi. The similarity of certain characteristics of the cases and decisions are as striking as the differences. Both judges conducted extensive hearings over the course of many months to review various complicated options for integrating schools. They sought to consider the local conditions while they assessed the relative risks and benefits of neighborhood schooling, freedom of choice, pairing, zoning, and busing. And, both examined the various plans that the plaintiffs, defendants, intervenors, and outside consultants proposed to them in light of rapidly evolving mandates and standards issued by the Fifth Circuit and Supreme Court. These were the familiar elements of federal judicial management of integration litigation in the 1970s.

Such parallels make divergences more telling. Connally and Seals each appointed local worthies, both to give voice to the concerns of their communities and to act as the judges' "eyes, ears and hands." The court-appointed citizens' committee was another familiar tool.[162] But where Seals specifically provided for a triethnic committee, Connally created a biracial committee.

In part, this fact reflects specific characteristics of the plaintiffs and also indicates the relative sizes of the three ethnic groups in the two cities. But African Americans constituted a significantly smaller percentage of the population in Corpus Christi than did the Mexican American community in Houston. Seals might therefore have created a biethnic committee of Anglos and Mexican Americans. The difference resulted from Seals's acceptance that de facto segregation was as large a problem as was de jure. Connally never discussed these concepts.[163]

The African American plaintiffs in Houston appealed, because Judge Connally had rejected their plan in favor of one that would achieve less integration. In their 25 August 1970 majority opinion, Fifth Circuit Judges Homer Thornberry and Lewis Morgan praised Connally's "learned, thorough, detailed consideration" of the legal and practical issues in *Ross v. HISD*.[164] They relied upon his analysis of the seven proposals. But the circuit judges were not satisfied with the predicted results of the equidistant zoning plan. A general rule had developed in school cases: "In the conversion from dual school systems based on race to unitary school systems, the continued existence of all-black or virtually all-black schools is unacceptable where reasonable alternatives exist."[165] The judges did not prefer the plaintiff-appellants' computer-generated plan to the equidistant plan. Instead, they created another plan by combining one plan Connally had approved with aspects of several proposals he had rejected. Thornberry and Morgan noted that the district's geographic capacity plan had been projected to eliminate every 100 percent black senior and junior high school, and also to eliminate senior and junior high schools that were more than 90 percent black. This would be a better result than that projected for the equidistant plan. Therefore the judges directed Connally to adopt the portion of the geographic plan which applied to the upper grade levels.

In HISD's elementary schools, the appellate judges agreed that the expected results of the equidistant zoning plan would be better than those projected for the geographic plan. The latter would leave 25,848 African American students enrolled in twenty-nine all- or nearly all-black elementary schools. Under the equidistant plan, only 21,418 African American students would attend twenty-seven segregated or nearly segregated schools. Morgan and Thornberry declared that "[n]either plan is acceptable."[166]

The judges directed Connally to use the equidistant zoning plan as the basis for elementary school assignments, but with certain modifications. They listed more than two dozen elementary schools to be arranged into one dozen pairs. The result would leave 11,982 African American students enrolled in fifteen virtually all-black elementary schools. Even if this might not be the best solution for HISD, Thornberry and Morgan left Connally the discretion to adopt "any other plan submitted by the school board or other interested parties, provided . . . that such alternate plan achieves at least the same degree of desegregation as that reached by our modifications." Finally, the judges modified the majority-to-minority transfer rule. They admitted that the rule Connally had already adopted was similar to the one the Fifth Circuit had accepted for Orange County. But in subsequent decisions the circuit had strengthened the requirements for integration. The latest version of an acceptable majority-to-minority rule mandated free transportation for any transferring student who wanted it. Also, the circuit judges required that a district give enrollment priority at any school to which the student wished to transfer, not only the next nearest school. Morgan and Thornberry therefore affirmed Connally's ruling in part, reversed it in part, and remanded the case to him with these stipulations.[167]

The third member of the panel, Judge Charles Clark, dissented. Nixon's first appointee to the Fifth Circuit, Clark harbored at least some of the president's reservations regarding the pace and direction of recent integration decisions. But Clark was a conservative judge who argued for caution, not a reactionary who called for the rollback of civil rights.[168] Clark suspected that the Fifth Circuit had gone too far in a quixotic attempt to integrate the public schools, and he worried that activists on the circuit would press ahead until they had reduced federalism to tatters. In his *Ross* dissent Clark's modest view of the function of the federal courts decried minute fiddling with students' assignments. This was not the courts' proper role. He had concluded that appellate judges "err when we substitute our judgment, based upon documents and maps, for that of the district courts whose decision is based upon flesh and blood contact with the real people and the real problems of the district."[169]

Clark charged that Thornberry and Morgan were inconsistent and disingenuous in their opinion. The Orange County plan had never been overturned, and the majority did not say why Connally was wrong to rely on it. So why did that recent ruling "still exist as the law of this circuit applicable to that county, to Tuscaloosa and Anniston, Alabama . . . but not in Houston, Texas?"[170] Of the circuit's vigorous but erratic efforts to integrate the schools, Clark declared: "It is rapidly becoming apparent that despite express disclaimers . . . the special school case panels of this circuit are now out ahead of the requirements laid down by the Supreme Court and have adopted sub silentio some unmentionable standard of numerical pupil racial balance to govern the affirmance or reversal of school case decisions."[171]

He suggested that the "true principle that underlies the reversal of the district court here is that the neighborhood school system ordered for Houston did not achieve that degree of racial balance some judges of this circuit have declared is 'enough.'" If his colleagues sought to meet a quota, Clark confessed that he did not understand why "the 'magic figures' must remain a mystery."[172]

The Orange County plan that Connally had adapted to HISD in *Ross* had complied with the legal standard in force when he ruled, Clark asserted. It was unfair to the district judges and the school districts for the Fifth Circuit to keep moving the target. "Unless someone would be boldly foolish enough to assert that courts can deprive school district patrons of their freedom," he said, "then it follows as the night follows the day that the courts will never finish litigating such 'numbers game' cases." If HISD was still not in compliance with constitutional mandates after more than a decade of continuous court oversight, then federal judges were at fault, not the HISD officials. The continual evolution in judicial policies simply proved that "the courts are totally inadequate . . . to deal with such numerous and complex interrelationships of rights . . . by remote control." But if the courts were to continue experimenting with new methods of introducing and evaluating integration of the schools, Clark declared, then it should follow what he called a "basic rule" of empirical procedure, to introduce new ingredients "singly, not in groups or bunches, lest the experiment fail because one new departure canceled out the benefits that came from another." School districts were still in the process of implementing the *Singleton* ratio, majority-to-minority transfers, and biracial committees. Cities and citizens were grappling with new prohibitions on racial discrimination in housing and employment. Clark declared that the circuit judges ought to allow the strong medicine they had already prescribed a fair chance to work before they applied a remedy as drastic as "student racial balancing."[173]

In one key area, however, Clark was the least conservative judge on the panel. He alone voiced concern that the Mexican American students were ignored in the integration plans. The panel majority had acknowledged that roughly thirty-six thousand Spanish-surnamed students were enrolled in the HISD schools, that they were counted as white, and that most lived in neighborhoods adjacent to traditionally African American neighborhoods.[174] But Morgan and Thornberry did not indicate that only one of the elementary schools they proposed to pair was mostly Anglo. Of the remaining schools, two-thirds were mostly black and one-third were predominantly Mexican American.[175] Clark was disturbed by the fact that this meant that with the Fifth Circuit's approval, Mexican American schools were to be paired with black schools in order to "integrate" them. The majority's tinkering with Connally's plan had not repaired this common flaw in Texas desegregation cases.[176]

Referring to Seals's *Cisneros* ruling, Clark asserted that "it is mock justice when we 'force' the numbers by pairing disadvantaged Negro students into schools with members of this equally disadvantaged ethnic group." He declared:

> I would be greatly surprised if a single school teacher could be found in the entire HISD who would testify that the educational needs of either of these groups is advanced by such pairings. We seem to have forgotten that the equal protection right enforced is a right to education, not statistical integration. Why, on this kind of a theory, we could end our problems by the simple expedient of requiring that in compiling statistics every student in every school be alternately labeled white and Negro! Then, you see, everything would come out 50–50 and could get our seal of approval once and for all.[177]

After this pointed ridicule, Clark "respectfully" dissented.[178]

African Americans and Mexican Americans considered the Fifth Circuit's modified zoning and pairing plan no better than Judge Connally's equidistant zoning plan, since both were essentially modified neighborhood schooling arrangements. In Houston as in Corpus Christi, the attendance zones and majority-to-minority transfer rules would lead to the integration of black with "white" students by assigning the Mexican American and African American students to the same schools. By accepting that result Connally, the Fifth Circuit majority, and the HISD board showed that they had not recognized the role the Mexican Americans' emerging ethnic consciousness and self-identification was beginning to play in integration politics.[179] Seals and Clark recognized the difference between biracial and triethnic desegregation. Soon after the *Ross* decision, more Mexican Americans in Houston demanded that Connally come to this recognition.[180]

No one in Houston was happy with the *Ross* plan. In late August 1970 the HISD board reluctantly prepared to implement the zoning and pairing ordered by the Fifth Circuit. The African American plaintiffs contemplated appealing to the Supreme Court. Several Mexican American civic, political, and religious groups formed an umbrella organization, the Mexican American Education Council (MAEC), to coordinate responses to *Ross,* including a school boycott. The group encouraged parents to keep students out of class on opening day of the new term. More than thirty-five hundred Mexican American students stayed home. The group also roused the Mexican American parents to picket elementary schools, bus stops, and the HISD administration building. MAEC organized more than two dozen *huelga* ("strike") schools staffed by volunteer teachers. Leonel Castillo, who would be named director of the federal Immigration and Naturalization Service (INS) by President Jimmy Carter, was an early MAEC leader. He was employed at the time of the protests as the community relations director for the Roman Catholic Diocese of Galveston and Houston.[181]

In mid-September the HISD board voted unanimously to seek a stay and to appeal the Fifth Circuit ruling to the Supreme Court. The vote apparently had more to do with the board's unease with the elaborate pairing than with the boycott, but the decision nevertheless opened the door for dialogue. MAEC suspended the boycott and encouraged students to return to their HISD schools by 21 September. The board agreed in principle to count Mexican Americans as an ethnic group separate from whites. HISD would hire more Mexican American teachers and counselors, bring Chicano perspectives into the curriculum, and appoint proportionate numbers of Mexican Americans to school committees. MAEC stayed active. It monitored HISD's adherence to the deal and turned *huelga* schools into after-school tutorial centers for Mexican American children.[182]

The board, the black plaintiffs, and the MAEC activists agreed that the *Ross* plan was not a suitable solution to segregation in HISD and resolved to delay court-ordered pairing.[183] The three-way bargain to delay was insupportable after the Fifth Circuit refused to grant a stay while the case was on appeal. At a meeting on 15 December, the HISD board approved a compromise plan to pair twenty-one elementary schools and assign students to them through a lottery. Mexican Americans declared the compromise solution to be as unacceptable as earlier plans. In January 1971, MAEC adopted a non-cooperation policy, and Mexican Americans resumed boycotting and picketing.[184]

Despite the parents' continued resistance and the board members' reluctance, court-ordered pairing began in February. HISD bused children to their new schools. In March the Supreme Court declined to stay the *Ross* ruling. In April the court firmly supported busing in *Swann*. The HISD board declared these questions closed.[185] Mexican Americans attempted to keep the questions open. In early 1971 MALDEF sought Connally's permission to intervene in *Ross*. He denied their motion on 24 May 1971. In a short memorandum opinion the judge noted that HISD and other school districts have "always treated Latin-Americans as of the Anglo or White race." In a reference to MALDEF's reliance on Seals's *Cisneros* ruling, Connally declared that even if Mexican Americans were an identifiable minority group, that fact did not entitle them "to escape the effects of integration" with African Americans. He contended—contradicting Seals's opinion—that Mexican Americans had never been subjected to "state-imposed segregation."[186]

FROM BIRACIAL DESEGREGATION TO TRIETHNIC INTEGRATION

In late April 1972 DeAnda informed the Fifth Circuit judges that Corpus Christi voters had recently approved bonds to fund school construction and renovation. DeAnda argued that CCISD should not be allowed the opportunity to reinforce a segregated system. The circuit judges agreed, and in a short per curiam enjoined the CCISD board from undertaking renovation and expansion projects until an appellate court decided *Cisneros.* The circuit judges assumed for the moment that Seals's evaluation of the CCISD's attitude toward integrating Mexican Americans was accurate: "Promoting integration of the Negro and Mexican-American students clearly was not considered by the [board] as a factor" in previous decisions regarding the location of new schools or which old schools should be renovated. The CCISD board did not consider, and "consequently did not pursue, viable alternative locations for schools which, even using a form of neighborhood plan, would have resulted in a much more favorable ethnic and racial balance." However, the circuit judges stated that, in issuing the injunction, they were not also deciding Mexican Americans' status.[187]

But resolution of the critical question of the role to be played by "national origin" minorities in "racial" school desegregation cases could not be delayed forever. Since Seals had ruled in June 1970, other federal judges had heard similar cases. U.S. District Judge William Wayne Justice of Tyler, in the Eastern District of Texas, had examined school segregation there and had also heard cases involving the San Felipe and Del Rio schools in the Western District. In *United States v. Texas,* a ruling with statewide implications, Justice had lined up with Seals and declared that Mexican Americans were an identifiable ethnic minority that had been denied equal protection.[188]

The U.S. Justice Department had also sued the Austin Independent School District (AISD), alleging that AISD maintained a dual school system. The government's major contention was that on Austin's east side most schools exclusively enrolled Mexican American and African American students. U.S. District Judge Jack Roberts's ruling in *United States v. Texas Education Agency* paralleled Connally's in *Ross v. HISD.* Roberts had ruled that although Mexican Americans did "constitute a separate ethnic group," the government had failed to prove that AISD had imposed de jure segregation upon them.[189]

Since the Texas federal district courts had not conveniently settled the biracial versus triethnic, de facto versus de jure questions among themselves, the Fifth Circuit judges had finally to confront the problem. In July 1972 the Fifth Circuit judges announced that they had decided on their own motion to hear the *Cisneros* appeal en banc. They did not grant a rehearing. Instead, the circuit court would reconsider the case on the basis of the existing hearing records, previous briefs, and transcripts of the earlier appellate arguments.[190]

Circuit Judge Dyer spoke for the Fifth Circuit majority on 2 August. The *Cisneros* case had raised a novel question, namely, whether the nonstatutory segregation of Mexican Americans was constitutionally permissible. The Fifth Circuit judges had decided that it was impermissible. Dyer said that, although the *Brown* decision dealt with statutory segregation, the definition of unlawful segregation included racial or ethnic isolation created or perpetuated by school boards' decisions, actions, and policies. *Brown* required only that a judge determine two facts to declare segregation unlawful. First, a judge must find that segregation, whether racial or ethnic, denied equal educational opportunity. Second, a judge must find that the segregation was the result of state action. Therefore "[w]e need not define the quantity of state action or the severity of the segregation necessary to sustain a constitution violation."[191]

The appellate judges would not declare that a dual school system was more tolerable because it had developed without legislative "insistence." Dyer denounced the CCISD's continued effort to characterize the Corpus Christi situation as de facto segregation that was the result of housing patterns beyond school board control and therefore beyond the federal courts' remedial authority. That contention, Dyer said, was "no longer entitled to serious consideration."[192]

Continuing, the circuit majority affirmed Seals's "explicit holding" that school board policies had created and maintained racial and ethnic segregation in Corpus Christi. Like Seals, they viewed reliance on neighborhood schools as the "direct and effective cause of segregation" and referred to the same evidence Seals had used in his ruling, that is, the minority "corridor" running through the central city. The fact that obvious state action was involved in creating the segregated housing patterns was not significant, Dyer said. By its "rigid superimposition" of a neighborhood school concept on the historic pattern, the school board had "equated the residential homogeny to ethnic and racial homogeny" and had produced "inevitable segregation. . . . We need find nothing more."[193] Discriminatory motives might have reinforced the segregated patterns, but such motives were "not necessary ingredients of constitutional violations in the field of public education." The circuit judges held that "the racial and ethnic segregation that exists in [CCISD] is unconstitutional—not *de facto,* not *de jure,* but unconstitutional."[194]

Not one of the fourteen Fifth Circuit judges who participated disagreed with Dyer's erasure of the distinction between de facto and de jure segregation. After affirming Seals's rulings in almost every detail, however, the circuit majority remanded the *Cisneros* case to Cox for more analysis. They directed him to develop an integration plan for CCISD that "minimized" busing.[195]

The Fifth Circuit majority's decision to remand the case fractured the opinion into varied concurrences and dissents. A majority of the circuit judges, including Brown, Wisdom, Gewin, Thornberry, Goldberg, Simpson, and Ingraham, concurred with the portion of Dyer's opinion that upheld Seals's main point that Mexican Americans were entitled to *Brown* remedies. A smaller majority, including Judges Thornberry, Coleman, Ainsworth, Godbold, Morgan, Clark, Ingraham, and Roney, joined Judge Bell's concurrence in that part of Dyer's majority opinion which charged the district court to minimize the use of busing in desegregation.[196]

Judge Coleman concurred in the decision to remand but also dissented from the majority's initial decision to examine *Cisneros* at all until the Supreme Court ruled in a triethnic school case from Denver that the justices had already certified for review, *Keyes v. School District Number One.* The *Keyes* case, like *Ross* and *Cisneros,* involved attempts by a school board to "integrate" schools by enrolling blacks and Hispanos (as Mexican Americans were called in Colorado).[197] Judge Godbold, joined by Coleman, Morgan, and Clark, would have declined to consider the case, but directed by eight judges to seven to consider it, they concurred only in the remand.[198]

Judge Goldberg, by contrast, joined by Brown, Wisdom, Gewin, and Simpson, dissented from the decision to require the district court to modify the remedy. They argued that such a review would produce no substantial modifications and merely delay integration.[199] Judge Gewin, with Brown, Wisdom, Goldberg, and Simpson, dissented from what they called the "modification-by-deletion" of the district court's remedy. Gewin believed that the Fifth Circuit had already settled every possible issue to be raised in the new district court review, either in the present opinion or in the majority's opinion in the *Texas Education Agency* case, which the circuit decided the same day. The remand would only delay implementation of the remedy.[200]

Despite the multiple opinions, the Fifth Circuit's essential holding was that for the purposes of remedying public school segregation under *Brown,* Mexican Americans were to be considered separately from Anglos. On 16 August DeAnda requested that Judge Cox approve a majority-to-minority transfer rule applicable to Mexican Americans. Cox convened a hearing the next week, where he approved DeAnda's motion. Cox ordered the CCISD board to provide transportation for students who had sought transfers by 21 August, a cohort of 383 Mexican Americans, 25 blacks, and 10 Anglos. He did not order the board to institute a permanent majority-to-minority transfer rule. But Cox directed CCISD to "speed up" its student-assignment plan: "[The] collective activity of those in charge cannot now continue at what the Court considers to have been a dilatory pace." Cox commanded the board to prepare a plan, "in good faith," by 15 September.[201]

Several weeks after the Fifth Circuit ruled in *Cisneros,* an appellate panel resolved at least one element of the integration controversy in Houston. On 6 September the same panel that had heard the earlier *Ross* appeal, Circuit Judges Thornberry, Morgan, and Clark, vacated Connally's denial of MALDEF's motion to intervene. They directed Connally to reconsider his *Ross* rulings in light of the basic findings in *Cisneros* and the *Texas Education Agency* case.[202] Thereafter, the integration plans developed for HISD accounted separately for Anglo, African, and

Mexican American students. Moreover, a triethnic committee became the court's eyes and ears.[203]

In June 1973 the Supreme Court refused to review *Cisneros.*[204] Instead, the justices took up equivalent questions in *Keyes.* The court ultimately declared in that Denver school desegregation case that African Americans and Mexican Americans could suffer "identical discrimination."[205] Unfortunately, the resolution of the question of Mexican Americans' status within a triethnic setting did not herald the end of the school integration controversy in either Corpus Christi or Houston.[206]

In September 1972 the CCISD board proposed to reassign 3,665 students and to close one majority black school. Cox rejected this plan and ordered another. In October, Hector Garcia, the former civil rights commissioner, was arrested along with seventeen students for conducting a sit-in protest against the CCISD board's continued refusal to allow Mexican Americans the right to transfer under a majority-to-minority rule. In May 1973 Cox rejected the latest integration plan. The board responded in June with minor changes.[207] This seesaw pattern continued until mid-1975, when Cox ordered the board to use a computer to develop integration plans.[208]

In 1976 the U.S. Commission on Civil Rights held hearings in Corpus Christi, with the announced intent "to influence in a positive manner a future course of the school desegregation," to promote the responsiveness of the school administrators to the "the total community," "to assist in informing the community" about the need for effective bilingual and bicultural programs," and to promote awareness of the "unique problems" affecting Corpus Christi's integration.[209] By the late 1970s the Texas Advisory Committee to the Civil Rights Commission still complained of the slow pace of school integration in Corpus Christi.[210] So did resident Mexican Americans.[211]

Patterns of growth and demographic change in and around many American cities created practical difficulties in implementing the multiethnic school integration plans. Suburbanization occurred for varied reasons. Many middle-class families, especially white families, abandoned cities and moved to newly developed or rejuvenating older communities to escape the perceived moral and physical dangers of the urban environment. This migration had been going on for decades and was related to rising prosperity and improving transportation technologies. But the growth of suburbs became known as "white flight" during the 1970s, when federal judges demonstrated that they would no longer suffer the delay of integration because of opposition from parents and school boards. As a consequence of middle-class migration, whites became the minority in many large, urban school districts and the majority in the many small districts that ringed cities.[212]

This pattern of suburbanization emerged around Houston. The dozens of municipalities outside the city limits were often enmeshed in bitter contests with one another and with Houston over annexation plans, public services, resources, and tax bases. Now the local school districts became rivals as well.[213] Portions of the predominantly white suburban school districts in Harris County, including the Alief, Katy, Aldine, Galena Park, Spring Branch, Pasadena, and Cypress-Fairbanks (Cy-Fair) districts, overlapped Houston's city limits. But the boundaries of the city and school district were not coincident, and these districts were all beyond the jurisdiction of HISD.[214]

These communities were not immune from school desegregation lawsuits. During the many years Connally oversaw HISD, other Southern District judges presided in similar litigation filed against the suburban and rural districts. The problems associated with court-ordered school desegregation in HISD were repeated, albeit usually much later, on a smaller scale, and over fewer years, in most of these surrounding school districts.[215] Joe Reynolds, HISD's longtime defense attorney, had warned in the late 1960s that white exodus would follow court-ordered integration. Reynolds knew better than most that this migration would not solve the legal problems: he also represented most of these smaller districts in their desegregation cases.[216]

During the 1970s white retreat also erupted inside Houston and HISD. Several separately incorporated municipalities, including Bellaire, Southside Place, and West University, had survived annexation battles and continued to exist as island communities within the city of Houston. However, their schools were within the jurisdiction of HISD. Soon after Houston voters ousted the conservative bloc from the school board in 1970, some residents of these mostly white enclaves sought to create the Westheimer Independent School District (WISD). The so-called "breakaway" district presumably would not be subject to court orders concerning integration of HISD. The latter-day secessionists failed. Ironically, the attempt to create the WISD brought the HISD board and the *Ross* plaintiffs into the ongoing school litigation on the same side. The HISD board argued that the WISD's breakaway must be quashed because it would complicate and potentially doom HISD's integration. With the majority of the white students in Harris County already beyond the reach of HISD, the secession of the WISD would have reduced the remaining white population further. In 1973 Connally enjoined the WISD organizers from proceeding with the effort for three years, to give the HISD administrators time to comply with the pairing, transfer, and busing rulings he had issued during the latest round of *Ross*. The proponents of the WISD revived the plan in the late 1970s, once Connally was dead. Lawsuits, countersuits, and appeals followed until Connally's successors in the Southern District buried the would-be breakaway.[217]

The federal appellate courts had declared that fear of white flight was no excuse to avoid integration.[218] But once white flight had occurred, integration plans had to be reformulated. By late 1974 it was clear to HISD's new superintendent, Billy Reagan, that pairing and transfers had failed to bring integration. He recommended to the school board that HISD create a formal panel to review the situation and offer new ideas. The board authorized the creation of the triethnic Task Force for Quality Integrated Education in November 1974.[219]

In December 1974 Chief Judge Connally turned sixty-five years old, accepted senior judge status, and entered a semiretirement that allowed him to retain his judgeship but carry a reduced docket.[220] Among the immediate reductions that the senior judge requested was to be relieved of the HISD case. Connally's colleague from the Southern District's border divisions, Judge Reynaldo Garza, succeeded him as chief judge. Garza assigned the HISD case to their colleague in Houston, Judge James Noel.[221] Senior Judge Connally suffered a heart attack on 2 December 1975, while hunting on a ranch near Falfurrias, Texas. He was accompanied on the trip—and then to the Brooks County Hospital, where he died—by his wife, Chief Judge Garza, and Judge Cox.[222]

FURTHER EXTENDING WHAT HAS ALREADY BEEN AN OVEREXTENDED CASE

The HISD Task Force recommended in May 1975 that the board create a system of "magnet schools." An update of freedom of choice, the magnet schools concept was predicated on the idea that if HISD offered high-quality education in various special subjects, such as performing arts or math and science, the district could attract Anglos into integrated schools. Judge Noel conducted hearings, then approved the plan in July 1975.[223]

The school district implemented the latest plan over three years. In the meantime, after sixteen years on the bench in the Southern District, Judge Noel also accepted senior judge status. In May 1977 President Jimmy Carter named a Houston lawyer, Finis E. Cowan, to fill the vacant federal district judgeship. Cowan was confirmed by the Senate less than one month later and received his judicial commission on 14 June 1977. Cowan was born 16 October 1929 in Dallas. He attended Rice University in Houston, where he earned the B.A. in 1951. He served as a lieutenant in the U.S. Marine Corps from 1951 to 1953 and then earned his LL.B. at the UT law school in 1956. He joined Houston's prestigious Baker, Botts law firm and remained there until his appointment to the Southern District of Texas.[224]

Judge Cowan now assumed oversight of the twenty-year-old *Ross* case. In June 1978 he reviewed the progress of integration under the magnet schools plan. Judge Cowan concluded that the HISD board had "no definite, high priority, well conceived plan to chart this district to the accomplishment of unitary status." Cowan ordered the board to develop a new integration plan. Among other subjects, he specifically directed the school board to address the question whether the magnet program had been overemphasized.[225]

The judge also suggested that the HISD board collaborate with predominantly white suburban districts to bus more Anglo students to the Houston schools.[226] Such an interdistrict solution, however, would probably have to be voluntary, because in 1974 the Supreme Court had struck down a multidistrict school desegregation decree in *Milliken v. Bradley*.[227] Such cooperation between the central city and its suburbs on school desegregation was unlikely, especially if the solution required busing students across district lines. That idea had already been suggested as a method of reversing white flight and had been unpopular.[228]

By the 1978–79 school year, the district boasted sixty-two magnet schools.[229] But it did not have many integrated schools. White flight to Houston's suburbs was accompanied by an influx of minorities, especially Mexican Americans and other Hispanics.[230] The combination of growth and demographic changes created more difficulties in school assignments. During the 1969–70 term the ethnic composition of HISD was approximately 53 percent Anglo, 33 percent African American, and 13 percent Mexican American. By the 1978–79 school year HISD student population was 30 percent Anglo, 45 percent black, and 24 percent Hispanic. Moreover, since 1970 sixteen schools that were more than 90 percent Anglo had become more than 90 percent African American.[231]

As the 1970s ended, according to a preliminary report the HISD board filed with Judge Cowan in August 1978, the district was spending millions annually on magnet schools that had failed to attract whites in numbers sufficient to satisfy the plaintiffs, the federal government, and the federal district judges. Despite questions regarding its effectiveness as a tool of integration, the magnet school program remained the centerpiece of the HISD's integration strategy. In early 1979 the parties on both sides of the *Ross* litigation prepared for a return to court.[232]

Judge Robert O'Conor had transferred to Houston from the Southern District's Laredo division. He inherited the HISD case when Judge Cowan resigned his judgeship in June 1979 to resume his partnership at Baker, Botts.[233] In June 1979 O'Conor presided in hearings to assess the school district's progress. Superintendent Reagan testified that the board had already done everything possible to achieve racial balance in the schools, but with Anglos becoming the overall minority in the student population, HISD schools could never be fully integrated.[234]

O'Conor ordered the HISD board to continue its efforts. The district created another panel, the Magnet School Task Force. Meanwhile, in May 1980 the federal government moved to amend its complaint against HISD. The Justice Department lawyers, having also concluded that interdistrict remedies were necessary to accomplish integration, sought O'Conor's approval to add twenty-two suburban districts and several state education agencies as defendants to the lawsuit. In essence, the latest motion sought to erase the myriad school district boundaries for the purposes of integration. The plaintiffs soon copied the government's example. O'Conor took the opportunity to review the status of the entire case against HISD. In June 1981 he denied the motions to add the suburban districts as defendants. He declared that the addition of twenty-six new defendants "would inject as many more issues into an already complex case . . . thus further extending what has already been an over-extended case."[235]

O'Conor announced his conclusion that the HISD board had already eliminated all vestiges of segregation and was operating a unitary system. What racial imbalance remained in the schools was not the HISD board's creation and was beyond its power to eradicate. The judge announced that he was placing the twenty-four-year-old lawsuit on his inactive docket. O'Conor would retain jurisdiction for three years, during which the HISD board must report student enrollments by race and ethnicity every six months. After three years of passive judicial monitoring, he would hold another hearing to decide whether finally to dismiss the *Ross* case.[236] The plaintiff parents and the government intervenors appealed, but on 16 February 1983 the Fifth Circuit judges agreed with O'Conor that nothing remained of HISD's dual school system. He could review the case and dismiss it if he thought there was no purpose in continuing court oversight of the district.[237]

In September 1984 as O'Conor's three-year monitoring period ended, Superintendent Reagan announced a negotiated settlement of the *Ross* case, which averted the trial O'Conor had scheduled for October. The NAACP Inc. Fund and MALDEF attorneys had signed off on a five-year agreement which, among other conditions, required the HISD to develop remedial programs to reduce minority dropout rates to the percentage of minority students in the district. Another provision in the nineteen-page agreement increased the percentage of black and Hispanic students allowed to attend magnet schools.[238]

Judge John Singleton became chief judge when Judge Reynaldo Garza joined the Fifth Circuit in 1979. Singleton was the Southern District administrator who, in November 1984, was able in a two-page order finally to announce the court's approval of an "out-of-court" settlement of the twenty-eight-year-old desegregation suit against HISD. Under the final agreement an independent committee would monitor the educational achievement in the district for five more years. The committee members would be the Texas governor, the mayor of Houston, and the presidents of the city's institutions of higher education, including Rice University, the University of Houston, Texas Southern University, Houston Baptist University, and the University of Saint Thomas.[239]

By August 1989 African Americans constituted more than 90 percent of the student body in 42 of the 232 HISD schools. Hispanics made up more than 90 percent of the population in 25 schools. Approximately 16 percent of the student population in the HISD schools were Anglos. The litigants agreed, however, that HISD was powerless to accomplish anything more. All parties asked that the case be dismissed. Ruben Rendon, a Houston attorney who represented the Hispanic intervenors, admitted that "[HISD's] not integrated . . . but you can't do it."[240]

The rise of the Chicano movement in the late 1960s transformed the basis of Mexican Americans' civil rights effort, and lawyers, including James DeAnda, finally were able to adapt the changed cultural and political consciousness to their litigation strategy. Unfortunately, African Americans had made so little progress of their own during the first decade after *Brown* that the Mexican Americans in Texas and elsewhere had not missed out on much real desegregation. The barriers raised by complexity, complacency, and demographic shift, moreover, limited the success of both African and Mexican American civil rights efforts during the 1970s.

CHAPTER SIX

Federal Criminal Justice on Trial in the 1970s

ACCORDING TO THE FIRST RULE of civil procedure, the federal judiciary's primary goal in civil disputes is to facilitate "the just, speedy, and inexpensive determination of every action."[1] Yet the litigants in civil lawsuits in the Southern District of Texas, especially in the border divisions but not only there, often faced substantial delays in getting their cases heard by the judge. This was due to the federal trial judges' responsibility to clear their criminal dockets first. This order of priority was established by the Sixth Amendment of the U.S. Constitution, which provides that "[i]n all criminal prosecutions, the accused shall enjoy the right to a speedy and public trial."[2] That general constitutional promise was given concrete expression when the U.S. Congress, after years of debating the probable causes and possible remedies of delays, passed the Speedy Trial Act of 1974. The statute established time limits for disposition of criminal cases, required dismissal of charges after unjustified delays beyond the time limits, and authorized judges to sanction attorneys for creating delays.[3]

The Speedy Trial Act was not concerned specifically with the state of the federal judiciary in south Texas, nor was its impact limited to that region. But the law did have particularly acute effect in the Southern District of Texas, where the judges were seeing ever more narcotics and immigration cases as a result of increasingly energetic interdiction. Although the congressional concern for illegal immigration ebbed and flowed, concern continually escalated with regard to the war on drugs. The national attention given to the problem of narcotics trafficking was manifested in the statutes the Congress passed to expand and to strengthen the federal law enforcement efforts. These included the Comprehensive Drug Abuse Prevention and Control Act of 1970, which included the Controlled Substances Act,[4] the change that drafted Border Patrol officers into the drug war in 1971 by mandating that they act as customs agents,[5] and the merger of the Bureau of Narcotics and Dangerous Drugs (BNDD)with the president's Office of Drug Abuse in 1973 to form the Drug Enforcement Agency (DEA).[6] The expansion of law enforcement efforts, predictably, added to federal caseloads.[7]

With the passage of these new statutes and the redirection and reorganization of law enforcement agencies, Congress increased both judges' and prosecutors' business, and then the Speedy Trial Act made both the judges and prosecutors responsible for timely conduct of an ever rising number of trials. Yet in the interest of improving the efficiency and productivity of the courts that operated under increased caseloads, the lawmakers also sought to reduce the case management burden on the federal district judges. In 1968 Congress created U.S. magistrates, who were empowered to arraign defendants, issue federal search warrants, and administer oaths. Magistrates were also authorized to conduct the trials for minor criminal offenses, to revoke probation, to assist federal district judges in pretrial proceedings for civil and criminal trials, and to review appeals.[8] A later chapter will examine magistrates' contributions in the Southern District of Texas.

This chapter will discuss the effects of various legislative and executive actions on federal criminal justice during the 1970s, especially as they affected the ways in which court business was conducted jointly by judges and prosecutors. The first part of this chapter describes the changes that certain new laws, such as the Speedy Trial Act, demanded in the structure of judicial docket management of the Southern District. The final section will also focus on the work of the judges as they faced new challenges and opportunities late in the decade, especially after Congress nearly doubled their numbers with the 1978 Omnibus Judgeship Act.[9]

The central section of this chapter examines the causes and effects of the U.S. attorney's controversial decision late in the decade to prosecute local police officers for official misconduct. Allegations of police brutality had long plagued many cities and states,[10] but several of the most notorious incidents of the 1970s occurred in Texas.[11] One novel development in these cases was the lobbying that was undertaken to bring the federal criminal justice machinery to bear against the alleged abusers. Mexican Americans in Texas demanded, for example, that federal prosecutors respond to persistent allegations of brutality by resorting to criminal civil rights statutes usually employed against southern police charged with complicity in the oppression of African Americans.[12] Where earlier chapters have described separately the causes and consequences of increased federal judicial involvement in civil rights and criminal justice matters, the majority of this chapter will discuss how these two issues were linked through this series of controversial trials in the Southern District.

The Mexican Americans' community-based campaign was similar in inception and execution to the contemporaneous and successful effort to have Mexican Americans enumerated as a separate group in desegregation cases. The outcome of these prosecutions was quite disappointing to the community and to the prosecutors. The result illustrates, moreover, that, although federal district judges and prosecutors might find themselves all but allied in some matters, as in the border divisions' well-oiled production of plea bargains or the ready acceptance of Border Patrol officers' searches upon reasonable suspicion, they could be bitter adversaries under other circumstances. The use of federal criminal laws to sanction local law enforcement officers sorely tested the boundaries of the judicial-prosecutorial relationship.

OF SPEEDY TRIALS, WEIGHTED CASES, AND CRASH DOCKETS

Federal judges had received some general guidance on the meaning of the Sixth Amendment during the "due process revolution" of the 1960s.[13] In 1967's *Klopfer v. North Carolina,* for example, a divided U.S. Supreme Court held that the due process clause of the Fourteenth Amendment incorporated the right to speedy trial, and the majority ruled that state criminal proceedings therefore must guarantee timely disposition. The court declared that the right to a speedy trial was "as fundamental as any of the rights secured by the Sixth Amendment."[14] Even "fundamental" rights are not absolute. Just five years later, in 1972's *Barker v. Wingo,* Justice Powell wrote for a unanimous court, by then under its new chief justice, Warren Burger, and described the defendant's right to speedy trial as "generically different" from other due process protections. The justices now referred to the right to speedy trial as "amorphous," "slippery," and as a "more vague concept than other procedural rights." Powell said that, as with the other due process rights, the right to speedy trial is informed by the general concern that "all accused persons be treated according to decent and fair procedures." Undue delay might frustrate this due process. But, the court added, it was often in the interest of society to provide a speedy trial, and this concern existed "separate from, and at times in opposition to, the interests of the accused."[15]

Prosecutors who allowed delay risked losing their evidence, because human witnesses became less reliable as memories faded and physical, forensic evidence degraded over time. Because many trial courts—state as well as federal—suffered under crushing caseloads that made the "speedy" disposition of cases an improbable if not an impossible goal, delay could be a useful tool in the hands of either defense or prosecuting attorneys. A defendant could bargain to reduce charges, and harried prosecutors might agree to the plea simply to close a case without the necessity of going to trial. In that instance, the Supreme Court said, the "deprivation of the right may work to the accused's advantage."[16] Of course, these issues cut two ways. Prosecutors, as shown in an earlier chapter, might also manipulate pleas for their own benefit, and defense evidence also tended to degrade over time. To help trial judges sort out these tensions, the justices set out a "balancing test" in which the conduct of both the prosecution and the defendant were weighed.[17]

The "balancing test" the court prescribed took the form of a four-pronged "functional analysis" in which the circumstances of a case created the context for rendering judgment. To decide whether a particular delay was an unconstitutional deprivation of rights, the judge weighed each of four factors. These four criteria were the length of the delay, the reason for the delay, evidence of the defendant's timely effort to assert the right (or lack of effort to do so), and evidence of prejudice to the defendant that had resulted from the delay.[18] This was a broad guideline, and the court offered a number of exceptions or additions to illustrate how judges should continue to employ their own discretion. For example, the justices asserted that the length of delay was "to some extent a triggering mechanism." It was only an imprecise tool which could "provoke" judges into reviewing "other factors that go into the balance." They noted that the length of delay was related to the inquiry regarding the reasons for it and stated that any deliberate effort by the prosecution to hamper the defense through delay was to be "weighted heavily against the government."[19]

The court stated that none of the four factors alone was necessary or sufficient to establish whether a defendant had suffered from the deprivation of the right to speedy trial. Rather, they related conditions that were to be "considered together with other circumstances as may be relevant." In the end, as the justices admitted, judges must "still engage in a difficult and sensitive balancing process." None of the four factors listed in the opinion possessed "talismanic qualities" by which to guide a judicial compass.[20] The justices had all but admitted in their opinion that they had drawn a new map that indicated very few new landmarks. But they explicitly refused, as they expressed it in the *Barker* decision, to "engage in legislative or rulemaking activity, rather than in the adjudicative process to which we should confine our efforts." This statement may or may not indicate the reaction to the activism of the Warren court: it may only be a rhetorical bone the Burger court tossed to the critics of its predecessor.[21]

In either instance, the justices are clear in their belief that a resolution of the speedy trial question would not emerge in an inflexible schedule. For this reason, the rather restrained opinion is also perhaps an intended and mild rebuke to several state legislatures that, as the court also mentions, were already writing speedy trial timetables into law. The justices do not mention the highly publicized efforts by the president and the Congress to establish federal guidelines for speedy trials.[22]

The court did not suggest a schedule because the justices were aware that most of the delays in the criminal justice system were the result of burgeoning caseloads, which were a collective problem and beyond the direct control of a trial's participants. In concurring with the *Barker* opinion, Justice White wrote that he knew as well as anyone that the actors might rely on trial delays to win cases, because then one side might believe that "time was on their side." But if a defendant truly desired an early trial, he wrote, then "personal factors should prevail if the only countervailing considerations offered by the State are those connected with crowded dockets and prosecutorial caseloads."[23]

The *Barker* ruling, from the defendants' perspective, outlined a strategy of asserting the rights to a speedy trial, even if that assertion was intended actually to gain ultimate dismissal of the indictment. Under the new federal rules of criminal procedure that were revised the same year that *Barker* was announced, moreover, the nation's federal district judges were authorized—although not commanded—to dismiss charges when prosecution languished so long on the docket that the delay appeared to violate rights.[24]

Delay caused by caseload became an element in the defense strategy of a drug possession trial that Judge Carl Bue conducted in Houston in 1973. Federal agents, acting on an informant's tip, discovered 376 pounds of marijuana stored in a garage. Judge Bue discharged one jury that had deadlocked during its deliberations, but he empaneled a second jury, which in September 1973 convicted three defendants for possession with the intent to distribute. The defendants filed a motion for yet a third trial, however, alleging that the judge had erred along the way to their conviction.[25] The most serious allegation the defendants made was that the lag between arraignment on 12 February 1973 and commencement of trial on 9 July had been excessive and prejudicial to their case. Bue noted that the defendants had not asserted this claim earlier, or shown that the delay had any effect at all on their defense. The defendants, however, were not relying solely on the Supreme Court's *Barker* decision in their request for a third trial. They relied as well on the Southern District's own rules.[26]

In March 1973, to give effect to the *Barker* mandate, the judges had worked with the prosecutors and the clerk's office to construct a "Plan for Achieving Prompt Disposition of Criminal Cases," which thereafter required that the prosecutors commence a criminal trial within ninety days of arraignment.[27] This local plan was intended to be a "binding rule of court," yet a failure by the government to comply still did not require dismissal.[28] The judges decided, after deliberation among themselves and consultation with colleagues in other federal districts, that a trial commenced with the selection of a jury through the process known as voir dire. This definition enabled judges to "stop the clock" after swearing a particular jury panel to sit for a specific trial. Thereafter, a trial judge did not confront the possibility of dismissing serious cases. If a particular case was not expected to come before the judge for some time, the judge could even send the preselected, presworn jury home. The jurors could be recalled when they were needed. A pretrial reexamination by the judge and the attorneys, to determine if the individual jurors were still acceptable for service, was usually sufficient to begin.[29]

The defendants in Judge Bue's court claimed that the lengthy delay in their case violated the district's local guidelines. Bue deflected the procedural attack by noting that these rules were instituted to prevent mischief, inefficiency, or neglect by the prosecutor that might lead to prejudicial circumstances, such as the loss of a vital defense witness. Bue reminded the defendants that they had waited until the last minute before the scheduled trial date to file the complaint. In any case, the judge ruled, the district's local plan provided for continuance for "any period of delay occasioned by exceptional circumstances." The judge found that the delay was the fault of neither prosecutors nor defense attorneys. Rather, it arose solely from the court's "extremely" and "unavoidably congested" docket. On those grounds Judge Bue denied the motion for retrial.[30]

The defendants appealed on grounds similar to those that supported their earlier motion for a retrial. A Fifth Circuit panel emphasized that "plans for achieving prompt disposition" were in fact written, administered, and enforced to protect the "public's interest" in an efficient criminal justice system, not to safeguard the defendant's rights to a speedy trial discussed in the Sixth Amendment. The appeal therefore compelled the circuit judges to ask only whether it would be in the public interest to disregard the local plan's ninety-day limit. They declared that the plans placed an "affirmative duty on the government to bring the accused to trial" and that it was also "the duty of the prosecutor and the court to make these plans work."[31]

The circuit judges agreed that the Southern District, like most districts, suffered under the burden of crushing caseloads but stated that dismissal might still be warranted if the delay was caused by the court's failure to give scheduling preference to criminal trials.[32] They noted, as had Judge Bue, that the Southern District's plan provided for continuance for delay "occasioned by exceptional circumstances." A truly exceptional reason for delay might be a temporarily crowded docket due to a major trial or "unusually large numbers of criminal filings."[33]

The judges noted that Bue had not explicitly referred to the reasons behind the delay, although, according to the district's plan, the judge should have stated the specific facts behind his general comments regarding the "unavoidably congested" docket. Nonetheless, in *United States v. Rodriquez,* the appeals court affirmed the convictions. The Fifth Circuit judges declared that even in the "absence of explanatory comment," Judge Bue's ruling left it "sufficiently implicit that the crowded docket was one that resulted from inadequate judicial resources."[34]

When they upheld Judge Bue's decision, the Fifth Circuit judges suggested that if the Southern District of Texas's docket was perpetually overburdened, then the judges sitting there ought to amend their local plan "to accord with the realities of the situation."[35] The Southern District judges attempted to do that by raising the limit for delay between arraignment and trial from 90 to 120 days. They also amended the plan for prompt disposition to define "exceptional circumstances," but, even so, the plan had no more binding force on the judges than before.[36]

The Fifth Circuit panel was clearly in sympathy with the district judges. Despite their general vote of confidence, however, Chief Judge Connally noted in a July 1974 memorandum to the court clerk, Bailey Thomas, that, to the best of his knowledge, the *Rodriquez* decision marked the first time that the circuit judges had been concerned enough with delays to request an explanation of the district's inability to meet its self-imposed deadline.[37] But the decision apparently was not a sign of tension between the Fifth Circuit and Southern District courts. Judge Woodrow Seals later relied on the circuit's "affirmative duty" language from *Rodriquez* to dismiss a tax evasion case in which the defendant had waited two years and seven months between indictment and trial. A Fifth Circuit panel, noting that the delay was due both to continuances that had been requested by the defendant and the case overload, maintained that Judge Seals had erred. He had failed, the appellate judges ruled, "to appropriately exercise" his discretion under the local plan for prompt disposition. The circuit court reversed the dismissal and remanded the case to the district for a trial on the merits.[38]

The Supreme Court's decisions regarding proper criminal trial procedures and proper criminal investigations intersected at the border. On 7 February 1973 U.S. Border Patrol agents stopped and searched a car for illegal aliens at a temporary border checkpoint near Sarita, Texas. The driver, Manuel Maizumi, and his female companion both claimed to be U.S. citizens. They appeared nervous when questioned, however, and one of the border agents smelled the odor of marijuana through the vehicle's open window. He requested that Maizumi open the trunk and discovered that one of the three suitcases inside contained eighty-four pounds of marijuana. Maizumi was arrested and charged with possession with intent to distribute.[39]

At his trial before Judge Owen Cox in Corpus Christi, Maizumi contended that the warrantless search of his vehicle was illegal according to the Supreme Court's then-recent landmark holding in *Almeida-Sanchez*.[40] Cox ruled that the court's decision, announced 21 June 1973, need not be applied retrospectively to criticize an arrest made in February. Because the government allowed more than ten months to lapse between arraignment and trial, Maizumi claimed that the judge should dismiss the charges because the government's delay deprived him of the right to speedy trial. He sought relief under both the *Barker* doctrine and the district's plan for prompt disposition. Cox rejected these claims and convicted Maizumi. On Maizumi's appeal the Fifth Circuit upheld Judge Cox's rulings.[41]

These cases illustrate that the judges in the Southern District were able to fill a large discretionary space the Supreme Court left open to them. Under "extraordinary" and "exceptional" circumstances, which by the 1970s were familiar, compliance with the Sixth Amendment—or the illusion of compliance—required little more than lip service and judicial sleight of hand. As long as the *Barker* criteria and procedural rules allowed exceptions, the ideal of speedy trials remained an unmet goal in the Southern District.

The Speedy Trial Act authorized judges to impose sanctions on the attorneys for failure to meet deadlines, but the act would not become effective until July 1979.[42] During the multiyear period of transition, however, the act called upon judges to develop new plans and required the creation of a planning group that would include the U.S. attorney, the clerk of the court, and the chief judge, who would chair the panel. The Southern District judges also invited Thomas Black, a law professor from Saint Mary's University in San Antonio, to be their planning group's reporter. This group studied its options and consulted with the experts at the Federal Judicial Center in Washington, D.C., in order to develop a districtwide plan that would comply with the statute.[43]

Judge Reynaldo Garza became chief judge in December 1974, upon Connally's accepting senior status. The Supreme Court ruled in a 1975 case from another district court that, at least for the purposes of applying the *Barker* balancing criteria, the time to trial ought to be measured from the date of the arrest.[44] But the decision did not settle the question of which timetable was to be applied under the Speedy Trial Act. Once again, that key piece of the puzzle was left to the construction of the district courts, because, although the plan's content was specified in the statute, the act still did not define when the clock began ticking. Garza suggested in a memorandum to Bailey Thomas in March 1975 that, as the clerk staff prepared monthly lists for the district judges that alerted them to the cases that were approaching a deadline, they should record a variety of milestones. Garza noted in this memorandum that both the Administrative Office of the United States Courts and the Federal Judicial Center were inclined to accept that the Speedy Trial Act's timeline began with the arrest, while Garza and the other federal trial judges he had conferred with regarded arraignment as the logical starting point.[45] The planning group that Garza chaired ultimately developed a plan that was similar to the plan already in place under the rule of criminal procedure. It continued to define trial delay in terms of days elapsed between arraignment and jury selection.[46]

As the Southern District's chief judge during the second half of the 1970s, Garza worked with the court's clerk and the other judges to develop and implement a variety of docket management innovations that were related to but not necessarily dependent on speedy trial issues. One was the introduction of a system of "weighting" cases before assigning them to individual judges' dockets. He wrote to the four Houston-based judges as soon as he became the chief, for example, to schedule a meeting to discuss a system of classifying civil and criminal cases. The purpose of classification, as Garza reminded his colleagues, was "to avoid a Judge getting five straight bankruptcy cases in which he very seldom participates, and another Judge getting five straight antitrust suits, which we all know are time consuming."[47]

Proper classification would be followed by random assignment, and this system would, he hoped, help to equalize the dockets in the long run. Chief Judge Garza wrote to Bailey Thomas shortly after the judges' meeting to confirm that, once weights were assigned, the cases ought to go onto a judge's docket as the result of a double-blind system. This required the clerk of the court to choose a case number and a judge's name from a stack of cards. To accomplish this end, only Thomas and two of his deputy clerks were to have access to the card files listing the cases.[48]

This was the system Thomas relied on to effect the division of work that he and Garza established for 1975. The assignments gave Judge Garza all of the responsibility for Brownsville and Judge Cox all of the responsibilities for cases in Corpus Christi and Victoria. Senior Judge Connally was to keep the criminal cases in Laredo. Judge Noel was to hear all of the cases in Galveston. The Houston assignments were only slightly more complicated. Judge Hannay was to receive 10 percent and Noel 14 percent of the criminal cases filed there. Judges Seals, Singleton, and Bue were each to be assigned 25.33 percent of the criminal cases. These three also each received 24 percent of the civil cases, while Hannay had 17 percent and Noel 11 percent. The judges also passed around a miscellaneous docket.[49]

The next year's assignments, of course, reflected the changed composition of the Southern District court. Garza decided to cut his responsibility for the Brownsville dockets to only 60 percent, with Cox taking 12 percent and the late judge Connally's replacement, Judge O'Conor, handling 28 percent. O'Conor also assumed full responsibility for the Laredo dockets. Cox kept all cases in Corpus Christi and Victoria. Noel continued to dispose of all cases on the Galveston docket. But, because the eighty-three-year-old Hannay had taken senior judge status, he was to be assigned no new cases. Instead, he was expected to clear his docket of pending cases. Noel was to receive 15.4 percent of the criminal cases filed in Houston, and Seals, Singleton, and Bue were each to be assigned 28.86 percent. They also got 28.2 percent of the civil cases, with Noel taking the remaining 13.42 percent.[50]

The percentages for 1976 had to be amended in the spring to give work to Ross N. Sterling, Senior Judge Hannay's replacement in Houston. Sterling was born in Houston on 18 January 1931. He was the grandnephew of Ross S. Sterling, a Texas oil magnate who was elected governor of Texas the same year his grandnephew was born. Sterling spent a term in the U.S. Army, from 1951 to 1954, before attending the University of Texas (UT). He earned his B.A. in 1956 and stayed to earn his LL.B. at the law school in 1957. Sterling clerked for one year for Fifth Circuit Judge John R. Brown and then joined the Vinson and Elkins law firm in Houston. He was made a partner there in 1969. Sterling was active in the state Republican Party. He was a precinct chair in Houston; was a delegate to every county, district, and Republican state convention since 1962; and, in 1966, chaired the senatorial district caucus. His nomination in 1976 by President Gerald Ford was supported by the Republican U.S. Senator John Tower as well as by John Connally, the former Texas governor who had become a Republican to serve as U.S. treasury secretary. Connally was also a partner in Sterling's firm.[51]

Sterling was commissioned to the federal bench on 18 May 1976, and within a matter of weeks Chief Judge Garza had ordered the necessary adjustments to judicial work assignments. He would thereafter accept 70 percent of the Brownsville work, with Cox taking the remaining 30 percent. O'Conor continued to hear all of the criminal and civil cases in Laredo. Hannay still handled only pending cases in Houston. In addition, Noel had also become a senior judge and was to receive no new cases. Sterling would begin to accept 15 percent of the criminal matters in Houston, with Judges Seals, Singleton, and Bue handling 28.33 percent each. These three each would receive 25 percent of the civil cases in Houston. Sterling would handle 14 percent, and O'Conor would come to Houston to cover the remaining 11 percent.[52]

Judge Garza usually remained in Brownsville, as the work assignments indicated, and he traveled to Houston only when that was necessary to attend to district business. He had appointed his Houston colleagues to be liaison judges to work with the Southern District's internal offices, such as the probation office, or the local branches of federal government agencies, such as the Internal Revenue Service. After some of the judges complained about particular assignments, Chief Judge Garza reset the duties in December 1976. He asked Senior Judge Noel, who, Garza wrote, "has done a magnificent job reorganizing our Clerk's office," to continue to serve as liaison there for another six months, or at least until his successor was appointed and on board. Judge Seals, naturally enough for the former federal prosecutor, would be the court's liaison with the U.S. attorney, the U.S. marshal, and the public defender. Judge Singleton would be the liaison with both the probation office and with the clerk's office, especially for space and facilities matters. Judge Bue would be liaison with the U.S. magistrate's office and the staff attorneys. Bue would also manage the court's central library. Judge Sterling would work with the bankruptcy judges and court reporters.[53]

For 1977, in addition to these miscellaneous administrative jobs, the judges would carry essentially the same percentages of cases that they had been assigned in the spring of 1976.[54] There were two other personnel-related matters that Chief Judge Garza had to manage. The first was the request by Judge O'Conor to have his official station moved to Houston. O'Conor told Garza that he was spending more time in Houston than in Laredo and had come to prefer living in Houston.

Garza agreed that the switch would not disrupt the court's business, and he wrote to the Administrative Office to start this process.[55] The second matter was the necessary realignment of the caseload after Judge Finis Cowan took over for Judge Noel in Galveston. Garza arranged for Bue, Seals, Singleton, and Sterling each to give Cowan twenty cases, in a mix of heavy, light, and average weights.[56]

With plans to comply with the Speedy Trial Act in the works, and a full complement of judges and two senior judges in Houston, Chief Judge Garza authorized a "crash" or "blitz" docket call in September 1977. It would be the civil docket analogue to the jail delivery days that cleared the criminal dockets on the border. The goal of the crash docket was to eliminate dozens of older civil cases that had never been tried, settled, or dismissed. The oldest case on the list had been filed in 1970. Disposing of the docket required the attention of several of the judges, who kept hundreds of lawyers waiting in the halls of the courthouse. The judges also kept hundreds of jurors on call. The judges imposed a no-excuses and no-continuances rule. Lawyers who settled a case *after* a jury had been called were charged for the jurors' time.[57]

The Houston civil docket's "spring cleaning" was no doubt a bracing experience for all involved, yet the event could close only a small fraction of the thirty-five hundred civil cases that were pending on the Southern District dockets. Nevertheless, by identifying and eliminating dead weight, the Southern District judges could begin to see the true extent of their civil case backlog. The "crash docket" became a recurring event in the Southern District. After the new year Garza decided to put off the usual cycle of docket equalization until a crash docket could be arranged for February 1978.[58] To prepare for that event, Garza sought new funding from the Administrative Office to enable the Southern District's clerk to contract for the temporary services of the necessary number of professional court reporters.[59]

THE POLITICS AND PROCESS OF FEDERAL CIVIL RIGHTS PROSECUTIONS

The Southern District judges faced a much different problem of administering criminal justice when the U.S. Attorney committed his office to using federal criminal statutes with antecedents in the Reconstruction era to prosecute several local police officers for depriving individuals of their civil rights.[60] The prosecutions unfortunately pitted several judges' views of law and social order against prosecutors' views of social justice, with the result that the legitimacy of both perspectives was publicly called into question. The Mexican American community's emergent activism played a large part in the affair. Mexican American civil rights groups in Texas, including the oldest, the League of United Latin-American Citizens (LULAC), and the newest, the Mexican-American Legal Defense and Education Fund, filed civil rights claims in federal courts with increasing frequency.[61] Like their African American counterparts, these activists employed private civil suits, usually seeking equitable injunctions, to fight discrimination. Mexican Americans used these legal weapons, for example, to combat patterns of abuse like the strike breaking by the Texas Rangers. They enjoyed greater success in this effort than many other plaintiffs who brought police forces into the federal courts.[62] During the 1970s Mexican Americans began to demand, however, that federal prosecutors respond to allegations of police brutality made by Mexican Americans in Texas. They asked specifically to have applied to southwestern officers extant criminal statutes previously employed against southern police in the 1960s.[63] Mexican American leaders discovered, however, that the proven strategies for private civil rights lawsuits—where plaintiffs asked not only for an equitable remedy in the courtroom but also appealed to community conscience in the streets—were not useful in criminal trials, even when those trials involved civil rights violations. What follows examines the obstacles the criminal "plaintiffs" faced.

The resort to prosecution under civil rights laws had recent precedents in the Southern District of Texas, but that particular legal attack on official misconduct was rare before the 1970s. In 1966, for example, Woodrow Seals, then U.S. attorney, prosecuted two Galveston officers who had, in the words of the indictment Seals secured against them, imposed "summary punishment" upon two prisoners by beating them. A jury acquitted those officers in a trial presided over by Judge Noel.[64] Five years later, in 1971, a state jury acquitted two Houston Police Department (HPD) officers charged with murder in the beating death of Bobby Joe Conner, an African American man who had been detained in the HPD's Galena Park substation. U.S. Attorney Anthony J. P. Farris indicted them in the Southern District court, and Seals, now a judge, presided. The outcome was the same as before; a jury acquitted the officers. The acquittal came, however, only after Judge Seals characterized a defense motion to dismiss the case, on grounds that it exposed the defendants unconstitutionally to double jeopardy, as "erroneous" and "superficial."[65]

Erroneous or not, the question of double jeopardy—especially as it related to state versus federal power and authority—was not superficial. That issue had remained politically charged in the South since the 1950s. To avoid conflicts with state governments, the U.S. attorney general rarely authorized "dual prosecutions," unless there had been clear evidence of bad faith or incompetence in a case previously prosecuted by a state. Before 1977, moreover, the Department of Justice almost never pursued dual prosecution if the state had obtained a conviction in a case.[66] But sustained lobbying by Mexican Americans in the 1970s ultimately overcame the federal government's reluctance.[67]

Mexican American activists had been pressing unsuccessfully for greater federal attention to abuses by Texas law enforcement for years, but they finally persuaded Attorney General Griffin Bell to revise the policy on dual prosecutions. The event that triggered Bell's decision to alter the dual prosecution policy was Richard Morales's gruesome shotgun death near the central Texas town of Castroville in September 1975.[68] Frank Hayes, the marshal of Medina County, suspected the twenty-seven year-old construction worker of involvement in a string of local burglaries. Hayes and two other officers arrested Morales and drove him to an isolated road, where Hayes struck Morales with the stock of his shotgun, menaced him with the barrel, and threatened to kill him if he failed to answer questions. During this "interrogation," the shotgun discharged and killed Morales. To hide his actions, Hayes recruited his wife and her sister to help him transport the body four hundred miles east to Carthage, Texas, where they buried Morales in a shallow grave in the pine woods near the Louisiana border. Two days later, after receiving tips from a series of witnesses along this mysterious burial route (including one from the clerk at the hardware store where Hayes bought shovels), investigators recovered Morales's body and arrested Hayes. Hayes claimed that the shotgun had discharged accidentally, but the grand jury indicted him for murder. The trial jury convicted him on a lesser charge of aggravated assault and sentenced Hayes to ten years in state prison. Under Texas law that sentence made him eligible for parole after six years.[69]

Civil rights leaders claimed that the incident was only an extreme example of the constant intimidation Mexican Americans suffered at the hands of Anglo peace officers in Texas and complained that Hayes's punishment was too light for such egregious behavior. Ruben Sandoval, a San Antonio attorney who during the 1970s made a name for himself by denouncing the brutality of Texas police, became the legal advisor and spokesperson for the Morales family. He wanted federal authorities to prosecute Hayes under criminal civil rights laws. Sandoval had championed this same strategy as early as 1973, in the case of a Dallas police officer, Darrell Cain. Cain had held a pistol to twelve-year-old Santos Rodriguez's head while the boy was handcuffed in the back seat of Cain's patrol car. After Cain had threatened to pull the trigger, the gun discharged and killed Rodriguez. The state prosecuted Cain for murder, a state jury convicted him on that charge, and the jurors sentenced him to serve five years in prison. Dallas officials later pointed to the fact that Cain was arrested the same night, dismissed from the Dallas Police Department (DPD), and served time after conviction as evidence that the system of self-policing actually worked in Dallas, as it did not in Houston. Minorities disagreed. Sandoval urged the Justice Department to investigate the Rodriguez case as well as the Morales case, but the standing policy all but prohibited federal prosecution after a state prosecution ended in conviction.[70]

Sandoval consistently pressed for federal intervention in such cases, and after

Hayes's trial he redoubled his efforts. He was motivated in this crusade by the knowledge that if Cain, Hayes, and other police officers were convicted under federal criminal civil rights statutes, federal trial judges, rather than local state juries, would pass sentence. And under the civil rights laws, judges could impose maximum sentences of life imprisonment. Prominent Texas politicians, including Governor Dolph Briscoe, Attorney General John Hill, and U.S. Representative Henry B. Gonzalez of San Antonio, ultimately joined Sandoval in efforts to persuade the federal government to loosen restrictions on dual prosecutions. Bound by the existing policy, however, the U.S. attorney in San Antonio, John Clark, declined even to open a federal grand jury probe. As of 20 January 1977, the Ford administration's last day in office, the outgoing attorney general, Edward H. Levi, had refused to authorize federal action in the case.[71]

The lobbying effort benefited from the change of administration. Griffin Bell, who abandoned a secure seat on the U.S. Court of Appeals for the Fifth Circuit to accept the top post at the Justice Department, examined the record of the Hayes trial. On 11 February 1977 he relaxed his department's dual prosecution guidelines.[72] In explaining his decision, Bell noted that "[i]n this instance, the allegations of abuse of authority by a law enforcement officer are so serious that they would merit presentation to a federal grand jury, even had death not resulted and even had there been no other alleged common law violation."[73]

Bell's new policy gave the assistant attorney general for civil rights more discretion to undertake dual prosecutions. This policy change implied that lawyers working in the Civil Rights Division could act independently of a state investigation, and, although in practice federal agents still paused to "monitor" events while a state acted, federal contemplation of simultaneous prosecutions became "the rule rather than the exception."[74]

Longtime U.S. Representative Henry B. Gonzalez, who, after resisting the militant activism of the 1960s, now seemed to speak for the Mexican American masses in Texas, noted that "[i]f this hadn't happened there would have been a constant festering feeling of injustice for Mexican Americans." Sandoval declared with satisfaction that Bell's decision demonstrated that the new attorney general was "on the right side."[75]

The Carter administration made minority civil rights a priority, but because deference to state administration of justice was still practiced in most instances, the chances of federal action after successful state prosecutions remained slim.[76] If a state prosecuted an officer for civil rights violations under a statute essentially equivalent to a federal law, for example, federal action would follow only if the state trial left "substantial federal interests demonstrably unvindicated." The criteria for making this decision included such factors as "ineffective" prosecution, court or jury nullification in "blatant disregard of the evidence," or unavailability of some key evidence at the time of the state trial. As a result of these official reservations, Drew S. Days III, assistant attorney general for civil rights from March 1977 through September 1980, still approved during his tenure only seven federal prosecutions of previously tried state cases.[77]

Then an even more egregious incident of police abuse than the Morales and Cain cases came to light and increased the momentum for prosecutions. When Jose "Joe" Campos Torres returned to civilian life in Houston in late 1976, after serving three years in an elite combat unit of the U.S. Army, he retained the vestiges of military-style discipline. Before exercising, the twenty-three-year-old donned olive-drab fatigue pants and combat boots. But positive habits he learned in the service were offset by destructive behavior. Reportedly, Torres's heavy drinking led to his discharge from military service in September 1976. After jogging on Thursday afternoon of 5 May 1977, Torres began a drinking binge that ended in a barroom brawl and his arrest by HPD officers.[78] Three days later, passers-by found Torres's drowned body drifting in Houston's Buffalo Bayou.[79]

After these bystanders reported their discovery to the police, Carless Elliott, a twenty-year-old rookie officer who had taken part in the arrest, quietly contacted his police department superiors and informed them he had witnessed his partner and other HPD officers beat Torres and then push him into the Bayou.[80] His disclosures led the state to prosecute two of the officers for murder, but the jurors convicted the two for the lesser offense of negligent homicide. Two weeks after these convictions, a federal grand jury in Houston indicted the same defendants, as well as two of the other officers, for violating Torres's civil rights, and causing his death, while acting "under color of law."[81]

The Torres episode and the ensuing criminal trials became landmarks, not because police brutality against minorities was unusual, or because prosecutions for misconduct were unknown, or even because federal prosecution of local law enforcement officers was unprecedented,[82] but because the federal criminal prosecution of the officers involved in the Torres incident became a central goal of the Mexican American community in Houston and much of Texas. This section of the chapter describes the ways in which Mexican Americans' hopes were frustrated.

During a press conference in Houston on Friday, 6 May, HPD Chief "Pappy" Bond described his plans to create an Internal Affairs (IA) Division. The police department's professional reputation, low under Bond's predecessors, had sunk lower by the spring of 1977, after incidents involving a black motorist whom officers allegedly brutalized after a high-speed chase, and a white lawyer police shot to death during a botched drug raid.[83] Fred Hofheinz criticized the HPD during his unsuccessful campaign for mayor in 1971. In the years after Hofheinz won the office in 1974, however, more than two dozen cases in which police killed or injured citizens came before Harris County grand juries. Before the Torres incident, the grand jury indicted an officer only once: that defendant was an off-duty policeman who shot and wounded a man after their cars collided on the freeway.[84]

After the lawyer's death Bond reluctantly seconded Mayor Hofheinz's proposal that Houston's police cadets receive better training in the use of deadly force. Bond hoped his announcement of the IA unit's impending formation would satisfy critics who called for an independent citizen's review board to investigate cases of seeming police misconduct.[85]

On Monday morning, after the discovery of Torres's drowned body, Bond called another press conference to announce that he had formed an ad hoc IA division, and that its investigators were already looking into "a very serious problem."[86] Chief Bond assigned Lieutenant Don J. McWilliams of the HPD to lead the new division. Guided by Officer Elliott's shocking admissions, McWilliams soon pieced together the details of Torres's last night. Late on 5 May—the night before Bond's first press conference—Antonio Bela, the manager of Club 21, a neighborhood bar on Houston's predominantly Mexican American east side, tried to eject Torres for fighting with the other patrons. After pinning Torres to the bar's pool table, Bela asked someone to call the police.[87]

Officer M. G. Oropeza was already nearby, writing out a traffic citation. At approximately 11:35 P.M., Oropeza radioed his dispatcher to request assistance from back-up officers and proceeded to Club 21. He entered just ahead of Officers Elliott and Stephen Orlando, who arrived by car. The three officers wrestled the struggling Torres to the floor, handcuffed him, and dragged him outside. Oropeza returned to his traffic duties once four more officers, Terry Denson, Joseph Janish, Louis Kinney, and Glenn Brinkmeyer, arrived in two police cruisers.[88]

Elliott subsequently testified that Torres stopped struggling once they had him in handcuffs, but he continued to curse the officers. Janish suggested that the officers try to pacify their prisoner on the way to jail. The officers drove to a warehouse district near the 1200 block of Commerce Street, two blocks north of the Harris County Criminal Courts building, and parked below street level on a concrete bank on the south side of Buffalo Bayou. This was a "hole," an area where police officers knew they could take a break during a long shift but remain out of public view. The five senior officers pulled Torres from the car, but left him handcuffed as they insulted, slapped, and shoved him. Elliott said he stood aside, "trying not to look." He told McWilliams's investigators he saw no blood on Torres after the bar scuffle but did after the officers beat him.[89]

Orlando and Elliott returned Torres to the backseat of their squad car and drove him to the city jail. The desk sergeant refused to admit the obviously injured prisoner and told the officers to take Torres to an emergency room. Rather than face several dull hours at the hospital, only to charge him later with relatively minor offenses such as public drunkenness and resisting arrest, Orlando resolved to set Torres free, without filing any charges. Once he was back in the squad car, however, Torres resumed his cursing of the officers. Orlando radioed Janish and Denson to suggest they meet again at the "hole," this time to teach Torres respect for the police. Kinney and Brinkmeyer also heard the call and returned to the bayou. During the first beating, Denson had confessed to the others that he had always wanted to watch a prisoner swim the bayou. Orlando now suggested that this second session on the embankment presented Denson his opportunity to fulfill his desire. Denson then seized Torres by the arms, led him to the edge, twenty feet above the murky water, and reportedly remarked, "Let's see if the wetback can swim."[90]

Elliott had removed Torres's handcuffs but then stayed in the vehicle to respond to a dispatcher's radio call. He rejoined the others just as Torres dropped into the bayou. Elliott had also brought Torres's wallet from the car; Orlando pitched it into the water after its owner. The officers briefly tracked their former prisoner's progress with spotlights, and several later testified that Torres swam away "in total control."[91] In his own earliest account Elliott agreed that Torres seemed to be "swimming smoothly." He later testified under oath, however, that Torres only "looked like he was treading water to stay afloat."[92]

Because the wallet was not with the body when it was found, investigators could not immediately identify Torres. As news of the discovery spread, several of the officers involved used the delay to settle on a common story if they were ever questioned. They agreed to claim that they had released Torres at Saint Joseph's Hospital. Elliott later testified that Denson, Orlando, and Kinney had urged silence, Denson telling him, "Remember, you're just as guilty as I am. . . . You pushed him in the bayou just like I did."[93] Elliott then decided that the proposed conspiracy of silence was an impossible burden, and he told his father, an HPD veteran, about the incident. The elder Elliott contacted Assistant Chief B. K. Johnson, who passed the news to Bond.[94]

The investigation proceeded rapidly. After an eight-hour, predawn, closed-door meeting with HPD administrators, Bond authorized a murder investigation against Denson and relieved the remaining five officers of duty, but with pay. Bond passed the evidence to Harris County Assistant District Attorney Sam Robinson, who predicted that the grand jury would file charges within a week. Denson retained prominent defense attorney Robert Bennett[95] and posted a ten-thousand-dollar personal bond upon being charged. When confronted by reporters, he said merely, "I'm tired now . . . I prefer to say nothing whatsoever."[96] By the end of the week, Bond had fired everyone but Elliott, who remained on "relieved-of-duty" status. Bond told reporters he could not say why the rookie merited special treatment, but since HPD sources had already confirmed to reporters that the investigation began with a tip from an officer, Elliott seemed the one most likely to have been the whistle-blower.[97]

Chief Bond had responded to the Torres tragedy with dispatch, in contrast to his actions in other recent episodes of alleged HPD misconduct, and clearly was attempting to limit damage to HPD's image. But as details of Torres's ordeal emerged, administrative sanctions against the officers seemed too little, too late. After Bond's initial announcement that Denson alone faced the charges, dozens of protesters, including Torres's mother, Margaret, assembled at city hall to demand that the state prosecute all six officers for Torres's murder. And after burying their son, with a military-style honor guard provided by the local chapter of the Veterans of Foreign Wars,[98] Torres's parents retained attorney Percy Foreman to examine options for filing a private civil rights lawsuit. Foreman—ironically, the father of a Galveston police officer—had previously defended policemen charged with brutality. But now he called Houston a "police state," where officers were more violent and unchecked than in any comparable police force in the country. He placed the blame on Frank Briscoe, who served as district attorney from 1961 to 1966, and the incumbent district attorney, Carol Vance, who "whitewashed every charge against policemen" and so encouraged police violence by letting the officers believe that they were above the law.[99]

Mexican American activists concerned by the civil rights situation in Texas called for federal authorities to file criminal charges. Even after Bond had announced the pending charge against Denson, Mamie Garcia, director of Houston's LULAC chapter, sent a telegram to U.S. Attorney General Griffin Bell to request that he immediately authorize a federal probe of the Torres incident. Garcia received no quick reply from Washington, and the victim's father, Jose Luna Torres, sent a similar request to the local Federal Bureau of Investigation (FBI) office. A Justice Department spokesperson responded that federal investigators would take no active role in the case until a county grand jury completed deliberations.[100]

Notwithstanding all remaining limitations, Bell's announcement that federal authorities would at least investigate Hayes's role in Morales's death was a major breakthrough for Mexican American civil rights activists. Ruben Sandoval celebrated Bell's conversion by traveling to Houston and agitating for preemptive federal intervention in the Torres case.[101] Exactly one week after Torres's death, Sandoval participated in a rally arranged by the Houston LULAC chapter. Framed by signs referring to "killer cops" and "racist cops," he demanded federal action in what he saw as a clear-cut violation of Torres's civil rights. Sandoval predicted that if the Mexican American community waited for the state to indict the HPD officers, they would only face charges of "involuntary manslaughter" or "assault" for causing Torres's death. The state jury, he continued, would give Torres's assailants only "a two- to ten-year slap on the hand." But if the community pressed for federal action, Sandoval said, "we can get any number of years up to life." The crowd applauded that prospect. Johnny Mata, director of LULAC's affirmative action program, agreed that the Torres matter demanded federal attention. Bob Cortez, an administrative aide to state legislator Ben Reyes, assured the crowd that Reyes intended to confer with Attorney General Bell about the case. Then Margaret Torres, speaking in Spanish, tearfully asked for justice for her son. The assembly resolved to call for federal investigation of racism in the HPD and circulated a petition demanding a civilian review of the Torres case.[102]

The next day, 13 May, Joseph Jachimczyk, the Harris County medical examiner who performed the autopsy on Torres's body, submitted his report. Although Chief Bond instructed Jachimczyk and his assistant, Eduardo Bellas, not to discuss the findings, the press soon learned, and reported, that Torres's body had shown bruises on the head, body, stomach, and shins. Moreover, toxicology tests revealed a high blood alcohol count at the time of death. The medical examiners concluded that Torres never had a chance to survive a dive into the bayou in that drunken, beaten condition, and therefore they reported the cause of death as "drowning, homicide." Denson's attorney, Robert Bennett, sought to limit such sensational publicity and especially wanted to keep any more damaging details from Elliott's allegations from the press. He and Michael Ramsey, whom Orlando retained, asked State District Judge Allen Stilley to issue a "gag order" against Bond and other personnel with knowledge of the case. To forestall an official gag, Bond circulated a memo to officers warning them to refrain from making public comments without his approval.[103]

Hofheinz praised Bond's handling of the Torres case, claiming that "Pappy Bond is the best thing to come along in a long time." Of the allegations of police brutality, the mayor admitted he had believed that earlier cases of police misconduct were "isolated events." Instead, he said, "there is something loose in this city that is an illness . . . the attitude of some people—including a lot of community leaders, people in charge of mass communications—believing that whatever a Houston police officer does is okay." Hofheinz had thought "we had it licked, only to . . . find out we seem to be back in the 1960s after all."[104]

Critics of the HPD, agreeing with Hofheinz that Houston harbored an "illness," were unwilling to stand idle while the federal government considered its options, and they pressed for civilian review. Texas House Speaker Billy Clayton promised to appoint an interim committee to investigate the HPD, which "probably" would include a half dozen representatives from Harris County. Ben Reyes, Houston's representative in the legislature, expected to be on the committee. Reyes implied that among his aims for the investigation would be deterrence. Of abusive officers he said, "[W]e need to take away that 'safe' feeling from them, so they will know that they're going to be judged by someone other than an internal affairs division." But, he added, "we're not after a witch hunt. . . . We're trying to solve a problem."[105]

Bond had agreed in principle to meet with Houston's ministers and minority leaders even before Torres's death but decided that improving minority community–police relations had become urgent enough actually to schedule the meeting. As Bond greeted a delegation on 17 May, dozens of protesters, with Margaret Torres again in attendance, demonstrated for two hours in front of the police station, chanted "Equality not brutality," "We want justice," and "Stop the war against Chicanos." They demanded unsuccessfully to see Bond. Torres complained that since her son had been killed by his officers, she should have been invited to the meeting ahead of all the others. Bond later claimed that he planned to meet with Torres but office protocol precluded his admitting uninvited participants to a scheduled appointment.[106]

Eugene Mendoza, president of the Mexican American Council, said that community leaders were willing to give Bond time to respond to their concerns, because they had "never worked with any police chief who was so candid." But he also noted that none of the HPD representatives had been Spanish speakers or blacks, which, he said, illustrated "the type of thing that has to change." He suggested that HPD officers should become more aware of Hispanic culture and the Spanish language.[107]

Nevertheless, Bond could not resolve one of the delegation's major concerns. Attorney Frumencio Reyes, chair of Houston's Political Association of Spanish Speaking Organizations (PASSO) chapter, suggested that Bond supplement HPD's IA unit by accepting the oversight of a citizen's review board.[108] Bond declared that he lacked the authority to create such a board, and admitted he actually opposed the idea, since IA could do the job. Marcario Ramirez, a spokesperson for the Mexican American Service Organization, said that Houston's Spanish speakers would organize their own review panel whether or not the city council approved an official review board. Ramirez promised that Mexican Americans would make a show of force at the next meeting. At that meeting six spokespersons, accompanied by fifty raucous protesters, criticized HPD racism and forced Hofheinz to admit that Torres's death was a "black mark" on his administration. The mayor accepted "the blame that three years of work on the subject was not enough to prevent" such tragedies from happening.[109]

Public support for a federal civil rights investigation expanded to include Carol Vance, the Harris County district attorney. Because he believed the "best interests of justice" would be served if the HPD officers were prosecuted under the applicable federal laws, Vance said he would be willing temporarily to defer state indictments, so that the Justice Department could step in. Vance noted that among the advantages of a federal prosecution was that the officers' violation of Torres's civil rights seemed clear, while Vance, in order to convict on a state murder count, had the heavier burden of proving Denson *intended* to kill Torres. Vance said he was not abandoning the state investigation but stressed that he did not want to "foul up" a future federal case, for example, by granting immunity to witnesses, which might thwart their subsequent prosecution on federal charges. Hofheinz agreed, and the mayor enlisted his friend Lloyd Bentsen, U.S. senator from Texas, to spur federal prosecutors into action.[110] Two weeks after Torres plunged into Buffalo Bayou, Hofheinz changed his diagnosis of Houston's malady from an "illness" to a "cancer" and said that he ultimately wanted the case tried in both federal and state courts. Moreover, if the federal authorities hesitated too long, Hofheinz promised he would personally request that the state prosecute immediately. He was "interested in swift and effective justice in this case."[111]

Hofheinz had hoped to persuade Bond to reconsider his announced retirement and would keep Bond on the job if he decided to seek another term as mayor.[112] Ultimately, Hofheinz chose not to run for reelection. On 9 June he announced he would not seek a third term. Bond resigned the next day and announced that he would run for mayor in November. However, several days later Bond reconsidered, retracted his candidacy announcement, and accepted a position as Tenneco's chief of security. HPD Captain Harry Caldwell succeeded to the embattled position of chief as the Torres case entered a new phase.[113]

On 28 June 1977, after a three-week investigation, the Harris County Grand Jury indicted Denson and Orlando for murder and Janish for misdemeanor assault.[114] The district attorney gave Kinney and Brinkmeyer immunity in exchange for their testimony, but Chief Caldwell nevertheless declared that their dismissal was final. The chief returned Elliott to patrol duty. An assistant city attorney told reporters that the investigation and indictments had demonstrated that the HPD was able to police itself and called this the "most significant aspect of the case."[115]

Defense attorneys Bennett and Ramsey successfully sought a transfer of Denson and Orlando's trial to Huntsville, the site of the state's main prison complex and a city where the Texas Department of Corrections was the major local employer.[116] It was also home to Sam Houston State University, which had large law enforcement and criminal justice programs. School administrators actively promoted Huntsville as a change of venue city for controversial trials; the trial of the Torres defendants was the third case transferred there in 1977. The Criminal Justice Center staged these high-profile trials in a courtroom-style auditorium, so criminology students could attend and observe. In the two earlier cases in 1977, the juries proved more partial to the defense's point of view, delivering one acquittal and one negligent homicide conviction rather than the murder conviction sought by the prosecution.[117] Defense attorneys who came to Huntsville were less interested in promoting education than with protecting the interests of their clients by gaining a sort of "home-field advantage": defense teams hoped to seat a jury accustomed to the rough realities of law enforcement and the intricacies of dominance and submission behavior inherent in police-prisoner relations. In short, defense attorneys expected that the predominantly white, conservative panels in Huntsville would give police officers the benefit of their doubt in cases of alleged brutality.[118]

Ramsey had experience with this kind of defense maneuver. In 1971 he was the defense attorney in the state murder trial of officers accused of killing Bobby Joe Conner. That case had many similarities with the Torres case. For example, the victims were minorities (Conner was African American) and approximately the same age as their accused killers, and both were not sober (Conner probably used heroin the night he died, and Torres was drunk); in both cases there were six officers involved, who did not immediately learn of the death (the officers who had been interrogating Conner in the Galena Park substation rushed him to the hospital, when he collapsed with a ruptured spleen); when they did learn of the death, they met to "get the story straight"; and, a twenty-year-old rookie accused his colleagues after talking to a senior officer. The Conner incident also resulted in a federal civil rights trial, which Ramsey successfully transferred to New Braunfels, a small town in central Texas with a large population of retired military personnel. The officers were acquitted there in 1972. Richard "Racehorse" Haynes, the other defense attorney in the federal case, later declared, "I knew we had the case won . . . when we seated the last bigot on the jury."[119]

Bennett and Ramsey must have been disheartened when, as they were making final preparations for the state trial of the Torres matter, Sandoval's long cultivation of the Justice Department finally bore fruit in the Morales case. On 29 September 1977 a federal jury sitting in Waco, the conservative home of the historically Baptist church–affiliated Baylor University, convicted Frank Hayes of acting under color of law to deprive Richard Morales of his civil rights. The jury also convicted Hayes's wife and her sister for their part in transporting the body. The ex-marshal faced the possibility that the federal judge in Waco would sentence him to spend the rest of his life in prison.[120]

Prosecutors probably interpreted the Hayes verdict as a good omen. Ted Poe, a twenty-nine-year-old assistant district attorney who had never lost in a felony case, led the prosecution team.[121] Bert Graham, the second prosecutor, had won the longest sentence ever attained by the Harris County district attorney's office: he convinced a state jury in 1972 to sentence a convicted rapist to one thousand years in state prison.[122] Erwin Ernst, the district attorney for Huntsville's Walker County, frequently sat in with Poe and Graham and offered them advice on a range of topics from jury selection to cross-examination.[123] Convicting Denson and Orlando of murder necessitated showing that they intended to cause Torres's death when they beat him and pushed him into Buffalo Bayou. That difficult task was complicated by the fact that the only eyewitnesses, the former officers themselves, recalled details differently, and some were either unable to recall or unwilling to swear to key statements attributed to them by other eyewitnesses.[124] Given the tangle of testimony coming from the witness stand, Graham employed a simple psychological tactic to reinforce the humanity of the absent victim. He ensured that Torres's weather-beaten boots were visible to the jury whenever a prosecutor examined a witness. Also, in their scale model of the crime scene, the prosecutors placed a red plastic doll, representing Joe Torres lying face down in the bayou, while six blue plastic HPD officers looked on. But the defense attorneys were also experienced in courtroom stagecraft. Ramsey just as carefully ensured that the boots were under the table and out of sight whenever he cross-examined a witness.[125]

Bennett and Ramsey did not deny their clients' willing involvement in the Torres incident, which would have been all but impossible after testimony from Brinkmeyer and Elliott. But they did attempt to show that Denson and Orlando had not acted as ringleaders or with particular malice or deadly intent against Torres. For example, the defense team called Kinney to the stand to testify that Torres was taken to the "hole" at Janish's suggestion.[126] The defense called nine witnesses who testified to Orlando's good reputation, and Bennett called Denson to testify that he had never been rough on any other prisoner.[127] But during his cross-examination of Denson, Poe reminded the jury of earlier testimony, that Denson had warned the belligerent Torres before the beating: "If you act like a human being we'll treat you like one." With Denson on the stand, Poe said, "You kept that promise didn't you . . . you didn't treat him like one, did you?"[128]

Ramsey hinted early on that he would close the defense's case with a "bombshell," which was the "expert" testimony of a private investigator, Ed Pankau. Pankau, who wore dark sunglasses during his testimony, told jurors that he had recently visited the "hole," consumed eight cans of beer, pulled on a pair of combat boots, and then jumped into the bayou. He testified he could still swim with no difficulty and had even made it to the opposite bank in fifty-eight seconds. Poe established by cross-examination that Pankau, a former Green Beret, considered himself a strong swimmer. He next asked, "[D]id anybody beat you up before you jumped in?" Pankau quipped, "Not at this time . . . but I had several volunteers." Ramsey claimed he considered Pankau's testimony worthy because it demonstrated, he said, that the bayou was not necessarily dangerous; and if the bayou was not dangerous, then leaving Torres to swim there could not be construed as an act intending to kill. After dropping their dubious "bombshell," the defense rested.[129]

On 30 September, prosecution witnesses rebutted Denson's claims of past good behavior. For example, Brinkmeyer returned to the stand and gave his alternative account of Denson's five years on the force, much of it based on HPD gossip or Denson's own alleged bragging about prior bad acts. Brinkmeyer delivered this "sweeping testimony" out of the presence of the jury, because State District Judge James "Bud" Warren had not yet ruled whether the jury would be allowed to hear such evidence. Bennett and Ramsey objected to allowing "scurrilous" tales, because the alleged episodes, which Brinkmeyer recounted without dates or names, could not be refuted. Poe countered, "[I]t happened so many times that it's not possible for Brinkmeyer to recall the details."[130] Warren excluded much of Brinkmeyer's testimony but allowed him to state that there was "no doubt" in his mind that Denson deliberately pushed Torres into the bayou.[131] The defense attorneys recalled Denson, who once again denied under oath that he had *pushed* Torres into the bayou. Torres, Denson always maintained, had jumped.[132]

Then the jury listened to closing arguments. Ernst, who had joined the prosecution team to offer his own summation, wanted the jury to remember the courage Elliott showed in resisting peer pressure to keep quiet. Poe expressed his own anger that the two defendants had "tarnish[ed] the badge that every good cop wears" when they took it into their own hands to try and convict Torres and to sentence him to death for public drunkenness. He struck a table with a heavy police flashlight, to remind the jurors that witnesses testified that Orlando hit Torres with such a flashlight, and called it the gavel "Judge Orlando" used during the fifty-eight-minute "trial" he gave Torres. Instead of courage or anger, Ramsey and Bennett focused their summation on the legal requirement that in order to find the two defendants guilty of murder, the jury must decide beyond reasonable doubt that they intended to kill Torres. Ramsey referred to Orlando's testimony about the decision to take Torres to a "hole" and asked whether it had been unreasonable for Orlando to try to "calm down a madman." And in his last effort to minimize the testimony of eyewitnesses Elliott and Brinkmeyer, who both claimed Denson pushed Torres into the Bayou, Bennett told jurors it did not really matter, since "[w]hether you believe push or jump . . . Terry Denson did not intend to cause great bodily harm."[133]

On 4 October, Judge Warren instructed the seven-woman, five-man jury that they must either acquit a defendant or convict him of one of four possible offenses. They must convict for murder if they believed beyond a reasonable doubt that a defendant intended to "cause serious bodily injury" to Torres and caused death by committing an act "clearly dangerous to human life." If they decided that Torres's death was due to reckless behavior, that a defendant disregarded a substantial risk of injury, they could convict of involuntary manslaughter. A conviction of negligent homicide was proper if jurors decided a defendant caused Torres's death by ignoring dangers of which he should have been aware. Finally, jurors had an option to convict a defendant of simple assault, for beating Torres.[134]

Jury deliberations continued longer than many observers expected, and the jurors asked to reexamine most of the evidence. Bennett and Ramsey expressed satisfaction that the panel was being very methodical. On 6 October the jurors announced they had reached a verdict.[135] They found both Denson and Orlando guilty of negligent homicide. Ramsey said that this misdemeanor conviction "complicate[d]" the issue, since he was already preparing for a possible federal trial.[136] Graham disagreed with the decision but admitted that the verdict at least fit the facts of the case; he said that distinguishing among murder, manslaughter, and negligent homicide was a matter of how a jury used its discretion to view victim and perpetrators. If the jury truly believed the defendants when they testified they thought Torres was capable of swimming to safety, then they could not convict for murder.[137]

Margaret Torres attended the trial and soon appeared in the hall with a typed press release. She blamed the all-white jury for the verdict and thought that Poe and Graham had done a good job. Regarding the possible punishments for negligent homicide, she said, "If Jose had killed one of those cops or if five Mexican Americans had killed one cop, then they all would be on Death Row,"[138] but "I heard all they can get is one year in jail, and I'm disgusted." She said, "The Mexican-American community will continue to fight for justice."[139] Ruben Bonilla, executive director of LULAC, projected that "this message should extend to the White House. . . . If the federal government takes no action, we will know that Washington does not give a damn about our interests and we will remember that in the next election." Bonilla planned to meet with Justice Department officials in Washington, to repeat demands for federal prosecution of Orlando and Denson.[140] But Antonio Bela, the manager of Club 21, where Torres was arrested, expressed puzzlement. Of the verdict, he reportedly asked: "[I]t's not a felony to kill?"[141]

The punishment phase of the trial commenced immediately with the same jury. Bennett argued, "These circumstances do not cry out for revenge." But because he got a "compromise" verdict from the jury regarding guilt, Poe was determined to get the maximum penalty. He placed a chair in the middle of the courtroom—mimicking Ramsey's gesture during summation of placing Orlando where he could sit in clear view of the jury—and stated, "My client, Joe Torres, can't sit there." Poe turned the tale on its head, asking, "What if Torres had been with his East End buddies against Denson and Orlando and had negligently thrown them in. . . . You'd be looking for the nearest pine tree to hang him on. Is that a double standard? I hope not." He argued that the jury should give the officers jail time, if for no other reason, then because "[a] year from now, they'll still have their whole lives ahead of them. . . . But this chair will still be sitting here . . . empty."[142]

The jurors soon declared themselves to be deadlocked, but the judge, who did not want to declare a mistrial over the sentencing, told them to continue deliberating. At five o'clock the jurors asked to use the restroom, and as they filed out of the jury room, the foreman slipped a note to the bailiff, which informed him that the jury had agreed on a sentence. By then the crowd had dispersed, because it seemed likely that the deliberations would drag into the weekend. Only the defendants and their families, the attorneys, and court officials were in the auditorium to hear the two identical sentences of "$2000 fine with one year in jail, probated." Those jurors willing to be interviewed explained that the prosecution had simply failed to prove that Denson pushed Torres, and so they obviously could not convict him or Orlando of murder. Also, many of the jurors reportedly disregarded Brinkmeyer's rebuttal testimony as unreliable. Some jurors doubted Kinney's testimony, as well, especially after he admitted on the witness stand that he was testifying to "save my hide." Ultimately, half of the panel favored acquittal, but their fellow jurors persuaded them Denson and Orlando were not blameless in Torres's death. One juror admitted she initially favored acquittal and changed her mind only when another reasoned that the HPD officers showed neglect by not staying nearby long enough to confirm that Torres made it out of the bayou alive. Some jurors were convinced the officers should serve jail time, but all ultimately agreed that the maximum, but with probation, would be most just. The jurors' final compromise was that both Denson and Orlando would receive the same sentence.[143]

Ben Reyes said he was saddened but not surprised at the verdict, and called the change of venue to Huntsville "the worst miscarriage of justice" he had ever seen. Ruben Bonilla agreed that it would have been naive to expect a fair and impartial decision from a jury selected from the inhabitants of Huntsville. Noting that "what little we . . . have gotten in Texas in the way of education and voting rights has come through the federal process,"[144] Reyes resumed his calls for federal intervention and declared that the probated sentences only "add[ed] insult to injury for this community. . . . We knew all along that our only relief is on the federal level. I'm reminding everyone I see of that."[145] Sandoval, Bonilla, and Antonio Morales of the American G.I. Forum (AGIF) joined forces to visit Washington, D.C., to urge a prompt federal response.[146] In addition to personal appeals from those prominent private emissaries, Griffin Bell received pleas to prosecute from both U.S. senators from Texas, Republican John Tower and Democrat Lloyd Bentsen, several of the state's U.S. representatives, Texas Attorney General Hill, and Governor Briscoe. Bell promised a prompt decision on whether to authorize the federal dual prosecution.[147]

During a news conference the morning after the sentences were announced, local LULAC spokespersons called on the state legislature to enact its own, stronger civil rights laws, modeled on the federal statutes. A LULAC volunteer asked: "Why is it we have to feel more comfortable with the federal government than we do our own courts? . . . We need something to keep the Torres case from happening again and again."[148] Two hundred protesters assembled in Houston's Moody Park, where Margaret Torres and other speakers denounced the Walker County jury through a portable public address system. The speakers were continually seconded by chanting protesters, who waved a variety of placards criticizing the police. Among the signs was a parody of the HPD's public relations slogan, "The Badge Means You Care," which the demonstrators had altered to "The Badge Means You Kill." The protesters marched to police headquarters, where they changed their chants from "We Want Justice" to "We Want the Feds."[149] Chief Caldwell remained inside the station. He told the press it would make more sense to protest in Huntsville but added, "[S]ense doesn't always seem to have a lot to do with these things. . . . This department is the only agency administering justice that couldn't have influenced that trial in any way." Caldwell declared that he was angry about the sentences as well. But he lashed out at the "demagogic, self-serving rhetoric in the community." Denunciations of the police and the criminal justice system had caused, he implied, a jury backlash. He was glad that the case was finally going to a federal court, "where it belonged all the time."[150]

J. A. "Tony" Canales took the oath of office as U.S. attorney for the Southern District of Texas on 23 September 1977, one week before state prosecutors opened the case against Denson and Orlando. It was a controversial appointment. As a criminal defense attorney in south Texas, Canales had often represented accused drug dealers, successfully, and he was also no stranger to minority politics or civil rights causes. Conservative critics delayed his confirmation by noting that during a rally in May 1976 Canales reportedly had declared, "[Mexican Americans] say now to the Anglo, 'Open up your arms and welcome us because if you close your arms and we have to go in there knocking heads, there's going to be a lot of people getting hurt for a long time, and it ain't going to be us."[151] The confirmation controversy cemented his credentials with his fellow Mexican Americans.

Canales immediately displayed his intention to pursue dual prosecution in the Torres matter when, upon taking control of the district's organization, he convened a federal grand jury to review the evidence. He invited representatives from civil rights organizations to come to his office and confer about Mexican American issues and attitudes. He also created his own Civil Rights Division, the nation's first within a U.S. attorney's office. During Canales's three-year tenure, his internal Civil Rights Division prosecuted, among other matters, six major police misconduct cases, three involving the HPD. The resources Canales committed to his division, when compared to those being made available nationally, indicated the priority Canales placed on civil rights prosecutions (or it demonstrated that item's relative lack of priority in the overall federal government).

During the weeks of ferment over the state sentences,[152] Canales told reporters he was "not happy" with the situation but noted that his personal feelings could not accelerate the pace of progress in Washington, where the question whether the Justice Department would seek a federal trial would have to be decided. But other concerned observers were committed to affecting the federal process. National, state, and local leaders of Mexican American groups planned to meet immediately with Terry Adamson, special assistant to Attorney General Bell, to urge a federal investigation. Richard Baca, general counsel for the U.S. Civil Rights Commission, said that the commission had already dispatched a letter urging Bell to intervene and would now follow up with personal requests. Baca confirmed that the Torres incident, and several similar events in Denver, Philadelphia, and Chicago, might lead the commission to have hearings in Houston and those cities to examine police misconduct.[153] Canales could only reassure the public, especially uneasy Mexican Americans, that the case had the "highest priority in my office and in the Civil Rights Division of the Justice Department."[154] As U.S. attorney, Canales could initiate civil rights prosecutions for misdemeanors, that is, statutory violations not resulting in death. For fatal cases, like the Torres incident, Justice Department guidelines required that the assistant attorney general for civil rights, Drew Days, authorize the prosecution.[155] Reportedly, Canales privately contacted the division's attorneys the moment he learned of the state verdict, to discuss the possibility of a federal criminal trial, but he publicly stressed that his personal emotions would not affect the pace of the official decision-making process. The high number of police misconduct complaints in the Southern District of Texas rendered formal oversight difficult, however, and Canales eventually developed an "informal understanding" with Days, who authorized him to "present cases that need to be presented." Canales soon claimed that "it's all my show, so I'm happy with it. I don't think [Days's people] are [happy] with it; it doesn't make any difference to me."[156]

TEXAS IS OUR MISSISSIPPI

Torres's death was not an unprecedented or isolated incident. If raw numbers of complaints to the Southern District's U.S. attorney's Civil Rights Division, roughly thirty to fifty per month, can be taken as an estimate of the true state of affairs, police misconduct was ongoing and pervasive in Houston and its surrounding region. The vast majority of the complaints did not spawn federal trials, which are expensive and time-consuming whether they concern civil rights or other crimes. Even an aggressive prosecutor must undertake only the most serious cases.[157]

The Torres trial was only the first of three infamous HPD misconduct cases of the period. The remaining two HPD trials also became famous, for providing examples of the long-rumored practice by police of planting so-called "throwdown" guns to justify questionable uses of deadly force. One incident involved the victim in a two-year-old case. After midnight on 11 July 1975, about 1 A.M., a deputy constable saw an Anglo American youth, later identified as eighteen-year-old Billy

Keith Joyvies, and a teenage girl removing a tool box from a truck in the parking lot of a club in northern Harris County. The constable (and eventually six additional law enforcement officers from Harris County's various overlapping jurisdictions) chased the pair's car onto the freeway. They chased Joyvies some thirty miles, at speeds approaching one hundred miles per hour. While in pursuit, five of the officers began firing their weapons at the car; a total of sixteen shots had been fired by the end of the chase. Joyvies was hit once in the head by a .45 caliber bullet and died in the hospital without regaining consciousness. The officers justified the shooting by claiming they saw Joyvies reach behind the seat, presumably for a gun, and they reported finding a .25 caliber pistol in the teenager's car. After a routine investigation, which followed all incidents of discharging of weapons by police officers, a Harris County grand jury cleared the officers of any fault in the shooting.[158]

The victim in the other incident became nearly as well known as Joe Torres. Eighteen months after the Joyvies incident, shortly before the death of Joe Torres, Houston police shot and killed another teenager after a high-speed highway chase. Randall Alan Webster, a seventeen-year-old high school dropout from Shreveport, Louisiana, came to Houston for his scheduled induction into the U.S. Navy. After midnight on 8 February 1977, Webster broke into the display floor of an automobile dealership and drove a customized van through the windows. He led the HPD on a lengthy high-speed chase up and down Interstate Highway 45 (known locally as the Gulf Freeway). According to a witness to the chase, the police fired at the van during the pursuit, in violation of HPD policy, which had been changed in 1976 in the aftermath of the Joyvies incident. Webster finally ceased his joy ride when he came to a roadblock. HPD Officer Danny Mays, who had radioed the dispatcher he had seen a rifle in the van (the police never found one), approached on foot as the young man climbed out of the stolen van. A moment later, Mays fired a single shot. Webster died at 4:30 A.M. at Houston's Ben Taub Hospital from a gunshot wound to the head.[159]

Canales made veteran Assistant U.S. Attorney (AUSA) Mary Sinderson the supervisor of the Southern District's Civil Rights Division, and she investigated these episodes. Webster and Joyvies were Anglo American youths; Conner, the Galena Park victim, was African American, and Torres was Mexican American. The cases may demonstrate that, despite charges of racism, some HPD officers were equal opportunity assailants. The fact that Canales authorized investigations into the questionable use of deadly force by the police without regard to the race or ethnicity of the victim indicates that he was an equal opportunity prosecutor. Not race but abuse of power was at the core in many of these incidents. Nonetheless, the almost casual brutalization of Torres, the officers' manifest disregard for his civil rights, and the apparently racist attitudes exhibited by the officers during the notorious encounter justified placing him high on the catalogue of civil rights martyrs, and high on Canales's list of prosecutorial priorities. Perhaps Mexican American leaders would rank Richard Morales above Joe Torres on their register of victims, because his example motivated Attorney General Bell to relax the decades-old federal policy regarding dual prosecutions. Absent that previous effort by the civil rights community, it is likely Canales would have faced a protracted struggle to convince Days and then Bell to allow the federal government to take a "second bite from the apple." The success of earlier political action on behalf of Morales eased the way for Canales, who now stood poised to pursue the criminal civil rights charges in the Torres affair.[160]

On 20 October 1977, five weeks into Canales's tenure, the federal grand jury in Houston returned indictments against Denson, Orlando, and Kinney, who were charged in four counts with violations of the deprivation of rights statutes, and Janish, who was charged in only three counts. The grand jury also named Brinkmeyer an unindicted coconspirator.[161] The first three counts alleged that the officers deprived and conspired to deprive Joe Torres of his civil rights while acting "under color of law" as police officers.[162] The fourth count charged Denson, Orlando, and Kinney with conspiring to prevent Elliott from communicating information about the case to the FBI.[163]

The timing of the federal indictments came as a surprise. Assistant Attorney General Days had said earlier that week that a decision might be ten days away. One of Days's prosecutors from the Civil Rights Division, C. Brian McDonald, had come to Houston to confer with Canales only a few days before.[164] Once the indictments were announced, Frumencio Reyes of PASSO said that the "community will be a lot calmer now. . . . I'm glad they came in came in before the weekend. . . . I doubt there'll be any march or incident between now and the time the trial starts."[165]

This reassurance had political overtones. Since the 1976 national election Mexican Americans had criticized President Jimmy Carter for his failure to appoint significant numbers of Hispanics to his administration, and also for supporting only a limited amnesty for undocumented aliens in the United States, which many regarded as unfair to Mexicans. The Justice Department's decision to proceed swiftly and to indict the Torres defendants on federal civil rights charges, coupled with Bell's decision in the Morales case, seemed to repair the rift.[166] Mexican Americans' satisfaction deepened on 23 October, when the federal judge in Waco sentenced Frank Hayes to life in prison.[167]

The long-anticipated federal trial of Torres's assailants began on 23 January 1978, with U.S. District Judge Ross N. Sterling presiding. The crowd never reached unmanageable size, as it did in Huntsville, and, with heightened security measures provided by U.S. marshals, Sterling had no difficulty maintaining order.[168] During opening statements Mike Andrews, representing Janish, reminded the jury that "the government must show that the defendants specifically intended" to violate Torres's civil rights and "also must show that the defendants knowingly entered into a conspiracy."[169] The prosecution team's task actually was more difficult than that: they had to persuade a jury that the benefit of the doubt that law-abiding citizens ordinarily extend to policemen was misdirected in the case of these four alleged rogue officers.

On 26 January, the first day of witness testimony, Sinderson and McDonald called Elliott to the stand. Over two days, Elliott repeated the story he told during the state trial, that is, that the other officers helped Denson and Orlando beat Torres and then failed to stop Denson from pushing Torres into the bayou.[170] Under cross-examination, one of the defense attorneys asked Elliott if he was a conspirator himself. Elliott answered that he was not guilty of a criminal act but admitted he was too scared to stop the other officers from mistreating Torres.[171]

The prosecution then presented the results of the HPD's Internal Affairs investigation. HPD detective Larry Ott quoted from Brinkmeyer's written statement, taken three days after the incident, which supported Elliott's version of events. In it Brinkmeyer stated that Denson pushed Torres. Ott next testified that Kinney, who initially had denied involvement, admitted after being shown Brinkmeyer's statement: "That's exactly what happened." Ott also read aloud from Janish's statement, in which Janish claimed that Torres jerked away from Denson and jumped into the bayou. But the detective noted that Janish had given this version only after conferring with Denson. In their statements all three of the officers agreed that Torres was "slapped several times" and also agreed he seemed to be swimming away after plunging into the water. Kinney and Brinkmeyer, however, said in their statements that they were unable to see Torres a few minutes later when they stopped at two nearby bridges and scanned the surface of the bayou.[172]

A second HPD detective, Ed Whitehead, read Orlando's signed statement, in which Orlando admitted suggesting that he and his colleagues should scare Torres before letting him go and asking if anyone still wanted to throw Torres into the bayou. Finally, IA leader McWilliams read the statement Denson signed, in which he admitted that Torres had been "brutalized" while in custody, and that the prisoner's nose was "bloodied in some manner." But Denson's version of the final moments of the incident diverged from all of the other officers' accounts. According to Denson, "[Torres] was shouting. . . . A scuffle ensued. The next thing I knew, he jumped in the Bayou. He seemed in total control."[173]

On 31 January the prosecution closed its case. Judge Sterling granted Kinney's motion to have his case severed from the other but denied the remaining three defendants' motion for a directed verdict of acquittal.[174] The defense opened its case the next day, on 1 February, when Denson testified in his own defense. To explain why in his earlier sworn statement he said that Torres was "brutalized," Denson said that "brutality is just another word officers tag on any type of physical confrontation when they have to arrest somebody. . . . It's a joke . . . because to some people, even putting on handcuffs and sitting a person down in the back of the car is brutalizing." Denson reaffirmed his Huntsville testimony that the officers took Torres to the Commerce Street location to calm him, to "reason" with him. He claimed they returned there intending "to scare him or impress upon him certain facts." Denson said that he jumped backwards when Torres attempted to grab him, because the prisoner had bragged about his army service in a unit that specialized in the Eastern martial arts. "The next thing I knew," Denson stated, "he was going down into the water." McDonald cross-examined Denson and asked him to confirm that the officers joked about Denson's pushing Torres into the water, as he had testified in Huntsville. Denson said he had not challenged that impression at the time, because he took their joking to be "a form of hero worship." McDonald asked if he meant that it was a cause for "hero worship to the police department to push a person into the Bayou?" Denson replied, "[N]ot exactly . . . I don't know how to express it." Spectators in the gallery murmured in disbelief at some of Denson's statements. U.S. deputy marshals stood between the rows of seats to restore order.[175]

Orlando next testified that in the days after the incident, he worried about losing his job for breaking HPD regulations. Under them the officers had no discretion to release a prisoner once he was arrested. Orlando denied being concerned about a regulation against "use of unnecessary force." He contradicted his earlier statement that he and his fellow officers had "slapped around" Torres. Instead, he testified that when Torres kicked at the officers, Denson "slapped him down on the hood . . . [and] the others just shoved him around." Orlando said he did not interfere when Denson took Torres to the edge of the bayou, because "I was going to let him go anyway."[176]

Janish next testified that by employing the word "slap" in his early statement, he had really meant "push." He reiterated his belief that Torres had jumped into the water but allowed that he might actually have fallen. Janish explained that he "saw a lot of movement just in a split second . . . I saw hands in the air, then I saw Torres go off the side." But Janish still contended that Torres had no problems swimming in the bayou. Rather, he told Andrews that his "hands were coming out over his head" and that as Torres swam, he "looked like Mark Spitz." During his cross-examination of Janish, McDonald recalled that Spitz, who had won seven gold medals in the 1972 Olympics, "could really chug across the water," but the he asked Janish if he had ever seen "Mark Spitz swimming in combat boots and fatigue pants?" Janish agreed that Spitz wore a swimsuit. McDonald referred once again to Janish's signed statement and noted that of the officers present at Torres's drowning, only Janish and Denson, who were able to confer alone before giving their statements, maintained that Torres jumped. Janish declared that he stood by his statement.[177]

The trial continued in a rare Sunday session. The defense team, again hoping to raise the issue of self-defense, wanted to call several witnesses who could either attest to Torres's belligerent past behavior or testify to his prowess as an army paratrooper. Judge Sterling ruled that such testimony was inadmissible. The defense rested, after calling to the stand only the defendants (again, Kinney was no longer connected to the case) and two officers as character witnesses. The defense attorneys had attempted to show that either the facts of the event as recalled by the various witnesses could not be reconciled with sufficient clarity to prove intent, or, in the alternative, show that the testimony proved only that the officers suffered a lapse of better judgment. No one, the defense insisted, intended to deprive Torres of his federally guaranteed civil rights.[178]

On 6 February Judge Sterling presided over a day of closing statements by the attorneys and instructed the jury on the relevant federal law.[179] During the first full day of deliberations, jurors sent four notes to the judge. One suggested a jury visit to the "hole" where Torres had been beaten, a request Sterling denied. Another note asked for a clarification of the legal definition of the charge "assault." Sterling provided the law on the subject.[180] The jury deliberated for two days and announced on 8 February that it had decided that Orlando, Janish, and Denson were all guilty of conspiring to deprive Torres of his right to due process, which resulted in his death. The conviction could result in a possible sentence of life imprisonment.[181] The jurors also convicted all three defendants on the second count.[182] But they acquitted on count number three, indicating that jurors were not convinced that Denson actually *pushed* Torres into Buffalo Bayou. This was a major victory for Denson. Conviction on this charge carried a possible maximum penalty of life in prison.[183] Finally, the jury acquitted Denson and Orlando on count four, conspiracy.[184]

Sterling had instructed the jury that the government did not have the burden of proving that the officers intended for Torres to die. He informed the jury, in answer to a query, that "[i]f they engaged in a conspiracy to violate Torres' civil rights and Torres died as a result, then they are guilty" on count number one. Therefore, the jury did not have to find that the officers "engaged in overt acts" such as actually pushing Torres into the water. Sinderson said, "When he came out with that, I knew we were going to get Count 1." She had hoped for a conviction on the cover-up count, "because we wanted to break that code of silence." But she admitted that the staff of the fledgling Civil Rights Division was "happy." "Considering this was our first case and our first conviction," Sinderson announced, "I think it was a feather for our division." Canales agreed, and declared that he was proud of the new group. He said, "Justice was served. . . . The verdict speaks to me very loudly."[185]

Mexican American activists took the opportunity afforded by the convictions, as they had with the earlier decision to prosecute Hayes for killing Morales, to build support for their greater cause. A. Miguel Romo, director of the National Congress of Hispanic American Citizens (El Congreso), an umbrella organization representing thirty groups, announced that the coalition was asking President Carter to create a national commission to investigate the "genocide being waged on Hispanics" by law enforcement officers. Romo was pleased that Annie Guiterrez, associate director of Carter's Domestic Council, had agreed to meet with his group and discuss the issue. In Washington, Ruben Sandoval and Antonio Bustamante, a spokesman for El Congreso, testified before a Senate committee that was then considering legislation to expand federal jurisdiction over police brutality cases by defining a state as a "person" for the purposes of prosecution and therefore holding state officials responsible for subordinate misconduct. In his testimony Sandoval also called for an end to the police's "genocide" of Chicanos.[186]

Ruben Bonilla of LULAC noted that during the previous ninety days alone, four Mexican Americans had died "under mysterious circumstances" in the custody of Texas law enforcement officers. He commended the Houston jury for "overcoming the injustice" that had occurred in Huntsville, but Bonilla added that only a life sentence would persuade other violent officers to abjure brutality. Ben Reyes agreed. He was "certainly encouraged by the jury decision. . . . But we have to have some faith in the entire system and that will only come by sending the policemen to jail for the rest of their lives."[187]

On 28 March 1978, after he reviewed sentencing memoranda and briefs prepared by attorneys in the case, Judge Sterling conducted a sentencing hearing.[188] He interviewed each of the three former officers, heard statements from and asked questions of character witnesses, and listened to the attorneys' summary statements. McDonald declared that the three purposes of criminal sentences were punishment, rehabilitation, and deterrence. He argued that Sterling should impose a "substantial period of incarceration," not only to punish the individual defendants, but because the "deterrent effect is significant in a case that has attracted this kind of attention, [and] involves this kind of criminal act." A stiff sentence would send a powerful message to potential violators still working in law enforcement.[189] Naturally, the defense argued the opposite, that long prison sentences would send no signals and accomplish nothing to change the culture of the HPD.[190]

Before pronouncing sentence, Sterling declared that the Torres incident represented "a situational offense which these defendants will never encounter again. They will never again be police officers, and . . . a long period of confinement would have little impact upon the operation of the Houston Police Department, where I conceive the heart of the trouble to lie." The judge sentenced each defendant to serve one year in prison for the misdemeanor and ten years for the felony conspiracy, and directed that the sentences be served consecutively. Then Sterling shocked the prosecutors by immediately suspending the latter sentence, and imposing instead five years' probation. The judge explained his decision by noting that two juries had failed to find the defendants *intended* for Torres to die.[191]

After Sterling announced these sentences, McDonald attempted over the clamor of the crowd to remind him that probation was not among the authorized punishments for these particular convictions. McDonald shouted "[T]here is some question about whether or not a probated sentence . . ." The judge responded, "I have resolved that question to my own satisfaction. We will be in recess."[192]

Mexican Americans cried foul. Margaret Torres said, "I thought the [federal] government was going to take care of everything. . . . It's just a slap in the face. It's just getting away with murder."[193] Ben Reyes, who had called for calm before the federal trial, now declared that Sterling had "made it impossible to convince people that there is equal justice for all. We told them we lost the first round but wait until the federal court is done. What the hell can we tell them now?" He took special exception to the "damn asinine" assertion that the problem was within the HPD but not with the individual officers, and said, "What a poor excuse for a judge he had to be to make that kind of judgment. . . . To say a person is not accountable to the law because of a social condition shows that he just doesn't understand or doesn't want to understand the law."[194] Bonilla of LULAC said, "The progress Mexican-Americans had made in seeking the administration of justice has been lost."[195] Mamie Garcia, LULAC's district director, asserted that "we can only hope that the predominantly white society will be able to live with its conscience."[196]

Richard Vara, a Mexican American columnist, argued for continued restraint and condemned Judge Sterling for testing the limits of that restraint. He urged Mexican Americans to retain their respect, trust, and faith in the system that "just kicked [them] in the teeth." But, he wrote, "perhaps now the majority of those in Texas who argue that minorities do not need extra protection under the law in employment, education and other areas will see that what is food for the goose is not necessarily given to the gander, particularly if that gander happens to be a shade dark."[197] A primary motivation for the crusade for federal intervention in police brutality cases was the fact that in the federal courts, life-tenured federal district judges, rather than local state juries guided by elected state judges, sentenced the convicted. Texas attorneys and minority leaders now began to argue that, since it appeared federal justice had its own limitations, they should now lobby to strengthen the state civil rights laws.[198] Texas Attorney General Hill announced, during a press conference at his gubernatorial campaign headquarters, that he was disappointed with the sentences and was "willing to lead" the effort to revise state civil rights laws so future cases could be handled by state courts.[199]

Sterling now became a major target of scorn.[200] Hector Garcia, founder of AGIF and Tony Canales's uncle, asked Judge Singleton to convene a commission to censure Sterling. Failing that action, Ruben Sandoval assured a Mexican American crowd that civil rights leaders would ask Attorney General Bell to appoint a three-judge panel to consider Sterling's censure. Ed Peña, vice president of the Washington-based La Raza National Lawyers Association, said he planned to analyze Sterling's sentencing of Chicano defendants, to learn if his decisions demonstrated a pattern of discrimination.[201] Frumencio Reyes of PASSO wondered "whether [Sterling] is under some sort of pressure."[202] Reyes labeled Sterling "a racist, red-neck judge."[203]

Many activists who had led the protests against the state sentences but had counseled patience until the outcome of the federal case now regretted that advice. Hector Garcia, not the AGIF founder but the chair of the Coalition for Responsible Law Enforcement,[204] lamented that "maybe what was going on in the streets made more sense in terms of saying what needed to be said." Garcia said he had "yet to see how the Coalition was useful . . . I don't know how close we ever got to solving any problems. It's up to the police department now." Travis Morales, leader of the newly-organized group "People United against Police Brutality," thought the Mexican American community activists actually had gotten all they could realistically hope for from federal justice, namely, a hearing that publicized the problem. Morales said, "[W]e never expected much more than what we got out of the feds. There is no way to expect justice from those that don't care. . . . We have gotten indictments, though, and started a movement against police brutality. That's a real victory."[205]

Mexican Americans arranged a march and rally to call for more minority representation in the federal judiciary. The city council approved the event but refused to issue a parade permit, which meant the participants would have to remain on sidewalks. Travis Morales announced that his group was planning a separate march. He said PASSO, LULAC, and AGIF had "led us down too many blind alleys."[206] Approximately five hundred demonstrators marched through downtown Houston and gathered in front of city hall to protest the sentences given the Torres defendants. Garcia of PASSO and other minority leaders, including state legislator Mickey Leland, an African American, called for unity in seeking tougher state civil rights laws and also demanded a state human rights commission. Ruben Bonilla, Ben Reyes, and Ruben Sandoval called on Mexican Americans to use their growing political power in the Southwest to vote out of office the politicians who "appoint insensitive people to state and federal benches."[207] Seventy-five supporters of Morales's People United briefly attended, chanted "The people fight back when the cops attack," and urged a march on police headquarters. Among the placards was one that declared, "It's the whole damn system, not a couple of bad cops."[208]

After Sterling's granting of probation, Ruben Sandoval commented on a curious inconsistency: Sterling had assessed jail time for a misdemeanor but probation for a felony.[209] Neither Canales nor Sinderson had commented publicly on the sentences, but Canales's team soon focused their attention on the inconsistency that Sandoval had described. On 5 April, one week after the sentencing, Sinderson moved to correct the sentences. It was not that probated sentences were inconsistent or unjust, but rather that they were "illegal and not within the scope of the court's discretion." According to the research Sinderson marshaled in support of the motion, the federal sentencing laws excluded probation for offenses punishable by death or life imprisonment.[210]

The prosecution then adopted a risky strategy. Sinderson appealed to equitable notions of justice, and explicitly linked the outcome of the case to its symbolic importance to Mexican Americans in Texas. In addition to raising the question of strict legality, therefore, the prosecution's motion called broadly for justice. Sinderson wrote: "The fundamental concept of equal justice requires that the rights of minority victims be vindicated and that those who would cause such deprivations be deterred from such misconduct. The fundamental concept of equal justice also requires that those who are given the special authority of police officers be held at least equally accountable for their criminal acts as those who are not accorded such a position."[211] She concluded with an even more ringing extralegal argument:

> The United States has grave concern that the imposition of probation in this case will cause citizens of all races and backgrounds to believe that the sentence was a result of the continuing inequality of treatment accorded to minorities. This public perception of inequality, and the belief that the life of a Mexican-American citizen has little value, can only do damage to the respect for the laws and for the belief in justice which must be the mortar which binds our nation together.[212]

These comments were out of place in a motion to a federal district judge who was preparing to assess a criminal sentence, because a prosecution, unlike civil rights litigation, is at least formally concerned only with the legal relationships between the defendant and the government. Sinderson apparently intended her statements, however, not to persuade Sterling but to reassure Mexican Americans who threatened to take to the streets.[213]

The defense responded to the prosecution's motion to correct the sentence on 11 April and simply restated a reading of the law that agreed with Sterling's own interpretation, that probation was unavailable only in those cases where life imprisonment or a death penalty was *mandatory.* The response did not appeal to sentiment but to statistics, citing the previous three years of sentence profiles gleaned from the annual reports of the director of the Administrative Office. The defense attorneys responded to the extralegal appeals by characterizing them as such. When they disputed Sinderson's presentation of the case law, for example, they wrote that the "[a]uthorities cited by the Government on this point *(in that portion of their motion dealing with the law)* are not directly in point."[214]

On 17 April, in refusing to correct the sentence, Judge Sterling cited Administrative Office annual statistics. In 1977 four persons convicted of second degree murder, thirty-three convicted of rape, and six convicted of kidnapping had received probation. In 1976 those receiving probation after conviction of these same offenses were two, twenty, and five, respectively. And, similarly, in 1975 the numbers were three, twenty-eight, and ten.[215] Judge Sterling concluded, "[T]hroughout the nation, the Federal Judiciary has interpreted the language 'imprisonment (or imprisoned) for any term of years or for life' to be consistent with the [statutory] language authorizing the granting of probation. Probation is prohibited when a punishment of death or life imprisonment is *mandatory*." Sterling made no comment on the nonlegal portions of Sinderson's motion, unless that is what he referred to in calling the request to amend sentence an "entirely unprecedented motion" filed by the government.[216]

Less than three weeks after Sterling issued the denial, on 7 May 1978, fifteen hundred people converged in Houston's Moody Park to protest and to commemorate the one-year anniversary of Torres's death. Travis Morales of People United passed out pamphlets to the families who also came to the park to celebrate a Mexican holiday, Cinco de Mayo. A fight erupted, which police attempted to stop. Their intervention precipitated a riot that resulted in the arrest of forty people, the hospitalization of fifteen, and half a million dollars in property damage. Morales and two others were later charged with inciting the so-called Moody Park Riots.[217]

The U.S. attorney's office filed a notice of appeal of the judge's denial ten days after the riots and indicated an intention to seek a writ of mandamus, an injunction used to compel a lower-court judge to execute a legal duty.[218] Mandamus was usually applied to correct egregious abuses of power. For example, federal district courts have original jurisdiction to compel an officer or employee of the United States to perform a nondiscretionary duty owed to a plaintiff. Under the same principle, the federal courts of appeals can compel action in a district court.[219]

On 19 May 1978 Sterling entered an order for "Judgment and Probation/Commitment" for Denson, Orlando, and Janish. He also issued a second order, which stayed the sentences until the question of their validity was determined. In the order the judge also announced he would attempt "to set forth upon the record the reasons, which stem from the unprecedented procedural posture of this case," for his decision.[220] Sterling revealed that he had not been entirely forthcoming in his earlier statements and had "not heretofore articulated the most cogent reason for the sentences imposed." This was because he had vainly attempted "to depoliticize what has become an almost intolerable situation of attempts to interfere with the independence of this court." After summarizing motions the lawyers had been trading, the judge stated that his main reason for deciding that the defendants deserved probation was that "the Government entered into a plea agreement with one of the former police officers not on trial in this case that if he would testify against those on trial here, he would be permitted to plead guilty to the same actions upon which the jury found these Defendants guilty under a different statute carrying a maximum penalty of one years imprisonment and further that in his case the Government would recommend probation."[221] Sterling's admissions were as startling in a judicial order as Sinderson's earlier appeal to sentiment had been in a prosecutor's motion.[222]

Sterling wanted to do more than reject the government's motion to correct the sentence; he wished to repudiate the prosecutorial tactic used to secure the convictions. He perceived inequality in the deal Canales offered Brinkmeyer, as opposed to the public demonization thrust upon the other HPD officers because they had chosen to exercise their right to mount a vigorous legal defense. In short, Sterling did not approve of Canales's strategy of offering immunity and plea bargains to break the police officers' code of silence. These bargains are standard tools of prosecution, and Canales authorized the same arrangements for some of the officers implicated in the Webster and Joyvies deaths. Sterling was not the first to complain that the practice tainted criminal convictions. Canales experienced criticism from another quarter around the same time. Reportedly, he went to the Department of Justice headquarters expecting to receive an award for his actions in the police cases, and instead received a written reprimand for granting immunity to an officer without prior approval from Washington. Canales's response was to turn to a colleague and say: "[S]ee this letter. I don't agree with this letter. This is the kind of thing I use to wipe my ass with."[223]

The judge seemed to believe that brokering plea agreements in return for testimony, which meant unequal punishment for equal criminal acts, did not serve justice. But because Canales had limited Sterling's options by manipulating the indictments to allow Brinkmeyer to plead guilty to a lesser charge in a separate proceeding, there was only one way for the judge to render justice, and that was to sentence the convicted officers to the minimum jail time, which conveniently matched Brinkmeyer's sentence. Moreover, Sterling was well aware of the political undertones that tainted every aspect of the case, including the prosecution's appeals to the "public perception of inequality." The judge chose to stand against political machinations.

Canales did not accept defeat; instead, after this last repudiation, he decided to go over Sterling's head. On 23 May the U.S. attorney filed an amended notice of appeal, and on 14 July he executed a petition for mandamus.[224] Judge James C. Hill of the U.S. Court of Appeals for the Fifth Circuit delivered the majority's opinion on 5 February 1979. The substantive issue in the appeal, Hill noted, was whether the federal probation statute authorized a suspended sentence and probation for a conviction under the federal deprivation of civil rights conspiracy statute, in a case in which the victim of the constitutional deprivation was killed. This was a straightforward factual question with a straightforward factual answer: according to Hill, because the defendants Denson, Orlando, and Janish had been duly convicted of offenses for which death or life imprisonment may be imposed as a sentence, the "ordinary plain meaning" of the sentencing statute was that Sterling lacked the authority to suspend punishment and grant probation.[225] Judge Sterling was wrong in his interpretation of his discretion under the law. He had no power to depart from the statute and grant probation in this case. The circuit judge believed that there was "no ambiguity in the language of the statute that would justify such a departure."[226]

With regard to Sterling's "most cogent reason" for granting probation, the Fifth Circuit judges found that judicial independence did not mean freedom from the duty to apply clear statutory language. Moreover, Judge Hill stated, "it is inappropriate for the sentencing court to attempt to harmonize the fate of convicted defendants with the fate of witnesses with whom the Government has struck a bargain. The executive has the discretion to refrain from even prosecuting lawbreakers as part of its efforts at investigation of law enforcement." Hill said that the "authority of the federal courts to order probation comes from Congress, not plea bargains." Sterling erred in giving probation.[227]

The authority of the Fifth Circuit to issue the writ of mandamus was unquestioned, and this could have ended the Torres matter. However, as in situations in which jurors tended to give the benefit of their doubt to policemen, the appellate judges now hesitated to second-guess the trial judge. Judge Hill noted that Sterling had constructed a matrix of punishment, consisting of a year in prison and five years on supervised probation, which could be revoked and replaced with a ten-year sentence. The sentence was illegal but it was not arbitrary, and it was firm and fair enough to be just. Moreover, because the circuit judges could only direct the district judge to impose a *new* sentence, but not a *particular* sentence, Hill warned that a writ of mandamus might actually defeat the intent of the appeal by opening the door to a less onerous, albeit legal sentence.[228] The Fifth Circuit, having declared that the government's attorneys were correct in asserting that Sterling owed the defendants a *legal* sentence, declined to force him to impose one.[229] For the sake of judicial harmony, the circuit judges deferred to Judge Sterling's imagined possession of discretion, rather than exercise their actual authority.[230]

The appeal victory, unaccompanied with a reward, typified the pattern of unsatisfying "paper" victories the Southern District's civil rights attorneys won during the summer of 1979. While waiting for the result of the appeal in the Torres case, Sinderson completed trials in the Webster and Joyvies cases. In the former, the prosecutors proved that two HPD officers planted a gun to justify the shooting of the unarmed Webster. After deliberating for six days, the jury convicted the officers on charges relating to their concealing the "throwdown" but not of conspiring to deprive Webster of his civil rights. Canales claimed he was not disappointed, since "this was a cover-up case and the jury found that. . . . We are happy with the verdict."[231]

The resultant sentences punctured his satisfaction. The Webster defendants received probation. Not only this, but during the sentencing hearing on 14 May 1979, Judge Finis Cowan echoed Sterling's criticism of Canales's tactics. Cowan noted that defendants "faced the awesome, enormous power of a government legally authorized to purchase testimony by grants of immunity and prosecute them with unlimited resources." The judge assessed sentences of five years' probation. The outcome was so similar to that in the Torres case that Sinderson predicted that HPD officers were "already laughing about what happened to us." An angry Canales merely told reporters, "We didn't purchase any testimony."[232]

LULAC leaders declared they were "appalled" at the Webster sentences. They called for better screening of candidates for federal judgeships. Sandoval said, "We have a bunch of gutless wonders on the bench." He called Cowan's sentence "irresponsible" and claimed, "There is undeniably a dual system of justice, not only in this state but throughout the U.S. . . . For so long there's been a great laxity on prosecution of police officers." LULAC's Johnny Mata noted that this might have been the first time his organization spoke out on a civil rights case involving a nonminority. Sandoval declared, "This gives us a new dimension, but it's not a new endeavor. . . . We have been talking about human rights, not ethnic rights." Sandoval said Judge Cowan's criticism of "purchased testimony" was a "smokescreen to evade his failure to meet up to his responsibilities."[233]

After the Webster verdict, Frumencio Reyes of PASSO said, "I don't know what the government has to prove to find someone guilty of violating someone's civil rights. . . . we're going to have one hell of a time trying to contain any demonstrations this summer." Reyes said that Mexican Americans already knew there was little justice available for them in court, but most thought that because Webster was white, the chances of conviction were greater. Instead, he said, the verdict proved only that police officers were judged differently than ordinary citizens. Whites should also be disturbed, Reyes said. Hector Garcia of the Coalition for Responsible Government said that the verdict proved that the public still had a "tendency to support the police regardless of how questionable their action may be." He added that the nation was in the midst of a "backlash," and although Webster was white, he was a victim of a growing disregard for civil rights.[234]

Sinderson insisted that "[a]nyone who does civil-rights work is prepared to take a loss without folding up his tent and stealing away into the night. . . . We will still continue to present cases . . . without any expectation that task will be easy."[235] On 25 July Judge Singleton granted the defense's motion for a directed verdict of acquittal in the Joyvies case. He declared that the officers' "possibly illegal" actions after shooting Joyvies without justification were intended "to protect themselves" and

> to protect the Houston Police Department from public criticism . . . [but their] conduct—improper, shocking—does not constitute a violation [under the] charge brought against them . . . [the] bizarre facts [cannot] condone the improper, and possibly illegal, behavior of [the defendants]. . . . However, our system of justice demands that no person be convicted of a crime of which he is not guilty—even though the conduct of those accused is bad, illegal, improper and reprehensible.[236]

Singleton said that the "government has the duty to produce sufficient evidence to prove beyond a reasonable doubt that each of them had the specific intent to violate a right Billy Keith Joyvies was guaranteed." He did not believe the prosecution proved that case.[237]

Sinderson "respectfully disagree[d]," insisting that if there was any weakness in the case it was that the government "had to depend on members of a closed fraternity whose motivating desire was to protect one another." She said, "We are, of course, disappointed to lose . . . but it will not slow down our investigations."[238] But the Joyvies loss did signal the conclusion of the Southern District's two-year experiment with individual criminal civil rights prosecutions. When asked about the possibility of pursuing civil lawsuits against the police department, Canales implied that he had not ruled out seeking an injunction against the city of Houston. Perhaps not realizing the irony in his words, he said that "[i]f the police chief is held in contempt, then he'd *slap his men* into line."[239]

Canales had not given up in the Torres matter, however. The government's appeal had been heard by a panel of three federal judges, and one had dissented. Therefore, when Circuit Judge Hill delivered the opinion of the court, he had spoken for the majority of the U.S. Court of Appeals for the Fifth Circuit on the basis of his vote and that of one other judge. Canales filed a request for a rehearing by the full Fifth Circuit. The circuit court granted the request on 30 March but stipulated that it would consider the case solely on the transcripts, that is, without new oral arguments.[240] On 4 October Fifth Circuit Judge Alvin B. Rubin issued a majority opinion to reverse the earlier denial of mandamus. Rubin wrote that, although a federal trial judge has some discretion in sentencing, "[t]he imposition of a sentence that is illegal is a manifest transgression," and therefore the earlier panel should have issued the requested writ "as a matter of course." He reiterated that the circuit judges could not impose their own sentence, but they could and would direct Judge Sterling to impose a sentence that was within the statutory limits.[241]

Mexican Americans were wary. LULAC's Johnny Mata admitted, "[The decision] certainly has restored some of the integrity of the federal court and restored some of the community's faith." He hoped Sterling would "follow the proper judgment," but he remained skeptical because "the problem started with him in the first place."[242] On 30 October 1979 Sterling fulfilled Mata's gloomy expectations.[243] The judge resentenced Denson, Orlando, and Janish to one year and one day on the felony count and ordered the sentence to be served concurrently with the misdemeanor sentence. This sentence was legal, but by adding that extra day Sterling made the men eligible for parole, which was unavailable to federal prisoners serving one year or less. The former officers could be released after serving one-third of their terms, and perhaps less with "good-time." Ruben Bonilla called the sentences a "contemptuous act in defiance of an appellate court order." He noted that "once again [Sterling] has shown he has no conception of fairness or equality or justice. He has earned the contempt and disrespect of the Hispanic Americans of this country. . . . [He] should be censured, reprimanded, impeached, or otherwise removed from the bench."[244]

Judge Sterling, protected by tenure, remained on the bench in the Southern District of Texas until his death in 1988. On the other hand, Canales left office with the president who appointed him. When Canales stepped down in late 1980, still the only U.S. attorney who had established a local Civil Rights Division, he was so frustrated by his experience that he declared in no uncertain terms that he would not return to public life. When news reporters asked if he had plans to seek future office, he replied, "None. . . . Let me repeat. None. None. None. Never. Never. Never. *Nunca. Nunca. Nunca.*"[245]

Mexican American civil rights activists did not anticipate the frustration the federal criminal justice system would create for their constituents. They had become expert at filing civil actions in federal courts and requesting equitable injunctions, but the quest for criminal sanctions was different from the pursuit of equitable remedies. A legal strategy that had been increasingly effective on the civil side of the federal court proved to be counterproductive on the criminal side. These frustrations did not lead Mexican Americans to abandon their search for justice in the federal courts. Ruben Sandoval, for example, had continued all along to lobby for a dual prosecution in the Darrell Cain–Santos Rodriguez case. In July 1978 the Justice Department decided that the case did not meet the standards for dual prosecution, because police officer Cain's state trial had been fair and proper.[246]

The final insult in the Torres trial convinced Mexican American leaders that they should try again, because Cain's actions resembled those of Marshal Hayes. They asked federal authorities to review the five-year-old incident once more, before the statute of limitations elapsed.[247] This last-ditch effort also failed, but Mexican Americans had not yet given up hope on the federal criminal justice system. They concentrated on political appeals, however, such as demanding tighter screening of judicial candidates in order to eliminate those with "latent prejudices."[248] As one protester explained, the Mexican American community must continue its activism because "Mr. Carter doesn't understand Texas is our Mississippi."[249]

The Southern District judges seemed in many instances, especially in the border divisions, to be enthusiastic partners of the prosecution. In the police misconduct cases, by contrast, the judges and prosecutors were clearly adversaries. Of the several possible explanations for this outcome—that the judges were, in fact, just as racist as the community charged, or that they were strict law and order types unwilling to give the enemies of the police a weapon—the most likely is the latter. Given the dilemma of choosing sides in what appeared to be an internecine battle between two natural allies—the prosecution and the police—the federal district judges, whether they were linked to liberal or conservative politics before their appointment, opted for a conservative interpretation of the law, a studied neutrality to outcomes reminiscent of the formalist era. That the judges were not neutral is shown by their varied, passionate condemnations of the prosecutors' decisions that put them on both horns of the dilemma. The judges who presided in the police brutality cases did find the entire affair to be "an almost intolerable situation."

REGARDLESS OF RACE, COLOR, SEX, RELIGION, OR NATIONAL ORIGIN

The political pressures on the Southern District judges during the police prosecutions were anomalous, in that the usual business of the court—developing plans to manage criminal cases under the Speedy Trial Act, working through crash dockets to keep up with the civil case backlogs—was accomplished out of the public eye. But the media and community attention given to the federal district courts during the late 1970s enabled minority activists to remind President Carter that he had not yet fulfilled a campaign promise to appoint women and minorities to the federal judiciary.[250]

Some of the president's supporters blamed this lapse on the lifetime tenure enjoyed by the sitting judges, which kept turnover slow. Yet Carter had named another white male, Cowan, to the bench when Judge Noel had stepped down. Carter's best opportunity to make good on his pledge came when Congress resolved to increase, substantially, the total number of federal judgeships. The Omnibus Judgeship Act of 1978 instantly opened 150 positions on the federal bench. The expansion offered Carter the opportunity to transform the character of the entire national judiciary. The changes would be especially significant in the Southern District of Texas, because the legislation increased the total number of positions there from 8 to 13.[251]

The 1978 act contained an explicit invitation from Congress to the president to make a revolution in the judiciary. Section 8 announced that the Congress "(1) takes notice of the fact that only 1 percent of Federal judges are women and only 4 percent are blacks; and (2) suggests that the President, in selecting individuals for nomination to the Federal judgeships created by this Act, give due consideration to qualified individuals regardless of race, color, sex, religion, or national origin."[252] Carter seized the opportunity. During his entire term as president, more than 15 percent of his judicial appointees were female, and more than 21 percent were minorities.[253]

U.S. Senator Lloyd Bentsen of Texas, who had succeeded Ralph Yarborough in 1970 but then served his first six-year term under Republican presidents, finally was able to reward a select few of his friends and supporters by recommending them to the president for federal judgeships.[254] With Bentsen's advice and the consent of the rest of the Senate, Carter appointed James DeAnda to be one of the five new federal district judges in the Southern District of Texas. After thirty years of litigating in its courts, DeAnda became the district's second Mexican American judge.[255]

The next nominee, Gabrielle Anne Kirk McDonald, was born on 12 April 1942 in Saint Paul, Minnesota. She was brought up in Manhattan, New York, and Teaneck, New Jersey. McDonald attended both Boston University and Hunter College but never earned an undergraduate degree. She earned her LL.B. at Howard University, finishing first in her class, in 1966. She worked for two years in New York City, for the National Association for the Advancement of Colored People (NAACP) Legal Defense and Education Fund. In 1967 she was the lead NAACP staff attorney on the first significant win by plaintiffs on an employment discrimination claim, filed under Title VII of the Civil Rights Act (CRA) of 1964, in a case against Philip Morris.[256] In 1969 McDonald entered private practice in Houston, where she continued to build a reputation for effectiveness in Title VII and other civil rights litigation. With her appointment McDonald became the first black judge to serve on any U.S. district court in Texas. She was also the first woman on the Southern District bench and only the third woman to serve on a federal court in Texas.[257]

The three remaining new judicial seats went to white men, but they also brought a measure of diversity to the district. George P. Kazen was born 29 February 1940 in Laredo, into a prominent Lebanese American family. He earned his B.B.A. at UT in 1960 and his J.D. at UT law school in 1961. After one year as a briefing attorney for the Texas Supreme Court, Kazen began a three-year term in the U.S. Air Force, where he was a captain in the Judge Advocate General Corps from 1962 to 1965. As described in an earlier chapter, Kazen had then entered private practice in Laredo.[258]

Norman William Black was born in Houston on 6 December 1931. Perhaps no one since Judge James Allred—that is, upon his second appointment to the bench—boasted such pertinent experience to be a federal judge in the Southern

District. Black attended UT in Austin, where he earned his B.B.A. in 1953 and his LL.B. in 1955. He served in the U.S. Army Military Police from 1955 to 1957. After his discharge from the army, Black spent the next year as a law clerk for Judge Ben Connally in Houston. He spent two years, from 1958 to 1960, as AUSA in Houston. He spent the next sixteen years in private practice, with his own firm, Black, Hebinck, Hargrove, and Clark. He became a U.S. magistrate in the Southern District in 1976. Black was in that position when the president named him to the district bench. He was the first Jewish person to become a federal district judge in the Southern District.[259]

The president appointed George E. Cire, a state associate justice, to the fifth new judgeship. Cire was born on 29 September 1922 in Houston. He attended Saint Edward's University in central Texas, where he earned his B.S. in 1943. He served in the U.S. Marine Corps from 1943 to 1946 and then attended the UT School of Law, where he earned his LL.B. in 1948. After only one year in private practice, however, Cire resumed his career in the marines. He returned to Houston and private practice in 1951. Cire was later elected to the 165th District Court in Houston, where he was a judge for twelve years. In 1976 Cire became an associate justice of the 14th Court of Civil Appeals, also in Houston.[260]

All five of the nominees were confirmed by the Senate on 11 May 1979.[261] Chief Judge Garza had already introduced himself. In January 1979 he had written to "My dear Judges and Judges-To-Be," suggesting a court meeting in February in Houston. He invited all of the nominees to the new judgeships because he was confident of their imminent confirmation and commissioning, and he wanted them to take part in decisions at the earliest opportunity. Among the matters Garza hoped they would discuss were the standards and procedures for appointing U.S. magistrates, whose status was soon to change due to new legislation by Congress. Garza also wanted to apprise both old and new judges of the necessity to be prepared to try defendants who would be coming up on the sixty-day limits of the Speedy Trial Act, which was soon to go into full effect. Finally, the chief judge wanted to discuss the selection of the next judge to assume the oversight of the venerable HISD desegregation case. Judge Cowan, who had inherited the case from Judge Noel, had told Garza he intended to resign after only two years on the bench.[262]

Cowan made this decision official at the end of March, when he announced that he would resign on 30 June. Citing concerns for the soon-to-be-in-force strictures of the Speedy Trial Act, Cowan suggested that Garza instruct the clerk to assign no new cases to his docket.[263] The chief judge agreed, and he also decided that the newly appointed Judge Cire would inherit responsibility for the resigning Judge Cowan's civil docket in Houston. Cowan would keep all of his cases in Galveston, however, and Garza suggested that Cowan concentrate on disposing of the outstanding criminal trials before leaving the bench, so that the court would not "run into Speedy Trial problems."[264] When Cowan did leave at the end of June, Garza asked the clerk to assign the Galveston docket to Sterling.[265]

Garza ordered further revisions in work assignments that would be in effect as soon as the five new judges arrived in May. Docket equalization across the newly expanded district court was to be accomplished by shifting of weighted cases. Judge Singleton, for example, would give incoming Judge McDonald 10 heavy cases and incoming Judge Black 99 heavy, 121 average, and 66 light cases. The other sitting judges were to transfer to one or more of their new colleagues similar numbers of cases. As a result, Garza hoped, each of the eight full-time active Houston judges would have a civil docket consisting of either 428 or 429 cases.[266] The numbers would have to be revised upon Cowan's departure, but, for the time being, the clerk's duty to assign cases on a percentage basis was substantially easier than ever before. Judge DeAnda, for example, would be assigned 50 percent of the criminal and civil cases filed in Brownsville, Judge Kazen 25 percent of both categories there, and Judge Garza the remaining 25 percent. In Houston, Judges Singleton, Seals, Bue, O'Conor, Sterling, Cire, McDonald, and Black each received 12.5 percent of the criminal and civil filings.[267]

President Carter appointed a Galveston lawyer, Hugh Gibson, to replace Cowan. Gibson was born on 8 November 1918 in Cameron, Texas. He attended the Rice Institute, now Rice University, where he earned his B.A. in 1940. Like so many men of his generation, Gibson was in the military during World War II. He served as a sergeant in the U.S. Army from 1942 to 1945. Gibson returned home to Texas to attend the Baylor University School of Law, earned the LL.B. in 1948, and then stayed on for one more year to teach. Although he remained in private practice, Gibson became assistant district attorney in Galveston in 1949, then assistant city attorney in 1951. From 1954 to 1968, he was judge of the Probate Court of Galveston County. For the next decade, until his appointment to the federal bench, he was a state judge in the Fifty-sixth Judicial District in Galveston. Judge Gibson assumed Cowan's vacant seat on 5 October.[268]

President Carter's opportunities to appoint judges in the Southern District of Texas were still not exhausted. In his May 1979 equalization memorandum, Chief Judge Garza explained to his fellow judge that, because he was anticipating his own appointment to the Fifth Circuit, he had, for the time being, assigned himself only one-half of his normal docket.[269] Garza had earlier turned down Carter's offer to become U.S. attorney general, but he accepted when the president offered him one of the newly created seats on the Fifth Circuit.[270] This appointment, of course, left yet another judicial vacancy on the district bench. Carter's last appointment in the Southern District was Filemon B. Vela. Vela was born 1 May 1935 in Harlingen, a border town in far south Texas. After serving as a U.S. Army private from 1957 to 1959, he attended law school at Saint Mary's University in San Antonio, where he earned his J.D. in 1962. He briefly entered private practice in Harlingen, then moved his practice to Brownsville in 1963. Vela served as a city commissioner there in the early 1970s. In 1975 he became a state judge for Cameron and Willacy Counties, in the 107th District. He was still there when the president appointed him to Garza's old seat in Brownsville, which he assumed on 18 June 1980.[271]

With Garza's move to the Fifth Circuit, Judge Singleton, with one day of seniority over Judge Seals, became the chief judge of the Southern District of Texas. He inherited a much expanded and diversified court from Garza. Singleton did not inherit Garza's clerk of the court to guide him through the new decade. V. Bailey Thomas, who had served the Southern District judges since December 1951, retired in December 1979. Thomas's chief deputy clerk, Jesse E. Clark, who had been a probation officer in the district before moving into the clerk's office, assumed the top job there.[272]

One of the first challenges Singleton and Clark faced was the implementation of the rather slow-moving Speedy Trial Act. After making their extended preparations, the district judges waited for the new regime. An amendment to the act in August 1979 delayed its full force by another year. The amendment allowed the Southern District judges further to refine their approach to the complex chronology of criminal cases. The basic strategy, stopping the clock if possible, remained essentially unaltered for years.[273] The district's "final" plan was promulgated in April 1980.[274]

CHAPTER SEVEN

Adjuncts and the Oversight of Corporate Misconduct

IN HIS DECEMBER 1978 MEMORANDUM setting out the judicial work assignments for 1979, Chief Judge Reynaldo Garza informed the judges of the Southern District that no new criminal cases were being assigned to Judge John Singleton after 1 January, until further notice. This was at the request of Singleton, who reported that he would soon begin "a long-winded criminal case involving containers."[1] The criminal trial evolved into a related civil action known generally as *In re Corrugated Container Antitrust Litigation,* and Singleton continued to preside over the case well after he succeeded Garza as chief judge. Singleton's tenure as chief of the district was fraught with administrative and especially personnel upheaval. Yet he was lauded as an expert administrator, and he was praised by the bar and the bench in the Southern District for eagerly tackling complex cases that nobody else wanted.[2]

The *Corrugated Container,* or "cardboard box," case proved to be complex as well as "long-winded," and at times it seemed to try Judge Singleton just as much as he tried it. But he could not put off disposing of his full docket forever, and he assumed his additional duties as chief judge in 1980. The judge could, however, arrange for assistance in sorting through the details of the civil case by appointing a special master according to Rule 53 of the Federal Rules of Civil Procedure.[3] The master was a judicial adjunct who could act as an auditor, examiner, or referee in a complex bundle of cases or serve in a specific capacity in a single case, such as supervising discovery or developing remedies.[4]

The appointment of masters was one tactic increasingly employed by federal district judges to assist them in managing complex, protracted litigation, especially class-action suits. The master's function was similar to the role played by the biracial or triethnic panels in desegregation cases. They were a trial judge's eyes and ears outside the courtroom. The first section of this chapter examines Singleton's management of the record-breaking cardboard box case that opened his tenure as the chief judge of the district. The enormously complex case illustrates how the nation's business can be bound up with law and politics. The point is made again in the last part of the chapter, through an examination of the government's interest in sorting out the banking scandals of the 1980s. Federal government regulators and prosecutors filed a series of complex involuntary bankruptcy proceedings and securities prosecutions that continued to bedevil the Southern District judges into the 1990s.[5]

Before the 1980s the judges would have either presided in these actions or employed a "referee," such as a special master, but in thc Bankruptcy Reform Act of 1978, the Congress created a system of separate bankruptcy courts and judges in each federal district. By 1984, after a period of transition, and after an amendment was enacted in response to an adverse U.S. Supreme Court decision, the federal bankruptcy tribunals were in full operation.[6] They were, like masters, subordinate adjuncts whose rulings could be appealed to federal district judges. In most cases, however, a district judge approved the reorganization plans that had been painstakingly brokered by a bankruptcy judge.[7]

In "average" economic times, when businesses fail at a more or less steady and predictable rate, bankruptcy cases are routine and a "final judgment" by a bankruptcy judge is for all practical purposes truly final, because bankruptcies are usually uncontested. Most cases are negotiated between voluntary bankrupts and claimant creditors.[8] During times of extraordinary economic distress, however, stakes are high and claimants usually desperate. In the 1980s, for the first time since the bank failures of the Great Depression, a large share of cases in Texas involved commercial banks and so-called "thrift" institutions, especially savings and loan (S&L) associations.[9] Bankruptcy judges presided over forced or involuntary cases filed by the creditors rather than the debtors. The federal district judges in the Southern District were called upon to preside in an array of civil suits spawned by the widespread insolvency. Many cases transpired over years and metamorphosed into multiple-courtroom incarnations that were managed by district and bankruptcy judges working in tandem.

The availability of court adjuncts was not a new development.[10] During the 1980s, however, all of the Southern District judges, not just the chief, came to rely more heavily than ever before on special masters and bankruptcy judges, and, as will be examined in the next chapter, on the magistrates as well, whose availability was relatively recent. To use them effectively, the judges learned more lessons in managerial judgeship.[11]

THE MOST BEAUTIFUL TRIAL THAT YOU CAN PRESIDE OVER

The U.S. Department of Justice's Antitrust Division opened its investigation of the cardboard box industry in late 1975.[12] The prosecutors convened a grand jury in July 1976 in Houston, where Judge Singleton presided over the deliberations. The consolidated, multidistrict, class-action, antitrust civil suit, *In re Corrugated Container Antitrust Litigation,* grew out of the criminal investigation. Singleton attempted to streamline the case from the very beginning. He encouraged the litigants to negotiate, reminding them that the best strategy for resolving highly complex suits was to settle, "whenever possible, as soon as possible."[13]

The judge's enthusiasm for pretrial dealing did not emerge solely or even principally from his concern for saving litigants' time and money, but rather from his hope that settlement would save him the time and trouble that would be consumed by his having to try the larger case. Singleton, like other federal judges in the Southern District of Texas and elsewhere in the nation, faced a tremendous and constant backlog of cases. U.S. District Judge Hubert L. Will of the Northern District of Illinois advised his newly appointed colleagues attending a 1976 training seminar, for example, that a full-blown trial was a "last resort resolution of a controversy." Judge Will suggested instead that they adopt procedures to "maximize the possibilities of settlement," because "it is the rare case in which there isn't justice in some degree on both sides, and most cases, therefore, are better disposed of, in terms of highest quality of justice, by a negotiated—freely negotiated—settlement, than by the most beautiful trial that you can preside over."[14]

The federal courts of appeal, moreover, maintained that, as long as the results were fair, reasonable, and adequate, it lay within the discretion of the district judge to promote settlements in the legitimate interest of "judicial economy." The prevailing view of the federal judiciary supported Singleton's later assertion in the cardboard box case that the "compromise of complex litigation is favored both by strong judicial policy and public policy."[15]

In addition to the caseload pressure, other, more immediate concerns motivated Singleton to promote early resolution of the cardboard box case. As the criminal case concluded and the parties focused their attentions on the civil suit, the federal judiciary entered a period of institutional growth after the passage of the Omnibus Judgeship Act of 1978. One result of these changes, of course, was that Singleton became chief judge of a much-expanded Southern District in 1979, after Chief Judge Garza was appointed to the Fifth Circuit Court of Appeals. The longer the cardboard box suit continued, the more its demands distracted his attention from his overloaded docket and the responsibilities of his new post. He was therefore especially anxious to drive the litigation to its conclusion. He was generally successful: all but one of the thirty-seven defendants were able to "buy peace" from the plaintiffs by the summer of 1980.[16]

The government's prosecution strategy in the criminal cases complicated Singleton's efforts to settle the civil lawsuits. To obtain key evidence, for example, the justice department investigators sought to compel industry insiders to testify before the grand jury. At the government's request Singleton granted a handful of key witnesses limited "use" immunity.[17] Thereafter, during an eighteen-month inquiry grand jurors heard testimony from nearly one hundred witnesses, the majority of whom were not immunized against future prosecution, and examined or read excerpts from approximately one hundred depositions. Much of the evidence seemed to indicate that plant managers and regional representatives from competing container companies frequently compared and discussed prices.[18]

The grand jury finally issued two indictments—one listing felony charges and one listing alleged misdemeanor violations—on 25 January 1978. It named fourteen corrugated and sheet cardboard manufacturers and twenty-six present or former executives of these implicated companies as conspirators. The indictments alleged that their conspiracy had begun as early as 1960 and had continued to the present. Because the Congress had upgraded violations of the Sherman Antitrust Act's price-fixing provisions, from misdemeanors to felonies, in a statutory change that had become effective 1 January 1975, the prosecutors sought the dual indictments in order to include appropriate charges over the entire span of years.[19]

The indictments alleged that several of the industry's largest manufacturers, including Mead Corporation, International Paper, and the Weyerhaeuser Company, had disclosed to one another the prices to be charged or quoted for their products, and therefore "various buyers of corrugated containers and corrugated sheets have been deprived of free and open competition." A spokesperson for the justice department noted that, in terms of the business volume controlled by the companies charged with criminal violations, these combined cases represented the largest antitrust action in the Antitrust Division's history.[20]

Months before the grand jury issued the indictments, however, rumors of the government's action in convening a grand jury spawned dozens of civil lawsuits, each alleging substantially the same behavior described in the criminal indictments. The civil suits collectively named more than three dozen cardboard box manufacturers. The civil litigation began when the Adams Extract Company of Austin, Texas, perhaps best known as a maker of flavoring agents such as vanilla extract, filed a federal civil action on 7 March 1977. The Adams Extract suit—the first of fifty-five separate civil actions eventually filed by corrugated cardboard customers—charged the suppliers of its cardboard boxes with conspiring to fix prices.[21] At the request of the lawyers, these fifty-five suits against various box makers were consolidated in Houston by the Judicial Panel on Multi-district Litigation.[22]

On 6 December 1977, one week after the consolidation, Singleton directed the dozens of plaintiffs' attorneys to form a steering committee that could commence negotiations to settle out of court with the defendants.[23] The attorneys elected Stephen D. Susman, a Houstonian who initially represented Adams Extract, to chair the steering committee. Because the goal of the committee was to create a "favorable psychological climate," Susman announced, it would be offering "discounts" to early settlers.[24]

The plaintiffs therefore indicated that the defendants could save themselves time, trouble, and money, by coming to terms sooner rather than later. This negotiating strategy yielded its first results during the summer of 1978, when the steering committee settled with the St. Regis Paper Corporation, a company that had not been indicted in the criminal case. St. Regis agreed to "buy peace" from the plaintiffs for $1.7 million, which represented approximately $428,000 for each percentage point of its estimated share of the cardboard box market. To emphasize the attraction of a quick settlement, the plaintiffs demanded successively higher rates in later agreements, eventually up to ten times the initial per point multiplier. For example, the International Paper Company—only the second defendant to settle—paid more than twice St. Regis's rate. International pleaded nolo contendere ("no contest") to the felony charge, and Singleton fined the company $617,000. International then agreed to pay the civil plaintiffs $8.3 million, or $1 million per point.[25]

The plaintiffs' committee negotiated from these "per point" demands because, although they had access to some important public documents, including the two criminal indictments, and to general financial data, such as estimated market share, they relied on little more than an educated guess regarding the probable extent of a particular defendant's actual liability. During the settlement negotiations the plaintiffs usually requested the settling defendant's continued cooperation during civil discovery, a condition to which both St. Regis and International agreed.[26] The committee had requested transcripts of grand jury testimony, a potentially valuable source of information, but the judge refused to release these while the criminal suit was pending. Singleton recognized that the needs of general discovery were insufficient justification for violating the customary secrecy of grand jury proceedings.[27] The committee expected to engage the more orthodox mechanisms of discovery after the criminal trial, which was scheduled to commence in January 1979.[28]

In the meantime, the plaintiffs' steering committee requested that Singleton certify their consolidated litigation as a class action. The committee intended to present a unified front during their negotiations. However, because the plaintiffs included so many sizes and kinds of cardboard consumers (as a group, they ranged from equipment manufacturers to "mom and pop" grocers), they lacked the necessary solidarity. In July 1978 a group of cardboard "sheet" purchasers, who had only recently consolidated with the original plaintiffs, filed a request for their own separate class certification. They argued that the first group of plaintiffs did not encompass all consumers of corrugated cardboard, but only those who purchased finished containers. The sheet purchasers doubted container buyers could represent them during negotiations.[29] Singleton believed that the parallel negotiations would lead to duplication of effort. On 6 September, therefore, he certified as the plaintiff class all persons in the United States who had purchased corrugated containers from any of the defendants between 1 January 1960 and 25 January 1978.[30]

One month after certification of a single class, the sheet purchasers tried once again to distinguish their interests from the larger group of container consumers. They asked the judge to clarify the class definition and requested that he either make their relationship to the class more explicit, if they were excluded, or create a subclass of sheet purchasers within the overall class, if they were not.[31] Singleton believed that "although differences may exist between the sheet plants and other corrugated purchasers, there are no inherent conflicts between them."[32] He agreed to this second request because he did not consider himself familiar enough with the cardboard industry to second-guess the sheet purchasers if they were determined to maintain a separate identity. On 26 December, Singleton reluctantly divided the plaintiffs into subclasses, the first composed of sheet purchasers and the second including all other consumers of corrugated products.[33]

After creating the subclasses Singleton designated several companies and their attorneys to be the representatives of each. The original unitary steering committee had already agreed to settle with twenty-four of the defendants for damages totaling more than $300 million. In December 1978 the committee had reached seven additional agreements, including five deals with unindicted defendants in which settlements had ranged from $2 million to $2.75 million per market point. The plaintiffs also convinced a misdemeanor indictee to pay $3.5 million per point, for example, and a felony indictee to settle for $4.5 million per point.[34]

The new representatives declared a moratorium on settlement negotiations, to last through the several weeks following Christmas 1978, to take stock of these agreements and to recast separate strategies. When the plaintiffs' representatives resumed the negotiations on 5 January 1979, they did so strictly on behalf of their subclasses. As Singleton had dreaded, the defendants had difficulties negotiating in parallel, and the discussions initially broke down. Within a few weeks the subclasses compromised in the interest of reviving the process. The container subclass allowed the sheet subclass to reserve the option either to enter agreements jointly with them, and share a designated portion of the settlement proceeds, or to opt out, accept nothing, and proceed to trial with that defendant. The defendants accepted the arrangement because it provided at least the possibility that they could settle claims of both subclasses in one negotiation. Negotiations got back on track under this new scheme, and the plaintiffs reached additional settlements. Eleven defendants paid between $1.5 million and $4 million per point of market share. However, two other companies that were willing to settle declared that they were at "borderline insolvency." After seeing the auditors' reports, the plaintiffs agreed to accept lower rates from these defendants.[35]

Throughout these joint negotiations, some individual companies, members of the sheet purchaser subclass, maintained their opposition to the two dozen deals made before their separation from the larger plaintiffs' class. They considered the deals to be illegitimate because they were negotiated without access to data or sworn testimony, and as a result were more a matter of blind faith than of hard fact. In addition, the sheet purchasers felt that offering per-point discounts to the earliest defendants, without regard to actual liability, had been misguided and had reduced the plaintiffs' overall recovery. More important, they believed the per-point rates negotiated before division into subclasses did not reflect the fraction of market share consisting of sheet sales. For example, in settling so cheaply with St. Regis, which was not a large manufacturer of containers, the committee did not take into account the fact that the firm was the nation's third largest producer of corrugated sheets. On these grounds, the sheet buyers argued, the discounted early settlements were inadequate to cover the damages caused specifically to sheet purchasers.[36] Notwithstanding these individual objections, on 16 April 1979 the class representatives filed a motion requesting preliminary approval of the settlements.[37]

Singleton chose to wait until the criminal trial, in which he also was presiding, concluded before he acted on the request for approval. In the criminal proceedings, as in the civil case, there was a premium on avoiding trial. Seven defendant companies and three executives had quickly pleaded "no contest" to charges of felony price fixing. Five companies and fifteen individuals pleaded guilty to misdemeanor violations of the antitrust laws. The remaining defendants—the Mead Corporation, a second company, and six individuals—pleaded not guilty to felony price-fixing, alleged grand jury abuse by the Justice Department, and moved to dismiss the criminal charges.[38] The defendants claimed that the coercive interviews with the reluctant witnesses exhibited the "trappings" of grand jury proceedings—in that they featured subpoenas, immunity offers, and sworn testimony—even though the interviews took place outside the presence of grand jurors. And because witnesses' attorneys and government investigators *were* present, the defendants argued the interviews violated the prohibition against unauthorized persons' hearing grand jury testimony. The defendants further argued that interviews that were summarized before the grand jurors by an investigator should have been presented as full transcripts instead. Finally, because the government offered immunity only for information that promised to lead investigators into "new fields," the defendants believed that the fear of indictment may have led some witnesses to color their testimony in order to receive immunity.[39] On 7 July 1978 the judge held that none of these alleged facts were grounds for dismissal. Singleton denied the motion and set the case for trial.[40] The trial lasted three months, but the six-woman, six-man jury deliberated just three and one-half hours before it acquitted all felony defendants on 27 April 1979.[41]

One month later, on 30 May, Singleton turned his attention back to the civil case. He declared that because the proposed agreements were "within the range of possible approval . . . notification of them should be given to the class members."[42] On 1 August, he also rejected the objections to the earliest settlements. He granted preliminary approval to the plaintiffs' motions to dismiss the class actions against the settling defendants.[43] At the judge's direction, the plaintiffs sent approval notices to three hundred thousand potential members of their class, stating the nature of the claim and the options regarding participation in settlement.[44] Singleton conducted hearings to consider whether he should "finally" approve the initial settlements, now that thousands of class members around the country were aware of their provisions. He announced he found the agreements to be fair, adequate, and reasonable, and therefore granted his approval on 21 December.[45]

The plaintiffs were motivated just as much by economic concerns as were the defendants, and all parties eventually came to realize that peace might be bought and sold more cheaply than justice.[46] The three dozen box makers who had agreed to settle with the plaintiffs' committee had continued to maintain their innocence, but, because they also sought to avoid the uncertainties, delays, and expenses of a jury trial, they agreed to pay into a plaintiffs' damages fund. With the accumulated interest the plaintiffs' nest egg eventually totaled several hundred million dollars. Even so, some individual plaintiffs were dissatisfied, and it came as no surprise when these dissenters appealed; they argued that the judge could not have examined the earliest settlements in any meaningful way, because they were based on the steering committee's guesses and compromises. Singleton, they said, could only accept the committee's word that it had protected all interests equally. Moreover, they noted that the judge's "justification" for his decision consisted of bland restatements of the basic legal questions, simply "boiler-plate."[47] Proponents of the settlements suggested that, given Singleton's familiarity with the case, by then extending four years, his ruling was no doubt well reasoned, but the rationale, literally, went without saying.[48]

Considering the long list of motions on which the judge ruled, and the deep pool of potential critics, appeals were to be expected. But Singleton—given his commitment to the goal of maximizing judicial economy—must have been extremely frustrated when a unanimous panel of three judges from the Fifth Circuit agreed with the appellants that he rushed to judgment, rebuked him, and remanded his ruling. On 3 April 1981 Circuit Judge Tjoflat, for a unanimous panel of three Fifth Circuit judges, remanded Singleton's approval of the early settlements. Their wide-ranging decision rebuked both the judge and the appellants. On the one hand, in answer to the various appellants' complaints regarding the supposed flaws in the settlement process, the judges held that there was no evidence of conflict of interest among negotiators, that an absence of presettlement discovery alone did not invalidate the agreements, that a district judge could release a defendant from state antitrust claims, that an allegedly defective notice of a settlement did not moot the settlement itself, and that it was proper for the judge to consider the settlements even though his ruling regarding cross-claims and contribution were on appeal. The opinion therefore generally vetted the integrity of the process as it had been managed by Singleton. The circuit judges noted that the appellate courts had only a limited function in questioning the validity of class action settlements approved by a district judge, especially "in light of the strong judicial policy favoring settlement of disputes."[49] On the other hand, the circuit judges agreed with the appellants that the approval order was flawed, because the judge's rationale for the approval was missing. Even the limited role they had was impossible to play without Singleton's justification.

The single complaint from the dissenting plaintiffs with which the appeals judges felt compelled to agree was that Singleton apparently ruled on the early settlements without taking the necessary deliberations. Agreement on that single point was not sufficient to invalidate the ruling outright. However, absent the rationale, it was possible to declare that Singleton's order was incomplete. Although the judges admitted they were reluctant to delay the resolution of the case any further, they remanded the approval. In essence, they directed Singleton to provide them with the detailed results of a thought experiment, and they put the judge on notice that he would be given no credit for doing the work in his head.[50] The appellate judges stated that although none of the appellants' arguments persuaded them that agreements should be set aside, the panel members were nonetheless "in agreement with certain objectors that the district court's findings are insufficiently detailed to allow us to determine whether the district court abused its discretion in concluding that the terms of the settlements . . . are fair, reasonable, and adequate." The circuit judges shared Singleton's taste for compromise. But they rejected his order on the grounds that Singleton did not demonstrate to their satisfaction that he had rendered his pragmatic decisions only after sufficient mental struggle—in short, the circuit refused to "grade" Singleton's homework until he documented the reasoning that led him either to grant or deny the settlement.[51]

The heart of the remand was the circuit judges' description of the simple, three-step thought process that an ideal district judge would employ to evaluate settlements. First, the judge was to establish the range of the plaintiff's possible recovery in a full-dress trial. Then, the judge was to consider, on the basis of an evaluation of the apparent strength of the plaintiff's evidence, the likelihood of prevailing in such a trial. Clearly, the judge could determine whether a proposed settlement was fair, adequate, and reasonable, from the standpoint of a plaintiff, only after completing the first two steps. The fairness of an actual, proposed settlement could be weighed only if the judge had constructed a hypothetical settlement and placed it on the second pan of the judicial assayer's balance. Each step was, quite literally, a "judgment call," which required the district judge to exercise discretionary powers to speculate. But it was a necessary part of the judicial function.[52]

On 4 June 1981 Singleton filed additional findings of fact and conclusions of law, in which he described in detail how he came to his conclusion that the settlements were fair, adequate, and reasonable.[53] The Fifth Circuit declared themselves to be satisfied with the effort and affirmed his approval of the settlements on 29 October 1981.[54] Of course, that affirmation only applied to the initial twenty-four settlements. The second dozen required Singleton's imprimatur as well, and by this time he apparently expected to be continually second-guessed by the plaintiffs, if not by appellate judges. When the plaintiffs placed the next several proposals before him, he approved them just as readily, but he provided short summaries of the financial arrangements that led him to believe the assessments were fair, adequate, and reasonable.[55]

The first defendant to be considered in this group, Southwest Forest Industries (SFI), had not been indicted for any criminal antitrust violations but now paid a substantial premium to settle. The firm's business accounted for less than 1.5 percent of the total sales of the civil defendants, but it settled for $2,925,000, that is, about $2,000,000 per point of market share. This total included an October 1979 deal with the container subclass for $2,490,000, and another with the sheet subclass in May 1980, for $435,000. The deals were concluded after the plaintiffs used discovery to obtain twenty depositions from key current and former SFI employees, which Singleton described as an "extensive record."[56]

The next defendant, Packaging Corporation of America (PCA), presented a more difficult case, because the evidence the plaintiffs obtained through discovery, records as well as ten depositions, was mixed. If there was a conspiracy to violate antitrust laws, it varied from one fabrication plant to another. One individual admitted to participating in price fixing. The others convincingly denied the allegation. PCA was also investigated but not indicted by the grand jury. When the plaintiffs realized they faced a substantial challenge to prove wrongdoing in court, they decided a settlement would be preferable. The judge noted in his approval notice that the total $8 million PCA agreed to pay was the largest of the postacquittal group, that is, it came after the initial twenty-four settlements, and represented 14.3 percent of PCA's total *profits* between 1973 and 1975. Unlike the SFI deal, the PCA settlement was not divided into portions for each subclass. According to Singleton, the agreement came after "several months of hard, arms-length bargaining," during which "[b]oth sides were forced to move away from their original positions."[57]

Three of the settling defendants, the Georgia-Pacific, Fibreboard, and Potlatch Corporations, were in a category by themselves. Only Georgia-Pacific was named as a potential target of the government's original investigation, but it was not charged. Not only did the grand jury not indict them; it never subpoenaed any of their employees, and it did not place any of the three on the list of unindicted coconspirators in the bill of particulars accompanying the criminal indictments. Nevertheless, the plaintiffs subsequently filed suit against the three. During civil discovery the companies willingly opened their files and made their employees available for depositions. No employee from these defendant firms ever asserted the Fifth Amendment, and many would agree to act as witnesses at the civil trial. Consistently, the employees denied ever communicating their pricing policies to competitors. In fact, according to the evidence of millions of pages of documents and the testimony of dozens of witnesses, none of these companies seems to have participated in the alleged conspiracy in any capacity whatsoever. Therefore, a few months before the beginning of the civil trial on 2 April 1980, the whole plaintiffs' class, not the subclasses separately, agreed to settle jointly with these three companies, for a sum of $3 million.[58]

In his summary Singleton wrote that there were three benefits to settling with these firms, besides the obvious, which was the probability that the plaintiffs would lose the case at trial. First, removing three more names simplified the case to be made before the jury. Second, the evidence against these firms was so weak, if not actually nonexistent, that their being at the trial might even be detrimental. Third, and most immediately significant, the defendant firms agreed to the immediate release of $187,500. This cash infusion came at a crucial juncture. The plaintiffs' "trial preparation costs were mounting rapidly."[59]

The next two settlements Singleton examined were finalized with the defendants that dropped out of the civil trial. It is odd that Alton Box Board was among the last to settle, because the firm was willing to buy peace from the earliest days of the litigation. Alton pleaded nolo to the criminal charge, paid a fine of $143,000, and had entered negotiations with the plaintiffs during the summer of 1979. Discussions dragged on for a full year, because Alton claimed financial hardship and was angling for a discount. The plaintiffs waited to consummate the deal until an outside accounting firm completed an audit, and until key evidence had been introduced at trial. The accountant (Price, Waterhouse) concluded that Alton was suffering financially. On 11 July 1980, after the trial had gone on for six weeks, Alton agreed to pay a total of $5.4 million in three annual installments. This was a discount, but it still equaled Alton's combined profits after taxes for the years 1977 to 1979. It represented $1.9 million per point of market share.[60] Predictably, Singleton listed enhanced discovery as a key benefit of this settlement, because Alton agreed for the first time to cooperate with the plaintiffs' efforts. Also, Alton agreed to cease cooperating with the defense in the civil trial. The settlement also included yet another cash windfall, an immediate payment of $920,000 to reimburse costs.

Finally, the judge believed that halfway into the trial, a positive outcome remained in doubt, even if the plaintiffs prevailed. Given Alton's "weakened financial condition," a large liability judgment might simply drive the losing defendant into bankruptcy.[61]

Westvaco Corporation also waited until the last moment to settle for $975,000. The company dropped out after twelve weeks of trial, one day before Mead rested its case in defense, and before Westvaco presented its own defense. Singleton noted that he faced a unique situation in considering this approval, because all the plaintiffs' evidence against Westvaco was out in the open prior to the deal. He had information enough to assess the strength of a case against the defendant. He did not regard the evidence as particularly solid; in fact, the judge declared that the plaintiffs' chances of recovering against Westvaco were "remote." The plaintiffs' witnesses had undercut their case by providing exculpatory evidence concerning Westvaco's participation in a price-rigging conspiracy. Singleton saw the defense's case as stronger. Considering this, and the fact that hard bargaining brought the settlement up from the low figure Westvaco offered to open negotiations, Singleton had few qualms about the deal.[62]

Singleton's summaries document the working dynamics between the plaintiffs and the defendants, but his assessments did not conform exactly to the three-step plan enumerated by the circuit. That ideal model was difficult to build in an actual case, where evidence was messy. But Singleton's assessments, impressionistic renderings more often than logical constructions, revealed the basic outlines of his thought processes, which provided the critical piece missing from the earlier approvals. Overall, they did not prove much about the adequacy of the settlements, but they did reinforce the image of Singleton as pragmatist. The judge's assessments were abstracts, not detailed accounting reports. In fact, he rarely went so far as to take the first step, and he skipped evaluating the possible range of recovery. He started with the second step, assessing the likelihood of the plaintiffs' prevailing in a trial. When he attempted to guess the future, Singleton often declared that the plaintiffs' prospects ranged from dim to dismal. And in the third step, the judge seemed merely to conclude that any settlement was fair, reasonable, and adequate, if the plaintiffs' case was a loser. Although Singleton seemed to take the circuit's rebuke seriously, he tended to end up where he began, maintaining the position that, as long as the parties agreed to it, it was fine with him. On 17 May 1982 he filed the opinion approving the settlements.[63]

Singleton completed the drill the circuit judges assigned to him, and they subsequently upheld the rulings. But his order approving the twenty-four earliest agreements did not mark the end of the case. In the interim between the criminal and civil trials, negotiations with another dozen defendants were underway or completed. If the parties reached settlement, the terms would require the judge's preliminary, and then final, approval. In early 1980, however, talks broke down and many of the negotiations required Judge Singleton's intervention instead. The discovery efforts proved to be less fruitful than the steering committee had hoped, and discovery stalled when a number of witnesses, including several who had accepted "use" immunity as the price of an appearance before the grand jury, asserted Fifth Amendment privileges against self-incrimination in the conference room. The confrontations over discovery and evidence that occurred after the criminal trial demonstrated the limits of federal judicial power.

Philip Fleischacker, Charles J. Franey, and Alex Hopkins were all employees of defendant companies during the period of the alleged price-fixing conspiracy. Hopkins and Fleischacker both testified before the grand jury under "use" immunity. Franey was neither subpoenaed nor immunized, but submitted to an interview with Justice Department investigators in exchange for a letter promising that no information he revealed would be used against him in any criminal action; effectively, it was an informal immunity grant. The government transcribed the interview and presented it to the grand jury. During the criminal trial the Justice Department obtained orders granting Franey and Hopkins "use" immunity, and they testified for the prosecution.[64]

At the conclusion of the trial the civil plaintiffs' steering committee subpoenaed a number of witnesses from the criminal proceedings, including Fleischacker, Franey, and Hopkins. On 22 January 1980, while being deposed in New York City, Fleischacker asserted his Fifth Amendment privileges rather than respond to questions regarding knowledge of or participation in the alleged conspiracy. A week after Fleischacker took the Fifth, Hopkins claimed the same privilege in Houston.[65] Confronted with the real possibility that a wall of silence might block the suit's steady progress toward ultimate resolution, Singleton reconsidered his earlier refusal to open materials from the grand jury investigation. In a pair of orders he issued after Fleischacker refused to testify, the judge released the transcripts of the grand jury testimony given by 135 witnesses.[66]

When Franey refused to answer the questions posed to him in Houston on 4 March, the plaintiffs obtained a court order from Singleton compelling him to testify. Franey appeared for the deposition in open court the next day. By then, the plaintiffs' attorneys could depose the witness with the aid of questions and answers either taken verbatim or derived from his own grand jury testimony. As Singleton explained, the privilege against self-incrimination was no longer available to Franey, because he did not face criminal sanctions based on the immunized testimony, and his present answers were so clearly derived or closely related to that testimony as "to be thoroughly tainted and inadmissible against him in any conceivable future prosecution."[67] Nonetheless, Franey once again invoked the Fifth Amendment in the face of the plaintiffs' questions. When he refused to answer after being directly ordered to do so, the judge declared the witness to be in contempt, sentenced him to sixty days in prison and fined him five thousand dollars.[68]

The steering committee—apparently reinvigorated by the courtroom drama—obtained new subpoenas for Fleischacker and Hopkins. The witnesses, now confronted not only with their own transcribed testimony, but also with an impatient Judge Singleton, persisted in asserting the Fifth Amendment privilege. On 10 March, Singleton presided by speakerphone over Fleischacker's deposition in New York. Then, on 19 March, the judge presided in person over Hopkins's questioning. In both instances, these sessions simply echoed Franey's experience: upon their refusal to answer, Singleton found the witnesses in civil contempt.[69] Rather than disputing the judge's interpretation of his immunity grant, Fleischacker appealed the contempt citation on the basis of the fact that he was not a resident of the Southern District of Texas. He asserted that Singleton lacked jurisdiction either to preside over his deposition or to order him to answer the plaintiffs' questions, and argued that these facts rendered invalid the contempt citation that resulted.[70]

Although the judges of the Fifth Circuit agreed with Singleton insofar as he claimed the purpose of the multidistrict statute was to streamline litigation, and the statute authorized him temporarily to act as a judge in another district, the appeals judges supported Fleischacker regarding jurisdiction. In this specific case Singleton's orders under the statute conflicted with a strong court policy minimizing inconvenience, particularly to a nonparty witness, as Fleischacker was in the civil suit. The judges noted in particular the procedural rule that a recalcitrant witness could be sanctioned only in the district where a deposition was taken.[71] Given this rule, Singleton's order to answer was probably invalid, as was the contempt citation. On 19 June, Fifth Circuit Judge Tjoflat concluded that, for the same reasons Singleton could not rule as he had, the Fifth Circuit also lacked jurisdiction to hear the appeal of those orders.[72]

The judges of the Fifth Circuit suggested that Fleischacker direct his appeal to the judges of the Second Circuit, who then accepted jurisdiction without commenting on the correctness of the other circuit's ruling regarding procedure.[73] In an opinion delivered on 2 March 1981, Circuit Judge Meskill for the court affirmed Singleton's power to compel Fleischacker's testimony over his Fifth Amendment invocations and remanded the case back to the Southern District of Texas, where it would proceed. But the circuit judges vacated Fleischacker's contempt citation, on the grounds that Singleton had occasionally allowed the plaintiffs' counsel to pose questions during deposition that were overbroad and encompassed matters well outside the text of the grand jury transcript. In these instances assertion of Fifth Amendment privilege was only appropriate.[74]

Hopkins and Franey fared much better with their appeal, which the Fifth Circuit retained under its jurisdiction. Circuit Judge Tjoflat held for the court that

Singleton had only asserted, not established, that the witnesses were safe from further prosecution. As examples, they stated that no one had shown in court that all the applicable criminal statutes had run, and they noted that a federal court in Ohio had undertaken its own investigation of the corrugated container industry.[75] The circuit judges rejected Singleton's reasoning that any testimony the witnesses gave in his court proceedings would be "tainted" by their immunized grand jury testimony, because it was guided by the transcript thereof. Any legal effect of this "taint" would have to be established by a hearing in a future criminal case, the judges reasoned, and could not be predetermined by Singleton; therefore, Franey and Hopkins had correctly asserted their rights by taking the Fifth.[76] The judges added, moreover, that in trying to compel them to testify, Singleton was attempting unilaterally to establish immunity that he lacked authority to grant. Therefore, holding that Singleton lacked power to issue those orders, the judges vacated them.[77] The split decisions in the bifurcated appeals demonstrated how the circuits remained divided on the issue of judicial power, and future decisions continued the pattern.

John A. Conboy, a former employee of the Weyerhaeuser Company, was at the center of the next case to ask the question whether Singleton could compel a previously immunized witness to testify, and in many ways that case was a replay of the Fleischacker case. But in the end it resembled Hopkins's and Franey's cases. The judge granted Conboy immunity to testify before the grand jury in January 1978, only a few weeks before the panel issued the criminal indictments. On 20 May 1981 the plaintiffs attempted to depose him with the aid of a transcript of his grand jury testimony, and he asserted his privileges under the Fifth Amendment. Conboy was a resident of Illinois at the time the plaintiffs subpoenaed him, and as soon as he balked, the plaintiffs' counsel called to obtain a ruling from Singleton, who then ordered the witness to answer and found him in contempt for refusing, all by long-distance telephone.[78] The trajectory of events was similar to Fleischacker's appeal. On 17 July 1981 Senior Seventh Circuit Judge Swygert affirmed Singleton's power to compel Conboy to testify.[79]

On rehearing by the Seventh Circuit, however, Conboy's case took on the character of the appeal by Franey and Hopkins. Circuit Judge Sprecher, who dissented in the first opinion, now spoke for the majority and reversed the earlier ruling. On 16 October 1981 he held for the court that Singleton could only speculate, not dictate, that a witness was safe from future prosecution. In essence Sprecher declared there were too many uncertainties in the law to discount the possibility that Conboy might face a criminal trial. The Seventh Circuit then vacated Singleton's order, closely following the reasoning of the Fifth Circuit.[80] But the appeals of the recalcitrant witnesses resulted in conflicting decisions across circuits. The U.S. Supreme Court agreed to consider the issue.[81]

In the course of the corrugated container litigation, Singleton saw several of his orders appealed and remanded or vacated. The judge's ego was probably not as severely assaulted by these outcomes as was his sense of "judicial economy." The circuits affirmed many of his decisions as well, but awaiting even a positive outcome on appeal delayed final resolution of the case. For example, on 14 January 1982 the Fifth Circuit remanded his orders to release additional grand jury transcripts to "assist" witnesses in recalling their long ago testimony, so that he could "rebalance" the need for disclosure against the need for grand jury secrecy. The remand was based on the fact that the plaintiffs had learned much information since the original orders two years earlier, and it might not be necessary to release the new transcripts.[82] On remand Singleton rebalanced and decided that the need for additional discovery still outweighed the court's interest in secrecy. The Fifth Circuit affirmed his decision on 13 September.[83]

Before the civil trial commenced, the steering committee experienced major upheaval. Steve Susman, who had done so much to make the settlements possible, himself disputed the division of legal fees among the partners of his employer, the law firm Mandell and Wright. Susman argued that as the leader of the plaintiff's legal team, he worked harder on the case and deserved a greater share of its rewards. Susman eventually left Mandell & Wright to found his own firm, Susman, Godfrey, and McGowan, and he invited veterans of the ongoing corrugated container litigation to be his partners.[84]

On 9 June 1980, the plaintiffs' case finally proceeded against the three remaining nonsettling defendants. Two of the three, Alton and Westvaco, settled after the trial started. The Mead Company stood alone, the only defendant in the protracted civil suit to proceed to judgment rather than agree to settlement.[85] On 13 September the company was not rewarded for its perseverance: the jury decided that Mead and eighteen other companies had conspired to raise and to maintain the price of corrugated cardboard sheets and containers at approximately 5 percent above their fair market value. The jury further held that during Mead's participation in the conspiracy, which began sometime before 1 January 1964 and continued at least until 31 December 1975, the conspirators had bilked their unwary customers of at least $350 million.[86] Because every other company had settled before the trial, and Singleton had already ruled that defendants could not file cross-claims, Mead alone was liable for the full sum of damages.[87] Under the treble damage provisions of the Clayton Act, these could exceed $1 billion.[88] Damages did not automatically treble, however, and it was not within the jury's purview to decide this liability; that decision lay within the judge's discretion.[89]

As he entered this next phase of the litigation, the judge arranged for continued support. The Administrative Office had, at Singleton's request in February 1978, authorized his hiring an extra law clerk and secretary to assist him in the consolidated case management. In October 1980, as the settlement meetings were under way, he wrote to request an extension of this authorization.[90] Then, over Mead's objections, Singleton on 27 January 1981 gave oversight of the next phase of the case to a special master.[91] The accounting analysis of Mead's liability was beyond Singleton's expertise, and the *Manual for Complex Litigation,* a publication he referred to fairly often throughout the trial, recommended the use of a master to untangle especially complicated fact-dependent questions. A master relieved a judge of the onerous duty of crunching numbers.[92] Singleton directed the special master to conduct the postverdict proceedings, gather evidence, and establish the monetary figure to which the 5 percent overcharge could be applied.[93] The special master served Singleton much as the steering committee had served the plaintiffs, that is, as the mediator of settlement. The difference was that Mead, unlike earlier settlers, appeared to have few remaining alternatives to submission.[94]

The master conducted hearings from March 1981 through August 1982 and collected detailed financial data on Mead's corrugated-product sales. With the plaintiffs' assistance he assembled evidence of purchases made by 160,000 class members during the thirty-three-month period between early 1973 and late 1975. An additional proceeding was to be scheduled by the special master when the settlement was reached. Within a matter of months, he would make this information available in the final report.[95] On 14 September 1982 the plaintiffs agreed to settle with Mead, and the master's discovery process abruptly ended. Under the terms of the proposed agreement, the Mead Company agreed to pay $45 million, plus the accumulated interest on that principal sum accruing at 9.5 percent. Mead would pay in installments over six years, beginning 1 October 1982.[96] The Mead settlement was larger, both in total dollars and in dollars per point of market share, than that paid by any other defendant.[97]

If Singleton approved the deal, he would be taking steps toward concluding the corrugated container class-action litigation.[98] The judge gave preliminary approval to the settlement at a hearing on 14 September, where he heard no objections. Three days later, Singleton ordered that the plaintiffs notify class members of the terms.[99] Singleton voiced his own concerns about continuing the litigation until the master established an "objective" settlement. One was the risk of reversal, especially on matters of evidence and testimony. He had presided over innovations, and his orders had been appealed. The Supreme Court might overturn his rulings on the matter of self-incrimination.[100] Another concern was reform and rumors of reform in the controversial realm of antitrust legislation. Congress was at the time considering several bills that might have changed the rules of plaintiffs' recovery, cross-claims, contribution, and other key tools.[101] If any of these parameters changed while the case was open, the cause of resolution might suffer a major setback.

Although for some reason no plaintiffs raised the issue, Singleton realized that there might be questions in the future about a settlement that let Mead off the hook for 5 percent of the potential treble damages. In ruling on this, Singleton came the closest yet to constructing the ideal model of a settlement justification. He recalled that the jury in the civil trial had estimated a range of damages between $300 million and $400 million, and the treble recovery would then be $900 million to $1.2 billion. The recovery might be less if Congress acted soon: one of the pending bills would allow claims against a settlement. The fund the corrugated container defendants paid into, with accumulated interest, was approaching $700 million, the level of the treble damages. In that case, Mead's liability would be diluted by the huge fund already paid by the entire group of settling defendants, to about the level it settled. Another law might reduce Mead's payment to triple its true share of the damages. If so, Mead's liability would be the industry's ill-gotten profits of $300 million, multiplied by the 5 percent overcharge the jury had found, and then trebled. That would be $45 million, the amount of the settlement, again. In short, Singleton believed the settlement to be fair, reasonable, and adequate. He granted a motion to enter the final judgment approving all of the settlements on 30 November 1982.[102]

By separate order Singleton entered a final judgment to dismiss all claims and close the action, except that he retained jurisdiction for the purpose of directing the distribution of the settlement fund.[103] He now turned his attention to assessing who actually deserved a share of the very large pie the plaintiffs accumulated.[104] The lawyers were first in line. During the five years of litigation, thirty-nine law firms represented some nine thousand box buyers, and at settlement these firms claimed approximately $50 million of the $500 million, plus interest, that the defendant companies had placed in the settlement fund. Susman, the lead lawyer for the plaintiffs, claimed the largest share of this sum; he requested $8 million for his firm, which included for himself $4 million, or approximately $800 per hour for work on the case. The cardboard box buyers believed their legal bill to be excessive, even "obscene," especially given the fact that the largest share to be taken by any plaintiff company was $15 million. Susman received a great deal of personal criticism, both from his clients and from attorneys for his opponents.[105]

Twenty-seven of the largest plaintiff firms, including General Motors and Beatrice Foods, were also among those standing to gain the most from the settlement. They hired a Dallas law firm to sift through Susman's records for evidence of overcharges. Clients were not pleased to find that he billed the $800 hourly rate "just for talking to congressmen on Capitol Hill." Thomas Long, the general counsel for Westvaco, agreed that Susman had charged a high hourly rate and declared, "I wouldn't pay him that." Another opponent lawyer noted that Susman had had his senior partners "running around doing work that less expensive associates could have done." A plaintiffs' attorney from Kansas City who worked alongside

Susman's firm—and whose firm stood to receive $2 million—countered that Susman kept a tight rein on expenses and apportioned the work among various firms to prevent duplication of effort. Susman defended himself by noting the hardship of the long hours he and the other attorneys had logged during the five years leading to settlement, risking both family tranquility and professional stability. He argued that his clients should consider it "the greatest thing on earth" that he and his colleagues had been willing to work for only 10 percent of the settlement, because lawyers' contingency fees were usually much higher.[106]

Two lawyers for the defendants—former U.S. Attorneys General Griffin B. Bell and Benjamin Civiletti—subsequently lobbied the Congress to limit damage awards in antitrust cases, encouraging lawmakers to enact the legislation to which Judge Singleton had referred in his final opinion. Susman soon became their whipping boy, and they cited his fees as compelling evidence of the need for reform. As an example, Bell noted to journalists that the tab for Susman's firm was 160 times the average $50,000 award to be received by a plaintiff company. Susman responded to their criticism by saying that it was "a sad day when these lawyers sell their reputations, which were gained by public trust." He and his defenders lobbied against new legislation, arguing that the proposed limitations on damage awards would only harm consumers and small businesses, by discouraging top lawyers from taking the risky, protracted class-action cases.[107]

Given the profitable, and mostly settled, outcome of the case, neither lawyers nor plaintiffs would be discouraged so long as Congress maintained the status quo of the antitrust laws. Susman claimed that the future viability of his recently founded firm depended on the judge's agreeing to his $8 million fee. His firm had already become involved in some thirty other antitrust cases, despite the publicity over Susman's fee, and graduates of the country's top law school were seeking jobs from him, because of the same publicity. After all, he crowed, he had won "against the most expensive lawyers in the country." In the process, he had became one of them.[108]

The critics, and even the defenders of the fees, seemed to agree that in a complex case with nine thousand clients, no single company was in a position to watch over attorneys. It became Singleton's task to rule whether the requests for fees were reasonable, just as he approved settlements.[109] He had initially hoped to rule within a month but soon decided to appoint a commission to review the reasonableness of the lawyer's requests and report back to him with recommendations. Bob Lanier, a Houston businessman who at that time was chairman of the Texas Highway Commission and later was elected Houston's mayor, chaired the review committee that the judge appointed.[110]

On 2 September 1983 Singleton awarded $40.7 million in fees and expenses to the fifty-five law firms involved in the litigation and ordered that the money be taken out of the $550 million he approved in the earlier settlement. Even reduced from the $51 million initially sought, this sum still worked out to be more than twice the hourly rate regularly charged by many attorneys and represented 7.4 percent of the total settlement. The judge said in his order that he allowed these "high multipliers" because the firms had worked six years without any fees, on a risky case, and that it was justified given the "quality of work, efficiency in action, substantial recovery obtained and success at trial." In the end, Singleton approved 115,000 hours of work billed by more than three hundred lawyers.[111]

Lanier noted that in the final tally approved by the judge, thirteen firms received more than two and a half times their regular hourly rate, and forty-two received less than two and a half times their going rate. The court order allowed the sixteen lawyers in Susman's firm, Susman and McGowan, to multiply their regular hourly rate by four times, and they received $6.7 million of the $9.4 million requested. Susman, then forty-two years old, said he was "delighted."[112] He noted that the firm's approximately $7 million was "the largest fee that's ever been awarded in any kind of class action case." He would personally receive $3.2 million for his service as chair of the steering committee. Susman said that "I guess I'm happy. . . . You're always a little disappointed when you don't get more."[113]

Singleton noted that the plaintiff's lawyers had all been from small to medium-size firms, and they had competently opposed lawyers from large law firms, such as Vinson and Elkins, and Baker, Botts.[114] The judge justified a portion of the total by noting that it had been necessary to include the expenses of lobbying U.S. senators and representatives. He said lobbying by the plaintiffs' lawyers had become necessary to counter a lobbying effort, mounted by at least one of the defendant box manufacturers during the litigation, to convince the Congress to alter federal antitrust laws and thereby reduce the manufacturer's liability to customers.[115] Even after high-profile pleas by Bell and Civiletti, however, the antitrust "reform" legislation failed.[116]

The judge's work was not yet at an end: after all of the money due to the lawyers and owed to the nine thousand class claimants had been distributed, approximately $1 million remained uncollected and drawing interest. In order to dispose of these leftover funds, Singleton established a program to fund scholarships in various law schools, for the purpose of furthering research and education in litigation practices. The judge eventually supported scholarship programs at law schools at the University of Houston, Texas Southern University, Texas Tech University, University of Texas (UT), Stanford University, and University of Pennsylvania. The funds also benefited education efforts of the National Association of Attorneys General, the Packaging Education Foundation, and the International Corrugated Packaging Foundation.[117]

Judge Singleton oversaw the corrugated container antitrust litigation for more than six years. He showed that he could be contemptuous of legal details if he thought they obscured the fundamental issue, he was known to snap at witnesses as well as attorneys who tried his patience, and his behavior could seem downright rude.[118] But the judge all along had been less interested in projecting a public image of judicial detachment and dispassion than in pursuing judicial efficiency. Although it is possible to speculate, from the evidence of multiplying appeals, that his policy of constantly striving to maintain the momentum of the case actually strengthened forces resisting its resolution, it is worth noting that the appellants in the case—perhaps more so than in most other cases—were inclined to resist a compromise.

Recalcitrant witnesses, who believed that their testimony could and would be used against them, obviously had little to gain by meeting the judge halfway. Sheet cardboard purchasers were from the start only reluctant participants in the settlement process. Singleton's impatience with these parties' concerns increased their alienation, although it is unlikely that a more sensitive approach would have proven any more productive. If trial judges took deliberate care that rulings were never at risk for reversal and saw to it that all parties got everything they wanted, then complex cases such as the box case would only rarely be resolved.

Singleton's efforts to facilitate settlement were in line with the case management approaches that were being promoted by the leading reformers of the early 1980s, who were just beginning to tout the benefits of extrajudicial "alternative dispute resolution." Rule 16 of the Federal Rules of Civil Procedure was amended in 1983, for example, to make "facilitation of settlement" an explicit goal of the venerable pretrial conference.[119] Singleton's particular devotion of time and energy to the case, however, and the skills he displayed in keeping the contentious parties moving steadily toward conclusion earned him lasting praise, and several award nominations for service to justice, from the legal profession.[120]

The judge had so devoted his industry to the cardboard box criminal trial that he had continued into 1980 to limit his new criminal cases.[121] But his duties as chief judge demanded ongoing attention. These involved his attempt to justify his suggestion to the relevant Judicial Council committees, almost immediately after the Southern District's expansion to thirteen judges in May 1979, that the court be allocated two additional judgeships. The reason they needed more judges, as Singleton wrote to the chair of the Subcommittee on Judicial Statistics, Fourth Circuit Judge John Butzner, was that the Southern District had yet to receive the full benefits of the thirteen judgeships listed. Judge Finis Cowan had resigned soon after the five new judges arrived, and Judge Hugh Gibson, his replacement, was not able to start his duties until November of 1979. Judge Garza had moved up to the appellate court, and, as Singleton wrote in early March 1980, no replacement seemed likely to arrive until late spring or early summer. The district's strength was further diminished when newly appointed Judge George Cire suffered a heart attack on 5 September 1979. He underwent open-heart surgery and was unable to resume the "full exercise of his docket," as Chief Judge Singleton termed it, until February 1980.[122]

There were continual personnel difficulties during the whole of Singleton's tenure as chief judge, but the Southern District was allocated no additional judgeships until 1990. When Judge Owen Cox announced in late 1980 that he would take senior judge status and would receive no new filings after 1 January 1981, Clerk of the Court Jesse Clark worried that the necessary shifting of Cox's caseloads from Victoria and Corpus Christi to the Brownsville and Laredo judges, George Kazen, James DeAnda, and Filemon Vela, would disrupt the balance in what he and Judge Singleton referred to as the district's "Southern Constellation."[123]

Hayden Wilson Head Jr., the Corpus Christi attorney whom President Ronald Reagan appointed to replace Judge Cox, did not enter on duty until the end of October 1981. Head was born 12 November 1944, in Sherman, in north Texas. He attended UT, where he earned his B.A. in 1966, and stayed to earn his LL.B. at the law school there in 1968. He practiced privately in Corpus Christi for one year and then served a three-year term in the U.S. Navy, from 1969 to 1972. He resumed his Corpus Christi practice after his discharge.[124]

Judge Woodrow Seals accepted senior judge status on 25 December 1982. President Reagan appointed Ricardo H. Hinojosa, a native of the border town of Rio Grande City, to replace Seals. Hinojosa, born 24 January 1950, attended UT, where he earned his B.A. in 1972. Rather than staying in Austin, however, Hinojosa opted to earn his J.D. at the Harvard Law School. After graduation in 1975, he clerked for the Texas Supreme Court for one year and then entered private practice on the border, becoming a partner at Ewers, Toothaker, Ewers, Abbott, Talbot, Hamilton, and Jarvis in McAllen. He received his appointment in 1983, partly, it was reported, because while in Cambridge, Massachusetts, he had befriended a Harvard business school graduate named George W. Bush, oldest son of Vice President George H. W. Bush.[125]

The welcome additions of Judges Head and Hinojosa were balanced by Judge O'Conor's unexpected resignation in September 1984. O'Conor, dispirited from the heavy workload in the Southern District and also concerned that his judicial salary could never provide for his family's needs, wished to enter private practice in Houston. He gave Chief Judge Singleton two weeks' notice.[126] This compounded disruptions that had developed in the spring of 1984, after Judge Cire's health began once again to suffer. Cire underwent surgery to repair damage caused by an infection associated with his first surgery and had to be put on a reduced workload from that time forward.[127] As O'Conor's final day approached, Chief Judge Singleton wrote to the chief of the Personnel Division of the Administrative Office, requesting the continued authorization to employ O'Conor's staff. Singleton also announced in the same letter his intention to seek the help of the Judicial Councils in enlisting senior or active federal judges "who might be willing to sit in Houston for periods of at least one month."[128]

In December 1984 Chief Singleton and Clerk Jesse Clark made out the judicial work assignments for 1985. The welcome changes of 1984—new judges on board in the "Southern Constellation" and Judge DeAnda moved to Houston—had to offset the difficulties created by Judge O'Conor's sudden resignation and Judge Cire's lingering illness. Singleton would retain all of the pending cases on his docket and would handle 10 percent of the new criminal and civil filings in Houston. Judges Bue, DeAnda, Black, McDonald, and Sterling each would have 18 percent of the criminal cases and 15 percent of the civil cases filed in Houston. Judge Cire would retain the cases then pending on his docket and also handle 15 percent of the Houston civil docket. Judge Gibson handled all cases in Galveston. In the "Southern Constellation" Judge Kazen took the complete dockets for both Laredo and Victoria. Judge Hinojosa would split the Brownsville docket with Judge Vela, and Judge Head would have responsibility for all Corpus Christi filings.[129]

The judgeship that O'Conor had resigned remained vacant for fifteen months. Judge Cire's health continued steadily to decline throughout 1984, and he died in May 1985. The chief judge and the clerk distributed the work among the Southern District's judges and, occasionally, to visiting judges willing to come to Houston. The average load per judge was approximately seven hundred pending cases.[130]

Judge O'Conor's long-awaited successor finally joined the Southern District in December 1985. Lynn Nettleton Hughes was born in Houston on 9 September 1941. He earned his B.A. in 1963 at the University of Alabama, Tuscaloosa, but returned to Texas to attend law school. He earned his J.D. at UT in 1966. Thereafter Hughes was in private practice in Houston until 1979, when he was elected state judge for the 165th Judicial District. The next year he was elected a judge in the 189th Judicial District. He was in that position when President Reagan appointed him, on the recommendation of U.S. Senator Phil Gramm, to the Southern District of Texas.[131]

David Hittner was born on 10 July 1939, in Schenectady, New York. He attended New York University as an undergraduate, earning the B.S. in 1961, and as a law student, earning the J.D. in 1964. He served in the U.S. Army for two years, achieving the rank of captain. Apparently because he was one of the rare Jewish officers in his division, his commanding officer appointed him an acting chaplain. Hittner was in private practice in Houston for a dozen years, until 1978, when he was elected judge of the 133d District Court of Texas. Hittner was a state judge when the president appointed him to succeed Judge Cire in June 1986.[132]

By the mid-1980s the need for these new full-time judges in the district was acute. Many Texans spent at least a part of the raucous decade in court, it seemed, and many were there to attack their debtors or to defend themselves against creditors. The United States had emerged from a brief recession that lasted from 1980 to 1982, but Texas was out of step with the rest of the nation. The state's energy-dependent economy had greatly expanded in response to the rise of petroleum prices during the 1970s, but the economy then contracted as prices plummeted during a worldwide oil glut in the 1980s. By mid-decade not only the oil and gas companies but also the real estate, construction, and financial firms that shared the benefits of earlier expansion remained mired in a deep regional recession. Bank- and bankruptcy-related litigation swamped Texas's state and federal court systems during the last part of the decade.[133] In March 1986 Jesse Clark sent Chief Judge Singleton a graph of the bankruptcy cases pending on the Southern District's docket at the end of each year from 1980 to 1985. From 4,509 cases pending in 1980, the number climbed to 20,977 in 1985.[134] Judges Hughes and Hittner soon assumed responsibility for managing their share of these many cases.

AS REASONABLE A SOLUTION AS IS PLAUSIBLE

Stability in banking had since World War II enabled Texas's steady rise to prosperity. No Texas bank failed during the nearly four decades following the creation of the Federal Deposit Insurance Corporation (FDIC).[135] But when the worst national financial crisis since the Great Depression developed during the 1980s, with lingering effects into the 1990s, Texas suffered more institutional failures than any other state. Many factors fueled the statewide crisis, but "public confidence" to the point of foolhardiness, bolstered by federal deposit insurance, an effect observers have labeled the "moral hazard," increased the devastation.[136]

The institutions that had underwritten the economic expansion during the oil boom were among the insolvent businesses after the oil bust. In general, the Texas credit failures conformed to the pattern of overextension that doomed its other industries. Many business owners, made dizzy by the spiraling rise and decline of oil profits, accepted risks they might have avoided in a more stable era, in the hope that potential gains could offset mounting losses. Bankers loaned desperate or deluded businessmen the money they needed to undertake these gambles.[137] Managers of some banks and thrifts were further intoxicated, and the depth of the future distress compounded, when regional economic reversal combined with apparent national legislative advances.

As the economy slumped in 1980, federal legislators, acting in the name of market reform, lifted some long-standing regulatory burdens. For example, thrifts traditionally were limited to lending to homeowners, who undertook long-term, low-interest-rate mortgages. This limitation prevented S&Ls from competing for new depositors on equal terms with commercial banks. The latter loaned to a wider variety of investors and charged higher interest rates on shorter-term loans. In 1980 lawmakers relaxed restrictions on thrifts, which could then make higher interest consumer loans.[138] Deregulation of the lending industry resulted in lower interest rates for consumers' loans and sparked a recovery, as lawmakers intended, but the increased competition for customers in the financial industry also drove lenders to support even riskier investments, especially in high-dollar commercial construction.[139] Many of these speculative ventures failed in the still-depressed Texas real estate market. Lenders gained little for shareholders when they foreclosed on empty office towers or deserted suburban shopping malls, and the losses sustained from this gambling triggered the bankruptcies of many of the lending institutions themselves.

Ill-considered and, often, allegedly fraudulent lendings forced both the commercial banks and the traditionally stable but newly deregulated S&Ls to fail, at unprecedented rates.[140] Some observers had identified troubling signs earlier in the decade, but few expected the widespread problems that occurred.[141] When the crisis came, the Congress, courts, and claimants reacted, each in its own way, to a rapidly deteriorating situation. But by the end of the 1980s, it was probably too late to save many of the victims of the "tragedy."[142] Federal regulatory agencies were under pressure to stem the tide of failures and to assign blame and to punish those institutions and individuals deemed responsible for what was being called a "bailout," "scandal," or, most often, simply "the debacle."[143]

Unfortunately, temptations to folly were not unique to such Sunbelt boomtowns as Houston.[144] Bankers succumbed elsewhere as well, even in thrifty New England.[145] By 1989 bank and S&L failures were a national scandal. It was increasingly clear that Congress had contributed to the crisis through its earlier deregulation. The lawmakers had not retracted federal deposit insurance, the carrot extended to bankers during the New Deal, in exchange for the stick of oversight. Instead, Congress had raised the dollar figure of the maximum account insured. The government was obligated to assume responsibility for bad debts and worthless properties owned by hundreds of insolvent banks and thrifts. As the scale of the crisis swelled, lawmakers reasserted control, both to stabilize the lending industry, especially wayward S&Ls, and to limit political damage to themselves. In August 1989 President George Bush signed the Financial Institutions Reform, Recovery, and Enforcement Act (FIRREA), which formally separated federal regulatory and insurance functions and imposed new regulations to be administered by the Federal Reserve, the Office of the Comptroller of the Currency (OCC), and the FDIC.[146] Newly empowered by FIRREA, and pressed by the anxious lawmakers, FDIC became more aggressive in its attacks on what it deemed poor management practices. Seeking vigorously to enforce banking laws new and old, regulators offered the carrot less often, and applied the stick earlier, than ever before.

As a result of the legal flux, federal judges grappled with elements of law and fact that were far more fluid than usual. Although judges engage in potentially controversial but necessary acts whenever they mediate disputes between national and local interests, they can usually rely on the stability of either law or facts, and often both, to maintain the delicate balance the federally organized American legal and political systems require. This stability is relative: controlling legislation is subject to repeal; judicial precedent is subject to reversal; and settlements reached between litigating parties are subject to changed conditions. These very shifts are often grounds for further litigation even in ordinary times. But during the bankruptcy crisis of the 1980s, the law's unsettled quality likely prolonged the agony of insolvent institutions.

Among the most contentious of these bankruptcy-related cases was the complex litigation arising from the collapse of MCorp, a national bank holding company that operated twenty-five branches in Texas. The MCorp bankruptcy suggested that Texas was not falling behind the rest of the country but leading the way. The failure merited mention as one of three "most significant failures" in the federal government's self-study of the crisis.[147] Starting in 1989, Judge Hughes presided in a number of civil actions related to the MCorp bankruptcy, in which the failing financial empire not only found itself pitted against its debtors and creditors, but also opposed to its erstwhile rescuer, the federal government.[148] The federal regulatory agencies responsible for managing the mess contributed to the litigative confusion and garnered their share of blame and criticism. During the four years that Judge Hughes managed the judicial autopsy of MCorp, its corporate dismemberment became apparently an end in itself for "arrogant and inept" regulators. He grew disgusted by "a spectacle of expensive litigation."[149] To the judge, the regulators' search for scapegoats rather than solutions fed the debacle.

In 1864 the U.S. Congress overcame lingering Jacksonian fears, bypassed states-rights obstructions,[150] and established a system for regulation of national banks through a National Bank Act.[151] But the national banking system then created was strong only in comparison to the vacuum of authority it filled. The treasury's comptroller of the currency was titular regulator and supervisor of national banking but had to rely on persuasion rather than coercion to bring members into the voluntary system.[152] State banking systems survived into the twentieth century and retained a powerful, often disruptive influence on the national economy. When financier and private banker J. Pierpont Morgan, an unlikely and, some thought, embarrassing white knight, was called on to rescue the economy from a financial panic in 1907, some reformers challenged the remaining American taboo against vigorous central banking.[153] In 1913 Congress created the Federal Reserve System, charging its governing board of money experts with rationalizing the nation's banking system through studied manipulations of interest rate.[154] But the

First World War initiated a new cycle of boom and bust. The war not only crippled European political and financial systems but also delayed effective federal management of the American economy for a generation.

The next major change in the banking system was a reaction to another crisis. Between 1930 and 1933, more than nine thousand banks—30 percent of those doing business in 1929—failed. The mass failure, begun with a "run" on deposits in February 1933, ended when, in early March 1933, the newly inaugurated president, Franklin Roosevelt, ordered remaining institutions to close for a four-day national "bank holiday."[155] By then all of the forty-eight state governors already had declared moratoria on withdrawals. Nonetheless, Roosevelt's act seemed bold, vigorous, and imaginative, a stark contrast to the public's perception of the conservative efforts of the departed Hoover administration. When some banks reopened on 13 March, enough confidence had been restored that customers, who had been withdrawing and hoarding money against the expected total collapse of the banking system, fed a "massive return flow" of cash into banks.[156]

The new president's conviction that the national financial crisis was sustained by "fear itself" contrasted sharply with the lack of focus demonstrated by the federal officials formally charged with overseeing the banking system. Neither the regulators of the Federal Reserve nor the voluntary business association of the National Credit Corporation (NCC), for example, was able to calm the economy through the manipulation of credit availability. Neither body possessed the prestige, power, or resources to do so, and they could not agree on the division of responsibility for managing aspects of the rapidly multiplying crises. Both reacted too conservatively to do much good. A new agency, the Reconstruction Finance Corporation (RFC), replaced the NCC in February 1932. Although the RFC was more liberal than its predecessor in its lending policies, it too engaged in mostly "stopgap measures."[157]

As Roosevelt alloyed economics and politics in the crucible of his New Deal, he and his supporters in Congress sought to give federal officials both the power needed to end the Great Depression and the tools necessary to prevent another such disaster.[158] The federal government at last exercised extensive, although still not exclusive, authority in the national and, increasingly, global economy, especially the credit economy. The OCC, for example, already entrusted with general supervision, gained more regulatory power to create but also to close nationally chartered banks. If, upon examination, the comptroller determined that a bank was insolvent, he or she placed it in receivership to preserve any remaining assets.[159]

Congress carried the nation farther along the path of bank reform than Roosevelt had been prepared to travel. For example, in one of the most significant provisions in the sweeping Banking Act of 1933, also known as the Glass-Steagall Act, Congress created federal deposit insurance despite the president's own stated resistance.[160] The FDIC would be the limited insurer of deposits.[161] The idea of insurance, regulators hoped, would attract depositors to the national banking system, keep the banks stable, and prevent more panic-driven runs.[162] The FDIC had a second role in regulation: under the Federal Reserve Act of 1933, it was to be the receiver for insolvent national banks.[163] When this "stepchild" of the New Deal proved both to be more successful and more popular than some of its legislative siblings, Roosevelt adopted the idea as if it were his own. Wisely so; in the estimation of one prominent historian of the New Deal, writing thirty years after the orphan's birth, federal deposit insurance was a "brilliant achievement."[164]

MCorp Financial, Incorporated, evolved from a Dallas establishment, the Mercantile Bank, into a national bank holding company which did business across Texas through eighty-five branches. MCorp helped to fund Texas's economic boom through twenty-five subsidiary MBanks.[165] When oil prices collapsed at the end of 1985, the value of real estate, normally a hedge against recession, eroded as well. The twin calamities undermined the finances of many Texas banks. Approximately one-third failed during the 1980s. In the midst of these upheavals, MCorp purchased and absorbed Southwest Bancshares, a rival bank holding company that was near insolvency.[166]

As economic reversals ended the boom, business partners became adversaries. In 1985 five plaintiffs sued MBank Abilene, complaining of promissory estoppel, fraud, tortious interference with business relations, defamation, and violation of the Texas Deceptive Trade Practices Act (DTPA). A central claim was that the bank's director had breached an oral promise to lend $3 million to a distressed oil and gas company. After a five-week trial, a jury returned a ten-to-one verdict for the five plaintiffs and assessed total damages of more than $100 million. The state trial judge entered a revised judgment against MBank Abilene of approximately $69 million and granted the bank's motion to stay the judgment, pending exhaustion of appeals, but then withdrew the order.[167]

MBank sought to reinstate the stay by petitioning for a writ of mandamus in both the Texas Court of Appeals and the Texas Supreme Court.[168] It also sought protection from its status as a national banking association, basing its motion for mandamus on a century-old clause in the "Banks and Banking" portion of the United States Code, known as section 91. It provided that "no attachment, injunction, or execution shall be issued against such association or its property before final judgment in any suit, action or proceeding, in any state, county, or municipal court."[169] The judicial interpretation of this clause, the meaning of "final judgment," and several other, more affirmative federal banking laws played a large role in litigation arising from the 1980s banking crisis. This was rarely trodden ground; although the provision was enacted in 1873, the U.S. Supreme Court had considered the practical meaning of section 91 only three times in the next one hundred years, in 1887, 1900, and 1905.[170] In 1977 the court considered the clause a fourth time and held that it did not apply to an action by a debtor "seeking a preliminary injunction to protect its own property from wrongful foreclosure" but did prevent the "prejudgment seizure of bank property by creditors of the bank."[171]

These few interpretations did not unequivocally support MBank. Both Texas appellate courts refused the bank's petitions. The state trial court denied MBank's motion for a new trial, and the victors filed writs of garnishment against MBank Dallas, MBank Fort Worth, a subsidiary of MBank Abilene named Anbore, Incorporated, and the Federal Reserve Bank of Dallas.[172] In the Abilene division of the U.S. District Court for the Northern District of Texas, federal attorneys sought a temporary restraining order (TRO) and preliminary injunctions both against execution of the state court judgment and against claims by the plaintiff victors in the state action.[173] The court granted the TRO, then twice extended it, until the judge heard oral arguments on the government's motion for declaratory relief.[174]

In addition to the United States's general interest in ensuring that federal laws such as section 91 were properly understood and enforced, the government had a substantial pecuniary interest in the outcome of the case. The federal comptroller of the currency regulated and supervised national banks, and FDIC insured their deposits. If MBank Abilene became insolvent, a situation that an immediate payment of $69 million might precipitate, FDIC would be obliged to compensate depositors for a sum greater than $218 million.[175] To forestall those consequences, the government, as had MBank Abilene, sought a construction of section 91 precluding payment until the bank exhausted its appeals.[176]

The federal district judge noted that the United States sought the injunction after the completion of a state trial on the merits, which the government contended was not a "final judgment" because it was subject to appeal. The defendants countered that "final judgment" meant a self-contained final decision by a particular judge, even though an appeal could follow. None of the previous four Supreme Court decisions had touched the "precise question raised here, that is the meaning of the term 'final judgment.' " Therefore, the federal district court had the responsibility to interpret the meaning of the statute.[177] The judge believed that Congress intended the law to prohibit premature claims on assets by one creditor to the detriment of others, and decided that "final judgment" meant a ruling from which no further appeal can be taken, because that construction promoted the intent.[178] The defendants' preferred interpretation "could cause havoc," said the court, because even though an appellate court might later overturn the judgment, the national bank might have little recourse in regaining the assets. The government's argument prevailed; if MBank Abilene paid the judgment immediately it might become insolvent and be unable ever to recover.[179]

The federal district court granted the government the declaratory relief it sought, finding section 91 to preclude attachment of MBank Abilene's assets until it had exhausted all routes of appeal.[180] To grant a preliminary injunction, however, the court also had to establish four factors in the government's favor: (1) a substantial likelihood of success on the merits; (2) a substantial threat of irreparable injury if the injunction did not issue; (3) that the threatened injury outweighed danger the injunction might cause to the defendant; and (4) that the injunction would not "disserve the public interest."[181]

Conceding the first factor, the district judge decided that the U.S. government would prevail. On the remaining points the government introduced evidence that MBank Abilene lacked sufficient funds from which to pay the judgment and would probably become insolvent, harming the bank's depositors. Even if the state judgment was overturned or modified, the defendants might not repay to the FDIC the money expended to pay secured deposits. More important perhaps, the court thought the bank's failure would also affect the community, causing the public "to lose confidence in the national banking system."[182] The judge wrote: "No amount of money could restore the public's confidence in MBank Abilene . . . no amount of money could rebuild MBank Abilene into the viable financial institution it presently is. . . . As a practical matter, it would be impossible to reconstitute and reopen the bank."[183] Federal regulators had testified that 109 banks had already failed in 1986, and further insolvency would certainly be a disservice to the public interest.[184] The potential harms, the court ruled, far outweighed the defendants' stated concern that after the appeals process was exhausted, MBank Abilene would have no money left to pay their judgment. In late October 1986 the district judge issued the preliminary injunction.[185]

Two and one-half years later, the federal regulators substantially repeated this performance on behalf of another MCorp subsidiary, MBank Greens Parkway of Harris County, Texas. The bank sued in state court to recover on two promissory notes executed by Susan E. Taylor, the owner of an oil-related business, Exploration Services. She filed counterclaims, alleging damages under the DTPA.[186] In late February 1989, after the jury trial, the state trial judge entered in Taylor's favor a "final judgment" of $9.6 million. The court denied MBank's requests for an order prohibiting Taylor from filing an abstract of the judgment before exhausting the appellate process.[187]

On 1 March, Taylor recorded her abstract with the Harris County clerk. The same day, the United States, again on behalf of the OCC, filed an action in the federal district court for the Southern District of Texas, seeking a TRO and a preliminary injunction.[188] The government argued on the same grounds as in the MBank Abilene case but now had the victory's precedential support.[189]

In late March 1989 Judge James DeAnda granted the preliminary injunction and ordered Taylor to withdraw her abstract of judgment.[190] In response, Taylor filed notice in the Harris County property records announcing her *involuntary* withdrawal of the abstract of judgment, subject to appeal. In April, Judge DeAnda ordered Taylor to release the abstract *completely,* or be held in contempt.[191] Taylor appealed to the Fifth Circuit, arguing, as had the Abilene defendants, that the United States lacked legal standing to bring the case because no sufficient governmental interest was at stake. The U.S. government asserted once more that its interest stemmed from the OCC's obligation to ensure the safety and soundness of the national banking. The only fresh argument was Taylor's contention that her abstract of judgment was not specifically described in the language of section 91. The government answered by stressing that the effect of the abstract was the same as injunction, in that it prevented free transfer of property. The Fifth Circuit agreed with the regulators on this second issue. Relying heavily on the reasoning in the Abilene case, the circuit judges affirmed DeAnda's judgment and order.[192]

One factor that made the Taylor case more than a repeat of Abilene was that the federal government, in particular FDIC, was less abstractly involved in the general financial health of MBank Greens Parkway. One week after Judge DeAnda granted the preliminary injunction, federal regulators had declared the insolvency of MBank Greens Parkway's parent company, MCorp. The FDIC then intervened in the Taylor cases (state and federal), in support of the existing pleadings but in its own name, after its appointment as the bank's receiver. These continuing controversies included the MBank's original motion for a new state trial and a motion to modify, correct, or reform the state judgment, actions that FDIC successfully removed to the Southern District of Texas shortly before the state court ruled on the pending motions.[193]

The leaders of the MCorp financial empire continued to litigate claims for several more years, until all of the MBanks were absorbed through the mergers and buyouts that complicated the already complex roster of claimants in the banking crisis. Further to confuse the issue, as the decade waned MCorp no longer considered government regulators as allies: the company's managers resisted coming under FDIC receivership, claiming it was an unnecessary expedient, and the Federal Reserve Board (Fed), as official superiors to FDIC, became targets of MCorp's most important and longest-running lawsuit. This reversal of fortune occurred because, in a calculated recanting of the arguments made in the Abilene case some thirty months earlier, the board of FDIC decided that it had become in the public's interest for many MBanks to fail. MCorp later argued persuasively that FDIC had conspired to hasten insolvencies. By 1989 the banking crisis entered a critical phase.

The seeds of the transformation in the federal regulator's attitudes toward MCorp were rooted in earlier policy developments. In 1984 the Federal Reserve Board revised its regulations to add the "source of strength" rule, which required that a member holding company should "serve as a source of financial and managerial strength to its subsidiary banks and shall not conduct its operations in an unsafe or unsound manner."[194] To clarify its policy, the Fed published in the *Federal Register* a statement effective 24 April 1987, which provided that,

> in serving as a source of strength to its subsidiary banks, a bank holding company should stand ready to use available resources to provide adequate capital funds to its subsidiary banks during periods of financial stress or adversity and should maintain the financial flexibility and capital-raising capacity to obtain additional resources for assisting its subsidiary banks. [The] company's failure to meet its obligation to serve as a source of strength to its subsidiary bank(s), including an unwillingness to provide appropriate assistance to a troubled or failing bank, will generally be considered an unsafe and unsound banking practice.[195]

The Fed solicited comments on this definition of terms, and apparently was willing to revise the statement, but in fact it published no revisions in subsequent editions of the *Register.*[196]

These amendments became a live issue for MCorp (the parent corporation as well as two wholly owned subsidiaries, MCorp Financial, Incorporated, and MCorp Management) during the summer of 1988. Gene H. Bishop, chairman and chief executive officer of MCorp, began requesting "open-bank" assistance for distressed MBanks in Dallas, Houston, and Abilene.[197] As a condition for its aid, FDIC regulators demanded that MCorp agree to a so-called "standstill agreement." Under it the company would maintain the funding of its banks at levels consistent with those existing at the time MCorp first sought assistance.[198] This meant that healthy MBanks that had been lending millions of dollars in federal funds to MBanks Dallas and Houston would continue shoring up those troubled sibling banks. Meanwhile, FDIC would seek a buyer for the faltering MBanks.[199]

According to Chairman Bishop, a timely infusion of cash would have stabilized the banks. But he believed this arrangement was designed instead to cause even more MBanks to become insolvent, which would allow FDIC to seize control of the entire network. Bishop noted that FDIC had earlier refused even to negotiate a bailout for the MBanks unless MCorp "downstreamed" funds, meaning that any dividends and profits due to the owners of shares in the holding company would be diverted into distressed MBanks rather than distributed to the shareholders. But upon hearing rumors of this plan, representatives from Shearson Lehman Hutton, one of MCorp's largest creditors and also one of its major stockholders, told MCorp's board of directors that they believed downstreaming the holding company assets would violate MCorp's fiduciary duties to the shareholders.[200]

William Seidman, chairman of the FDIC's board during this phase of the banking crisis, actually agreed that the proposed downstreaming of MCorp assets to the MBanks would create the conflict of interest described by Shearson. The directors of bank holding companies could accumulate enormous profits from the healthy banks. But not only were they not obliged to use that money to save sick banks; they risked sanctions for attempting to do so. Seidman considered this to be a "basic defect" in the American banking system: under the source of strength doctrine, duties to shareholders conflicted with obligations under the banking laws. The directors risked lawsuits by stockholders on the one hand and regulators on the other, whatever they decided. Nevertheless, as chairman, Seidman acted on his perceived duty to the stockholders in the FDIC insurance fund, that is, American taxpayers, and opted to sue MCorp.[201]

Seidman's explanation of the dilemma MCorp faced does not address Bishop's charge that FDIC schemed to force his banks into bankruptcy. However, MCorp's conspiracy theory is apparently substantiated by the minutes of an FDIC board meeting that contain statements indicating that FDIC officials believed the entire network of MBanks would be more attractive to prospective buyers than would a handful of individual banks. That the bank's chairman was not paranoid is attested by the fact that a federal judge later agreed that the evidence of the board minutes seemed to support the inference. Subsequent actions by FDIC were consistent with these statements. It is possible to infer that regulators actually planned to render insolvent as many MBanks as possible by forcing the company to "downstream" its funds.[202]

The seeds of the "scheme" apparently were planted in October 1988. The FDIC's senior national bank examiner for the Southwestern Region reported to the OCC that twenty of twenty-five MBanks both did not meet statutory minimum capital levels for member banks and had failed to maintain the lower capital requirement MCorp had negotiated with FDIC.[203] After receiving this report, the Fed's board of governors notified MCorp that the company was being investigated for possible violations of the "source of strength" regulation. The board was concerned that the company's business practices were "likely to cause substantial dissipation of the assets" that MCorp needed to serve as a source of strength for its subsidiary MBanks. The board quickly issued an amended notice of its charges and ordered the company to implement "an acceptable capital plan" that promised that all of MCorp's assets were to be used to recapitalize the MBanks "suffering capital deficiencies," that is, the large banks that were taking heavy losses from real estate– and energy-related loans.[204]

The amended notice also instituted three temporary orders. The first forbade MCorp to pay any dividends, the second forbade MCorp "to dissipate" any assets without prior board approval, and the third reiterated the regulator's command that MCorp use "all of its assets" to support subsidiary banks in need of capital.[205] MCorp challenged these orders in federal court in the Northern District of Texas. The Fed agreed to suspend the third order, pending the outcome of the ongoing negotiations between MCorp and FDIC regarding efforts to aid the several distressed MBanks.[206]

While these negotiations continued, MBanks in Dallas and in Houston would have failed outright if they were not allowed to borrow the funds at the Federal Reserve discount rate and if regular cash infusions they received from sister MBanks were unavailable. MBank Abilene did become insolvent, and several other MBanks failed by the end of the year. With the failures looming, FDIC contacted several companies interested in buying MBanks.[207]

In a meeting of the FDIC Board of Directors in late October, member William Roelle distributed reports on both MCorp and another distressed bank holding company, Texas American Bancshares (TAB). Roelle noted that if the federal funds loaned among the MBanks were valued at 70 percent of their actual amount, an accounting item FDIC could control, the result would be the failure of many of the MBanks, enabling FDIC to "grab a great number. . . . We would end up with a great number of the subsidiary banks in both TAB and MBank."[208] In November 1988 Director of Bank Supervision Paul Fritts explained at another board meeting how the FDIC board might resolve the MCorp matter. He noted that if

> they had a liquidity squeeze . . . we would capture 16 of the banks as of October 31 and control 75 percent of the total assets . . . [if we] look for the first time individually at . . . MBanks Fort Worth and MBank Austin . . . if we analyzed and found them to be insolvent . . . you get 18 of the 25 banks, and you get 82 percent plus of the total assets. And the remaining seven banks are not really significant in the big picture. . . . [A] pretty good package, and all you really need to do to get that much—and I hate to say it this way but—[is] to have a liquidity insolvency at Dallas and Houston, and I don't think that's a very far-fetched thing, *as long as the other banks aren't allowed to pull their money out.*[209]

Fritts then suggested that it would be possible to ensure that the "other" MBanks did not withdraw their funds from the Dallas and Houston MBanks, if "you stepped right in and said, you know, 'The Fed's not going to fund you anymore. You're up to "X" dollars.' Those two banks [would] close."[210] Other board members, including FDIC Chairman Seidman, indicated that they were amenable to this method of achieving the MBanks' insolvency.[211]

At this meeting the FDIC board decided to demand that MCorp enter into the previously mentioned standstill agreement as a condition for the government's providing open-bank assistance to the troubled MBanks. Some board members harbored doubts about the fairness of that agreement. Also, they wondered whether MCorp would interpret the plan as a predatory scheme, because in the summer of 1988 a similar arrangement between FDIC and the Dallas bank of First RepublicBank Corporation had led to the closure of the Dallas bank and to the insolvency of all forty of First RepublicBank's Texas subsidiaries. One board member wondered if the proposed agreement would "be a red flag to MCorp . . . because they know how it was used in the First Republic situation." The board spent a significant portion of that meeting on phrasing the letter to MCorp outlining the aid agreement. For example, Seidman asked, "Okay, then why does the next sentence say, 'We believe that it is in our interest to explore open bank assistance.' Because we're exploring all kinds of assistance: open and closed. That sounds to me to be kind of affirmatively misleading." A member responded, "That was just a little sugar coating . . . it's not essential." Seidman concluded, "We're not going to fool these people in my opinion."[212] Seidman was correct that MCorp was not fooled, because these discussions outlined the essential elements of Bishop's alleged conspiracy. However, the FDIC board, which included the comptroller of the currency, with the cooperation of the Fed, put aside doubts and enacted the plan to require the standstill agreement.[213]

If the regulators' intent was to bring MCorp to crisis, then the scheme bore fruit on 21 March 1989, when three creditors filed an involuntary bankruptcy proceeding against MCorp in the U.S. Bankruptcy Court for the Southern District of New York. One week later, on 27 March, MCorp informed managers of individual MBanks about the litigation and issued a press release announcing its intention to convert the suit to a voluntary bankruptcy and to reorganize the holding company under Chapter 11.[214] The same day, the smaller MBanks began to demand the return of federal funds, amounting to more than $502 million, that they had loaned to MBank Dallas. The Dallas bank honored the $46.9 million request of the first affiliate to call in its loan, MBank New Braunfels, but as similar demands mounted throughout the day, the president of MBank Dallas advised employees to withhold payment.[215]

Since November 1988 the government's scrutiny had included monitoring MCorp's finances on a daily basis. Just before 7 P.M. on 27 March 1989, an OCC employee who had been assigned to monitor MBank Dallas's liquidity reported electronically to his supervisor in Washington, D.C., that several MBanks had made unsatisfied demands on Dallas, and that some banks, including MBank New Braunfels, refused to sell overnight federal funds to MBank Dallas.[216] Next morning, the directors of both MBank Dallas and MBank Houston, through counsel, informed Chairman Seidman officially of the crisis and requested assistance. The same day, the senior deputy comptroller of the currency advised the Federal Reserve Bank in Dallas that the OCC believed MBank Dallas "no longer viable from either a capital or liquidity standpoint." That is, failure was imminent. The letter added that FDIC had decided against providing open-bank assistance and concluded that, without aid from FDIC or the Fed, MBank Dallas would become "liquidity insolvent." The Federal Reserve Bank in Dallas immediately closed

MBank Dallas's line of credit and demanded immediate repayment of all outstanding loans, which totaled approximately $1.425 billion.[217] On the next day, FDIC personnel entered the twenty-five MBanks to assess the solvency of each. By the next morning, the FDIC regulators declared twenty of the MBanks to be insolvent.[218]

The regulators placed the insolvent banks' remaining assets in receivership, to be managed by a new, specially chartered statewide national bank association, owned by FDIC, known as the Deposit Insurance Bridge Bank (DIBB).[219] The DIBB soon changed its name to Bank One, Texas, when the BancOne Corporation of Ohio began to manage DIBB for FDIC. Bank One subsequently purchased the assets and assumed the liabilities of the former MBanks, under an agreement specifying that FDIC retained the rights to pursue all claims against the deceased banks' debtors.[220]

The only MBanks survivors were those in Brownsville, Corpus Christi, El Paso, and Waco. They had traded federal funds among themselves, but not to the MBanks in Dallas or Houston. The lucky MBank New Braunfels had been quick enough off the mark to recover its $46.9 million from MBank Dallas before that bank suspended payments. Before the FDIC actions, MCorp and all its subsidiary MBanks had assets of more than $17 billion. Although the closure left the five remaining MBanks with deposits totaling some $2.3 billion, the disaster was so complete that on 31 March, MCorp's two subsidiaries, MCorp Financial, Incorporated, and MCorp Management, filed voluntary Chapter 11 petitions in the U.S. Bankruptcy Court for the Southern District of Texas.[221] The involuntary bankruptcy proceeding filed against MCorp in New York was subsequently transferred and consolidated with the related cases in Texas.[222]

To complete its housecleaning, the Fed commenced a second proceeding against MCorp, alleging that the company violated the Federal Reserve Act when it required subsidiaries MBank Houston and MBank Preston to extend to the holding company an unsecured credit line of more than $63 million.[223] Maintaining that the regulators closed twelve of the twenty MBanks "illegally or improvidently," MCorp went on the offensive in May 1989, filing an adversarial bankruptcy proceeding against the Fed's board of governors, again in the Southern District of Texas.[224] MCorp sought a TRO, and a preliminary injunction, to stay the Fed's two administrative proceedings, that is, the latest statutory charge and the original source-of-strength action. The company also sought to prevent the Fed from taking further actions against it without prior approval of the bankruptcy court. MCorp argued that the proceedings should have been stayed automatically under the federal bankruptcy code.[225] But a bankruptcy judge denied the company's requests. The Fed then filed a successful motion to have the case removed from the bankruptcy court and transferred to the district's civil docket.[226]

Judge Hughes of the Southern District drew the duty to preside in the civil controversy between MCorp and the Fed. The issue for him to decide, Hughes concluded, could be narrowed to a single question. Should a "nonbank corporation," specifically a holding company that owns banks but also other nonbank subsidiaries, be required to have its bankruptcies administered by a banking agency such as FDIC, or be entitled to the protections afforded by the presence of a federal bankruptcy judge?[227] Any decision, noted Judge Hughes, would have broader impact than a "normal" preliminary injunction, which maintained the legal status between litigants until their claims could be heard on the merits. Instead, his decision would be analogous to a declaratory judgment, because, in effect, he would be assigning an authority, either judicial or administrative, to supervise MCorp's restructuring.[228]

The judge had to choose from among several apparently conflicting federal statutes. MCorp asserted that federal bankruptcy judges had been given exclusive jurisdiction over all property in the bankrupt's estate, under the bankruptcy code.[229] Also, the Fed's attempt to gain control of MCorp assets prior to bankruptcy proceedings violated the automatic stay provisions of that code. Even if the Fed was exempt from observing the automatic stay, MCorp argued, the bankruptcy code still authorized injunctions to protect debtors from interference from third parties.[230] The Federal Reserve countered MCorp's arguments by noting that the Congress eliminated federal court jurisdiction over the Fed by enacting the Financial Institutions Supervisory Act (FISA). It provided that "[n]o court shall have jurisdiction to affect by injunction or otherwise the issuance or enforcement of any notice or order under this section, or to review, modify, suspend, terminate, or set aside any such notice or order."[231] According to the Fed's interpretation, the automatic stay that would have been imposed under the bankruptcy code was superseded by FISA.[232]

In making his decision, Judge Hughes estimated the probable effects of giving priority to either statute. If he issued the injunction, Hughes would effectively be allowing MCorp to reorganize under the protection afforded by a bankruptcy judge. If, on the other hand, the district judge withheld the injunction, FDIC would administer the bankruptcy. He gave more weight to the bankruptcy laws. Their primary object was to maintain the viability of the nation's businesses, "so that they may make a contribution to the economic vitality of the country."[233] Hughes noted that bankruptcy jurisdiction had been granted by Congress "for the restricted purpose of facilitating the reorganization of the debtor." If the FISA provisions apparently trumped that jurisdiction, the importance of the bankruptcy court's task was cause enough to supersede the conflicting statute.[234] To continue the Fed's proceedings would only delay or derail the company's reorganization, as it would "oblig[e] MCorp to respond in multiple forums to multiple agencies, each with its own internal and external priorities." This lagging could prove fatal. If MCorp was "to survive to the benefit of the creditors and the government, it must act quickly, for a lingering Chapter 11 case inevitably becomes a liquidation."[235]

On 19 June 1989, after weighing the effects of ruling in favor of either party,

Judge Hughes determined that the risk of harm to MCorp "in both probability and magnitude" exceeded the danger to the government, whose "interests . . . can adequately be represented in the bankruptcy proceedings."[236] The judge enjoined the Fed from pursuing its goals for MCorp except under the aegis of the bankruptcy court.[237] Under the injunction, the Fed was prevented from using either its regulatory or supervisory authority "to attempt to effect, directly or indirectly, a reorganization of the MCorp group or its components or to interfere, except through participation in the bankruptcy proceedings, with the restructuring." The order embraced the governors of the Federal Reserve System, its employees and agents, and "those acting in concert with them."[238]

Ultimately, Judge Hughes's decision in favor of MCorp may have been most influenced by his perception that the Fed's only plan for reorganization consisted of selling MCorp's dead or dying members to the highest bidder, rather than attempting to revive the company. Throughout his opinion Hughes was unsympathetic to the federal regulators. For example, in addition to its statutory arguments, the Fed claimed that in proceeding against MCorp it was merely performing its normal regulatory and supervisory functions, which were not in the class of third-party actions that the Congress intended to be automatically enjoined.[239] In his response to the Fed's self-characterization as a disinterested party, the judge noted that "[b]oth the Board's generalized, diffuse interest in the holding company as well as [its] duplicative, distracting hearings militate for its being not exempt from the stay."[240]

By contrast, Judge Hughes was apparently sympathetic to MCorp's theory that it was the victim of a government conspiracy, which he characterized as the claim that "the current state of regulatory orders issuing from the Board is effectively an attempt by the Board to control the estate . . . for the purpose of dictating MCorp's future structure." In his written opinion the judge referred to the administrative proceedings as "reorganization by subterfuge." However, Hughes noted that "[w]hile this appears plausible, it is unnecessary to address it in detail because the stay applies to most of the regulation and because the Board is subject to the anti-interference prohibition." In the end, Judge Hughes left it to a bankruptcy judge to scrutinize the "potential for undisclosed motivations," when the Fed presented its inevitable arguments to lift the stay.[241]

When Hughes issued his opinion in favor of MCorp, he made it clear that he remained not only unmoved by the regulators' concerns, both stated and allegedly unstated, but that he was also disdainful of their methods. Hughes noted that he was aware that the precedent held the potential to tempt other companies to abuse the bankruptcy code, a point that the Fed had argued. But the judge then declared that "[t]he court is also mindful of who was paid to prevent the bank practices that resulted in the collapse of the system in the Southwest." Judge Hughes concluded that, given the facts of the case, "[n]either side has an occasion for self-righteousness."[242]

Judge Hughes's preliminary injunction effectively authorized MCorp to reorganize in the Southern District of Texas. Bankruptcy proceedings soon commenced there before U.S. Bankruptcy Judge Letitia Z. Clark.[243] But MCorp had also already begun to pursue its complaint that the federal regulators acted unlawfully in closing a dozen of the twenty allegedly "insolvent" MBanks, by filing a civil action in the Northern District of Texas in March 1990.[244] And the Fed, still contending that Hughes had lacked jurisdiction to issue his injunction, immediately appealed to the Fifth Circuit.[245] Although channeled into separate legal forums, these tributary currents of the MCorp affair continued to ebb and flow in parallel with the bankruptcy case.[246]

After they emerged from their headwaters of the MCorp insolvency, the divergent courses of each of these three litigation streams can be mapped independently. Regarding the appeal of Judge Hughes's injunction, a panel of judges from the Fifth Circuit supported one of the federal government's contentions but frustrated the other. The circuit judges agreed with regulators that under the Administrative Procedure Act, a bank holding company was not "ordinarily entitled" to judicial review until the Fed's board issued a final order.[247] MCorp had continued to argue that the district courts had exclusive jurisdiction over its bankruptcy under the judicial code, but the appeals panel held that the code was intended to grant district courts *concurrent* jurisdiction with administrative agencies.[248] The circuit judges declared that Judge Hughes did not actually "harmonize" the conflict with FISA but effectively repealed it. As a result, his decision invested the district court with an "equitable power withheld from every other court by the language" of the statute.[249]

In addition, MCorp argued that because the district court enjoyed exclusive jurisdiction over its assets, the Fed's administrative proceeding should be stayed while the bankruptcy proceeded.[250] But the circuit judges noted that the Fed had not "sought control over the property of MCorp's estate." It sought permission to proceed with its own action. And, alluding to the company's conspiracy theory, they added: "Nor at this early stage do we find the Board's enforcement actions to be *sham proceedings*, brought as a means of controlling the debtor's assets." Unlike Judge Hughes, the appellate judges were not fully persuaded that the action was "simply an attempt to assist FDIC to obtain MCorp's property *under the guise* of remedying a violation" of the Federal Reserve Act. Indeed, the circuit noted the Fed was "well within its authority" to pursue the "self-dealing" allegations (that is, the section 23 action) and ruled that the government's notice of charges was "not on its face a *sham proceeding*."[251] In sum, by filing for bankruptcy, MCorp obtained protection from its creditors but not from the regulators.

However, the Fifth Circuit judges believed that regulators faced similar constraints, and they concluded that the district court had jurisdiction to review the Fed's actions. When the Fed asserted that it had been granted broad authority under FISA to order a holding company to cease any practice regulators judged "unsafe or unsound," such as failure to provide capital to troubled subsidiary banks, the appellate judges ruled that the order to downstream funds would have required MCorp's directors "to disregard [their] own corporation's separate status; it would amount to a wasting of the holding company's assets in violation of its duty to its shareholders." This had been MCorp's argument, and the appellate panel agreed that downstreaming holding company funds "could hardly be considered a 'generally accepted standard of prudent operation.'" The Fed relied on an "unreasonable and impermissible interpretation" of the term "unsafe or unsound."[252]

Finally, because a "fundamental" aim of the Bank Holding Company Act (BHCA) was "to separate banking from commercial enterprises," the panel reasoned that Congress's purpose was "obviously not served if the Board is permitted to treat a holding company as merely an extension of its subsidiary bank." Although BHCA had granted substantial authority, it did not allow regulators to reconsider financial and managerial soundness of subsidiary banks *after* approving a holding company's application to join the Federal Reserve System.[253]

On 15 May 1990 the Fifth Circuit judges remanded the case, with instructions to continue to enjoin the "source of strength" proceedings but to vacate the injunction related to "self-dealing."[254] This split decision satisfied no one: both parties appealed, and the U.S. Supreme Court granted certiorari to review the entire action.[255] Meanwhile, MCorp pressed its civil suit against the government in the Northern District of Texas. As a bellwether case in the emerging banking crisis, this second stream in the MCorp litigation forced judges there to grapple, as had Judge Hughes, with competing interpretations of the banking and bankruptcy statutes. In August 1989 Congress further complicated the judges' tasks by passing FIRREA.[256]

Enacted primarily to rationalize the financial industry's restructuring, FIRREA authorized the federal bailout of failed institutions and consolidated previously disparate regulatory authority under the FDIC. However, the actual extent of the new and apparently sweeping grant of authority was not immediately obvious. To allow FDIC to become accustomed to its new role, for example, the act authorized a ninety-day stay in any judicial proceeding in which an institution in FDIC receivership "is or becomes a party."[257] The lingering legal ambiguity was demonstrated when regulators requested a stay in Susan Taylor's suit against MCorp, which was then on remand to the Southern District.[258]

On 19 December 1989 Judge David Hittner entered what amounted to a split decision on FIRREA. On the one hand, the judge ruled that because FDIC had been appointed the receiver of MBank Greens Parkway on 28 March 1989, six months before the date of its request, the government was not entitled to stay the proceedings.[259] On the other hand, when Hittner addressed Taylor's objections to the methods by which FDIC originally removed the case from state court, the judge ruled that her arguments were mooted by FIRREA, which provided that "in the event of any appealable judgment, the [FDIC] as . . . receiver shall have all the rights and remedies available to . . . [FDIC] in its corporate capacity," including removal to federal court.[260] In concluding that under the "presently applicable statutes" FDIC was authorized to remove the case after the state court judgment had been entered but was not entitled to stay old proceedings, the judge seemed to imply that FIRREA was at least semiretrospective.[261]

The ruling did not greatly clarify FIRREA. Basic questions, precisely what powers the Congress intended to confer upon FDIC and exactly whose authority the lawmakers intended to override, continued to arise in the many lawsuits in which FDIC became enmeshed.[262] U.S. District Judge Robert W. Porter confronted FIRREA as he presided in MCorp's litigation in the Northern District of Texas.[263] In addition to its claims that the Fed exceeded its statutory authority by interfering with subsidiary relationships, the holding company argued that, by seizing the MBanks, regulators violated not only federal banking laws but also the takings clause of the Fifth Amendment and the equal protection clauses of both the Fifth and Fourteenth Amendments. MCorp claimed that twelve of the twenty subsidiary banks were effectively solvent when the government forced them to close, and because the banks' assets allegedly represented a net worth of more than $70 million, the directors sought to compel the government to compensate the company for the losses.[264]

The Fed contended that FIRREA merely "clarified" the laws on the books in March 1989. Therefore, the court should apply the act retrospectively to the actions that closed the MBanks.[265] Retrospection would benefit the government's defense, because FIRREA granted FDIC discretion to limit recovery by the creditors of a failed national bank to the assets they would recoup in a straight liquidation.[266] For example, FDIC valued claims by subsidiary MBanks against MBank Dallas at 80 percent of par, and claims on MBank Houston to 78 percent. Given the sums the smaller MBanks loaned to the larger banks, this left a significant shortfall. Moreover, FDIC promised depositors and non-MBank creditors compensation in full.[267] MCorp maintained that the MBanks could have remained solvent had FDIC agreed to reimburse them as well; in addition, the company argued that the pledge to satisfy the claims of some creditors, but not MBank's, violated the National Bank Act's mandate that "all creditors are to be treated alike."[268]

As before, the government questioned the federal court's jurisdiction in the matter, adding the contention that MCorp was barred from proceeding by the

Federal Tort Claims Act (FTCA).[269] However, the Fifth Circuit had held similar actions by analogous agencies to be beyond the protection of FTCA.[270] Also, MCorp sought to persuade the judge to allow the suit by producing transcripts of FDIC board meetings. Porter agreed that they showed FDIC apparently seeking to craft "an internal policy—not to be disclosed to the national banks under its control—of planning and timing declarations of insolvency so as to lasso as many banks [or] holding companies as possible, in order to create a more attractive package for resale." Concluding that the scheme was not the sort of regulatory action contemplated by FTCA, Judge Porter ruled that the lawsuit could continue.[271] Finally, the government contended that FIRREA precluded judicial review by its provision that "no court may take any action, except at the request of the [FDIC] Board of Directors by regulation or order, to restrain or affect the exercise of powers or functions of the [FDIC] as a conservator or a receiver."[272] This potentially serious challenge to MCorp's ability to pursue its claims faded when Judge Porter declined to apply FIRREA retroactively.[273]

Ultimately, Judge Porter concluded that none of the federal regulators' arguments merited keeping the proceeding out of the district court.[274] Having assumed jurisdiction, the judge finally considered the actual claims. Despite their extended wrangling over the proper forum and jurisdiction, the parties disputed no "genuine issue" of fact that would warrant undertaking the expense and delay of a trial. Instead, the plaintiffs and defendants had placed six motions and cross-motions before the judge, each of which sought either summary judgment, or dismissal.[275] Judge Porter decided, as had Judge Hughes before him, that the available evidence substantiated MCorp's allegation that the regulators had "plotted to close as many MBanks as possible."[276]

The Fed countered that the MCorp directors were the real conspirators, because they had illegitimately acted in concert with the separate MBanks like an illegal unitary network and were now attempting to gain preferential treatment for MBank creditors. The judge scoffed at the allegation and declared, "Considering the experience and sophistication of the Defendants' attorneys in this case, the sparseness of this potentially damaging evidence and counsel's failure to set forth a coherent argument detailing the conspiracy scenario, is puzzling." Regarding the cooperation between the MBanks, including habits of lending funds to one another, Porter added: "Inferences can be drawn, to be sure, that would cast a taint upon MCorp's actions . . . [however,] the package of inference upon inference that the Defendants need to support their allegations is weak and tenuous at best."[277] Discriminating between creditors, the judge declared, "flouted" the National Bank Act.[278] Judge Porter granted summary judgment in favor MCorp, on 1 February 1991.[279]

The FDIC had entered the third stream of the litigation, the bankruptcy proceedings in the Southern District of Texas, in September 1989, when it filed fourteen claims against MCorp, totaling $847 million. Because the total claim was large and its constituent parts complex, MCorp successfully moved in September 1990 to bring the government's claims before District Judge Hughes rather than Bankruptcy Judge Clark. Judge Hughes eventually dismissed the bulk of the case, because the statute of limitations had run out on questioned actions.[280] For example, with regard to the government's claim that MCorp had forced member banks to sell their credit-card operations at an unfair price, FDIC argued that the "limitations clock" had started when the agency seized the MBanks in March 1989, but the judge ruled that the regulators bore responsibility for actions occurring before the takeover. In a ruling in late May 1991, Hughes determined that since FDIC had been "[c]harged with overseeing the very transactions of which it now complains, [it] cannot maintain these claims as an ignorant third-party successor."[281]

By June 1991 Judge Hughes's rulings and the FDIC's withdrawal of many of its claims reduced the contested sums to $305 million and then $262 million.[282] Meanwhile, Hughes refused to grant the FDIC's motion for summary judgment or to dismiss MCorp's counterclaims against the government, which also had been reduced to several hundreds of millions from a high of some $1 billion.[283] Then, in an oral ruling from the bench in mid-November 1991, Judge Hughes dismissed most of the remaining $262 million FDIC sought, leaving just $2.2 million intact from the government's initial claims. And that amount, if it prevailed, was offset by Hughes's additional judgment that FDIC owed MCorp approximately $84 million.[284] The judge's decision allowed MCorp's case to resume its progress in Bankruptcy Judge Clark's court.[285]

Six weeks before Judge Hughes's rulings enabled MCorp's bankruptcy to proceed, attorneys finally argued the merits of his original injunctions before the justices of the U.S. Supreme Court.[286] On 3 December, Justice John Paul Stevens delivered the court's 8–0 opinion that District Judge Hughes had lacked jurisdiction to enjoin either of the Fed's regulatory proceedings.[287] The justices unanimously ruled that, according to the "plain, preclusive language" of FISA, "[n]o court shall have jurisdiction to affect by injunction or otherwise the issuance or enforcement of any notice or order under this section, or to review, modify, suspend, terminate, or set aside any such notice or order." FISA was not qualified or superseded, as MCorp had argued, by the general provisions governing bankruptcy proceedings. The court therefore found no merit in MCorp's argument that the district court's injunction was authorized either by the automatic stay provision in the bankruptcy code or by the provision of the judicial code authorizing district courts to exercise concurrent jurisdiction over certain civil suits, such as bankruptcy proceedings.[288]

Rather than "harmonizing" apparently conflicting provisions, the justices concluded that the Fed's oversight actions fell "squarely" within the bankruptcy code, which expressly precluded an automatic stay from enforcing a "governmental unit's police or regulatory power."[289] Moreover, the Fifth Circuit had erred in authorizing judicial review of the Fed's source of strength regulation, because FISA's language "expressly provide[d]" MCorp with a "meaningful and adequate opportunity" to review the regulations and "clearly and directly demonstrate[d] a congressional intent to preclude review." The district courts lacked jurisdiction to review or enjoin the Fed's ongoing administrative proceedings; it was as simple as that. The appellate court had been mistaken to decide that the district court had jurisdiction to consider the merits of MCorp's challenge to the source-of-strength doctrine. Therefore, the Supreme Court reversed the Fifth Circuit's remand. At the same time, the justices affirmed the vacating of Hughes's injunction of the section 23 proceeding.[290] The Supreme Court remanded the case, and in April 1992 the circuit judges vacated Judge Hughes's injunction and dismissed the entire action for lack of jurisdiction.[291]

After participating in the MCorp bankruptcy proceedings for more than two years, the federal government could not have regarded the Supreme Court's ruling as anything but a Pyrrhic legal victory. The Federal Reserve would hardly seek to resume administrative hearings to investigate the holding company, both because MCorp was effectively defunct and because the Fed had sparred with it so long that it knew all it needed to know about MCorp. The court's decision settled the issues for the future, and there would be no purpose to reopening the past. Instead, the regulators continued to engage themselves in the two remaining tributaries of the MCorp litigation: the civil case in the Northern District, where the regulators were considering filing an appeal; and the MCorp bankruptcy in the Southern District, over which Bankruptcy Judge Clark presided.[292]

MCorp's progress through bankruptcy in the Southern District of Texas had been neither swift nor smooth. By early 1992 the MCorp debtors continued to own one bank but remained liable for an outstanding indebtedness of approximately $470 million. They had yet to develop a reorganization plan acceptable to Judge Clark. The latest proposal was three plans combined in a single document entitled the "Revised Third Proposed Chapter 11 Plan." These reorganization plans required, among other actions, that outstanding claims against MCorp, in excess of $2 billion, be reduced to $120 million by 31 December 1991. It was an ambitious schedule, considering that the debtors submitted the proposal to the judge on 30 September 1991.[293] Before commenting on the plans, Judge Clark noted how previous proceedings had been "marred by broken edges and failed burdens of proof."[294] And after reviewing the proposal, Clark decided the plans were not "fair and equitable" to the parties. In January 1992 Clark refused to confirm the proposed reorganization plan.[295] MCorp must discover a more acceptable method to restructure its nearly half-billion-dollar debt.[296]

Instead, the MCorp debtors, and a committee of unsecured creditors, appealed Bankruptcy Judge Clark's denial of confirmation to District Judge Hughes.[297] However, three of the creditors, Principal Mutual Life Insurance Company, Shearson Lehman Hutton, and FDIC, moved to dismiss the appeal, which they considered improperly pursued under the federal bankruptcy code.[298] Hughes agreed, and ruled that the appeal of the bankruptcy court's denial did not meet standards for permissive review.[299] In April 1992 Hughes granted the motion of the second group of creditors; that is, he dismissed the appeal and remanded the case to Clark.[300]

After more negotiations, wrangling, and squabbles, the creditors agreed on a reorganization strategy that provided for distribution of more than $400 million in assets, and for the settlement of more than $300 million in bank regulators' claims.[301] Judge Clark therefore confirmed a revised third version of the proposed plans.[302] The plans next went before Judge Hughes, who noted that "[a]fter four years of complex bankruptcy litigation, the prospect of a vitalizing reorganization disappeared long ago." As long as the plan served the interests of the creditors, followed the law, and maximized the value of the estates' assets, Hughes was willing to confirm any stable, rational reorganization.[303]

On 1 October 1993, as Judge Hughes approved the MCorp bankruptcy settlement, he also summarized the affair. The judge noted that MCorp and associated debtors had faced two thousand claims totaling over $4 billion, in which MCorp successfully objected to more than $3.5 billion. In settling at least some of the claims, Hughes stressed, the parties settled for "all of the normal reasons people choose contract over trial. . . . Not all claims could be compromised, and the debtors have initiated or responded to numerous adversary proceedings."[304]

Regarding a specific adversary, the judge restated his conclusion that the litigation began when the government "engineered" MCorp's probably avoidable insolvency. The lesson Judge Hughes learned from the legal proceedings was that FDIC was "a political institution that is subject to different rules, including after-the-fact assistance from congress. . . . Although that kind of differential has no place in a republic, it is an operative fact in the real world."[305]

In the end, Judge Hughes considered that the MCorp case had become "a spectacle of expensive litigation." There was only one certainty about the prospect of continuing the litigation, he wrote, and that was that "it will take a long time. . . . Given that FDIC is not constrained by the ordinary economic forces that affect private parties, that it has resourceful counsel, that it has statutory exemptions, . . . and that courts tend to accommodate governmental power, its policy of litigating to the death must be taken as a substantial factor that obliterates illusions of quick, cheap resolution."[306]

After honest people faced the consequences of poor judgment and the bad luck of economic decline, he continued, their "existing losses and consequent disruptions were compounded" by "an arrogant and inept intrusion of the government. Into the debris rushed litigious rascals, whose idea of the public administration of civil justice is a cross between a poker game and the battle of the Somme. As is usually the case, the quiet, competent, cooperative actions of the great many are obscured by those few others."[307] Now that MCorp's former possessions had been "seized, partitioned, valued, claimed, analyzed, and marshalled," however, Judge Hughes believed that the plans for ending the litigation were "as reasonable a solution to this historic problem as is plausible."[308]

CHAPTER EIGHT

Masters, Magistrates, and Managerial Judges

IN THE LATE 1970S federal district judges began to pass on responsibility for monitoring school desegregation plans to task forces, expert panels, and multiethnic citizens' committees. This occurred in Houston, for example, where the parties agreed within a short time—at least, short relative to the total time consumed by the litigation—to the mediated settlement and dismissal of the three-decades-old HISD desegregation suit.[1] Another example of the structural or institutional reform case emerged just as the school desegregation cases were fading from federal judicial priorities, in the form of prisoners' civil rights litigation, through which either an incarcerated individual sought relief from a perceived abuse or else a class of plaintiffs sought court-ordered reform of policies at state prisons and even local jails.[2] Prisoners' cases arose in several states, but the phenomenon was particularly hard felt in the Southern District of Texas, because the overwhelming majority of the detainees in Texas were housed in facilities that were within the Southern District's boundaries.[3]

Prisoners' suits multiplied so rapidly during the 1980s that the Southern District judges in Houston instituted new management techniques specifically to address the high volume of complaints that prisoners filed in their division. The first part of this chapter examines the judicial response to early, large-scale, and long-lasting prison reform cases. The next section describes the judges' collective response to the docket management problems that were created by a proliferation of individual prisoners' suits. In both kinds of case, the routine delegation of oversight functions to judicial adjuncts, such as masters and magistrates, was key to the judges' ability to come to grips with the prisoners' problem. Perhaps more even than when they oversaw school litigation, judges who oversaw prisoners' litigation were "managerial" and took on the "additional functions of local legislator and executive."[4]

The final section of this chapter examines a different source of docket congestion with which the Southern District judges have continually struggled and over which they have had little means of control. This was a dramatic increase in the number of narcotics prosecutions that can be associated with the ratcheting up of the federal war on drugs since the early 1980s. Presidents from both of the major parties have supported increased federal enforcement and prosecutorial resources. Congress has usually seconded these goals, both by enacting tougher laws and by authorizing the hiring of more prosecutors, some of them hired specifically to bring more cases against drug offenders.[5] The Congress also shifted effective control over sentencing from the judges to prosecutors through the 1984 Sentencing Reform Act. When it took effect in November 1987, this act abolished parole, established mandatory minimum sentences for federal crimes—especially drug-related violations—and created formulas to be used for computing sentences.[6]

There is no doubt that the two "political" branches had the authority to revise the criminal statutes and to adjust priorities for enforcement and prosecution, but the executive and legislative exercises of authority during the 1980s had an extraordinarily negative effect on the ability of the judiciary—especially federal district judges in the Southern District of Texas—to keep either their criminal or civil dockets current. Many federal judges found the sentencing guidelines—coupled with the Speedy Trial Act, which took effect in the early 1980s—to be obnoxious infringements on their exercise of authority over their own dockets.[7]

AN ARM OF THE COURT

The activity of federal law enforcement, especially in the area of narcotics interdiction and prosecution, increased in the 1970s, when, predictably, it added to the burden of federal trial judges.[8] Yet, according to the statistics collected and published by the Administrative Office of the U.S. Courts, the number of criminal cases prosecuted in the Southern District of Texas fell substantially, from a high of 3,290 cases in 1972 to only 1,614 cases in 1973, then 1,116 in 1974, and, finally, 1,079 in 1975.[9] The decline in criminal filings was not a cause for celebration, however, because the statisticians of the Administrative Office worried that counterintuitive results simply indicated "serious problems in the base data."[10]

Because the Southern District's budget was tied to its needs, usually as those needs could be predicted by the observed trends in caseload, the numbers also alarmed Chief Judge Reynaldo Garza. He and Clerk Bailey Thomas decided that the data misrepresented the reality of the steadily rising caseloads in the district and could not go unchallenged. They wrote to the Administrative Office in the spring of 1976, to suggest that the data did not reflect the fact that federal magistrates had begun to try immigration defendants on complaints, when previously, the federal district judges had tried them on indictments. The clerk's office did not assign case numbers when these minor crimes were referred to the magistrates, and therefore they were no longer being reported to the Administrative Office under criminal filings. But court time and resources were nevertheless consumed in processing the minor criminal cases. The judge and the clerk estimated the true rate of growth in the Southern District's criminal caseload, especially drug-related filings, to be 15 percent per year.[11]

Judge Garza, already plagued and preoccupied with immigration and narcotics cases on the border, had joined other federal judges in lobbying for the passage of the Magistrates Act of 1968.[12] Under the statute, in addition to conducting trials for minor criminal offenses, magistrates were authorized to revoke probation,[13] assist judges in pretrial proceedings for both civil and criminal trials, and review posttrial appeal applications.[14] The act was not fully implemented until June 1971, but then, as indicated by the numbers above, the impact was dramatic. The author of a contemporaneous study of immigration control in the 1970s, for example, concluded from that the decline in certain immigration-related prosecutions early in the decade "was due to the tendency of the United States Attorneys to reduce felony charges to misdemeanor[s]," which had "greatly expedited the disposition" of violations by assigning them to magistrates. The magistrates were therefore available by the 1970s to take up the repetitious duty of arraigning immigration defendants under the plea-bargained docket calls that Judges Connally and Garza had handled themselves throughout the 1960s.[15]

Although Congress had increased the workload on the trial judges by adding criminal statutes and by expanding federal law enforcement agencies, it reduced the burden on federal district judges by creating the magistrates. Final authority in deciding cases was reserved for the judge, but, aside from the occasional confusion over statistics, this variety of judicial "adjunct," like special masters, referees, and bankruptcy judges, proved useful to the federal district judges as their workload diversified.[16] The addition of magistrates to the Southern District judges' support personnel was especially welcome when prisoners' complaints began to crowd the civil dockets in the 1970s.

The U.S. Supreme Court had declared as early as 1958 that the Eighth Amendment's proscription of "cruel and unusual" criminal punishments "must draw its meaning from the evolving standards of decency that mark the progress of a maturing society."[17] Under this unhelpful criterion, federal trial judges had adopted a "hands off" policy regarding prisons and jails. Throughout the 1960s, therefore, federal judges deferred to professional administrators in matters of discipline and punishment.[18] Late in the decade, however, "evolving standards of decency" and the rising number of prisoners' complaints inspired federal district judges to abandon the hands-off policy.[19] Fifth Circuit Judge Frank Hooper noted in 1968, for example, that there had been "phenomenal" growth in the number of civil rights suits filed by, or on behalf of, inmates.[20] Circuit Judge Hooper had identified the trend in its early stages. In 1966, when the federal judiciary first reported the statistic, prisoners filed 218 civil rights claims under section 1983. Twelve years later, inmates filed 9,730 section 1983 complaints.[21]

The increase in prisoners' civil rights litigation aggravated the already serious congestion of federal dockets.[22] Fortunately, many inmate complaints were uncomplicated and, when successful in court, required only that judges order prison administrators either to cease or to initiate specific practices. For example, in a 1967 decision the Fifth Circuit Court of Appeals established that it was inherently unfair to try a defendant wearing a prison uniform, because it could bias jurors against the prisoner by tainting the presumption of innocence.[23] In 1969 the Supreme Court invalidated a regulation that banned prisoners from assisting one another in the preparation of petitions. The court held that the rule denied indigent and illiterate inmates their rights to seek to redress of their grievances in court.[24] In the Southern District of Texas in 1972, Judge John Singleton condemned, on First Amendment grounds, prison officials' routine censorship and withholding of mail, including inmates' correspondence with their attorneys. James DeAnda, the veteran civil rights litigator and future Southern District judge, was among the prisoners' lawyers in these cases.[25]

The Southern District of Texas, where the judges saw between 250 and 400 section 1983 actions annually, was among the top five federal districts hearing prisoners' cases during the 1970s.[26] In a single four-month period in summer 1972, for example, plaintiffs of all kinds filed 548 civil actions in the Houston Division of the Southern District. Fifty-four were section 1983 complaints by inmates. Twenty-nine of these suits alleged that the plaintiff was a victim of unconstitutionally harsh conditions or arbitrary discipline. Taking note of these figures as he was scrutinizing conditions in the Harris County jails, Judge Carl Bue stated, or perhaps understated, the issue in this way: "It is clear that public and legal scrutiny of the prison systems is now underway in this country."[27]

In 1972 Lawrence Alberti and other county prisoners filed a section 1983 complaint in the Southern District, as a class action on behalf of past, present, and future Harris County jail inmates. Alberti alleged that crowding and poor conditions in the jails amounted to cruel and unusual punishment. The suit named as defendants members of the County Commissioners Court and the Sheriff's Department, which administered the county detention facilities. Bue drew the case and conducted extensive hearings; he also visited the jails. In 1975, in *Alberti v. Sheriff of Harris County,* the judge ruled in favor of the plaintiff prisoners. He declared that approximately 2,500 county inmates, some who had not yet been tried and others who were only awaiting transfer to a state prison, had seriously and unconstitutionally overcrowded the jail, which was designed to accommodate 1,150 inmates.[28]

Overcrowding was at the root of many complaints about Texas prisons. In 1971, for example, George J. Beto, the director of the Texas Department of Corrections (TDC), admitted to state and federal judges visiting a Huntsville prison that there was a "degree of preposterousness" in the fact that the TDC housed 14,700 prisoners, a figure that was second only to California's inmate population. Many of the inmates, Beto argued, should have received probation rather than being sentenced to prison time.[29] When Beto retired the next year, however, the TDC held more than 16,500 inmates in fourteen separate prison units located in the southern and eastern regions of the state.[30] There were 25,000 prisoners behind TDC bars in 1978. That year, U.S. District Judge William Wayne Justice of the Eastern District of Texas began hearings in *Ruiz v. Estelle,* one of the largest and most controversial prison cases ever. The Ruiz case was filed in the Eastern District, but the witnesses were most frequently housed in prison units in the Southern District. Therefore, Justice tried the case in the federal courthouse in Houston. Two years later, when the inmate population stood at more than 30,000, Judge Justice ruled that Texas's prisons were unconstitutionally overcrowded.[31]

The *Alberti* county jail and *Ruiz* state prison suits developed independently, but, in part because of similar issues, the cases eventually became linked during extended proceedings. The cases intersected as state and local officials each sought to resolve overcrowding by shipping inmates to the other's facility. Unlike the comparatively simple decrees that could resolve controversies concerning prisoners' clothing, freedom of association, and free speech rights, both Bue in *Alberti* and Justice in *Ruiz* placed the institutions under court control, ordered their reorganization, and directed administrators to spend millions of tax dollars to correct overcrowded conditions. Both judges retained oversight for years as they sought to meliorate overcrowding. To assist them, both Bue and Justice relied on court-appointed adjuncts to act as their advisors, mediators, and enforcers. Curiously, neither judge sought at that early juncture to designate a magistrate to serve as a special master in these cases.[32]

Judge Bue, for example, established an Office of the Ombudsman in December 1975. He named James Oitzinger, the lead plaintiffs' attorney in *Alberti,* to be the ombudsman.[33] Judge Justice, by contrast, established an Office of the Special Master, but with an equivalent mandate. He chose Vincent Nathan, a transplanted Texan, former professor at the University of Toledo, and experienced master in prison cases, to be the *Ruiz* special master.[34] The appointment of these adjuncts, whether called masters or ombudsmen, was not new in complex and controversial cases. The Federal Rules of Civil Procedure, as seen in previous chapters, authorized federal district judges to appoint and to define the duties of masters.[35] As Nathan wrote in 1979, before his involvement in Ruiz, a master's role varies with the needs of the court.[36] An adjunct was "an arm of the court" who, with a judge's approval, might exercise "quasi-judicial" powers.[37]

A master might convene separate evidentiary hearings, for example, mediate disputes between the parties to a suit, broker settlements and consent decrees, and then monitor a defendant's compliance with court orders. In prison reform litigation, this last function might entail inspecting facilities under injunction or interviewing guards and prisoners.[38] As "surrogate judges," special masters could be as controversial as the real thing.[39]

Judge Buc's introduction to problems brewing in the Texas prison system came through a strange 1972 lawsuit, which led him to review the extraordinary career of Frances Freeman Jalet, one of the single-minded individuals who can be credited with the reversal of the federal judicial hands-off policy in the 1960s. Jalet had earned liberal arts degrees at both Radcliffe College and Columbia Teachers College. She continued her studies as she brought up a family and earned law degrees from both Columbia University and Georgetown University. Jalet was on the New York State Law Revision Commission from 1959 to 1967. Then, at age fifty-seven, she was admitted to the Reginald Heber Smith Foundation's program for training attorneys in poverty law, landlord-tenant law, juvenile courts, and administrative law. After she completed the foundation's six-week course at the University of Pennsylvania Law School, Jalet was sent to Austin, Texas, to work with the Legal Aid and Defender Society (LADS), which received its main funding from the Office of Economic Opportunity (OEO), a federal agency created in the 1960s to fight President Johnson's war on poverty.[40]

Fred Arispe Cruz, a TDC prisoner in Huntsville, wrote to Jalet after he read a September 1967 newspaper story from Austin that labeled her the "Portia for the Poor." Cruz was then twenty-eight years old, but he had a long criminal record and substantial residence in the TDC. He had first been jailed in the TDC at the age of eighteen, after his conviction for marijuana possession in 1957. When Cruz wrote Jalet, he was serving a fifteen-year sentence for robbery by assault. He had acquired some expertise in drafting legal documents for himself and other inmates, and had become one of the more talented of the so-called "writ writers" in the TDC.[41] This advocacy earned Cruz a reputation among admiring inmates as the "Ralph Nader in the prison system." After learning that Cruz shared her interest in social justice, Jalet began to correspond with him and then to visit him in the Huntsville prison.[42]

Although not licensed to practice law in Texas until March 1968, Jalet began to advise Cruz and other TDC prisoners in legal matters. After TDC Director Beto wrote to complain about her prison activities, the Austin LADS supervisor admonished Jalet for not concentrating her efforts on the poor. He then transferred her to the Dallas Legal Aid Clinic, another OEO project. Beto removed Jalet's name from an approved visitor list at Huntsville's prison in October 1968. On 24 December, Jalet's supervisor fired her.[43]

Beto apparently had a hand in Jalet's dismissal. He had suggested to her Dallas superiors that her advocacy was causing unrest in TDC prisons. Jalet sued Beto and the Dallas Clinic's director in state district court, alleging a conspiracy to deprive her of access to her inmate clients. The suit was dismissed, and she joined the Legal Aid Clinic at Texas Southern University (TSU) in Houston. In January 1969 Jalet became a party to another lawsuit making similar allegations but filed in federal court against Beto and a TDC warden. As a consequence, Beto barred Jalet from seeing TDC inmates until March 1969, when the federal suit was also dismissed.[44]

Beto complained to the dean of the TSU law school about her continued work with prisoners, but the dean defended Jalet's actions and interests. He retained her at the TSU legal clinic. In February 1970 Jalet's Smith Foundation Fellowship ended. Lacking this support, she moved to New York City to work for the Queens Legal Services.[45] She periodically returned to Texas to maintain contact with her prisoner clientele. In March 1971 she obtained a position in Houston with the Volunteers in Service to America (VISTA), another federal agency created in the 1960s to aid the poor. The VISTA job allowed her to resume her work with prisoners. Jalet made 583 visits to see inmates between October 1967 and March 1972, when her VISTA position ended. Seventy visits were to see Cruz, but she gave legal assistance to more than one hundred inmates. Many of the prisoners filed habeas corpus petitions, others section 1983 civil rights complaints attacking prison conditions and procedures. And Beto continued to search for a way to end her career. In November 1971, allegedly because of her many visits and her large clientele, Beto prohibited Jalet from seeing any TDC inmates except those who were already her clients.[46]

Cruz was discharged from prison in early 1972. He and Jalet immediately married.[47] Jalet began working for Harris County Legal Assistance, Inc. Cruz found volunteer work with the National Association for the Advancement of Colored People (NAACP) Legal Defense and Educational Fund (LDEF, the renamed "Inc. Fund"). The pair continued advocating prisoners' rights. Shortly thereafter, the U.S. Supreme Court ruled, in *Cruz v. Beto*, that the TDC could not interfere with efforts by "writ writers" to reform prisons through litigation. The justices agreed with Cruz that prisoners retained their right as citizens to petition the courts.[48]

The honeymoon ended in spring 1972. Three inmates filed separate but strikingly similar federal class action lawsuits, under section 1983, in the Southern District. The plaintiffs alleged that Jalet had attempted to organize an inmate uprising aimed at the violent overthrow of the TDC. With the "unwitting acquiescence" of TDC officials who had permitted her to make more than five hundred prison visits, Jalet had supposedly succeeded in establishing "numerous ostensible attorney-client relationships in furtherance of her conspiratorial goals." Her activities led to the plaintiffs' being threatened and beaten because "they would not yield to such plans to promote unrest and violence." They claimed to have suffered "irreparable injury" as a consequence of the conspiracy. The plaintiffs had been deprived of their rights under the Eighth and Fourteenth Amendments "to be free from harassment, intimidation, personal injury, threats of death, and cruel and unusual punishment."[49] According to the complaint, the prisoners sought to enjoin Jalet's access to TDC facilities, because "as the plaintiffs profess to see it, the system can successfully operate only when its code of strict rules and regulations is rigidly enforced without interference, thereby permitting an inmate to serve his sentence without incident in the minimum time permitted under such rules."[50]

Jalet contended that the complaints were instigated by the plaintiffs as the result of either promises of benefits, including early paroles, or threats of reprisal by TDC officials. She charged that the lawsuits were part of Beto's ongoing efforts to deprive her of her right to practice law and to consult with clients who happened to be confined in the TDC. Jalet argued that Beto was using the prisoner plaintiffs as "mere unknowing conduits" in his own "unlawful conspiracy." She argued that the judge should dismiss the case.[51]

Sixty witnesses testified during the six-week trial. Forty-seven were inmates or former inmates of the TDC. Thirteen testified for the plaintiffs and thirty-four for Jalet. Judge Bue announced on 18 September 1972 that only one fact was undisputed, that fact being that Jalet and TDC officials were "bitter antagonists." But "apart from serious problems in determining credibility of the inmate witnesses on both sides," Bue found no convincing proof of illegal activity on Jalet's part and "certainly none that can satisfy the legal requisites of a conspiracy."[52] Therefore, Bue ruled for Jalet and dismissed the lawsuit.[53] The judge noted that, having found that Jalet had not engaged in a conspiracy, he could end his opinion. Instead, Bue offered, "at the risk of prolonging" his opinion and admittedly in dicta, his reflections on the testimony at the lengthy trial.[54]

Bue admitted that the testimony and documentary evidence had exposed to him the details of "a way of life little known to the 'free world.'" Although he still accepted the basic proposition that individuals who violated the law should serve time in prison, Bue noted that "the fact remains that our prisons are full." With large numbers of inmates housed in a limited number of facilities, there must be a system of rules as well as prescribed punishment to be properly administered when the rules were violated. The rules must be clear and must be enforced fairly. The evidence in the Jalet case was too muddled for Bue to judge whether the rules were being fairly applied.[55] Bue suggested that by providing an administrative mechanism to dispose of prisoner grievances short of legal action, a "satisfactory solution should be much more readily achieved."[56]

The judge proposed that the TDC provide for investigation of prisoners' complaints by "an outside person or agency as well as by the institution." This was a version of the "ombudsman" concept, which he noted was in the testing stages in some states. The ombudsman would be "a third force, neither allied with the inmates nor the prison administration," who would independently investigate allegations of administrative malpractice, with a view toward correcting abuses. The office of the ombudsman, Bue suggested, "thus becomes the mechanism whereby fair and objective review of alleged prison abuses is thoroughly undertaken." Bue noted that the ombudsman concept had its detractors, including Beto. But the "absolute independence of the ombudsman from a prison administration can be the guarantee which insures that the inmate grievances will be heard and accorded an objective review and, where meritorious, that something will be done about them." If properly constituted, Bue declared, then the

> very presence of the ombudsman can serve to eliminate or, at least, reduce the polarization of views of witnesses representing the prison administration vis-a-vis the inmates at court proceedings which, as this extended litigation has amply proven, may resolve nothing, either in ascertaining the truth of an individual incident or in identifying the root evil, if any, to be corrected. Instead, when instances arise in which hearings are ultimately required to air prisoner grievances, there would be another potential source of information, presumably highly reliable, which would be of assistance in the determination of the truth of the matter.[57]

A successful administrative mechanism like the one Bue suggested, moreover, available through the ombudsman's office, would help to alleviate the recurrence of these types of prisoners' complaints on the crowded federal court dockets. This alternative to federal suits, Bue concluded, would "diminish the multitude of charges so frequently voiced that the courts are taking over and are bent on dictating the administrative procedures to be followed in the prisons."[58]

Through the extensive and graphic testimony of the Jalet trial, Bue had glimpsed some of the hidden world of the criminal detention system in Texas. He boldly suggested the adoption of an ombudsman who could act as an independent "third force" to mediate conflicts between inmates and administration. It is ironic that so soon after, in the Harris County jail case, *Alberti,* Bue retained the title of ombudsman but kept none of the attributes he had enumerated in the Jalet dicta.

In August 1972, Lawrence Alberti filed his section 1983 action against the Harris County Commissioners Court and the Sheriff's Department. Bue conducted extensive hearings, during which the expert witnesses on both sides of the case painted a grim picture. A plaintiffs' witness estimated that more than twelve hundred acts of violence were reported by inmates every year in the jail. Another of the plaintiffs' experts testified that the true number of sexual assaults may be "five to six times greater" than the number reported. But rather than deny the truth of these assertions, an expert witness for the defense testified that, on the basis of his experience with similar institutions, "sexual abuse and threats of sexual abuse are high."[59] The testimony led Bue to conclude that "inmate beatings and homosexual rapes and attacks are prevalent."[60] The result, he said, was "a continuous pattern of deprivations which clearly reach constitutional dimensions."[61]

When the testimony illustrated that the prisoners had genuine complaints and would likely prevail, the county entered into a consent decree, which generally accepted the plaintiffs' complaints that the detention facilities were inadequate. The parties signed, and Bue approved the decree on 4 February 1975. The decree called for renovations of existing facilities, the development of a new central jail, and improvements in staff and security. The commissioners court and the sheriff's office agreed to provide enough guards and other professional staff so that the administrators did not rely on inmates for assistance in keeping order. Judge Bue retained jurisdiction in the case so that he could amend the judgment or issue interim orders as necessary. However, he defined his role in the litigation as limited. The parties were to work together to devise the detailed proposals for implementing the rather broad consent agreement.[62]

On 1 May the county submitted a preliminary plan containing descriptions of the proposed renovations of the old detention center and a discussion of the architectural features of the jail to be built. The plan also included a proposal to schedule a bond election to raise $15 million, the sum the county suggested was necessary for the project. But in August the plaintiffs' attorneys, Gerald Birnberg and James Oitzinger, contacted Bue and expressed doubts about the 1 May plan. They moved for supplemental relief, asking Bue to play a more active role in the case.[63]

Bue recognized that he needed better information about the state of the present jail and the adequacy of the county's proposal to fulfill the provisions of the consent decree. Therefore, he held another six days of hearings and then, on 24 September, personally toured several of the county jail facilities. These consisted of a central jail in downtown Houston, which had been designed to hold 1,150, and a detention center in Humble, designed to hold 810 inmates.[64] Both of the facilities were holding more than twice the intended number of prisoners. Because time was short, since the bond election was only days away, and because he quickly learned what he needed to know, Bue issued his decision one day after the tour. He ruled that the plaintiffs were correct to doubt the plan the county had submitted. The proposed renovations, new construction, and bond issue of $15 million were completely inadequate for comporting with the consent decree in the future, since the plan would not even solve the problems of the present. It would take more money than the county had estimated to bring the jails into compliance with the constitutional standards.[65]

After more consultation with the parties, Bue issued a new, broad remedial order on 16 December 1975. Among other findings the judge determined that guards and staff in the jails were insufficient in number and inadequately trained. He ordered the county to begin adequate training, to increase the pay of jail personnel, and to increase the staffing sufficient to provide one jailer for every twenty inmates. He also established the Office of the Ombudsman "to monitor defendants' efforts in complying with this order and in fulfilling the mandate and requirement of the consent judgment." Specifically, it was the ombudsman's duty to make sure that the county observed the federal district judge's orders to create a pretrial release program that would allow most detainees to make bail quickly, to eliminate jail overcrowding, and to improve "deplorable," "inhumane," and deteriorating jail conditions. The ombudsman was to submit periodic reports directly to the court on pretrial release, report to the court "at any time" on overcrowding, make recommendations for improvements, and "similarly monitor and report upon defendants' efforts" to improve jail conditions in general.[66]

These duties were rather typical for a court adjunct such as a master. But Judge Bue then appointed Oitzinger and Birnberg to be the ombudsmen. Moreover, Bue specified that they could continue to represent the plaintiffs.[67] This was not a decision calculated to meet the criteria he had set out in the Jalet case, namely, that the ombudsman should be "a third force, neither allied with the inmates nor the prison administration." But the county did not appeal the order creating the ombudsman's office or the appointment of the two plaintiffs' attorneys to lead it.[68]

There is no evidence that Oitzinger and Birnberg abused the power or access that the ombudsman's office gave them. They did not receive everything they asked for in the litigation. In 1978, for example, Bue reluctantly approved the commissioners court's plans for the new downtown jail. These plans provided for four-person cells to be arranged into twenty-four-person dormitories. The plaintiffs had called for the creation of single inmate cells. Bue ruled that the four-to-a-cell jail design did not itself violate the minimum constitutional standards. He warned, however, that the new jail might not be safely occupied without providing additional staff. Bue conditionally approved the plan, contingent upon the defendants' providing adequate staffing to comply with other constitutional requisites.[69]

Judge Bue's growing familiarity with the issues raised by prisoners' civil rights suits made him the Southern District's first resident expert on that subject. In August 1974 Bue agreed to Chief Judge Connally's request that he consult with the Texas attorney general to examine the use of three-judge panels in cases involving prisoners' claims.[70] Six months later, after Connally had accepted senior judge status, new Chief Judge Garza transferred another TDC lawsuit involving Fred Cruz, known as *Cruz v. Estelle,* from Connally's docket onto Bue's.[71]

There were in addition more facets of the earlier *Cruz v. Beto* case for Bue to consider. On 19 October 1976 President Gerald Ford signed the Civil Rights Attorney's Fees Awards Act of 1976.[72] This gave federal courts discretion to award "reasonable" attorney's fees to the prevailing party in certain civil rights suits, including actions under section 1983.[73] Judge Bue had in fact already granted fees—because he decided that the TDC had displayed "bad faith" during the litigation—to William Bennett Turner, the San Francisco–based director of the NAACP's LDEF, who had been Cruz's lead attorney of record as the case went to the Supreme Court, and to Turner's associates in Houston, the future Southern District Judge Gabrielle McDonald and her then-husband, Mark McDonald. The parties were unable to agree to a definition of a "reasonable" fee, however, and Bue conducted a hearing to resolve that issue. On 3 March 1977 he announced his decision that the plaintiffs' attorneys should receive a total of $27,760. The judge based this sum on "legal memoranda" prepared by the legal team and, "most importantly," Bue declared, on his own "in-depth familiarity with the nature of the prosecution and defense which have characterized this long pending litigation."[74]

In 1982, spurred by the consent decree and remedial orders, Harris County completed its new downtown jail, with a designed capacity of 3,505 inmates, and it closed the old jail. Harris County later authorized the construction of yet another detention facility, this with a capacity of 4,000, and the renovation of the old central jail, boosted to house 400.[75] The capacity still fell short of demand, especially in May 1982, when the TDC, in an effort to meet cell space requirements mandated by Judge Justice in the *Ruiz* case, began limiting its intake of inmates from Harris County.[76] The Harris County situation deteriorated further when it missed Judge Bue's 15 February 1985 deadline to hire 300 additional guards for its new jail. In March, the ombudsman Oitzinger filed a contempt motion and requested that Bue order the county to pay the prisoners $46,846 per day until it hired the needed guards. Oitzinger noted that the $46,846 daily figure was twice what it would have cost Harris County to hire the new guards.[77]

The county appealed a number of Bue's orders, and in June 1986 Fifth Circuit Judge Robert Hill declared for a three-judge appellate panel that "[w]e conclude, as a matter of law, that the level of violence and sexual assault found to be existing in the Harris County jails constitutes a violation of the Eighth Amendment." Hill added that it was "regrettable that a federal court is still deeply involved" in overseeing the Harris County jails after thirteen years of litigation. But it was "more regrettable," Judge Hill added, that "after thirteen years conditions in the jails are still in contravention of constitutional standards. Despite the efforts of the parties and the court, inmates continue to be beaten, raped, abused, and assaulted."[78] The district court, the appellate judges ruled, had acted properly in fashioning "new relief for an old malady." Accordingly, the panel affirmed Bue's order "in all respects."[79]

Judge John R. Brown was a member of the Fifth Circuit panel that affirmed his old protégé Bue in *Alberti*, but he wrote a separate concurring opinion. Brown wrote separately, he said, to address two issues in the case that he believed "may prove to be snares for the unwary in future cases." The first issue concerned the scope of remedial orders under the Eighth Amendment. Judge Brown thought that "care must be exercised lest we resort too easily to remedies for the ephemeral 'totality of the conditions' in our haste, as judges, to do the right thing as people." His second concern was more pointed in questioning Bue's decision to appoint the plaintiffs' counsel to be his own ombudsman. Although Brown agreed, as he said, that, "on consideration of the whole record, this has not resulted in a miscarriage of justice," he would "strongly discourage" such an appointment in future cases. The roles of counsel and ombudsman are antithetical, Brown thought, and, to combine them in a single attorney created at the least an appearance of unfairness.[80]

Brown reminded the parties, including his friend Bue, that, as "an arm of the court," an ombudsman is under an obligation to behave impartially and to report objectively. He recognized that the Fifth Circuit had previously endorsed the judicial appointment of an ombudsman as the kind of innovation necessary to relieve overcrowded federal dockets. But when the circuit had approved, he noted, the district judge had shown "the good judgment to appoint a magistrate as Ombudsman."[81] Perhaps desiring to soften the blow of this mild criticism, Brown added, "We, and the lower federal courts, are courts of limited jurisdiction. Our task is not to correct all social ills, however egregious they may seem to us as individuals. The keys to the Kingdom are not in our hands."[82] Brown concluded that Bue "[t]o his credit . . . never strayed from his very limited role [and] in this case, I believe that we [the Fifth Circuit Court of Appeals] have done likewise."[83]

By February 1987 Harris County had opened another detention facility in downtown Houston, and with it achieved the landmark of having the population of its jails be only 5 percent above their design capacity. The county tried to end the *Alberti* case at that point and asked the judge for a final judgment and dismissal.[84] Judge Bue denied the request. But in April 1987, in order to replace Oitzinger, who had by then resigned as ombudsman, Bue appointed three new adjuncts to inspect the jails, to assess the county's compliance with court orders, and to determine the maximum capacities of the jails. These judicial adjuncts were designated a special master, a medical monitor-assessor, and a jail monitor-assessor.[85]

Judge Bue retired soon after appointing these three new court officers. His successor judge on the Southern District bench did not inherit responsibility for the case. Instead, Chief Judge Norman Black, the former magistrate, oversaw the compliance of the Harris County jails. In March 1993 he set a fifty-dollar-per-day fine for every inmate above the 9,800 ceiling allowed in the county's four detention facilities, to be paid by the state of Texas for not transferring prisoners out of the jail into state prisons. Black gave the state until 1 April to bring the county prisoner population under the cap. Harris County held 12,500 inmates that week, which means the state would be fined $135,000 a day after 1 April.[86] In August 1995, however, Chief Judge Black finally ended the twenty-three years of federal judicial control over the Harris County jails. Black also closed the offices of the special master and jail monitors.[87] Federal District Judge Justice, however, continued to monitor TDC prisons into the late 1990s.[88]

In August 1995, after the Harris County case was dismissed, former court ombudsman James Oitzinger noted that the *Alberti* litigation had accomplished much more than the relief of chronic overcrowding. "Before this [case]," he told reporters, "a mother couldn't visit her son, a wife couldn't visit her husband more than once a week. Now, any day you can go over there and see hundreds of visitors waiting in line. I think that had the most dramatic effect on the day-to-day lives of the inmates."[89]

WITH THE HOPE THAT SPRINGS ETERNAL

Reform of state and county prisons had supplanted school desegregation from the 1970s into the 1990s as the main example of judicially managed public law litigation. Bue, Justice, and their successors in the prison cases, like federal district judges who had supervised school districts for decades, returned to the cases again and again as officials appealed, then delayed, and, finally, reluctantly submitted. Federal interventions in prisons and jails was as controversial and as long-lived as judicial intervention in the public schools. TDC prisons and Harris County jails were under federal court supervision until the 1990s. In addition to such big cases, however, the Southern District judges faced a simultaneous increase in individual civil rights complaints under section 1983, as well as habeas corpus filings, so-called section 2254 cases.[90]

Congress expanded magistrates' authority several times in the 1970s, enabling the federal district judges to lean more heavily on these adjuncts for docket management. In 1976, for example, the Congress empowered U.S. magistrates to undertake "such additional duties as are not inconsistent with the Constitution and laws of the United States." Federal district judges could delegate these "additional duties" to the magistrate without litigants' consent. But the magistrate could only render a final decision in a civil case with the parties' consent. The prospect of waiting months or even years before rising to the top of a federal district judge's civil docket encouraged many to opt for the quicker route through a magistrate's court.[91] Congress granted the magistrates yet more authority in 1979. Upon the request of a district judge, and with the consent of the parties, magistrates were authorized to conduct "any or all proceedings in a jury or nonjury civil matter."[92]

Under their enlarged authority in criminal matters, the magistrates performed duties that were basically "ministerial." They assisted district judges by assuming the burden of presiding over routine pretrial proceedings, such as arraigning defendants and scheduling felony trials to be conducted later by the judge. Magistrates rendered similar aid during posttrial proceedings by conducting the first review of applications for new trials submitted by the convicted.[93] The magistrate's authority in civil cases could be more sweeping, especially when judges designated them to act as special masters.[94]

In the fall of 1976 Judge Bue suggested to Chief Judge Garza that it would be useful to begin to assign the Southern District's magistrates to review the burgeoning load of prisoners' filings. Garza agreed, and he ordered Bue's idea into effect under local rules in November 1976.[95] After the 1979 revision became effective, and after consultation with the other Southern District judges, Chief Judge Singleton, Garza's successor, issued a general order of the court that formalized the jurisdiction and procedures to be used in assigning magistrates. In addition to hearing basic civil and minor criminal matters, magistrates soon became the first, and often the only, officers of the court in the Southern District to review a prisoner's civil rights or habeas petition. A magistrate issued preliminary orders, conducted hearings, and submitted to a federal district judge a report containing proposed findings of fact and recommendations for the disposition of a petition.[96] To avoid "forum shopping," the general order adapted the Southern District's existing practice of random selection of judges to the selection of the magistrate to be assigned a particular case.[97]

Chief Judge Singleton had inherited a growing problem in the disposition of prisoners' cases. In August 1981 he wrote to "my dear Judges" to suggest new procedures. He noted that at the time, the Southern District dockets listed approximately six hundred pending prisoner section 1983 cases, of which two hundred had been pending since 1976 or before. Singleton admitted to "a real concern that if we do not do something about these cases, we are open to severe criticism by the Judicial Conference. I am even concerned that the matter could be the subject of bad publicity for the court." He recommended that, when the judges hired their next new magistrate, which they would do in the next few months, all pending prisoner section 1983 cases be assigned as a group to that individual. That magistrate should be temporarily relieved of all other duties, and should be wholly dedicated to clearing the backlog.[98]

In the spring of 1982, Singleton issued another general order that made the timely disposition of prisoners' petitions a higher priority for all of the Southern District's magistrates.[99] By late 1982 there were 668 civil rights cases and 322 habeas corpus cases still pending. One-third of these cases were two years old, and, as Singleton noted in a letter to the other judges, a few cases were eleven years old. The chief judge was writing to announce that the Houston-based judges had recently met and had committed the court to solving this "serious problem." The judges made it the primary duty of the Houston magistrates to handle prisoner cases. Table 3 indicates the caseload at that time.

Singleton was hopeful that, by concentrating their magistrate's attention, the Houston judges would eventually resolve the matter. Nonetheless, "given the current backlog and the continual filing" of cases, he wrote, "the resolution of the 'backlog problem' will only be gradual."[100]

Under this stepped-up plan, the number of pending section 1983 cases dropped from 670 to 583 over the next year. But, at the same time, the number of pending habeas corpus petitions had risen from 322 to 411. As U.S. magistrate H. Lingo Platter pointed out in a September 1983 memorandum to Singleton, this meant that the total number of prisoner cases had not been reduced significantly. The pending cases had dropped from 1,021 to 1,016.[101]

The problem was that Texas prison populations had continued to rise throughout the 1980s, and new filings rose accordingly. By September 1984, as Singleton wrote to the Administrative Office of the U.S. Courts, the TDC had approximately thirty-six thousand inmates, most of them still located within the area served by the Houston Division of the Southern District of Texas. They filed approximately one thousand new cases each year under either section 1983 or section 2254. The chief judge had written to the Washington, D.C., office to explain the Southern District's procedures and to justify his request for funding of several new staff attorneys who would "centralize the prisoner cases, monitor multiple filings to eliminate duplicity of work and help develop the litigation into a recognizable and manageable form." The judges depended on these staff attorneys as well as magistrates, Singleton explained, because the "difficulty with moving, managing and disposing of this type of litigation by judicial officers would be tantamount to throwing sand in the gears of justice and would certainly result in a congestion and clogging of the pending serious litigation."[102]

Singleton closed this letter by advising the Administrative Office that the clerk of court, Jesse Clark, supervised the staff attorneys, and that Judge James DeAnda was the designated liaison for the Southern District's magistrates.[103] Judge DeAnda inherited this duty from Bue in the mid-1980s, and, working with Singleton and Clark, DeAnda expended a great deal of energy attempting to rationalize the timely processing of the district's backlogged prisoners' cases.[104] In October 1986 DeAnda wrote to Singleton to submit, "[w]ith the hope that springs eternal," a plan for a "pilot program" for the management of the prisoner civil rights cases. He first stated the district's problem in stark terms. There were at that time 1,014 pending prisoner civil rights cases, of which 193 (19 percent) were more than three years old. An additional 137 (13 percent) had been pending more than two years. To truly get control of the problem, DeAnda offered the following recommendations: first, to dispose of "frivolous and patently merit-less cases at a very early stage"; next, to

TABLE 3. Prisoner Civil Rights and Habeas Corpus Litigation, November 1981 to October 1982

MONTH	FILED	CLOSED	§ 1983	§ 2254
November 1981	64	23	24	22
December 1981	20	9	24	14
January 1982	27	22	38	20
February 1982	48	18	20	12
March 1982	42	20	51	20
April 1982	44	17	50	13
May 1982	31	19	52	12
June 1982	48	18	50	18
July 1982	39	19	54	10
August 1982	43	21	67	11
September 1982	48	15	61	18
October 1982	35	17	35	17
TOTAL	489	218	526	187
MONTHLY AVERAGE	41	18	44	16

Source: Chief Judge John V. Singleton to "Mesdames and Gentlemen," 19 November 1982, clerk's files of Chief Judge Singleton, folder 6, Office of the Clerk of the Court, U.S. District Court, Southern District of Texas.

identify cases that must be resolved by either trial or settlement and to summarily dispose of the rest; and, finally, to treat the remaining "viable" cases as part of the regular flow of civil cases, where they could be disposed of without further undue disruption to the remainder of the civil docket.[105]

These steps relied heavily on the magistrates to classify the cases as viable or nonviable, but once a viable case had been identified, DeAnda continued, a preliminary hearing on it would be set before a district judge in every prisoner case, "regardless of age, stage or condition" of the case. He envisioned that, at that point in the process, the new cases would have been on file for between sixty and ninety days. The older cases, the judge noted, "will be in varying stages of disarray." The final element in his suggested pilot program was a coordinated effort by the Southern District, the Texas attorney general, and the TDC, to prepare a special docket of a few dozen pending cases that had been filed by inmates who were all held in a particular TDC prison. Those cases would be set for hearing on a certain date, and the Southern District judge would go to the plaintiffs' place of incarceration.

This scheme would eliminate, DeAnda concluded, the "overwhelming logistical problems for the prison officials, which would otherwise make the procedure unworkable."[106]

The Southern District's staff attorneys would review and summarize the files of cases included on the special docket. The purpose of the summary would be to prepare a judge for a "one-on-one conference" with the plaintiff prisoner, during which the prisoner would state his case, under oath, in narrative form, by question and answer, or "by whatever method the court deems most expedient and effective." A prison medical officer, with all of the plaintiff's medical records, and a TDC administrative officer, with all of the plaintiff's administrative records, would be made available to provide relevant information. If, after this on-site hearing, the judge determined that a case should remain on the docket, the clerk of the court would issue a summons and the case, including a transcript of the hearing, would be returned to its assigned judge's civil docket for processing under the standard procedures.[107]

Chief Judge Singleton liked DeAnda's plan and ordered it into operation with four of the Southern District's judges on the roster to travel to the detention facilities as necessary. DeAnda chaired this new "Pilot Committee." In July 1986 Fifth Circuit Chief Judge Charles Clark had written to the chief judges of each district court in the circuit, to request that they establish some "realistic" guidelines for the processing of prisoner litigation. Singleton decided that DeAnda's idea fit that description, and in December he sent to Clark a summary of the early results of the pilot program. Judge Norman Black had conducted on-site hearings in 43 cases and was able to dismiss 39 of them, leaving just 4 cases for further action. Judge DeAnda had heard a similar number of cases with similar results. Singleton informed Clark that, after January 1987, two Southern District judges would be able to preside in hearings each month. Singleton anticipated, therefore, that, if 40 cases could be heard by each judge, for a total of 80 per month, then 60 would be dismissed. He concluded that the pilot program would be able to clear 720 cases from the Southern District dockets during the next year.[108]

During this same period, Singleton continued, it could be anticipated that approximately 600 new cases would be filed and that one-third could be disposed of by the staff in the office of the clerk. This would add approximately 400 cases to the docket during the same twelve-month period, resulting in a net reduction of 320 cases from the pending docket. Judge Singleton noted that, at that rate, balanced against new filings, it was possible that the Southern District could actually catch up on the pending section 1983 cases within three years.[109]

Judge DeAnda reported to Singleton on 28 April that the pilot program was "in full swing," and he shared the "good news" that 239 prisoners' cases had been closed during the first quarter of 1987, compared to 111 closed during a comparable period of 1986. "So," DeAnda concluded, "there is hope."[110] Six months later, with the program celebrating its first anniversary, he reported that 932 pending cases had been closed by 1 September 1987. There were 644 cases pending, of which 281 were more than two years old, but the judges had made substantial progress. In addition to reducing the pending caseload and lowering the number of old cases, DeAnda wrote, "many of the remaining suits were simplified by eliminating unnecessary parties, erroneous theories of recovery, and frivolous claims." Judge DeAnda stressed in his report the worthiness of the program in separating such chaff. He noted, for example, that the inmates would lose practically all of their cases, but a "small percentage have merit and evidentiary support." DeAnda concluded his annual report by suggesting that the Southern District should award its "Order of the Purple Heart . . . for wounds suffered and work above and beyond" to the members of the pilot committee, Judges Norman Black, Lynn Hughes, and David Hittner.[111]

Judge DeAnda would soon be in the position to award this medal himself, if it had actually existed. Chief Judge Singleton turned seventy on 20 March 1988, and he formally assumed senior judge status on 1 April. Judge Bue, who would have been in line for the office, had taken senior status on 2 September 1987. Judge Ross Sterling had died on 14 January 1988. Because the five Southern District judges appointed to the positions created in 1978 had all received their commissions on the same day in May 1979, seniority was by date of birth rather than by time in service. The chief judgeship fell to DeAnda, who had been born in 1925. He assumed the job with prisoners' civil rights cases well under control, in no small part due to his own initiative in conceiving of and implementing the pilot program. In June 1988, for example, Chief Judge DeAnda signed and returned a memorandum sent by Judge Justice of the Eastern District of Texas regarding the latter's efforts to resolve his own prisoners' case problem. DeAnda was proud to report at that time that the Southern District had managed to reduce its prisoner civil rights caseload from a high of approximately 1,200 pending cases to around 300.[112]

THE THOUGHTFUL PRIORITIZATION THAT IS THE ESSENCE OF GOVERNMENT

President Ronald Reagan sought to get the federal government out of the social and institutional reform business. One way to do that was to fill positions on the federal district and appellate courts with conservative jurists who agreed with his own views on the need for judicial restraint, both in the general realm of federalism, meaning limited national intervention in state and local matters, and in the specific area of federal protection of civil rights.[113] Another way Reagan sought to restrain the federal judiciary, however, was to rely more heavily on the judgment of lawyers in the executive branch. The Justice Department's Office of Legal Policy issued litigation guidelines in 1988, for example, that explicitly disparaged the role federal judges had played in public law litigation. The authors of these guidelines criticized judicial micromanaging of schools, hospitals, and prisons. They instructed department lawyers to brief and to argue constitutional cases in terms of the Framers' original intent, and, if they were engaged in ongoing institutional reform litigation, they were to "urge courts to use equitable relief sparingly."[114]

Concurrent with his administration's disavowal of federal responsibility for civil rights, Reagan presided over an expansion of the federal role in criminal justice. He announced early in his first term that narcotics law enforcement would become a national priority. This policy emphasis had a great impact on the workload of federal district judges, especially the judges who sat close to the border with Mexico, as they did in the Southern District of Texas. Soon after the president declared a war on drugs, Reagan's attorney general, Edwin Meese III, began publicly to link narcotics smuggling with the influx of illegal aliens. Meese asserted that drug smugglers "get lost in the crowd" crossing the border.[115]

This emphasis on the border was not only a policy of the Reagan administration. President Jimmy Carter had formed the U.S. Select Commission on Immigration and Refugee Policy in 1977. The commission's 1981 report recommended, among other things, increased resources for the traditionally underfunded Border Patrol. This report laid the foundations for the 1986 Immigration Reform and Control Act (IRCA). IRCA sanctioned employers who "knowingly" hired undocumented aliens but granted legal residency to several million aliens. These provisions made it necessary for Congress to increase the investigation and enforcement capability of the U.S. Immigration and Naturalization Service (INS). The Border Patrol in particular saw enormous growth after IRCA's passage, which enabled the Reagan administration to expand its role in the war on drugs.[116]

The legislative branch usually supported the executive branch initiatives against narcotics trafficking. In 1981, for example, the Congress amended the Posse Comitatus Act—a statute that had been in force since Reconstruction to prohibit the U.S. military from engaging in civilian law enforcement duties—to allow military personnel to supply intelligence, equipment, and training to civilian agencies.[117] The Defense Drug Interdiction Assistance Act subsequently further enlarged the military's authority to lend its resources to drug interdiction.[118] In the apt words of political scientist Timothy Dunn, this legislation, coupled with the growth of the Border Patrol and other federal law enforcement, has led inexorably to the "militarization" of the U.S.-Mexico border.[119]

One of the early signs of the changes the drug war brought in the Southern District came in 1984, when Congress removed Hidalgo and Starr Counties from the Brownsville Division and created a new border division at McAllen, halfway between Laredo and Brownsville. This made three border courthouses available for trials. Significantly, Congress did not create any new Southern District judgeships.[120] An indication of the congressional and presidential attitudes toward federal trial judges came through the 1984 Sentencing Reform Act, which abolished parole for federal inmates and established mandatory minimum sentences for federal crimes.[121] The criminal statutes to be enforced in the new McAllen courthouse were therefore more rigid than they had been during the 1960s and 1970s, when Judges Connally and Garza presided over so many plea-bargained drug trials in Laredo and Brownsville. This was precisely the intent of the statute. The new guidelines, which were developed by the members of an appointed commission and in place by late 1987, sought to achieve uniformity of sentencing where critics previously had seen judicial caprice.[122]

Congress did not wait for the sentencing commission's results to get tough on narcotics dealers. The 1986 Anti-Drug Abuse Act, for example, increased penalties and instituted mandatory minimum sentences for most drug violations.[123] The penalties were still tied to the quantity of the controlled substance. A first-time federal offender who was convicted of possessing with intent to distribute one hundred kilograms of marijuana was subject to a mandatory prison term for a minimum of five years.[124] A first-time offender convicted of the same basic crime but involving one kilogram of heroin, or five kilograms of cocaine, was subject to a mandatory minimum sentence of ten years.[125] If a convicted offender had two or more prior state or federal felony drug convictions, the penalty was a mandatory sentence of life in prison.[126]

In one respect, the border emphasis of the federal war on drugs brought little change to the Southern District of Texas. In July 1987, for example, Judge George Kazen presided over a trial in which a defendant sought to suppress evidence discovered when a roving Border Patrol agent stopped his vehicle. The arresting agent was able to articulate facts that convinced the judge that he had cause enough to suspect illegal activity. The vehicle in question was a rental truck with Pennsylvania license plates, traveling north on Farm-to-Market Road (FM) 1017 a few miles south of Hebbronville. The driver and his only visible passenger were young Hispanic males. As they neared Hebbronville, the driver did not continue north, toward Freer and the San Antonio area, but turned east on State Highway 285 to Falfurrias. This was not the most direct route to Falfurrias and other points east, but it might have been a route designed to avoid the stationary Border Patrol checkpoints on U.S. Highways 281 and 77. The last two times he had encountered rental trucks on that road, the officer testified, the trucks had been smuggling undocumented aliens.[127]

The Border Patrol officer testified to other factors that persuaded him to stop and search the truck. As it passed the well-marked Border Patrol vehicle, for example, the driver "appeared stunned and frightened." When the Border Patrol vehicle turned to follow the truck, moreover, the truck "jerked wildly" into the wrong lane and then swung back almost off the road in the other lane. Finally, when the truck stopped, the passenger stated to the officer that he was an undocumented alien and volunteered that there were nine others in the back. Based on "the totality of the foregoing circumstances," Kazen was convinced that the stop and subsequent search were justified by at least the reasonable suspicion that this vehicle contained undocumented aliens. He denied the motion to suppress and convicted the defendants.[128]

Incidents like this one involving Border Patrol stops and searches were typical in the Lower Rio Grande Valley.[129] Many of the vehicles contained aliens, but many contained narcotics. Defendants in either sort of case often sought to suppress the evidence against them, only to lose that bid in all but the rarest circumstances. But an increase in the number of law enforcement officers operating on the border, especially those in the rapidly expanding Border Patrol, and a simultaneous increase in the number of prosecutors multiplied the number of these otherwise routine trials. The rise in prosecutions was compounded, many federal district judges complained, by the creation of the mandatory minimum sentences, because such rigid guidelines contributed to a decrease in guilty pleas.[130]

The federal criminal justice initiatives of the 1980s were indications of a preference on the part of both the executive and the legislative branch for vigorous enforcement and prosecution over judicial discretion. The number of federal criminal cases tried in federal courts increased by 10 percent, with the result that, by the end of the decade, approximately 40 percent of federal trials were criminal prosecutions. In 1985 federal criminal filings were in the majority on the dockets of only five of ninety-six district courts. By 1989 criminal cases constituted more than half of the docket in twenty-five districts. The activity was greater still in the area of narcotics law enforcement. The number of drug-related cases filed in the federal district courts increased by more than 200 percent while Ronald Reagan was president.[131] To accomplish this transformation, Congress added more than 700 prosecutors to various U.S. attorney's staffs between 1984 and 1989, for a total of more than 3,100. President George Bush sought to continue the trend by requesting in his first antidrug bill that Congress add another 800 prosecutors to the rolls.[132]

Although Presidents Reagan and Bush both sought to appoint restrained judges, they looked for activist prosecutors to fight the war on drugs. Reagan found one in Henry K. Oncken, a former assistant prosecutor for Harris County and a state district judge whom U.S. Senator Phil Gramm of Texas recommended in 1985 for the job of U.S. attorney for the Southern District of Texas. Oncken became one of the nation's most aggressive federal prosecutors, and Bush kept him on after 1989, during his own administration. By 1990, the year Oncken resigned the office, his staff had more than doubled, from 52 to 110 assistant U.S. attorneys (AUSAS). Those AUSAS, in turn, more than doubled the number of prosecutions filed annually in the Southern District, from 828 to 2,072 cases.[133] In the months between June 1988 and September 1989 alone, Oncken's team of prosecutors filed 1,481 narcotics cases. This was more than were filed in any other federal judicial district, and more than twice as many as in the runner-up Western District of Texas, where the prosecutors filed 721 drug cases. The number of AUSAS in the Western District also grew, but only from 36 in 1987 to 56 in 1991.[134]

Oncken's hawkish stance on prosecuting a high number of narcotics violations, avoiding plea bargains, and seeking heavier sentences led to tensions between the prosecutors and the judges of the Southern District.[135] The judges complained that a high rate of prosecution simply indicated Oncken's own lack of judgment. His office filed charges in 66 percent of the criminal matters referred to them in 1988 by federal law enforcement agencies such as the Federal Bureau of Investigation (FBI) or the Drug Enforcement Agency (DEA). By contrast, federal prosecutors in Miami, the Southern District staff's closest competitors in terms of criminal referrals, filed charges in only 44 percent of referred cases. The national average was approximately 36 percent. By 1990 Oncken's prosecutors were twice as likely to file charges on a case a federal agency sent them as they had been in 1985.[136]

By June 1989 each of the Southern District's judges managed a combined civil and criminal docket of more than 600 cases. The next year, each of the judges managed approximately 800 cases. The figure for combined caseload, of course, obscured the reality that the judges in the border divisions, like their predecessor judges, focused almost entirely on criminal law. A better indication of the division of labor among the judges is the fact that, in 1989, the federal district judges sitting in Laredo, McAllen, Corpus Christi, and Brownsville presided in more than 11 percent of all of the federal narcotics cases tried nationwide. The Southern District judges and Clerk of Court Jesse Clark often reported, usually in correspondence seeking either relief or more resources, that their district was the "battleground" in the war on drugs.[137]

The overworked federal district judges and the underworked lawyers with civil cases pending in the Southern District of Texas complained that Oncken demonstrated too little discretion. Critics referred to the statistics on judicial efficiency that showed that the Southern District courts had become so clogged with minor drug prosecutions that important civil litigation languished. Oncken's mania for drug cases, moreover, forced his federal prosecutors to overlook the epidemic in white-collar crime, especially the fraud that many critics suspected played a major role in the failures of hundreds of Texas financial institutions during the 1980s. Oncken answered his critics by arguing that he had made narcotics cases a priority because the Southern District had more problems with drug trafficking than with bank fraud. The choice to emphasize one over the other, he said, was well within his prosecutorial discretion.[138]

Judge Lynn Hughes, whom Reagan had appointed to the Southern District bench just before he appointed Oncken as U.S. attorney, became one of the prosecutor's leading critics. Hughes stated in 1990, for example, that Oncken's policies lacked the "thoughtful prioritization that is the essence of government." He did not question the federal prosecutor's integrity or his motives, but Hughes said that "running twice as fast in the wrong direction is not a solution in criminal justice." There was no law mandating that prosecutors and judges agree on the court's priorities, but they did have to work together to get cases through the system. It was unfortunately true, moreover, that Oncken started his tenure under a cloud. Soon after he was appointed in 1985, he reportedly complained both that his prosecutors were too inexperienced and that the Southern District judges were too lenient. The judges had interpreted this comment, Hughes later said, to mean that the new U.S. attorney thought that they all ought to "work harder."[139]

The tension between the Southern District's judges and its prosecutors was aggravated by personnel shortages on the court. In January 1988 Judge Ross Sterling died and left a vacancy on the bench that remained open for seven months. Soon after his death, Judge Gabrielle McDonald—apparently out of financial concerns as well as because the reality of the job was incommensurable with her own ideal of justice—resigned her seat and reentered private practice. Chief Judge John Singleton stepped down to take senior judge status in April. Judge Carl Bue had already taken senior judge status the previous fall, and his replacement had not yet joined the court. These vacancies forced the clerk's office to distribute the rising caseload to fewer federal district judges.[140]

Kenneth M. Hoyt was born in San Augustine County, Texas, on 2 March 1948. He attended Houston's only historically black college, TSU, where he earned his A.B. in 1969. He then stayed in Houston to attend TSU's Thurgood Marshall School of Law, where he earned the J.D. in 1972. Hoyt practiced in Houston from 1972 to 1985 and was also city attorney of Kendleton, Texas, from 1975 to 1981. In that year he became city attorney of Prairie View, the home of another historically black state school, Prairie View A&M University. Hoyt then served one term as the presiding judge in the 125th Civil District Court from 1981 to 1982. He spent one year on the faculty at Houston's South Texas College of Law, and the next year at the law school at TSU. Hoyt returned to public office as a justice of the First District Court of Appeals of Texas. He served from 1985 to 1988, when Reagan named him to succeed the retired Bue. He was for a short time the second African American on the court, but with Judge McDonald's departure, he became the only black judge in the Southern District of Texas. Hoyt received his commission on 1 April 1988.[141]

Hoyt joined the court the same day that Singleton passed the chief judgeship to Judge DeAnda. Among the first steps DeAnda took as chief judge was to orchestrate a public relations campaign with the goal of attracting visiting judges to the Southern District of Texas. He then started working with Jesse Clark to reorganize and redistribute the pending caseloads that were either left or else would be left by the loss of judges.[142] Judge Sterling's successor finally arrived to join the court that summer. Simeon T. Lake III was born in Chicago, Illinois, on 4 July 1944. He moved to Texas for school, first to College Station, to attend Texas A&M University, where he earned his B.A. in 1966, then to Austin, to attend the University of Texas (UT) School of Law, where he earned his J.D. in 1969. He was in private practice in Houston for one year, then spent the year 1970 to 1971 in the U.S. Army. Lake returned to Houston and to private practice in 1972. He received his judicial commission in August 1988.[143]

Judge Singleton's position went to a member of his own judicial family. Melinda Harmon was born in Port Arthur, Texas, on 1 November 1946. She attended Radcliffe College, where she earned her A.B. in 1969, then attended UT law school, where she earned her J.D. in 1972. Harmon spent two years after graduation as a law clerk for Judge Singleton in the Southern District of Texas. She worked from 1976 to 1988 as a trial attorney in the litigation section of Exxon in Houston. Harmon became a state judge in 1988, in the 280th District, in Harris County. She had the unique opportunity to succeeded her old boss in May 1989, when George Bush nominated her to fill Singleton's seat after the latter took senior status.[144]

The increasing delay in filling judicial vacancies, due in large part to rising rancor over the partisanship associated with the appointment process, was a serious problem by the late 1980s. Singleton's position, for example, stood empty for nearly a year, as did the vacancy created when Judge Hugh Gibson became a senior judge on 1 November 1989. Gibson's successor, Samuel B. Kent, did not receive his commission until 1 October 1990. Kent was born 22 June 1949, in Denver, Colorado. He earned his B.A. at UT in 1971 and his J.D. at UT School of Law in 1975. Kent entered private practice in Galveston, remaining there until George Bush named him to Gibson's seat.[145]

Judge McDonald's seat remained vacant for more than a year. Her replacement, John David Rainey, was born 10 February 1945, in Freeport, Texas. He attended Southern Methodist University (SMU) in Dallas, where he earned his B.B.A. in 1967. After an intervening term in the U.S. Army, Rainey returned to Dallas to attend the SMU law school, where he earned his J.D. in 1972. Rainey entered private practice, first in Dallas from 1973 to 1979, then in Angleton, Texas, from 1979 to 1986. His political career began when he became director of the Angleton Chamber of Commerce in 1983. He became a judge of the 149th District Court, in Brazoria County, Texas, in 1987, where he remained until President Bush appointed him to succeed Judge McDonald. Rainey received his commission in May 1990.[146]

The new Southern District judges took their seats just as the friction between their fellow judges and the prosecutor reached a crucial period. Amid the growing chorus of criticism of Oncken's performance, Senator Gramm began quietly to interview candidates to replace him. The senator could contemplate this step because prosecutors lack even the formal independence granted to federal district judges under Article III of the U.S. Constitution. Gramm commenced the search in May 1990, and Oncken resigned the post in June.[147] The senator soon recommended Ronald Woods, a Houston attorney, as Oncken's replacement. Woods was a former FBI special agent who, in the late 1970s and early 1980s, had also served in the Southern District U.S. Attorney's Office as chief of the fraud, narcotics, and public integrity sections. He had been among those who had criticized Oncken for his lack of enthusiasm for prosecuting white-collar crimes. After taking his oath as the U.S. attorney in November 1990, Woods announced that he could make prosecuting bank fraud one of his highest priorities.[148]

Woods was the district's U.S. attorney until January 1993, and, as promised, he did preside over a shift in priorities from drugs to white-collar crime involving insurance companies, health care providers, real estate developers, and savings and loans.[149] Judge Hughes presumably was not pleased with this development. He later noted, obviously reflecting upon his experience presiding over the MCorp bankruptcy, that "[a]fter the bankers had followed government rules in their reckless expansion, the government decided to blame the bankers, endlessly prosecuting officers criminally for bad judgment, wasting judicial resources, destroying lives in a cruel, ugly gesture."[150]

IT'S GOING TO GET WORSE

The new U.S. attorney reduced the overall backlog of criminal cases in the Southern District of Texas by opting to file charges in fewer referred cases. Yet, although Woods was more selective in prosecutions than his predecessor, he could not abandon narcotics prosecutions. In 1990, the same year that Woods turned his staff's attention to white-collar crime, the federal government named the Southwest border as one of the nation's five "High Intensity Drug Trafficking Areas" (HIDTAS). The designation brought higher funding and increased coordination among various civilian law enforcement organizations, military units, and intelligence agencies that were by then involved in federal drug interdiction. The border was the only HIDTA that was a geographic region rather than a metropolitan area. Houston, moreover, was one of the remaining four HIDTAS.[151] The resulting concentration of interdiction and prosecution forces after 1990 was a major development for the Southern District. Once the political pressure to prosecute high-profile and high-dollar savings and loan fraud cases had abated, drug trials returned to their traditional dominance on the dockets in the district.[152]

The Border Patrol, as the civilian agency directly involved in domestic interdiction of both drug traffic and illegal alien migration, was the main beneficiary of federal money in general and the military's expertise in particular. The Border Patrol was by 1990 the leading federal law enforcement agency in the war on drugs.[153] The number of narcotics seizures made annually by Border Patrol officers in the southwestern region rose 50 percent between 1990 and 1993, from 4,200 to 6,400, and the total weight of cocaine the Border Patrol seized nearly doubled during the same years, from 14,000 pounds to 27,000 pounds. The Border Patrol's success encouraged federal policymakers, but also showed how much of their illicit product narcotics traffickers could put into the stream of international commerce. The implications of that fact worried government leaders in Mexico and the United States.[154]

The governments of both countries expected that legitimate international exchange would increase once the North American Free Trade Agreement became effective in 1994, but leaders of both Mexico and the United States also expected that smuggling of illicit drugs and undocumented immigrants would surge under the treaty's regime. In October 1994 U.S. attorneys from the districts along the border met with the DEA, the FBI, the Border Patrol, the U.S. Coast Guard, and the Criminal Division of the Justice Department to establish the Southwest Border Council. The council had the responsibility for developing and implementing the Southwest Border Initiative, a congressionally conceived project to coordinate regional interdiction and prosecution.[155]

At the same time, President Bill Clinton's attorney general, Janet Reno, announced a comprehensive southwestern border strategy, which was based on "prevention through deterrence." The basic aims of this latest strategy were, first, to deter illegal migration and narcotics trafficking, but, second, to accomplish that goal while avoiding interference with the flow of legal traffic through the ports of entry. According to Gustavo de la Vina, a Rio Grande Valley native who rose to become chief of the Border Patrol under Reno, the number of agents in 1993 as well as the number and age of their vehicles and equipment were insufficient "to bring integrity and safety to the Southwest border." The administration proposed vastly increased appropriations for the organization.[156]

Congress supported the Clinton administration's strategy. The Border Patrol's budget doubled, from $362 million in 1993 to $727 million by 1997, and the number of agents more than doubled, from 3,389 to 7,357.[157] Lawmakers supported increasing border enforcement in other ways as well. Among the various provisions of the 1994 Violent Crime Control and Law Enforcement Act, for example, was an authorization for the Justice Department to increase the number of Border Patrol agents and support staff by at least 1,000 persons each fiscal year 1995 through 1998.[158] Congress was more explicit the next year, when it appropriated $1.5 billion for the INS and specifically directed the INS Commissioner to hire 700 new Border Patrol agents.[159] The trend culminated when the Senate Judiciary Committee unanimously approved a proposal to require the attorney general to hire "not less" than 1,000 Border Patrol agents each year between 1997 and 2001. President Clinton signed this mandate into law in September 1996, as part of the Illegal Immigration Reform and Immigrant Responsibility Act.[160] The national and international border initiatives reinforce, according to political scientist Peter Andrea, the "apparent paradox of U.S.-Mexico integration that a barricaded border and a borderless economy are being created simultaneously."[161]

These developments in federal criminal justice inspired Southern District Judge George Kazen to predict in 1996, "It's going to get worse." He noted that both sides in that year's presidential race were saying that they wanted to get tougher on drugs and illegal immigration. But Kazen worred that "[e]very Border Patrolman you put out there is going to increase the number of arrests and stops made. . . . When they say they're going to get tough on drugs and immigration, it's the Southern and the Western districts of Texas that are going to feel that."[162]

The judge also worried that the "next wave" of backlogs was on the horizon, as the first of the convicts imprisoned under the federal sentencing guidelines finished their prison terms and many became subject to extended periods of "supervised release" similar to parole. Before the guidelines were instituted, cases of released convicts who violated parole were heard by the U.S. Parole Commission. Under the guidelines, however, the release was to be supervised by the judge who heard the original case. During the twelve months preceding 31 October 1996, probation officers in the Southern District of Texas filed approximately 1,200 reports on former prisoners who had violated terms of their parole or supervised release. McAllen had the most, with 393 reports filed. The Houston Division had 345, Laredo 180, Corpus Christi 139, and Brownsville 128. This new twist in prisoners' proceedings threatened to take up even more of Kazen's and the other Southern District judges' dockets.[163]

Conclusion: Just, Speedy, and Inexpensive Resolutions

IN THEIR 1927 STUDY of the federal judicial system, *The Business of the Supreme Court,* Felix Frankfurter and James Landis declared that "the business of the courts is determined by the nature and extent of the predominant activities of contemporary life."[1] In 1983 Professor Owen Fiss attributed "bureaucratization of the judiciary" to the "growing size and complexity of American society."[2] Both of these observations are certainly borne out by the history of the Southern District of Texas. The concerns and complexity of American society, taken together, provide only partial explanation for the changes in the district's business. The rise of public law litigation, as a form and as a forum of change, also partially explains the shift in the Southern District dockets that Charles Zelden noted and this book has supported. Yet the new commitments emerged slowly over the decades and did not displace established duties of the federal district courts. The judges continued to shepherd varied private cases through their civil dockets and processed large numbers of repetitive prosecutions on their criminal dockets. The goals of legal action have grown more direct and litigants have grown more demanding. These, too, have driven the growth of the judiciary.[3]

In his 1982 examination in the *Yale Law Journal* of "the origins of judicial activism in the protection of minorities," Robert Cover quipped that it seemed that, ever since the Supreme Court decided *Brown v. Board of Education,* the federal district courts had become "quasi-administrative bodies overseeing school desegregation and occasional other tasks."[4] Even as Cover wrote, the era of federal judicial oversight of school desegregation and other "structural reforms" was drawing to its close.[5] Contrary to views expressed in conservative academic circles, therefore, the judicial implementation of the *Brown* mandates did not result in "government by judiciary."[6] Instead, in 1986, near the end of the period studied in this history, Fifth Circuit Judge John R. Brown—one of the major proponents of federal judicial action, if not activism—noted, "We, and the lower federal courts, are courts of limited jurisdiction. Our task is not to correct all social ills, however egregious they may seem to us as individuals. The keys to the Kingdom are not in our hands."[7]

The keys were so far from judicial hands by the 1990s, moreover, that federal district judges were feeling more like much-put-upon pack mules than respected workhorses. Chief Justice William Rehnquist complained in a 1990 report, for example, that congressional policies had created an "hourglass-shaped" criminal justice system. At one end were large staffs of prosecutors who filed federal criminal cases. At the other end, the government had devoted abundant resources to build prisons to house the convicted offenders. But between the two, Rehnquist said, there had been no corresponding expansion in federal "judge power" to handle the increased workload. Rehnquist suggested that the result of this congressional neglect would be a "bottleneck" in the system that would reduce the nation's capacity to win the war on drugs.[8] The chief voiced this concern again in 1992, in an address to the American Bar Association. He warned that efforts to "get tough" on drug offenders threatened to transform the federal district courts into "national narcotics courts."[9]

The judges of the Southern District of Texas, like federal district judges across the nation, were alarmed when U.S. Senator Joseph R. Biden, the chair of the Senate Judiciary Committee, began to suggest in the late 1980s that federal courts ought to be trying more drug cases, rather than leaving so many for the state courts to prosecute. The judges were further disturbed when Biden and other prominent members of Congress complained simultaneously that federal district judges had been lax in clearing their civil dockets.[10] The comments and criticisms occurred within the context of debates over a Senate bill proposing "streamlining measures" aimed at reducing delays in civil cases in the federal courts. The good news in all this for the Southern District judges was that the bill promised the first additions to the court since 1984.[11]

The bill was passed and signed into law as the Civil Justice Reform Act (CJRA) of 1990. It provided that each federal district court generate a "civil justice expense and delay reduction plan." The plan could be written from scratch by the district judges or based on a model developed by the Judicial Conference of the United States. In either case, the purpose of the delay reduction plan, in the words of the statute, would be "to facilitate deliberate adjudication of civil cases on the merits, monitor discovery, improve litigation management, and," in an intentional legislative echo of the first goal of federal rules of civil procedure, to "ensure just, speedy, and inexpensive resolutions of civil disputes."[12]

CJRA created the Civil Justice Reform Advisory Group, a study panel charged to identify causes and remedies for delay in the federal district courts. The local CJRA advisory group for the Southern District of Texas was chaired by Harry M. Reasoner, the managing partner of Houston's venerable Vinson and Elkins law firm. The local group's official report, which it issued after Ron Woods had been the U.S. attorney for the Southern District for one year, recognized his achievements. The group noted, for example, that under his discriminating prosecution philosophy, criminal filings were down by one-third. As a result, the Southern District judges were able to focus more of their attention on clearing the civil dockets. The CJRA panel also critiqued the judges' management. It recommended, for example, that the judges delegate more pretrial criminal and civil matters, perhaps 5–10 percent of the cases, to the magistrates. To this end, the panel called on the Congress to authorize the hiring of additional support personnel.[13] This was in line, apparently, with the congressional intent. The magistrates were given more power, increased prestige, and higher pay by the Judicial Improvements Act of 1990, in which the Congress renamed them U.S. magistrate judges.[14]

The CJRA group's report also declared Congress to be guilty of causing or contributing to the delay in the federal courts. Truly to cut the costs and backlogs prevailing in federal civil litigation, the committee members declared, Congress should authorize more resources for the judiciary. It should certainly stop the trend toward "federalizing" crimes, such as minor drug offenses, that could be handled in state courts. Congress should stop authorizing new federal prosecutors without also adding new court personnel to balance the increased workload. Finally, the panelists complained about the effect of sentencing guidelines.[15]

The Federal Courts Study Committee, another congressionally created panel, submitted its own report around the same time. Its members also blamed the rising number of drug cases, the mandatory minimum sentencing guidelines, and even the Speedy Trial Act for contributing to trial backlogs and delays. The primary reason the panel gave for the effect of sentencing guidelines on the disposition of trials was that defendants facing the same punishment for a crime whether they face trial or accept a plea bargain had no incentive to plead guilty. This was especially true, the panel reported, in drug cases, where "draconian" penalties were mandated. Even small reductions in the number of plea bargains created problems for the federal courts. The committee estimated that a 5 percent drop in guilty pleas translated into at least a 33 percent increase in the number of criminal trials.[16]

Neither of the study panels, however, addressed the effect of mandatory minimum sentences on prosecutorial discretion. Federal prosecutors could increase or reduce the length of a "mandatory" prison sentence by manipulating the variables—such as the weight of drugs seized, or the use of a gun in a crime—that were factors in the formula federal district judges applied to set a sentence after a conviction. As before the guidelines, a prosecutor and a defense lawyer might cooperate on the specifics of the charge to arrive at a mutually agreeable solution. The trial judge, however, lacked oversight, input, or discretion in the matter.[17]

The federal sentencing guidelines shifted much of the power in the courtroom from judges to prosecutors and law enforcement. Instead of a judge's deciding the pertinent facts about a criminal and a crime and handing down a sentence based on them, prosecutors now make those calls. The charge they file, in essence, determines the sentence.[18] More significantly, as shown by the experience with U.S. Attorney Henry Oncken, as well as by the increased activity on the border, the judges have to be reactive rather than active. "The Department of Justice has a lot of control over what we do," Judge George Kazen noted, "because we have to react to the cases they file."[19] Judge Lynn Hughes, writing in 1997 on the problems created by the "nationalization of crime," named prosecutorial discretion the "most forceful, unchecked power in America."[20] This was an ironic thing for a federal district judge to assert. During the *Brown* era similar criticism had been directed against judges, who were often charged with abuse of discretion.[21]

In the same round of 1990 legislation, Congress authorized five new federal district judgeships for the Southern District of Texas, bringing the total to eighteen.[22] Partly because of partisan wrangling reminiscent of the 1950s, however, the president and Congress filled these positions slowly—so slowly that Chief Judge DeAnda decided to write Senator Biden to inquire after the absent judges.[23] This was to no avail. With various deaths or retirements, including DeAnda's own retirement, the Southern District of Texas remained at less than full strength until 1999.[24]

The effects on delay and caseload caused by congressional neglect in creating new judgeships was compounded by the fact that the Congress and president had been remiss in filling existing but vacant judgeships. In early 1990 there were fifty-seven judicial vacancies, including eight the judiciary classed as emergencies because the seats had been empty for more than eighteen months. Jesse E. Clark, the Southern District's longtime court clerk, did not see the problem as an hourglass. He chose a metaphor that, to him, more aptly described the effect of mixing lengthy judicial vacancies with overburdened court dockets. "It's like a traffic jam," he said. "There are too many cars and too little cement."[25]

Notes

INTRODUCTION

1. This includes every Texas county that touches the gulf but one: Jefferson County, which is adjacent to Louisiana, is in the Eastern District of Texas. See 28 U.S.C. § 124.

2. The U.S. Constitution extends federal judicial power to "all cases in law and equity" and grants federal jurisdiction in "all cases of admiralty." U.S. Const., art. III, § 2. In the Judiciary Act of 1789, the first Congress established the federal judiciary and authorized federal district courts to exercise "exclusive original cognizance of all civil causes of admiralty and maritime jurisdiction." Act of 24 September 1789, ch. 20, § 9, 1 Stat. 73–77; codified at 28 U.S.C. §§ 1331–33.

3. In 1845 Galveston became the seat of the first federal court in Texas by an act of 29 December 1845 (9 Stat. 1). The current Southern District of Texas was created when President Theodore Roosevelt signed the Act of 4 March 1902 (32 Stat. 65) to divide the state into four federal districts. The geographic jurisdiction of the Southern District included Galveston, but the island city was still rebuilding from the hurricane that had devastated it the previous year. Therefore, Congress designated Houston as the headquarters division by an act of 11 March 1902 (32 Stat. 68). Brownsville was already a federal district court (Act of 21 February 1857, 11 Stat. 164), as was Laredo (Act of 2 March 1899, 30 Stat. 1002). Congress later designated new Southern District court divisions in Victoria (Act of 18 April 1906, 34 Stat. 122), and Corpus Christi (Act of 29 May 1912, 37 Stat. 120). Erwin C. Surrency, "Federal District Court Judges and the History of Their Courts," 40 F.R.D. 139 (1967), 289. In 1984 Congress created another border division, in McAllen.

4. In large part, the regional boom resulted from the vigilance of leaders who sought to turn every contingent event, whether the discovery of oil locally or the outbreak of war internationally, to Texas's and therefore their own advantage. Their efforts brought Houston, the district's headquarters, such spectacular growth that it became known as the "golden buckle" of the nation's Sun Belt. See Kaplan, "Houston," 196–212; and Fisher, "Urban Sunbelt," 33–58.

5. See generally Davidson, *Race and Class.*

6. Carp and Stidham, *The Federal Courts,* 23. Also Lyles, *Gatekeepers.*

7. See the summary by Friedman, "Opening the Time Capsule," 229–40. For other social science based treatments of the lower federal courts, see Abraham, *Judicial Process;* Carp and Stidham, *Judicial Process in America;* Rowland and Carp, *Politics and Judgment;* and Carp and Rowland, *Policymaking and Politics.* For calls for, commentary regarding, and some critiques of the social science approach to studying trial courts, see Grossman and Sarat, "Litigation in the Federal Courts," 321; Sarat, "Understanding Trial Courts," 318; Saltzburg,

"American Trial Judge," 1; Jacob, "Travails of Exploration," 407; and Flemming, "Contested Terrains," 941.

8. See Erwin C. Surrency, *History of the Federal Courts* (New York: Oceana Publications, 1987).

9. Hall and Rise, *From Local Courts to National Tribunals,* 1.

10. Geographic size and diversity make the Southern District of Texas unusual among the federal judicial districts, but the range of court business that results from size and diversity renders it representative of many other districts. In 1789, when the Congress created the federal district courts, there were thirteen districts and thirteen judges. There are now nearly one hundred districts and more than six hundred federal district judges. The states of California, New York, and Texas are home to the largest and busiest federal courts in the nation. The U.S. District Court for the Southern District of New York, for example, which encompasses Manhattan and the Bronx, had twenty-seven judges in 1990, the largest number of any district.

11. Much of this work also tends to treat the district courts as subsets of the greater federal judiciary. See, for example, the papers collected in Levin and Wheeler, *The American Judiciary,* and Strazzella, *Federal Role in Criminal Law.* Also see Task Force on Administration of Justice, *Task Force Report: The Courts* (Washington, D.C.: U.S. Government Printing Office, 1967) [materials published in support of the *President's Commission on Law Enforcement and Administration of Justice*].

12. Zelden, *Justice Lies in the District.* Other exceptions to this neglect are Freyer and Dixon, *Democracy and Judicial Independence;* Larsen, *Federal Justice;* Fritz, *Federal Justice in California;* and Tachau, *Federal Courts.*

13. Members of the state's civic elite promoted the virtues of private initiative and free enterprise, and believed that government's only legitimate function with regard to commerce was to provide an infrastructure, physical and regulatory, that facilitated economic development. Feagin, *Free Enterprise City,* 46–72. Thomas and Murray, *Progrowth Politics,* 63–65. Shelton et al., *Houston,* 9–18.

14. Zelden, *Justice Lies in the District,* 11.

15. Zelden concluded that there were three reasons for the "remarkable continuity" of the court's priorities through six eventful decades: first, local business leaders looked to federal judicial rulings to foster stability during unsettled times; second, their near total reliance on the mechanisms of private development allowed business leaders to boost regional economic prospects without also confronting racial tensions exacerbated by urbanization and industrialization; and, third, the federal district judges sitting in the Southern District during this period shared the background and hence the outlook of the business class. These three factors combined to make the judges powerful allies of business. Ibid., 11–12.

16. Ibid., 11.

17. Some doubted that there was an explosion, or that Americans are particularly litigious. See Galanter, "Reading the Landscape," 26–36.

18. Friedman, *Total Justice,* 5.

19. U.S. Const., art. III, § 1. The Framers further guaranteed the independence of the judiciary through the prohibitions on bills of attainder (art. I, §§ 9, 10). The text of the Constitution does not include the words "judicial independence," but the concept was soon abstracted from these provisions. Zagel and Winkler, "The Independence of Judges," 799.

20. Bermant and Wheeler, "Independence and Accountability," 858.

21. Zelden, *Justice Lies in the District,* 34–37.

22. The office of clerk of court was created in tandem with the position of federal district judge in the First Judiciary Act, Act of 24 September 1789, 1 Stat. 73. The position is currently described at 28 U.S.C. § 751. See Wheeler, *Federal Court Governance,* 11.

23. Posner, *Federal Courts,* 102–29.

24. See Magistrates Act of 1968, Pub. L. No. 90–578, 82 Stat. 1107 [The office of U.S. commissioner, which was supplanted by the office of U.S. magistrate, was formerly described at 28 U.S.C. § 636]. Also see Federal Magistrate Act of 1979, Pub. L. No. 96–82, 93 Stat. 643, codified as amended at 28 U.S.C. §§ 631–39 (1985). For the creation and expansion of the duties of the magistrates, see Surrency, *History of the Federal Courts,* 361–69; and Carp and Stidham, *The Federal Courts,* 61–84.

25. The U.S. district courts have original jurisdiction in federal civil, criminal, and administrative law, in diversity cases, and in admiralty. See 28 U.S.C. §§ 1331–33. In addition, federal district judges have original jurisdiction, "exclusive of the courts of the states," in all matters of bankruptcy. 28 U.S.C. § 1334. art. I, § 8 of the U.S. Constitution authorized Congress to enact a "uniform" law of bankruptcy. The earliest comprehensive federal bankruptcy statute was the Bankruptcy Act of 1898, which is currently codified as Title 11 of the United States Code (11 U.S.C.). Federal laws concerning banks and banking are in Title 12 (12 U.S.C.).

26. Act of 6 November 1978, Pub. L. No. 95–598, codified at 28 U.S.C. §§ 151–58. In the 1978 law, bankruptcy judges could hear cases related to bankruptcy proceedings, such as a civil suit involving a company that had filed under Title 11, as well as cases actually brought under Title 11. The bankruptcy judges would be appointed by circuit judges to serve fourteen-year terms. They could be removed by the judicial council in that circuit. Moreover, their salaries could be reduced by an act of Congress. In a four-person plurality decision, the Supreme Court upheld a Minnesota district judge's ruling that the original 1978 act was unconstitutional. The justices held that Congress had vested the bankruptcy judges with the "power and prestige" of art. III federal judges, without giving them the necessary independence. The court stayed its judgment until 4 October 1982, to enable lawmakers to amend the laws. *Northern Pipeline Construction v. Marathon Pipeline,* 102 S.Ct. 2858 (1982). It was a "badly fragmented" ruling, because the distinction between art. III "constitutional" courts and art. I "legislative" tribunals was and is controversial. Wright, *The Law of Federal Courts,* 50–52. In response to the court's ruling in *Northern Pipeline,* Congress passed the Bankruptcy Amendments and Federal Judgeship Act of 1984 (Act of 10 July 1984, Pub. L. No. 98–353, 98 Stat. 338), which clarified that bankruptcy judges served fixed terms and were paid fixed salaries (which were tied to the salaries of district judges). Bankruptcy judges are paid 92 percent of what life-tenured district judges are paid. 28 U.S.C. § 153.

27. However, in many cases the federal district judge merely approves reorganization plans brokered by the bankruptcy judge. Neely, *Judicial Jeopardy,* 35–37. In addition to trial duties, bankruptcy judges may serve on bankruptcy appellate panels ("BAPS"), to review decisions by individual bankruptcy judges. 28 U.S.C. § 158. The response to the creation of these courts has not been overwhelmingly positive and is often ambivalent. See generally Seron, *Judicial Reorganization.* For a discussion of the rise of these specialized judges, see Resnik, "History, Jurisdiction, and the Federal Courts," 171, esp. nn. 65–76. For an exploration of the rationale for splitting federal jurisdictions among a proliferating variety of these less independent non–art. III judges, see generally Baum, "Specializing the Federal Courts," 217–24.

28. Federal Rules of Civil Procedure (hereafter Fed. R. Civ. P.), Rule 53. Vincent Nathan,

who gained prominence as a special master in prison reform cases during the 1970s, has noted that the master's role varies with the needs of the court. Nathan, "The Use of Masters," 421.

29. Wald, "Bureaucracy and the Courts," 1485–86.

30. See Fed. R. Civ. P., Rule 1 ("Scope of Rules").

31. Posner, *Federal Courts*, 224.

32. Administrative topics have received generous attention from both legal historians and social scientists, but again, the majority of these studies are too general or theoretical to be useful as anything but schematics of a particular approach, or as sources of statistics. See, for example, Saari, *American Court Management;* Belknap, *To Improve the Administration of Justice;* Weston and Wells, *The Administration of Justice;* Willoughby, *Principles of Judicial Administration;* Wheeler and Whitcomb, *Judicial Administration;* and Clark, "Adjudication to Administration," 65. A more specific study is Hellman, *Restructuring Justice.* Some of the otherwise fine studies are now a generation out of date: Fish, *Politics of Federal Judicial Administration.* Also old, but still useful, are Goldman and Jahnige, *Federal Courts as a Political System;* and Cole, *Administration of Justice.*

33. Surrency noted that "traditionally, the histories of courts have focused on one of three themes: 1) the organization; 2) the famous cases decided by the courts; or, 3) biographical sketches of the judges." Surrency, *History of the Federal Courts,* ix–xi, 81–93.

34. See Resnik, "Managerial Judges," 376; and Resnik, "From 'Cases' to 'Litigation,' " 5. For "umpires" see Chayes, "The Role of the Judge," 1282–86.

35. See Heydebrand and Seron, *Rationalizing Justice;* Clark, "Adjudication to Administration," 73–77; Peckham, "Federal Judge as a Case Manager," 770–71; and King, "Management of Civil Case Flow," 155–56.

36. Professional concerns regarding complexity emerged earlier in the century, when American industry and population boomed. These worries increased as the government's obligations and regulations expanded in the 1930s, under the New Deal. A surge of complex antitrust litigation also worried leading figures of the bar and the judiciary in the 1950s. The Judicial Conference of the United States adopted the "Prettyman Report" (of "Procedure in Antitrust and Other Protracted Cases") on 26 September 1951. Yankwich, " 'Short Cuts' in Long Cases." On the administrative developments earlier in the century, see Chandler, "Some Major Advances." For later progress, as well as plans for the future, see Clark, "The Sky is Falling," 998; and Jones, "Future of the Federal Courts," 17–20, 44–45.

37. Chayes, "The Role of the Judge," 1282–86. See also Chayes, "Supreme Court, 1981 Term," 51–55.

38. Fiss, "The Forms of Justice," 2. Also see Chayes, "The Role of the Judge," 1292–95. According to art. III, § 1, of the U.S. Constitution, federal courts may hear "all cases in law and equity." Since 1938, when the separate procedural regimes for law and equity were joined in the federal rules of civil procedure, federal district judges have been authorized to issue injunctions under Rule 65. The rules also govern other aspects of a case: Rule 23 permits class actions, Rule 18 allows the joinder of claims and remedies, and Rule 20 joins parties. As Roach noted, "The core elements of equity are the breadth and flexibility of equitable remedial powers which allow a trial judge to order remedies without careful attention to the demands of causation and restoration. . . . Both the theory and practice of equity fit the demands of structural reform. Equitable doctrine and theory can certainly explain those cases where courts did much less than restore rights. Equity can also justify those more rare cases where courts went beyond what was demanded by the restoration of rights." Roach,

"Limits of Corrective Justice," 862. Also McKnight, "How Shall We Then Reason?" 947–948.

39. As Fiss noted, the "first ploy of any manager is to induce collaboration; authoritative directives are reserved as a last resort." Fiss, "The Forms of Justice," 36–37. Fiss's article was part of the ongoing examination of the role of federal district judges in institutional reform litigation. In part, it was a response to Chayes's 1976 article. Diver, "Judge as Political Powerbroker," 43. "Note: Implementation Problems," 428. Buckholz et al., "Special Project," 784. Eisenberg and Yeazell, "The Ordinary and the Extraordinary," 465. Also see Fiss, *The Civil Rights Injunction,* 4–5. The civil rights injunction has taken and held center stage during the modern civil rights era (roughly defined as post–World War II). Hoffer, *The Law's Conscience,* 180. But the scope of the federal equitable grant with regard to its employment for judicial intervention in state institutions is disputed. See Nagel, "Separation of Powers," 661; and Fletcher, "The Discretionary Constitution," 635.

40. See Resnik, "Managerial Judges," 391. Also see Resnik, "From 'Cases' to 'Litigation,'" 5. Elliott counters Resnik's claim in her earlier article to identify judicial creativity when what actually occurred was the adaptation of "existing structures to new functions." Elliott, "Managerial Judging," 307. The distinction is worth noting, but it is not critical to my own examination.

41. *Brown v. Board of Education of Topeka,* 347 U.S. 483 (1954) [hereafter *Brown I*]. Also see 349 U.S. 294 (1955) [hereafter *Brown II*]; and *Bolling v. Sharpe,* 347 U.S. 497 (1954). And, generally, Kluger, *Simple Justice.* Greenberg, *Crusaders in the Courts.*

42. *Brown I,* 347 U.S., at 495.

43. *Brown II,* at 301. For the continuing role played by federal judges in the post-*Brown* civil rights era, see Peltason, *Fifty-eight Lonely Men;* Couch, *History of the Fifth Circuit;* Spivack, *Race, Civil Rights, and the United States Court of Appeals;* Bass, *Unlikely Heroes;* and Belknap, *Federal Law and the Southern Order.*

44. *Plessy v. Ferguson,* 163 U.S. 537 (1896).

45. The *Brown* decision was limited to schools. Civil rights activists next called on the federal government to outlaw racial discrimination in public accommodations, voting, employment, and housing. See Sitkoff, *Struggle for Black Equality,* 44–48.

46. Patterson, *Brown v. Board of Education,* xiv.

47. Mason, *Palladium of Freedom,* 170.

48. Patterson, *Brown v. Board of Education,* xxvii–xxix.

49. Chayes, "Supreme Court, 1981 Term," 6.

50. Under the terms of the U.S. Constitution, members of the federal judiciary, whether serving on the "inferior" tribunals or on the Supreme Court, are guaranteed both continuance in office and undiminished compensation "during good behavior." U.S. Const., art. III, § 1. In addition, the judiciary depends on the Congress and the president to set its budget and jurisdiction. The two "political" branches also influence the courts through changes in federal regulations or criminal laws. Bermant and Wheeler, "Independence and Accountability," 858.

51. Brown, "Hail to the Chief," 145. Judge Brown eventually served as chief judge of the U.S. Court of Appeals for the Fifth Circuit. He was one of the court's great protectors of civil rights. See Bass, *Unlikely Heroes,* 101–5; and Read and McGough, *Let Them Be Judged,* 52–54. John R. Brown was born in 1909, in Nebraska, and was educated there and in Michigan. He moved to Houston in 1932 and became a corporate attorney specializing in admiralty and maritime law. When appointed in 1955, Judge Brown was the youngest, at forty-five, to serve

on the Fifth Circuit. Couch, *History of the Fifth Circuit,* 92. He became chief judge in 1967. Spivack, *Race, Civil Rights, and the United States Court of Appeals,* 97–98.

52. For the role played by federal judges, both at the district (trial) and the circuit (appellate) levels in the post-*Brown* civil rights struggle, see generally Couch, *History of the Fifth Circuit;* Spivack, *Race, Civil Rights, and the United States Court of Appeals;* Bass, *Unlikely Heroes;* and Belknap, *Federal Law and the Southern Order.*

53. Peltason, *Fifty-eight Lonely Men.*

54. When scholars, especially conservative academics, pondered the legacy of the Warren court, they begin with an assessment of the legitimacy of the *Brown* decisions and examine it and other "activist" public law rulings in light of their perceived effects on law, society, politics, the courts, and the Constitution. See Bickel, *The Least Dangerous Branch;* Bozell, *The Warren Revolution;* Kurland, *The Warren Court;* Hall, *The Warren Court's Conceptions of Democracy;* Levy, *Supreme Court under Earl Warren;* and Berger, *Government by Judiciary.*

55. In 1938 multiparty litigation procedures were standardized through the adoption of the Fed. R. Civ. P. For example, Rule 23 governs class actions; Rule 18, joinder of claims and remedies; and Rule 20, joinder of parties. Finally, Rule 42(a) consolidates parties.

56. For an examination of the active role of federal judges from an insider's perspective, see Johnson, "Observation," 903. Also see Cooper, *Hard Judicial Choices,* 26–44, 85–102, 136–58, 205–27. Cooper considers the problem of the effects of federal, state, and local politics on the district judges as they use remedial decrees to enforce federal laws over the objections (or obstructions) of local majoritarian politics (3–9). The slow but steady progress of the African American civil rights movement inspired members of other disenfranchised, despised, or disillusioned groups to appropriate its rhetoric and style, and to sue their own perceived oppressors in federal court. Conservatives doubt the *constitutionality* of such federal intervention, but for liberal skepticism regarding the *capacity* of the courts to achieve a rights "revolution," see Glazer, "Should Courts Administer Social Services?" 64; and Rosenberg, *The Hollow Hope.*

57. Chayes, "The Role of the Judge," 1281. Chayes inspired many responses. See Fiss, "The Forms of Justice," 1; Diver, "The Judge as Political Powerbroker," 43; "Note: Implementation," 428; Buckholz et al., "Special Project," 784; and Eisenberg and Yeazell, "The Ordinary and the Extraordinary," 465.

58. Even at the peak of civil rights activity in the 1960s, when celebrated landmark decisions vindicated varied constitutional claims, federal district judges had continued to hear traditional civil suits and criminal cases. By and large, business continued as usual in the federal courts, despite the drama of the school desegregation cases. At the height of the civil rights movement, the cases related to *Brown* accounted for less than 3 percent of the Fifth Circuit's total appellate caseload. Bass, *Unlikely Heroes,* 19.

59. Chayes, "The Role of the Judge," 1284.

CHAPTER 1. The Varieties of Public School Desegregation

1. *Hernandez v. Driscoll Consolidated Independent School District* [hereafter *Hernandez v. Driscoll* CISD], Civil Action [Civ. A.] 1384, U.S. District Court, Southern District of Texas (S.D. Tex.), Corpus Christi Division, hearing transcript, 3:545 (1 November 1957). Case files for the U.S. District Court, S.D. Tex., and several other federal courts are preserved at the National Archives and Records Administration–Southwest Regional Archives (NARA-SWA), in Fort Worth. See Civil cases, S.D. Tex., Corpus Christi Division, 1938–69, Record Group

(RG) 21, boxes 232–33, folders for C.A. 1384 [the hearing transcript is loose in box 233]. All subsequent citations of files for this case will refer to this NARA-SWA record group. The final published decision for *Hernandez v. Driscoll CISD* may be found at 2 *Race Rel. L. Rptr.* 329 (S.D. Tex., 1957).

2. *Brown v. Board of Education of Topeka* (hereafter *Brown I*), 347 U.S. 483 (1954).

3. *Brown v. Board of Education of Topeka* (hereafter *Brown II*), 349 U.S. 294 (1955).

4. The Civil Rights Act (CRA) of 1875 gave federal judges, as chancellors in equity, the authority to issue injunctions to forestall future deprivations of rights. Hoffer, *The Law's Conscience*, 130–34.

5. See, generally, Tidwell, "James V. Allred." Allred was an associate attorney in Wichita Falls at the firm Martin and Oneal (1921–23), and was made a name partner in Martin, Oneal and Allred (1923–25). He was an assistant district attorney (1922–23), before becoming district attorney (1923–25). After moving to the governor's mansion, Allred received an honorary LL.D. in 1936 from Texas Christian University in Fort Worth. "Allred," in *Judges of the United States.*

6. The Framers of the U.S. Constitution entrusted the president with the power to appoint federal judges but balanced this power by mandating the "advice and consent" of the Senate. U.S. Const., art. II, § 2. The requirement gave rise to the current procedure by which all prospective judges are vetted by the Senate Judiciary Committee, often with the informal "advice and consent" of the party leaders and sometimes with that of the legal profession, before the whole Senate votes to approve or reject the nomination. Schuck, *The Judiciary Committees*, 222–41. Also see Chase, *Federal Judges;* and, for an earlier look, especially discussions of judicial appointments during the first half of the twentieth century, Harris, *Advice and Consent of the Senate*, 315–24.

7. When they are presented with an opportunity to appoint a judge, presidents normally defer to the senators of the host state, especially when they belong to the president's own party, who might suggest or informally veto nominations. The "courtesy" is commonly asserted with respect to district and circuit seats, because senators presumably better understand how a proffered judgeship will either exacerbate or pacify local rivalries, such as that existing between Allred and O'Daniel. Goldman, *Picking Federal Judges*, 42, 80–81. After resigning his first federal judgeship and losing his senate bid, Allred resumed a legal career in Houston, first in solo practice (1943–45) and later in association with other attorneys (Willian Z. Rozan [1946–47], Jack K. Ayer [part of 1948], then with Ayer and Levert J. Able [1948–49]). "Allred," in *Judges of the United States.*

8. Allred's second appointment conveniently removed this intermittent ally but potential political rival from Johnson's own "path to power." This political rivalry was serious, although not as nasty as Johnson's relationship with his subsequent Democratic rival in Texas, the more liberal Senator Ralph Yarborough. In the first installment of his multivolume biography of Johnson, Robert Caro describes Allred as withdrawing from the primary race as early as 1941, that is, prior to his leaving the bench. Caro, *The Path to Power*, 682–83. In the second volume, however, Caro describes Allred as in competition with the then-Representative Johnson for Roosevelt's endorsement for the Senate race well into 1942. Caro, *The Means of Ascent*, 17, 28. For Allred and Johnson, also see Zelden, *Justice Lies in the District*, 153, 177, and 271, n. 8.

9. *Hernandez v. Driscoll CISD;* Hearing transcript, 3:545–46.

10. Tom Connally served as a representative in the state legislature, then in the U.S. House of Representatives from 1914 to 1928, and finally in the U.S. Senate from 1928 to 1952. Senator

Connally was chair of the Foreign Relations Committee of the Senate from 1940 to 1952. In the 1930s one Democratic leader described Tom Connally, then serving his first term as a senator, as ambitious in the pursuit of his own career but "not unfriendly to the Roosevelt forces." Roosevelt was surprised and disappointed when "party regular" Senator Connally helped to bury the president's dead-on-arrival court-packing bill in 1937. Patenaude, "Garner, Sumners, and Connally," 43. Leuchtenburg, *The Supreme Court Reborn*, 137.

11. Connally also practiced law at Sewell, Taylor, Morris, and Garwood. He was a name partner at Sewell, Taylor, Morris, and Connally in 1942, when he resigned to join the service. "Connally," in *Judges of the United States*. Senator Johnson suggested Connally for the judgeship, it appears, to remove yet another potential rival in Texas politics. Zelden, *Justice Lies in the District*, 177 and 271, n. 8.

12. *Delores Ross et al. v. President of the Board of Trustees of the Houston Independent School District* [hereafter *Ross v. HISD*], Civ. A. 10444, S.D. Tex., Houston Division (1957). Various court decisions relating to this case were published. See, for example, *Ross v. Rogers*, 2 *Race Rel. L. Rptr.* 1114 (S.D. Tex., 1957); and *Ross v. HISD*, 5 *Race Rel. L. Rptr.* 703 (S.D. Tex., 1960), affirmed as *HISD v. Ross*, 282 F.2d 95 (5th Cir., 1960), stay and certiorari denied, 364 U.S. 803 (1960).

13. Kellar, *Make Haste Slowly*. Read and McGough, *Let Them Be Judged*, 92–93.

14. Chayes, "The Role of the Judge," 1281–84.

15. The relevant public school law stated: "The terms 'colored race' and 'colored children,' as used in the preceding, and elsewhere in this act, include all persons of mixed blood descended from negro ancestry." Act of 20 May 1893, 23rd Legislature, General Laws of Texas, ch. 122, "Public Free Schools," § 15. See Gammel, *The Laws of Texas*, 616. The Texas legislature reenacted the statute, including its definition of "colored children," by an act of April 1905, 29th Legislature, p. 263, §§ 93–96, 128. This was subsequently codified in the General Provisions, ch. 19, arts. 2897–99. *Complete Texas Statutes*, 491.

16. The state's history and geography combined to make Texas law and society reflective of regional prejudices from both the South and Southwest. Foley, *The White Scourge*, 1–12. Also, Vandiver, *The Southwest*. The term *Anglo* may need some clarification. In 1970 the U.S. Civil Rights Commission noted that, as it was customarily employed in the Southwest, *Anglo* referred "to white persons who are not Mexican Americans or members of some other Spanish surnamed groups" and that the word carried "no derogatory connotations in the Southwest or in the Report or in this Summary." U.S. Commission on Civil Rights, *Mexican Americans*, 2, plus note. However, since *Anglo* literally refers to those of English descent, it is inadequate to account for descendants of the Bohemians (Czechs), Germans, or other Europeans who settled in Texas. The problem of accounting for diversity and patterns or historical discrimination within European-descended populations has given rise to "whiteness" studies. See Roediger, *Toward the Abolition of Whiteness*.

17. The present study answers the challenge laid down by Ariela Gross, who has noted that—with the exception of Ian F. Haney Lopez and a few others—"legal scholars and historians . . . have paid scant attention to the records of trials in local courts." Gross, "Litigating Whiteness," 116.

18. The Fourteenth Amendment provides that "all persons born or naturalized in the United States, and subject to the jurisdiction thereof, are citizens of the United States and of the State wherein they reside. No State shall make or enforce any law which shall abridge the privileges or immunities of citizens of the United States; nor shall any State deprive any person of life, liberty, or property, without due process of law; nor deny to any person within its jurisdiction the equal protection of the laws." U.S. Constitution, amend. XIV, § 1.

19. *Plessy v. Ferguson,* 163 U.S. 537 (1896). Associate Justice John Marshall Harlan dissented from the court majority's approval of Louisiana laws establishing "Jim Crow" in public accommodations. For a classic treatment of the rise of racial segregation in southern culture, see Woodward, *Strange Career of Jim Crow.*

20. Riches, *The Civil Rights Movement,* chap. 1.

21. Du Bois, *The Souls of Black Folk,* 13. The book is a collection of Du Bois's miscellaneous writings. He used similar imagery of the "color line" in 1901 while discussing the race subordination that continued to be suffered by blacks in the United States since the end of the Civil War. Du Bois, "The Freedmen's Bureau," *Atlantic Monthly* 87 (1901): 354–65. I owe the credit for the latter reference to Gwen Hoerr McNamee, "Crossings of the Color Line: African American Women Lawyers in Illinois, 1894–1930" (paper presented at the annual meeting of the American Historical Association, Boston, 4 January 2001), 1 n. 1.

22. See generally Kluger, *Simple Justice.* Also Abraham and Perry, *Freedom and the Court,* 342–55.

23. Tex. Const., art. 7, § 7: "Separate schools shall be provided for the white and colored children, and impartial provision shall be made for both." Act of 20 May 1893, 23rd Legislature, General Laws of Texas, ch. 122, "Public Free Schools," § 15. Gammel, *The Laws of Texas,* 10:616. The Texas legislature periodically reenacted the statute. The final codification of Jim Crow school laws in Texas came in the Revised Statutes (R.S.), ch. 19, art. 2900 [combining former arts. 2897–98]. See Jenkins, *The Revised Civil Statutes,* 1:1036.

24. As the NAACP's chief litigator, Thurgood Marshall sought to get cases into federal court as rapidly as possible. Kluger, *Simple Justice,* 214–15. Greenberg, *Crusaders in the Courts,* generally. Federal trial court decisions in civil rights cases, even if adverse, forged the keys that opened the gates to the national legal arena. Hence the title of a recent study of federal trial judges' decision-making: Lyles, *The Gatekeepers.*

25. *Sweatt v. Painter,* 339 U.S. 629 (1950). A companion graduate desegregation case is *McLaurin v. Board of Regents,* 339 U.S. 637 (1950). For information about Heman Sweatt and the background on his case, see Barr, *Black Texans,* 213–15; and Jensen, "The Houston Sit-In Movement," 212.

26. *Brown v. Board of Trustees of La Grange ISD,* 187 F.2d 20 (5th Cir., 1951), 25.

27. Ibid., 24.

28. Hutcheson served as chief judge of the Fifth Circuit from 1948 to 1959. He remained active on the appellate court into the 1960s and died in 1973 at age ninety-four. Spivack, *Race, Civil Rights, and the United States Court of Appeals,* 91–92. Circuit Judge John R. Brown offered his observations regarding judicial tenure and independence in a 1959 address honoring Hutcheson on the occasion of the latter's stepping down from the chief judgeship. See Brown, "Hail to the Chief," 145.

29. *Brown v. Board of Trustees of La Grange ISD,* 187 F.2d 20, 24.

30. Ibid., 24.

31. *Brown I,* 495. The *Brown* decision joined various "school cases" from Kansas, South Carolina, Virginia, and Delaware. A federal judge found in 1952 that black schools in the segregated Topeka district were substantially equal to the white schools, and therefore were permissible under the "separate but equal" doctrine established by *Plessy.* The plaintiffs appealed on the grounds that separation *rendered* facilities unequal. The justices heard arguments in the case twice. NAACP attorneys, specifically chief counsel (and future associate justice of the U.S. Supreme Court) Thurgood Marshall, first argued the case on 9 December 1952. A reargument on 8 December 1953 was generally concerned with the historical context of the passage and ratification of the Fourteenth Amendment. In another companion case

to *Brown I* and the joined state cases, *Bolling v. Sharpe*, 347 U.S. 497 (1954), the court declared the segregated schools in the federal enclave of the District of Columbia to be unconstitutional. See generally Kluger, *Simple Justice.*

32. Derrick A. Bell Jr., "*Brown v. Board of Education* and the Interest-Convergence Dilemma," *Harvard Law Review* 93 (1980): 518.

33. Patterson, *Brown v. Board of Education,* xxvii–xxix.

34. The *Brown* decision was limited to schools. The court did not directly overturn *Plessy* until after the Montgomery, Alabama, bus boycotts sparked a new phase of the civil rights movement. *Gayle v. Browder*, 352 U.S. 903 (1956). Sitkoff, *The Struggle for Black Equality.*

35. Marshall, quoted in Kluger, *Simple Justice*, 736.

36. Powe, *The Warren Court*, 50–57; Kluger, *Simple Justice*, 736.

37. *Brown II*, 299–301.

38. Ibid.

39. Scholars have pondered the rationale underpinning the Supreme Court's decision to support desegregation in principle but to abandon it in fact by ordering that segregation be dismantled through individual lawsuits in the district courts. Many critics argue that the timid court simply passed the buck. Peter Hoffer has argued that *Brown II* was not, as is frequently contended, an instance of cynical compromise of principle in a difficult case. Hoffer noted that, if *Brown* was not "good constitutional law," the compromises it contained were "very good constitutional equity." The *Brown II* order was an equitable solution appropriate to the case. It was misinterpreted, often deliberately, by judges and local school boards choosing to read "all deliberate speed" as permission to delay. But, Hoffer concluded, the justices' decision to remand to the district courts was not a nod to federalism, a capitulation to state's rights, or a failure of nerve; rather, Hoffer believes, the court sought to achieve a fair decision that would respect the rights of all, even the segregationists. Hoffer, *The Law's Conscience*, xii, 180–91. Another scholar has argued, however, that the justices were concerned that a more "activist" decision would threaten the court's prestige, already at risk, and that they decided that the federal district courts could take the heat of the ruling without undermining faith in the system. Halpern, *On the Limits of the Law*, 74.

40. The provisions in question were part of the Foundation School Program, which, like other state educational programs, was limited to segregated schools. In 1949 the Texas legislature enacted the Gilmer-Aikin Act (Foundation School Program Act, 51st Legislature, ch. 334, art. 2922 §§ 11–22). The purpose of Gilmer-Aikin was "to guarantee to each child of school age in Texas the availability of a minimum Foundation School Program for nine (9) full months of the year, and to establish the eligibility requirements applicable to Texas public school districts." Ibid., § 11. The act also had provided that "the number of professional units [i.e., teachers] allotted for the purpose of this act to each school district, except as herein provided, shall be based upon and determined by the average daily attendance for the district for the next preceding school year, separate for whites and separate for negroes. Such allotments, based upon white attendance shall be utilized in white schools, and allotments based upon negro attendance shall be utilized in negro schools." Ibid., § 13

41. The final "Jim Crow" school law was in the Revised Statutes (R.S.) of Texas, ch. 19, art. 2900 [as previously noted, combining former arts. 2897–98], which provided: "All available public school funds of this state shall be appropriated in each county for the education alike of white and colored children, and impartial provision shall be made for both races. No white child shall attend schools supported for colored children, nor shall colored children attend schools supported for white children. The terms 'colored race' and 'colored children'

as used in this title, include all persons of mixed blood descended from negro ancestry." See Jenkins, *The Revised Civil Statutes,* 1:1036. The legislative history of public school segregation begins in the Act of 20 May 1893, 23d Legislature, Gen. Laws of Tex., ch. 122, "Public Free Schools," § 14: "The children of the white and colored races shall be taught in separate schools, and in no case shall any school consisting partly of white and of partly colored children receive any aid from the public school fund"; and, the legislature provided in § 94 that each child attend school in the district in which "it" resided, except that "white children shall not attend the schools supported for colored children, nor shall colored children attend the schools supported for white children." See Gammel, *Laws of Texas,* 10:614, 616, 637–38. In § 58 the lawmakers provided for "impartial provision" within these separate schools, with three white trustees elected or appointed for the white school districts and three "colored" trustees elected or appointed (upon written application by ten black residents of the affected district). If there were not enough African American children in a district to justify this, two or more districts could be consolidated, to be governed by the trustees of the district in which classes actually met. Ibid., 628. This section was amended by the next legislature, meeting two years later, in 1895, to define the power, authority, and responsibility of trustees for "the control and management" of the schools and to provide specific guidance on the selection of trustees. For example, trustees, both white and "colored," were to be elected "in all cases." However, in polling as in other public intercourse, separate but equal was still the rule. The 1895 amendment stated that the "election for white and colored trustees shall be held at the same times and places, and the ballots cast for white trustees shall be deposited in a separate box from that used for the ballots cast for colored trustees." The returns and official certification of results were also recorded on a separate basis. Amendment by Act of 21 March 1895, 24th Legislature, Gen. Laws of Tex., ch. 24, "Public Free Schools," § 1. Gammel, *Laws of Texas,* 10:759.

42. *McKinney v. Blankenship,* 154 Tex. 632 (Tex. Sup. Ct., 1955), 642–43; affirming 282 S.W.2d 691 (1955). See also Ladino, *Desegregating Texas Schools,* 28–33.

43. Read and McGough, *Let Them Be Judged,* 64–68.

44. Powe, *The Warren Court,* 60–69.

45. Kinch and Long, *Allan Shivers,* 3.

46. Ladino, *Desegregating Texas Schools,* 42.

47. Peltason, *Fifty-eight Lonely Men,* 25, 213. Read and McGough, *Let Them Be Judged,* 27–31. Judge Hutcheson was the second oldest active federal judge at the time. He served as the Fifth Circuit's chief judge until the summer of 1959, when the law forced him to step down from that position. He remained active for several more years. For Hutcheson, see Reed and McGough, *Let Them Be Judged,* 121–22. Ladino, *Desegregating Texas Schools,* 88–90 [Ladino incorrectly gives Hutcheson's name as John]. For Rives, see Couch, *History of the Fifth Circuit,* 82–94.

48. *Jackson v. Rawdon,* 135 F.Supp. 936 (N.D. Tex., 1956), reversed and remanded, 235 F.2d 93 (5th Cir., 1956), at 96, cert. denied, 352 U.S. 925 (1956). This was the first post-*Brown* African American school desegregation case to reach the Fifth Circuit.

49. Ladino, *Desegregating Texas Schools.*

50. See the Dallas County case *Brown v. Rippy,* 233 F.2d 796 (5th Cir.), cert. denied, 352 U.S. 878 (1956), and *Avery v. Wichita Falls Independent School District,* 241 F.2d 230 (5th Cir.), cert. denied, 353 U.S. 938 (1957). For detailed background material on the cases, see Read and McGough, *Let Them Be Judged,* 64–91. In each of these cases, the Fifth Circuit decided in favor of parties seeking to desegregate the local schools, but segregation continued de facto

for some time. In the Wichita Falls case, for example, the judges of the Fifth Circuit decided that *Brown* did not demand *integration,* just removal of existing segregation barriers.

51. Davidson, "Negro Politics," 50–51.

52. See Cole, *No Color Is My Kind,* 54–57; and Oppenheimer, *The Sit-In Movement,* 92–93. In 1963 the Board of Trustees of the Rice Institute, Houston's premier private institution, sought to desegregate the school. The board was motivated less by moral objections to segregation than by their concern that in the post-*Brown* era Rice would be unable to attract or to retain first-class faculty or to win lucrative federal grants for research to be conducted under the auspices of the Manned Spacecraft Center (later renamed Johnson Spacc Ccnter), which the National Aeronautics and Space Administration recently had established at Clear Lake, near Houston. This effort required state court intervention, because Rice's 1891 charter called for the trustees to maintain it for "white inhabitants" of Houston. Moreover, the board faced legal challenges from segregationist-minded alumni. Ultimately, with the aid of Baker and Botts, one of Houston's top law firms, the trustees successfully argued that maintaining Rice as a segregated southern university would never fulfill the founder's larger goal in endowing it, which was that Rice become a school of the "first rank." *Coffee v. Rice University,* 408 S.W.2d 269 (1966). During the legal proceedings, and on the same grounds, the trustees also convinced the courts to allow them to rename the institute "Rice University" and to change the charter to allow them to charge tuition. Pratt and Castaneda, *Builders,* 205–11. Hyman, *Craftsmanship and Character,* 339. Also Lipartito and Pratt, *Baker & Botts,* 61, 160–61.

53. *Ross v. Eckels,* 434 F.2d 1140 (5th Cir., 1970), 1142. Davidson, "Negro Politics," 51–52. Because the bimonthly meetings appeared on local television, the interested public could follow the progress of the board's study. Read and McGough, *Let Them Be Judged,* 92–93.

54. Peltason, *Fifty-eight Lonely Men,* 33.

55. Ellen Middlebrook, "Mrs. Rogers Asks Public Patience in Integration," *Houston Post,* 7 January 1956, 4A. Kellar, *Make Haste Slowly,* 78–80.

56. To ensure the children's protection, and his own, Nelson carried a pistol in a paper bag. Read and McGough, *Let Them Be Judged,* 93. In 1994 the Houston branch of the NAACP honored Nelson, then eighty-nine years old. The group noted that the past vice president accompanied Delores Ross to school. "Houston Chapter of NAACP Honors New Life Members," *Houston Post,* 14 February 1994, p. A-13.

57. Quoted in Read and McGough, *Let Them Be Judged,* 94. Also see Davidson, "Negro Politics," 53.

58. Read and McGough, *Let Them Be Judged,* 94, 95–110. See also Davidson, "Negro Politics," 52.

59. Davidson, "Negro Politics," 68. Bass, *Unlikely Heroes,* 117. For contemporary accounts by journalists who reported on the reaction to desegregation throughout the South, see the essays collected in Shoemaker, *With All Deliberate Speed.* There was a continuing controversy over the difference between the words *integration* and *desegregation.* In a rehearing of *Briggs v. Elliott,* one of the original school desegregation cases joined with *Brown,* the federal district judge declared that the Constitution "does not require integration. . . . It merely forbids [segregation]." 132 F.Supp. 776 (E.D.S.C., 1955), 777. In *Brown* the U.S. Supreme Court had employed neither term. The justices would not clarify the difference between them until late in the next decade. This allowed conservative judges, including the federal district judge in the South Carolina case, to give *Brown* a minimal reading, and many judges cited *Briggs* with approval in their rulings.

60. Susan Besze Wallace, "The Changing Complexion of HISD: As the Desegregation Legal Battle Wore On, Houston School Demographics Were Steadily Changing," *Houston Post,* 15 May 1994, A-16.

61. *Ross v. HISD,* 5 *Race Rel. L. Rptr.* 703 (S.D. Tex., 1960). Facets of this litigation were also in case reports as *Ross v. Dyer* (because, for example, Dyer was president of the board of trustees of HISD in 1957), *Ross v. Peterson,* and *Ross v. Eckels;* these refer to the same case and will be cited as appropriate.

62. Wallace, "The Changing Complexion of HISD."

63. Quoted in Zelden, *Justice Lies in the District,* 206. See also Read and McGough, *Let Them Be Judged,* 104.

64. *Plummer v. Casey,* 148 F.Supp. 326 (S.D. Tex., 1955); affirmed as *Derrington v. Plummer,* 240 F.2d 922 (5th Cir., 1956); cert. denied, 77 S.Ct. 680 (1957). See Kellar, *Make Haste Slowly,* 78.

65. Peltason, *Fifty-eight Lonely Men,* 122–23.

66. See Fed. R. Civ. P., Rule 16 ("Pre-Trial Procedure; Scheduling; Management"); Murrah, "Pre-trial Procedure," 14 F.R.D. 417 (1953); and Clark, "Objectives of Pre-trial Procedure."

67. Judith Resnik, "Managerial Judges," 376, 410–13.

68. The Legal Process movement was a creature of the 1950s. It tried to address the threat of judicial whim implied by Legal Realism, but without relying on formalist pretenses that had brought judicial review into bad repute during the previous generation. The scholars who might be collected under this "process" banner were few but influential. Laura Kalman named former students, clerks, or disciples of Professor-cum-Justice Felix Frankfurter, such as Henry Hart and Herbert Wechsler, as founders of "process jurisprudence." Kalman, *Strange Career,* 41–42. For another scholar's list of approximately one dozen apostles of the "legal process," see Ackerman, "Law and the Modern Mind," 123; and Duxbury, "Faith in Reason," 665. In 1953 Hart and Wechsler dedicated the first edition of their still influential casebook to Frankfurter; see Hart and Wechsler, *Federal Courts and the Federal System.* A second edition appeared in 1973. See Bator et al., *Federal Courts and the Federal System* (2d ed.). The third edition was published in 1988; see Bator et al., *Federal Courts and the Federal System* (3d ed.). Hart and Oliver Sacks, another Frankfurter adherent, completed in 1958, but failed to publish, their textbook on process jurisprudence, but the work is now available. See Henry M. Hart Jr. and Oliver M. Sacks, *The Legal Process: Basic Problems in the Making and Application of Law,* ed. William N. Eskridge Jr. and Phillip P. Frickey (Westbury, N.Y.: Foundation Press, 1994); also Eskridge and Frickey, "Making of the Legal Process," 2031.

69. After campaigning to reinvigorate principled judicial restraint by developing neutral rules, Kalman says, the "process theorists" became "obsessed with procedural issues, with limiting the role of the federal courts, with ensuring courts found and followed statutory purpose," and with establishing boundaries for legitimate judicial review. Kalman, *Strange Career,* 30. See Fallon, "Hart and Wechsler Paradigm," 970–71. See also Tribe, "Puzzling Persistence," 1063.

70. *Ross v. Rogers,* 2 *Race Rel. L. Rptr.* 1114 (S.D. Tex., 1957). See also Read and McGough, *Let Them Be Judged,* 99–101.

71. *HISD v. Ross,* 282 F.2d 95 (5th Cir., 1960), 96.

72. White was a graduate of Booker T. Washington High School. For White's campaign, see Davidson, "Negro Politics," 53–55. The main administration building of the HISD is now named in her honor.

73. Erna Smith, "Participants Recall Events of Desegregation in HISD," *Houston Post,* 17 May 1979, p. 4A.

74. Some NAACP leaders suggested appealing to the Fifth Circuit Court for a writ of mandamus, a rare order to compel a lower court judge to execute a legal duty. Read and McGough, *Let Them Be Judged,* 103–4. Mandamus was applied to correct egregious abuses of power. For example, federal district courts have original jurisdiction to compel an officer or employee of the United States to perform a nondiscretionary duty owed to a plaintiff. Under the same principle, the U.S. courts of appeals can compel action in a district court. The statute giving U.S. district courts this power is codified at 28 U.S.C. § 1361 (Compelling Performance). Technically, the writ of mandamus no longer exists in American law. Under the Federal Rules of Civil Procedure, "extraordinary" writs have been abolished in favor of a motion or complaint "in the nature of mandamus," which accomplishes the same legal object as the writ. Fed. R. Civ. Proc., Rule 81(b).

75. Peltason, *Fifty-eight Lonely Men,* 106.

76. Davidson, "Negro Politics," 107–8. See *Texas v.* NAACP (Smith County, 7th Judicial District, 1957). Ladino, *Desegregating Texas Schools,* 133–40.

77. Peltason, *Fifty-eight Lonely Men,* 122–23.

78. Read and McGough, *Let Them Be Judged,* 103.

79. Quoted in Read and McGough, *Let Them Be Judged,* 104. See also Peltason, *Fifty-eight Lonely Men,* 122–23.

80. Davidson, "Negro Politics," 67–68.

81. Quoted in Peltason, *Fifty-eight Lonely Men,* 124. Reynolds eventually defended most of the embattled Houston area school districts in their decades-long desegregation cases. Art Wiese, "Meet Joe Reynolds, Schools' Counsel in Desegregation Cases," *Houston Post,* 7 September 1969, "Insight," pp. 1–2.

82. *HISD v. Ross,* 282 F.2d 95 (5th Cir., 1960), 96. By then, Texas state law required that voters approve a salt-and-pepper scheme, and a low turnout of Houston voters approved the plan in a special referendum held on 5 June 1960. However, Texas Attorney General Will Wilson concluded that school districts could not be deprived of funds, merely because they desegregated, without a favorable result in a local referendum. "Opinion of Attorney General," 5 *Race Rel. L. Rptr.* 711 (1960). This may have persuaded the board that it really had no options for delay.

83. After the board asked Connally to clarify this order, he submitted a detailed desegregation plan on 12 August. *Ross v.* HISD, 5 *Race Rel. L. Rptr.* 703 (S.D. Tex., 1960).

84. The panel consisted of Circuit Judges Rives, Warren Jones, and John Minor Wisdom. *HISD v. Ross,* 282 F.2d 95 (5th Cir., 1960).

85. *HISD v. Ross,* 364 U.S. 803 (1960).

86. Kellar, *Make Haste Slowly,* 136–38.

87. Read and McGough, *Let Them Be Judged,* 108.

88. Kellar, *Make Haste Slowly,* 92.

89. Peltason, *Fifty-eight Lonely Men,* 123. For Peltason's discussion of Galveston, see p. 138.

90. Kellar, *Make Haste Slowly,* 151–77.

91. After the 1958 crisis in Little Rock, Arkansas, where nine black children were harassed and threatened for attending school, one Houston activist reportedly declared that "they had better not try that in Houston. Maybe they can get away with it in Arkansas. But they couldn't do that to us; remember we're Texans!" Quoted in Peltason, *Fifty-eight Lonely Men,*

137. For the Supreme Court's response to the Little Rock crisis, see *Cooper v. Aaron*, 358 U.S. 1 (1958).

92. *Ross v. Dyer*, 203 F.Supp. 124 (S.D. Tex., 1962), 125.

93. Ibid., 125. Although the new complaint was brought on behalf of Sheila Smith, district court treated it as a continuance of Delores Ross's case, because an alleged violation of Connally's August 1960 order was the basis of Smith's complaint. Principal counselors in both sides of this case are listed as in the original case: Weldon Berry of Houston for Ross, with Inc. Fund lawyers U. Simpson Tate of Dallas and Thurgood Marshall of New York listed on the appeal (although it is unlikely that Marshall participated in person). Joe H. Reynolds represented HISD. James J. Hippard of Houston was Smith's counsel in the intervening case.

94. F.Supp. 124 (S.D. Tex., 1962), 125.

95. Ibid., 125.

96. F.Supp. 124, 126.

97. Ibid., 126. During the course of hearing the arguments, Judge Connally "expressed some uncertainty as to the validity of the rule when applied to a peculiar situation." This record does not elaborate on this point, but Connally acknowledged that the HISD board "voluntarily modified" the rule in question to eliminate any doubt in the judge's mind.

98. Ibid., 126.

99. Ibid., 126.

100. *Ross v. Dyer*, 312 F.2d 191 (5th Cir., 1963), 194.

101. Ibid., 194.

102. Ibid., 195–96. Judge Brown noted that this biasing effect "is markedly illustrated in considering the undisputed fact of large families among Negroes."

103. Ibid., 197.

104. Ibid., 197–98. On 25 January 1963, the Fifth Circuit denied HISD's request for a rehearing.

105. For an interesting discussion of the benefits of this claim, see Harris, "Whiteness as Property," 1707, 1753.

106. *In re Rodriguez*, 81 Fed. 337 (W.D. Tex., 1897).

107. The right of individuals to U.S. citizenship as a consequence of birth on U.S. soil was clouded by the *Dred Scott* decision in 1857 but conferred and clarified by the ratification of the Fourteenth Amendment in 1868. The mechanism for extending citizenship rights to the foreign-born individuals remained the prerogative of Congress. The precedent for granting citizenship to Mexican nationals in Texas was established even before statehood. After Texas declared its independence from Mexico, the 1836 Texas Constitution recognized even the non-Anglos then living there to be citizens of the new "Lone Star" republic. The U.S. Congress recognized all citizens of that republic as citizens when Texas joined the Union in 1845. The Treaty of Guadalupe-Hidalgo—which set out the terms of Mexico's defeat in the Mexican-American War of 1846–48—gave Mexico's vast northern provinces to the United States but also stipulated that all inhabitants in the ceded territory who neither left the territory nor announced an intent to retain Mexican citizenship within one year would automatically become U.S. citizens. In 1849 the California state constitution granted Mexicans the same citizenship rights enjoyed by Anglo-Americans. See Ngai, "The Architecture of Race," 88, esp. n. 47.

108. *In re Rodriguez*, 81 Fed. 337 (W.D. Tex., 1897).

109. Ngai, "The Architecture of Race," 93.

110. Ibid., 88–90.

111. Ibid., 89.

112. Ibid., 91.

113. Lopez, "Race, Ethnicity, Erasure," 1148 n. 20, 1170–71, and 1179 n. 115.

114. Some persons of Mexican descent may also have an African descent; however, the "one drop rule" as described in the Texas statutes (and those of most other southern states) generally did not apply to Mexican Americans. Davis, *Who Is Black?,* 114–15, and generally.

115. See Greenfield and Kates, "Mexican Americans," 682, esp. n. 92.

116. Acts of 29th Legislature, ch. 124, § 102. Legislators later amended the law to prohibit the use of textbooks not printed in the English language. However, the statutes did not prevent *teaching* or *learning* languages other than English. For example, the English-only laws law did not prevent the "teaching of Latin, Greek, French, German, Spanish, Bohemian, or other language as a branch of study in the high schools grades as outlined in the state course of study." Acts of 1918, 4th Civ. Stat., ch. 80, § 1. Codified in the General Provisions, ch. 19, art. 2904(5a). The latter three languages are included because many Texans or their ancestors originally had emigrated from the regions of Bohemia (the present-day Czech Republic), Germany, and, of course, Mexico, during the nineteenth century, and linguistic enclaves persisted throughout the state. See, for example, Struve, *Germans and Texans;* Machann and Mendl, *Czech Voices;* and Montejano, *Anglos and Mexicans.* In 1918 patriotic lawmakers authorized *criminal* sanctions to be initiated against teachers who taught in a language other than English. Convicted violators were subject to fine and dismissal. Texas Penal Code, arts. 1038(a)–(f). *Complete Texas Statutes,* 492.

117. Montejano, *Anglos and Mexicans,* 160.

118. Ibid., 160. See Greenfield and Kates, "Mexican Americans" 682.

119. The Americanization movement was fed by World War I–era xenophobia aimed at "hyphenated" Americans of divided and therefore questionable loyalty. It sought to educate immigrants and transform the foreign-born into citizens who were both English-speaking and "100% American." John F. McClymer, "The Americanization Movement and the Education of the Foreign-Born Adult, 1914–1925," 105. At a conference on Americanization and citizenship, called by the U.S. Commissioner of Education, Dr. P. P. Claxton noted that "Americanization is a process that makes for the harmony of differences that are good only in their blending. It recognizes national equality as it does individual equality, but does not make equality another word for identity." Fredric P. Woellner, "The Teaching of American History as a Factor in Americanization," *School and Society* 13 (21 May 1921): 590.

120. San Miguel, *"Let All of Them Take Heed,"* 69–70, 116, 165–71. See generally Ramos, *The American GI Forum;* and Allsup, *The American GI Forum.* See, also generally, Hero, *Latinos and the U.S. Political System.*

121. Martinez, "Legal Indeterminacy," 555.

122. Montejano, *Anglos and Mexicans,* 191–96.

123. *Inhabitants of Del Rio ISD v. Jesus Salvatierra,* 33 S.W.2d 790 (Tex. Civ. App., 1930), dismissed for lack of jurisdiction, and cert. denied, 284 U.S. 580 (1931). [Some references cite the case as *Salvatierra v. Independent School District;* hereafter, I will refer only to *Salvatierra.*] The state judge in this case, pleased that he was the first to address the legality of segregating Mexican Americans, began his opinion by acknowledging: "It is to the credit of both races that, notwithstanding widely diverse racial characteristics, they dwell together in friendship, peace, and unity, and work amicably together for the common good and a common country." He added, "It is a matter of pride and gratification in our great public educational system . . . that the question of race segregation, as between Mexicans and other white races, has not heretofore found its way into the courts of the state." Ibid., 794.

124. The superintendent testified that he did not send English-speaking children "who came in late over to the school where I sent the Mexican or Spanish speaking children." Ibid., 792–93.

125. Emphasis added. Ibid., 794–95.

126. Ibid. The plaintiffs sought to bring this case before the U.S. Supreme Court, but the justices dismissed the appeal for lack of jurisdiction. 284 U.S. 580 (1931).

127. Martinez, "Legal Indeterminacy," 577–80.

128. The ruling bedeviled Mexican American civil rights litigants for decades. Forty years later, the federal courts decided that bilingual education might reduce the language and even culture problems better than segregation. In 1971's *United States v. Texas*, 342 F.Supp. 24 (E.D. Tex., 1971), U.S. District Judge William Wayne Justice ordered Texas school administrators to cease segregation of Mexican Americans and to institute bilingual and bicultural education. Judge Justice ruled that segregation because of linguistic differences created a stigma of inferiority. On the state's appeal, the Fifth Circuit affirmed Justice. 466 F.2d 518 (5th Cir., 1972). For Judge Justice's role in *United States v. Texas*, see Kemerer, *William Wayne Justice*, chap. 5.

129. *Mendez v. Westminster School District*, 64 F.Supp. 544 (S.D. Cal., 1946).

130. Glenn and de Jong, *Educating Immigrant Children*, 338.

131. *Mendez*, 64 F.Supp., 549. Regarding these Mexican American desegregation cases, one commentator noted how "strikingly similar" this 1946 pronouncement is to statements made by the Supreme Court eight years later, in *Brown*. Salinas, "Desegregation of Schools in the Southwest," 940. In fact, the case offered an example of cooperation between LULAC and the NAACP's LDF, in that Robert L. Carter, an LDF attorney, contributed an amicus curiae brief. The case was a "useful dry run," which allowed the LDF to test arguments it would later use in *Brown*, and without risking a reversal. Kluger, *Simple Justice*, 399–400. The civil rights litigators rarely coordinated suits with their counterparts, but organizations representing Mexican Americans and African Americans in civil rights litigation occasionally made common cause, either as intervenors in suits or as writers of amicus briefs in support of one another's positions. However, tension between Mexican Americans and African Americans over legal strategies continued, since leaders of the various organizations were often jealous of their perceived turf and reacted poorly to interference from other organizations. Wasby, *Race Relations*, 123–24.

132. *Mendez*, 64 F.Supp., 549.

133. *Westminster School District v. Mendez*, 161 F.2d 774 (9th Cir., 1947), 781.

134. *Mendez*, 161 F.2d, 780. See *Roberts v. City of Boston*, 59 Mass. (5 Cush.) 198 (1849), in which Massachusetts courts ruled that, in the absence of legislation, local school boards had discretion to segregate. *Mendez*, 161 F.2d, 779 n. 6.

135. *Mendez*, 161 F.2d 784.

136. State courts ruled against Mexican American efforts to desegregate public accommodations until forced to abandon the position by federal courts. As to restrictive covenants, the Supreme Court's decision in *Shelley v. Kraemer*, 334 U.S. 1 (1948) prevented the state courts from ruling against Mexican Americans. Martinez, "Legal Indeterminacy," 573.

137. Opinion No. V-128, *Digest of Opinions of the Attorney General of Texas* (Austin: Gammel, 1947), 39. See Rangel and Alcala, "De Jure Segregation," 335–36, esp. nn. 158–59.

138. *Delgado v. Bastrop ISD*, Civ. No. 388 (unreported: W.D. Tex., 15 June 1948).

139. Rice ultimately ruled that, if a school district provided for linguistic segregation, any separate facilities must be located on the same campus as other classrooms. Ibid., 1–2.

140. Woods, "Official Communication from the Superintendent," 1–3.

141. Ibid., 6–7.

142. Ibid., 1. No district needed to spend its budget on tests: instead, the superintendent supplied addresses of the Austin publisher of exams and informed local officials that they could "order [a] supply of tests [for a] price [of] not more than $1.25 for the instructions and tests for 25 pupils." In the spirit of local control, school district administrators retained discretion to segregate or not to segregate, and the decision was contingent on their willingness to spend their budget for that purpose. In addition, the superintendent would allow local officials to set their own standards for competency, "since the situation which we face requires immediate action." He noted, however, that "after one year of experimentation and adjustment, then we may be ready to fix a state-wide standard." Ibid., 8–9.

143. Ibid., 3.

144. Salinas, "Desegregation of Schools in the Southwest," 941. As noted, *Delgado v. Bastrop* was unpublished and so lacked much precendential weight outside Texas. But the next *reported* federal case involving segregation of Mexican Americans, in Arizona three years after *Delgado,* supported Judge Rice's essential findings. In *Gonzalez v. Sheely,* 96 F.Supp. 1004 (D. Ariz., 1951), the judge followed *Mendez* to find that a district that segregated Mexican American children into one school attended solely by Mexican Americans violated the children's Fourteenth Amendment rights. The court determined that the physical segregation harmed students' ability to learn English and retarded development of a common culture, which the judge thought was essential to full participation in American civic life. Further, the court found that the segregation fostered antagonism and wrongly suggested to the Hispanic children that they were inferior to Anglos. Ibid., 1005–7. The court enjoined discriminatory practices where the legislature had not specifically authorized segregation of students of Mexican descent. However, the *Gonzales* decision, once again following *Mendez,* did not forestall the probable result: continued separate classrooms for the language minority. The judge noted that "English language deficiencies of some of the children of Mexican ancestry . . . may exist to such a degree in the pupils in elementary schools as to require separate treatment in separate classrooms." Ibid., 1009. According to Martinez, even given this shortcoming, the decision represented a significant advance over *Salvatierra,* because the *Gonzalez* court was sensitive to the notion that segregation placed a "stamp of inferiority" on Mexican Americans, in anticipation of *Brown I,* in which the Supreme Court declared that segregation created feelings of inferiority "that may affect . . . hearts and minds in a way unlikely ever to be undone." 347 U.S. 483 (1896), 494. This rejected the reasoning in *Plessy* that if legally compelled segregation made minorities feel inferior, that result was not the fault of the law, but "solely because the colored race chooses to put that construction upon it." 163 U.S. 537 (1896), 551. The *Salvatierra* court, Martinez notes, remained "oblivious to such concerns." Martinez, "Legal Indeterminacy," 580.

145. "DeAnda," in *Judges of the United States.*

146. DeAnda recalled, years later, that he faced few obstacles in his college years that he could ascribe clearly to race prejudice. Yet he also made no effort to correct the assumption, made by at least a few of his fellow students (apparently based on his name and olive skin) that he was of Italian descent. Oral history interview with James DeAnda by Steven Wilson, 20 May 1998. For similar recollections in a more convenient format (although in a story that contains some minor inaccuracies regarding some of the cases discussed), see Student News Feature, "Judge James DeAnda: Graduate Blazed Trails in Texas Civil Rights," *Townes Hall Notes,* Fall 2000, 74–77. (This is the magazine of the UT School of Law.) For one firm's experiences with hiring Hispanic lawyers, see Hyman, *Craftsmanship and Character,* 412.

147. *Sanchez v. State,* 243 S.W.2d 700 (1951), 701; Case No. 25,496, Court of Criminal Appeals of Texas (also published at 156 Texas Cr. R. 468); November 21, 1951. See Lopez, "Race, Ethnicity, Erasure," 1169–70, esp. n. 83.

148. *Sanchez v. State,* 243 S.W.2d 700 (1951), 701.

149. *Hernandez v. State,* 251 S.W.2d 531 (1952), 533. Case No. 25,816, Court of Criminal Appeals of Texas, 18 June 1952.

150. Ibid. The qualifications for jury service in any Texas county included state and county citizenship, as well as qualifications to vote in the county; status as a freeholder within the state, or a householder within the county; possession of sound mind and good moral character; and ability to read and write (presumably in English). In addition, prospective jurors must not have been convicted of any felony and must not be under indictment or other legal accusation for theft or of any felony during the jury's term of service. See Vernon's Texas Code of Criminal Procedure (1948), arts. 333–50.

151. *Norris v. Alabama,* 294 U.S. 587 (1935). Also see *Powell v. Alabama,* 287 U.S. 45 (1932).

152. *Hernandez v. State,* 251 S.W.2d 531 (1952), 535.

153. *Serapio Sanchez v. State,* 147 Tex. Crim. 436 (1944), 443; Case No. 22,856, Court of Criminal Appeals of Texas (also published at 181 S.W.2d 87), May 17, 1944.

154. *Hernandez v. State,* 251 S.W.2d 531 (1952), 532–35.

155. *Hernandez v. Texas,* 347 U.S. 475 (1954).

156. Ibid., 479–81.

157. *Hernandez* immediately precedes *Brown* in the published decisions of the Supreme Court.

158. *Hernandez v. Texas,* 347 U.S., 475, 477–81.

159. Furthermore, the court held that even unintentional discrimination might constitute a denial of equal protection. Ibid.

160. Lopez, "Race, Ethnicity, Erasure" 1143–46, 1158–72, and 1187 n. 135. Also Lopez, *White by Law.* Scholars of African American civil rights efforts often exclude Mexican Americans, an exclusion that emerges as the absence of discussion of the their activities, or of *Hernandez,* even in works focused on desegregation battles in Texas. See Ladino, *Desegregating Texas Schools.* However, as previously noted, the LDF's Robert Carter filed an amicus brief in 1946's *Mendez.* Also, Kluger discussed the equal protection aspects of a later school-funding case with a Mexican American focus, *San Antonio ISD v. Rodriguez,* 93 S.Ct. 1278 (1973). See Kluger, *Simple Justice,* 399–400 (*Mendez*), 669–770 (*Rodriguez*).

161. *Hernandez v. Driscoll CISD* was not the first case after *Brown* was announced that was *filed* in a federal court by Mexican Americans after *Brown.* The first was *Romero v. Weakly,* 131 F.Supp. 818 (S.D. Cal., 1955), in which Mexican Americans filed suit against California's El Centro School District. Attorneys for the school district claimed that state courts had yet to apply and construe applicable state laws and argued the federal district judge should abstain. Under the *Pullman* abstention doctrine, federal courts seek to avoid premature interference with the state court's construction of state laws. See *Railroad Commission of Texas v. Pullman,* 312 U.S. 496 (1941), 501. The federal district judge agreed with the school district and dismissed the lawsuit. The judges of the U.S. Court of Appeals for the Ninth Circuit reversed. The appellate judges ruled that the plaintiff had raised no unadjudicated questions of California state law that justified *Pullman* abstention. The Ninth Circuit judges ordered the federal district court to hear the case. *Romero v. Weakly,* 226 F.2d 399 (9th Cir., 1955), 402. By the time *Romero* reached rehearing in the Southern District of California, however, *Driscoll CISD* was well under way in the Southern District of Texas. The Ninth Circuit judges

observed that the Mexican American plaintiffs might have justified federal intervention on the grounds of their belief that federal judges would be more open to their arguments than judges in state courts, because the state judges are subject to reelection while federal judges are appointed for life. Ibid., 401. George A. Martinez believes this to be a key point, because Mexican Americans had not enjoyed much success in the California state courts. Martinez, "Legal Indeterminacy," 581–82.

162. Allred, "Opinion," 3–6, NARA-SWA, RG 21, box 232, folder 1: "1384 *Herminio Hernandez v. Driscoll Consolidated ISD, et al.*"

163. Hearing transcript of *Hernandez v. Driscoll*, 1:6, 63–64, 93–95, NARA-SWA, RG 21, box 233.

164. Hearing transcript of *Hernandez v. Driscoll*, 1:6, 63–64, 93–95, NARA-SWA, RG 21, box 233.

165. DeAnda et al., "Complaint to Enjoin Violation of Federal Civil Rights and for Damages," 1–2, NARA-SWA, RG 21, box 232, folder 3: "1384 *Hernandez v. Driscoll.*" Specifically, the complaint referred to 42 U.S.C. §§ 1981–83 (formerly, 8 U.S.C. § 43). These statutes were codifications of the CRAS of 1870 and 1871, which provided as follows: "All persons within the jurisdiction of the United States shall have the same rights in every state . . . to the full and equal benefit of all laws . . . as is enjoyed by white citizens" (Act of 1870, § 16, codified 42 U.S.C. § 1981); and "every person who, under color of any statute, ordinance, regulation, custom, or usage, of any State or Territory, subjects, or causes to be subjected, any citizen . . . to the deprivation of any rights, privileges, or immunities secured by the Constitution and laws, shall be liable to the party injured" (Act of 1871, § 1, codified 42 U.S.C. § 1983). DeAnda also represented similarly situated plaintiffs in *Trinidad Villareal, et al. v. Mathis ISD of San Patricio City*, which he filed at the same time as *Hernandez v. Driscoll CISD*, and on the same grounds. Judge Allred granted the defendants' motion to dismiss the case in May 1957, after DeAnda's expert witness begged off. *Villareal v. Mathis ISD*, Civ. A. 1385 (S.D. Tex., Corpus Christi Division, 2 May 1957), NARA-SWA, RG 21, Civil cases of the S.D. Tex., Corpus Christi Division, 1938–69, RG 21, box 233, folder 1385.

166. DeAnda et al., "Complaint to Enjoin Violation of Federal Civil Rights and for Damages," 5. To make up for this deprivation, the plaintiffs also sought to obtain damages from the board. The requested damages, for each individual plaintiff, were as follows: four thousand dollars in actual damages for the estimated wages lost after the plaintiff was unnecessarily held back in school for two years and another four thousand dollars in punitive damages. Ibid., 7–8.

167. "Answer [of Driscoll Consolidated ISD, et al.]," NARA-SWA, RG 21, box 232, folder 2: "1384 *Hernandez v. Driscoll.*" The Cox of the firm's title is Owen D. Cox, who is listed as the defendants' cocounsel on the case. Cox, who also later became a judge in the Southern District, did not appear to take part in the suit, however. For biographical material, see "Cox" in *Judges of the United States.* Also on 22 December, the Texas attorney general's (AG) office moved to dismiss the case as it applied to J. W. Edgar, the state commissioner of education. The AG also moved (in the alternative) for a more definite statement, or for a summary judgment. John Ben Shepperd was still the AG; the motion for the state was filed by his assistant AG, Horace Wimberley. "Motion to Dismiss," NARA-SWA, RG 21, box 232, folder 2: "1384 *Hernandez v. Driscoll.*" Allred denied the motion on 21 February 1956, pending further hearings. Docket sheet, NARA-SWA, RG 21, box 232, folder 1: "1384 *Hernandez v. Driscoll.*"

168. *Race Rel. L. Rptr.* 329, 331.

169. "Preliminary Pre-trial Order," NARA-SWA, RG 21, box 232, folder 2: "1384 *Hernandez*

v. Driscoll." In the same order, Allred granted the defendant district's request to file a counter claim; see "Counter-Claim by Defendant," NARA-SWA, RG 21, box 232, folder 2: "1384 *Hernandez v. Driscoll.*"

170. Also, the plaintiffs had claimed the state commissioner as a defendant because Edgar "provid[ed] state funds . . . while being fully cognizant of the practices"; "Statement of Plaintiffs Claims," NARA-SWA, RG 21, box 232, folder 2: "1384 *Hernandez v. Driscoll.*" On 18 April, Wimberley argued that the commissioner of education had no discretion to withhold funds, whether he was cognizant of unlawful practices or not, because his certification of funding approved by the legislature was a purely ministerial and mandatory function (via art. 2922–20, Tex. Civ. Stat., art. 2663, Rev. Civ. Stat.); "Statement of Defendant J.W. Edgar in Reply to Plaintiffs' Claims," NARA-SWA, RG 21, box 232, folder 2: "1384 *Hernandez v. Driscoll.*" On 7 September, Allred granted Edgar's motion to be removed from the list of defendants. "Order Dismissing J.W. Edgar, State Commissioner of Education from the Cause," NARA-SWA, RG 21, box 232, folder 2: "1384 *Hernandez v. Driscoll.*" The list of defendants was again refined on 25 September, when the court substituted Kenneth Harlan for original named defendant Ed Pohlmeyer, who on 22 December 1955 notified Allred that he had resigned from board of trustees of Driscoll CISD on 11 October. Harlan had been appointed to serve out Pohlmeyer's unexpired term. "Answer of Defendant Ed. Pohlmeyer," NARA-SWA, RG 21, box 232, folder 2: "1384 *Hernandez v. Driscoll.*" Harlan filed his answer to the charges on 24 September, but merely adopted the previous defense. "Order of Dismissal as to Ed Pohlmeyer and Substituting Kenneth Harlan as Party Defendant," NARA-SWA, RG 21, box 232, folder 1: "1384 *Hernandez v. Driscoll.*"

171. "Reply to Plaintiffs' Claims by [Driscoll Consolidated ISD, et al.]," 4, NARA-SWA, RG 21, box 232, folder 2: "1384 *Hernandez v. Driscoll.*"

172. Ibid., 6.

173. DeAnda et al., "Plaintiffs' Pre-Trial Memorandum," 1, NARA-SWA, RG 21, box 232, folder 2: "1384 *Hernandez v. Driscoll*" (emphasis added; the reference is to *Mendez*).

174. Ibid., 1–2.

175. Hearing transcript of *Hernandez v. Driscoll,* 1:11–12, NARA-SWA, RG 21, box 233 (no folder).

176. Ibid., 1:4.

177. Ibid., 1:50–65.

178. Ibid., 2:228–30.

179. Ibid., 2:269–75.

180. Davis et al., "Brief for Defendants," 25–40, NARA-SWA, RG 21, box 233 (no folder). Curiously, when Davis refers to *Brown,* it is to disparage the opposing attorneys' imitation of the Supreme Court's reliance in that decision on "experts," who were cited in briefs but not entered as evidence where they could be properly cross-examined. Ibid., 25.

181. Davis et al., "Brief for Defendants," 14–15, NARA-SWA, RG 21, box 233 (no folder).

182. Hearing transcript of *Hernandez v. Driscoll,* 3:348–580, NARA-SWA, RG 21, box 233 (no folder).

183. Davis et al., "Brief for Defendants," 18–19, NARA-SWA, RG 21, box 233 (no folder).

184. Hearing transcript of *Hernandez v. Driscoll,* 1:118, NARA-SWA, RG 21, box 233 (no folder).

185. Davis et al., "Brief for Defendants," 36–37, NARA-SWA, RG 21, box 233 (no folder).

186. Allred, "Opinion," 6 n. 7, NARA-SWA, RG 21, box 232, folder 1: "1384 *Hernandez v. Driscoll.*"

187. Hearing transcript for *Hernandez v. Driscoll* (1 November 1957), 3:543, NARA-SWA, RG 21, box 233 (no folder).

188. Ibid., 544.

189. Ibid., 545–46.

190. Ibid.

191. Ibid., 548.

192. Docket log, NARA-SWA, RG 21, box 232, folder 1: "1384 *Hernandez v. Driscoll.*"

193. DeAnda et al., "Plaintiffs' Brief," p. 8, NARA-SWA, RG 21, box 233 (no folder).

194. Davis et al., "Brief for Defendants," 12–13, NARA-SWA, RG 21, box 233 (no folder). Davis, as evidenced by previous discussions, attempted to reargue rather than to summarize his case. He concluded that the "only question which the courts should decide" is whether the district acted in good faith (p. 6). Davis also contended that the plaintiffs did not represent a proper "class" with standing under Rules of Civil Procedure. Fed. R. Civ. P. Rule 23(a). Allred's reply was a curt: "This contention comes a bit late and is overruled." Allred, "Opinion," NARA-SWA, RG 21, box 232, folder 1: "1384 *Hernandez v. Driscoll.*"

195. DeAnda et al., "Plaintiffs' Brief," 8, NARA-SWA, RG 21, box 233 (no folder).

196. DeAnda et al., "Plaintiffs' Reply to Defendants' Brief," 6, NARA-SWA, RG 21, box 233 (no folder).

197. Allred, "Opinion," 12, esp. n. 13, NARA-SWA, RG 21, box 232, folder 1: "1384 *Hernandez v. Driscoll.*" See also 2 *Race Rel. L. Rptr.* 329, 332–33. The liberal Texas journalist and editor Ronnie Dugger had written to the judge to request a preview of his decision in the case. Allred replied to Dugger's letter but denied his entreaty. Dugger to Allred, 3 January 1957, and Allred to Dugger, 5 January 1957, NARA-SWA, RG 21, box 232, folder 3: "1384 *Hernandez v. Driscoll.*"

198. Allred, "Judgment," 2, NARA-SWA, RG 21, box 232, folder 1: "1384 *Hernandez v. Driscoll.*"

199. Martinez, "Legal Indeterminacy," 583–84. Among the stated goals of Martinez's article is his attempt "to demonstrate that courts' decisions either for or against Mexican-Americans were often not inevitable or compelled," and to expose the extent to which courts have exercised discretion and "helped or failed to help establish the rights of Mexican-Americans." Ibid., 559. Martinez analyzes (mostly published) decisions concerning Mexican American litigation of civil rights issues between 1930 and 1980. For the legal hurdles Mexican Americans faced before and after the *Brown* decisions, specifically, and how they could or could not aid the Mexican Americans' parallel struggle, see Martinez, "Legal Determinacy," 613. In particular, Martinez cites *United States v. Texas Education Agency*, 467 F.2d 848 (5th Cir., 1972), in which the Fifth Circuit Court of Appeals acknowledged that *Brown* did not permit linguistic difficulties or other "benign" justifications for segregating Mexican Americans.

200. Mexican Americans were bound by what critical legal and race scholar Richard Delgado has called the "Black-White Binary." Delgado, "Rodrigo's Fifteenth Chronicle," 1187.

201. Salinas, "Desegregation of Schools in the Southwest," 941; San Miguel, "Mexican American Organizations," *Social Science Quarterly* 63 (1982): 708–9.

202. For these events, see generally Ignacio M. Garcia, *Viva Kennedy;* and Quezada, *Border Boss.*

203. The vacant seat was originally created in 1949 as a temporary judgeship that would exist during the life of the incumbent and then expire, but the U.S. Congress made the position permanent in 1954. Zelden, *Justice Lies in the District,* 210–12; and Tidwell, "James V. Allred." Sheldon Goldman, *Picking Federal Judges,* 120–21.

204. Zelden, *Justice Lies in the District*, 210. Goldman, *Picking Federal Judges*, 133–34. Carp and Rowland, *Policymaking and Politics*, 58–59. This apparently was not the political dynamic that the Framers had hoped to produce. In the *Federalist* Alexander Hamilton described the ideal of the unequal division of appointment authority: "It will be the Office of the President to nominate, and, with the advice and consent of the Senate, to appoint. There will, of course, be no exertion of choice on the part of the Senate. They may defeat one choice of the Executive, and oblige him to make another; but they cannot themselves choose—they can only ratify or reject the choice he may have made." Hamilton, Madison, and Jay, *The Federalist*, essay no. 66.

205. Oral history interview with James DeAnda by Steven Wilson, 20 May 1998. Allsup, *The American GI Forum*, 133; and San Miguel, *Let All of Them Take Heed*, 164–65.

206. In 1953 and again in 1954, Garza was decorated by Pope Pius XII. See "Garza," in *Judges of the United States;* and Fisch, *All Rise*, 70–77 and generally.

207. This requires clarification. Garza was not actually first, but he was the first federal judge to be widely *recognized* as a Mexican American. In 1947 President Truman appointed Harold R. Medina, the son of a Mexican father and an Anglo mother, to the Southern District of New York. Medina was later promoted to the Second Circuit. Judge Medina dedicated a volume of his collected writings and speeches "to my father, Joaquin Adolfo Medina, born in the city of Merida, Yucatan, Mexico, on November 27, 1858." See Medina, *Anatomy of Freedom*, v. But Medina was not regarded as Hispanic by Anglo politicians and apparently was not raised as a Hispanic, and as a consequence, Medina's appointment is generally not regarded as being as politically significant as Garza's. The fact that an unrecognized or unremarked Hispanic sat on the federal bench underscores the fluidity of racial politics involving and ethnic identity claimed by Hispanics. Fisch, *All Rise*, 177 n. 1; also Goldman, *Picking Federal Judges*, 196, n. kk.

208. Pycior, *LBJ and Mexican Americans*, 116–24. The authors of two major histories of the Mexican American civil rights campaigns in Texas incorrectly identify the longstanding—albeit conservative—Democrat Garza as a Republican. This mistaken information might have become part the political lore of the state because Garza joined Governor Shivers in supporting Eisenhower against Stevenson. Allsup, *The American GI Forum*, 133; and San Miguel, *Let All of Them Take Heed*, 164–65. For a sympathetic view of Garza's career, but one that also notes the divisions his appointment created within the Mexican American community in Texas, see Fisch, *All Rise*, 70–77. As critical legal scholar Richard Delgado assessed Garza's career, "Garza began—and even ended—with good social instincts and a love of justice." But it was "difficult for him to think of himself or his group in effective legal terms—as a people with a history of conquest and brutal treatment in need of redress." According to Delgado, he ruled "against [his] people . . . and other minorities." Richard Delgado, "Book Review: Rodrigo's Fifteenth Chronicle," 1187. Delgado's article is a review of Fisch's biography of Garza.

209. Navarro, *The Cristal Experiment*, 17–51. For later political developments in the same city, in years after the Chicano movement emerged, see Navarro, *The Cristal Experiment*, generally; Trujillo, *Chicano Empowerment*, also generally; and Montejano, *Anglos and Mexicans*, 282–84.

210. Servín, "The Post–World War II Mexican-American," 144.

211. The Supreme Court first described de facto segregation in *Swann v. Charlotte-Mecklenburg Board of Education*, 402 U.S. 1 (1971), in which the justices upheld court-ordered busing. The court did not resolve the de jure–de facto distinction in *Swann*. As late as 1982, the justices upheld an amendment to California's state constitution that prohibited state

officials from employing busing to end de facto segregation. See *Crawford v. Board of Education of Los Angeles*, 452 U.S. 527 (1982).

212. *Cisneros v. Corpus Christi ISD*, Civ. No. 68-C-95 (S.D. Tex., 1970); and 467 F.2d 142 (5th Cir., 1972). See Gerald M. Birnberg, "*Brown v Board of Education*," 339. Also Delgado and Palacios, "Legally Cognizable Class," 393. This judicial recognition implied that Mexican Americans finally could commence what one scholar has labeled the "other struggle for equal schools." Donato, *The Other Struggle*, 12.

213. Sitkoff, *The Struggle for Black Equality*, generally. Also see Carson, *In Struggle;* and Blumberg, *Civil Rights*, rev. ed.

214. Wilkinson, *From Brown to Bakke*, 61–62, 111–12. Wilkinson was a legal academic who later became a federal district judge.

215. Pub. L. No. 88–352, §§ 201–7, 78 Stat. 241–46 (1964); codified as amended at: 42 U.S.C. § 2000(a)–(h). For proscriptions of discrimination in public education, 42 U.S.C. §§ 2000(c); for employment, 42 U.S.C. §§ 2000(e); and for housing, 42 U.S.C. §§ 3601–31. The CRA passed by majorities of 289 to 126 in the House and 73 to 27 in the Senate. Bipartisan support was solid. House Democrats voted 153 to 91 for the legislation and Republicans voted yes 136 to 35. The split in the Senate was 46 Democrats for versus 21 against. Senate Republicans voted in favor 27 to 6.

216. Graham, *The Civil Rights Era*, 262–67. Other significant initiatives against discrimination emerged from the executive and legislative branches. In 1962 President Kennedy issued Executive Order 11063, which prohibited racial, ethnic, and religious discrimination in federally subsidized housing. Congress enacted fair housing provisions in the CRA of 1968 (Pub. L. No. 90–284, 82 Stat. 73); codified as amended at: 42 U.S.C. §§ 3601–19. This "Fair Housing Act" prohibited the use of race, color, religion, or national origin in the sale or rental of most housing. Judges were also active in enforcing these provisions. To strengthen the act, Congress enacted legislation in 1988 to give the executive branch new authority to bring lawsuits when mediation efforts fail. By removing a one-thousand-dollar limit on punitive damage awards in housing bias cases, the new law permits government to seek large monetary damages for victims of housing discrimination. Fisher, "The Judge as Manager," 7.

217. *Singleton v. Jackson Municipal Separate School District*, 348 F.2d 729 (5th Cir., 1965).

218. *Singleton v. Jackson Municipal Separate School District*, 355 F.2d 865 (5th Cir., 1966). Meanwhile, the Supreme Court and political branches thrust federal district judges into the political thicket of voting rights. In 1962's *Baker v. Carr*, the justices charged the judges with the task of overseeing reapportionment of federal and state electoral districts until districts reflected substantially equal voter populations. *Baker v. Carr*, 369 U.S. 186 (1962). Two years later, in *Reynolds v. Sims*, the justices directed federal district judges to allow no further elections under apportionment schemes they found to be unconstitutional. *Reynolds v. Sims*, 377 U.S. 533 (1964), 585–87. Congress subsequently passed the Voting Rights Act (VRA) of 1965 (Pub. L. No. 89–110, 79 Stat. 437); codified as amended at 42 U.S.C. §§ 1971–73. The act was extended by the Voting Rights Act Amendment of 1970, Pub. L. No. 91–285, 84 Stat. 314; the Voting Rights Act Amendments of 1975, Pub. L. No. 94–73, 89 Stat. 400; and the Voting Rights Act Amendments of 1982, Pub. L. No. 97–205, 96 Stat. 131. The VRA did not apply in Texas until 1975. For that reason, voting rights and reapportionment, though important, are not a major factor in developments in the Southern District examined in this chapter. But see Davidson, "The Voting Rights Act," 34–35; and Scher, Mills, and Hotaling, *Voting Rights and Democracy*, 26–29.

219. Bass, "Faces Turned to the Future," *Houston Law Review* 34 (1998): 1498 (this was a contribution to "Dedication: The Judge John R. Brown Papers" in the same volume). For Bass's more complete discussion of the Fifth Circuit's role in enforcing *Brown,* see Bass, *Unlikely Heroes,* 299 and generally.

220. *United States v. Jefferson County Board of Education,* 372 F.2d 836 (5th Cir., 1966), 847.

221. Peltason, *Fifty-eight Lonely Men,* 244. Also Hoffer, *The Law's Conscience,* 180–211.

222. See *Baker v. Carr,* 369 U.S. 186 (1962), in which the court mandated the remapping of federal and state legislative districts to achieve substantial equality of voter population; and *Reynolds v. Sims,* 377 U.S. 533 (1964), which affirmed federal judicial orders for legislative reapportionment.

223. After gaining experience and frustration in the 1960s civil rights and protest movements, for example, advocates of women's rights initiated their own campaign of "public law litigation" in the 1970s. See Evans, *Personal Politics,* chap. 9; O'Connor, *Women's Organizations' Use of the Courts,* generally; Mezey, *In Pursuit of Equality,* generally; and Ginsburg, "Grappling with Sex Discrimination," 132.

CHAPTER 2. Legislation, Litigation, and Judicial Economy

1. Quoted in Farrand, *Records of the Federal Convention,* 120.

2. See generally Fisch, *All Rise.*

3. "Hannay," in *Judges of the United States.* Zelden, *Justice Lies in the District,* 153. Also "Texas News Briefs," UPI, 24 October 1983.

4. The federal district judge with the longest service on a court becomes the chief judge of the district. The U.S. Congress created the position in 1948, when around half of the districts sat only one judge. For the statute directing that the chief judge be the most senior active judge serving in the district, see 28 U.S.C. §§ 136–37. Unlike the chief judgeships of federal district and circuit courts, the chief justice of the U.S. Supreme Court is specifically appointed to that position.

5. Joe M. Ingraham attended National University from 1924 to 1927. In Fort Worth, Ingraham was at Zweifel and Tuohy, (1928–35). In Houston he was first at Baker, Botts, Andrews, and Wharton (1935–42) and after his wartime service returned for one year to the same firm, which was then Baker, Botts, Andrews, and Walne (1946–47). Judge Ingraham was sixty-six years old, and still the sole Republican on the Southern District bench, when President Richard Nixon elevated him to the Fifth Circuit court in 1969. "Ingraham," in *Judges of the United States;* and Zelden, *Justice Lies in the District,* 177–78.

6. Circuit Judge Ingraham took senior status when he became eligible to do so at age seventy, in 1973. Couch, *History of the Fifth Circuit,* 148, 161.

7. During the John Adams administration, for example, the lame-duck Federalist Congress passed, and the ascendant Republicans subsequently repealed, the Judiciary Act of 1801, which created so-called midnight judges. Passed by Act of 13 February 1801, 2 Stat. 89; repealed by Act of 8 March 1802, 2 Stat. 132. The Federalist William Marbury's judgeship (a magistracy) was at issue in *Marbury v. Madison.* Chief Justice John Marshall asserted the federal judiciary's power to review congressional legislation but used that power to declare that his jurisdiction in the Marbury case, which was authorized by the 1789 Judiciary Act, was actually proscribed by the Constitution. As a result, Marshall never directly addressed the validity of the 1801 legislation. *Marbury v. Madison,* 5 U.S. (1 Cranch) 137 (1803).

8. According to many commentators, the appointment process is and has always been a blend of patronage and ideology. Judgeships are powerful bargaining chips in political battles. Carp and Rowland, *Policymaking and Politics*, 53–62. See, generally, Goldman and Jahnige, *Federal Courts as a Political System;* and Cole, *Administration of Justice.*

9. Goldman, *Picking Federal Judges*, 112, 126–31, 152–53. For a sense of the Byzantine, and even Machiavellian, aspects of the federal judicial environment before, during, and after these administrations, see Chase, *Federal Judges.* For an earlier look, especially discussions of judicial appointments during the first half of the twentieth century, see Harris, *Advice and Consent of the Senate*, 315–24.

10. No one had expected Earl Warren to demonstrate a progressive character. After speaking with Warren, President Dwight D. Eisenhower concluded that he held a moderately conservative ideology. But soon Warren "was in the process of providing leadership for a libertarian-activist approach to public law and personal rights." Eisenhower later remarked that appointing the California governor to be chief justice of the Supreme Court was one of the worst mistakes he made as president. Riggs and Westerberg, "Judicial Independence," 353 (citations omitted).

11. In 1922, at the urging of William Howard Taft, former president and current chief justice, the Congress took the first steps to rationalize, centralize, and bureaucratize the administration of the federal courts. The Congress established the Judicial Conference of the United States (formerly the Conference of Senior Circuit Judges) to survey annually the "condition of business" in the federal courts. The conference was directed to suggest improvements in the administration of justice and to develop timely recommendations regarding when, where, and how much to increase the number of federal judgeships. Act of 14 September 1922 (Pub. L. No. 67–298, ch. 306, §2, 42 Stat. 838), currently codified at 28 U.S.C. §§ 331–34. The Judicial Conference is chaired by the chief justice of the U.S. Supreme Court and includes the chief judge and one district judge from each of the circuits. This innovation had a significant impact on the overall judiciary, because the Judicial Conference gives federal judges a formal mechanism to effect changes in administration. Congressmen frequently refer to conference reports during hearings and debates regarding the problems of the judiciary. Carp and Stidham, *The Federal Courts*, 64–65. Also Clark, "Adjudication to Administration," 111. For the legislative history of the Judicial Conference, see 28 U.S.C. § 331.

12. Conservative politicians, however, were not the only opponents of administrative reforms and expansion of the judiciary. The renaissance of judicial activism also disturbed a small but influential group of academic "legal liberals," who had been advocates of judicial restraint since the 1930s. Although they applauded the progressive conclusions of *Brown*, they were troubled that the Warren Court had failed to supply coherent constitutional arguments to justify the decision. The liberal academics proposed to eliminate Warren Court–style activism by constraining judicial discretion through a *new* kind of formalism, and conservative politicians sought the same ends simply by restricting judicial numbers. Kalman, *Strange Career of Legal Liberalism*, 27–28.

13. See generally Juan Ramon Garcia, *Operation Wetback;* and Meier and Ribera, *Mexican Americans/American Mexicans*, 189–90. Also Fitzgerald, *Face of the Nation*, 219–20. The term *wetback* appeared frequently in the press, government publications, and judicial opinions. For example, see the remarks of Fifth Circuit Judge John R. Brown, a Texan, in a labor case in 1961. Brown explains that "migrant Mexican workers [are] referred to traditionally as

'wetbacks.'" Brown is not promoting the term but does not condemn "tradition," either. *Johnson v. Kirkland,* 290 F.2d 440 (5th Cir., 1961), 441.

14. Stat. 415 (1958) (amending 28 U.S.C. §§ 1331–32).

15. Friendly, *Federal Jurisdiction,* 15–18.

16. The district total of 170 pending cases included the following: 63 contract actions; 38 land condemnations; 10 other real property actions; 14 personal injury tort actions; 17 personal property tort actions; 16 patent suits; 4 tax suits; and 8 miscellaneous civil actions. "Summary of Civil Cases Pending September 30, 1961, Filed Prior to January 1, 1959, by Nature of Suit," clerk's files of Chief Judge Ben C. Connally, folder 1.

17. This fact allowed Houston's mainline corporate law firms to undertake some admiralty practice, usually in the area of maritime insurance, rather than leaving this lucrative business to the admiralty "boutique" firms. Because much of the maritime traffic on the Gulf Coast involved the transport of oil and petroleum products, this was a natural development. Baker and Botts, one of the larger firms in Houston, followed this route into admiralty, since it was already involved in Texas's oil and gas industries. Lipartito and Pratt, *Baker & Botts,* 120–21. James Elkins, founder of Vinson and Elkins, another large Houston firm, long resisted creating a separate admiralty division or hiring admiralty lawyers. In part, this was because he considered it an arcane specialty, akin to patent or bankruptcy, and in part it was because admiralty seemed to be merely a variation of insurance law. Hyman, *Craftsmanship and Character,* 120, 338–39, 482–95. Although weighted with a special vocabulary, admiralty trials were actually relatively simple and nontechnical. They frequently employed depositions rather than live testimony, because actors and witnesses were often unavailable to appear because of the nature of their maritime professions. That the court was sitting in admiralty was often signaled by the fact that the judge was authorized to decide admiralty cases without a jury. In the unification of procedures, the courts created the availability of jury trials in some cases but not all. For example, amended Rule 38(e) provided that "These rules shall not be construed to create a right to trial by jury of the issues in an admiralty or maritime claim." Fed. R. Civ. P., Rule 38(e). On the absence of a jury, see Friedman, *A History of American Law,* 551–53. Thackston, "Seamen's Remedies," 354–59.

18. During President Woodrow Wilson's administration, for example, Congress authorized only one judgeship, because the Republican-controlled House was reluctant to create positions only to have them filled by a Democratic president. Chandler, "Some Major Advances," 320. American entry into World War I also interrupted the congressional authorization of new district judges, which usually occurred in pace with caseload. Frankfurter and Landis, *Business of the Supreme Court,* 230–31.

19. Frankfurter and Landis noted that, due in large part to Prohibition, the district courts were also swamped with "petty criminal" prosecutions. Ibid., 293.

20. Act of 14 September 1922 (Pub. L. No. 67–298, ch. 306, §2, 42 Stat. 837), currently codified at 28 U.S.C. § 331. See Erwin C. Surrency, "A History of the Federal Courts," *Missouri Law Review* 28 (Winter 1963): 239, esp. n. 130.

21. Goldman, *Picking Federal Judges,* 64.

22. This raised to four the total number of judgeships in the Southern District. Act of 3 August 1949 (63 Stat. 493), amending 28 U.S.C. § 133.

23. Goldman, *Picking Federal Judges,* 112.

24. Congress authorized three new circuit judgeships, twenty-one new permanent district judgeships, and six temporary district seats (which would expire with the death of the

occupant). Act of 10 February 1954, 68 Stat. 9, ch. 6 § 2(a)(3), amending 28 U.S.C. § 133. Congress did not expand the field further until 1961.

25. Zelden, *Justice Lies in the District,* 177.

26. This legislative history was related by Senate minority leader Everett Dirksen (R-Ill.). *Congressional Record* [hereafter CR], 3 March 1961, vol. 107, pt. 3, p. 3160.

27. Goldman, *Picking Federal Judges,* 140–41, 153.

28. Senator Dirksen attributed the "50–50" comments to Eisenhower via the Attorney General. The comments are printed as quotes in the *Congressional Record,* but they are probably paraphrased. *CR,* 3 March 1961, vol. 107, pt. 3, p. 3160.

29. The conference had revised the recommendation at the most recent meeting, 21–23 September 1960, and now suggested that fifty new judges were required to break the caseload logjam. See *CR,* 2 Mar 1961, vol. 107, pt. 3, pp. 3067–68. Rather than expand the number of judgeships, the Congress continually fiddled with administrative and jurisdictional boundaries, often at the suggestion of the Conference. Surrency, *History of the Federal Courts,* 81–93.

30. The legal and scholarly communities were deeply concerned at the congestion and delay in the courts. See, for example, *Lagging Justice,* a special issue of the *Annals* of the American Academy of Political and Social Science. The following essays are included in *Annals* 328 (1960): Green, "The Situation in 1959," 7–28; Johnsen, "Judicial Manpower Problems," 29–36; Kalven, "The Bar," 37–45; and Chandler, "Congestion and Delay," 144–52.

31. This had become a familiar process during the previous seven years, as legislators typically cited statistics proving a growing caseload crisis back home, noted that many cases took several years to come to trial, and proposed bills authorizing judgeships in their own states or districts. The Texas delegation of both houses took part in this early scramble for spoils. Rep. Rogers introduced H.R. 150 to add one district judge in the Northern District of Texas. *CR,* 3 Jan 1961, vol. 107, pt. 1, p. 38. Sen. Ralph Yarborough introduced S. 494 to add three judges, one each in the Southern, Northern, and Western Districts. Ibid., 879. Rep. Kilday introduced H.R. 3774 to add one judge to the Western District. Ibid., 1705.

32. *CR,* 3 March 1961, vol. 107, pt. 3, pp. 3156–61.

33. Ibid., 3217–18.

34. *CR,* 4 May 1961, vol. 107, pt. 6. Senate report at p. 7324; House report at pp. 7371–74.

35. The House accepted the report after a short debate. Ibid., 7374–78.

36. *CR,* 20 June 1961, vol. 107, pt. 10, pp. 10784–87. The American Bar Association exercised some influence in the appointing process throughout this period, by rating the qualifications of judicial nominees. However, by far the greatest influencing factor, perhaps even more important than the will of the president himself, was the opinion of the senators from the state with the vacant judgeship. Many senators regarded the nominating process in reverse to that set out in the Constitution and thought it was their right to appoint lower federal judges with the "advice and consent" of the president. Corsi, *Judicial Politics,* 117–32.

37. *CR,* 19 May 1961, vol. 107, pt. 7, p. 8492. The 1961 Omnibus Judgeship Act became Pub. L. No. 87–36.

38. Peltason, *Fifty-eight Lonely Men,* 7. Eisenhower reportedly took his judicial appointments very seriously, while Kennedy was criticized for not realizing how important the selection process could be, especially for the progress of civil rights in the South. Bass, *Unlikely Heroes,* 154. Eisenhower's judicial appointments generally stood up better than Kennedy's picks to scholarly scrutiny. This may be a factor of swamping: Eisenhower appointed Earl Warren to be chief justice of the U.S. Supreme Court, while Kennedy clearly appeased the segregationist senators in the South when appointing the judges for that region. Carp and

Rowland, *Policymaking and Politics,* 54. For another interesting look at the statistical background of presidential appointees, from the Johnson through the Reagan administrations, see Carp and Stidham, *The Federal Courts,* 87–100. Carp and Stidham's general evaluation of Eisenhower's habit of making "apolitical" appointments is compatible with the preceding discussion. They also discuss the political tone of several other presidential administrations as reflected in lower court appointments (100–118). Eisenhower achieved balance in the district courts, however, just by appointing a large number of Republicans to the bench to counter the lopsided Democratic tally with which he started. Every president from Eisenhower through Carter, with the exception of Gerald Ford, appointed judges from their own party at a rate above 90 percent. Ford's rate was around 80 percent Republican. See Corsi, *Judicial Politics,* 132–42, esp. the statistical tables on 134–35.

39. Texas politics were more complicated after the Republican John Tower won a special election for Johnson's Senate seat. Yet Tower's election left intact the rough parity that had developed between the Democratic factions. Tower held the seat until the 1980s. Zelden, *Justice Lies in the District,* 210. Davidson, *Race and Class,* 29–32, 166.

40. "Noel," in *Judges of the United States.* Noel was in Washington, D.C., on state business when the Japanese attacked Pearl Harbor on 7 December 1941. Rayburn arranged for Noel and his boss, Texas Attorney General Gerald Mann, to be seated in the House chamber to hear President Roosevelt's address requesting that Congress declare war. Noel found a Washington recruiting office and joined the U.S. Navy. "Ex-U.S. District Judge Noel, Who Ruled in School Cases, Dies at 87," *Houston Chronicle,* 30 August 1997, p. A40.

41. To ensure the smooth functioning of government when Congress is out of session, the Constitution gives the president authority to appoint judges with neither the advice nor the consent of the Senate. Art. II, § 2, cl. 3 states: "The President shall have power to fill up all Vacancies that may happen during the Recess of the Senate, by granting Commissions which shall expire at the End of their next Session." Congress has attempted to restrict the use of the recess authority by limiting salary payments to recess appointees. 5 U.S.C. 5503 (1966). Thomas A. Curtis, "Note, Recess Appointments to Article III Courts: The Use of Historical Practice in Constitutional Interpretation," 84 *Colum. L. Rev.* 1758 (1984).

42. CR, 16 March 1962, vol. 108, pt. 4, pp. 4342–44. Kennedy also appointed state judge Sarah T. Hughes, only the second woman ever appointed and confirmed to be a U.S. district judge, to one of the two new judgeships in the Northern District.

43. Ibid., pp. 4343–44. Sen. Stennis of Mississippi, in commentary printed in the *Congressional Record,* also endorsed the new judge. Stennis declared that he "had the pleasure of serving a few years ago on a commission with Judge Noel. I was very much impressed with him." This must refer to the Commission on Government Security. Stennis noted that Noel was the nephew of a former governor of Mississippi and that "it is another illustration of the soundness and high qualities of Texas because of the contributions made thereto by the State of Mississippi." See CR, 16 March 1962, vol. 108, pt. 4, pp. 4342–44.

44. Lawrence Friedman observed, primarily with regard to the nineteenth century, that admiralty cases were "staples of the docket of all federal courts." Friedman, *A History of American Law,* 260.

45. *Annual Report of the Director of the Administrative Office of the U.S. Courts.* In 1960 the district was authorized four judges, but only three were sitting. Whether total admiralty cases (361) are divided by authorized (four) or by sitting judges (three), the Southern District of Texas ranked third in cases per judge (90 or 120 per judge). The busiest district was the Southern District of New York (encompassing Manhattan and the Port Authority of New

York), with sixteen authorized judges and 2,294 admiralty cases, followed by the Eastern District of Louisiana (New Orleans), with two judges and 434 cases. The Eastern District of Pennsylvania (Philadelphia) ranked third, with 485 cases heard by eight judges. The fifth busiest admiralty jurisdiction was the Northern District of California (San Francisco), with seven judges and 261 cases filed. For authorized judgeships, see 28 U.S.C. § 133. For admiralty filings, see *1960 Annual Report*, Dir. Admin. Office, U.S. Courts, Table c-3a, "Civil Cases Pending in the United States District Courts," pp. 240–47; cited in Fiddler, "The Admiralty Practice in Montana," 17.

46. Maritime torts were distinguished simply as those torts committed on navigable waters. This traditional definition was amended by the U.S. Congress to include cases where a waterborne vessel causes damage or injury on dry land. A ship may run aground to cause property damage, for example, and recovery for the tort is still available in admiralty. Admiralty Extension Act (62 Stat. 496 [1948], 46 U.S.C. § 740). Even in the nineteenth century, many of the peculiarities of admiralty were often "more a difference in style than in substance." Friedman noted "strong parallels between admiralty and tort law, despite their traditional differences." Friedman, *A History of American Law*, 553.

47. These are essentially industrial accident cases, and the nautical elements do not logically set admiralty in "a world all its own" or mark it as an esoteric subject. Instead, seaman's personal injury suits fit neatly within the generic categorization of a leading text on the federal courts, which consigned admiralty disputes to the mundane-sounding realm of "private civil litigation"; Schill, "Moragne-Gaudet," 917; Wright, *The Law of Federal Courts*, 97; Bator et al., *Federal Courts and the Federal System*, 3d ed., 32. This assessment of admiralty as almost wholly civil and private seems to be a twentieth-century bias. According to one recent scholar, the "Founding Generation's paradigm of federal admiralty jurisdiction is best described as public—not private—litigation," because of its criminal law elements. Castro, "Federal Admiralty Jurisdiction," 118.

48. Maritime remedies differed according to the nature of the work being performed when the injury occurred. Custom guided practice; however, statutory relief was also well-established. Thackston, "Seamen's Remedies," 319–20. Although the U.S. Supreme Court had rulemaking power in admiralty since 1792, the court did not promulgate admiralty rules until 1844. These were superseded by the Admiralty Rules of 1920, which, as amended, remained in effect until 1966. Admiralty and civil procedures were unified on 1 July 1966. Thereafter, admiralty cases were brought within the Federal Rules for Civil Procedure, and treated as civil actions, with certain minor variations for admiralty and maritime claims identified by the designation under Rule 9(h). The variations relate to third-party practice (Rule 14[c]), deposition procedure (Rule 26[a]), jury trial (Rule 38[e]), and venue (Rule 82). If a claim is filed with a Rule 9(h) declaration and based on the federal court's jurisdiction specified in 28 U.S.C. § 1333, then Rule 14 permits a defendant to "pass on" to a third party (such as an insurance company) all or part of the liability to the plaintiff, but the plaintiff may not recover judgment directly against the third party unless the defendant amends the complaint to assert a claim against the third party. There are also six "Supplemental Rules for Certain Admiralty and Maritime Claims." The Supplemental Rules, for example, apply to in rem and quasi in rem actions. Wright, *The Law of Federal Courts*, 408. Until the 1966 unification courts usually docketed their admiralty cases separately, but the Administrative Office published its last separate statistics for admiralty cases in 1960, perhaps in anticipation of unification. Fiddler, "The Admiralty Practice in Montana," 16.

49. Gilmore and Black, *The Law of Admiralty*, 248.

50. *The Sea Gull*, 21 Fed. Cas. 909 (C.C.D. Md., 1865), 910. Comment, "Admiralty," 1516.

51. Thackston, "Seamen's Remedies," 319–21, esp. nn. 1, 3. Beer, "Keeping Up," 398–99. Beer, a federal district judge in the Eastern District of Louisiana, is a harsh critic of the juridical expansion of the terms *seaman* and *vessel* to encompass anyone or anything coming into contact with water. Ibid., 379.

52. Bue, "Admiralty Law in the Fifth Circuit," 350. This is one of several influential law review articles by Bue. In it he is primarily concerned with personal injury cases. Bue specialized in admiralty as a partner of the Houston firm Royston, Rayzor, and Cook. Attorneys who practice admiralty law have long considered the U.S. Court of Appeals for the Fifth Circuit to be the nation's premier forum for their specialty. Until 1981 the Fifth Circuit included the entire American Gulf Coast, from Brownsville, Texas, to Key West, Florida. Brown, "Another Maritime Anomaly," 1318 [the referenced case is *Penrod Drilling Corp. v. Williams*, 868 S.W.2d 294 (Tex., 1993)]. In 1981 Congress split the Fifth Circuit to create the Eleventh. Even after this division, the Fifth Circuit still encompasses several of the busiest ports in the United States, including New Orleans, the circuit's headquarters. Barrow and Walker, *A Court Divided*, 1–2; also Couch, *History of the Fifth Circuit*. The reconstituted Fifth Circuit contains Texas, Louisiana, Mississippi, and the Panama Canal Zone. The Eleventh Circuit consists of Florida, Georgia, and Alabama. Fifth Circuit Court of Appeals Reorganization Act of 1980. Pub. L. No. 96–452 (amending 28 U.S.C. § 41).

53. Quoting Gilmore and Black, *The Law of Admiralty*, 248. As an admiralty lawyer, and later as a federal district judge who presided over many admiralty cases, Bue belonged to the generation preoccupied with "filling in the details." In 1970 President Nixon appointed Bue to the bench of the Southern District. Zelden, *Justice Lies in the District*, 215.

54. Admiralty was "left behind" in 1938, when judicial reformers attained a long-sought goal and unified the separate law and equity procedures under the new Federal Rules of Civil Procedure. The proponents of complete unification persisted in their efforts. See Currie, "Civil and Admiralty Rules," 1. See the proposed amendments at 34 F.R.D. 325 (1964), and the Supreme Court's official notice of the new rules at 86 S.Ct. 1 (1966). Prior to procedural unification in 1966, American admiralty practice retained much of the traditional terminology and procedures from British practice, as supplemented by the Admiralty Rules occasionally promulgated by the Supreme Court. For example, an admiralty complaint was a "libel"; a plaintiff was a "libellant"; a defendant was a "respondent." Members of the admiralty bar (one of the oldest specialized bars) were traditionally called "proctors." On the unification in the Federal Rules of Civil Procedure, see Surrency, *History of the Federal Courts*, 150–51.

55. Bue, "Admiralty Law in the Fifth Circuit," 350.

56. Ibid., 360–62.

57. In the same opinion Story noted that seamen acquired "habits of gross indulgence, carelessness, and improvidence," and therefore required a guardian. *Harden v. Gordon*, 11 Fed. Cas. 480 (C.C.D. Me., 1823), 483. Justice Story expressed similar sentiments in other opinions; see *Reed v. Canfield*, 20 Fed. Cas. 426 (C.C.D. Mass., 1832). It is apparent that the perceived necessity for a ward-guardian relationship is based on a stereotype (which is not to dispute its historical validity) of the sailor and his life aboard ship. Throughout the nineteenth century it was believed that mariners were drunk, depressed, and violent, perhaps because they were away from home and family for years at a time, and also lacked the education and the sense to save money for their return. Jarvis, "Rethinking the Meaning," 468 n. 16.

58. This included a "maintenance" stipend, physician's bills until "maximum cure" is

reached, and wages payable through the terms of the sailing contract. By the 1960s this could be as much as twenty dollars a day, but it was still eight dollars in some courts. Jarvis, "Rethinking the Meaning," 469 n. 20.

59. Because of these special considerations, admiralty law provided remedies for injuries sustained at sea that seemed infinitely kinder to the sailor than the contemporary land-based tort law was to the brakeman, miner, and machinist. The law of industrial accidents lagged far behind the guardian-ward relationship established in admiralty law. Tort actions expanded tremendously during the nineteenth century, as larger, faster, and more dangerous machines were developed. Unlike sailors subject to maritime practice, the industrial employees of America found little economic, medical, or moral support from employers or judges until the turn of the twentieth century. The most famous example of the high hurdles faced by workers during this period, the "fellow servant" doctrine as propounded by the U.S. Supreme Court, usually prevented an injured worker from gaining support or recovering damages from his employer whenever an accident had been caused by another employee. Eventually, a few states enacted workmen's compensation laws to rectify the perceived social injustices of the tort system of the era. Friedman, *A History of American Law*, 484–85. Also see White, *Tort Law in America*.

60. Schill, "Available Forums and Recoverable Damages," 1 n. 2.

61. Occupations connected to the still expanding railroad system were among the most dangerous in the nation. FELA abrogated both that rule and the doctrine of "assumption of risk," and replaced the common law principle that held contributory negligence a complete defense in tort cases with a new rule of comparative negligence. The statute provided that "[e]very common carrier by railroad . . . shall be liable in damages to any person suffering injury while he is employed by such carrier . . . for such injury . . . resulting in whole or in part from the negligence of any of the officers, agents, or employees of such carrier, or by reason of any defect or insufficiency, due to its negligence, in its cars, engines, appliances, machinery, track, roadbed, works, boats, wharves, or other equipment." 35 Stat. 65, ch. 149 (now codified as 45 U.S.C. §§ 51–60). See Surrency, *History of the Federal Courts*, 149–51; Jarvis, "Rethinking the Meaning," 472–74; and Sims, "The American Law," 987–89. The 1908 law was actually the second attempt to pass a federal liability act. After an adverse Supreme Court decision, Congress narrowed the scope of the act to compensation for injuries suffered while a rail worker was engaged in interstate commerce. The first FELA, passed 11 June 1906, as 34 Stat. 232, did not distinguish between intrastate and interstate commerce. The decision overturning the law came in *First Federal Employers' Liability Cases*, 207 U.S. 463 (1908). The second liability act referred to "liability of common carriers by railroad, in interstate or foreign commerce, for injuries to employees from negligence . . ." and stated that "[e]very common carrier . . . shall be liable in damages to any person suffering injury while he is employed by such carrier . . . for such injury . . . resulting in whole or in part from the negligence of any of the officers, agents, or employees of such carrier." The court subsequently sustained the second FELA. Passed 22 April 1908, it is now 45 U.S.C. § 51. This version of FELA was sustained in *Second Federal Employers' Liability Cases*, 223 U.S. 1 (1912).

62. Stat. 1164. One of the reasons for the revival in congressional interest in maritime matters was the tragic sinking of the RMS *Titanic* in 1912, which left many widows of lost British crewmen uncompensated. Beer, "Keeping Up," 384–85.

63. *Chelentis v. Luckenbach S.S. Co.*, 243 Fed. 536 (2d Cir., 1917), affirmed: 247 U.S. 372 (1918). Some scholars have interpreted this ruling as part of the apparent "crusade" the U.S.

Supreme Court had embarked on against *state* maritime legislation. The court also seems to have intended the decision to goad the Congress to write a better piece of legislation. See Jarvis, "Rethinking the Meaning," 469–71.

64. Merchant Marine Act, 41 Stat. 1007, § 33, now codified at 46 U.S.C. § 688. The most useful and most controversial innovations of the act regard trial by jury and the absorption of a wrongful death action into admiralty. This was by way of a piece of companion legislation, the Death on the High Seas Act (DOHSA) (41 Stat. 537, currently 46 U.S.C. §§ 761–68). The Judiciary Act of 1789 also provided admiralty remedies in maritime matters, except "saving to suitors, in all cases, the right of a common law remedy where the common law is competent to give it." Ch. 20, § 9, 1 Stat. 73–77; codified at 28 U.S.C. § 1333(1). This "savings to suitors" clause contains an important distinction, because although admiralty jurisdiction was "exclusive" to the federal courts, Congress at least potentially undermined much of the court's authority with this language. The plaintiff could bring an in personam maritime action on the "law," rather than "admiralty," side of the federal courts, or even in state court. Federal courts have retained exclusive jurisdiction over in rem claims, that is, suits against the ship by maritime lien, and various other claims not covered by the "savings" clause. If some other basis for federal jurisdiction exists in addition to the maritime nature of the suit, such as diversity or a federal statute, a person could bring the suit in the federal courts without an admiralty designation. A maritime suitor who met the criteria of the savings clause could therefore "forum shop" based on an estimation of the chances of winning before a jury or a judge. The "saved" right to bring maritime cases in state court has become increasingly important in recent years. Watson, "Modern Practice Considerations," 474–77. Also see Friendly, *Federal Jurisdiction*, 129–31. At the time of his publication, Friendly was chief judge of the U.S. Court of Appeals for the Second Circuit. He was critical of the continued separation of railway workers' compensation law from remedies available to all other interstate transportation workers, such as bus drivers, truckers, and airline crew, because he believed compensation laws of the states were mature enough to be satisfactory in all cases. This now-artificial distinction, he said, creates a disparity of benefits and invites maneuvering to take advantage of the most favorable law and venue available. Procedural delays and costs grow because of this forum shopping.

65. *Vickers v. Tumey*, 290 F.2d 426 (5th Cir., 1961), 429–30.

66. Recovery by a seaman for illness and injury is currently governed both by the Jones Act and by the general maritime law. Moreover, the Supreme Court has consistently held that the state and federal courts have concurrent jurisdiction under the Jones Act. Watson, "Modern Practice Considerations," 474–77. Healy, "Remedies for Maritime Personal Injury," 313, 359–60. The general maritime law did not provide remedies for wrongful death, because an action for injury dies with the person, as it does in the common law. Unseaworthiness was therefore a maritime cause for personal injury compensation but not for wrongful death indemnity. Bue, "Admiralty Law in the Fifth Circuit," 375.

67. In 1922, through an amendment of the Federal Judicial Code, Congress had extended to harbor workers legal coverage that reserved "to claimants the rights and remedies under workmen's compensation laws of any state." The Supreme Court subsequently held that because working the docks was a maritime trade and hence a matter for admiralty law, it was unconstitutional to extend coverage of the act to a longshoreman. However, in its decision the court hinted that the Congress could enact its own specific compensation rather than piggybacking on the state laws. Congress responded by enacting the LHWCA. 44 Stat. 1424; currently, 33 U.S.C. §§ 901–50. In 1940 the Supreme Court declared the 1938 rules of civil

procedure applied to suits brought under the LHWCA. 308 U.S. 642 (1940). Surrency, *History of the Federal Courts*, 192.

68. Sims, "The American Law," 1001.

69. Ibid., 973.

70. *Mike Hooks, Inc. v. Pena*, 313 F.2d 696 (1963), 697. Nevertheless, Judge Brown continued to profess the belief that whenever admiralty judges "declare the governing principles of admiralty and maritime law, they are doing more than carrying out their Constitutional duty. The admiralty law that they declare carries the authority of the . . . Constitution itself." Brown, "Admiralty Judges," 250–51 [Brown gave this address at the Inaugural Nicholas J. Healy Lecture on Admiralty Law, held at New York University School of Law, 5 November 1992]. The constitutional provision for admiralty jurisdiction in art. III is the only grant to the federal judiciary that specifically identifies an area of substantive law. Congress expected the federal courts to conform to the principles and procedures of admiralty law as it had developed over many centuries in England. But in addition, federal district judges necessarily assumed the historical leadership role in adapting English practices, or even older principles inherent in the international maritime law, to the conditions in the United States. Congress has a major role in developing admiralty law as well. Although the Constitution does not contain a specific extension of admiralty power to the legislative branch, Congress logically enjoys this authority through its constitutionally granted power to regulate interstate and foreign commerce. U.S. Const., art. I, § 8. Therefore, the judiciary and Congress exercise a form of concurrent jurisdiction over the law of admiralty: the "general maritime law" is defined by the courts, unless superseded or controlled by statute. New applications, especially in response to changes in the state of the art in nautical technology, ordinarily are left to the discretion of judges, but Congress controls their jurisdiction. For example, in 1875, rather than increase the size and cost of the judiciary to match demand, Congress narrowed jurisdiction, by eliminating some types of cases that could be brought in admiralty. Congress also raised the monetary limit on federal controversies from two thousand to five thousand dollars and restricted jurisdiction over some patent and bankruptcy cases, both also highly technical areas of the law. Act of 16 February 1875; 18 Stat. 315. For all of these reasons, the First Judiciary Act's distinction between admiralty and maritime law is significant. As a practical matter, the Congress and the courts do not always serve the same interests, and the struggle to reconcile the competing interests involved in maritime commerce may produce "both brilliant and erroneous decisions, depending to some degree on the viewpoint of the beholder." Healy, "Remedies for Maritime Personal Injury," 313.

71. *Morales v. City of Galveston*, 181 F.Supp. 202 (S.D. Tex., 1959); also 364 U.S. 295 (1962).

72. *Tipton v. Socony Mobil Oil Co., Inc.*, 315 F.2d 660 (5th Cir., 1963); also 375 U.S. 34 (1963).

73. *Haire v. Isthmian Lines, Inc.*, 231 F.Supp. 606 (S.D. Tex., 1963).

74. The absence of a jury was an admiralty practice retained for most instances when the admiralty and civil procedures were unified. When admiralty merged with civil procedure, substantive maritime law survived, but its special procedures and language were reduced to a handful of distinctive admiralty remedies (such as in rem actions, foreign attachments, and limitations of action), which were invoked if the plaintiff filed the claim as admiralty or maritime in nature, under Fed. R. Civ. P., Rule 9(h). Admiralty libels could be taken in personam (against a person, whether natural or corporate) or in rem (against goods and property, such as a named ship or a quantity of, say, cotton or tobacco). The suit in rem is rare outside the admiralty court, and when it does appear, it is clearly guided by admiralty

practice. For example, the Federal Food, Drug, and Cosmetic Act of 1938 (52 Stat. 1044, § 304) provides that forfeiture cases "shall conform, as nearly as may be, to the procedure in admiralty." This resulted in curiously named cases such as (the hypothetical) *United States v. 300 Bottles of Aspirin.* See Gilmore and Black, *Law of Admiralty,* 30–31; and Jarvis, "Rethinking the Meaning," 479 n. 58. For the procedure by which a libellant in rem resorts to the fiction that a vessel is a person and the admiralty court "arrests" the vessel to gain jurisdiction, see Thackston, "Seamen's Remedies," 321–23.

75. Although the hierarchy of maritime workers was a central fact of traditional admiralty jurisprudence, these distinctions were fluid in an era of equitable jurisprudence. Some maritime workers, including longshoremen and machinists on offshore oil-drilling platforms anchored in the Gulf of Mexico, also suffered job-related injuries and sought benefits in court. Schill, "The Unsolvable Puzzle," 635–39.

76. *Morales v. City of Galveston,* 181 F.Supp. 202 (1959), at 204.

77. The U.S. Supreme Court confirmed these principles in *Mitchell v. Trawler Racer, Inc.,* 362 U.S. 539 (1960).

78. *Morales v. City of Galveston,* 181 F.Supp. 202, at 205–7.

79. Ibid., 208.

80. *Morales v. City of Galveston,* 275 F.2d 191 (1961). On certiorari, 364 U.S. 295 (1962), the U.S. Supreme Court vacated the judgment and remanded the case to the court of appeals for consideration in the light of *Mitchell v. Trawler Racer,* which the justices had decided in the interim. The Fifth Circuit court found that *Mitchell* was inapplicable to the case and again affirmed District Judge Connally's judgment. *Morales v. City of Galveston,* 291 F.2d 97 (1962). Circuit Judge Rives, in dissent, thought that the ship and its equipment were not "reasonably fit for their intended use," since as much as 10 percent of the grain loaded from the elevator was fumigated, and because the owners had knowledge of similar past accidents. Ibid., 99.

81. *Morales v. City of Galveston,* 368 U.S. 816 (1962).

82. *Morales v. City of Galveston,* 370 U.S. 165 (1962), 171. Douglas wrote for himself and Justices Clark, Harlan, Brennan, and White; Justice Frankfurter did not participate in the case. Arthur J. Mandell of Houston's Mandell and Wright had argued the cause and filed the brief for the longshoremen. Preston Shirley of Galveston argued the cause and filed briefs for the city of Galveston. Edward W. Watson, also from Galveston, argued the cause for the Cardigan Shipping Co., Ltd.; Clarence S. Eastham authored the briefs with Watson.

83. *Morales v. City of Galveston,* 370 U.S. 165 (1962), 172. Chief Justice Warren and Justice Black concurred in this dissent.

84. Justice Stewart did discuss the issue in the court's majority opinion, and he noted that this was the correct conclusion. *Morales v. City of Galveston,* 370 U.S. 165 (1962), 168. Stewart cited *Seas Shipping Co. v. Sieracki,* 328 U.S. 85.

85. OCSLA; 43 U.S.C. § 1333. The complexity of this situation further increased in 1953, when proliferating oil-drilling rigs in the Gulf of Mexico and elsewhere inspired Congress to extend personal injury and wrongful death remedies to offshore oilworkers in the OCSLA. See Sims, "The American Law," 1001. For the offshore industry, see Pratt, Priest, and Castaneda, *Offshore Pioneers.*

86. U.S.C. § 1333(c)(1).

87. *Tipton v. Socony Mobil Oil Co.,* 315 F.2d 660 (1963), 661–62, esp. n. 3.

88. Ibid., 662.

89. Ibid., 663, esp. n. 1.

90. *Tipton v. Socony Mobil Oil Co., Inc.*, 375 U.S. 34 (1963), 35. Houston's Clyde W. Woody appeared for Tipton. George B. Matthews represented the oil company.

91. Ibid., 37. Justice Harlan dissented, stating that "the admission of this evidence in the circumstances of this case did not prejudice the petitioner and was, therefore, harmless error." Moreover, he did not believe the case was, as he wrote, "certworthy." Ibid., 38.

92. *Haire v. Isthmian Lines, Inc.*, 231 F.Supp. 606 (S.D. Tex., 1963); Galveston Division; Civ. A. No. 2841, 18 January 1963.

93. The "Articles of Agreement" is the seaman's formal employment contract, generally a standard form with blanks for specific dates and destinations. In the past, breaking articles (for example, by deserting the ship) was a serious crime. Under the various congressional merchant marine acts, a seaman must sign and register his articles before the U.S. shipping commissioner before each voyage. Healey, *Foc's'le and Glory-Hole*, 13–15, 150–52. For an example: Ibid., 193–98.

94. F.Supp., at 607.

95. In this context, a colloquialism for a refrigerated ("reefer") storage compartment.

96. The U.S. PHS provides hospital care and outpatient service for sick and disabled seamen. The service is administered by the surgeon general and is an agency akin to the VA (Veterans Administration). Healey, *Foc's'le and Glory-Hole*, 114, 120.

97. There was no medical evidence that Haire would suffer any permanent disability from the accident. 231 F.Supp., at 607. But Haire was evidently an extremely unlucky person: during this same period, he reentered the hospital with a broken leg (apparently unrelated to his other injury).

98. F.Supp., 607. The *Steel Seafarer* ended its voyage on 4 January 1962; ibid., 608.

99. Ibid., 608.

100. Again, by the 1960s this election was somewhat unimportant. The case was tried without a jury, at the close of the evidence and after the arguments of counsel Newton B. Schwartz of Houston's Schwartz and Lapin, for Haire; and Edward W. Watson of Galveston's Eastham, Watson, Dale, and Forney, for Isthmian Lines. Ibid., 607.

101. F.Supp., at 607.

102. Under 46 U.S.C. § 594, if Haire had been discharged *before* embarking, he would be due just a month's pay. The statute protects seamen against wrongful discharge, but not injury once articles are signed and the ship underway. The judge therefore found that the statute did not apply to Haire's claim. 231 F.Supp., at 608. Moreover, Judge Noel found "good cause" for setting aside the release Haire had signed.

103. F.Supp., at 608. The decision was subsequently affirmed. *Haire v. Isthmian Lines, Inc.*, 334 F.2d. 521 (5th Cir., 1963).

104. *Pyles v. American Trading and Production Corp.*, 244 F.Supp. 685 (S.D. Tex., 1965); Galveston Div. [Civ. A. 64-G-66, 10 August 1966].

105. He added to this claim for maintenance and cure, as well as attorney's fees, in an amended petition filed 10 May 1965. The company had only paid maintenance to Pyles for the twelve days from 5 August to 17 August. Ibid., 686.

106. Ibid., 686.

107. The case was tried before the court, and lawyers (Sidney Ravkind of Mandell and Wright of Houston, for plaintiff; Edward W. Watson of Eastham, Watson, Dale, and Forney, of Houston, for defendant) submitted briefs. Ibid., 686.

108. Ibid., 686.

109. *Vaughan v. Atkinson*, 369 U.S. 527 (1962), 531.

110. 244 F.Supp., 687. However, Pyles was not entitled to maintenance for periods he actually spent in hospitals. Judge Noel noted that the court had held that maintenance could be claimed only for the period of convalescence until the maximum cure was obtained. *Farrell v. the United States,* 336 U.S. 511 (1949), 516.

111. F.Supp., 687.

112. Ibid., 687.

113. *Moore v. O/S Fram,* 226 F.Supp. 816 (S.D. Tex., 1963).

114. U.S.C. § 761. Many states had their own wrongful death statutes, but the federal DOHSA superseded them. Thackston, "Seamen's Remedies," 365–73. Also Jarvis, "Rethinking the Meaning," 487 n. 92. Unfortunately, the DOHSA did not define "spouse" or "representative." The acceptance, regulation, and privileges of common law marriage vary by state, further clouding the issue of who is eligible to bring suit under the Jones Act. Ibid., 490–94, esp. nn. 104, 122. Jarvis raises the question of "domestic partnership" between homosexual sailors as a wrinkle to be ironed out by the courts. Ibid., 499 n. 132.

115. F.Supp., 817.

116. The Jones Act ensures that an employer can be held liable if his or her negligence plays the slightest part in bringing about an injury or death aboard the vessel. The Jones Act allows wrongful death suits for negligence but not unseaworthiness. Bue, "Admiralty Law in the Fifth Circuit," 375. As a matter of law, a seaman cannot be contributorily negligent for following orders that result in his own injury even if he recognizes the possible danger of doing so. However, the "essence" of a Jones Act suit is negligence. Strictly speaking, a seaman bringing a Jones Act negligence suit, like his common law counterpart, bears the burden of proving the essential elements of a negligence action: the existence of a duty, the negligent breach of that duty by the defendant, and some causal relationship between the breach and injury. Thackston, "Seamen's Remedies," 352–53, 349, esp. n. 140.

117. F.Supp., 818.

118. There were limits to this indulgence. Drunkenness was one thing, but recovery after illicit sexual activity (or injuries sustained escaping from a brothel window) is quite another. See *Farrell v. the United States,* 336 U.S. 511 (1949), 516. See more examples in Thackston, "Seamen's Remedies," 363–64.

119. For a discussion of the legal meanings of "proximate cause" and "negligence," see Thackston, "Seamen's Remedies," 349–53.

120. Garza also examined and approved the Moore's deal with their "proctor," Benjamin S. Hardy of Sharpe and Hardy of Brownsville. Hardy was to receive one-third of the award to each member of the family. Wilhelm Foods was represented by Tom Clendenin Jr., of Cox and Wilson, also of Brownsville. 226 F.Supp., 818.

121. *Farmer v. O/S Fluffy D,* 220 F.Supp. 917 (S.D. Tex., 1963). Not only did Garza preside again, but the same attorneys also repeated their roles.

122. When catches are good, a shrimp boat may stay out of port as long as a month. But because shrimp will not keep longer than a few weeks, captains may send their catch back with a returning boat. 220 F.Supp., 918–19.

123. F.Supp., 919–20.

124. Farmer's body was sent to Brownsville and later buried in Georgia. After receiving medical treatment in Mexico, Hebert returned to Brownsville. He was tried and acquitted for Farmer's murder. The jury, in a criminal trial that took place in Garza's court, apparently found that he had acted in self-defense. 220 F.Supp., 920–21.

125. Of this sum, the widow received nine thousand dollars, the daughter twenty-five hundred dollars, and the son fifty-five hundred dollars. Farmer was survived by his parents, but they were independent of him and so were not considered for the damage award. 220 F.Supp., 921.

126. For example, a decade earlier, a circuit court of appeals had written that "while the gravamen of a Jones Act suit is negligence, it is not the relatively narrow common law concept of negligence, but a more liberal one commensurate with the broad purposes of the . . . Act." *Forgione v. United States,* 202 F.2d 249 (3d Cir., 1953), 252, cert. denied, 345 U.S. 966 (1953), 640 [citations omitted]. This was in line with an earlier decision of the Supreme Court, which stated that the Jones Act was "not to be narrowed by refined reasoning or for the sake of giving 'negligence' a technically restricted reading. It is to be construed liberally to fulfill the purposes for which it was enacted." *Jamison v. Encarnacion,* 281 U.S. 635 (1930), 640.

127. *Vickers v. Tumey,* 290 F.2d 426 (5th Cir., 1961), 434–35.

128. For more lurid tales of the shrimpers, see Maril, *Texas Shrimpers,* esp. chaps. 5 ("When the Frenchmen Came: A Social History of Shrimpers in Texas Ports") and 6 ("At the Dock: Drinking and Deviance"). In another case featuring seaborne assault, *Boudin v. Lykes Bros. S.S. Co.,* 348 U.S. 336 (1955), the Supreme Court determined that in the warranty of seaworthiness, there could be no distinction between defective ship's equipment and defective ship's personnel, including those with "a proclivity for assaulting people," who after all could be more dangerous than a "rope with a weak strand." However, the court continued to assume the worst regarding the lifestyles of merchant seamen, to wit: "The problem, as with many aspects of the law, is one of degree. *Was the assault within the usual and customary standard of the calling?* Or is it a case of a seaman with a wicked disposition, a propensity to evil conduct, a savage and vicious nature? If it is the former, it is one of the risks of the sea that every crew takes. If the seaman has a savage and vicious nature, then the ship becomes a perilous place. A vessel bursting at the seams might be a safer place than one with a homicidal maniac as a crew member." Ibid., 339–40 [emphasis added]. See also Thackston, "Seamen's Remedies," 339–40, nn. 32–37. Mere shipboard "horseplay" has not usually been construed as misconduct that forfeits a right to remedy. The behavior exhibited in this case was clearly outside of that line. The Supreme Court does recognize that, at least while on shore leave, a sailor forfeits rights to maintenance and cure by his own willful misconduct. As one justice put it, "the traditional instances are venereal disease and injuries received as a result of intoxication, although on occasion the latter has been qualified in recognition of a classic disposition of sailors ashore." *Aguilar v. Standard Oil Co.,* 318 U.S. 724 (1943), 731. That is, a drunk sailor may not be capable of "willful" misconduct. Soldiers also have this reputation: in the army contracting a venereal disease is not misconduct, but failing to report it is. Gilmore and Black, *Law of Admiralty,* 258–60. Also Thackston, "Seamen's Remedies," 363–64.

129. *Fair v. Mississippi Valley Barge Line Co.,* 239 F.Supp. 158 (S.D. Tex., 1965); Corpus Christi Div. (Civ. A. 63-c-14, 16 March 1965).

130. F.Supp., at 159.

131. Ibid., 159.

132. Ibid., 160.

133. The widow sued under the Jones Act, but also under the Texas state "survival statute" (V.A.C.S., art. 5525), which provided remedies similar to those available under the Jones Act. The case was tried before the judge, and lawyers submitted briefs. Sidney Ravkind and

John N. Barnhart, of Mandell and Wright, for plaintiff; R. W. Woolsey, of Kleberg, Mobley, Lockett, and Weil of Corpus Christi, for defendant. Ibid., 159.

134. Ibid., 160.

135. Ibid., 160.

136. The judge also considered the time Fair spent in personal and "charitable pursuits": Fair had been an alcoholic but joined Alcoholics Anonymous and had been sober for seven years before his death. Garza noted that he devoted time to helping others with this problem. Ibid., 160.

137. The Jones Act does not explicitly limit damages, but the federal courts have ruled that recovery is limited exclusively to pecuniary damages. This is because the Jones Act links seamen's remedies to FELA. The Supreme Court held that FELA provided damages for pecuniary loss only. *Michigan Central Railroad v. Vreeland,* 227 U.S. 59 (1913), 69–71. Brown, "Another Maritime Anomaly," 1332.

138. Judge Connally's efforts in the late 1950s had not totally eliminated this variety of case from the dockets.

139. See *Stone v. Reynolds Metals Company,* 233 F.Supp. 440 (S.D. Tex., 1964); affirmed: 355 F.2d 934 (5th Cir., 1966). Also see *Vasquez v. Glens Falls Insurance Company,* 426 F.2d 296 (5th Cir., 1970).

140. Act of 25 June 1938, 52 Stat. 1060; codified as amended at 29 U.S.C. §§ 201–19. Wage and hour provisions appear at §§ 206–7.

141. U.S.C. § 217.

142. *Farmers Reservoir & Irrigation Co. v. McComb,* 337 U.S. 755 (1949); Frankfurter concurring, 770.

143. *H. B. Zachry Co. v. Mitchell,* 262 F.2d 546 (5th Cir., 1959). Until 5 May 1962 the minimum wage specified by FLSA was $1 per hour. From 6 May 1961 through 26 March 1963, the minimum wage was $1.15 per hour.

144. Both 29 U. S. C. § 203(j), emphasis added. In more detail, the 1938 FLSA provided: "'Produced' means produced, manufactured, mined, handled, or in any other manner worked on in any State; and for the purposes of this Act an employee shall be deemed to have been engaged in the production of goods if such employee was employed in producing, manufacturing, mining, handling, transporting, or in any other manner working on such goods, or in any process or occupation necessary to the production thereof, in any State." As amended, this section provided that: "an employee shall be deemed to have been engaged in the production of goods if such employee was employed in producing, manufacturing, mining, handling, transporting, or in any other manner working on such goods, or in any closely related process or occupation directly essential to the production thereof, in any State." Therefore, in 1949 federal lawmakers amended the last clause of § 203(j). See *Mitchell v. H. B. Zachry Co.,* 362 U.S. 310 (1960), 312 n. 2.

145. *H. B. Zachry Co. v. Mitchell,* 262 F.2d 546 (5th Cir., 1959), 548.

146. Ibid., 552.

147. *Mitchell v. H. B. Zachry Co.,* 362 U.S. 310 (1960), 321. Frankfurter was joined in the opinion by Justices Clark, Harlan, Whittaker, and Stewart.

148. *Mitchell v. Vollmer & Co.,* 349 U.S. 427 (1955), 429. Under these "practical considerations," the federal court defined a variety of apparently local occupations as "engaged in commerce." For a sample of the range of these occupations, see *Hayden v. Bowen,* 404 F.2d 682 (5th Cir., 1968), 683–84, esp. n. 5; and *Goldberg v. Wade Lahar Construction Co.,* 290 F.2d 408 (5th Cir., 1961), 416–17 n. 6.

149. *Mitchell v. H. B. Zachry Co.*, 362 U.S. 310, 326.

150. Ibid., 325. Douglas was joined in his dissent by Justices Black and Brennan, and Chief Justice Warren.

151. *Goldberg v. Wade Lahar Construction Co.*, 290 F.2d 408 (5th Cir., 1961), 420.

152. The P. & L. Equipment Company requested a rehearing en banc; after the Fifth Circuit denied the request, the firm did not appeal the decision. *Goldberg v. P. & L. Equipment Co.*, 311 F.2d 88 (5th Cir., 1962), 89.

153. *Wirtz v. Wohl Shoe Co.*, 382 F.2d 848 (5th Cir., 1967), 850.

154. *Wirtz v. Valco, Inc.*, 280 F.Supp. 449 (S.D. Tex., 1968), 452.

155. *Wirtz v. Valco, Inc.*, 407 F.2d 1322 (5th Cir., 1962).

156. The apparently probusiness ruling in the 1959 *Zachry* case is among the evidence recently marshaled to argue against the Fifth Circuit's lingering reputation for liberality, which is based mostly on the circuit judges' action with regard to desegregation. See Waltman, "Minimum Wage Litigation," 52. The swift broadening of FLSA after the *Zachry* decision narrowed the act, however, indicates that the reputation may have been deserved even in economic matters.

157. See *Hodgson v. Ewing;* 1971 U.S. Dist. LEXIS 14882; 64 Lab. Cas. (CCH) P32,451, at 6–7.

158. The FLSA exempted agricultural wages at 29 U.S.C. § 213(a)(6); agricultural workers are exempted from the hours provisions at § 213(b)(12).

159. *Wirtz v. Boyls*, 230 F.Supp. 246 (S.D. Tex., 1964); affirmed 352 F.2d 63 (5th Cir., 1965).

160. *Wirtz v. Fortuna Broom Company;* S.D. Tex., 1966; Corpus Christi Division, Civil No. 64-C-77); 1966 U.S. Dist. LEXIS 7136, 53 Lab. Cas. (CCH) P31,785, at 1–2.

161. Under §§ 6, 7, 11(c), 12, and 15(a) of FLSA; that is, 29 U.S.C. §§ 206, 207, 211(c), 212, and 215(a). *Wirtz v. Fortuna Broom Company*, 5.

162. *Wirtz v. Fortuna Broom Company*, 5.

163. *Wirtz v. Fortuna Broom Company*, 6–7. Beck then pleaded poverty and personal hardship. He claimed that his corporations had been losing money for years and presented evidence that the Fortuna Broom Company had an income of only $17,569 in 1962, that in 1963 it took a loss of $18.64, and that its 1964 income was only $533.05. The South Texas Broom Corn Company had seen even worse business. In 1962 it had a loss of $2,844.44, in 1963 it lost $288.75, and the company's 1964 income was only $684.19. Beck's personal income was only $1,084.89 in 1962, $1,489.43 in 1963, and $5,075.43 in 1964. Finally, Beck's wife had died recently, and because of community property laws and laws of inheritance, descent, and distribution, other parties had legal claims against his assets. As a result of these misfortunes, the defense urged, Beck would be unable to discharge the liability for unpaid minimum wages and overtime compensation, should Garza grant that part of the Labor Department's requested injunction. Again, Garza was skeptical of the defense claims. He noted that the evidence showed that Beck, through his corporations, owned assets sufficient to fulfill any obligations that were due to the employees. *Wirtz v. Fortuna Broom Company*, 9.

164. I have rounded the final figure. *Wirtz v. Fortuna Broom Company*, 13–14, 21.

165. *Wirtz v. Fortuna Broom Company*, 21. See *Fortuna Broom Company v. Wirtz*, 379 F.2d 327 (1967).

166. U.S.C. §§ 1461–68.

167. For the history of the bracero agreements, see generally Calavita, *Inside the State;* Craig, *Bracero Program;* and Kirstein, *Anglo over Bracero.* Also see Zelden, *Justice Lies in the District*, 176–77, 192–93.

168. See Act of 4 August 1942, 56 Stat. 1759, as amended by Act of 26 April 1943, 57 Stat.

1152; renewed as Act of 12 July 1951, Pub. L. No. 78, ch. 223, 65 Stat. 119, as amended by Act of 13 December 1963, Pub. L. No. 88–203, 77 Stat. 363, expired 31 December 1964. Although the discussion focuses on labor in Texas, the bracero program extended into other states.

169. U.S.C. § 1461. *Johnson v. Kirkland,* 290 F.2d 440 (5th Cir., 1961), 441–42 nn. 2–3.

170. U.S.C. § 1463. *Johnson v. Kirkland,* 290 F.2d, 442, esp. n. 4. On 28 June 1960, for example, after the Texas Employment Security Agency reported that a "reasonable effort" had been made to fill open farm jobs with domestic workers, the Labor Department's regional director in Dallas announced that the July 1960 quota in the Rio Grande Valley would be fifty-five thousand bracero workers. Under the MLA the director established the quota contingent upon the following: (1) growers' continued efforts to recruit domestic workers; (2) domestic workers' replacing the guest workers wherever possible; (3) domestic workers' wages being equal to or better than wages of bracero workers; and (4) the public posting of the quota and its conditions at local employment offices. Ibid., 443.

171. The Border Patrol acts under supervision of the U.S. attorney general (8 U.S.C. § 1103). The Congress created the Border Patrol with the INA of 1924 (currently codified at 8 U.S.C. § 1357). The Deportation Act of 4 March 1929 amended the 1924 act to streamline the deportation process. The new law also made it a federal felony for a deported alien to reenter the U.S. (under 8 U.S.C. § 1326). The INS, the Border Patrol's parent agency, was not originally within the Justice Department. On 10 June 1933 Congress merged the Bureau of Immigration with the Bureau of Naturalization to create the INS. Because the federal government expected immigrants to join the work force, lawmakers originally put the INS under the authority of Secretary of Labor Frances Perkins. By the end of the decade, however, high-ranking diplomats in the State Department were unhappy with Perkins's efforts on behalf of refugees from war-torn Europe and encouraged President Franklin D. Roosevelt to support the transfer of the INS to the Department of Justice, where it would operate under Attorney General Robert Jackson. The Congress enacted the transfer on 14 June 1940. Thereafter, an immigration service that was created to enforce domestic racial policy during a period of extreme nativism was to be associated with national security, because the mission of the INS and its Border Patrol were linked to the Federal Bureau of Investigation's (FBI) job of keeping out foreign spies and saboteurs. As a result of its wartime responsibilities, INS budgets increased, its personnel more than doubled (to 8,500) by 1942, and the service was poised to respond when FDR signed an executive order authorizing the internment of Japanese Americans. Fitzgerald, *Face of the Nation,* 164, 173, 184–85. Many Mexican Americans considered the Border Patrol to be a historically abusive and racist organization. Rendón, *Chicano Manifesto,* 200–202. Alleged Border Patrol abuses include "breaking," the psychological or physical abuse by officers to obtain information regarding immigration status. Texas Advisory Committee, *Sin Papeles,* 46. For more sympathetic yet not wholly positive views of the Border Patrol, see U.S. Department of Justice, *1970 Annual Report,* 11; and Ehrlich, Bilderback, and Ehrlich, *The Golden Door,* 286–92.

172. Fernandez, *Mexican-American Border Region,* 70. Immigration to the United States was largely unrestricted until the twentieth century, and *illegal* immigration was therefore a relatively new problem. Congress enacted the first federal immigration regulation, which barred entry by convicts and prostitutes, in 1875 (Act of 3 March 1875, ch. 141, § 5, 18 Stat. 477). An earlier law, defining human contraband related to labor exploitation, had prohibited immigration or importation of Chinese and Japanese servants (Act of 19 February 1862, §§ 2158–64, 18 Stat. 379). The modern era of immigration legislation commenced when Congress passed the 1921 Quota Act (ch. 8, 42 Stat. 5; formerly codified at 8 U.S.C. §§ 229–31).

In areas where Mexican immigrants formed a large part of the traditional labor force, such as the states in the American Southwest, capitalism overcame nativism. To protect the economic interests of ranchers and farmers who depended on Mexican labor, Congress exempted the Western Hemisphere from the quota formulas. However, although Mexicans were excluded from quotas, they were subject to fees, such as a ten-dollar charge for a visa and an eight-dollar head tax. Heer, *Immigration in America's Future,* 45–48. Widespread legal Mexican migration into the U.S. Southwest occurred in three waves, which describe three major historical epochs: the era of railroad and industrial development (especially in the 1880s, after the Chinese were excluded); the era of agricultural development (1910–30, which also was the era of the Mexican Revolution); and the bracero period (1942–64). In each case, social, political, or economic conditions in Mexico propelled working-class people north into the U.S. Jones, "Undocumented Mexican Migration," 103. The term *illegal alien* has been criticized by the United Nations, which resolved in 1975 to employ instead the term *nondocumented migratory worker* whenever possible. See Salinas and Torres, "Undocumented Mexican Alien," 863 n. 1; also Oren, "Status of Undocumented Aliens," 667.

173. The "Texas Proviso," in paragraph 4 of the law, explicitly provided that employing an illegal alien was not the criminal act of "harboring," which was condemned in paragraph 3. Act of 27 June 1952, 66 Stat. 163; 8 U.S.C. § 1103 (1952). Because President Truman thought it was a racist and shortsighted law, Congress passed the McCarran-Walter Act over his veto. Heer, *Undocumented Mexicans,* 12–13; and Heer, *Immigration in America's Future,* 58.

174. *Johnson v. Kirkland,* 290 F.2d 440 (5th Cir., 1961). Judge Ingraham subsequently dismissed two similar suits for not naming a different indispensable party, specifically, the director of the Bureau of Employment Security at Washington. See *McBride Farms Marketing Association v. Johnson,* 290 F.2d 474 (5th Cir., 1961); and *Rio Hondo Harvesting Association v. Johnson,* 290 F.2d 471 (5th Cir., 1961).

175. The employers could recruit foreign workers under Public Law 144, of the McCarran Act. See Mooney and Majka, *Farmers' and Farm Workers' Movements,* 155. For illegal immigration, see Fitzgerald, *Face of the Nation,* 180–91; Salinas and Torres, "Undocumented Mexican Alien," 868–75; and Texas Advisory Committee, *Sin Papeles,* 7. See U.S. Department of Justice, *1970 Annual Report,* 11. The number of undocumented Mexican nationals arrested north of the border sharply increased in 1965, and total arrests climbed each succeeding year. Salinas and Torres, "Undocumented Mexican Alien," 863. Toney, *Control of Illegal Mexican Migration,* 55.

176. For labor organizers' efforts in the valley, see Rhinehart and Kreneck, "Minimum Wage March," 29.

177. For a variety of organizing campaigns, see Zamora, *Mexican Worker in Texas,* 162–72; Cockcroft, *Outlaws in the Promised Land,* 176–77; and Nelson-Cisneros, "UCAPAWA Organizing Activities," 81–82. Above all, labor supporters blamed the failure of agricultural organization on the presence of "guest workers," who distorted the domestic labor market, depressed wages, and stifled farm workers' freedom to organize. Mooney and Majka, *Farmers' and Farm Workers' Movements,* 150–54. Also see Craig, *Bracero Program,* 150–97.

178. Davidson, *Race and Class,* 123–32. See, for example, *Lodge No. 12, District No. 37, International Association of Machinists v. Cameron Iron Works, Inc.,* 257 F.2d 467 (5th Cir., 1958); and *Galveston Maritime Association v. South Atlantic & Gulf Coast District, International Longshoremen's Association,* 234 F.Supp. 250 (S.D. Tex., 1964).

179. U.S.C. § 206(5). Subsection 5 was added by Pub. L. No. 89–601, § 302; 80 Stat. 830.

180. Rendón, "The Long Road," 35.

181. *Hodgson v. Ewing*, S.D. Tex., 69-B-108; 1971 U.S. Dist. LEXIS 14882; 64 Lab. Cas. (CCH) P32,451, at 1–2.

182. 64 Lab. Cas. (CCH) P32,451, at 4–5.

183. Ibid., 6–7.

184. Ibid., 8.

185. Ibid., 9–11.

186. *Farmers Reservoir & Irrigation Co. v. McComb*, 337 U.S. 755 (1949); Frankfurter concurring, 770.

187. Judicial Conference Report, September 1964, p. 52. Quoted in "Procedures and Standards Used in Conducting United States Court Judgeship Surveys, 1964–1980," report, clerk's files of Chief Judge John V. Singleton, folder 5.

188. Burger, "The Courts on Trial," 71.

189. Ibid., 74. The relevant statute provided that "[e]ach judicial council shall make all necessary order for the effective and expeditious administration of the business of the courts within its circuit. The district judges shall promptly carry into effect all orders of the judicial council." 28 U.S.C. § 232.

190. Burger, "The Courts on Trial," 82. See Nelson, *Administration of Justice.*

191. Fed. R. Civ. P. (Rule 1: "Scope of Rules").

192. Fish, *Politics of Federal Judicial Administration*, 228–68.

193. Pub. L. No. 88–139, dated 16 October 1963.

194. Judge Connally, "Order: Terms of Court Abolished," 4 December 1963, clerk's files of Chief Judge Ben C. Connally, folder 1.

195. Judge Hannay remained on the court, however, and did not choose to assume the semiretired status of a senior judge until 1975. In 1958 Congress mandated that a chief serve only until the age of seventy. See 28 U.S.C. §§ 136–37 (1958 amendment, Pub. L. No. 85–593).

196. U.S.C. §§ 136–37. The clerk of court is appointed by the district court judges, with duties established by the judges and by statute. The first clerk, Christopher Dart, served from 1 July 1902 to 28 April 1913. The second, L. C. Masterson, served from 3 May 1913 to 7 May 1940. The fourth, Hal V. Watts, served from 1 July 1940 until he was succeeded by V. Bailey Thomas on 15 December 1951.

197. U.S.C. 1445(c). As amended 25 July 1958, Pub. L. No. 85–5545, 72 Stat. 415. See Judge Connally, "Comparison Study as to the Percentage of Workmen's Compensation Cases Filed for the Four United States District Courts of the State of Texas against the Total of Civil Cases Filed for the Periods Fiscal Year 1956, Fiscal Year 1957, First Three Quarters of Fiscal Year 1958," undated tables, clerk's files of Chief Judge Ben C. Connally, folder 1.

198. "Connally," in *Judges of the United States.*

199. Fifth Circuit Chief Judge Elbert Tuttle to "The District Judges Addressed, Re: Cases Pending over Three Years in District Courts," 10 September 1964, clerk's files of Chief Judge Ben C. Connally, folder 1.

200. Warren, "Address," 182.

201. Between 1960 and 1983, district court filings rose 250 percent, and cases docketed in the courts of appeals surged 686 percent. The increasing complexity of cases brought in federal courts amplifies the burden generated by caseload growth. Levit, "Caseload Conundrum," 323. Also see Clark, "Adjudication to Administration," 125–48; Heydebrand and Seron, "Demand for Court Services," 303; and Resnik, "Managerial Judges," 393–94.

202. Oral history interview (OHI) with Judge John V. Singleton Jr., by Steven H. Wilson, 15 July 1996.

203. "Singleton," in *Judges of the United States.*

204. Bill Lee, "Singleton: Spectator to Bar to Bench," *Houston Chronicle,* 10 July 1966, 1C. In 1963 Governor Connally appointed Singleton to the State Depository Board. John Mort, "Six Texans Nominated to U.S. Judgeships," *Houston Chronicle,* 29 June 1966, 22A.

205. "Seals," in *Judges of the United States.* "Woodrow B. Seals, 72, Federal Judge in Texas," *New York Times,* 30 October 1990, p. B7. Bob Tutt, "Seals: Church, Civic Work and Politics," *Houston Chronicle,* 10 July 1966, 1C. See "Resolution in Memory of Judge Woodrow Seals," in the scrapbook of Judge Seals compiled by the clerk of court, S.D. Tex.

206. Leslie Carpenter, "Houston Attorney Serves as Texas Contact Man at Demo Headquarters," *Dallas Times Herald,* 16 September 1964, p. A11. Bob Tutt, "The Day before Dallas: Kennedy Got Big Welcome in Houston," *Houston Chronicle,* 21 November 1993, p. C1.

207. Leslie Carpenter, "Houston Attorney Serves as Texas Contact Man at Demo Headquarters," *Dallas Times Herald,* 16 September 1964, p. A11. Also see CR, 22 July 1966, vol. 112, pt. 13, p. 16723–27.

208. CR, 9 February 1966, vol. 112, pt. 2, p. 2808. CR, 2 March 1966, vol. 112, pt. 4, p. 4554.

209. CR, 2 March 1966, vol. 112, pt. 4, pp. 4555, 4560.

210. CR, 21 March 1966, vol. 112, pt. 5, p. 6324. The 1966 Omnibus Judgeship Act is Pub. L. No. 89–372.

211. See the report, and Senator Yarborough's comments, in CR, 22 July 1966, vol. 112, pt. 13, pp. 16723–27. Johnson also appointed Irving Goldberg, who had served on Johnson's congressional staff during the 1940s, to the Fifth Circuit. Also "Seals, Singleton Approved," *Houston Post,* 22 July 1966, 20C; Lee, "Singleton: Spectator to Bar to Bench," and Tutt, "Seals: Church, Civic Work and Politics," both articles under the single heading "New U.S. Judges Both Worked Their Way to the Top," *Houston Chronicle,* 10 July 1966, 1C.

212. OHI, Singleton, 15 July 1996.

213. She also noted that with the U.S. attorney's position open in the Northern District, "Seal's appointment . . . creates a second district attorney's vacancy, perhaps opening a 50–50 way for agreement on the northern district appointment." See Margaret Mayer, *Dallas Times-Herald,* 29 June 1966. Also see "Judgeship Compromise," *Texas Observer,* 8 July 1966, p. 12.

214. This fact comforted commentators who surveyed the Texan's appointees during the Reagan Administration. McFeeley, *Appointment of Judges,* 133–39.

215. For the switch of the HISD case from Ingraham to Connally, see Read and McGough, *Let Them Be Judged,* 454 [Read and McGough identify both Connally and Ingraham incorrectly, as sitting in the *Eastern* District of Texas].

216. Chief Judge Connally, Judicial Work Assignments, memorandum, 14 January 1963, clerk's files of Chief Judge Ben C. Connally, folder 1.

217. Chief Judge Connally, Judicial Work Assignments, memorandum, 2 January 1964, clerk's files of Chief Judge Ben C. Connally, folder 1. Chief Judge Connally, Judicial Work Assignments, memorandum, 1 January 1966, clerk's files of Chief Judge Ben C. Connally, folder 2.

218. Chief Judge Connally to "Dear Judges," 12 August 1966, clerk's files of Chief Judge Ben C. Connally, folder 2. Judge Ingraham to Chief Judge Connally, 25 August 1966, clerk's files of Chief Judge Ben C. Connally, folder 2. Judge Noel to Chief Judge Connally, 29 August 1966, clerk's files of Chief Judge Ben C. Connally, folder 2.

219. Judge Hannay also retained the bar admission proceedings, and Judge Ingraham

kept the naturalization proceedings. Chief Judge Connally, Judicial Work Assignments, memorandum, 25 November 1966, clerk's files of Chief Judge Ben C. Connally, folder 2.

220. Once more, cases in which the United States was a party went to Judge Singleton. Chief Judge Connally to V. Bailey Thomas [clerk], 10 January 1967, clerk's files of Chief Judge Ben C. Connally, folder 2. The 1968 assignments showed only minor changes from 1967. Judge Ingraham was to be assigned 25 percent of the civil cases in Houston during 1968, Judges Seals and Noel 10 percent each, and Judge Singleton 27 percent of the total. Chief Judge Connally, Judicial Work Assignments, memorandum, 22 December 1967, clerk's files of Chief Judge Ben C. Connally, folder 2.

221. OHI, Singleton, 15 July 1996.

222. Fifth Circuit Chief Judge John R. Brown to "The Chief Judges of the District Courts Concerned: Three-Year-Old Cases," 18 September 1969, clerk's files of Chief Judge Ben C. Connally, folder 2.

223. Ibid.

224. Chief Judge Connally to V. Bailey Thomas, 12 August 1966, clerk's files of Chief Judge Ben C. Connally, folder 2.

CHAPTER 3. The Rules and Exceptions of Border Justice

1. Fisch, *All Rise*, 70–77. Zelden, *Justice Lies in the District*, 34.

2. Zelden, *Justice Lies in the District*, 50–53; Fisch, *All Rise*, 119.

3. Griffin, "Drugs and Political Corruption," 3–4.

4. The office of U.S. attorney is defined in Chapter 35 of Title 28 of the U.S. Code (Judiciary and Judicial Procedure). The president appoints one U.S. attorney for each federal judicial district, subject to confirmation by the Senate (28 U.S.C. § 501), but only the president can remove the U.S. attorney from office (28 U.S.C. § 504). Within his or her district the U.S. attorney has the power, discretion, or duty to: (1) prosecute offenses against the United States; (2) prosecute for or defend the federal government in all civil actions in which the United States is concerned; (3) appear in behalf of the government defendants in federal tax, customs, or other revenue-related civil actions; (4) institute collection proceedings and prosecute for violations of federal revenue laws; and (5) report as the U.S. attorney general directs (28 U.S.C. §§ 541–50). For political challenges inherent in the office, see generally Eisenstein, *Counsel for the United States;* and Seymour, *United States Attorney.*

5. The total cases are available in the *1964 Annual Report of the Director of the Administrative Office of the U.S. Courts* (Washington, D.C.: U.S. Government Printing Office, 1965). For local annual totals, I rely on the case numbers on the files at the National Archives and Records Administration–Southwest Regional Archives, in Fort Worth, Texas [hereafter NARA-SWA], which keeps the files for the federal courts in Texas. In 1962 clerks in the Southern District of Texas adopted the following straightforward method of case number assignment, to reflect the year, division, and sequence in which a case was entered on the court docket: the first part of any case number represents the year, the second part is a letter that represents the city, and the final part records the actual order of filing. For example, Crim. No. 65-L-1 represents the first criminal case filed in Laredo in 1965 (dates on the files generally reflect the accuracy and reliability of the system). In more recent cases the clerks have reversed the initial two fields, but the general filing system is as I have described. For totals claimed above: NARA-SWA, Record Group (RG) 21, S.D. Tex., Laredo Criminal Docket,

1964–66, box 713. Box 713 contains Crim. No. 64-L-255, the last case of 1964; it is followed by Crim. No. 65-L-1. [This is also the system for civil dockets, where "Civ." replaces "Crim."] See *United States v. Hanna et al.*, Crim. No. 64-C-41; Corpus Christi Criminal Docket, 1964–69, box 270. In this Corpus Christi case, filed 28 October 1964, Judge Garza examined three defendants charged on an information for two counts under the Federal Juvenile Delinquency Act (18 U.S.C. § 5031 et seq.). All three pled guilty; therefore, Garza found them to be juvenile delinquents and consigned them to the custody of the U.S. attorney general during their minority, and recommended that they be committed to separate facilities. However, all went to the Federal Correctional Institution at Englewood, Colorado. The last 1965 case in Laredo is Crim. No. 65-L-280; the next case in this box is Crim. No. 66-L-1; for both, see NARA-SWA: RG 21, S.D. Tex., Laredo Criminal Docket, 1964–66, box 722. For other cases, see *United States v. Sustaita*, Crim. No. 69-L-819. NARA-SWA: RG 21, S.D. Tex., Laredo Criminal Docket, September–December 1969, box 804; and *United States v. Sanchez*, Crim. No. 69-B-858. NARA-SWA: RG 21, S.D. Tex., Brownsville Criminal Docket, September–December 1969 (no separate box numbers, but folders are arranged by case name and number).

6. These violations included, for example, interstate transportation of stolen vehicles, assault on federal officers, counterfeiting of federal securities, and even robbery of federally insured banks. For transportation of a stolen motor vehicle in foreign commerce (18 U.S.C. § 2312), see *United States v. Tijerina*, Crim. No. 69-L-382. NARA-SWA: RG 21, S.D. Tex., Laredo Criminal Docket, June–August 1969, box 789. For possession and concealment of a counterfeited security (18 U.S.C. § 472), see *United States v. Zurndorfer*, Crim. No. 69-L-766. NARA-SWA: RG 21, S.D. Tex., Laredo Criminal Docket, September–December 1969, box 802. For willfully and forcibly assaulting a federal officer (18 U.S.C. § 111), see *United States v. Pardo et al.*, Crim. No. 69-B-673. NARA-SWA: RG 21, S.D. Tex., Brownsville Criminal Docket, September–December 1969, box labeled "69B657 to 69B688." Finally, on 12 August 1969, federal prosecutors in Brownsville obtained indictments in two unrelated bank crime cases. The first indictment charged twenty-two-year-old Juan Jesus Mireles Garcia with bank robbery (under 18 U.S.C. § 2113[a]). Garcia pled guilty when he was arraigned on 3 February 1970, and on 27 February, Judge Garza sentenced Garcia to fifteen years to be served concurrently with a state sentence then in effect. See *United States v. Garcia*, Crim. No. 69-B-581. The second indictment charged twenty-seven-year-old John Harvey Filberth and forty-three-year-old Jose Gonzales Gonzales with three bank crimes: conspiracy to commit bank robbery (18 U.S.C. § 371), embezzlement (18 U.S.C. § 2113[b]), and possession of stolen money (18 U.S.C. § 2113[c]). The case disposition shows the prosecutor's strategy of managing the docket. When he was arraigned on 14 August 1969, Gonzales pled not guilty to all counts. When Filberth was arraigned the next day, however, he pled guilty to the conspiracy count. Gonzales then sought rearraignment, and on 2 September he also pled guilty to conspiracy, but still not guilty to all other charges. On 6 October, Judge Garza sentenced both to five years on the conspiracy count, and the government dismissed the remaining counts. On 2 December, Garza denied Filberth's and Gonzales's motions to reduce the sentences. See *United States v. Filberth et al.*, Crim. No. 69-B-582. Both cases, NARA-SWA: RG 21, S.D. Tex., Brownsville Criminal Docket, June–August 1969, box 69B578 to 69B599.

7. Transportation of a stolen motor vehicle in foreign commerce is prohibited under 18 U.S.C. § 2312, with the possible penalty of five years imprisonment and/or a five-thousand-dollar fine.

8. Forgery of a U.S. Treasury check is a crime under 18 U.S.C. § 495. It carries the possible penalty of ten years' imprisonment and/or a one-thousand-dollar fine.

9. Heer, *Immigration in America's Future,* 45–48; Heer, *Undocumented Mexicans,* 12–13. Congress allowed the bracero system to expire on New Year's Eve 1964 (see Act of 4 August 1942, 56 Stat. 1759, as amended by the Act of 26 April 1943, 57 Stat. 1152; renewed by the Act of 12 July 1951, Pub. L. No. 78, ch. 223, 65 Stat. 119, as amended by the Act of 13 December 1963, Pub. L. No. 88–203, 77 Stat. 363). Subsequently, the lawmakers also abolished the national origins quota in the immigration system. Under the provisions of the Immigration Act of 1965, every country outside of the Western Hemisphere received unlimited visas for relatives of citizens and twenty thousand visas for ordinary immigrants. For the first time, the 1965 act set quotas on immigration from nations in the Western Hemisphere (Act of 3 October 1965, Pub. L. No. 89–236, 79 Stat. 911; as amended at 8 U.S.C. §§ 1–14354). Heer, *Immigration in America's Future,* 55–56. Salinas and Torres, "Undocumented Mexican Alien," 863.

10. Mexico had long been a source of both marijuana and heroin, but the country became a newly important trafficking, staging, and transit area in the 1960s, and by the 1970s the U.S.-Mexico border emerged as the most embattled front in the emerging federal "war on drugs." Ultimately, the U.S. government attempted to stem the tide by enacting a succession of laws to strengthen federal enforcement efforts in the 1980s. For the emergence of the federal "war," see Marion, *Federal Crime Control Initiatives;* Johns, *War on Drugs;* and Bertram et al., *Drug War Politics.* Also see Zeese, "Drug War Forever?" 252.

11. The Prohibition experience (1919–33) strained resources in the Southern District of Texas, which because of its geographic conjoining to the international border, already handled a large number of smuggling cases. The addition of bootlegged liquor dramatically increased the criminal docket, which during the 1920s made up between one-half and two-thirds of the district's business. Unlike the many overawed and overworked judges in some jurisdictions, the Southern District's judge during the Prohibition era, Joseph C. Hutcheson Jr., handled these routine cases efficiently. Also, Judge Hutcheson was generally lenient when prohibition offenders came before him, because he recognized that they were "not people set apart, public enemies, but average, ordinary, underprivileged common men" who did not deserve long prison terms. Zelden, *Justice Lies in the District,* 67–69. The border continued to provide the district with the majority of its criminal cases well after the repeal of liquor prohibition, because traffic in drugs, aliens, and other contraband remained illegal.

12. The Border Patrol acts under supervision of the U.S. attorney general. 8 U.S.C. § 1103.

13. Customs agents operate under the supervision of the treasury secretary. 19 U.S.C. § 6.

14. Lyles, *Gatekeepers.*

15. Alschuler, "Prosecutor's Role," 52–55; Langbein, "Short History of Plea Bargaining," 261; and Feeley, "Perspectives on Plea Bargaining," 199. Local variations of the discretionary policies are rarely articulated and rarely published, but the *U.S. Attorneys Manual* described possible criteria. Abrams, "Internal Policy," 13–25.

16. Federal Rules of Criminal Procedure (Fed. R. Crim. P.), Rule 11.

17. Institutionalized plea bargaining in the 1960s was neither unique to the legal culture of the border divisions, nor even unprecedented in the Southern District. Early in the century, when smuggling usually involved livestock or small amounts of *mescal* (a Mexican liquor), it was common for a Southern District judge to reward a guilty plea with a light sentence or probation. During World War I judges matched guilty pleas with light sentences in draft evasion cases, many of which involved recent refugees from the Mexican Revolution who—perhaps understandably given the U.S. Army's 1917 intervention in Mexico, itself a police action against Pancho Villa—were reluctant to be inducted into the U.S. military. In the 1950s the federal government's "Operation Wetback" forced Southern District judges and

prosecutors to dedicate whole days or weeks to the disposition of routinely plea-bargained undocumented alien cases. Zelden, *Justice Lies in the District,* 50–53, 62–72, 98–100, 191–93. In 1954 the U.S. government conducted mass arrests and deportations in a quasi-military action organizers dubbed "Operation Wetback." See Juan Ramon Garcia, *Operation Wetback;* Fitzgerald, *Face of the Nation,* 219–20; and Meier and Ribera, *Mexican Americans/Americans,* 189–90.

18. Enker, "Perspectives on Plea Bargaining," 110–11. Some scholars question the conventional wisdom that plea bargaining and case pressures "go together," because settlement practices based on other factors recur even in less congested state and federal courts. However, few dispute that caseload and bargaining are often linked in the busiest courts. Heumann, "Plea Bargaining and Case Pressure," 524–27.

19. Since their presence is believed to be "inherently coercive," trial judges are usually not participants in plea negotiations (depending on local or state rules). Although judges may review a proposed bargain before accepting a plea of guilty during the arraignment process, they effectively have no more than a veto, which may be further constrained by case pressure. Heinz and Kerstetter, "Pretrial Settlement Conference," 350. Some commentators conclude that judges ought to play a larger and more positive role in pretrial proceedings. See Alschuler, "Trial Judge's Role," 1154; Alschuler, "Defense Attorney's Role," 1179.

20. The U.S. Department of Justice receives criminal referrals from other government agencies and then applies discretion in the disposition of a case, ranging from decisions to plea bargain or to prosecute. In the fiscal year ending 30 June 1970, the Justice Department filed 38,079 criminal cases in the U.S. courts. The leading category was motor vehicle thefts (referred by the FBI), the second most frequent category was draft violations (from the Selective Service Administration), and the third was Immigration Act violations (referred by the Immigration and Naturalization Service). Most often, referrals were filed directly to the U.S. attorney of the district where the offense allegedly occurred. There was little bureaucratic review of local decisions, except with regard to decisions to dismiss a previous indictment, which is supposed to be with prior approval. Rabin, "Agency Criminal Referrals," 1037–38.

21. Note the frequent references to Leary, as a scientist and intellectual as well as a popular media personality, scattered throughout the following disparate sources: Becker, "History, Culture and Subjective Experience," 163–76; Mooney, "Popular Music," 67–85; Chenoweth, "Rhetoric of Hope and Despair," 25–45; Berki, "Crisis of the New Radicalism," 56–92; Jaros, "Biochemical Desocialization," 1–28; and Purcell, "Social Thought," 80–100.

22. For further discussion of plea bargaining due to heavy caseloads, and for comparisons to an assembly line: Abrams, "Internal Policy," 1–2, esp. n. 2.

23. AUSAS are formally appointed by the president, but they are ordinarily subject to removal by the attorney general (28 U.S.C. § 503). Eisenstein, *Counsel for the United States,* 35.

24. Heer, *Immigration in America's Future,* 120–21. The apprehension statistics compiled by the INS illustrate the phenomenon. In 1964, when the INS arrested 86,597 undocumented aliens, 43,844 (51 percent) were Mexican nationals. The service apprehended 283,557 aliens in 1969, including 201,636 (71 percent) Mexicans. U.S. Department of Justice, *1964 Annual Report,* 7–8; *1969 Annual Report,* 12. Total *convictions* for violations reflected the vastly lower number of detainees formally prosecuted. In 1964 the courts convicted 2,882 defendants. In 1969 the number was 4,623. Moreover, there were 154 convictions for illegal entry in fiscal year 1964, but the number of convictions only grew to 5,084 in 1971, and to 10,292 in 1972.

According to one author who has examined this practice, "over ninety percent of Mexican 'wets' arrested are allowed to 'voluntarily' depart." Toney, *Control of Illegal Mexican Migration,* 14–15, 20–21, 55, and especially table 54: "Convictions for Immigration and Nationality Violations, Years Ended June 30, 1963–72," at 108–11.

25. AUSA Morrill sought the indictments from a federal grand jury in Brownsville, but he sent the cases to be tried in Laredo. Morrill acted locally on behalf of U.S. Attorney Woodrow B. Seals, who officially directed the prosecutions from the Southern District's Houston headquarters. AUSA Ronald J. Blask is listed as the prosecutor in a few of the cases.

26. In 1896 the U.S. Supreme Court declared that the Fourteenth Amendment did not limit its protection to U.S. citizens. *Wong Wing v. United States,* 163 U.S. 228 (1896). The primary difference in alien defendants' legal standing is that, if convicted, they will be deported after serving a criminal sentence. Heer, *Immigration in America's Future,* 122. However, throughout the twentieth century, aliens (like many other "persons," including many American citizens) have been obliged to undertake litigation to establish the scope of these protections. Oren, "Status of Undocumented Aliens," 669–73. Oren dedicates much discussion of the right to an education, but her analysis is grounded in the idea that courts often illegitimately muddle the categories used in immigration law (for example, an aliens' breach of the laws of illegal entry) with other legal rights. As a result, courts too often treat aliens as an "outlaw" class without any rights at all. Ibid., 709. Other critics of the government's immigration policies argue that the United States has a moral obligation to serve the needs of undocumented Mexicans. Lopez, "Undocumented Mexican Migration," 695–707.

27. Under 18 U.S.C. § 911 (which carried the possible penalty of two years' imprisonment and/or a one-thousand-dollar fine). See *United States v. Cano,* Crim. No. 65-L-76. NARA-SWA: RG 21, S.D. Tex., Laredo Criminal Docket, 1964–66, boxes 715 and 716.

28. U.S.C. § 1326 (possible penalty: two years' imprisonment and/or one thousand dollars).

29. *United States v. Delgado,* Crim. No. 65-L-85. NARA-SWA: RG 21, S.D. Tex., Laredo Criminal Docket, 1964–66, box 715.

30. *United States v. Gallegos,* Crim. No. 65-L-86. NARA-SWA: RG 21, S.D. Tex., Laredo Criminal Docket, 1964–66, box 716.

31. U.S.C. § 1546 (possible penalty: five years and/or two thousand dollars).

32. *United States v. Salazar,* Crim. No. 65-L-100. NARA-SWA: RG 21, S.D. Tex., Laredo Criminal Docket, 1964–66, box 716.

33. U.S.C. § 1324 (a); possible penalty: five years and/or two thousand dollars for each alien. This was also an emerging problem. The INS reported 525 cases of alien smuggling in 1965, and 4,564 cases in 1972. The number of smuggling cases reached 8,074 by 1974. *1965 Annual Report,* 9; *1972 Annual Report,* 9; and *1974 Annual Report,* 11.

34. Because Leal was a U.S. citizen, probation was condition of good behavior. *United States v. Leal,* Crim. No. 65-L-103. NARA-SWA: RG 21, S.D. Tex., Laredo Criminal Docket, 1964–66, box 716.

35. U.S.C. § 751 (the "escape act").

36. *United States v. De Leyna,* Crim. No. 65-L-104. The earlier conviction is in 65-L-12. Both: NARA-SWA: RG 21, S.D. Tex., Laredo Criminal Docket, 1964–66, box 716.

37. Under statute 8 U.S.C. § 1325; *United States v. Gonzales,* Crim. No. 69-L-484, NARA-SWA: RG 21, S.D. Tex., Laredo Criminal Docket, June–August 1969, box 795. Judge Connally presided over many day-long docket calls in 1969 that seemed to feature this marvel of efficient administration. Given the number of defendants involved in the system, it is unlikely

that the organization of the Southern District of Texas was as finely tuned as the dates indicate, and it is difficult to determine three decades after the fact whether they are accurate representations. There are instances during this period of docket calls occurring one or two days after indictments, which is plausible. It is likely that administrators prepared the documents nearly simultaneously. The details aside, it is clear that the assembly line had been accelerated since 1965, when a month had passed between indictment and arraignment.

38. Under statute 8 U.S.C. § 1326; *United States v. Hernandez-Vasquez*, Crim. No. 69-L-508, NARA-SWA: RG 21, S.D. Tex., Laredo Criminal Docket, June–August 1969, box 795.

39. Under statute 18 U.S.C. § 911; *United States v. Palomo*, Crim. No. 69-L-512. Ibid.

40. Under statute 18 U.S.C. § 1546; *United States v. Campos*, Crim. No. 69-L-518. Ibid.

41. *United States v. Flores*, Crim. No. 69-L-523. Ibid.

42. Under statute 8 U.S.C. § 1324 (a)(2); *United States v. De La Cruz*, Crim. No. 69-L-529. Ibid. For similar facts and disposition, *United States v. Juan Donato Saucedo Ramirez*, Crim. No. 69-L-530. Ibid.

43. Under statute 8 U.S.C. § 1325; *United States v. Adenas*, Crim. No. 69-L-531. NARA-SWA: RG 21, S.D. Tex., Laredo Criminal Docket, June–August 1969, box 796.

44. *United States v. Barrera*, Crim. No. 69-L-575. NARA-SWA: RG 21, S.D. Tex., Laredo Criminal Docket, June–August 1969, box 796; *United States v. Villagomez*, Crim. No. 69-L-598, NARA-SWA: RG 21, S.D. Tex., Laredo Criminal Docket, June–August 1969, box 797.

45. Under statute 8 U.S.C. § 1326; *United States v. Davila*, Crim. No. 69-L-599. NARA-SWA: RG 21, S.D. Tex., Laredo Criminal Docket, June–August 1969, box 797.

46. *United States v. Flores*, Crim. No. 69-L-600. Ibid.

47. *United States v. Garcia*, Crim. No. 69-L-601. Ibid.

48. *United States v. Manzanares*, Crim. No. 69-L-604. Ibid.

49. *United States v. Hurtado*, Crim. No. 69-L-602; *United States v. Lopez*, Crim. No. 69-L-603. Both Ibid.

50. Chief Judge Garza to "My Dear General Kirks," n.d., clerk's files of Chief Judge Reynaldo G. Garza, folder 1. More than thirty years later, Judge Garza was still proud of the efficiency of this innovation. See oral history interview with Reynaldo G. Garza by Steven H. Wilson, 30 March 1998. Fisch, *All Rise*, 94–95. Garza has received some criticism for his complicity in these mass hearings in a book review of Fisch's biography, which also does double duty as a fictionalized musing on race and politics. But the author of the review, a prominent critical legal studies scholar and a law professor at UT, concluded that "Judge Garza's legal training did not equip him with a theory for understanding [the undocumented aliens'] predicament in any other terms," and "[i]t would have taken a judicial genius to pioneer a new approach, especially back then." Delgado, "Rodrigo's Fifteenth Chronicle," 1192.

51. U.S.C. § 482. See also 19 U.S.C. § 1581.

52. The Fourth Amendment states: "The right of the people to be secure in their persons, houses, papers, and effects, against unreasonable searches and seizures, shall not be violated, and no Warrants shall issue, but upon probable cause, supported by oath or affirmation, and particularly describing the place to be searched, and the persons or things to be seized." Waples, "From Bags to Body Cavities," 56. For constitutional status of border searches prior to the beginning of the war on drugs, see "Note, Search and Seizure at the Border—The Border Search," *Rutgers Law Review* 21 (1967).

53. *Terry v. Ohio*, 392 U.S. 1 (1968), 19. See also *Carroll v. United States*, 267 U.S. 132 (1925).

54. The federal lawmakers allowed another early exception. Congress passed an act that authorized the warrantless entry and inspection of distilleries and liquor warehouses, if they

were federally licensed or subject to federal taxation. Act of 3 March 1791, ch. 15, § 24, 1 Stat. 199. See also Act of 18 February 1793, ch. 8, § 27, 1 Stat. 305, 315; and Act of 2 March 1799, ch. 22, §§ 68–71, 1 Stat. 627, 677–78. The current statute allowing the "border search" exception is derived from a Reconstruction-era law that made the Customs Bureau part of the Treasury Department (Act of 18 July 1866, 14 Stat. 178). However, judges ordinarily defer to an enabling clause of the statute, under which the customs statutes are to be given the broadest possible scope. See 19 U.S.C. §§ 1581–1582. The courts have held that border searches "are not limited to searches at an international boundary though they must have a relation to it." Ittig, "Rites of Passage," 329. Also Sims, "Recent Developments," 1647.

55. Act of 31 July 1789, ch. 5, §. 24, 1 Stat. 29. Congress repealed the original statute in 1790, but replaced it with a similar law (Act of 4 August 1790, ch. 35, §§ 48–51, 1 Stat. 145, 170). When subsequent Congresses revised the statutes, they preserved collectors' unique authority to conduct border searches. See Yale, "Beyond the Border," 739–52.

56. For example, the 1789 statute provided that "if [officers] shall have cause to suspect a concealment thereof, in any particular dwelling-house, store, building, or other place, they or either of them shall, upon application on oath or affirmation to any justice of the peace, be entitled to a warrant to enter such house, store, or other place (in the day time only) and there to search for such goods, and if any shall be found, to seize and secure the same for trial." Act of 31 July 1789, ch. 5, § 24, 1 Stat. 29.

57. *Weeks v. United States*, 232 U.S. 383 (1914). Yet, law professor Akhil Amar has argued that a "reasonable" search does not necessarily require a warrant. Amar, *Constitution and Criminal Procedure*, 4–6. State judges were not bound by the requirements of the Fourth Amendment. However, in general they were bound by state constitutions and bills of rights. Nineteenth-century state legislators often regulated search warrants by statute. Dinan, *Keeping the People's Liberties*, 53.

58. Ch. 1, 38 Stat. 785. For the genesis of the Harrison Act, see Musto, *The American Disease*, 59–65. The Harrison Act was only the first act in a long, ongoing drama; the federal government began to regulate, tax, and prohibit an ever-growing list of narcotics and "dangerous drugs." Walker, *Drug Control*, 29–30.

59. Pub. L. No. 66–66, 41 Stat. 305. Congress passed the Volstead Act over President Woodrow Wilson's veto, and the act took effect in 1920. See U.S. Constitution, amend. XVIII.

60. *Carroll v. United States*, 267 U.S. 132 (1925), 147, 153.

61. For an analysis of the *Carroll* decision and its role in prohibition enforcement, see Murchison, *Federal Criminal Law Doctrines*, 52–59.

62. Walker, *Drug Control*, 192.

63. The Narcotic Drugs Import and Export Act of 1922 added cocaine to the list of prohibited drugs. Ch. 202, 42 Stat. 596 (1922). For Anslinger's role in the development of federal narcotics law enforcement, see Kinder and Walker, "Stable Force," 908; Walker, *Drug Control*, 99–117; Musto, *The American Disease*, 210–29; and Morgan, "Public Problem," 246–48.

64. *United States v. Lane*, Crim. No. 65-L-106. NARA-SWA: RG 21, S.D. Tex., Laredo Criminal Docket, 1964–66, box 716. *United States v. Galaviz*, Crim. No. 69-L-772. NARA-SWA: RG 21, S.D. Tex., Laredo Criminal Docket, September–December 1969, box 802. Federal narcotics experts estimated that one brick, which often came wrapped in "characteristic" Mexican paper (usually this meant a newspaper from a marijuana-rich province) provided enough marijuana to make approximately 3,300 cigarettes. Federal Bureau of Narcotics, *Report on the Traffic in Opium and Other Dangerous Drugs* (Washington, D.C.: U.S. Government Printing Office, 1966), 17.

65. The relevant portions of the Narcotic Drugs Import and Export Act (70 Stat. 570), 21 U.S.C. § 176(a) stated: "Notwithstanding any other provision of law, whoever, knowingly, with intent to defraud the United States, imports or brings into the United States marijuana contrary to law, or smuggles or clandestinely introduces into the United States marijuana which should have been invoiced, or receives, conceals, buys, sells, or in any manner facilitates the transportation, concealment, or sale of such marijuana after being imported or brought in, knowing the same to have been imported or brought into the United States contrary to law, or whoever conspires to do any of the foregoing acts, shall be imprisoned."

66. Also under: 21 U.S.C. § 176(a).

67. The relevant part of the Marijuana Tax Act (26 U.S.C. § 4741 et seq.) is § 4744(a), which provided: "It shall be unlawful for any person who is a transferee required to pay the transfer tax imposed by § 4741 (a): (1) to acquire or otherwise obtain any marijuana without having paid such tax, or (2) to transport or conceal, or in any manner facilitate the transportation or concealment of, any marijuana so acquired or obtained."

68. See 26 U.S.C. § 7237.

69. The Marijuana Tax Act of 1937 (26 U.S.C. § 2593[a]) was the predecessor statute of the 1960s-vintage "tax count." It had been originally targeted at Mexican immigrants, who were generally associated with marijuana use. Marion, *Federal Crime Control Initiatives,* 24. According to the interpretation of the Supreme Court, the legislative history indicated that the act was intended "merely to impose a very high tax on transfers to nonregistrants and not to prohibit such transfers entirely." See *Leary v. United States,* 395 U.S. 6 (1969), at 22–25.

70. The statute proscribing importation and transportation and concealment of heroin was also a part of the Narcotic Drugs Import and Export Act (21 U.S.C. § 174). This was subsequently repealed and its substance recodified (at 21 U.S.C. § 801 et seq.) by the "Controlled Substances Act" of 27 October 1970 (Pub. L. No. 91–513, 84 Stat. 1242). Purchase "not in or from the original stamped package" was prohibited to distinguish narcotics smuggling from the legal importation of legitimate medical narcotics derived from opium, such as morphine.

71. As late as 1963, President Kennedy's Advisory Commission on Narcotic and Drug Abuse described this drug, the original illicit cash crop to come through Texas from Mexico, as relatively harmless. The report suggested, for example, that the lack of addiction associated with marijuana made it less harmful than opiates. Himmelstein, *Strange Career of Marihuana,* 90–91. Unlike Himmelstein, I have adopted the spelling "marijuana." The spelling "marihuana" seems to have predominated in the official literature during the 1960s. My preference will necessitate changing spelling in some quotes, especially statutes, but I will not burden the reader further with intrusive notices to this effect.

72. The prosecution's management machine worked less well when the defendant faced charges that resulted from a vehicle search conducted by the Border Patrol, because there was less room for maneuver. Federal prosecutors charged these defendants under statutes that proscribed unlawful importation of marijuana (18 U.S.C. §§ 952 and 960[a][1]), but there was no tax count associated. The pungent odor of marijuana often led to its discovery during these types of searches. In these cases, as we will see, the defendants often moved to suppress the evidence, and when that strategy failed, they usually requested a bench trial rather than a jury trial. The odor of marijuana was ordinarily sufficient to establish probable cause for a search of the vehicle. See *United States v. Perez,* 364 F.Supp. 1217 (S.D. Tex., 1972), 1218 [Corpus Christi Division; Crim. No. 72-C-31]; *United States v. Wright,* 476 F.2d 1027 (5th Cir., 1973), cert. denied, 414 U.S. 821 (1973); and *United States v. Alderete,* 546 F.2d 68 (5th Cir.,

1977). Later, judges determined that a discernible odor of freshly applied air freshener (which marijuana smugglers learned to apply to cover the odor) might also establish probable cause to search a vehicle. *United States v. Reyna*, 546 F.2d 103 (5th Cir., 1977).

73. *United States v. Rodriguez* (S.D. Tex., 1956; Houston Division, Crim. No. 12772).

74. *United States v. Rodriguez*, 195 F.Supp. 513 (S.D. Tex., 1960; Laredo; Crim. No. 17857), 514.

75. The narcotics violator registration statute provided, in relevant part: "(a) . . . no citizen of the United States . . . who has been convicted of a violation of any of the narcotics or marihuana laws of the United States, . . . the penalty for which is imprisonment for more than one year, shall depart from or enter into or attempt to depart from or enter into the United States, unless such person registers, under such rules and regulations as may be prescribed by the Secretary of the Treasury with a Customs official, agent, or employee at a point of entry or a border Customs station . . . (b) Whoever violates any of the provisions of this section shall be punished for each such violation by a fine of not more than $1000 or imprisonment for not less than three years, or both." (18 U.S.C. § 1407). For questions and critical analysis of registration statutes, see Suiter, "Self-Incrimination and Registration Statutes," 507.

76. Rodriguez spent the night in jail, and was arraigned before a municipal judge the next afternoon. The United States Commissioner in Laredo was unavailable for the arraignment. *United States v. Rodriguez*, 195 F.Supp. 513, 514–15. Some legal scholars questioned the use of registration statutes as justifications of other investigation. See Suiter, "Self-Incrimination and Registration Statutes," 507.

77. Ibid., 516. In 1960, before the Warren Court's "due process revolution," the admissibility of confessions was controlled by the "McNabb-Mallory" rule, which was named for two cases: *McNabb v. United States*, 318 U.S. 332 (1943), and *Mallory v. United States*, 354 U.S. 449 (1957). Under the "McNabb-Mallory" rule, law enforcement officials had no positive duty to inform suspects of their rights against self-incrimination, but a judge could scrutinize the "voluntariness" of an admission offered in police custody with an eye to the "totality of the circumstances," and might suppress evidence if it was obtained through intimidation or coercion. The rules for "voluntary" admission became problematic after the Supreme Court's decision in *Miranda*.

78. *United States v. Rodriguez*, 195 F.Supp. 513, 515–16.

79. Ibid., 516.

80. *Rodriguez v. United States*, 292 F.2d 709 (5th Cir., 1961).

81. During the 1960s the revolution in police procedure respecting the civil rights of the criminally accused occurred in parallel with the race-oriented civil rights revolution, and it usually advanced by the same means, through civil litigation. Like school desegregation and other civil rights cases, Chief Justice Warren is credited with (or, alternatively, excoriated for) fostering the criminal rights revolution symbolized by such landmarks as *Mapp v. Ohio*, 367 U.S. 643 (1961), concerning the exclusionary rule; *Gideon v. Wainwright*, 372 U.S. 335 (1963), affirming the right of the indigent to counsel in a criminal case; *Escobedo v. Illinois*, 378 U.S. 438 (1964), establishing the right to have counsel present during police questioning; and *Miranda v. Arizona*, 384 U.S. 436 (1966), confirming the right to have counsel and the right to withhold testimony that may self-incriminate. Friedman, *Crime and Punishment*, 300–304. In the years since what some believe was the "failure" of the revolution, critics have complained that the Supreme Court draws exceptions less carefully than it should. According to one accounting, as of 1985, the court had enumerated twenty-six exceptions to

the Fourth Amendment. Bradley, *Criminal Procedure Revolution,* 165–66. The list of legitimate warrantless searches includes inventory searches, searches incident to arrest (including "frisking" a suspect), "plain-view" searches, "hot-pursuit" searches, and "consent" searches. Mabry, "*United States v. Ross,*" 1245.

82. U.S. 83 enters Texas in the northern Panhandle region, adjacent to neighboring Oklahoma, and runs generally north–south, approximately bisecting Texas until the highway reaches the U.S.-Mexico border at Laredo. From Laredo the highway runs generally east–west along the border and the Rio Grande River for some two hundred miles, until the road terminates near the Gulf of Mexico at Brownsville, Texas. The Falcon Heights area is sparsely populated. Judge Connally noted that the region contained "large ranches and few persons," "the towns—and even habitations—are few and far apart," and while there, "a visitor hears Spanish spoken as often as English." *United States v. Brett* (Laredo Division; Crim. No. 65-L-275), 290 F.Supp. 929 (S.D. Tex., 1966), 931.

83. Agents "patted down" Brett; he was not carrying a weapon at the time, but investigators later found a pistol in the car. *United States v. Brett,* 290 F.Supp. 929, 931–32.

84. Ibid., 932.

85. Ibid. However, he believed the evidence did not support convictions on all three counts. The judge decided that circumstances indicated that "in all probability" the defendants purchased the heroin on the American side of the border, and he acquitted Brett and Cruz of the charge of importing it. But he found both to be guilty, "as undoubtedly they are," of the remaining charges of transporting and concealing narcotics, and purchasing them out of the original package. *United States v. Brett,* 290 F.Supp. 929, 933–34. The defendants appealed; on 8 May 1967 the Fifth Circuit affirmed Connally's judgment. *Brett v. United States,* 377 F.2d 520 (5th Cir., 1967).

86. Ibid., 932. Again, Connally refers to the power of customs officers to search a vehicle if there is "reasonable cause" to suspect there is merchandise that was imported contrary to law (19 U.S.C. § 482).

87. *United States v. Brett,* 290 F.Supp. 929, 933. Taking the "reasonable cause" quote from the long-standing legal precedent in *Carroll v. United States,* 267 U.S. 132, 158.

88. *United States v. Brett,* 290 F.Supp. 929, 933–34.

89. U.S.C. § 4737(a).

90. *United States v. Isquierdo et al.,* Crim. No. 65-C-45. NARA-SWA: RG 21, S.D. Tex., Corpus Christi Criminal Docket, 1964–69, box 272. See also 69-B-124.

91. *United States v. Mack et al.,* Crim. No. 65-L-277. NARA-SWA: RG 21, S.D. Tex., Laredo Criminal Docket, 1964–66, box 722.

92. *United States v. Hayes,* Crim. No. 65-L-274. NARA-SWA: RG 21, S.D. Tex., Laredo Criminal Docket, 1964–66, box 722.

93. Emphasis in original; see Matusow, *The Unraveling of America,* 290–91 (Matusow credits Leary for the statement but does not quote Leary directly and includes no citation).

94. Testimony of Timothy Leary, *United States v. Leary,* transcript, pt. 1, § 2, p. 254. NARA-SWA: RG 21, Laredo Criminal Docket, 1964–66, box 725, "Appeal" folder.

95. "LSD" is the abbreviation for lysergic acid diethylamide, a powerful hallucinogen similar to that found in ergot (a type of cereal-grain fungus), psilocybin is the synthesized version of the active compound in the "sacred mushroom," and mescaline is derived from peyote cactus. Leary's instant enthusiasm appears to have been a common response to a psychedelic drug experience. LSD first gained prominence in the 1950s among a well-

respected, well-educated elite of medical researchers and their close friends. Gray, "Religious Freedom Act Amendments," 795–96.

96. The judges of the U.S. Court of Appeals for the Fifth Circuit, basing their summary on Leary's own trial testimony, given in 1966, agreed that he possessed "an impressive academic background." Leary was born in 1920, briefly attended West Point and the University of Alabama (he was ejected from both), and then received a Ph.D. in clinical psychology from the University of California in 1950. During his eight years at the Kaiser Clinic, Leary received and administered nearly five hundred thousand dollars in federal grants to support his research on mental illness. From 1953 to 1956, he served on the University of California medical faculty. *Leary v. United States,* 383 F.2d 851 (1967), 856–57.

97. *Leary v. United States,* 383 F.2d 851 (1967), 857.

98. For Leary's own assessment of his academic career, his work at Harvard, and, finally, events surrounding his dismissal, see Leary, *Flashbacks,* 187–98, and generally (caution: the events depicted are not arranged chronologically, and the book is not indexed; however, a selected bibliography is included as the frontispiece). For examples of the variety of topics that captured Leary's interest before and after the Harvard years, see Leary, *Changing My Mind.*

99. Leary argued later that there must have been a conspiracy to search his vehicle, that he had been set up for an arrest because of his notoriety. This is vain nonsense; under the "border search" doctrine, the customs officers needed no reason at all.

100. This summary is reconstructed from testimony, judicial findings, and various court documents from the trial in the U.S. District Court for the Southern District of Texas: *United States v. Leary et al.,* Crim. No. 66-L-37. NARA-SWA: RG 21, S.D. Tex., Laredo Criminal Docket, 1964–66, boxes 724–25.

101. Testimony of Herbert O. Best, *United States v. Leary,* transcript, pt. 1, § 1, p. 74. NARA-SWA: RG 21, Laredo Criminal Docket, 1964–66, box 725, "Appeal" folder.

102. Testimony of Helen M. Loftis, *United States v. Leary,* transcript, pt. 1, § 1, p. 109. NARA-SWA: RG 21, Laredo Criminal Docket, 1964–66, box 725, "Appeal" folder.

103. Testimony of Timothy Leary, *United States v. Leary,* transcript, pt. 1, § 2, pp. 323–27. NARA-SWA: RG 21, Laredo Criminal Docket, 1964–66, box 725, "Appeal" folder. Also Leary, *Flashbacks,* 236.

104. Testimony of Rey L. Hatch, *United States v. Leary,* transcript, pt. 1, § 1, p. 136. NARA-SWA: RG 21, Laredo Criminal Docket, 1964–66, box 725, "Appeal" folder.

105. Testimony of Rey L. Hatch, *United States v. Leary,* transcript, pt. 1, § 2, p. 149. NARA-SWA: RG 21, Laredo Criminal Docket, 1964–66, box 725, "Appeal" folder.

106. Testimony of Rey L. Hatch, *United States v. Leary,* transcript, pt. 1, § 1, p. 137. NARA-SWA: RG 21, Laredo Criminal Docket, 1964–66, box 725, "Appeal" folder.

107. Leary realized that his U-turn changed his life. He recounts the arrest in the chapter "Busted at Laredo" and also devotes many pages to the legal repercussions. Leary, *Flashbacks,* 232–43.

108. Record of proceedings, *United States v. Leary,* transcript, pt. 1, § 1, p. 3. NARA-SWA: RG 21, Laredo Criminal Docket, 1964–66, box 725, "Appeal" folder. In addition to materials available in court documents, Leary recounts the arrest and the legal advice he received in: Leary, *Flashbacks,* 234–39.

109. Leary, *Flashbacks,* 241. Also, Testimony of Timothy Leary, *United States v. Leary,* transcript, pt. 1, § 2, pp. 298–99. NARA-SWA: RG 21, Laredo Criminal Docket, 1964–66, box 725, "Appeal" folder.

110. Leary, *Flashbacks*, 237–38. In fact, at fifty-six years of age, Judge Connally, who was born on 28 December 1909, was only eleven years senior to Leary.

111. Testimony of Timothy Leary, *United States v. Leary*, transcript, pt. 1, § 2, p. 272. NARA-SWA: RG 21, Laredo Criminal Docket, 1964–66, box 725, "Appeal" folder.

112. During Testimony of Timothy Leary, *United States v. Leary*, transcript, pt. 2, § 1, pp. 346–47. NARA-SWA: RG 21, Laredo Criminal Docket, 1964–66, box 725, "Appeal" folder.

113. Under the federal Youth Corrections Act, 18 U.S.C. § 5010(a).

114. *Leary v. United States*, 383 F.2d 851 (5th Cir., 1967), and *Leary v. United States*, 392 F.2d 220 (1968). Susan Leary was tried at the same time as her father, but she waived trial by jury and accepted Connally's judgment in a bench trial. Connally found her guilty on the tax count and not guilty on the narcotics-smuggling counts. He suspended imposition of sentence and placed her on unsupervised probation while she was a minor, under the federal Youth Corrections Act, 18 U.S.C. § 5010(a). She then moved to dismiss her appeal. Record of proceedings, *United States v. Leary*, transcript, pt. 1, § 1, pp. 4–5. NARA-SWA: RG 21, Laredo Criminal Docket, 1964–66, box 725, "Appeal" folder.

115. *Leary v. United States*, 383 F.2d 851 (5th Cir., 1967), and *Leary v. United States*, 392 F.2d 220 (1968). Record of proceedings, *United States v. Leary*, transcript, pt. 1, § 1, pp. 4–5. NARA-SWA: RG 21, Laredo Criminal Docket, 1964–66, box 725, "Appeal" folder.

116. In a chapter chronicling the "Rise and Fall of the Counterculture," Matusow writes that Leary lost credibility with the "heads" (members of the drug culture) when he went "Hollywood" during these years after the arrest, and few of the younger generation were old enough to remember that he "had ever been a serious man." Leary might have agreed with Matusow's judgment, rendered in Matusow's account of America's "unraveling," that "[f]ew lines of the sixties wore so badly" as Leary's famous rallying cry to American youth that they "turn on, tune in, drop out," which inevitably is invoked in nostalgic, journalistic, or scholarly accounts of the "summer of love." Matusow, *The Unraveling of America*, 291. In his memoirs, however, Leary claimed to be flattered when the phrase was co-opted in a soft-drink advertising campaign. Leary, *Flashbacks*, 253. For additional illustrations how the "turn on" line is used to invoke Leary's contributions to the era, see Gitlin, *The Sixties*, 206–7.

117. Chief Judge Connally to V. Bailey Thomas [clerk], 10 January 1967, clerk's files of Chief Judge Ben C. Connally, folder 2. Also Chief Judge Connally, Judicial Work Assignments, memorandum, 22 December 1967, clerk's files of Chief Judge Ben C. Connally, folder 2.

118. Jonnes, *Hep-Cats, Narcs, and Pipe Dreams*, 255–70; Sharp, *Dilemma of Drug Policy*, 20–27.

119. Under the Drug Abuse and Control Amendments of 1965 (Pub. L. No. 89–74, 79 Stat. 226; 21 U.S.C. § 360[a], "Food and Drugs").

120. "Special Message to the Congress on Crime and Law Enforcement: 'To Insure Public Safety,' 7 February 1968," and "Special Message to the Congress Transmitting Reorganization Plan I of 1968 Relating to Narcotics and Drug Abuse Control, 7 February 1968," both in *Public Papers of the Presidents of the United States* (Washington, D.C.: National Archives, 1970), Lyndon B. Johnson, 1968, at 190, 197–98. Johnson noted that his reorganization plan "moves in the direction" of earlier "distinguished groups," such as the 1949 Hoover Commission and the 1963 Presidential Advisory Commission on Narcotics and Drug Abuse. Johnson's "Reorganization Plan No. 1 of 1968" became effective 8 April 1968; see 3 C.F.R. Comp., 1968, 149. Presidents had often expressed their interest in crime through expert commissions, blue-

ribbon panels, or grant subsidies to state and local law enforcement agencies. See Gordon and Morris, "Presidential Commissions," 122–29.

121. See 28 U.S.C. § 509, "Functions of the Attorney General." Brickey, "Criminal Mischief," 1149 n. 109; generally, Rachal, *Federal Narcotics Enforcement.*

122. Friedman, *Crime and Punishment*, 274. For Nixon's 1968 strategy, see Matusow, *The Unraveling of America*, 427–29.

123. "Special Message to Congress on Control of Narcotics and Dangerous Drugs, 14 July 1969," *Public Papers of the Presidents*, Richard Nixon, 1969, at 514.

124. G. Gordon Liddy was a key member of the "Special Presidential Task Force" that conceived and planned Operation Intercept in 1969. But his activities in subsequent posts, first as one of the White House "plumbers" and then as one of Nixon's domestic operatives in the 1972 reelection campaign, made Liddy one of the most notorious figures in the Watergate scandal. Liddy, *Will*, 201–13, 251–338.

125. Juan de Onis, "Drug Watch on Mexico Adding to Latin Disillusion with Nixon," *New York Times*, 8 October 1969, p. 17. Pike, *FDR's Good Neighbor Policy.*

126. Liddy, *Will*, 185–86. See also Barry, Browne, and Sims, *The Great Divide*, 59–60.

127. See "Remarks at a Bipartisan Leadership Meeting on Narcotics and Dangerous Drugs, 23 October 1969," in *Public Papers of the Presidents*, Richard Nixon, 1969, at 831.

128. Ibid., p. 838.

129. Walker, *Drug Control*, 192; and Vallance, *Prohibition's Second Failure*, 66–67.

130. "Remarks at a Bipartisan Leadership Meeting on Narcotics and Dangerous Drugs, 23 October 1969," in *Public Papers of the Presidents*, Richard Nixon, 1969, at 831. Nixon was unhappy with the domestic performance of BNDD, and in 1972 he established a White House–based Office of Drug Abuse to concentrate on urban drug problems. BNDD was still focused on international trafficking. Walker, *Drug Control*, 191–92. In 1973 Nixon issued Reorganization Plan No. 2, which called for BNDD and the Office of Drug Abuse to merge and form the Drug Enforcement Agency (DEA) (5 U.S.C. § 906 [App. II]; also 28 U.S.C. § 509 [note]). See *U.S. Code Cong. & Admin. News*, 28 March 1973, p. 912. Congress established the DEA to be the principal federal agency concerned with narcotics interdiction, but its agents coordinated with other law enforcement personnel such as customs agents and Border Patrol officers. Brickey, "Criminal Mischief," 1149.

131. *United States v. Bright et al.*, Crim. No. 69-L-658. NARA-SWA: RG 21, S.D. Tex., Laredo Criminal Docket, September–December 1969, box 799.

132. *United States v. Walters et al.*, Crim. No. 69-L-659. Ibid.

133. *United States v. Galaviz*, Crim. No. 69-L-772. NARA-SWA: RG 21, S.D. Tex., Laredo Criminal Docket, September–December 1969, box 802.

134. *United States v. Hunter et al.*, Crim. No. 69-L-820. NARA-SWA: RG 21, S.D. Tex., Laredo Criminal Docket, September–December 1969, box 804.

135. During this period Leary issued his "new commandments for the Nuclear Age," which included: (1) "Thou Shalt Not Alter the Consciousness of Thy Fellow Man"; and (2) "Thou Shalt Not Prevent Thy Fellow Man from Altering His Own Consciousness." See Leary, "Meaning of Marijuana," 130, 139.

136. *Leary v. United States*, 395 U.S. 6 (1969).

137. *Leary v. United States*, 431 F.2d 85 (5th Cir., 1970).

138. Leary was a fugitive for several years during the early seventies but was eventually arrested and extradited to the United States. Leary, *Flashbacks*, 287–310. See Chepesiuk, *Sixties Radicals*, 149.

139. *Leary v. United States,* 544 F.2d 1266 (1977).

140. *Leary v. United States,* 544 F.2d 1266 (5th Cir., 1977).

141. Leary, *Flashbacks,* 242–43.

142. Ibid., 239.

143. For example, *Miranda v. Arizona,* 384 U.S. 436 (1966), which established, among others, the right to remain silent and to have counsel present during interrogation. See Baker, *Miranda;* and Amar, *Constitution and Criminal Procedure.*

144. *Byers v. United States,* Civ. A. 69-L-16 (opinion: 3 September 1969; affirmed 24 August 1971, 5th Circuit No. 71–2560); *Rubenstein v. United States,* Civ. A. No. 69-L-17 (opinion: 3 September 1969); *Lewis v. United States,* Civ. A. 69-L-18 (opinion: 26 August 1969; affirmed 24 August 1971, 5th Circuit No. 71–2558); *Ramirez v. United States,* Civ. A. 69-L-19 (opinion: 1 July 1969); *Downey v. United States,* Civ. A. 69-L-20 (opinion: 1 July 1969). NARA-SWA: RG 21, S.D. Tex., Laredo Civil Docket, 1969, box 82. Also, the Fifth Circuit ruled that the Leary decision was not prospective. See *United States v. Scardino,* 14 August 1969, 5th Circuit No. 27171, 414 F.2d 925 (5th Cir., 1969).

145. *Moore v. United States,* Civ. A. 69-L-22 (opinion: 10 September 1969); the same bargain on a three-count indictment was upheld, on 20 February 1969: *McClain v. United States,* Civ. A. 69-L-24 (opinion: 3 December 1969); indicted 22 November 1967 (Crim. No. 67-L-365), same deal on three-count for seven pounds, on 8 March 1968: *Patterson v. United States,* Civ. A. 69-L-25 (opinion: 3 December 1969); "making the now familiar contention—which has been decided adversely . . . by the Court of Appeals" (p. 2). NARA-SWA: RG 21, S.D. Tex., Laredo Civil Docket, 1969, box 82.

146. Leary, *High Priest.* See the chapter on Leary entitled "From High Priest of LSD to High-Tech Guru," in Chepesiuk, *Sixties Radicals,* 147. Leary wrote a succession of memoirs intended to burnish this image and to ensure that his tribulations secured his residence in the pantheon of countercultural pioneers. His efforts at self-justification largely succeeded. For example, two investigators who "revisited" the decade returned convinced that Leary could be ranked among the "seven who created the sixties counterculture that changed America." Whitmer, with Wyngarden, *Aquarius Revisited,* 13–46. The authors of *Aquarius Revisited* also include such literary figures as William S. Burroughs, Allen Ginsberg, Ken Kesey, Norman Mailer, Tom Robbins, and Hunter S. Thompson, but the book begins with Leary (acknowledgments and 8–12). Another author included Leary on a longer list, of eighteen influential "radicals" who "shaped the era." Chepesiuk, *Sixties Radicals,* 147–57. Chepesiuk also accorded this distinction to the MIT linguistics professor and longtime political gadfly Noam Chomsky (133–46). Leary died of prostate cancer in 1996, and his cremated remains were launched into orbit in April 1997, along with those of Gene Roddenberry (creator of the 1960s television series *Star Trek*), and twenty-two other space enthusiasts. "LSD Guru Takes Trip of His Dreams," *Herald* (Glasgow), 12 May 1994, p. A2.

147. The federal interest in crime and its roots primarily was manifested through studies and subsidies for state and local law enforcement agencies. Gordon and Morris, "Presidential Commissions," 122–29.

148. Under the Dyer Act, 18 U.S.C. § 2312.

149. Under 8 U.S.C. § 1326.

150. Under various statutes; defendants indicted under the Comprehensive Drug Abuse Prevention and Control Act of 1970, which became effective 1 May 1971, would not yet appear in this data.

151. Musto, *The American Disease,* 247–57. For the National Commission on Reform of

Federal Criminal Laws, see Pub. L. No. 89–801; also see U.S. Senate, Committee on the Judiciary, *Reform of the Federal Criminal Laws*, pt. 1, p. 40. "The President's News Conference, 24 March 1972," *Public Papers of the Presidents*, Richard Nixon, 1972, at 495. The conflicts indicated that, briefly in the early 1970s, a "policy window opened" for researchers and lobbyists who argued that the federal government should relax the prohibition on marijuana. DiChiara and Galliher, "Dissonance and Contradiction," 47–48, 62.

152. The new statute passed in October 1970, and became effective on 1 May 1971. The Comprehensive Drug Abuse Prevention and Control Act of 1970, Pub. L. No. 91–513, 84 Stat. 1236 (codified, as amended, at 21 U.S.C. §§ 801–971).

153. Regarding heroin, this meant repealing proscriptions against unlawful importation, unlawful transportation and concealment, and unlawful purchase of narcotics "not in or from the original stamped package" (21 U.S.C. § 174).

154. Also Pub. L. No. 91–513, as for the Comprehensive Act, but the Controlled Substances Act was 84 Stat. 1242 (27 October 1970); see 21 U.S.C. 812 (1988).

155. The Controlled Substances Act provided, in part: "(a) Except as authorized by this subchapter, it shall be unlawful for any person knowingly or intentionally—(1) to manufacture, distribute, or dispense, or possess with intent to manufacture, distribute, or dispense, a controlled substance" (21 U.S.C. § 841[a][1]).

156. Leary, *Flashbacks*, 265. Leary's assessment of the era's amateurish smuggling accords with the results of contemporary analysis of Houston's marijuana suppliers. Two researchers determined that many marijuana importers were young people whose first and perhaps sole crime, if it was not reported, entailed a road trip to Mexico. Sayer and Rotenberg, "Houston High Schools," 760.

157. Grinspoon, *Marihuana Reconsidered*, 359–60. Another factor which increased the participation of organized crime in large-volume marijuana smuggling was the concurrent boom in the American demand for Mexican heroin. John Moore and Reed Holland, "The Laredo–San Antonio Heroin Wars," *Texas Monthly*, August 1973, 46–51; Moore and Holland, "Carrasco Revisited," *Texas Monthly*, September 1973, 41–42; and David Harris, "The Dark and Violent World of the Mexican Connection," *New York Times Magazine*, 18 December 1977. Also see Walker, *Drug Control*, 193. Mexico had long been a minor source of heroin, but it became America's largest source during the 1970s, as federal narcotics agents steadily closed off other sources and routes. See Zeese, "Drug War Forever?" 252. These efforts included the successful campaign to break the fabled "French Connection," which for many years channeled Turkish heroin into the United States, primarily into the port of New York, from Corsica and Marseilles. For a description of the origin and end of the "French Connection," see Walker, *Drug Control*, 191–192; also President's Commission on Organized Crime, *America's Habit*, 105–32. By 1973 the DEA noticed that Mexican "brown" heroin had replaced Turkish heroin in major American cities. U.S. Department of Justice, Drug Enforcement Administration, *Fact Sheet* (1978), 3; Ruiz-Cabañas, "Illicit Drug Supply Role," 44, 53.

158. "Nixon Condemns 'Permissive' Judges: President Says Leniency Harms Drive on Drugs," *New York Times*, 23 September 1972, pp. 1, 14. For Nixon's contributions to the federal "war on drugs," see Bertram et al., *Drug War Politics*.

159. "Remarks to Customs Agents and Inspectors after a Tour of the Laredo Customs Facility, 22 September 1972," in *Public Papers of the Presidents*, Richard Nixon, 1972, at 886.

160. "Statement about Drug Abuse Law Enforcement, 22 September 1972," in *Public Papers of the Presidents*, Richard Nixon, 1972, at 887–88.

161. Simon, *In His Own Image*.

162. Circuit Judge Ingraham was sixty-six years old when appointed, and he took senior status when he became eligible to do so, at age seventy, in 1973. Couch, *History of the Fifth Circuit,* 148, 161.

163. "Bue," *Judges of the United States.*

164. But Brown, who was by 1970 the chief judge of the Fifth Circuit, had traveled in those circles and probably thought Bue would make the perfect federal judge. See Speech by Judge Brown, printed in the Proceedings of the Presentation of the Portrait of Hon. Carl Olaf Bue Jr., 28 August 1987, included in 680 F.Supp. (1987), at 77. In 1977, Bue was awarded the Texas Municipal Courts Association's Chief Justice Joe R. Greenhill Award, as the "Outstanding Jurist contributing to the judicial process in Texas." Bue was a member of the Houston, Federal, and American Bar Associations, the Maritime Law Association, the American Judicature Society, the English Speaking Union, the Houston Philosophical Society, and several honor societies. "Bue," *Judges of the United States.*

165. Mark Obbie, "The Judges," *Houston Post,* 5 January 1986, D.

166. Transcript of the proceedings of Bue's swearing in (no title), p. 24. This document is held by the Houston Metropolitan Research Center, in the HMRC's collection of the papers of Carl O. Bue Jr. In addition to the district judges, Chief Judge Connally solicited remarks from Fifth Circuit Chief Judge John R. Brown and from Leon Jaworski, the 1970 president-elect of the American Bar Association. Transcript of the proceedings, generally.

167. *Jones v. United States,* 357 U.S. 493 (1958), at 499.

168. *Mapp v. Ohio,* 367 U.S. 643 (1961). Dinan, *Keeping the People's Liberties,* 159–60.

169. Allen, "Investigation and Police Practices," 883.

170. *Lane v. United States,* 321 F.2d 573 (5th Cir., 1963).

171. *Marsh v. United States,* 344 F.2d 317 (5th Cir., 1965).

172. Waples, "From Bags to Body Cavities," 56–57.

173. Coast Guard officials were also included with customs and immigration agents in the group of law enforcement officers authorized to conduct versions of the border search. See Yatter et al., "Investigation and Police Practices," 968.

174. According to the relevant immigration statute in the United States Code: "(a) Any officer or employee of the Service defined under regulations prescribed by the Attorney General shall have power without warrant—(1) to interrogate any alien or person believed to be an alien as to his right to be or to remain in the United States. . . ." 8 U.S.C. § 1357(a)(1). Immigration agents are authorized by the same statute to search any compartment where an unauthorized alien might be concealed: "within a reasonable distance from any external boundary of the United States, to board and search for aliens any vessel within the territorial waters of the United States and any railway car, aircraft, conveyance, or vehicle." Moreover, "within a distance of twenty-five miles from any such external boundary" the officers were authorized "to have access to private lands, but not dwellings, for the purpose of patrolling the border to prevent the illegal entry of aliens into the United States." 8 U.S.C. § 1357(a)(3). To implement the statute, the attorney general issued a statement in the code of federal regulations that defined the term "reasonable distance" as "within 100 air miles from any external boundary of the United States or any shorter distance which may be fixed by the District Director." 8 C.F.R. § 287.1 (a)(2).

175. See the examination of Agent Aker, in trial transcript, pp. 8–9, in *United States v. McDaniel,* Crim. No. 71-L-329. NARA-SWA, RG 276, U.S.C.A., 5th Circuit, case/folder 71–2810.

176. According to the relevant statute, "any officer of the Bureau of Customs of the Trea-

sury Department . . . or any commissioned, warrant, or petty officer of the Coast Guard, or any agent or other person authorized by law or designated by the Secretary of the Treasury to perform any duties of an officer of Customs Service" serves as a customs agent. 19 U.S.C. § 1401(i). The treasury secretary issued a directive (see 19 Fed. Reg. 7241) to empower the commissioner of customs to act on his behalf, and delegated to customs agents the authority to designate border patrol officers as "acting Customs Patrol officers." The designation came without compensation. 36 C.F.R. 13,410 (1971). On 14 July 1971 the assistant commissioner of customs designated all Border Patrol officers to be acting customs patrol officers. See *United States v. Thompson,* 475 F.2d 1359 (5th Cir., 1973), 1362. Timothy Dunn has investigated, among other things, the relationship of cross-designations of law enforcement officers to the later militarization of the southwestern border. Dunn claimed that before 1986 the Border Patrol was "concerned almost exclusively with immigration enforcement" and that, although the Border Patrol's move into narcotics interdiction "reportedly had already been under way in some areas for several years," that shift occurred early in the 1980s. Dunn, *Militarization of the U.S.-Mexico Border,* 80–83, 52–53, and see 221 n. 93. Case studies to be presented in the present text will illustrate that the shift occurred much earlier.

177. *Almeida-Sanchez v. United States,* 413 U.S. 266 (1973).

178. For a discussion of this judicial function, see Scalia, *A Matter of Interpretation,* 7–9.

179. Insisting on fine distinctions did not violate standards of "good behavior." The clause relating to judicial tenure provides: "Judges, both of the supreme and inferior Courts, shall hold their Offices during good Behaviour." U.S. Const., art. III, § 1.

180. *United States v. Thompson,* 390 F.Supp. 337 (S.D. Tex., 1974), 339–40.

181. The majority of border search cases in the 1970s arose in the Fifth and Ninth Circuits. Other federal courts looked to these circuits for guidance on the issues. Waples, "From Bags to Body Cavities," at 55 n. 10.

182. *United States v. Hart,* 506 F.2d 887 (5th Cir., 1975), at 889–91 n. 1. Some of the cases mentioned in this Fifth Circuit opinion arose before the 1971 extension of customs power to the Border Patrol, but nonetheless seemed relevant to the question in 1975.

183. See 36 C.F.R. 13,410 (1971).

184. Toney, *Control of Illegal Mexican Migration,* 24, 41–42. The INS budget figures (rounded to nearest $100,000), are taken from: "Table 2: Immigration and Naturalization Service Appropriations" (25). Compare this Nixon-era event to the crisis sparked in the 1990s when the press discovered that Zoë Baird, President William Clinton's first nominee to be U.S. attorney general, employed an undocumented Peruvian couple as servants. Heer, *Immigration in America's Future,* 65–66.

185. See examination of Agent Aker, in trial transcript, pp. 8–9, in *United States v. McDaniel,* NARA-SWA, RG 276, U.S.C.A., 5th Circuit, case/folder 71–2810.

186. Among these was the right to remain silent. *Miranda v. Arizona,* 384 U.S. 436 (1966).

187. The government later dropped the tax charge. Docket sheet, p. 2 (20 July 1971), in *United States v. McDaniel,* Crim. No. 71-L-329. NARA-SWA, RG 276, U.S.C.A., 5th Circuit, case/folder 71–2810.

188. See cross-examination of Aker in the trial transcript, pp. 13–15, *United States v. McDaniel,* Crim. No. 71-L-329. NARA-SWA, RG 276, U.S.C.A., 5th Circuit, case/folder 71–2810.

189. Judgment and Commitment, 26 August 1971 *United States v. McDaniel,* Crim. No. 71-L-329. NARA-SWA, RG 276, U.S.C.A., 5th Circuit, case/folder 71–2810. After being indicted with McDaniel and undergoing most of the trial with him, Canada requested and received from Connally a severance from McDaniel's case on 20 July 1971 (docket sheet, p. 2). Canada

was convicted in a separate trial and lost his appeal. *United States v. Canada,* 459 F.2d 687 (5th Cir., 1972), 688.

190. *United States v. McDaniel,* 463 F.2d 129 (5th Cir., 1972), 131.

191. Ibid., 131–32.

192. Ibid., 132–33.

193. Ibid., 135–36. The Fifth Circuit denied a rehearing en banc.

194. Ibid., 134

195. Ibid., 133–34; cert. denied, 413 U.S. 919 (1973).

196. Scc, c.g., *United States v. Storm,* 480 F.2d 701 (5th Cir., 1973) 702–3. For the trial, pp. 49–62, and docket sheet, p. 2. *United States v. Storm,* Crim. No. 72-L-463. NARA-SWA, RG 276, U.S.C.A., 5th Circuit, case/folder 72–3138.

197. *Marsh v. United States,* 344 F.2d 317 (5 Cir., 1965).

198. *United States v. Storm,* 480 F.2d 701, 702. Circuit Judges Dyer and Simpson completed the three-judge panel.

199. *United States v. Storm,* 480 F.2d 701, 703. For Brown's discussion of precedents, 702–4.

200. Ibid., 705.

201. *Almeida-Sanchez v. United States,* 413 U.S. 266 (1973), 269.

202. Ibid., 272.

203. Ibid., 281.

204. Ibid., 273.

205. Yale, "Beyond the Border," 733–34; and Compton and Wells, "Constitutionality of Search and Seizure."

206. *United States v. Jackson,* 825 F.2d 853 (5th Cir., 1987), 855, cert. denied, 484 U.S. 1011 (1988), and 484 U.S. 1019 (1988).

207. Rosenzweig, "Functional Equivalents," 1125. See *United States v. Bowen,* 500 F.2d 960 (9th Cir. 1974). Cited in *United States v. Fuentes,* 379 F.Supp. 1145 (S.D. Tex.; Crim. No. 74-B-69), 1146–47.

208. *United States v. Bowen,* 500 F.2d 960 (9th Cir., 1974), 984, pt. 2 n. 5.

209. *Bowen v. United States,* 422 U.S. 916 (1975), 918n. 1.

210. For a catalogue of cases in which federal courts considered which elements constituted the "functional equivalent" of the border: Compton and Newland, "The Functional Border Equivalent."

211. *United States v. Conner,* 364 F.Supp. 1168 (S.D. Tex.; Crim. No. 73-B-247).

212. Judge Garza noted that the Ninth Circuit had held that a stop by the Border Patrol might be based on a "founded suspicion," which may be less than probable cause. See *United States v. Bugarin-Casas,* 484 F.2d 853 (9th Cir., 1973). After a valid stop, the probable cause to search for contraband also arose. *United States v. Conner,* 364 F.Supp. 1168, 1169.

213. *United States v. Conner,* 364 F.Supp. 1168, 1169–70.

214. Ibid., at 1169–70. Judge Garza drew on this opinion in a similar case to quote his statement on the need to "make up our minds" about protecting the border. *United States v. Zamora,* 364 F.Supp. 1170 (S.D. Tex., 1973; Brownsville Division; Crim. No. 73-B-230), 1171–72.

215. *United States v. Fuentes,* 379 F.Supp. 1145 (S.D. Tex., 1974), 1151.

216. Ibid., 1147. Other judges of the Southern District subsequently declared (although without explicit reference to a "second river") these Border Patrol checkpoints were permanent, and therefore functional equivalents of the border: Falfurrias, in *United States v. Leal,*

547 F.2d 1222 (5th Cir., 1977); and Sarita, in *United States v. Reyna,* 572 F.2d 515 (5th Cir., 1978), rehearing denied, 575 F.2d 881 (5th Cir., 1978), and certiorari denied, 439 U.S. 871 (1978).

217. *United States v. Fuentes,* 379 F.Supp. 1145, 1146.

218. Ibid., 1146–47. In addition, he cited Southern District trial decisions recently reversed by the Fifth Circuit. U.S. District Judge Owen D. Cox of the Corpus Christi Division (appointed in 1970), for example, noted that the checkpoint at Falfurrias, sixty-five miles north of the border, was "non-permanent," in that it was not staffed at all hours of the day and was shifted up and down the same stretch of the highway. *United States v. Speed and Rainer* (S.D. Tex., 1973; Corpus Christi Division; Crim. No. 72-C-70). The circuit used *Almeida-Sanchez* to reverse the conviction, ruling that the temporary checkpoint could not be a functional border equivalent. *United States v. Speed,* 480 F.2d 478 (5th Cir., 1973).

219. Garza noted federal courts had previously determined that in extended border search cases the odor of marijuana was sufficient to establish probable cause for a search. See *United States v. Perez,* 364 F.Supp. 1217 (S.D. Tex., 1972; Corpus Christi Division; Crim. No. 72-C-31), at 1218; *United States v. Wright,* 476 F.2d 1027 (5th Cir., 1973), cert. denied, 414 U.S. 821 (1973); and *United States v. Alderete,* 546 F.2d 68 (5th Cir., 1977). In this last case, the Fifth Circuit declared that the search would have been valid anyway, since the checkpoint in question had been determined to be a functional equivalent of border, at which probable cause (that is, the odor of marijuana) was not required.

220. *United States v. Fuentes,* 379 F.Supp. 1145, 1148.

221. Ibid.

222. Judge Garza used a Spanish term, *los mojados* ("the wet ones"), derived from the common derogatory stereotype of all undocumented immigrants as "wetbacks." Note the pervasiveness of the term—and the author's negative view of Mexican American border culture—in Madsen, *The Mexican-Americans of South Texas.* For a sympathetic view, see Samora with Bustamante and Cardenas, *Los Mojados.*

223. *United States v. Fuentes,* 379 F.Supp. 1145, 1149.

224. Ibid., 1150.

225. *United States v. Byrd,* 483 F.2d 1196 (5th Cir., 1973).

226. *United States v. Fuentes,* 379 F.Supp. 1145, 1152.

227. Ibid., 1145, 1150.

228. Fuentes appeared with his attorney, waived a jury, and submitted to a bench trial in 31 May 1974. Ibid., 1153. *United States v. Fuentes,* 517 F.2d 1401 (5th Cir., 1975).

229. *United States v. Alvarez-Gonzalez,* 401 F.Supp. 931 (S.D. Tex., 1975; Brownsville; Crim. No. 74-B-277).

230. *United States v. Gonzalez-Alvarez* [*sic*], No. 75–3537. (The original opinion of the appeal was reported at 528 F.2d 1056 [5th Cir., 1976], but this was later withdrawn by the Fifth Circuit.) Alvarez-Gonzalez waived his right to be sentenced within sixty days of the date of his conviction. This limit was established under the Federal Rules of Criminal Procedure, Rule 50(b). *United States v. Alvarez-Gonzalez,* 401 F.Supp. 931, 932.

231. *United States v. Ortiz,* 422 U.S. 891 (1975). The Fifth Circuit held that *Ortiz* applied retroactively. *United States v. Martinez,* 526 F.2d 954, 955 (5th Cir. 1976). The remaining cases, which according to Garza did not affect his decision, were *Bowen v. United States,* 422 U.S. 916 (1975); and *United States v. Brignoni-Ponce,* 422 U.S. 873 (1975).

232. *United States v. Alvarez-Gonzalez,* 401 F.Supp. 931, 932–33.

233. Ibid., 933.

234. Ibid., 934.

235. Ibid. The opinion cited was *United States v. Santibanez,* 517 F.2d 922 (5th Cir., 1975).

236. *United States v. Alvarez-Gonzalez,* 542 F.2d 226 (5th Cir., 1976), at 227. The original written opinion, *United States v. Gonzalez-Alvarez,* No. 75–3537, was previously reported at 528 F.2d 1056 (5th Cir., 1976), but it was withdrawn by the court.

237. Ibid., 228.

238. Ibid., 229. The Fifth Circuit had previously considered these factors, in another case, but wished to make the criteria more explicit. See *United States v. Hart,* 506 F.2d 887 (5th Cir., 1975), vacated and remanded, 422 U.S. 1053, and reaffirmed on remand, 525 F.2d 1199 (5th Cir., 1976). See *United States v. Reyna,* 572 F.2d 515 (5th Cir., 1978), cert. denied, 439 U.S. 871 (1978).

239. Alvarez-Gonzalez's lawyer attempted to prove that the permanent fixtures were not yet erected when the search took place in 1974; Garza ruled that they were, and the circuit judges did not dispute this. *United States v. Alvarez-Gonzalez,* 561 F.2d 620 (5th Cir., 1977), 622 n. 4.

240. Ibid., 622.

241. Ibid., 622–23.

242. Ibid., 624 n. 8.

243. Ibid., 623.

244. Ibid., 625.

245. *United States v. McDaniel,* 463 F.2d 129, 132–33.

246. *United States v. Alvarez-Gonzalez,* 561 F.2d 620, 626.

247. *United States v. Calvillo,* 537 F.2d 158 (5th Cir. 1976), 160.

248. *United States v. Alvarez-Gonzalez,* 561 F.2d 620 (5th Cir., 1977), 629–30.

249. Ibid. The decision was not reversed, and in 1978 the Fifth Circuit referred to the La Gloria Border Patrol checkpoint as both "permanent" and the "functional equivalent of border." *United States v. Robinson,* 567 F.2d 637 (5th Cir., 1978), rehearing denied, 570 F.2d 949 (5th Cir., 1978), cert. denied, 439 U.S. 819 (1978). Moreover, without a demonstration of changed circumstances, the circuit declined to reevaluate a checkpoint location once a judicial determination had been made that it met the criteria to be a functional border equivalent. See *United States v. Dreyfus–de Campos,* 698 F.2d 227 (5th Cir., 1983), cert. denied, 461 U.S. 947 (1983).

250. For attempts by other courts within the Fifth Circuit to define the "functional equivalent," see "Note, Border Zone Search Law," 264–71.

251. Senior judges were retired but continued to draw salary and could be called back to assist the court if the judge wished to serve temporarily. Judges were eligible at seventy years of age (after ten years' service), or sixty-five years of age (after fifteen). 28 U.S.C. § 371. Judge Connally died at age sixty-five, on 2 December 1975. "Judge Ben Connally Dies of Heart Attack," *Houston Post,* 3 December 1975, pp. 1A, 19A; "Judge Ben C. Connally, Who Presided over Houston's School Integration Battles," *New York Times,* 4 December 1975, p. 44.

252. "O'Conor," in *Judges of the United States.*

253. Oral history interview with Robert J. O'Conor Jr. by Steven H. Wilson, 2 January 1998.

254. *United States v. Wilson,* 553 F.2d 896 (5th Cir., 1977), 898–99.

255. *United States v. Wilson,* 432 F.Supp. 223 (S.D. Tex., 1976; Laredo Division; Crim. No. 75-L-44).

256. *United States v. Wilson,* 553 F.2d 896 (5th Cir., 1977), 896–97.

257. *United States v. Ramsey,* 431 U.S. 606 (1977), 616. Moreover, Justice Rehnquist noted, the border search exception was "as old as the Fourth Amendment itself" (619). The court has often put great stock in the fact that the same Congress enacted both the Fourth Amendment and the "exception." For example, see *Boyd v. United States,* 116 U.S. 616 (1886), 623. Critics of the modern border search have noted, however, that no evidence exists that the first Congress "ever measured the searches authorized by the Customs act against the standards set by the proposed fourth amendment." Waples, "From Bags to Body Cavities," 54 n. 7. Also "Note: Border Searches and the Fourth Amendment," *Yale Law Journal* 77 (1968): 1001.

258. *Johnson v. United States,* 333 U.S. 10 (1948), at 14–15.

259. "Chicanos to Confer on Aliens," *Houston Post,* 21 October 1977, p. 5A. "Border Patrols by KKK Rapped," *Houston Post,* 29 October 1977, p. 6B.

260. Castillo, "Hispanic Political Power," 98–99. Also see the interview with Castillo published in the collection by Terkel, *My American Century,* 77–82. Castillo had been active in local and regional politics in Texas before taking over at the INS. He had been elected Houston's city controller in 1971 and was the community relations director for the Roman Catholic diocese of Galveston and Houston in the late 1960s. De León, *Ethnicity in the Sunbelt,* 186–87, 192–93.

261. "Castillo Says Mexican Shunned Citizenship because of Past Abuses," *Houston Post,* 9 April 1978, p. 20C. "Castillo Tries to Head Off KKK Patrols," *Houston Post,* 21 October 1977, p. 5A.

262. "Carter Asks Congress to Decriminalize Marihuana Possession; Cocaine Law Is Studied," *New York Times,* 15 March 1977, p. 15; Bertram et al., *Drug War Politics,* 93–97. Johnson and Uppal, "Marihuana and Youth," 101.

263. Fisch, *All Rise,* 142–45, 149–54, 162.

264. Beale, "Federalizing Crime," 48–49.

CHAPTER 4. Managing "Our Federalism" in the Southern District

1. Cooper, *Hard Judicial Choices,* 12–44, and generally.

2. U.S. 167 (1961).

3. Act of 20 April 1871 (ch. 22, § 1, 17 Stat. 13; formerly codified as R.S. Sect. 1979, then as 8 U.S.C. § 43; currently codified as amended at 42 U.S.C. §§ 1981–83). This first section of the bill merely added civil and equitable remedies to the criminal penalties already established in the CRA of 1866, and so it was the least controversial part of the 1871 act. This section was left intact, although it was narrowly interpreted, when the Supreme Court stripped the original act of much of its efficacy in the 1883 *Civil Rights Cases,* by overturning provisions for the freedmen's equal access to the nation's public accommodations, entertainment, and transportation. 109 U.S. 3 (1883). See Nelson, *The Fourteenth Amendment,* 194–97; also Hyman, *A More Perfect Union,* 529. For the Supreme Court's views on the legislative history of the Ku Klux Klan Act, see *Monroe v. Pape,* 365 U.S. 167 (1961), 171; and *Monell v. Department of Social Services,* 436 U.S. 658 (1978), 665.

4. U.S. 496 (1939). Previously, federal courts frequently had issued injunctions against labor organizers.

5. The key to the *Monroe* ruling was that the equal protection section (§ 1983) required

no proof of willful misconduct, while the conspiracy section of the act did (§ 1981). The officers, although not the city of Chicago itself, were made liable to pay civil damages. "Note: Developments in the Law," 1169–72. See Hess, "Good Cop–Bad Cop," 154.

6. Friedelbaum, "Warren Court and American Federalism," 68, esp. n. 80. Less than a decade after *Monroe,* some critics claimed that the expansion had already gone too far, because federal court jurisdiction in civil rights claims had grown to include situations that were arguably never intended to be subjects for equitable relief. At the least, critics suggested, some of the cases were better suited for state courts. "Note: Limiting the Section 1983 Action," 1487. Others celebrated the trend and called for more of the same, claiming that only federal judges, by dint of experience, temperament, and tenure, could adequately right society's moral wrongs by conscientiously attending to individuals' civil rights. Chevigny, "Section 1983 Jurisdiction," 1357. The court overruled parts of *Monroe,* but only to find that cities could be held liable for civil damages. *Monell v. Dept. of Social Services,* 436 U.S. 658 (1978).

7. Prohibitions of discrimination in employment, housing, and education were extended through subsequent amendments to the CRA of 1964. See 42 U.S.C. § 2000(a)–(h).

8. U.S.C. § 1983, describing "Actions for Deprivations of Civil Rights under Color of Law."

9. The 1964 CRA reaffirmed and expanded the U.S. attorney general's authority to enforce civil rights laws through litigation undertaken by the Justice Department's Civil Rights Division. See Landsberg, *Enforcing Civil Rights,* 50–51; and Days, "In Honor of *Brown v. Board of Education,*" 991. Congress followed the 1964 CRA with the 1965 Voting Rights Act (VRA). The 1965 VRA was subsequently strengthened and extended. The VRA and its amendments are currently codified at 42 U.S.C. §§ 1971–73. Congress enacted fair-housing provisions in a 1968 CRA at 42 U.S.C. §§ 3601–19, 3631.

10. U.S. 479 (1965).

11. Three-judge courts are empowered to enjoin allegedly unconstitutional state laws in 28 U.S.C §§ 2281–84 (the "Three Judge Court Act"). This law was enacted by the Congress at the turn of the twentieth century, in an attempt to temper the perceived imprudence of district judges in issuing the unpopular injunctions in labor cases. The legislators apparently thought that a judicial panel would act more "reasonably" than a solo judge. With the rise of civil rights consciousness and federal willingness and authority to enforce civil rights during the 1960s, the number of cases heard by three-judge panels also increased dramatically; they doubled between 1963 and 1973. Under the statute, panel decisions could be appealed directly to the Supreme Court. In time, these panels became widely regarded as wasteful of time and manpower. During the Supreme Court's October 1969 term, approximately 22 percent of the docket concerned appeals from three-judge courts. In 1976 Congress limited the jurisdiction of three-judge courts to cases concerning congressional districts and apportionment matters, or "when otherwise directed by Congress." Surrency, *History of the Federal Courts,* 249–50. Cases heard annually by three-judge courts declined from 208 in 1976 to 9 in 1990. Carp and Stidham, *Judicial Process in America,* 2d ed., 46–47. For a historical treatment of the three-judge courts written during the height of the civil rights revolution, see Currie, "Three-Judge District Court," 30–31.

12. *Dombrowski,* 380 U.S. 479, at 487. The court held that the "chilling effect" was substantial in those states with laws against organizing civil rights protests. The case "unleashed a torrent" of suits seeking protection from state prosecution. Schauer, "Unraveling the 'Chilling Effect,' " 685. See Amsterdam, "Criminal Prosecutions," 828; and Maraist, "Federal Injunctive Relief," 535–607.

13. "Note: The Federal Anti-injunction Act," 1871–72.

14. Between 1871, the year the Klan law was enacted, and 1939, the year the court decided *Hague,* the federal courts reported nineteen cases filed under the equivalent of § 1983. Bator et al., *Federal Courts and the Federal System,* 2d ed., 950 n. 3. Also, see Blum and Urbonya, *Section 1983 Litigation,* 1–6; and Zagrans, " 'Under Color of' What Law," 499.

15. Kurland, "Enter the Burger Court," 80.

16. The California statute prohibited circulating or publicly displaying any written or printed matter containing advocacy for the commission of a crime "as a means of accomplishing a change in industrial ownership or control, or effecting any political change." *Younger v. Harris,* 401 U.S. 37 (1971), 39 nn. 1–3.

17. *Younger v. Harris,* 401 U.S. 37 (1971), 43–45.

18. The federal district courts have jurisdiction in § 1983 cases under 28 U.S.C. § 1343. An indication of the importance to the principle of "Our Federalism" was that the court majority relied on it, rather than the Anti-injunction Act, the statutory bar to federal action that the state lawyers had cited. *Younger v. Harris,* 401 U.S., at 40. See Baird, "Federal Court Abstention," 519–20.

19. Under the long-standing *Pullman* abstention doctrine, for example, federal courts should seek to avoid premature interference with the state court's construction of state laws; see *Railroad Commission of Texas v. Pullman,* 312 U.S. 496 (1941), at 501.

20. The *Younger* decision became the leading case in a cohort of six similar cases. The other five cases, decided the same day as *Younger,* were *Samuels v. Mackell,* 401 U.S. 66 (1971); *Boyle v. Landry,* 401 U.S. 77 (1971); *Perez v. Ledesma,* 401 U.S. 82 (1971); *Dyson v. Stein,* 401 U.S. 200 (1971); and *Byrne v. Karalexis,* 401 U.S. 216 (1971). Also on that day, the justices relied on *Younger* to issue summary decisions in an additional sixteen cases. See 401 U.S., 984–90. In *Samuels v. Mackell,* the court refused to permit federal declaratory relief, which the justices said had "virtually the same practical impact as a formal injunction." 401 U.S. 66 (1971), 72. See Zagrans, " 'Under Color of' What Law," 503–4. Before these decisions, Prof. Kurland noted that the court under Chief Justice Burger had so far exhibited few significant differences from its immediate predecessor. He declared in 1970 that his impression after reading cases was that the court had not changed with the appointment of a new chief in 1969, and concluded the "Court's major theme remained equality and its major function continued to be the centralization of power in one branch or another of the national government." Accordingly, Kurland wrote, "precedents were treated cavalierly; both new ones and old ones were readily overruled or distinguished to death." Kurland, "Enter the Burger Court," 91–92. These concerns paralleled commentators of a decade earlier. In 1960 Stanley Friedelbaum noted that "attacks upon the Supreme Court during the past half-decade have centered about judicial pronouncements which, critics contend, reflect an excessively narrow view of state powers." The critics usually focused on particularly obnoxious rulings, but Friedelbaum contended that the Warren court had been fairly balanced with regard to federalism. The court usually abstained from exercising diversity power, for example, whenever it would disrupt federal-state relations for no good reason. However, he admitted that federal courts had "not been inclined to apply the abstention doctrine consistently." Friedelbaum, "Warren Court and American Federalism," 53, 86–87.

21. Wasby, *Continuity and Change,* 40–45. For support of the argument that the court's decision was partly an effort "to contain the explosive growth of section 1983 litigation," see Baird, "Federal Court Abstention," 520.

22. Lyndon B. Johnson remained a strong supporter of the bracero system, often against

the preferences of his Mexican American constituents. See Pycior, *LBJ and Mexican Americans,* 104–7, 146–46.

23. Throughout the 1950s Chávez had been a leader in the Community Service Organization (CSO). Nelson, "Who Is César Chávez?" 232–33.

24. Mooney and Majka, *Farmers' and Farm Workers' Movements,* 154–58; Pulido, *Environmentalism and Economic Justice,* 70–71.

25. Bailey, "The Starr County Strike," 47.

26. During the interview Nye reportedly told Nelson that the FBI was in town, to investigate an alleged threat to blow up the courthouse or to destroy the buses used to transport Mexican laborers, and he warned Nelson that they would be watching him. See *Francisco Medrano et al. v. A.Y. Allee et al.,* 347 F.Supp. 605 (S.D. Tex., 1972), 612 [Brownsville Division; Civ. No. 67-B-36]. Also Bailey, "The Starr County Strike," 48.

27. Art. 5154(s), Tex. Rev. Civ. Stat.

28. Bailey, "The Starr County Strike," 48–49. Ronnie Dugger, " 'A Long Struggle with La Casita,' " *Texas Observer,* 24 June 1966, p. 1.

29. Rhinehart and Kreneck, "Minimum Wage March," 33–39; Bailey, "The Starr County Strike," 49–53. Also see "The Valley Strikers Are Walking to Austin," *Texas Observer,* 22 July 1966, pp. 7–8; and, *Texas Observer,* 5 August 1966, p. 6.

30. Rhinehart and Kreneck, "Minimum Wage March," 35; Bailey, "The Starr County Strike," 50.

31. *Medrano v. Allee,* 347 F.Supp. 605 (S.D. Tex., 1972), 609–12.

32. Peña subsequently testified that Chandler and the other protesters employed abusive and vulgar language, but he ultimately recanted his charge, contained in his official complaint, that the union members had used "obscene language, vulgar language, indecent language, swearing and cursing, yelling and shrieking, exposing the person, and rudely displaying a weapon." *Medrano v. Allee,* 347 F.Supp. 605 (S.D. Tex., 1972), 612.

33. The county filed this charge as a violation of art. 474 of the Texas Penal Code.

34. *Medrano v. Allee,* 347 F.Supp. 605 (S.D. Tex., 1972), 613.

35. Ibid.

36. The *empresario* Stephen F. Austin founded the Texas Rangers in 1823 to help protect settlers. The Rangers, officially organized in 1835, are stationed across the state and assist local authorities in investigating major crimes. For a laudatory account of Ranger history, see generally Webb, *The Texas Rangers.* For a generally condemnatory account, see Samora, Bernal, and Peña, *Gunpowder Justice,* chap. 8. For a contemporary view of the intervention of the Rangers in the Starr County strikes, see Procter, "The Modern Texas Rangers," 218–20. Since 1935 the state's legendary and controversial enforcers of frontier justice have been an elite division of the Department of Public Safety (DPS). For the modern investigative enforcement authority of the Rangers, see art. 4413(11), Tex. Rev. Civ. Stat.

37. Art. 5154(f), Tex. Rev. Civ. Stat. A primary strike or boycott is aimed directly at the employer whose labor policies are being protested. A secondary strike or boycott aims to pressure another party to agree to cease doing business with the primary target. The National Labor Relations Act prohibited secondary strikes or boycotts, and under the so-called "hot cargo" provisions, the statute also prohibits businesses from agreeing not to deal with the products of an employer involved in a labor dispute. 29 U.S.C. § 158(e). The U.S. Supreme Court, relying on the rational basis test, has upheld the ban on secondary boycotts and sympathy strikes. See *Electrical Workers v. National Labor Relations Board,* 341 U.S. 694 (1951), 705.

38. *Medrano v. Allee*, 347 F.Supp. 605 (S.D. Tex., 1972), 612–15.

39. Ibid., 616–17.

40. Ibid.

41. *La Casita Farms, Inc. v. United Farm Workers Organizing Committee;* District Court of Starr County, Texas, No. 3809. *United Farm Workers Organizing Committee v. La Casita Farms, Inc.*, 439 S.W.2d 398 (1967), at 403.

42. *Medrano v. Allee*, 347 F.Supp. 605 (S.D. Tex., 1972), 611.

43. The subsequent appeal to the Supreme Court consumed another year. See *Allee v. Medrano*, 416 U.S. 802 (1973).

44. See *Balderas v. La Casita Farms*, 8 Fair Empl. Prac. Cas. 683 (S.D. Tex., 1973), at 688; 500 F.2d 195 (5th Cir., 1974).

45. Chávez, quoted in Cockcroft, *Outlaws in the Promised Land*, 175.

46. Navarro, *Mexican American Youth Organization*, 22–36; Quiñones, *Chicano Politics*, 101–5.

47. See Quiñones, *Chicano Politics*, 118–19; Ignacio M. Garcia, *Chicanismo*, 1–4; and Rendón, *Chicano Manifesto*, 200–202. For a discussion of the generational issues that led to the rise of the Chicano challenge to the "Mexican American Generation," see Gutiérrez and Hirsch, "Challenge to the American Ethos," 86–103; Mario T. Garcia, *Mexican Americans*, 13–22; and Munoz, *Youth, Identity, Power*, generally.

48. Navarro, *Mexican American Youth Organization*, 174, 198. Gonzalez, "An Attack on Chicano Militants," *Congressional Record*, 91st Cong., 1st sess., 22 April 1969, 358. Also, see Hero, *Latinos and the U.S. Political System.*

49. Gonzalez, *Mexicanos*, 219.

50. Servín, "Post–World War II Mexican-American," 144. See "Latin Leaders Walk Out on U.S.," *Texas Observer*, 15 April 1966, p. 5. Quiñones, *Chicano Politics*, 106–8. For the significance of this event, see Allsup, *The American GI Forum*, 160–61. For tensions and jealousies between African and Mexican Americans in the mid-1960s, see Barbaro, "Ethnic Resentment," 77–79.

51. Rowan, "A Minority Nobody Knows," 29.

52. San Miguel, *"Let All of Them Take Heed,"* 164–69; and San Miguel, "Mexican American Organizations," 708–9. Ramos, *The American GI Forum.*

53. In late September 1966 Congress had amended FLSA, ending agricultural workers' blanket exemption from the statute. 29 U.S.C. § 206(5). Subsection 5 was added by Pub. L. No. 89–601, § 302; 80 Stat. 830. But a Senate subcommittee, studying recommendations further to amend the FLSA, visited the valley in July 1967 after the state judge's injunction ended the strike. The senators took testimony from participants on both sides of the wage controversy. The panel's investigation focused new attention on the patterns of discrimination the Anglo majority in Texas maintained against Mexican Americans. The tone of the questions and the comments made by one of the panel's leading members, Senator Edward M. Kennedy, made it clear that he favored the cause of the farm workers over that of the growers. See "Little People's Day," *Texas Observer*, 21 July 1967, p. 5.

54. *Hernandez v. Texas*, 347 U.S. 475 (1954).

55. For discussion of variations on these "transfer" and "choice" rules, see Rangel and Alcala, "De Jure Segregation," 327–29.

56. See "Testimony of Pete Tijerina," 13 December 1968, in U.S. Commission on Civil Rights, *Hearing Held in San Antonio*, 653–55. Richard L. Dockery, the Southwest regional director of the NAACP, had also testified in support of similar proposals. He told the com-

mission his organization included many Mexican American members and had recently established offices in San Antonio. See "Testimony of Richard L. Dockery," 9 December 1968, in U.S. Commission on Civil Rights, *Hearing Held in San Antonio,* 92–93. Richard Alatorre, a staff member of the Southwest office of the NAACP's Legal Defense Fund, Inc. (or the "Inc. Fund"), followed Tijerina on the program in San Antonio. He testified that the two legal defense organizations were making common cause to fight discrimination against all minority groups in the Southwest. See "Testimony of Richard Alatorre," 13 December 1968, in U.S. Commission on Civil Rights, *Hearing Held in San Antonio,* 656–57. Tijerina consciously modeled MALDEF on the Inc. Fund after meeting and discussing the need for such an organization with Jack Greenberg, who was the LDF's chief litigator during the 1960s. Tijerina sought funding from the Ford Foundation at Greenberg's suggestion. See O'Connor and Epstein, "A Legal Voice," 284–85; San Miguel, "*Let All of Them Take Heed,*" 169–72; and Quiñones, *Chicano Politics,* 110–12. African and Mexican American litigators had rarely coordinated strategies before the late 1960s, but by the time of MALDEF's founding, they saw the wisdom in mutual legal support, either as intervenors in lawsuits or as writers of amicus briefs. For the dynamics of coalitions the various organizations built to accomplish their goals (with each other and with other minorities), and of rivalries that occasionally prevented their accomplishing these goals (within and without their own group), see Wasby, *Race Relations,* 123–24.

57. See "Testimony of Pete Tijerina," *Hearing Held in San Antonio,* 653–55. The civil rights commissioners also heard testimony from an education professor named George I. Sanchez, of UT, who had testified as an expert witness during DeAnda's 1957 case. Like DeAnda and Tijerina, Sanchez described persistent discrimination against Mexican Americans that resulted from historical and cultural conditions specific to the Southwest. See "Testimony of George I. Sanchez," 9 December 1968, *Hearing Held in San Antonio,* 90–101. Garcia and the other commissioners also decided to hear testimony from union leaders, then in the early stages of their suit, as well as from officials. See "Testimony of Rev. Edgar A. Krueger," *Hearing Held in San Antonio,* 419; and "Testimony of Alfred [Y.] Allee, Sr.," 13 December 1968, *Hearing Held in San Antonio,* 715. Also see "Staff Report: Farm Workers," *Hearing Held in San Antonio,* 953; and "Staff Report: The Commuter on the United States-Mexico Border," *Hearing Held in San Antonio,* 982. The commission hearings were summarized in "New Accent on Civil Rights: The Mexican American," *Civil Rights Journal* 2 (winter 1969): 16–23.

58. This ultimately proved to be a wise decision, because the U.S. attorney general waited until late 1969 before joining in a Mexican American lawsuit. *Perez v. Sonora Independent School District,* Civ. No. 6–224 (N.D. Tex, 1969). Noted in Birnberg, "*Brown v. Board of Education,*" 339 n. 10.

59. Navarro, *Mexican American Youth Organization,* 80–87. For the critical importance of student activists for the growth of the Chicano movement, see Smith, "Mexicano Resistance," 288–97. Also Gonzalez, *Mexicanos,* 208–18.

60. Navarro, *Mexican American Youth Organization,* 115–18, 120–24; and Rendón, *Chicano Manifesto,* 174–94. Also Exhibits 12–16, in U.S. Commission on Civil Rights, *Hearing Held in San Antonio,* 881–92. California saw the same kind of student unrest. Torgerson, " 'Brown Power' Unity," 279.

61. The isolation and alienation of the Mexican American community, which was subsumed in the cultural nationalism of the Chicano youth movement, left T. R. Fehrenbach, author of a noted history of Texas published in 1968, wondering whether south Texas was on the verge of becoming the Quebec of the United States. Fehrenbach, *Lone Star,* 698–701.

That separatist end was the announced goal of the most militant of the Chicanos, but most of the activists were willing to proclaim a symbolic homeland in the Southwest they called *Aztlán*. García, *Chicanismo*, 94–98.

62. Navarro, *Mexican American Youth Organization*, 118–20. The "agitation" condemned by the school board was a critical tool for the coordination of the Chicano movement. Tirado, "Mexican American Community Political Organization," 105–27.

63. The typical demands testify to the restlessness and emerging self-consciousness of students in general and attest to the *Chicanismo* informing Mexican American youth in particular. For a "laundry list" of typical walk-out demands, see Rendón, *Chicano Manifesto*, 177–79. For origins and ultimate abandonment in 1969 of "no Spanish" rules, see Carter, *Mexican Americans in School*, 97–98; and Rangel and Alcala, "De Jure Segregation," 310 n. 20.

64. Navarro, *Mexican American Youth Organization*, 120–23.

65. Ibid., 120–23.

66. Ibid., 124.

67. Quoted in Navarro, *Mexican American Youth Organization*, 124.

68. *Ramirez v. Edcouch-Elsa Independent School District*, unpublished (S.D. Tex., 1969), Brownsville Division, Civ. No. 68-B-116. The students prevailed in December 1968, the same month the civil rights commissioners held hearings in San Antonio. San Miguel, *"Let All of Them Take Heed,"* 172–73; and San Miguel, " 'The Community Is Beginning to Rumble,' " 135–36.

69. Rangel and Alcala, "De Jure Segregation," 369.

70. Navarro, *Mexican American Youth Organization*, 125–48.

71. Critics of the American policy in Vietnam argued that the undeclared war there was either unconstitutional or immoral, and probably both. In any case, they believed that the government should end its military commitments in that country. Many protesters refused to register for the draft, burned their draft cards after registering, or simply resisted induction when they called. In each instance, these individuals risked incarceration in a federal prison. See, for example, *Schacht v. United States*, 398 U.S. 58 (1970); *Gee v. United States*, 319 F.Supp. 581 (S.D. Tex., 1970); and *Clay*, AKA *Ali v. United States*, 403 U.S. 698 (1971). The last case involved the appeal of the boxer Muhammad Ali, born Cassius Clay, to overturn his conviction for refusal to submit to military induction in Houston. Judge Ingraham presided in the original trial in the Southern District of Texas. Failure to report for and to submit to induction into the armed forces was a violation of 50 App. U.S.C. § 462(a). As with many political and social controversies of a tumultuous era, the issues were translated into legal questions and spilled over into the nation's courtrooms. Whether the issue was the propriety of peaceful protest, civil disobedience, or even violent resistance to U.S. government policies, state and federal judges were called on to identify a bright line that separated the citizen's responsibility to follow the law from the right to dissent. For the generation of younger Americans asked to fight, the collective political goal of ending the war depended on an even more personal decision: whether to submit to induction into the military and risk death, or to resist the draft and risk prison. Certainly, this is an oversimplification of the political and moral choices facing the generation of draft-age citizens. The implications of the ongoing involvement of American troops were also issues among the even younger generation, still in high school but approaching draft age. Their efforts to protest the Vietnam War led to a landmark case before the Supreme Court, which asserted that even high school students did not "shed their constitutional rights to freedom of speech or expression at the schoolhouse

gate." *Tinker v. Des Moines*, 393 U.S. 503 (1969), at 506. See Johnson, *The Struggle for Student Rights*. See also Matusow, *The Unraveling of America*, 394.

72. This was an issue that MAYO raised frequently in the late 1960s. The mimeographed leaflets announced the time, place, and reason of the rally on one side, in Spanish, and listed the relevant draft statistics in English on the reverse side. The information seems to be based on an article by Prof. Ralph Guzman of the University of California at Santa Cruz, which Representative Edward R. Roybal of California entered into the *Congressional Record*. See "Mexican-American Casualties in Vietnam," *Congressional Record*, 91st Cong., 1st sess., 8 October 1969; Rep. Roybal's entry has been reprinted in Moquin and Van Doren, *A Documentary History*, 371–73.

73. The two other students, Ortiz and Trevino, were also suspended for leafleting, but they do not play a large part in the subsequent case, because they declined to join Escalante's lawsuit. One effect of their brief participation in the protest is that their refusal to join the suit persuaded Judge Garza to deny Escalante's request to expand the suit into a class action. See *Escalante v. La Feria Independent School District*, unpublished (S.D. Tex., 1970), Civ. A. No. 69-B-163, S.D. Tex., Brownsville Division, NARA-SWA, RG 21, box 491, folder for Case No. 69-B-163 [hereafter cited as *Escalante v. La Feria ISD*]. See Memorandum and Order, 1 August 1970, pp. 1–4.

74. She did not mention the possibility that she had been singled out by an Anglo principal because she was a Chicana. See Escalante's letter, dated 14 November 1969, labeled "Defendants Exhibit No. 2," in *Escalante v. La Feria ISD*.

75. *Tinker v. Des Moines Independent Community School District*, 393 U.S. 503 (1969), 506 [hereafter *Tinker*].

76. In *Tinker*, announced 24 February 1969, the justices supported the students' claim that they were citizens under the Constitution and therefore entitled by the Fourteenth Amendment to equal protection under the law. See Johnson, *Struggle for Student Rights*, ix–x, and generally.

77. *Escalante v. La Feria ISD*. See Escalante's deposition, filed 20 May 1970, pp. 9–10, 15–16, 40–41. The date of the deposition session is not provided, but it must have been 5 February 1970: during the proceedings Escalante referred to her eighteenth birthday "two days ago" and gives her birthday as February 3; see deposition, p. 4.

78. The declaratory judgment was available under the Declaratory Judgment Act, 28 U.S.C. § 2201.

79. *Escalante v. La Feria ISD*. See Complaint, 19 December 1969, 1–4; Defendant's Motion to Dismiss, 26 January 1970.

80. Ibid.; see Complaint, 19 December 1969, 1; Defendant's Original Answer, 26 January 1970, pp. 1–2.

81. Ibid., see Complaint, 19 December 1969, 1; Defendant's Original Answer, 26 January 1970, pp. 3–9.

82. *West Virginia State Board of Education v. Barnette*, 319 U.S. 624 (1943).

83. See *Escalante v. La Feria ISD*. See Trial Brief, filed 15 May 1970, pp. 3–10.

84. *Escalante v. La Feria ISD*; see Defendant's Trial Memorandum, filed 20 June 1970, p. 7, 17–18. The school district sought to have the case dismissed because Escalante had not exhausted her administrative options before filing the federal case. Garza admitted that recent Fifth Circuit decisions suggested that he should have sent Escalante to negotiate further with the La Feria Board of Education. However, he decided that this would have been futile; the two other students suspended with Escalante, Ortiz and Trevino, used the administrative

channels, but their suspensions remained in full effect. On this ground, Garza denied the district's motion to dismiss the case. See Ibid., Memorandum and Order, 1 August 1970, p. 5.

85. Ibid., Memorandum and Order, 1 August 1970, p. 6.

86. Fisch, *All Rise*, 115–17.

87. Navarro, *Mexican American Youth Organization*, 157–58. In its early years MALDEF also accepted minor claims of the "legal aid" variety, concerning minor disputes, which did not actually require legal counsel. O'Connor and Epstein suggest that, despite some victories, MALDEF was not an effective constitutional litigator until at least 1973; moreover, even then it lost more often than it won. O'Connor and Epstein, "A Legal Voice for the Chicano Community," 285.

88. F.Supp. 1328 (S.D. Tex., 1969). See *Escalante v. La Feria ISD*. Post-trial Memorandum, filed 1 June 1970, p. 1.

89. F.Supp. 1034 (S.D. Tex., 1970). Johnson cites the case number (Civ. No. 69-[H]-185), because the decision had not yet been published when he wrote the brief. See *Escalante v. La Feria ISD*. Defendant's Post-Trial Memorandum, filed 1 June 1970, p. 10.

90. Sharpstown was actually a junior/senior high school; it maintained seventh and eighth grades.

91. *Sullivan v. Houston ISD*, 307 F.Supp. 1328 (S.D. Tex., 1969), 1328–30 [Houston Division; Civ. A. No. 69-H-266].

92. Ibid., 1330–31.

93. Ibid., 1331–32.

94. Ibid., 1332–33.

95. Ibid., 1328. See Federal Rules of Civil Procedure, Rule 23. In 1966 Rule 23 had been broadened to ease class actions in civil rights matters.

96. *Sullivan v. Houston ISD*, 307 F.Supp. 1328 (S.D. Tex., 1969), 1334.

97. Matusow, *The Unraveling of America*, 311–42. The American Civil Liberties Union (ACLU), which had been involved in the *Tinker* case, was busy fighting this surveillance and persecution of student dissent. Walker, *In Defense of American Liberties*, 280–88. For the SDS and other radicals in context of the 1960s, see generally Gitlin, *The Sixties*. Also Lipset, *Rebellion in the University*, 197–98.

98. *Sullivan v. Houston ISD*, 307 F.Supp. 1328 (S.D. Tex., 1969), 1334–36.

99. To expedite the final determination of the case, Judge Seals entered an order under Rule 65(a)(2) of Federal Rules of Civil Procedure, to consolidate the application for a preliminary injunction with the hearing on 9 April. *Sullivan v. Houston ISD*, 307 F.Supp. 1328 (S.D. Tex., 1969), 1334–36.

100. Fed. R. Civ. P., Rule 23.

101. *Sullivan v. Houston ISD*, 307 F.Supp., 1337.

102. *Tinker*, 393 U.S. 503 (1969), 511.

103. *Sullivan v. Houston ISD*, 307 F.Supp., 1339.

104. Ibid., 1340–41.

105. As is obvious by this line of cases, the issue of due process for students was under much scrutiny at the time. See generally Wright, "Constitution on the Campus," 1027. Some observers were unhappy with the "contemporary phenomenon of litigious libertarianism" that led to the multiplication of school-related lawsuits. See Haskell, "Judicial Review of School Discipline," 211–13.

106. *Sullivan v. Houston ISD*, 307 F.Supp., 1342–45.

107. Seals said that when a high school student was facing dire consequences, he or she had as much a right to expect "a clear, specific normative statement which does not infringe on free expression than does a university student or possibly even the accused in a criminal case." Seals ruled that school regulations "probably do not need to be as narrow as criminal statutes," but if school officials could threaten a severe punishment like expulsion, then they must do it under a rule which reasonably informed the students what specific conduct was proscribed. *Sullivan v. Houston ISD*, 307 F.Supp. 1328, 1342–45.

108. Judge Seals derives for his "chill" language from *Dombrowski v. Pfister*, 380 U.S. 479 (1965).

109. *Sullivan v. Houston ISD*, 307 F.Supp., 1345. In assembling his list of procedures, Judge Seals relied heavily on the U.S. Court of Appeals for the Fifth Circuit's 1961 landmark decision in an African American student's "sit-in" case, *Dixon v. Alabama State Board of Education*, 294 F.2d 150 (5th Cir., 1961). Some civil libertarians believed that by the late 1960s *Dixon* needed updating in light of the Warren court's "due process" revolution and the rise of campus protests. Wasserstein, "The Courts and the Campus," 38–39, 47. The U.S. Supreme Court finally examined and upheld due process rights of students in 1975's *Goss v. Lopez*, 419 U.S. 656 (1975); see esp. 572–76. For a review of the developments in due process in schools between *Dixon* and *Goss*, and an estimation of the impact of the latter decision, see Kirp, "Proceduralism and Bureaucracy," 841–42.

110. A committee of students, administrators, parents, attorneys, and others held hearings to discuss aspects of school discipline. The final version of the rules required prior submission to principals of all nonschool publications that were to be distributed either on campus or off campus in a manner "calculated" to result in presence on the campus. The principal enjoyed one working day to review the publication before distribution. If the principal and HISD attorneys believed that the publication contained "libelous or obscene language or advocate[d] illegal action or disobedience to published rules on student conduct," the principal could withhold approval and material could not be distributed. Beyond these libel, obscenity, and advocacy conditions, however, the rules provided that denials were to be content-neutral: distribution could not be prohibited simply because the proposed publication "contained the expression of any idea, popular or unpopular." In addition, to conform with Judge Seals's order, the new regulations contained specific provisions governing suspension procedures. Upon violating the regulations, a student could be suspended for a "reasonable" time not exceeding three school days, and only upon written notice of the reasons for the suspension to parents or guardians. For longer suspensions or for indefinite suspensions, the student, parent, or guardian was entitled to written notice as well as a prompt hearing with the principal, if he or she wanted one. At the meeting, the accused student could produce witnesses and be assisted by counsel. Also, a suspended student had the right to appeal, first to the assistant superintendent and then to the HISD Board. *Sullivan v. Houston ISD*, 333 F.Supp. 1149 (S.D. Tex., 1971), 1154; also 475 F.2d 1071 (5th Cir., 1973), 1073–74.

111. In 1969 judges of the U.S. Court of Appeals for the Seventh Circuit overturned the suspensions of several SDS members at the University of Wisconsin at Madison, after deciding that university rules against "misconduct" were constitutionally defective. See *Soglin v. Kauffman*, 418 F.2d 163 (7th Cir., 1969). See Haskell, "Judicial Review of School Discipline," 215–18. The doctrine of "in loco parentis," which held that administrators acted in the place of parents to protect and instruct students, is rarely if ever mentioned in these cases. Ibid., at 235 n. 63.

112. *Sullivan v. Houston ISD*, 333 F.Supp. 1149 (S.D. Tex., 1971), 1159 [citations omitted]. See *Griswold v. Connecticut*, 381 U.S. 479 (1965).

113. *Schwartz v. Galveston Independent School District*, 309 F.Supp. 1034 (S.D. Tex., 1970) [hereafter cited as *Schwartz v. Galveston ISD*]; Civ. No. 69-G-185. See also case records in S.D. Tex., Galveston Division, NARA-SWA, RG 21, box 348, folder for Case No. 69-G-185. See especially Judge Noel's Memorandum Opinion, 2 February 1970, as corrected 16 February, as supplemented 18 February and 10 March 1970.

114. The code also allowed black students to wear "Afros." See *Schwartz v. Galveston ISD*, 309 F.Supp., 1035–1936, esp. nn. 1–2.

115. For Senator "Babe" Schwartz's liberal politics, see Davidson, *Race and Class*, 54, 150.

116. *Schwartz v. Galveston ISD*, 309 F.Supp., 1036–37. The same day, a fourteen-year-old freshman in La Porte, Texas, maintained his right to grow a mustache against school rules and also filed suit in Judge Noel's court. "School Getting Lip in Mustache Case," *Houston Post*, 9 December 1969. For the ACLU's support of high school students as well as college students, see Walker, *In Defense of American Liberties*, 306–7. A Houston native, Berg attended Tulane University in New Orleans, then transferred to UH, where he earned a law degree in 1967. In 1969 he had successfully appealed the case of Danny Schacht, a war protester convicted of misusing a military uniform during a demonstration, to the U.S. Supreme Court. See *United States v. Schacht*, 397 U.S. 58 (1969). When he won the *Schacht* appeal, Berg became, at the age of twenty-seven, the youngest attorney since Daniel Webster to win a reversal from the court. Gary Taylor, "Mogul's Case Just a Notch in His Belt," *National Law Journal*, 28 October 1991, p. 8.

117. *Schwartz v. Galveston ISD*, 309 F.Supp., 1036, 1049–50.

118. Ibid., 1048.

119. Ibid., 1048–50.

120. *Tinker*, 393 U.S. 503 (1969), 507–8.

121. Fifth Circuit Judge Elbert Tuttle dissented, on the grounds that the disruptions were because other students disliked the Beatle style and had disrupted classes with name-calling and threats. Judge Tuttle thought the regulations should have prevented the chilling, not the expression. *Ferrell v. Dallas Independent School District*, 392 F.2d 697 (5th Cir., 1968) 704–5. The Supreme Court had denied certiorari; 393 U.S. 856 (1968). For more on the *Ferrell* case, see Haskell, "Judicial Review of School Discipline," 233–34.

122. Judge Allan B. Hannay considered another "hair case" on 22 January 1970. See *Pritchard v. Spring Branch Independent School District*, 308 F.Supp. 570 (S.D. Tex., 1970).

123. John Quigley, "3 Bellaire Students Ousted over Paper," *Houston Post*, 23 October 1969, 23A.

124. Ibid.

125. John Quigley, "Pupil Sues Over Haircut Order," *Houston Post*, 26 November 1969. Seventeen "long-haired" boys and three girls showed up at the courthouse to show support. They reportedly missed school with their parents' permission. John Quigley, "Judge Rules Schools Can Ban Long Hair," *Houston Post*, 3 December 1969.

126. John Quigley, "Judge Rules Schools Can Ban Long Hair," *Houston Post*, 3 December 1969.

127. Also, members of San Jac's board of regents visited California and saw for themselves what large numbers of "those people" did to the peaceful atmosphere of a college campus. The prevalence of a conspiracy theory of the origin of the antiwar protest explained the response to militant groups such as MAYO and SDS. See, for example, Faser, *1968*, 51–54.

128. *Calbillo v. San Jacinto Junior College,* 305 F.Supp. 857 (S.D. Tex., 1969), 859.

129. Berg filed a motion to have the *Plain Brown Watermelon* case consolidated with Calbillo's. John Quigley, "3 Bellaire Students Ousted over Paper," *Houston Post,* 23 October 1969, 23A.

130. *Calbillo v. San Jacinto Junior College,* 305 F.Supp., 858 n. 2.

131. "SJC Must Readmit Bearded Student," *Houston Post,* 21 October 1969, 3A.

132. Spencer and the academic dean, O. W. Marcom, admitted that Calbillo had not previously been disciplined by college authorities. *Calbillo v. San Jacinto Junior College,* 305 F.Supp., 858. Spencer also acknowledged that he was present at a board meeting when a petition, signed by eleven hundred San Jac students, requesting that the ban be dropped was presented, but that he had recommended that the ban be retained. Fred Harper, "Judge Rules College Ban on Beards Illegal," *Houston Chronicle,* 31 October 1969.

133. Bob Cargill, "San Jac College Beard-banning Rule Sheared by Judge," *Houston Post,* 1 November 1969.

134. *Calbillo v. San Jacinto Junior College,* 305 F.Supp., 861 n. 4.

135. Ibid., at 859–60, 861 nn. 5, 6. Newspaper photographs support the judge's evaluation. Calbillo had fairly short hair and a cropped "van-dyke" beard and mustache. See photos accompanying Fred Harper, "Judge Rules College Ban on Beards Illegal," *Houston Chronicle,* 31 October 1969; and Bob Cargill, "San Jac College Beard-banning Rule Sheared by Judge," *Houston Post,* 1 November 1969.

136. Bob Cargill, "San Jac College Beard-banning Rule Sheared by Judge," *Houston Post,* 1 November 1969.

137. *Calbillo v. San Jacinto Junior College,* 305 F.Supp., 858–59, 861.

138. Ibid., 858–59, 861.

139. Ibid., 861.

140. Ibid., 861–62. The Calbillo case made national news, although only in a short blurb. See "Judge Backs Bearded Youth," *New York Times,* 2 November 1969. The San Jac administrators appealed, and on 5 November 1970 the Fifth Circuit vacated the *Calbillo* case as moot. Calbillo had persuaded the board of regents to clear his record and had withdrawn from San Jac to enroll elsewhere (reportedly after shaving his beard). Also, the circuit judges remanded the case, and, although Calbillo had not filed the case as a class action, they directed Singleton to decide whether the injunction applied to all students at San Jac "both now and in the future." The appeals court also gave the school the opportunity to revise its regulations so that they were "clearly related to the maintenance of reasonable discipline and decorum." *Calbillo v. San Jacinto Junior College,* 434 F.2d 609 (5th Cir., 1969), 610, esp. n. 1. See also "Student's Hair Case Again up to Court," *Houston Post,* 5 November 1970. Some citizens had complained that it was a waste of taxpayers' money for the state-supported college to appeal, but at least one Houstonian disagreed and wrote to the *Houston Post,* "I can't think of a better or more productive use for tax money than fighting federal nincompoopery. . . . The people of this country are fast getting a bellyful of soft-hearted civil libertarians who are continually telling the majority of citizens to go to . . . because one individual gets his feelings hurt." Lee W. Thompson, letter to the editor, "A Bellyful, Says Lee W. Thompson," *Houston Post,* 17 November 1969.

141. *Calbillo v. San Jacinto Junior College,* 305 F.Supp., 862 n. 7.

142. Tom Curtis, "Debate on Dress Code Revived by School Transfers," *Houston Chronicle,* 20 September 1970, 1A, 5A.

143. Singleton made these remarks in declining to set an immediate hearing on a suit

protesting the Cypress-Fairbanks School District's closing its all-black school. Fred Harper, "Judge Urges Less Note of Race, Hair in Schools," *Houston Chronicle,* 6 October 1970. This is an unreported case. One commentator suggested at the time: "Someone ought to build a monument to U.S. Judge John Singleton, who said school people ought to quit litigating over hair and short skirts, race and other nonessentials, and get on with educating. He said this in refusing to close an all-black school in view of the fact that the U.S. Supreme Court is expected to act on busing and neighborhood schools." From the weekly newsletter *Austin Report* 22, no. 48 (11 October 1970). This is an unreported case.

144. As noted, the regents were continuing their appeal to the Fifth Circuit. "San Jacinto Drops Hair, Beard Rule," *Houston Post,* 10 July 1970.

145. *Hander v. San Jacinto Junior College,* 325 F.Supp. 1019 (S.D. Tex., 1971), 1019–20.

146. Finally, Hander did not claim that he had been denied due process; like Calbillo, he had counsel during the administrative hearing regarding his dismissal. *Hander v. San Jacinto Junior College,* 325 F.Supp., 1020.

147. Ibid., 1020.

148. Ibid., 1021.

149. *Younger v. Harris,* 401 U.S. 37 (1971), 44.

150. *Hander v. San Jacinto Junior College,* 325 F.Supp., 1021–22.

151. Associate Justice William O. Douglas dissented from the majority's refusal to review a case involving the length of a student's hair in 1972, and he noted the more than fifty "hair cases" on the books. *Olff v. East Side Union High School District,* 404 U.S. 1042 (1972), cert. denied; but see dissent at 1045–46, incl. n. 5. Friedman's estimate was seventy-five federal cases on high school hair. He noted that this was an issue that would have been inconceivable to the lawyers, judges, and citizens in the nineteenth century. That it became such a pressing issue in the late 1960s is an example of the demand for relief in the courts that Friedman called the concern for "total justice." Friedman, *Total Justice,* 13.

152. Burger, quoted in *Press v. Pasadena Independent School District,* 326 F.Supp. 550 (S.D. Tex., 1971), 552; Houston Division, Civ. A. No. 71-H-187.

153. Ibid., 557–58.

154. U.S. 45 (1905).

155. *Press v. Pasadena Independent School Dist.,* 326 F.Supp., 565.

156. See *Karr v. Schmidt,* 460 F.2d 609 (5th Cir., 1972).

157. *Karr v. Schmidt,* 401 U.S. 1201 (1972), 1203.

158. Ibid., 1203. In fact, as of the mid-1970s, four federal circuits (Fourth, Eighth, First, and Seventh) had upheld the right of students to wear their hair as they chose, one (the Second) recognized the right by implication in a police grooming case, four upheld school grooming codes (Third, Fifth, Ninth, Sixth), and one (the Tenth) refused to intervene, calling it a state matter. In the order described, these cases were *Massie v. Henry,* 455 F.2d 779 (4th Cir., 1972), *Bishop v. Colaw,* 450 F.2d. 1069 (8th Cir., 1971), *Richards v. Thurston,* 424 F.2d. 1281 (1st Cir., 1970), *Breen v. Kahl,* 419 F.2d. 1034 (7th Cir., 1969), *Dwen v. Barry,* 483 F.2d. 1126 (2nd Cir., 1973), *Zeller v. Donegal School Dist. Bd. of Educ.,* 517 F.2d. 600 (3rd Cir., 1975), *Karr v. Schmidt,* 460 F.2d. 609 (5th Cir.), cert. denied, 409 U.S. 989 (1972), *King v. Saddleback Junior College,* 445 F.2d. 932 (9th Cir.), cert. denied, 404 U.S. 979 (1971), *Jackson v. Dorrier,* 424 F.2d. 213 (6th Cir.), cert. denied, 400 U.S. 850 (1970), and *Freeman v. Flake,* 448 F.2d. 258 (10th Cir., 1971), cert. denied, 405 U.S. 1032 (1972). Howard, "State Courts and Constitutional Rights," 927 n. 293. After a few years of the "new federalism," Professor Howard selected four areas (hair length, motorcycle helmet laws, sexual acts between consenting adults, and marijuana)

through which to explore state courts' responses to regulation of "lifestyles and autonomy." He notes that although myriad state courts employed various federal constitutional arguments both to uphold and to overturn school appearance regulations, only one state court, in Alaska, struck down a school rule by relying solely on analysis of liberty protected by the Alaska state constitution (see *Breese v. Smith,* 501 P.2d 159 [Alaska, 1972]). Howard further notes that state courts most often (with exceptions such as Alaska's court) follow the U.S. Supreme Court's lead in "autonomy and lifestyle" cases, rather than exploiting the opportunity to "weigh values" under their own constitutions. Some state courts devolved the responsibility even further. At least one state court cited Justice Black's notion that hair length cases should be left to the states and refused to intervene on the grounds of what might be called "intrastate federalism." The case was *Dunkerton v. Russell,* 502 S.W. 64 (Ky. App. 1973) 65 [the Kentucky court cited Justice Black's opinion *Karr v. Schmidt*]. Howard calls this "false logic" and notes that "[t]here may be good reasons for a state court not to decide hair length cases, but a mechanical use of Justice Black's judgment, whose basis was federalism, is surely not one of them." See Howard, "State Courts and Constitutional Rights in the Day of the Burger Court," 927–28, 933, 941.

159. *Lansdale v. Tyler Junior College,* 470 F.2d 659 (5th Cir., 1972), 662–663. See *Karr v. Schmidt,* 460 F.2d 609 (5th Cir., 1972). With this distinction clearly articulated by the Fifth Circuit judges, Singleton dismissed another high school hair case in December 1974. "Suit Over Hair Length Dismissed," *Houston Post,* 11 December 1974, 12A.

160. *Hander v. San Jacinto Junior College,* 468 F.2d 619 (5th Cir., 1972).

161. *Hander v. San Jacinto Junior College,* 519 F.2d 273 (5th Cir., 1975), 281–82 (Judge Brown concurring). The Fifth Circuit denied rehearing the case en banc, 522 F.2d 204 (5th Cir., 1975).

162. By the mid-1970s the court had developed the implications of *Younger* into "a doctrine of devolution of judicial power to state courts," and the justices apparently attached to the *Younger* abstention doctrine the "imperative dignity previously accorded substantive due process and the civil rights of blacks." Soifer and Macgill, "The *Younger* Doctrine," 1141–43.

163. In *Roth v. United States* (1957), a case concerned with a state prohibition on the advertisement of pornographic books through the mail, the court majority reaffirmed that obscene material was "utterly without social importance" and was not protected by the First Amendment. The *Roth* decision fixed the modern definition of obscenity as that which "deals with sex in a matter appealing to prurient interest," where "prurient interest" meant "[h]aving a tendency to excite lustful thoughts" or exhibiting "shameful and morbid interest in sex." Finally, the court established the legal test of obscenity as "whether to the average person, applying contemporary community standards, the dominant theme of the material taken as a whole appeals to prurient interest." See *Roth v. United States,* 354 U.S. 476 (1957), 484, 487, 489. Although the *Roth* opinion clearly excluded obscenity from the First Amendment, it also declared that the definition of obscenity must be established on the basis of the First Amendment rather than the common law. Under the 1868 British case *Regina v. Hicklin,* which established a common-law standard, prosecutions were allowed on the basis of the tendency of a work to "deprave and corrupt" the most susceptible segments of an audience. This lowest common denominator standard of *Regina* was overturned by *Roth.* In another major case, *Memoirs v. Massachusetts* (1966), the court augmented *Roth* with a three-pronged legal test. Under *Memoirs* material could be judged obscene if its dominant theme was "prurient," "patently offensive because it affronts contemporary community standards," and "utterly without redeeming social value." See *A Book Named "John*

Cleland's Memoirs of a Woman of Pleasure" v. Massachusetts, 383 U.S. 413 (1966), 419–20. This was known as the "Fanny Hill" case, because in the book, the "woman of pleasure" purported to have written the memoirs was named Fanny Hill. Three years later (twelve years after *Roth*), the court overturned as unconstitutional a state criminal prohibition of the possession of "obscene" home movies, as a matter of privacy. *Stanley v. Georgia,* 394 U.S. 557 (1969).

164. Many conservatives blamed the coarseness of the 1960s on liberal legal organizations, such as the ACLU, which often defended the rights of artists to free sexual expression. Walker, *In Defense of American Liberties,* 231–36, 318–20.

165. See *Universal Amusement Co. v. Vance,* 404 F.Supp. 33 (S.D. Tex., 1975) [Houston Division; Civ. A. No. 73-H-528].

166. The state law was art. 527 of the Texas Penal Code ("Obscene Matters"). Houston, like other large cities across America, had a history of regulating moral turpitude, especially prostitution. This history consisted of alternating periods of suppression and accommodation. A vice district existed in Houston after 1908, but in 1917 morals crusaders joined their cause to the patriotic concern with protecting soldiers from disease and degradation, and finally convinced city leaders to extinguish the "red-lights." See Mackey, "Red Lights Out."

167. The complaint claimed that, in all, the arrests and seizure violated no fewer than six amendments of the U.S. Constitution. The disputed state law was Article 527 of the Texas Penal Code.

168. "Theatre Obscenity Raids Halted," *Houston Post,* 1 November 1969.

169. "Movie Men Granted Hearing in Effort to Kill Obscenity Law," *Houston Post,* 17 October 1969, 15A.

170. The suit had been expanded to include the complaints of several owners and operators who were raided and arrested in previous weeks. "Adult Movie Raid Hearing to Continue," *Houston Chronicle,* 20 October 1970; "Panel: Adult Movie Arrests Needn't Stop," *Houston Chronicle,* 15 November 1970.

171. The Anti-Injunction Act provided in part that: "[a] court of the United States may not grant an injunction to stay proceedings in a State court except as expressly authorized by Act of Congress, or where necessary in aid of its jurisdiction, or to protect or effectuate its judgments." 28 U.S.C. § 2283.

172. *Academy v. Vance,* 320 F.Supp. 1357 (S.D. Tex., 1970), at 1358 [Houston Division; Civ. A. No. 70-H-1115]. See *Dombrowski v. Pfister,* 380 U.S. 479 (1965).

173. *Sheridan v. Garrison,* 415 F.2d. 699 (5th Cir., 1969), 709.

174. Judge Seals noted that the claim that the prosecution had been pursued in bad faith could be disregarded after examining the HPD's elaborate preparations for the raid. He declared that the vice squad's investigation and arrest procedures, planned by the police at the direction of the district attorney, testified to their good faith. Although the judge also noted that the Northern District of Texas had declared unconstitutional § 9 of art. 527 of the Texas criminal code, which had allowed seizure of property without an adversarial hearing, he saw this as no reason to grant the requested injunctions. See *Newman v. Conover,* 313 F.Supp. 623 (N.D. Tex., 1970). Seals further noted that the U.S. Supreme Court was preparing to hear an appeal from Massachusetts, *Karalexis v. Byrne,* 306 F.Supp. 1363 (D. Mass., 1969), which might clarify the murky constitutional boundaries of state obscenity law, and so refused to consider Texas art. 527's ultimate constitutionality. The very nature of the ongoing confusion, however, led Seals to believe that he could not declare the law unconstitutional "on its face." 320 F.Supp. 1357, at 1358–59, 1362–63.

175. Moreover, Singleton considered that in light of the *Newman* decision regarding property seizure, the defendants/plaintiffs deserved an adversarial hearing before their arrests. Unless adversarial hearings established the fact of obscenity before arrests, Singleton believed that the state authorities would be illegally seizing a business and therefore doing "by means of a back door the very thing a federal three-judge-court said they could not do by a constitutionally protected front door." 320 F.Supp. 1357, at 1363.

176. Ibid., 1365. Harris County District Attorney Carol Vance subsequently said the arrests were permitted "under ordinary criminal procedures" and that the films in question were "so obscene, depraved and sick" that they were not the type of pornography that was constitutionally protected. "Panel: Adult Movie Arrests Needn't Stop," *Houston Chronicle*, 15 November 1970. Vance also noted that patrons could be arrested in the raids, although making an obscenity case against them might be difficult, since patrons go to movies assuming that the films are lawful. "Raids on Sex Movies to Resume," *Houston Post*, 16 November 1970. Clearly, Judge Singleton was frustrated at the majority's refusal to intervene immediately in the Cinne Arts case. Singleton did get a chance to voice his opinion on free expression. During the same year the city council of Pasadena, under a public nuisance ordinance, wanted to prohibit "nudie movies" at the drive-in on Red Bluff Lane. Singleton guided them to a constitutionally acceptable licensing ordinance. The movies in question, including *Suburban Pagan* and *Hot Skin and Cold Cash*, were not found to be obscene, but drivers had risked being endangered by the unexpected sight of "bare female breasts and buttocks," which were visible from the road. See "Drive-in Theatre Sues for Damages, Return of Films," *Houston Post*, 26 February 1970; "Nude Film Case Up in Bare Air," *Houston Post*, 2 March 1970, 8A; "Trial Set in Drive-in Movie Quarrel," *Houston Post*, 29 April 1970, 9A; "Nudie Movie Law Voided by Judge," *Houston Chronicle*, 3 June 1970, 1A; "Pasadena Drivers' Fun May End," *Houston Post*, 3 June 1970; "Pasadena Must Try Again on Movie Law," *Houston Post*, 4 June 1970; "Pasadena OKs Nudie Movie Ordinance," *Houston Chronicle*, 9 June 1970, 12A; and "Pasadena Council OKs New Movie Law," *Houston Post*, 10 June 1970.

177. Most of the firsthand knowledge of the "simulated" nature of the staged acts comes from Montgomery's occasionally graphic testimony. The court record does not identify the playwright, but it can be assumed that Montgomery, the owner and stage manager of the theater, and its female star, was obviously enough of a multitalented *auteur* to write the scripts as well. *Montgomery v. Short*, 327 F.Supp. 726 (S.D. Tex., 1971), 727 [Houston Division; Civ. A. No. 71-H-181]. The relevant Texas statutes were art. 607 of the Texas Penal Code, §§ 16, 19, and 20, and §§28–42 of the City Ordinance of Houston. Under Texas's art. 607, "vagrants" included those engaged in prostitution, lewdness, or assignation, as well as those aiding and abetting such activities. The Penal Code's authors construed "lewdness" to "include any indecent or obscene act." Houston's § 28–42 defined unlawful indecent exposure circularly, as "expos[ing the] . . . person in an indecent manner," but also included "any obscene or indecent act in any street or other public place, or in the presence of any person." It was also indecent, according to this ordinance, to appear in public in a state of nudity, or "appear in public in the dress of the other sex." It is unclear from the record if this prohibition of transvestism, a common provision in municipal ordinances, was to be construed to include cross-dressing as a gorilla. See 327 F.Supp. 726; the statutes are discussed in app. A, at 729.

178. *Montgomery v. Short*, 327 F.Supp., 728.

179. U.S. 37 (1971).

180. F.Supp., 728.

181. Specifically, art. 607 of the Texas Penal Code, § 18, art. 667–19B of the Penal Code

(making criminal any lewd or obscene conduct at places licensed to serve liquor), and §§36–43 of the City Ordinance of Houston (prohibiting "any person to dance any indecent or immodest dance" within a license-holder's property). *Hearn v. Short,* 327 F.Supp. 33 (S.D. Tex., 1971), 34 [Houston Division; Civ. A. No. 70-H-1376].

182. Ibid., 34.

183. Ibid., 35.

184. However, because consideration of the municipal ordinance was outside the purview of the three-judge panel, Ingraham remanded the plea for relief from the ordinance back to a single-judge federal court for disposition, which presumably would dismiss it along similar lines. Ibid., 36.

185. Ibid.

186. Ibid. Singleton specifically mentioned *Redrup v. New York,* 386 U.S. 767 (1968).

187. Ibid., 36.

188. Ibid.

189. Ibid.

190. Finally, Judge Bue reproduced portions of the transcript of the hearing testimony as it had unfolded before the *Younger* announcement. Bue's recounting of the "dancing" makes for interesting reading. Ibid., 37–41. Bue noted as well that the admission charge for the My-O-My was a steep $3.00, and that beer and wine cost $1.55.

191. Bue felt compelled to write another angry thirty pages in an attempt to analyze federal obscenity precedents. Beginning with *Roth* and leading inexorably to the present case, he intended to demonstrate that the Supreme Court, by promulgating an unbroken series of splintered and confused decisions, had failed to establish a firm and unequivocal standard to guide lower federal judges. Essentially, Bue's opinion indicted the higher court for not meeting the issue head on, until it finally gave up and closed the federal route in *Younger.* Bue concluded that although "[i]t is unlikely after all of these years that there exists any historical or legal source which, by itself, would constitute a clear, unerring signal, heretofore unheard, as to the meaning of the First Amendment freedoms," the facts of the cases before his were "not so difficult . . . that they conceivably would meet one professed test of obscenity and fail another." Judge Bue's comments throughout his detailed history of state and federal obscenity cases leaves no doubt regarding his frustration about the creeping tide of judicial timidity. Ibid., 41–71.

192. F.Supp. 33, 71. The citizenry was divided on the rights of expression, but also on the rights of consenting adults to enjoy privacy. In 1965 the court defined a right to privacy, specifically the right for a married couple to use contraceptives at home, which emanated from the "penumbras" of the Ninth Amendment. *Griswold v. Connecticut,* 381 U.S. 479 (1965). Finally, twelve years after *Roth,* in 1969's *Stanley v. Georgia,* the court overturned as unconstitutional a state criminal prohibition of possession of "obscene" home movies, as a matter of privacy. *Stanley v. Georgia,* 394 U.S. 557 (1969). In these opinions the Supreme Court had variously mentioned "redeeming social importance," "social value," and then "patent offensiveness" in elaborating the legal test for obscenity. These terms, as well as the original *Roth* formulas such as "taken as a whole," "appeal to the prurient interest," and even the "average person," continued to cause problems of definition. For the justice's claims of clarity in the presence of demonstrated ambiguity, see Vines, "The Role of Courts of Appeals," 96–98.

193. The next day, the *Post* reported the dismissal in a 125-word blurb (counting the headline), which noted only that "a Feb. 23 U.S. Supreme Court decision in similar cases

was involved in the order to dismiss." See "U.S. Court Frees Police to Raid Nude Act Clubs," *Houston Post,* 17 April 1971, Courts/police section.

194. Captain Allbright later cited as the impetus of his action a New York opinion provided by the Houston district attorney's office. "Sex Film Loses Fight in Court," *Houston Post,* 3 May 1973.

195. *Universal Amusement Co. v. Vance,* 404 F.Supp. 33 (S.D. Tex., 1975), 39. In his lawsuit Spiegel challenged the constitutionality of the same Texas statute that had been invoked against the Cinne Arts manager and projectionist in 1969: art. 527 of the Texas Penal Code ("Obscene Matters"). Spiegel also claimed that his hearing before a state district judge had been defective. In his suit Spiegel requested ninety thousand dollars in damages and twenty-five thousand dollars in attorney's fees. "Sex Film Loses Fight in Court," *Houston Post,* 3 May 1973.

196. Over the course of two years, he joined twenty cases to the Houston litigation. Ibid., at 36–37. Only one of the additional suits was another case from the Southern District of Texas: *Hargrove v. Hill,* unpublished [Houston Division; Civ. A. No. 73-H-1114]. In the published opinion for *Universal Amusement Co. v. Vance,* Judge Singleton describes the circumstances in only the three representative cases.

197. *Universal Amusement Co. v. Vance,* 404 F.Supp., 37.

198. The judge declared that, although he believed that a Supreme Court ruling required the state court to return the film pending another trial, Spiegel must first seek relief in an appeal to the Texas Court of Civil Appeals before asking the federal courts to rule on the matter. Clyde Woody, Spiegel's attorney, said he would immediately make the request, but visiting state judge Stanley Kirk of Wichita Falls had already denied an earlier request to have the film returned. "Judge Refuses to Order Court to Return 'Deep Throat' Film," *Houston Chronicle,* 17 December 1973, 10A. The *Chronicle* article neglected to cite the specific Supreme Court ruling to which Singleton might have been referring, but it was probably *Younger.*

199. *Miller v. California,* 413 U.S. 15 (1973). The remaining cases of the *Miller* quintet were: *Paris Adult Theater I v. Slayton,* 413 U.S. 49; *Kaplan v. California,* 413 U.S. 115, *United States v. 12 200-Foot Reels,* 413 U.S. 123; and *United States v. Orito,* 413 U.S. 139 (all 1973).

200. This is often referred to as the LAPS test. *Miller v. California,* 413 U.S. 15 (1973), at 24. In practice, the court had still not made the job easier. The justices soon clarified the new standard in several other important cases, including *Heller v. New York,* 413 U.S. 483 (1973) and *Roaden v. Kentucky,* 413 U.S. 496 (1973). These latter cases dealt not with substantive obscenity laws but with the procedures to bring into court those who are alleged purveyors of obscenity. *Universal Amusement Co. v. Vance,* 404 F.Supp., 37.

201. Texas Penal Code, § 43.21, pt. 1 (a) and (d). Much of this language was taken from the *Roth-Memoirs* line of cases, rather than *Miller.* Pt. 1 (b) refers to "community standards," but pt. 3 defined "prurient interests" as material defined for a "specially susceptible audience," a contradictory anachronism from common-law definitions. The new § 43.21 retained the earlier art. 527 requirement that to be found obscene, material must be found to be "utterly without redeeming social value." At the same time, Texas legislators repealed art. 513 of the Penal Code ("Disorderly House"), which defined a disorderly house as a "any house, building, theater or other structure where obscene motion pictures are displayed, exhibited or shown to person under twenty-one (21) years of age." Art. 513 had also defined "obscene motion picture" and "prurient interest" in language virtually identical to the old art. 527, that is to say, in the language of *Roth* and *Memoirs.* In addition, however, art. 513 had included a sentence defining "contemporary community standards." The lawmakers replaced this with

a revised version of art. 4667 of Tex. Civ. Stat. ("Injunctions to abate public nuisances"). The old art. 4667 provided for the enjoining of "the habitual use, actual, threatened, or contemplated, of any premises, place or building or part thereof . . . [f]or keeping, being interested in, aiding or abetting the keeping of a bawdy or disorderly house, as those terms are defined in the Penal Code." The new art. 4667 specifically provided for enjoining the "habitual use, actual, threatened, or contemplated, of any premises, place or building or part thereof . . . [f]or the commercial manufacturing, commercial distribution, or commercial exhibition of obscene materials." Tex. Civ. Stat., art. 4667, pt. (d), *Vernon's Annotated Civil Statutes.* Statutes quoted in *Universal Amusement Co. v. Vance,* 404 F.Supp., 37–40.

202. George Flynn, "Theater Owner 'Upheld,'" *Houston Post,* 9 July 1975, p. 1A.

203. Attorneys for these three plaintiffs submitted joint briefs. Two of the three cases had remaining factual disputes, but Judge Singleton considered these immaterial to the determination of the cases. *Universal Amusement Co. v. Vance,* 404 F.Supp., 37.

204. "Panel Hears Obscenity Law Debate," *Houston Post,* 15 November 1974.

205. Texas Penal Code, art. 4667.

206. At the same time, Singleton maintained that the *threat* of a future prosecution under the nuisance statute was enough to present the actual controversy required by art. III of the Constitution. The original case is captioned *King Arts Theatre v. McCrea,* CA-6–345 (N.D. Tex.), but it is included and described in *Universal Amusement Co. v. Vance,* 404 F.Supp., 37–38.

207. *Dombrowski v. Pfister,* 380 U.S. 479 (1965), 487.

208. *Universal Amusement Co. v. Vance,* 404 F.Supp., 38–39.

209. That is, at Section 43.21, which defined obscenity in virtually the same terms as the old art. 527. The original charges were brought under the old language, but King Arts continued its complaint against the revised statutes. Ibid., at 39. The original obscenity statute, with its "sexual matters" language intact, had recently been challenged in the Texas Court of Criminal Appeals as *West v. State of Texas* and upheld, only to be appealed to the U.S. Supreme Court, which vacated and remanded the case to the Court of Criminal Appeals for further consideration in light of *Miller.* See Order for certiorari, granted, vacated and remanded in *West v. Texas,* 414 U.S. 961 (1973). On 9 October 1974, in a post-*Miller* rehearing of *West,* the court of criminal appeals held that although art. 527 was perhaps deficient, it had been authoritatively construed by Texas courts, and these constructions supplied any constitutional deficiencies. Therefore, the defendant in the *West* case derived no benefit from *Miller.* See *West v. State of Texas,* 514 S.W.2d 433 (Tex. Cr. App., 1974), at 448. Given these fresh tracks, Judge Singleton confidently believed that the court of criminal appeals, although it had only glossed the original "sexual matters" construction, would apply the same gloss to the new words and thereby provide authoritative guidance on the interpretation of Texas law in light of the *Miller* standard. *Universal Amusement Co. v. Vance,* 404 F.Supp., 40.

210. Judge Singleton noted that a federal obscenity statute, 18 U.S.C. § 1461, which had been challenged as unconstitutionally vague in *Miller,* had repeatedly been upheld. *Universal Amusement Co. v. Vance,* 404 F.Supp., 40–42.

211. If the county attorney proved a nuisance in these terms, for example, the statutes allowed the premises to be enjoined for one year unless the owner, tenant, or lessee makes a bond of at least one thousand but not more than five thousand dollars, with the condition that "the acts prohibited in this law shall not be done in said house." See Texas Penal Code, arts. 4665 ("Nuisance: evidence") and 4666 ("Nuisance: prosecution").

212. *Universal Amusement Co. v. Vance,* 404 F.Supp., 42–46. The classic cases of prior

restraint law are *Near v. Minnesota,* 283 U.S. 697 (1931) and *Freedman v. Maryland,* 380 U.S. 51 (1964).

213. Singleton accepted that the Supreme Court had allowed that some forms of prior restraint, operating under very special circumstances, might be acceptable, but only if the burden of proof remained with the censor and the statutes provided for a short, fixed interval to determine the obscenity of questionable material. *Universal Amusement Co. v. Vance,* 404 F.Supp., 42–46.

214. The original case was captioned *Dexter v. Butler* [SA-74-CA-168 (W.D. Tex.)]. See *Universal Amusement Co. v. Vance,* 404 F.Supp., 46–47.

215. *Universal Amusement Co. v. Vance,* 404 F.Supp., 46–47.

216. Texas Penal Code, § 43.23 ("Commercial Obscenity"), carried a possible penalty of a fine not to exceed one thousand dollars, or confinement not to exceed 180 days, or both. But Section 16.01 ("Unlawful use of criminal instrument") carried a penalty of a fine not to exceed five thousand dollars and confinement not more than ten nor less than two years. § 16.01, pt. (a), made it unlawful to possess, manufacture, or sell a criminal instrument, and pt. (b) defined "criminal instrument" to mean "anything that is specially designed, made, or adapted for the commission of an offense."

217. See *Universal Amusement Co. v. Vance,* 404 F.Supp., 47.

218. Ibid., 48.

219. As a result of four arrests, Dexter was responsible for fifty-five thousand dollars in personal recognizance bonds. Ibid., 46–47.

220. In addition, Judge Singleton said that the in-theater evaluations did not rise to the level of an adversarial hearing, particularly one aiming to assess the possible obscenity of *Deep Throat.* He added: "We assume that San Antonio is asking us to hold that their procedures are something more than an inquiry into the probable obscenity of the film. . . . The court will not so hold." See *Universal Amusement Co. v. Vance,* 404 F.Supp., 48–49.

221. Ibid., 50–51.

222. The Texas legislature had also amended the state's code of criminal procedure in January 1974. Art. 18.02 ("Search and Seizure"), § 2, allowed a warrant to be issued for this purpose.

223. On 1 May the Ellwest prosecution became one of the twenty cases consolidated under the original complaint in Houston. The original case was captioned *Ellwest v. Byrd,* CA-3-74-130-E (N.D. Tex.). The date of the first raid on the Ellwest is given as both 24 and 27 January in the opinion. See *Universal Amusement Co. v. Vance,* 404 F.Supp., 51–53.

224. Ibid., 51–53.

225. Ibid.

226. Ibid., 53.

227. Ibid., 54.

228. Ibid., 54–55.

229. Ibid., 56.

230. If the judges found bad faith, harassment, or special circumstances, they were to send the cases back to the three-judge panel to be disposed of according to the rules in the opinion. Ibid., 57. The state appealed but ultimately lost. A Fifth Circuit panel overturned Judge Singleton's opinion for the three-judge district court panel. One of the issues that the Fifth Circuit decided, which Singleton had not touched on in the district opinion, was the award of money damages. According to Singleton's opinion, damages would be the provenance of

the original judges. *Universal Amusement Co. v. Vance,* 559 F.2d 1286 (5th Cir., 1978). On a rehearing en banc, the full court of appeals overturned the Circuit panel, and strongly upheld the district decision. *Universal Amusement Co., Inc. v. Vance,* 587 F.2d 159 (5th Cir., 1978). Finally, five years after Judge Singleton and the other two judges delivered their original opinion, the Supreme Court also upheld the panel's findings. *Vance v. Universal Amusement Co.,* 445 U.S. 308 (1980). By 1980 the video cassette recorder had been introduced, and *Deep Throat* was available on home videotape.

231. Vance, quoted in "Ruling on Obscenity Law Has Little Effect Here," *Houston Chronicle,* 9 July 1975, 8A.

232. Vance claimed that only movies or magazines that featured pedophilia or bestiality were apparently fit for prosecution. Vance, quoted in "Ruling on Obscenity Law Has Little Effect Here," *Houston Chronicle,* 9 July 1975, 8A.

233. Spiegel, quoted in George Flynn, "Theater Owner 'Upheld'," *Houston Post,* 9 July 1975. In the Southern District as elsewhere, the question of obscenity continued to evolve. In recent years not only conservative religious, but also radical secular activists, and feminists who may be either pro- or antiporn, have debated theories of responsibility and public responses to pornography. See, for example, Baird and Rosenbaum, *Pornography;* Moretti, *Obscenity and Pornography;* de Grazia, *Girls Lean Back Everywhere;* Lacombe, *Blue Politics;* Kobylka, *The Politics of Obscenity.* And see *The Report of the Commission on Obscenity and Pornography.*

234. *Younger v. Harris,* 401 U.S., at 43.

235. In the early 1970s the court extended the basic rationale of *Younger* to bar federal injunctions against civil proceedings that a state had initiated "in aid of and closely related to criminal statutes." They next discouraged federal intervention into any civil proceeding brought by a state. Zeigler, "Reassessment of the *Younger* Doctrine," 988. In addition to *Younger,* Judge Singleton noted the more recent *Huffman. v. Pursue, Ltd.,* 420 U.S. 592 (1975). *Huffman* established that the *Younger* doctrine of noninterference in state criminal prosecutions applied equally well to civil cases. Pursue, Ltd. owned an adult film theater. After conducting civil proceedings, an Ohio state judge had declared the movies to be obscene. The declaration authorized the closing of the theater and sale of personal property used in the theater's operation. Rather than appealing the state court decision, Pursue, Ltd. filed a § 1983 suit seeking a declaratory judgment against the state public nuisance law and injunctive relief from the state court order. Relying on the "Our Federalism" rationale of *Younger,* Justice Rehnquist wrote for the court that civil proceedings that were "akin to a criminal prosecution" were subject to *Younger* restrictions, and therefore the federal courts were required to abstain from interfering. This decision established what Rehnquist termed the "civil counterpart to Younger." 420 U.S. 592 (1975), 604. According to Bryce Baird, *Huffman* represented "a new direction in abstention doctrine that has developed almost exclusively through Rehnquist's opinions into the doctrine of civil rights abstention." He notes that the doctrine "encompasses, but is much broader than, *Younger* abstention." Baird, "Federal Court Abstention," 526–27.

236. Zeigler, "Accommodation of the *Younger* Doctrine," 269–70. In its 1967 opinion in *Zwickler v. Koota,* the Supreme Court reaffirmed the duty of the federal courts to hear civil rights cases. The justices noted: "Congress imposed the duty upon all levels of the federal judiciary to give due respect to a suitor's choice of a federal forum for the hearing and decision of his federal constitutional claims." *Zwickler v. Koota,* 389 U.S. 241 (1967), 248 (ci-

tations omitted). Even after *Younger* marked a change in direction, the justices continued to support the basic right of a civil rights plaintiff to have access to the federal courts. For example, in a 1972 case involving police officers who had closed down an adult bookstore as a public nuisance, the Supreme Court held that with § 1983, Congress expressly created a statutory exception to the Anti-injunction Act. The federal district judge ruled that the anti-injunction statute applied to the case. The Supreme Court reversed. *Mitchum v. Foster,* 407 U.S. 225 (1972), 227–228, 242. See Baird, "Federal Court Abstention," 511–12.

237. The plaintiffs, in addition to the UFWOC, AFL-CIO, included Francisco Medrano, Kathy Baker, David Lopez, Gilbert Padilla, Magdaleno Dimas, Benjamin Rodriguez. The defendants included Texas Ranger Captain A. Y. Allee, five of his Rangers, employees of the state of Texas and residents of Dimmitt County, Sheriff Solis of Starr County, Deputies Raul Peña and Roberto Peña, Justice of the Peace Lopez, and "Special Deputy" Rochester. *Medrano v. Allee,* 347 F.Supp. 605 (S.D. Tex., 1972), 611. The Texas statutes challenged were Texas Penal Code, art. 439 (prohibiting unlawful assembly), art. 474 (breach of the peace), and art. 482 (abusive language); and Tex. Rev. Civ. Stat., arts. 5154[d–f] (regulating mass picketing, secondary picketing, and boycotting).

238. *Medrano v. Allee,* 347 F.Supp. 605 (S.D. Tex., 1972), 618.

239. Ibid., 618. For example, Starr County deputies reportedly assisted in the distribution of *La Verdad* ("the Truth"), an antiunion newspaper. As Judges Seals noted, a typical headline was "Only Mexican Subversive Group Could Sympathize with Valley Farm Workers." Ibid., 617, plus appendix. Also noted at 416 U.S. 802 (1973), at 807, 826.

240. *Medrano v. Allee,* 347 F.Supp., 618.

241. Ibid., 634.

242. Ibid., 618.

243. See the denial at *Allee v. Medrano,* 414 U.S. 1020 (1973).

244. *Allee v. Medrano,* 416 U.S. 802 (1973), 810–11.

245. Ibid., 815–21.

246. Ibid., 821. Justice Powell did not participate in the decision.

247. For a discussion of the *Allee v. Medrano* case in terms of its relation to federalism and *Younger,* see Cooper, *Hard Judicial Choices,* 287–88.

248. Wasby, *Continuity and Change,* 7–8.

249. Kurland, "1971 Term," 210. For a critique that *Younger* abstention contradicted the Reconstruction Congress's intent in adopting the Fourteenth Amendment and enacting the predecessor statute of § 1983, see Zeigler, "Reassessment of the *Younger* Doctrine," 987–88.

250. Hufstedler, "Comity and the Constitution," 166; Blackmun, "Section 1983 and Federal Protection," 228; and Gibbons, "Legacy of the Burger Court," 310–11.

CHAPTER 5. Judicial Management of Triethnic Integration

1. The U.S. Supreme Court deferred to congressional intent in an important voting rights case, *Katzenbach v. Morgan,* 384 U.S. 641 (1966). See Pole, *Pursuit of Equality,* 421–23.

2. Funston, *Constitutional Counterrevolution?* 347–48; and O'Hara, "Introduction," 3. Also, for continued enforcement of civil rights statutes and decision under the early Nixon administration, see Landsberg, *Enforcing Civil Rights,* 141–42.

3. *Brown v. Board of Education of Topeka,* 349 U.S. 294 (1955), 295 [hereafter *Brown II*].

4. *Green v. County School Board of New Kent Co.,* 391 U.S. 430 (1968), 439.

5. *Alexander v. Holmes County Board of Education,* 396 U.S. 19 (1969), 20. See Melvin I.

Urofsky, *The Continuity of Change: The Supreme Court and Individual Liberties, 1953–1986* (Belmont: Wadsworth, 1991), 223–25; Wilkinson, *From Brown to Bakke,* 119–27; and Funston, *Constitutional Counterrevolution?* 40–55.

6. *Younger v. Harris,* 401 U.S. 37 (1971). Soifer and Macgill have noted that since the *Younger* decision was announced, Justice Hugo Black's slogan "Our Federalism," rather than legislative history or intent, has dominated the federal judicial development of federalism. See *Younger,* 401 U.S. 37, at 44; and Soifer and Macgill, "The *Younger* Doctrine," 1165.

7. Zelden, "From Rights to Resources," 484–89.

8. In 1954 the Supreme Court had condemned the exclusion of Spanish-surnamed citizens from juries as a violation of a Mexican American criminal defendant's due-process rights. The justices had accepted arguments that the Anglos in Texas treated Mexican Americans as a group that was distinct from "whites." However, the court maintained that the mere existence of local prejudice did not make Mexican descent a protected status in constitutional terms. See *Hernandez v. Texas,* 347 U.S. 475 (1954) 478–79, esp. n. 9.

9. See Allsup, *The American GI Forum,* 94–97; and Ramos, *The American GI Forum,* 22, 58–63.

10. *Hernandez v. Driscoll CISD,* 2 *Race Rel. L. Rptr.* 329 (S.D. Tex., 1957). For the practice of "tracking," see Rangel and Alcala, "De Jure Segregation," 331–33, esp. n. 139.

11. *Chapa v. Odem Independent School District* (S.D. Tex., 1967) [Corpus Christi Division, Civ. No. 66-C-72].

12. Ibid. However, Judge Seals requested additional evidence to support the validity of the ability testing in general. See Rangel and Alcala, "De Jure Segregation," 347–48, incl. nn. 241–45.

13. Ibid., 342–43 n. 216, and 348–49; Birnberg, "*Brown v. Board of Education,*" 339; and Levin and Moise, "School Desegregation Litigation," 76–80.

14. U.S.C. § 2000(a); see Salinas, "Desegregation of Schools in the Southwest," 939.

15. See "Comment: The Courts, HEW, and Southern School Desegregation," *Yale Law Journal* 77 (1967): 321. Also see Fisher, "The Judge as Manager," 7; and Wilkinson, *From Brown to Bakke,* 102–7.

16. *Singleton v. Jackson Municipal Separate School District,* 348 F.2d 729 (5th Cir., 1965). The case is known as *Singleton I.* In *Singleton II,* which followed the next year, the Fifth Circuit judges declared the HEW guidelines to be minimum standards and made it clear that judges should not "abdicate" their responsibilities regarding desegregation merely by conforming to the guidelines. 355 F.2d 865 (5th Cir., 1966).

17. San Miguel, "*Let All of Them Take Heed,*" 175–77.

18. Noted in Rangel and Alcala, "De Jure Segregation," 365–66 nn. 352–69. Also see Testimony of Jerold D. Ward, 11 December 1968, in U.S. Commission on Civil Rights, *Hearing Held in San Antonio,* 331–39.

19. Carlos Guerra, "Discourse by an Other," *Texas Observer,* 27 October 1967, p. 14.

20. In addition to the proliferation of official statements that recognized Mexican Americans as a distinct group, political activists associated with the Chicano movement rejected "white" status. They preferred to celebrate the "brown" identity they constructed for themselves. Meier and Ribera, *Mexican Americans/American Mexicans,* 211. Also Montejano, *Anglos and Mexicans,* 262–87. See Smith, "Mexicano Resistance," 288–97; and U.S. Commission on Civil Rights, *Mexican-American Educational Study, Report I,* 26.

21. San Miguel, "*Let All of Them Take Heed,*" 175.

22. See Rangel and Alcala, "De Jure Segregation," 342, 359.

23. *Cisneros v. Corpus Christi ISD*, 324 F.Supp. 599 (S.D. Tex., 1970). See Greenfield and Kates, "Mexican Americans," 662.

24. Salinas, "Desegregation of Schools in the Southwest," 951.

25. For the general theory and practice of these managerial activities, see Resnik, "Managerial Judges," 410–13.

26. The Fifth Circuit judges had authorized fair and nondiscriminatory "freedom of choice" plans among the preferred options for school desegregation. See *Singleton I–II;* supra, and *United States v. Jefferson County Board of Education*, 372 F.2d. 836 (5th Cir., 1966); en banc, 380 F.2d 385 (5th Cir., 1967). See also Gozansky, Gignilliat, and Horwitz, "School Desegregation," 946–66.

27. *Cisneros v. CCISD*, 330 F.Supp. 1377 (S.D. Tex., 1971).

28. *Swann v. Charlotte-Mecklenburg Board of Education*, 402 U.S. 1 (1971), 31. See Zelden, "From Rights to Resources," 519–23; and Bass, *Unlikely Heroes*, 308–9.

29. Chayes, "Supreme Court, 1981 Term," 47–48; also Fisher, "The Judge as Manager," 7. According to Judge McKnight, "Courts must decide if an institution or its practices violates the Constitution and, if so, how much authority courts can exercise in changing it." McKnight, "How Shall We Then Reason?" 921.

30. Orfield, "Anti-busing Legislation," 81–85. For presidential claims and disclaimers, see U.S. Commission on Civil Rights, *Federal Civil Rights Enforcement Effort*, 27–29, 66–70. As late as 1982, the justices upheld an amendment to the California state constitution that prohibited state officials from employing busing to end de facto segregation. See *Crawford v. Board of Education of Los Angeles*, 452 U.S. 527 (1982). Many of the initiatives against housing discrimination came from the executive and legislative branches. Fisher, "The Judge as Manager," 7.

31. Salinas, "Desegregation of Schools in the Southwest," 941; San Miguel, "Mexican American Organizations," 708–9.

32. Fees for counsel were provided in some employment discrimination cases under Title 7 of the CRA of 1964. 42 U.S.C. § 2000e-5(k). Congress later enacted provisions similar to those DeAnda suggested. These statutes authorize and even encourage the award of attorney's fees to the prevailing parties in school desegregation cases. The case for court-ordered imposition of attorney's fees is particularly strong where the plaintiffs have incurred substantial expense because of the obstinate refusal of a school board to recognize and comply with its legal obligations. See the Emergency School Aid Act of 1972, 20 U.S.C. § 1617. On 19 October 1976 Congress enacted the Civil Rights Attorney's Fees Awards Act of 1976, 42 U.S.C. § 1988. This provided for prevailing plaintiffs to recover reasonable attorney's fees in § 1983 actions. The trial judge has discretion to decide what is a "reasonable" fee. 42 U.S.C. § 1988(b), as amended by Pub. L. No. 104–317, tit. 3, § 309(b), 110 Stat. 3853 (119), describing "Attorney's fees." Also, see generally Hirsch and Sheehey, *Awarding Attorney's Fees.*

33. DeAnda, "Civil Rights," 220–21. President Lyndon B. Johnson created the Inter-agency Committee in response to Mexican American complaints that his administration had ignored their community's problems. The El Paso meetings became yet another point of contention, however, when the committee excluded the "militant" Mexican American leaders. See Allsup, *The American GI Forum*, 136–41; and Ramos, *The American GI Forum*, 99–106. In 1969 Congress established the Committee on Opportunities for Spanish Speaking People to succeed the Inter-agency Committee. Pub. L. No. 91–181, 83 Stat. 838 (1969). Ultimately, the U.S. attorney general waited until late 1969 before joining in a Mexican American lawsuit. *Perez v. Sonora Independent School District*, Civ. No. 6–224 (N.D. Tex., 1969). Noted in Birnberg, "*Brown v. Board of Education*," 339 n. 10.

34. O'Connor and Epstein, "A Legal Voice," 284–85. For planned litigation, see Wasby, *Race Relations*, 195–202.

35. See Texas Advisory Committee, *School Desegregation in Corpus Christi*, 42. For majority-to-minority transfer rules, see *Swann*, 402 U.S. 1 (1971), 26–27.

36. *Cisneros v. CCISD*, Civil Action (Civ. A.) No. 68-C-95, S.D. Tex., Corpus Christi Division; docket sheet, p. 2. Case files for the federal courts in Texas are held at (NARA-SWA), in Fort Worth. This case may be found in Civil cases, U.S.C.A., Fifth Circuit, RG 276, box 6104, folder for Case No. 71–2397, "1 of 2."

37. See Texas Advisory Committee, *School Desegregation in Corpus Christi*, 8–14, 42–43; and "Testimony of Paul Montemayor," in Texas Advisory Committee to the U.S. Commission on Civil Rights, *Hearings in Corpus Christi, Texas, 4–5 May 1976*, 3 vols. (Washington, D.C.: U.S. Government Printing Office, 1976), 1:67–68. Also noted in U.S. Commission on Civil Rights, *Fulfilling the Letter*, 108. Finally, see Allsup, *The American GI Forum*, 144.

38. See *Francisco Medrano et al. v. A. Y. Allee et al.*, 347 F.Supp. 605 (S.D. Tex., 1972) [Brownsville Division; Civ. No. 67-B-36], and Bailey, "The Starr County Strike," 47–48. The intersection of the goals of organized labor with the cause of Mexican American civil rights was a recurrent theme during the 1960s. The brief domination by Mexican Americans of the Crystal City municipal council in the early 1960s, was another example. The electoral takeover was orchestrated by PASSO, but the group received key support from the Teamsters Union. Montejano, *Anglos and Mexicans*, 282–84; and Navarro, *The Cristal Experiment*, 17–51. For later political developments in the same city, in years after the Chicano movement emerged, see Navarro, *The Cristal Experiment*, generally; and Trujillo, *Chicano Empowerment*, also generally.

39. Docket sheet, p. 2; *Cisneros v. CCISD*. NARA-SWA: Civil cases, Fifth Circuit, RG 276, box 6104, folder for Case No. 71–2397, "1 of 2."

40. *Cisneros v. Corpus Christi ISD*, 324 F.Supp. 599 (S.D. Tex., 1970), 601–2.

41. In the junior highs, one-third of the Mexican American and black students attended schools where the non-Anglo enrollment was greater than 90 percent. One-quarter of the Anglo students attended schools where the non-Anglo enrollment was less than 10 percent of the student body. Finally, in the CCISD elementary schools, 41 percent of the Mexican Americans and African Americans attended schools where over 90 percent of the students were non-Anglo. Thirteen percent of the Anglo children attended elementary schools with less than 10 percent non-Anglo enrollment. *Cisneros v. Corpus Christi ISD*, 324 F.Supp. 599 (S.D. Tex., 1970), 608. All of the figures in the text are approximate in the case record, and I have further rounded the numbers.

42. *Cisneros v. Corpus Christi ISD*, 324 F.Supp. 599 (S.D. Tex., 1970), 608.

43. For the quoted passages, and other excerpts of Carter's testimony regarding the history of discrimination in social and economic areas, see *Cisneros v. Corpus Christi ISD*, 324 F.Supp. 599 (S.D. Tex., 1970), 612 n. 38.

44. *Cisneros v. Corpus Christi ISD*, 324 F.Supp. 599 (S.D. Tex., 1970), 606 n. 30.

45. Ibid. Judge Seals quoted Carter from the hearing transcript, at 52–54.

46. *Cisneros v. Corpus Christi ISD*, 324 F.Supp. 599 (S.D. Tex., 1970), 603 n. 26. At the conclusion of this testimony, DeAnda offered as a plaintiffs' exhibit and Seals took judicial notice of Carter's recently published book. See Carter, *Mexican Americans in School*. DeAnda also called Hector Garcia to testify as an altogether different kind of expert witness. The AGIF founder, longtime Corpus Christi resident, and outspoken former member of the Civil Rights Commission vividly described his experiences with and personal observations of the forms of discrimination and segregation Mexican Americans experienced in schools, jobs,

homes, and hospitals. For excerpts of Garcia's testimony, see *Cisneros v. Corpus Christi* ISD, 324 F.Supp. 599 (S.D. Tex., 1970), 612–14 n. 39.

47. Ibid., 602 n. 11, 616–17 n. 49.

48. Ibid., 606.

49. Docket sheet, p. 3; *Cisneros v. CCISD.* NARA-SWA: Civil cases, Fifth Circuit, RG 276, box 6104, folder for Case No. 71–2397, "1 of 2."

50. *Cisneros v. Corpus Christi* ISD, 324 F.Supp. 599 (S.D. Tex., 1970), 603 n. 26. Judge Seals quoted Haskew from the hearing transcript, at 1223.

51. The hearings had continued daily after 14 May, except for 25–29 May, when Judge Seals had attended the Fifth Circuit's annual judicial conference in Miami, Florida. *Cisneros v. Corpus Christi* ISD, 324 F.Supp. 599 (S.D. Tex., 1970), 600–601, esp. n. 1. Before closing the proceedings, Seals heard and approved the application of an antibusing group, Concerned Neighbors, Inc., to join the case as amicus curiae. The organization's sixty-five hundred members complained that the destruction of neighborhood schools would harm students. See "Motion to Intervene or in the Alternative for Leave to Appear as Amicus Curiae," 5, and "Intervenor's Complaint," 1, both for Concerned Neighbors, Inc.; *Cisneros v. CCISD.* NARA-SWA: Civil cases, Fifth Circuit, RG 276, box 6104, folder for Case No. 71–2397, "1 of 2." The Concerned Neighbors group also suggested that court-ordered busing would deny parents' and students' civil rights, which might be grounds for a countersuit under § 1983. For background on the Concerned Neighbors, see Texas Advisory Committee, *School Desegregation in Corpus Christi,* 54–55; and Allsup, *The American GI Forum,* 146. On 2 June, Judge Seals rejected the bid to intervene of a nonprofit group of 200 parents and 450 children. In an in-chambers meeting Seals told the group's lawyer, Jack Pedigo, that the motion was untimely. Docket sheet, p. 3; *Cisneros v. CCISD.* NARA-SWA: Civil cases, Fifth Circuit, RG 276, box 6104, folder for Case No. 71–2397, "1 of 2."

52. *Cisneros v. Corpus Christi* ISD, 324 F.Supp. 599 (S.D. Tex., 1970), 600–601. Also, docket sheet, p. 4; *Cisneros v. CCISD.* NARA-SWA: Civil cases, Fifth Circuit, RG 276, box 6104, folder for Case No. 71–2397, "1 of 2."

53. See Amendments to the Federal Rules of Civil Procedure (Rule 23), 383 U.S. 1029 (1966), 1047. Chayes, "The Supreme Court, 1981 Term," 6. For a history and an expert's evaluation of the Rule 23 amendment's effect on the rise in litigation in the federal courts, see Miller, " 'Class Action Problem,' " 664.

54. See *Tijerina v. Henry,* 48 F.R.D. 274 (D. N.Mex., 1969); appeal dismissed, 398 U.S. 922 (1970). Noted in Birnberg, "*Brown v. Board of Education,*" 342 n. 29. Also, see Delgado and Palacios, "Legally Cognizable Class," 393.

55. *Cisneros v. Corpus Christi* ISD, 324 F.Supp. 599 (S.D. Tex., 1970), 604.

56. Ibid., 605.

57. Ibid., esp. n. 28. Judge Seals noted that "[i]t was decided as early as 1886 that although the Fourteenth Amendment may have been primarily concerned with Negroes, its protection is certainly not limited to them." See *Yick Wo v. Hopkins,* 118 U.S. 356 (1886). Moreover, he quoted Justice Miller's opinion for the Supreme Court in *The Slaughter House Cases,* to the effect that if "Mexican peonage or the Chinese coolie labor system" in U.S. territory evolved into a variety of slavery, then the Thirteenth Amendment would outlaw it. And, Miller had continued, "if other rights are assailed by the States which properly and necessarily fall within the protection of [the Reconstruction Amendments], that protection will apply, though the party interested may not be of African descent." See *The Slaughter House Cases,* 83 U.S. (16 Wall.) 36 (1873), 72.

58. *Cisneros v. Corpus Christi ISD*, 324 F.Supp. 599 (S.D. Tex., 1970), 605 n. 28.

59. Ibid., 606–7.

60. Ibid., 607.

61. Ibid., 608 n. 34. Judge Seals also took "judicial notice" of the 1960 U.S. Census of Population, and a special study by the Bureau of the Census, entitled "Persons of Spanish Surname," was based on the 1960 census. These documents indicated the following with respect to the five southwestern states, where the Mexican American population (i.e., persons with Spanish surnames) was largest. Arizona: in 1950, 128,580 inhabitants with Spanish surnames, out of a total population of 749,587; in 1960, 194,356 out of 1,302,161. California: in 1950, 758,400 out of 10,586,223; in 1960, 1,426,538 out of 15,717,204. Colorado: in 1950, 118,715 out of 1,325,089; in 1960, 157,174 out of 1,753,947. New Mexico: in 1950, 248,560 out of 681,187; in 1960, 269,122 out of 951,023. Texas: in 1950, 1,027,455 out of 7,711,194; in 1960, 1,417,810 out of 9,579,677.

See *Cisneros v. Corpus Christi ISD*, 324 F.Supp. 599 (S.D. Tex., 1970), 608 n. 31. Also see Plaintiffs' Exhibit 8, a copy of the 1960 census of Corpus Christi, Texas. The census shows the following with respect to Nueces County and Corpus Christi. The white population, other than those with Spanish surnames, numbered 126,794 in Nueces County and 98,504 in Corpus Christi (a difference of 28,290). The African American population numbered 10,108 in Nueces County and 9,156 in Corpus Christi (a difference of 952). Whites with Spanish surnames numbered 84,386 in Nueces County and 59,859 in Corpus Christi (a difference of 24,527). Inhabitants of other races numbered 285 in Nueces County and 171 in Corpus Christi (a difference of 114). The total population of Nueces County was 221,573; that of Corpus Christi was 167,690 (a difference of 53,883).

See *Cisneros v. Corpus Christi ISD*, n. 33.

62. Judge Seals further noted that "young Mexican-Americans have recently begun to call themselves Chicanoes [*sic*], and their movement, La Roza [*sic*]. During the pendency of this suit, these Chicanoes have been trying to get La Roza on the Texas ballot as La Roza Unida Party." *Cisneros v. Corpus Christi ISD*, 324 F.Supp. 599 (S.D. Tex., 1970), 615, esp. n. 39. For the creation of the La Raza Unida Party, see Quiñones, *Chicano Politics*, 158–59.

63. *Cisneros v. Corpus Christi ISD*, 324 F.Supp. 599 (S.D. Tex., 1970), 615–16.

64. Ibid., 616–17, esp. n. 48.

65. Ibid., 617–620, esp. nn. 50–57. For this "calculated" segregation, see also Rangel and Alcala, "De Jure Segregation," 326.

66. *Cisneros v. Corpus Christi ISD*, 324 F.Supp. 599 (S.D. Tex., 1970), 620, incl. n. 58.

67. Ibid., 627.

68. The Fifth Circuit judges announced this decision on 1 December 1969 and set a deadline of 1 February 1970 for full desegregation in five key areas of school business: student enrollment, faculty and staff, transportation, extracurricular activities, and facilities. *Singleton v. Jackson Municipal Separate School District*, 419 F.2d 1211 (5th Cir., 1969), 1217–18 [*Singleton III*], cert. denied, 396 U.S. 1032 (1970). A subsequent en banc proceeding is usually styled *Singleton IV*, 425 F.2d 1211 (5th Cir., 1970).

69. *Cisneros v. Corpus Christi ISD*, 324 F.Supp. 599 (S.D. Tex., 1970), 623, esp. n. 65. For criteria similar to *Singleton*, see also *Ellis v. Board of Public Instruction of Orange County, Florida*, 423 F.2d 203 (5th Cir., 1970).

70. *Cisneros v. Corpus Christi ISD*, 324 F.Supp. 599 (S.D. Tex., 1970), 623, esp. n. 65.

71. Ibid., 627.

72. Ibid., 628. Judge Seals suggested a majority-to-minority transfer along the lines described in *Singleton v. Jackson School District,* 426 F.2d 1364 (5th Cir., 1970) [*Singleton IV*].

73. The Fifth Circuit denied the defendants' appeal for a stay on 16 July 1970. *Cisneros v. CCISD,* 330 F.Supp. 1377 (S.D. Tex., 1971), 1378.

74. Any individual who declined to serve would be replaced by the person named on the next card in the stack. Judge Seals did not define "patron." He probably expected the parties to choose citizens of Corpus Christi who were already active in the controversy over the desegregation of CCISD. *Cisneros v. Corpus Christi ISD,* 324 F.Supp. 599 (S.D. Tex., 1970), 628.

75. *Cisneros v. CCISD,* 330 F.Supp. 1377 (S.D. Tex., 1971), 1379. On 18 March 1971 Seals granted CCISD leave to restore schools damaged by Celia, with certain exceptions. Docket sheet, p. 10; *Cisneros v. CCISD.* NARA-SWA: Civil cases, Fifth Circuit, RG 276, box 6104, folder for Case No. 71–2397, "1 of 2."

76. *Cisneros v. CCISD,* 330 F.Supp. 1377 (S.D. Tex., 1971), 1379.

77. Judge Seals was also concerned about being fair to Concerned Neighbors, Inc. On 24 July the group once again had tried to intervene in the case. The plaintiffs filed a motion in opposition to the intervention on 3 August. The defendant CCISD responded on 11 August. Judge Seals ultimately rejected the Concerned Neighbors group's request to become intervenors. Docket sheet, pp. 4–8; *Cisneros v. CCISD.* NARA-SWA: Civil cases, Fifth Circuit, RG 276, box 6104, folder for Case No. 71–2397, "1 of 2." In the meantime, at DeAnda's request, Judge Seals took judicial notice of a recently released report of the Civil Rights Commission detailing the "ethnic isolation" of Mexican Americans in education. *Cisneros v. CCISD,* 330 F.Supp. 1377 (S.D. Tex., 1971), 1379. See U.S. Commission on Civil Rights, *Mexican-American Educational Study.*

78. Docket sheet, p. 8; *Cisneros v. CCISD.* NARA-SWA: Civil cases, Fifth Circuit, RG 276, box 6104, folder for Case No. 71–2397, 1 of 2.

79. Docket sheet, pp. 9–10; *Cisneros v. CCISD.* NARA-SWA: Civil cases, Fifth Circuit, RG 276, box 6104, folder for Case No. 71–2397, "1 of 2." *Cisneros v. CCISD,* 330 F.Supp. 1377 (S.D. Tex., 1971), 1379–80. The Justice Department officially intervened, under Title 9 of the 1964 CRA, on 15 January 1971. See "Memorandum for the United States" (August 1971), 2, n. 3, in *Cisneros v. CCISD,* 330 F.Supp. 1377 (S.D. Tex., 1971). For executive branch participation in the controversy, see Wasby, *Continuity and Change,* 112–14.

80. U.S. 1 (1971).

81. Ibid., 28.

82. Ibid., 28–29, 31. Chayes, "Supreme Court, 1981 Term," 48.

83. Docket sheet, p. 10; *Cisneros v. CCISD.* NARA-SWA: Civil cases, Fifth Circuit, RG 276, box 6104, folder for Case No. 71–2397, "1 of 2."

84. *Cisneros v. CCISD,* 330 F.Supp. 1377 (S.D. Tex., 1971), 1380–86.

85. Ibid., 1386–89.

86. Ibid., 1390–92.

87. Judge Seals hypothetically compared this to a school district in which only 15 percent of the students were members of a minority group. In that school district, attendance by minority students at a single school of from 3 percent to 5 percent "may not be regarded as insignificant." Ibid., 1393.

88. Ibid., 1393–95; for options, see n. 7.

89. Ibid., 1396.

90. Ibid., 1396–97.

91. Ibid., 1397. Also, Seals directed that, due to the heavy workload, the human relations committee would to be expanded in May 1972 from twelve to eighteen members. Ibid., 1378–79 n. 1.

92. Ibid., 1392 n. 6.

93. The eighth seat in the Southern District was created by 84 Stat. 294 (1970). "Cox," in *Judges of the United States*. This was an ironic turn of events. Cox's Corpus Christi law firm, Boone, Davis, Cox and Hale, had defended the Driscoll CISD against DeAnda's complaint. Allan Davis, another partner, had filed the answer on behalf of the school district, and Cox was listed as the defendants' cocounsel on the case. Cox apparently did not take part in the suit, however. See "Answer [of Driscoll Consolidated ISD, et al.]" (22 December 1956); NARA-SWA: Civil cases, S.D. Tex., Corpus Christi Division, 1938–69, RG 21, box 232, folder 2: "1384 *Hernandez v. Driscoll*."

94. Chief Judge Connally to "Dear Bailey, Re: Corpus Christi School Desegregation Case," 28 July 1971, clerk's files of Chief Judge Ben C. Connally, folder 3.

95. Docket sheet, p. 12, *Cisneros v. CCISD*, NARA-SWA: Civil cases, Fifth Circuit, RG 276, box 6104, folder for Case No. 71–2397, "1 of 2." Also "Affidavit of Richard A. Hall" (3 August 1971), Exhibits A and B of "School District's Reply to Motion for Expedited Hearing and Summary Reversal of Stay Order and Request for Additional Relief Pending Appeal," p. 33; *Cisneros v. CCISD*. NARA-SWA: Civil cases, Fifth Circuit, RG 276, box 6104, folder for Case No. 71–2397, "2 of 2."

96. "Plaintiff-Appellees' Motion for Expedited Hearing and Summary Reversal of a Stay Order" (27 July 1971); *Cisneros v. CCISD*. NARA-SWA: Civil cases, Fifth Circuit, RG 276, box 6104, folder for Case No. 71–2397, "1 of 2." Also *Cisneros v. CCISD*, 448 F.2d 1392 (5th Cir., 1971), 1394.

97. See "Memorandum for the United States" (August 1971), 3; *Cisneros v. CCISD*. NARA-SWA: Civil cases, Fifth Circuit, RG 276, box 6104, folder for Case No. 71–2397, "1 of 2." When Justice Black reinstated the stay, he did so "without expressing any view as to the wisdom or propriety" of the solicitor general's position. *Corpus Christi ISD v. Cisneros*, 404 U.S. 1211 (1971), 1211–12. President Nixon made no secret of the fact that he was against busing. He directed members of his administration to resist attempts to speed the implementation of busing plans. He apparently pressured HEW's OCR, in its role as expert advisor to courts and school district, to slow down the pace of integration through "forced" busing. See Orfield, "Anti-busing Legislation," 94–99; and Panetta and Gall, *Bring Us Together*, 285–88.

98. See "Order" (23 August 1971); *Cisneros v. CCISD*. NARA-SWA: Civil cases, Fifth Circuit, RG 276, box 6104, folder for Case No. 71–2397, "1 of 2." *Cisneros v. CCISD*, 448 F.2d 1392 (5th Cir., 1971), 1394–95.

99. See Hyman, *Craftsmanship and Character*.

100. See "Plaintiffs-Appellees Brief" (26 August 1971); and "Appellants' Brief" (16 August 1971); *Cisneros v. CCISD*. NARA-SWA: Civil cases, Fifth Circuit, RG 276, box 6104, folder for Case No. 71–2397, "2 of 2." The "Concerned Neighbors," group also filed an *amicus* brief for the defendants. See "Brief of Concerned Neighbors, Inc." (31 August 1971); *Cisneros v. CCISD*. NARA-SWA: Civil cases, Fifth Circuit, RG 276, box 6104, folder for Case No. 71–2397, "2 of 2." *Cisneros v. CCISD*, 448 F.2d 1392 (5th Cir., 1971), 1395.

101. "Motion for Leave to File Brief Amici Curiae on Behalf of the NAACP Legal Defense and Educational Fund, Inc. and the Mexican-American Legal Defense and Educational Fund, Inc. and Statement of Interest of the Amici Curiae" (25 August 1971); *Cisneros v. CCISD*. NARA-SWA: Civil cases, Fifth Circuit, RG 276, box 6104, folder for Case No. 71–

2397, "1 of 2." Also see "Brief of the NAACP Legal Defense and Educational Fund, Inc. and Mexican-American Legal Defense and Educational Fund, Inc. as Amici Curiae" (25 August 1971); *Cisneros v. CCISD.* NARA-SWA: Civil cases, Fifth Circuit, RG 276, box 6104, folder for Case No. 71–2397, "2 of 2." The African American and Mexican American civil rights litigators saw the wisdom in mutual legal support in the CCISD case and coordinated their strategies. Wasby, *Race Relations,* 123–24. See also O'Connor and Epstein, "A Legal Voice," 284–85; and Quiñones, *Chicano Politics,* 110–12.

102. "Brief for the United States" (26 August 1971), 10–12; *Cisneros v. CCISD.* NARA-SWA: Civil cases, Fifth Circuit, RG 276, box 6104, folder for Case No. 71–2397, "2 of 2." The Justice Department was rarely an effective intervenor for Chicanos during this period. See Rangel and Alcala, "De Jure Segregation," 344 n. 220, 357, 373–74.

103. "Appellants' Reply to Motion for Assignment of Case upon Return of Mandate" (11 November 1971), 3–4; *Cisneros v. CCISD.* NARA-SWA: Civil cases, Fifth Circuit, RG 276, box 6104, folder for Case No. 71–2397, "1 of 2." See also: San Miguel, *Brown, Not White,* 166–67. San Miguel, in earlier work, misstated that Judge Cox, rather then Judge Seals, made the original finding that Mexican Americans were an identifiable minority. San Miguel, "*Let All of Them Take Heed,*" 178.

104. *Cisneros v. CCISD,* 448 F.2d 1392 (5th Cir., 1971), 1395–96. The issues needed resolving. On 14 September 1971, as *Cisneros v. CCISD* was on appeal, Judge Garza ordered busing in Brownsville, another Texas city with a large Mexican American population. See *Uresti v. School Board,* Civ. No. 70-B-100 (S.D. Tex., 1971). Noted in Rangel and Alcala, "De Jure Segregation," 359 n. 317.

105. See Transcript of Hearing (16 November 1971); *Cisneros v. CCISD.* NARA-SWA: Civil cases, Fifth Circuit, RG 276, box 6104, folder for Case No. 71–2397, "2 of 2." Allsup, *The American GI Forum,* 144–45.

106. For example, in his 1971 study of Houston's politics, Davidson takes into account the Mexican American community's access or lack of access to political power. In general, however, he treats racial politics, especially school desegregation, in terms of a black-white binary. See Davidson, *Biracial Politics,* 130–32, esp. table 5.4, "Racial Integration in Houston Independent School District, 1960–1971." Compare this approach to the same author's chosen title and expanded emphasis on white-black-Hispanic minority politics in a more recent work. See Davidson, *Race and Class,* 56–57, esp. table 3.4, "Relative Voter Turnout among Texas Minorities, General Gubernatorial Elections, 1978 and 1982."

107. *Ross v. Eckels,* 11 *Race Rel. Law Rep.* 216 (S.D. Tex., 1965). Also 434 F.2d 1140 (5th Cir., 1970), 1142. The circuit also authorized desegregation according to various "freedom of choice" plans in *Singleton II,* 355 F.2d, at 870, and in *United States v. Jefferson County Board of Education,* 372 F.2d 836 (5th Cir. 1966); and 380 F.2d 385 (5th Cir., 1967), en banc. For Judge Connally and "freedom of choice," see Couch, *History of the Fifth Circuit,* 141.

108. Allen B. Hannay was born in Hempstead, Texas, on 14 February 1892. The son of a U.S. attorney, Hannay attended Texas A&M University, received the LL.B. from the UT law school in 1913, and served as a county judge in Waller County from 1915 to 1917. Hannay enlisted in the U.S. Army during World War I and trained military pilots. After the war ended, he played professional baseball for the Houston Buffs. Hannay served twelve years as a state district judge in the 113th District, from 1930 to 1942. In 1942 President Franklin Roosevelt appointed Hannay to replace Judge Allred (who had resigned the seat) in the Southern District. Biographical material from: *Judges of the United States,* 239; and Zelden, *Justice Lies in the District,* 153.

109. *Broussard v. HISD*, 262 F.Supp. 266 (S.D. Tex., 1966), 266–68; Civ. Docket No. 66-H-334.

110. F.Supp. 266 (S.D. Tex., 1966), 268–71. This was the first time that Judge Connally had not presided over a desegregation complaint in Houston. All the players in this particular twist of the desegregation tale had changed, with one exception: Joe H. Reynolds continued to represent HISD. Arthur J. Mandell, William L. Wood, and Joseph L. Tita, all from Houston, represented Broussard.

111. The CRA of 1957 (Pub. L. No. 85–315, 71 Stat. 634). This was the first major federal civil rights legislation since Reconstruction. For executive branch enforcement of civil rights statutes and federal judicial decisions, see Landsberg, *Enforcing Civil Rights*. In 1958 the division had 15 attorneys and a budget of $180,000, and in 1965 it had 105 attorneys and a budget of just under $2 million. By 1980 the division's budget was approaching $17 million, and approximately 200 lawyers were on staff. Days, "In Honor of *Brown v. Board of Education*," 991.

112. The major exceptions were criminal prosecutions under 18 U.S.C. §§ 241 and 242. Other federal agencies operated under similar constraints: until 1972, EEOC had no power to sue employers that it felt had violated Title 7. Instead, EEOC referred matters to the Civil Rights Division. See the Equal Employment Opportunity Act of 1972. Pub. L. No. 92–261, § 4, 86 Stat. 103; codified at 42 U.S.C. § 2000(e)–(f). Days, "In Honor of *Brown v. Board of Education*," 991–94.

113. *Ross v. Eckels*, 317 F.Supp. 512 (S.D. Tex., 1970), 513; and *Ross v. Eckels*, 434 F.2d 1140 (5th Cir., 1970), 1142.

114. Emphasis in original. *Broussard v. HISD*, 395 F.2d 817 (5th Cir., 1968), 820.

115. Ibid., 820.

116. Ibid., 821. For Judge Connally and construction, see Read and McGough, *Let Them Be Judged*, 475.

117. F.2d 817 (5th Cir., 1968), 822–28. Judge Wisdom wrote the opinion in *United States v. Jefferson*.

118. *Broussard v. Houston ISD*, 395 F.2d 817 (5th Cir., 1968), 828–31. Subsequently, the Fifth Circuit dismissed the appeal as moot and denied rehearing; see 403 F.2d 34 (5th Cir. 1968).

119. *Ross v. Rogers*, 2 *Race Rel. L. Rptr.* 1114 (S.D. Tex., 1957); *Ross v. HISD*, 5 *Race Rel. L. Rptr.* 703 (S.D. Tex., 1960); *Ross v. Dyer*, 203 F.Supp. 124 (S.D. Tex., 1962); *Ross v. Dyer*, 312 F.2d 191 (5th Cir., 1963); *Ross v. Eckels*, 11 *Race Rel. Law Rep.* 216 (S.D. Tex., 1965); *Ross v. Eckels*, 12 *Race Rel. Law Rep.* 2005 (S.D. Tex., 1967). See Kellar, *Make Haste Slowly*, 151–55, and generally. For Judge Connally and the development of "freedom of choice" in Houston, see Couch, *History of the Fifth Circuit*, 141. Also, *United States v. Jefferson County Board of Education*, 380 F.2d 385 (5th Cir., 1967), en banc, then cert. denied, 389 U.S. 840; *Green v. County School Board of New Kent Co.*, 391 U.S. 430 (1968); *Alexander v. Holmes County Board of Education*, 396 U.S. 19 (1969), discussed above.

120. *Ross v. Eckels*, 317 F.Supp. 512 (S.D. Tex., 1970); and 434 F.2d 1140 (5th Cir., 1970).

121. As the population grew, the Mexican American community was also transforming into an emerging "Hispanic" community. Some of the population increase came from Central and South America, rather than Mexico, especially after 1980. In the 1970s, however, the overwhelming majority of the Hispanic minority was still Mexican American. Also, it is difficult to account for the number of undocumented Mexican/Hispanic residents of Houston. See Shelton et al., *Houston*, 98.

122. The five demands ARMAS submitted to the principal of Jefferson Davis High School

on 16 September 1969 were (1) add to the curriculum Chicano history and culture courses, to be taught by Chicano teachers; (2) eliminate the practice by counselors of encouraging students who were discipline problems to drop out of school; (3) hire more Chicano counselors "who understand the special problems of Chicanos in high schools"; (4) end the practice of posting a list of the girls who left school due to pregnancy; and (5) extend the lunch period from twenty to thirty minutes, as they had at "[a]ll other schools." San Miguel, "The Community Is Beginning to Rumble," 137–38.

123. San Miguel, *Brown, Not White*, 65–84, and generally.

124. The full list is reproduced in San Miguel, "The Community is Beginning to Rumble," 146.

125. Ibid., 147.

126. *Ross v. Eckels*, 317 F.Supp. 512 (S.D. Tex., 1970), 513.

127. The city's population had increased by one-half million. Shelton et al., *Houston*, 10; also Thomas and Murray, *Progrowth Politics*, 30–32.

128. *Ross v. Eckels*, 317 F.Supp. 512 (S.D. Tex., 1970), 513–14; *Ross v. Eckels*, 434 F.2d 1140 (5th Cir., 1970), 1141.

129. *Ross v. Eckels*, 317 F.Supp. 512 (S.D. Tex., 1970), 518; *Ross v. Eckels*, 434 F.2d 1140 (5th Cir., 1970), 1142–43.

130. *Ross v. Eckels*, 317 F.Supp. 512 (S.D. Tex., 1970), 514. By 1970 the case's African American namesake, Delores Ross, was approximately twenty-two years old and was no longer mentioned in the proceedings. Robert Eckels was president of the Board of Trustees of the HISD. That office had been occupied by Dallas Dyer in earlier proceedings (i.e., *Ross v. Dyer*). The court continued to track the case under Civ. No. 10444.

131. *Ross v. HISD*, 457 F.Supp. 18 (S.D. Tex., 1977), 26.

132. *Ross v. Eckels*, 317 F.Supp. 512 (S.D. Tex., 1970), 514. See Art Wiese, "Meet Joe Reynolds, Schools' Counsel in Desegregation Cases," *Houston Post*, 7 September 1969, "Insight," pp. 1–2.

133. *Ross v. Eckels*, 317 F.Supp. 512 (S.D. Tex., 1970), 513.

134. Ibid., 513–14, incl. n. 6.

135. Ibid., 513 n. 2.

136. Ibid., 514 n. 4. On 23 July 1969, when Judge Connally directed the parties to submit the alternative desegregation plans, he had called for HISD to reassign approximately twenty-five hundred black teachers to white schools. The so-called crossover teachers were to be in place by the opening of the next school term, 1 September 1969. The outgoing HISD board apparently ignored this deadline. The new board first discussed the crossover plan at its 5 February 1970 meeting. At a board meeting on 23 February, the HISD administrators admitted that this crossover had not been accomplished. Finally, at the 25 May meeting, the school administrators presented to the school board a plan for the racial mixing of staff and faculty. See the discussion in *Wright v. HISD*, 393 F.Supp. 1149 (S.D. Tex, 1975), 1160–61 [Houston Division, Civ. A. No. 72-H-1484].

137. *Ross v. Eckels*, 317 F.Supp. 512 (S.D. Tex., 1970), 514. During the summer of 1970, the school board instituted the new desegregation plan for the faculty. On 31 August 1970, the day the Houston schools opened for the new term, the faculty of the HISD was integrated under the *Singleton* ratio, which on a percentage basis was taken as 35:65 black to white. *Wright v. HISD*, 393 F.Supp. 1149 (S.D. Tex., 1975), 1163.

138. *Ross v. Eckels*, 317 F.Supp. 512 (S.D. Tex., 1970), 514.

139. Judge Connally is quoting from the opinion of Fifth Circuit Judge James Coleman, dissenting in part, in *Singleton IV,* 425 F.2d 1211 (5th Cir., 1970).

140. *Ross v. Eckels,* 317 F.Supp. 512 (S.D. Tex., 1970), 515.

141. Ibid., 514.

142. The locator map had limitations. As Judge Connally noted, there were discrepancies in counting the students in the various proposals. The figures for the equidistant zoning plan and for the geographical-capacity zoning plan are both projections based on an actual count of dots, each smaller than the head of a pin, which indicated the residence of each of almost 240,000 HISD students. The judge allowed that "[n]o two counts result in quite the same answer. For practical and comparative purposes, however, I think these inaccuracies may be disregarded." Judge Connally summarized these seven plans in more detail at *Ross v. Eckels,* 317 F.Supp. 512 (S.D. Tex., 1970), 515–21, esp. n. 13. Also, the judge appended charts showing the number of schools with the indicated ratio of white to black students under the preferred proposals. Ibid., 525–30. Also, see Kellar's discussion of the proposals and the basis for Connally's decision. Note, however, that rather than making reference to the Fifth Circuit's decision, Kellar mistakenly credits Connally's colleague in the Southern District, U.S. District Judge John V. Singleton, with establishing the *Singleton* ratio for faculty integration. Kellar, *Make Haste Slowly,* 155–58.

143. *Ross v. Eckels,* 317 F.Supp. 512 (S.D. Tex., 1970), 516.

144. Ibid., 516, n. 8.

145. Ibid., 515, 521.

146. Ibid., 516–17, incl. n. 10.

147. Ibid., 517–18, 521–22.

148. Ibid., 521–22.

149. Ibid., 522.

150. Judge Connally had not yet absolutely dismissed the Ted-Tac and Stolee plans, but they were clearly not his preference. Ibid., 522.

151. *Bivins v. Bibb County Board of Education,* 424 F.2d 97 (5th Cir., 1970).

152. *Ross v. Eckels,* 317 F.Supp. 512 (S.D. Tex., 1970), 521. That is, the majority-to-minority transfer rule described in *Singleton IV,* supra.

153. *Ross v. Eckels,* 317 F.Supp. 512 (S.D. Tex., 1970), 522–23.

154. *Ellis v. Board of Public Instruction of Orange County, Florida,* 423 F.2d 203 (5th Cir., 1970).

155. The lines would necessarily be drawn separately for high schools, junior highs, and elementary schools. *Ross v. Eckels,* 317 F.Supp. 512 (S.D. Tex., 1970), 519.

156. Ibid., 520.

157. Ibid., 522–24.

158. See Salinas, "Desegregation of Schools in the Southwest," 945; and Shelton, et al., *Houston,* generally.

159. *Ross v. Eckels,* 317 F.Supp. 512 (S.D. Tex., 1970), 523.

160. Furthermore, in addition to allowing transfers under the majority-to-minority rule, the HISD board had the authority to transfer students for other legitimate reasons. For example, physically handicapped, mentally retarded, or highly gifted children, or students seeking to enroll in vocational or other special courses, presumably would be permitted to attend schools with the appropriate facilities and courses. As Connally noted, "It goes without saying that all such transfers will be on a non-discriminatory basis." Ibid., 524.

161. Ibid.

162. Zelden offers an interesting interpretation of the "eyes, ears and hands" role. He notes that the reliance on judicial adjuncts in desegregation cases resembled the federal courts' use of receivers in bankruptcies or trustees in equity cases. Zelden, "From Rights to Resources," 499–502.

163. Judge Connally's appended analysis of the plans does not account for citizens with Spanish surnames. He is concerned only with black, white, and "unknown." *Ross v. Eckels,* 317 F.Supp. 512 (S.D. Tex., 1970), 525–30.

164. *Ross v. Eckels,* 434 F.2d 1140 (5th Cir., 1970), 1146.

165. The circuit judges quoted from *Allen v. Board of Public Instruction of Broward County, Florida,* 432 F.2d 362 (5th Cir., 1970).

166. *Ross v. Eckels,* 434 F.2d 1140 (5th Cir., 1970), 1147.

167. Ibid., 1148. See, for example, *Allen v. Board of Public Instruction of Broward County,* 432 F.2d 362 (5th Cir., 1970).

168. For example, he had also written a dissent in the latest en banc rehearing of the *Singleton* case. See *Singleton IV,* 425 F.2d 1211 (5th Cir., 1970). Clark was already well known to his new Fifth Circuit colleagues. And, despite having defended Governor Ross Barnett before the Fifth Circuit during the 1962 desegregation showdown over James Meredith's registration for classes at "Ole Miss," he was well respected. See *Meredith v. Fair,* 305 F.2d 345 (5th Cir., 1962), cert. denied, 371 U.S. 828 (1962). Read and McGough, *Let Them Be Judged,* 228–32, 346–47, 453–58. Also, see Bass, *Unlikely Heroes,* 176–77, 312–13, 331.

169. *Ross v. Eckels,* 434 F.2d 1140 (5th Cir., 1970), 1149.

170. Ibid., 1149. Further, Clark declared, the Fifth Circuit's rulings that tightened the integration tolerances for some districts merely widened the distance between the school districts under court order and those that were not. There were nearly two dozen separate school districts in Harris County. As he suggested, there were some areas within Houston's city limits that were not part of the HISD and not subject to ever-climbing but mysterious numerical standards. Judge Clark wondered why the circuit allowed such disparities to exist. He inquired, "Is the equal protection clause of the Constitution too impotent to reach the all-white 'cut-glass' set in Spring Branch and the predominantly Negro area in Northeast Houston?" Moreover, he asked, "why would a document as all-pervasive as our Constitution allow the imaginary boundary lines of Pasadena or Galena Park (or even the contiguous all-white Alief or Katy districts) to thwart racial balance if that balance be constitutionally required?" Ibid., 1150. In fact, within a short time the federal government filed suit to integrate several of these districts, including those in Katy, Galena Park, Klein, Madisonville, and Crosby. See *United States v. Katy Independent School District, et al.,* 333 F.Supp. 1325 (S.D. Tex., 1971); and *United States v. Board of Trustees of Crosby Independent School District, et al.,* 333 F.Supp. 1325 (S.D. Tex., 1971).

171. *Ross v. Eckels,* 434 F.2d 1140 (5th Cir., 1970), 1149. For these "disclaimers," see *Allen v. Board of Public Instruction of Broward County,* 432 F.2d 362 (5th Cir., 1970).

172. *Ross v. Eckels,* 434 F.2d 1140 (5th Cir., 1970), 1149.

173. Ibid., 1150–51.

174. Ibid., 1141.

175. De León, *Ethnicity in the Sunbelt,* 186.

176. *Ross v. Eckels,* 434 F.2d 1140 (5th Cir., 1970), 1150.

177. Ibid., 1150.

178. Ibid., 1151. For comments on Judge Clark's dissent, see Salinas, "Desegregation of Schools in the Southwest," 943, 949–50.

179. Judge Connally was at least being consistent. He discussed this problem of self-identification in a letter to Fifth Circuit Judge Walter Gewin, for example, to explain why the official figures on the racial balance of the juries in the Southern District were useless. The figures were tabulated based on questionnaires, and some potential jurors of Mexican descent identified themselves as "White," and others checked the box for "Latin." Connally wanted to dispense with the racial question altogether. Chief Judge Connally to "Dear Judge Gewin," 7 March 1969, clerk's files of Chief Judge Ben C. Connally, folder 2. In the late 1970s Judge Garza was still wrangling with this problem of judicial versus legislative/administrative versus self-identified distinctions. Chief Judge Garza to "Dear Mr. Shepard," 5 June 1978, clerk's files of Chief Judge Reynaldo G. Garza, folder 4.

180. San Miguel, " 'The Community Is Beginning to Rumble,' " 147.

181. San Miguel, *Brown, Not White*, 98–103. Castillo entered mainstream politics in Houston in 1971 and was elected the city controller. See Castillo, "Hispanic Political Power," 98. De León, *Ethnicity in the Sunbelt*, 186–87, 192–93. San Miguel, "*Let All of Them Take Heed*," 179. Kellar, *Make Haste Slowly*, 158. At a school board meeting during this period, fourteen people were arrested for inciting a riot. Most of those arrested were members not of MAEC, but of two militant groups, the Mexican-American Youth Organization and the Chicano Student Committee. Guadalupe San Miguel, "A Struggle in Vain; Ignoring Ethnicity Is a Slap in the Face of All Colors by HISD," *Houston Chronicle*, 28 September 1997, "Outlook," p. 1. As originally published, this article indicated that fourteen hundred people were arrested at the board meeting. The editors printed a correction to fourteen arrested protesters two days later. See *Houston Chronicle*, 30 September 1997.

182. De León, *Ethnicity in the Sunbelt*, 187–88. In Cotulla, Texas, Mexican American parents resorted to similar mass protest exercises in September 1970, and they forced their local school district to initiate the pairing they demanded. Rangel and Alcala, "De Jure Segregation," 327–29.

183. For other attempts in Houston to form multiethnic or multiracial solutions, see Quiroz, "Black, White, and Brown," 66–82, and generally.

184. De León, *Ethnicity in the Sunbelt*, 188–89. Dworkin, "Hispanics in the Houston Schools," in *Hispanics in Houston and Harris County*, ed. Caram, Dworkin, and Rodriguez, 100.

185. See *Ross v. Eckels*, 434 F.2d 1140 (5th Cir., 1970); and 91 S.Ct. 924. Susan Besze Wallace, "The Changing Complexion of HISD: As the Desegregation Legal Battle Wore On, Houston School Demographics Were Steadily Changing," *Houston Post*, 15 May 1994, p. A16. There were few violent confrontations between the proponents and opponents of busing in Houston. This was unfortunately not true elsewhere in the state. In Longview, in the Eastern District of Texas, several white men were convicted for conspiring to "booby trap" with dynamite the buses to be used in transporting black children to white schools. See *United States v. Hayes and McMaster*, 444 F.2d 472 (5th Cir., 1971), cert. denied, 404 U.S. 882 (1971); *Hayes and McMaster v. United States*, 464 F.2d 1252 (5th Cir., 1972). Several black extremists were also convicted for conspiring to bomb school administration buildings in Tyler, also in the Eastern District. See Barr, *Black Texans*, 211.

186. See "Memorandum on Motion to Intervene," quoted in Rangel and Alcala, "De Jure Segregation," 349 n. 254. The biracial committee's statistics from June 1971 revealed that the fifteen schools that the Fifth Circuit accepted would be all or nearly all black *were* all black.

The figures for the other elementary schools, however, showed that nineteen additional schools still had fewer than 10 percent white students. *Wright v. HISD*, 393 F.Supp. 1149 (S.D. Tex, 1975), 1163 n. 2 [Houston Division, Civ. A. No. 72-H-1484].

187. *Cisneros v. CCISD*, 459 F.2d 13 (5th Cir., 1971), 14.

188. *United States v. Texas*, 342 F.Supp. 24 (E.D. Tex., 1971). The Fifth Circuit affirmed but transferred the San Felipe–Del Rio cases to the Western District. 466 F.2d 518 (5th Cir., 1972). For the earlier procedural and legal rulings in this case, see 321 F.Supp. 1043 (E.D. Tex., 1971), affirmed and modified, 447 F.2d 441 (5th Cir., 1971), cert. denied, 404 U.S. 1016 (1972). Also, San Miguel, "Mexican American Organizations and the Changing Politics of School Desegregation in Texas, 1945–1980," 711–12. For Judge Justice's continuing role in the evolution of *United States v. Texas*, see Kemerer, *William Wayne Justice*, chap. 5.

189. *United States v. Texas Education Agency*, 467 F.2d 848 (5th Cir., 1972), 853–54. The Texas Education Agency (TEA) was a defendant in the federal government's suit because it had allegedly allowed school boards to adopt policies that perpetuated segregation. This was another consolidated case. In the Southern District of Texas, Judge James Noel heard the portion regarding the Katy ISD. See *United States v. Katy Independent School District et al.*, 333 F.Supp. 1325 (S.D. Tex., 1971); and *United States v. Texas Education Agency*, 443 F.2d 1372 (5th Cir., 1971).

190. Memo (12 July 1972); *Cisneros v. CCISD*. NARA-SWA: Civil cases, Fifth Circuit, RG 276, box 6104, folder for Case No. 71–2397, "1 of 2."

191. *CCISD v. Cisneros*, 467 F.2d 142 (5th Cir., 1972), 148.

192. Ibid., 147–48.

193. Ibid., 149.

194. Ibid., 148–49.

195. Ibid. Also, Read and McGough, *Let Them Be Judged*, 575–76.

196. Judge Bell, joined by Ainsworth, Morgan, and Roney, also specially concurred in that result. *CCISD v. Cisneros*, 467 F.2d 142 (5th Cir., 1972), 152–54. Judge Ainsworth, joined by Bell and Roney, concurred in the result, and also in the remand. Ibid., 160.

197. Ibid., 156–57. See *Keyes v. School District Number One, Denver*, 313 F.Supp. 61 (D. Colo., 1969), 69, 82–83, 98.

198. *CCISD v. Cisneros*, 467 F.2d 142 (5th Cir., 1972), 160.

199. Ibid., 157–59.

200. Ibid., 154–56. Judges Brown, Wisdom, Gewin, Thornberry, Goldberg, Dyer, and Simpson formally reiterated their opinions in *United States v. Texas Education Agency*. Ibid., 160.

201. This is "Plaintiffs' Post Appeal Motion No. 1." Noted in *CCISD v. Cisneros*, 350 F.Supp. 1241 (S.D. Tex., 1972), 1243.

202. *Ross v. Eckels*, 468 F.2d 649 (5th Cir., 1972).

203. The Supreme Court's subsequent ruling in *Keyes* was also a factor, see *Ross v. HISD*, 699 F.2d 218 (5th Cir., 1983), 221 n. 5.

204. See 413 U.S. 920 (1973).

205. *Keyes v. School District Number One, Denver*, 413 U.S. 189 (1973), 198. See Kenneth J. Meier and Joseph Stewart Jr., *The Politics of Hispanic Education: Un Paso Pa'lante y Dos Pa'tras* (Albany: State University of New York, 1991), 69–70; and San Miguel, "*Let All of Them Take Heed*," 180–81.

206. Jorjanna Price, "June Hearing Another Step in Long Hunt for Solution," *Houston Post*, 13 May 1979, p. 2A.

207. Allsup, *The American GI Forum*, 145.

208. Zelden, "From Rights to Resources," 534. Also, Dolezal, Gross, and Howard, "The Use of Computers," 91–97.

209. See Statement of Milton Tobian, in U.S. Commission on Civil Rights, *Hearing Held in Corpus Christi*, 3.

210. See Texas Advisory Committee, *School Desegregation in Corpus Christi*, 14–18.

211. In September 1977 Judge Cox rejected new efforts of another parents' group to intervene, and the Fifth Circuit affirmed. See *CCISD v. Cisneros*, 560 F.2d 190 (5th Cir., 1977). Also, San Miguel, "*Let All of Them Take Heed*," 185–86. For a short discussion and partial chronology of the *Cisneros* case, see Allsup, *The American GI Forum*, 145–46.

212. Weaver, "Suburbanization of America," introduction, 31–43, and 1–13.

213. Thomas and Murray, *Progrowth Politics*, 112–13, and generally. Many independent suburbs found themselves in a constant struggle to maintain their autonomy from Houston. Shelton et al., *Houston*, 28–40.

214. There were more than twenty separate school districts in Harris County. *Ross v. Eckels*, 434 F.2d 1140 (5th Cir., 1970), at 1142.

215. The Justice Department was often a plaintiff-intervenor in the suburban suits. For example, the U.S. filed what Judge Noel referred to as an "eleventh hour" desegregation suit against the Katy School District on 7 August 1970. Noel ruled on the case on 26 October 1971. See *United States v. Katy Independent School District, et al.*, 333 F.Supp. 1325 (S.D. Tex., 1971). The government filed suit in Crosby, Texas, in April 1970. *United States v. Board of Trustees of Crosby Independent School District et al.*, 333 F.Supp. 1325 (S.D. Tex., 1971). There was also a suit in Aldine, Texas. "Aldine Integration Suit Reopened in U.S. Court," *Houston Post*, 17 May 1977, p. 24C. Plaintiffs filed a desegregation suit in Galveston in 1959, and it was also reactivated in the late 1970s, after several dormant years. See *Smiley v. Vollert*, 453 F.Supp. 463 (S.D. Tex., 1978); *Smiley v. Blevins*, 514 F.Supp. 1248 (S.D. Tex., 1981). Also "Desegregation Plan: U.S. Judge Hears Galveston Proposal," *Houston Post*, 22 March 1978, p. 4A.

216. Art Wiese, "Meet Joe Reynolds, Schools' Counsel in Desegregation Cases," *Houston Post*, 7 September 1969, "Insight," pp. 1–2.

217. *Ross v. HISD*, 457 F.Supp. 18 (S.D. Tex., 1977) [Civ. A. No. H-77–92]; 559 F.2d 937 (5th Cir., 1977); 583 F.2d 712 (5th Cir., 1978), and 81 F.R.D. 532 (S.D. Tex., 1979). The WISD litigation also raised voting rights issues. See also *Coalition to Preserve Houston v. Interim Board of Trustees of the Westheimer Independent School District*, 454 F.Supp. 143 (S.D. Tex., 1978), and 494 F.Supp. 738 (S.D. Tex., 1980). For the WISD developments, see Kellar, *Make Haste Slowly*, 158–62, and generally. Also, Janet Sanders, "WASP Nest?" *Texas Monthly*, October 1976, pp. 93–94; and "HISD Trustee, Two Others File Suit against WISD," *Houston Post*, 15 February 1977, p. 5A. A similar movement for a "breakaway" district emerged in Fort Bend County, which is adjacent to Harris County. See *Fort Bend Independent School District v. City of Stafford*, 449 F.Supp. 375 (S.D. Tex., 1978), 594 F.2d 73 (5th Cir., 1979), and 507 F.Supp. 211 (S.D. Tex., 1980). See "Legal Action Set to Begin Oct. 21 on Stafford, FBISD School Suit," *Houston Post*, 13 October 1977, p. 8B; "Federal Judge Asked to Halt Stafford Move," *Houston Post*, 19 October 1977, p. 5A.

218. *Ross v. HISD*, 699 F.2d 218 (5th Cir., 1983), 226, citing *United States v. Scotland Neck City Board of Education*, 407 U.S. 484 (1972), 491.

219. *Ross v. HISD*, 699 F.2d 218 (5th Cir., 1983), 222.

220. "Judge Ben Connally Dies of Heart Attack," *Houston Post*, 3 December 1975, 1A, 19A; "Judge Ben C. Connally, Who Presided over Houston's School Integration Battles," *New York Times*, 4 December 1975, 44.

221. V. Bailey Thomas to "Gentlemen, Re: Civil Action 10,444 *Ross v. Houston Independent School District*," 17 January 1975, clerk's files of Chief Judge Ben C. Connally, folder 4.

222. See "Judge Ben C. Connally," scrapbook of Judge Connally compiled by the clerk of court, Office of the Clerk of Court, S.D. Tex.

223. *Ross v. HISD*, 699 F.2d 218 (5th Cir., 1983), 222. See also: Jim Craig, "Court Tentatively OKs Magnet Schools Plan," *Houston Post*, 11 July 1975, p. 1A; Jim Craig, "Magnet School Plan Ordered Implemented," *Houston Post*, 12 July 1975, p. 3A; Jim Craig, "Will People Buy Plan?" *Houston Post*, 13 July 1975, p. 1A; Jim Craig, "HISD Predicts 13-Year Enrollment Low," *Houston Post*, 16 July 1975, p. 1A; and Jim Craig, "Magnet Schools Provide Opportunity to Shop Around," *Houston Post*, 20 July 1975, p. 1A.

224. "Cowan," in *Judges of the United States.*

225. *Ross v. HISD*, 699 F.2d 218 (5th Cir., 1983), 222.

226. Ibid., 222. See Kellar, *Make Haste Slowly*, 162–64. Also see Susan Besze Wallace, "The Changing Complexion of HISD; As the Desegregation Legal Battle Wore On, Houston School Demographics Were Steadily Changing," *Houston Post*, 15 May 1994, p. A16.

227. *Milliken v. Bradley*, 418 U.S. 717 (1974) [*Milliken I*]. This was another ruling that demonstrated the court's support for federalism. A federal district judge had ordered the Detroit school board to purchase 295 school buses as part of a multidistrict strategy, with the cost borne by the state. The justices ruled that federal judges could not specifically direct state expenditures. See Fisher, "The Judge as Manager," 7; and Wolohojian, "Judicial Taxation," 339–41.

228. Arthur Wiese, "Busing across School District Lines Urged," *Houston Post*, 16 February 1977, p. 3A. Jim Asker, "School Chiefs Cool to Idea of Busing," *Houston Post*, 16 February 1977, p. 1A.

229. *Ross v. HISD*, 699 F.2d 218 (5th Cir., 1983), 222. Kellar, *Make Haste Slowly*, 162–64.

230. In 1980 the population of Houston was 14 percent Hispanic. Mexican Americans counted for 88 percent of this group. Most of the rest were immigrants from Central and South America. Thomas and Murray, *Progrowth Politics*, 70–71.

231. *Ross v. HISD*, 699 F.2d 218 (5th Cir., 1983), 220.

232. Ibid., 220. See "HISD Plans Magnet Recruiting Program," *Houston Post*, 2 April 1978, p. 24C; "HISD '78–'79 Integration Costs in Tens of Millions," *Houston Post*, 13 May 1979, p. 2A; and Jorjanna Price, "June Hearing Another Step in Long Hunt for Solution," *Houston Post*, 13 May 1979, p. 2A.

233. Carter appointed Hugh Gibson of Galveston to Cowan's vacant seat on 5 October 1979. In 1981 Cowan took command of the legal team representing the owners of a proposed nuclear power plant, the controversial South Texas Project (STP). The STP owners wished to replace the project's contractors, Brown and Root, which was defended in the massive litigation by Baker, Botts's longtime rival, Vinson and Elkins. After four years, during which the STP case became Cowan's "entire occupation," the litigation ended in favor of the owners, who received a $750 million cash settlement, possibly the largest cash settlement ever in a construction-related lawsuit. Lipartito and Pratt, *Baker & Botts*, 209.

234. Bill Coulter, "Pasadena Trustees Decide Not to Send Records to HISD," *Houston Post*, 18 May 1979, 14A. Jorjanna Price, "Future Monitoring of HISD Needed, Reagan Testifies," *Houston Post*, 21 June 1979, 23A. Jorjanna Price, "Reagan Sees No Integration for Inner City," *Houston Post*, 22 June 1979, 22A. "Trial to Resume," *Houston Post*, 19 July 1979, 28C. Jorjanna Price, "Judge Wants Plan for Inter-district School Programs," *Houston Post*, 6 October 1979, 1A, 27A. Jorjanna Price, "HISD Bias Complaints Expected," *Houston Post*, 21 October 1979, 3D. Jorjanna Price, "Justice Dept. Witness Says HISD Has Far to Go on Integration," *Hous-*

ton Post, 23 October 1979, 1A, 23A. Jorjanna Price, "HISD Refuses to Open Desegregation Research," *Houston Post,* 24 October 1979, 9A. Jorjanna Price, "HTA Blames City, HISD for Housing Segregation," *Houston Post,* 25 October 1979, 26A. Jorjanna Price, "HISD Says It Needs Whites from Suburbs for Integration," *Houston Post,* 26 October 1979, 20A.

235. *Ross v. HISD,* 699 F.2d 218 (5th Cir., 1983), 223, quoting Judge O'Conor's memorandum order.

236. *Ross v. HISD,* 699 F.2d 218 (5th Cir., 1983), 223. See Thomas and Murray, *Progrowth Politics,* 114–16. Also, "Judge Backs Houston Effort to Desegregate Its Schools," *New York Times,* 18 June 1981, 20A, col. 6; Sharon Herbaugh, "Federal Judge Says Houston School District Properly Integrated," Associated Press, 17 June 1981; Rocky Scott, "Government Motion Rejected In Desegregation Case," AP, 10 June 1981; Bruce Nichols, UPI, 17 June 1981.

237. *Ross v. HISD,* 699 F.2d 218 (5th Cir., 1983), 230.

238. Betty Luman, "Another Settlement Reached in HISD,"UPI, 10 September 1984.

239. "Desegregation Suit Settled in Houston," *Washington Post,* 28 November 1984, A12. "Judge Approves HISD Out-of-Court Settlement," UPI, 27 November 1984. "Judge Approves Settlement, Dismisses 28-Year-Old Lawsuit," AP, 27 November 1984.

240. "HISD Freed from Desegregation Suit," UPI, 31 August 1989. Susan Besze Wallace, "The Changing Complexion of HISD: As the Desegregation Legal Battle Wore On, Houston School Demographics Were Steadily Changing," *Houston Post,* 15 May 1994, p. A16. Melanie Markley, "Will Ethnic Diversity Suffer As HISD Rezones Schools?" *Houston Chronicle,* 5 April 1995, 1A.

CHAPTER 6. Federal Criminal Justice on Trial in the 1970s

1. Fed. R. Civ. P. (Rule 1, "Scope of Rules.").

2. The full text of the amendment provides: "In all criminal prosecutions, the accused shall enjoy the right to a speedy and public trial, by an impartial jury of the State and district wherein the crime shall have been committed; which district shall have been previously ascertained by law, and to be informed of the nature and cause of the accusation; to be confronted with the witnesses against him; to have compulsory process for obtaining witnesses in his favor, and to have the assistance of counsel for his defence." U.S. Const., amend. VI.

3. U.S.C. § 3162. The Speedy Trial Act of 1974 is codified as 18 U.S.C. §§ 3161–74 (ch. 208); added by Pub. L. No. 93–619, 88 Stat. 2076 (3 January 1975). The statute grew out of efforts by several presidents and successive U.S. Congresses to establish federal guidelines for speedy trials. For example, see the "model timetable for the processing of criminal cases" prepared by the President's Commission on Law Enforcement and Administration of Justice, published as *Task Force Report: The Courts,* 84–90; and materials collected during the first session of the 92d Congress to accompany the Senate Judiciary Committee's hearings on S. 895, "a bill to enforce the Sixth Amendment right to speedy trial," conducted in July and September 1971, and published as *Hearings before the Subcommittee on Constitutional Rights.*

4. The new statute became effective on 1 May 1971. The Comprehensive Drug Abuse Prevention and Control Act of 1970, Pub. L. No. 91–513, 84 Stat. 1236 (codified, as amended, at 21 U.S.C. §§ 801–971).

5. U.S.C. § 1401(i).

6. U.S.C. § 906 [App. II]; also: 28 U.S.C. § 509 [note]). See *U.S. Code Cong. & Admin. News,* 28 March 1973, p. 912.

7. Beale, "Federalizing Crime," 48–49.

8. U.S. magistrates replaced weaker U.S. commissioners. See the Magistrates Act of 1968 (Pub. L. No. 90–578, 82 Stat. 1108). 28 U.S.C. § 636. Also see 18 U.S.C. § 3401. Finally, Sear, "Supporting Personnel," 250–52.

9. Pub. L. No. 95–486 (revising number of judgeships allocated in 28 U.S.C. § 133). See also: "House OKs More Courts, 12 in Texas," *Houston Post*, 8 February 1978, p. 7A.

10. For the results of federal government's contemporary studies of this issue, see U.S. Commission on Civil Rights, *Who Is Guarding the Guardians?* 3–4. U.S. Commission on Civil Rights, *Federal Role in the Administration of Justice;* and U.S. Commission on Civil Rights, *Police Practices and Civil Rights.*

11. Unfortunately such cases are too familiar two decades later. Police misconduct cases still often require resort to both state and federal courts, as successive prosecutions of Rodney King's Los Angeles Police Department (LAPD) assailants in 1992 demonstrated. On 3 March 1991 LAPD stopped an African American motorist, Rodney King, after an eight-mile chase. Four officers repeatedly clubbed and kicked King. A bystander captured the event with a video camera. Four officers were subsequently acquitted of filing a false report and assault with a deadly weapon. One of the officers was also charged with using excessive force and being an accessory after the fact, for hiding his conduct from his superiors. Martin Berg, "Chronology of the Case," *L.A. Daily Journal*, 3 February 1992, p. 8. Martin Berg, "A Case Filled with Twists and Turns," *L.A. Daily Journal*, 30 April 1992, p. 9. Also, Skolnick, *Above the Law*, 1–22; and Lawrence, *The Politics of Force*, generally.

12. That is, under 18 U.S.C. §§ 241–42.

13. The federal courts did not give many of the deceptively simple statements of the Bill of Rights, especially the rights of the criminally accused, significant attention or articulation until Chief Justice Earl Warren led the U.S. Supreme Court in a "due process revolution" during the 1960s. For example, the Warren court relied on the Due Process Clause of the Fourteenth Amendment to "incorporate" the Fourth, Fifth, and Sixth Amendments, and to require state criminal trials to conform to federal standards of due process, in 1961's *Mapp v. Ohio* (367 U.S. 643 [1961]), 1963's *Gideon v. Wainwright* (372 U.S. 335 [1963]), and 1966's *Miranda v. Arizona* (384 U.S. 436 [1966]).

14. *Klopfer v. North Carolina*, 386 U.S. 213 (1967), 223. In *Klopfer* the prosecutor in a North Carolina state criminal trial was unable to obtain a conviction against Klopfer. The prosecutor refiled charges, but instead of undertaking a trial, he suspended (but did not actually terminate) the prosecution without providing a reason to the court, an action he could take under the state's "nolle prosequi with leave" law. Klopfer, frustrated at being consigned to legal limbo, pressed for a second trial or a final dismissal of the charges against him, but the state declined either course. Klopfer then appealed to the federal courts. After tracing the right to the "very foundation of our English law heritage," the U.S. Supreme Court ruled (six to three) that the North Carolina law enabled prosecutors to deny defendants their rights to a speedy trial. Commonly called "nol-pros," the usual application of nolle prosequi, or "to be unwilling to prosecute," is to volunteer to withdraw an indictment. Under federal procedural rules, a criminal prosecution terminates upon the granting of a government's motion to nol-pros an indictment (Fed. R. Crim. P. Rule 48[a]).

15. *Barker v. Wingo*, 407 U.S. 514 (1972), 519–22.

16. Ibid., 519–21. This potential defensive advantage was not present in Barker's case. In September 1958 Willie Mae Barker was indicted as an accomplice in a brutal tire-iron murder of a Kentucky couple. The state believed it had the stronger case against the other defendant, Silas Manning, and wished to prosecute him first (after which the state would then try to per-

suade Manning to testify against Barker). Accordingly, the state filed successive continuances in the Barker case while it was preoccupied with Manning's trial. Because of two hung juries, two reversed convictions, and then, finally, two successful convictions, this delay lasted until December 1962, and in the interim the state filed a total of sixteen continuances in Barker's case. In February 1962, after the state's request for a twelfth continuance, Barker moved to dismiss the indictment, but the motion was denied. He was also unsuccessful in objecting to subsequent continuances. In late 1963 the trial finally commenced, with Manning as the chief witness for the prosecution. Barker was convicted and given a life sentence, which the Kentucky Court of Appeals upheld while rejecting his claim that he had been denied a speedy trial. Barker filed for habeas corpus relief in the federal courts, then appealed to the U.S. Supreme Court. Ibid., at 516–19.

17. Ibid., at 530. Court delays increase the costs of a criminal proceeding as well, and both the defense and the prosecution share an interest in reducing these costs. The clear economic element renders the right to speedy trial exceptional among due-process protections, and demonstrates how it is a right girded on all sides by pragmatic considerations. See Freedman, *Constitutional Right,* 6, and generally.

18. *Barker v. Wingo,* 407 U.S. 514, at 530–33. On 22 June 1972 Justice Powell delivered the court's decision to affirm the lower federal courts' rejection of habeas corpus. He first established the four-pronged criteria for assessing what *was* a violation, and then accepted the state's arguments that the five-year delay between indictment and trial was "extraordinary" but not necessarily a violation of the guarantee to a speedy trial (at 533–36).

19. Ibid., at 530–31.

20. Ibid., at 533.

21. The court noted, however, that some of the federal circuit courts of appeal had already adopted their own timelines to guide the district courts under their jurisdiction. For example, the Second Circuit had mandated (barring "unusual" circumstances) that the government must be ready for trial within six months of an arrest, or dismiss the charges. The virtue in this approach, as the justices saw it, was a clarified and simplified application of the right, but they did not consider themselves constitutionally authorized to impose procedural rules, either on the federal courts or the state courts. The justices also rejected the adoption by several states of a rule under which a defendant's failure to demand a speedy trial was taken to be a waiver of the right. The court held that this option would be inconsistent with the established methods for waiving constitutional rights (e.g., those set forth in *Miranda*). Ibid., at 523–29.

22. Ibid., at 523. See the "model timetable for the processing of criminal cases" in President's Commission on Law Enforcement and Administration of Justice, *Task Force Report,* 84–90; and the materials collected during the first session of the 92d Congress to accompany the Senate Judiciary Committee's hearings on S. 895, "a bill to enforce the Sixth Amendment right to speedy trial," conducted in July and September 1971, and published as *Hearings before the Subcommittee on Constitutional Rights.*

23. Justice Brennan joined in the concurrence. *Barker v. Wingo,* 407 U.S. 514, at 537.

24. Under the Federal Rules of Criminal Procedure, the court may dismiss an indictment, information, or complaint if there has been an "unnecessary" delay in bringing the case to a grand jury, filing an information, or bringing a defendant to trial (Fed. R. Crim. P., Rule 48[b]).

25. *United States v. Rodriguez,* 375 F.Supp. 589 (S.D. Tex., 1974), at 591–92 [Houston Division; Crim. No. 73-H-7]. The allegations of error included the charge that Judge Bue improp-

erly admitted hearsay evidence, that the evidence was inadmissible due to lack of probable cause, and that Bue's refusal to order the first jury to continue deliberating placed the defendants in double jeopardy before a second jury. The defendants also claimed errors in Bue's refusal to acquit them with a directed verdict, and in his allegedly improper charge to the jury regarding the amount of marijuana indicating an intent to distribute. Bue rejected each allegation and denied the motion for a new (effectively third) trial. Ibid., at 596. On appeal, specifically for delay, double jeopardy, and admissibility of evidence claims, the Fifth Circuit affirmed Judge Bue. *United States v. Rodriguez,* 497 F.2d 172 (5th Cir., 1974) [No. 73–4020].

26. *United States v. Rodriguez,* 375 F.Supp. 589, at 591–93.

27. The ninety-day rule applied if the defendant was not in custody. The time limit was sixty days if the defendant was incarcerated while awaiting trial. *Plan for Achieving Prompt Disposition of Criminal Cases in the Southern District of Texas,* par. 2(b) [adopted 9 March 1973]. This plan was written in accordance with a federal procedural rule which provided that each district court "shall conduct a continuing study" of its administration of federal criminal justice and then "prepare plans for the prompt disposition of criminal cases" (Fed. R. Crim. P., Rule 50[b]). In *Barker,* the justices explicitly declined to set fixed timetables. *Barker v. Wingo,* 407 U.S. 514, at 523.

28. The "binding rule" language is from a Fifth Circuit opinion regarding the local plan established in the Middle District of Louisiana. *United States v. Bullock,* 551 F.2d 1377 (5th Cir., 1977), 1381.

29. Oral history interview with Senior Circuit Judge Reynaldo G. Garza by Steven H. Wilson, 18 March 1998.

30. *United States v. Rodriguez,* 375 F.Supp. 589, at 591–92.

31. *United States v. Rodriguez,* 497 F.2d 172, at 175.

32. A related federal criminal procedural rule provided that in preparing their court calendars, district courts were to give preference to criminal proceedings, at least "as far as practicable" (Fed. R. Crim. P., Rule 50[a]).

33. *United States v. Rodriguez,* 497 F.2d 172, at 176.

34. Ibid., at 176.

35. *United States v. Rodriguez,* 497 F.2d 172, at 176.

36. But even after Richard Garcia waited more than one year after his arraignment to face federal criminal charges for allegedly making false statements on his tax returns, District Judge Ross N. Sterling refused Garcia's request to dismiss the indictment and convicted him of the charges. The criminal statute governing the veracity of statements on tax returns is 26 U.S.C. § 7206(1). On appeal the Fifth Circuit affirmed that Sterling was well within his discretionary powers. *United States v. Garcia,* 553 F.2d 432 (5th Cir., 1977) [No. 76–4255].

37. Chief Judge Connally to "Dear Mr. Thomas," 25 July 1974, clerk's files of Chief Judge Ben C. Connally, folder 4.

38. *United States v. Clendening,* 526 F.2d 842 (5th Cir., 1976), 848.

39. The statute proscribing possession of marijuana with intent to distribute (the Comprehensive Drug Abuse Prevention and Control Act of 1970) provided: "Except as authorized by this subchapter, it shall be unlawful for any person knowingly or intentionally—(1) to manufacture, distribute, or dispense, or possess with intent to manufacture, distribute, or dispense, a controlled substance" (21 U.S.C. § 841[a][1]).

40. *Almeida-Sanchez v. United States,* 413 U.S. 266 (1973).

41. *United States v. Maizumi,* 526 F.2d 848 (5th Cir., 1976), 850–51. In two later cases Judge Cox heard involving marijuana seizure at the border, *Almeida-Sanchez* was no longer an

issue because the Border Patrol no longer used roving patrols or temporary checkpoints. But both defendants unsuccessfully sought relief under *Barker.* The Fifth Circuit upheld Judge Cox in both cases. In the first case, *United States v. Rankin,* 572 F.2d 503 (5th Cir., 1978), Cox rejected claims that a seven-month delay was explainable and not prejudicial to the defendants. In the second case, *United States v. Canales,* 573 F.2d 908 (5th Cir., 1978), Cox rejected the contention that a twenty-seven-month delay was prejudicial. In *Canales* the border checkpoint was also at Sarita (as in *Maizumi*), but it had already been declared to be a "functional equivalent" according to *Almeida-Sanchez* criteria in *United States v. Reyna,* 572 F.2d 515 (5th Cir., 1978).

42. The act allowed judges four calendar years after 1 July 1975 to prepare for its effect. 18 U.S.C. § 3163(c).

43. U.S.C. §§ 3165, 3168. The act demanded that the judges compile a list of the particular reasons for continuances that would be deemed acceptable by the court and provided for the creation of an elaborate system of statistical accounting of delays. 18 U.S.C. § 3166.

44. *Dillingham v. United States,* 423 U.S. 64 (1975).

45. Chief Judge Garza to "Dear Mr. Thomas," 24 March 1975, clerk's files of Chief Judge Reynaldo G. Garza, folder 1.

46. Oral history interview with Senior Circuit Judge Reynaldo G. Garza by Steven H. Wilson, 18 March 1998. For similar concerns over the impact of the Speedy Trial Act, see also Walter E. Hoffman, "Purposes and Philosophy of Sentencing," in *Proceedings of Seminar for Newly Appointed United States District Judges,* 13–18 September 1976, Washington, D.C., 75 F.R.D. 89 (1977), 287, 324–29.

47. Judge Garza to "My dear Judges," 17 December 1974, clerk's files of Chief Judge Reynaldo G. Garza, folder 1.

48. Chief Judge Garza to "Dear Mr. Thomas," 4 February 1975, clerk's files of Chief Judge Reynaldo G. Garza, folder 1.

49. Chief Judge Garza, Judicial Work Assignments, memorandum, 30 December 1974, clerk's files of Chief Judge Reynaldo G. Garza, folder 1.

50. Chief Judge Garza, Judicial Work Assignments, memorandum, 19 December 1975, clerk's files of Chief Judge Reynaldo G. Garza, folder 1.

51. "Sterling," in *Judges of the United States.* Also, Pete Wittenberg, "Who Is Ross Sterling? Man Who Shuns the Press Now the Center of Attention," *Houston Post,* 8 April 1978, 1A, 27A.

52. Chief Judge Garza, Judicial Work Assignments, memorandum, 29 May 1976, clerk's files of Chief Judge Reynaldo G. Garza, folder 1.

53. Chief Judge Garza to "My Dear Judges," 22 December 1976, clerk's files of Chief Judge Reynaldo G. Garza, folder 2.

54. Chief Judge Garza, Judicial Work Assignments, memorandum, 22 December 1976, clerk's files of Chief Judge Reynaldo G. Garza, folder 2.

55. Chief Judge Garza to "My dear Judge Brown and General Kirks, In re: Change of Official Station of Judge Robert O'Conor, Jr.," 23 February 1977, clerk's files of Chief Judge Reynaldo G. Garza, folder 2.

56. Rose B. Bart [administrative assistant to Judge Garza] to "Dear Mr. Thomas," note and attached order, 19 October 1979, clerk's files of Chief Judge Reynaldo G. Garza, folder 3.

57. Jorjanna Price, "Houston's Federal Judges Trying to Clear Overloaded Docket," *Houston Post,* 4 September 1977, p. 4A.

58. Chief Judge Garza to "My dear Judges," 22 December 1977, clerk's files of Chief Judge Reynaldo G. Garza, folder 3.

59. Judge Garza to "Dear Mr. McCabe," 7 February 1978, clerk's files of Chief Judge Reynaldo G. Garza, folder 3.

60. See 18 U.S.C. §§ 241 and 242.

61. These were the primary Mexican American organizations operating in Texas. San Miguel, *"Let All of Them Take Heed,"* 69–70, 116, 165, and 169–71; generally, Ramos, *The American GI Forum.* The San Antonio lawyer Pete Tijerina established MALDEF in 1967. He modeled MALDEF's organization and its goals on the NAACP Legal Defense Fund, Inc. (or the "Inc. Fund"). O'Connor and Epstein, "A Legal Voice," at 285. See generally Hero, *Latinos and the U.S. Political System;* and Wasby, *Race Relations.*

62. When police officers allegedly use excessive force, private citizens, individually or as a class, can seek federal protection under the 1964 CRA, specifically under 42 U.S.C. § 1983. "Note: Developments in the Law," 1155. In Texas "Chicano" civil rights activism was highlighted by a march to Austin in 1966, and by the south Texas farmworkers' strikes in 1968. The latter ended when the Texas Rangers intervened to arrest strike leaders. Meier and Ribera, *Mexican Americans/American Mexicans,* 211. Captain A. Y. Allee, commander of the south Texas unit of the Texas Rangers, was a defendant in the leading case to enjoin this activity by the Rangers. *Allee v. Medrano,* 416 U.S. 802 (1974), affirming in part, vacating in part, and remanding 347 F.Supp. 605 (S.D. Tex., 1971). The Texas Ranger case was the exception in the 1970s. Other U.S. Supreme Court decisions hindered private civil rights suits against police officers. In Philadelphia, African Americans challenged police misconduct, including searches and seizures directed against minorities allegedly for the purpose of harassing them. The court found no liability on the part of Philadelphia officials, and the justices distinguished *Allee* on the ground that the plaintiffs had not shown a pervasive pattern of abuse that would indicate a policy to violate rights. *Rizzo v. Goode,* 423 U.S. 362 (1975), 373–76. See Meltzer, "Deterring Constitutional Violations," 314–15. Adverse court decisions, such as *Rizzo,* had by the mid-1970s convinced the LDF of the NAACP to abandon police brutality cases as an unfruitful use of limited litigation resources. Wasby, *Race Relations,* 40–41. Before this abandonment, African American civil rights groups, such as the Congress on Racial Equality (CORE), organized school boycotts and rent strikes, but also focused on exposing police brutality or harassment perpetrated against minorities. Sitkoff, *Struggle for Black Equality,* 146.

63. The reluctance on the part of federal lawyers to act against the states was widespread but not universal. In November 1965 U.S. Solicitor General Thurgood Marshall argued before the Supreme Court that the justices should uphold the federal government's power to punish "lynch mob murder." Belknap, *Federal Law and the Southern Order,* 172–82. The court agreed and held that the federal government may prosecute state police officers who violated federal constitutional rights, if officers acted under "color of authority" of the state or under "color" of state law. *United States v. Price,* 383 U.S. 787 (1966).

64. *United States v. James George Beatty and Karl Lee Phillips,* Crim. No. 65-G-16, case files, U.S. District Court for the Southern District of Texas (S.D. Tex., Galveston Division, 1965), NARA-SWA, RG 21, box 216, folder 65-G-16.

65. *United States v. McMahon,* 339 F.Supp. 1092 (S.D. Tex., 1971) Cr., Crim. No. 71-H-260.

66. The Justice Department rule, referred to as the "Petite policy" (after *Petite v. United States,* 361 U.S. 529 [1960]), discouraged and in some instances barred "dual prosecution" when a state had already prosecuted and won its case, even if the state conviction was for a lesser charge and the resultant sentence was inadequate. Under the policy federal attorneys "had a very heavy burden to carry in initiating second prosecutions." See "Testimony of

Drew S. Days III," 16 September 1980, in U.S. Commission on Civil Rights, *Federal Role in the Administration of Justice,* 30. Also see Miller, *Double Jeopardy.*

67. The standard justification for federal deference to the states was the effort to maintain comity in the federal system, but another reason federal prosecutors might not seek to take a "second bite at the apple" was that proving criminal civil-rights violations was difficult. Landsberg, *Enforcing Civil Rights,* 54–55. The DOJ ordinarily indicted only if the state failed to respond to deprivations of civil rights within its borders; except in egregious cases of official misconduct, even a token prosecution was usually adequate to forestall the federal intervention. Belknap, *Federal Law and the Southern Order,* 76, 115.

68. The town is two dozen miles west of San Antonio (which is in neighboring Bexar County). In the mid-1970s Castroville's resident population was approximately two thousand.

69. Arthur Wiese, "Bell OK's Investigation by Federal Grand Jury into Morales Slaying," *Houston Post,* 12 February 1977, 20A.

70. See Gene Lyons, "Passion Play: Dallas Blacks Force a Showdown over Police Review," *Texas Monthly,* October 1980, pp. 131–32.

71. Arthur Wiese, "Bell OK's Investigation by Federal Grand Jury into Morales Slaying," *Houston Post,* 12 February 1977, 20A.

72. Professor Wasby refers to changes in attitudes or policies, when caused by changes in administration, as policy "flip-flops." Wasby, *Race Relations,* 247–51.

73. Arthur Wiese, "Bell OK's Investigation by Federal Grand Jury into Morales Slaying," *Houston Post,* 12 February 1977, 20A.

74. "Prepared Remarks of Drew S. Days III," in U.S. Commission on Civil Rights, *Federal Role in the Administration of Justice,* 126.

75. "Morales Slaying Probe Pleases Family Lawyer," *Houston Post,* 13 February 1977, 7E.

76. According to Drew Days, President Carter's assistant attorney general for civil rights, the Justice Department policy that several offenses arising from a single transaction should not lead to multiple prosecutions remained intact. However, federal-state dual prosecution on substantially the same evidence, but under a different statute and different jurisdiction, did not constitute double jeopardy, even if the two jurisdictions cooperated to achieve the dual prosecutions. "Testimony of Drew S. Days III," in *Federal Role in the Administration of Justice,* 28–31.

77. "Prepared Remarks of Drew S. Days III," in U.S. Commission on Civil Rights, *Federal Role in the Administration of Justice,* 126–27.

78. Tom Curtis, "Support Your Local Police (Or Else)," *Texas Monthly,* September 1977, p. 85.

79. "Bulletin," *Houston Post,* 10 May 1977, 1A.

80. Larry Troutt, "Bond Talks with Death Probe Jury," *Houston Post,* 11 May 1977, 1A, 19A.

81. Gary Taylor, "Two Ex-officers Convicted of Misdemeanor: Punishment Deliberations Will Resume Today," *Houston Post,* 7 October 1977, 1A, 19A. Any identity of federal prosecution of defendants who had been convicted in a state criminal trial, a so-called "dual prosecution," with the constitutionally prohibited "double jeopardy" is illusory. The Fifth Amendment of the U.S. Constitution provides, in relevant part, "[N]or shall any person be subject for the same offense to be twice put in jeopardy of life or limb[.]" U.S. Const., amend. V. In two cases decided in 1959, the U.S. Supreme Court held that a second prosecution under a different statute does not constitute double jeopardy (*Bartkus v. Illinois,* 359 U.S. 121 [1959]), and that a federal prosecution after an earlier conviction by a state court was not

necessarily barred by the Fifth Amendment's double jeopardy clause (*Abbate v. United States,* 359 U.S. 187 [1959]). As a result of these decisions, federal vindication of civil rights cannot be frustrated by the completion of a "sham" or deeply flawed prosecution. See "Note: Double Prosecutions," 1551–54. Also, under the federal arrangement's principle of "dual sovereignty," a criminal act is punishable by both state and federal governments. If this were not true, the prosecutorial action by one would interfere with the other's "sovereign" rights to employ its own criminal law. Hess, "Good Cop–Bad Cop," 178–81. See Indictment, *United States v. Denson,* Crim. No. H-77–107; criminal docket, S.D. Tex., 1977, Houston Division. The docket sheets (a chronological record of development in the case from the filing forward) and much other documentation for the federal case and its related appeals are in (NARA-SWA). See case files of the U.S. Court of Appeals for the Fifth Circuit (U.S.C.A., 5th Cir.), Record Group (RG) 276, box 142, folder 78–2102. Judicial decisions for the case, *United States v. Denson,* discussed below, are reported at 588 F.2d 1112 (5th Cir., 1979); 593 F.2d 3 (5th Cir., 1979); and 603 F.2d 1143 (5th Cir., 1979). In cases where police officers are suspected of harassing, injuring, or even killing while depriving or conspiring to deprive someone of their civil rights, U.S. attorneys may prosecute the alleged violations under two federal criminal statutes. The first statute criminalizes any "conspiracy against rights" (18 U.S.C. § 241). The second statute makes it a crime actually to deprive another citizen of rights while acting "under color of law" (18 U.S.C. § 242). This was a misdemeanor and carried a maximum sentence of one year in prison and a one-thousand-dollar fine.

82. Skolnick, *Above the Law,* 195–216.

83. Larry Troutt and Ann James, "Attorney Shot Dead during Police Raid on Hotel Suite Here," *Houston Post,* 12 February 1977, 1A, 23A. Curtis, "Support Your Local Police," 83–84.

84. Throughout the 1960s HPD Chief Herman Short was notorious for racism, and his officers were criticized for a propensity for questionable use of deadly force. For Chief Short and the HPD, see generally Justice, *Violence in the City.* Also, Curtis, "Support Your Local Police," 83, 158–60.

85. At the Houston Police Academy a cadet received only two hours of training, out of a total of 640 hours, regarding the proper use of deadly force. Reportedly, HPD officers joked that the mayor was misguided on the issue of better training; they claimed they were already "hitting everything [they were] shooting at." Curtis, "Support Your Local Police," 158–61. On 15 June the HPD formally established the permanent IA Division. Within six weeks the IA unit received more than 180 citizen complaints. Curtis, "Support Your Local Police," 83.

86. "Bulletin," *Houston Post,* 10 May 1977, 1A. Larry Troutt, "Bond Will Form Internal Affairs Division," *Houston Post,* 7 May 1977, 1A, 19A.

87. Larry Troutt, "Bond Talks with Death Probe Jury," *Houston Post,* 11 May 1977, 1A, 19A.

88. Curtis, "Support Your Local Police," 85. All the officers implicated in Torres's death were young and had clean disciplinary records; each had been rated highly by HPD superiors. Terry Wayne Denson, a twenty-seven-year-old member of the HPD's Radio Patrol Division who emerged as the ringleader of the Torres incident, was considered a model police officer by his superiors. His personnel file contained letters from citizens praising him for his promptness, helpfulness, and courtesy. Moreover, Denson had never fired his gun on duty and had drawn it only once during his five years with the HPD. Glenn Lee Brinkmeyer, also twenty-seven, had been in Denson's cadet class at the academy. Louis Glenn Kinney, twenty-seven, joined the force in 1973. The other officers were younger, and several had close family ties to the police department. Joseph James Janish, twenty-two, had been on the force for one year. Stephen Orlando, twenty-one, was the son of an HPD detective, and his mother

and two brothers were all members of the HPD. Elliott also followed his father onto the force. Phil Hevener, "'There's Been a Lot of Heartbreak,' Says Father of Ex-officer," *Houston Post,* 7 October 1977, 19A.

89. Pete Wittenberg, "City Police Rookie Recounts Testimony in Torres Death," *Houston Post,* 27 January 1978, 3A.

90. Pete Wittenberg, "Police Chief Critical of Violence," *Houston Post,* 31 January 1978, 16A.

91. Tom Curtis, "Support Your Local Police," 87.

92. Pete Wittenberg, "City Police Rookie Recounts Testimony in Torres Death," *Houston Post,* 27 January 1978, 3A.

93. Pete Wittenberg, "Elliott Recounts Chain of Events in Torres Death," *Houston Post,* 28 January 1978, 4A.

94. Curtis, "Support Your Local Police," 87.

95. Before becoming involved in the Torres case, Bennett was already prominent in Texas legal and political circles. He was the former chief of the Harris County district attorney's Special Crimes Division. Bennett was a major player in the murder trial of the hit man accused of killing John Hill, a prominent Houstonian. Tom Curtis, "Reporter," *Texas Monthly,* January 1978, p. 62. See Thompson, *Blood and Money.*

96. "Bulletin," *Houston Post,* 10 May 1977, 1A; Larry Troutt, "Officer Charged with Murder," *Houston Post,* 10 May 1977, 1A.

97. Larry Troutt, "Five of 6 Officers Fired in Torres Death Case," *Houston Post,* 13 May 1977, 1A, 21A.

98. Torres's father claimed his son was "a good swimmer and he loved karate, but he never fought nobody." Burke Watson, "Slain Man's Brother Asks 'Why' of Death," *Houston Post,* 11 May 1977, 19A. Torres's cousin agreed that Joe Jr. "never laid a hand on anybody" and "knew what would happen if he hit a policeman." The Harris County DA revealed, however, that Torres had several arrests on his record, including one from 1971 that led to a guilty plea on a charge of assaulting a highway patrolman; Torres had paid the fine of twenty-five dollars. Larry Troutt, "Bond Talks with Death Probe Jury," *Houston Post,* 11 May 1977, 1A, 19A. Larry Troutt, "Five of 6 Officers Fired in Torres Death Case," *Houston Post,* 13 May 1977, 1A, 21A.

99. Curtis, "Support Your Local Police," 83.

100. Larry Troutt, "Bond Going 'in Direction' of Firing 5 in Torres Case," *Houston Post,* 12 May 1977, 1A, 27A. The press and other interested parties frequently identified the victim as "Jose Campos Torres," or "Jose Campos Torres Jr." Although "Jose" was often Anglicized to "Joe," the mother's middle name was almost always employed in print, except when the case went to the U.S. Court of Appeals for the Fifth Circuit. The Fifth Circuit Court substituted the father's name: "Joe Luna Torres Jr." See *United States v. Denson,* 588 F.2d 1112 (5th Cir., 1979).

101. Activists also sought federal charges against Cain for shooting Rodriguez in Dallas, but this effort proved unsuccessful. "Texas 'Justice': Civil Rights Laws Too Weak, Minorities Say," *Houston Post,* 2 April 1978, 9D. However, federal lawyers tried four of the seven cases Days approved in Texas. The first was Hayes's case, eventually tried in Waco; the remaining three cases concerned various alleged transgressions of HPD officers, and federal prosecutors tried the cases in Houston. The first of these HPD cases, of course, concerned the death of Joe Torres.

102. The activists had assembled in the gymnasium of Our Lady of Guadalupe Catholic

Church. Organizers planned to present the document at LULAC's state convention, to be held that weekend in Lubbock. Terry Kliewer, "Federal Probe of Slaying Urged," *Houston Post*, 13 May 1977, 16A. This goal to create a review board paralleled efforts by minority groups in many large cities. Browning, Marshall, and Tabb, *Protest Is Not Enough*, 152–56.

103. Ann James, "Body Bruised, Autopsy Shows," *Houston Post*, 15 May 1977, 1A, 2A. Jachimczyk later testified as an expert witness that Torres had no chance to survive in the bayou. Gary Taylor, "Orlando, Denson Get Probated Sentences," *Houston Post*, 8 October 1977, 1A, 27A. Larry Troutt, "Five of 6 Officers Fired in Torres Death Case," *Houston Post*, 13 May 1977, 1A, 21A.

104. Frank Davis and Larry Troutt, "Mayor Calls Police Image 'Illness,'" *Houston Post*, 17 May 1977, 1A, 19A. By the late 1970s Houston suffered a soaring crime rate that worried longtime residents, who argued that the dramatic rise in allegations of police brutality showed only that society itself was out of control and law enforcement had to get tougher, to match increasingly deviant behavior exhibited by criminals. Under such conditions, some scholars posit, police abuse was perhaps "unofficially tolerated as the price we pay for law and order." Hess, "Good Cop–Bad Cop," 149.

105. Jon Standefer, "Clayton Promises Probe by Interim House Panel," *Houston Post*, 19 May 1977, 1A, 27A.

106. Mike Avalos, "Protesters March: Minority Leaders Meet Bond," *Houston Post*, 18 May 1977, 1A, 23A. "Vance Wants U.S. Probe of Torres Death Case," *Houston Post*, 19 May 1977, 1A, 27A.

107. Mike Avalos, "Protesters March: Minority Leaders Meet Bond," *Houston Post*, 18 May 1977, 1A, 23A.

108. Ann James, "Body Bruised, Autopsy Shows," *Houston Post*, 15 May 1977, 1A, 2A.

109. One of these speakers, Alfred Leal, vice president of the Mexican-American Bar Association of Harris County, told the council that the only way to restore respect between the community and the police was through the creation of a citizens review board. "Hispanics Organizing Police Review Board," *Houston Post*, 18 May 1977, p. A4.

110. "Vance Wants U.S. Probe of Torres Death Case," *Houston Post*, 19 May 1977, pp. A1, A27.

111. "Hofheinz, Vance Wait for Justice," *Houston Post*, 20 May 1977, A3.

112. Frank Davis and Larry Troutt, "Mayor Calls Police Image 'Illness,'" *Houston Post*, 17 May 1977, 1A, 19A.

113. A Houston social-gossip columnist later referred to exchief Bond as the Houston-based energy firm's "security czar." Marge Crumbaker, "Late-snacking Quentin Perry, Lost Cash Reunited," *Houston Post*, 29 March 1978, p. A22.

114. "Acquittals Wind Up 2 Years of Probes, Trials," *Houston Post*, 26 July 1979, A22.

115. Curtis, "Support Your Local Police," 87.

116. The Texas Department of Corrections (TDC) has since been renamed the Texas Department of Criminal Justice (TDCJ).

117. Gary Taylor, "'Bullwhip Case' Recalled," *Houston Post*, 9 October 1977, 1A, 2A.

118. Gary Taylor, "Denson Slapped Others, Former Officer Testifies," *Houston Post*, 1 October 1977, 1A, 27A.

119. Fred King, "Torres Case Recalls Earlier Verdict: Both Trials Had Similarities, but Officers Convicted in This One," *Houston Post*, 7 October 1977, 3A. Haynes quoted in Curtis, "Support Your Local Police," 164.

120. All three defendants appealed, but the Fifth Circuit affirmed their convictions.

United States v. Hayes, 589 F.2d 811 (5th Cir., 1979); cert. denied, 444 U.S. 847 (1979). Also, "Hayes Faces Possibility of Life Term," *Houston Post*, 1 October 1977, 4A.

121. Poe was reportedly known as "Toothbrush" around the county jail, because inmates told their cellmates to pack one if they went to trial facing him, as they would be going straight to prison. He enjoyed the reputation and once set a toothbrush on the defendants' table at the beginning of a trial as a warning. Gary Taylor, "Movie-like Atmosphere Surrounds Torres Case," *Houston Post*, 2 October 1977, 1A, 2A.

122. Gary Taylor, "Torres Case Jurors Meet Again Today," *Houston Post*, 6 October 1977, 1A, 27A.

123. Ernst was for many years the key trial attorney for the Harris County district attorney's office, and he was the prosecutor who lost to Ramsey in the 1971 Galena Park case. Gary Taylor, "Jury Set to Begin Deliberating Today in Trial of Officers," *Houston Post*, 4 October 1977, 1A, 21A.

124. Gary Taylor, "Movie-like Atmosphere Surrounds Torres Case," *Houston Post*, 2 October 1977, 1A, 2A.

125. On one occasion someone apparently sympathetic to the defense moved the red doll onto the opposite bank of the "bayou," suggesting the possibility that Torres could have survived to escape from the water. Gary Taylor, "Movie-like Atmosphere Surrounds Torres Case," *Houston Post*, 2 October 1977, 1A, 2A.

126. Janish was awaiting trial on his misdemeanor charge and was not at risk in their trial.

127. Gary Taylor, "Denson Slapped Others, Former Officer Testifies," *Houston Post*, 1 October 1977, 1A, 27A.

128. Gary Taylor, "Movie-like Atmosphere Surrounds Torres Case," *Houston Post*, 2 October 1977, 1A, 2A.

129. Gary Taylor, "Denson Slapped Others, Former Officer Testifies," *Houston Post*, 1 October 1977, 1A, 27A.

130. Some of Brinkmeyer's memories did make it into the record of the proceedings, but the judge ruled that the most inflammatory remarks were inadmissible. Ibid.

131. Gary Taylor, "Jury Set to Begin Deliberating Today in Trial of Officers," *Houston Post*, 4 October 1977, 1A, 21A.

132. Ibid.

133. Gary Taylor, "'Pride' Blamed for Death: Torres Case Jury Deliberates," *Houston Post*, 5 October 1977, 1A, 23A.

134. Gary Taylor, "Torres Case Jurors Meet Again Today," *Houston Post*, 6 October 1977, 1A, 27A.

135. Under Texas law negligent homicide was a Class A misdemeanor and carried a possible punishment ranging from probation to one year in jail, or a maximum two-thousand-dollar fine, or both. Gary Taylor, "Two Ex-officers Convicted of Misdemeanor: Punishment Deliberations Will Resume Today," *Houston Post*, 7 October 1977, 1A, 19A.

136. "Federal Trial Possible," *Houston Post*, 7 October 1977, 1A, 19A.

137. Apparently, Graham said, the jury had believed that the drunken, injured Torres was more like Daniel Boone than a little girl lost in the woods. "Torres 'More Like Daniel Boone,'" *Houston Post*, 7 October 1977, 1A.

138. Rob Wood, Associated Press, 6 October 1977.

139. Gary Taylor, "Two Ex-officers Convicted of Misdemeanor: Punishment Deliberations Will Resume Today," *Houston Post*, 7 October 1977, 1A, 19A.

140. Rob Wood, Associated Press, 6 October 1977.

141. Jim Maloney, "Bitterness Greets Verdict: 'It's Not a Felony to Kill?'" *Houston Post*, 7 October 1977, 3A.

142. Gary Taylor, "Two Ex-officers Convicted of Misdemeanor: Punishment Deliberations Will Resume Today," *Houston Post*, 7 October 1977, 1A, 19A.

143. Gary Taylor, "Orlando, Denson Get Probated Sentences," *Houston Post*, 8 October 1977, 1A, 27A. Gary Taylor, "No Evidence, Jurors Claim," *Houston Post*, 8 October 1977, 1A, 27A.

144. Ed Jahn, "Mexican-American Groups Looking to Federal Process," *Houston Post*, 7 October 1977, 3A.

145. "U.S. Courts Seen As 'Only Recourse,'" *Houston Post*, 8 October 1977, 22A.

146. Reyes dispatched an aide to Washington to accompany them. Ed Jahn, "Mexican-American Groups Looking to Federal Process," *Houston Post*, 7 October 1977, 3A.

147. This was essentially the same political coalition that had successfully called for the federal prosecution of Frank Hayes for killing Richard Morales. Bill Curry, "Three Ex-Policemen Draw 1-Year Terms; Mexican-Americans Bitter Over Sentences in Houston Death," *Washington Post*, 29 March 1978, 7A.

148. Ken Grissom, "LULAC Will Lobby for Civil Rights Laws," *Houston Post*, 9 October 1977, 12A.

149. Jim Asker, "About 200 Protest Torres Case Verdict," *Houston Post*, 9 October 1977, 1A, 2A.

150. "Caldwell Blames 'Rhetoric' For Ex-officers' Sentences," *Houston Post*, 8 October 1977, 22A. Mayor Hofheinz, although publicly stating his assumption that the state prosecution had proceeded properly, nonetheless added his voice to those calling for federal intervention. "Mayor Asks U.S. to Proceed in Case," *Houston Post*, 7 October 1977, 3A. State prosecutor Ernst, who had lost to Ramsey in the Conner case, took comfort in the fact that the Torres defendants were convicted, even if only for misdemeanors. He said it suggested that brutality was less tolerated than earlier, and officials more suspect. He also noted the New Braunfels jury consisted of eleven men and one woman, rather than seven women to five men in Huntsville; Ernst thought women were likely to be less tolerant of brutality. He took the verdict as evidence that "slowly . . . perhaps we're becoming more civilized." Fred King, "Torres Case Recalls Earlier Verdict: Both Trials Had Similarities, but Officers Convicted in This One," *Houston Post*, 7 October 1977, 3A.

151. At thirty-three years old, he was one of the youngest persons in the nation to hold that office. Tony Canales was born in 1944 in Brownsville and grew up in Mercedes, Texas, until his mother began practicing medicine in Corpus Christi. Two of Canales's uncles were also doctors, but he chose a career in law. After attending UT in Austin, Canales graduated from Saint Mary's University School of Law in San Antonio, in 1969. Canales returned to Corpus Christi and—thanks to the proximity of the U.S.-Mexico border—he began to build a major criminal defense practice. Walt Borges, "Tony Canales: Going against the Grain," *Texas Lawyer*, 6 May 1996, p. 1. The district director of the Corpus Christi chapter of the Conservative Caucus vigorously opposed the appointment and reminded the press of Canales's fiery statements. Pete Wittenberg, "Outspoken Civil Rights Advocate Is New U.S. Attorney," *Houston Post*, 9 October 1977, 21A.

152. For the ferment in Houston, see the editorials "The Torres Case Verdict," *Houston Post*, 12 October 1977, 3B; "The Torres Unhappiness," *Houston Post*, 13 October 1977, 3D; and "The Torres Case, Cont'd," *Houston Post*, 18 October 1977, 3C.

153. "Federal Trial Possible," *Houston Post,* 7 October 1977, 1A, 19A.

154. Gary Taylor and Pete Wittenberg, "Officers to Appeal Verdict," *Houston Post,* 15 October 1977, 1A.

155. Even limited discretion was available only after a September 1976 change in the guidelines. In contrast, Canales could initiate any other, non–civil rights prosecutions under their own authority. "Testimony of J. A. Tony Canales," 11 September 1979, in U.S. Commission on Civil Rights, *Hearings on Police Practices,* 129–20, 139.

156. Days's team of prosecutors in the Civil Rights Division pursued civil lawsuits, such as public accommodation and housing discrimination cases, as well as criminal cases. Canales's local group would also press civil suits, but during the first year the four AUSAs assigned to full-time work in the local division were wholly preoccupied with criminal cases. "Testimony of J. A. Tony Canales," in *Hearings on Police Practices,* 129–131. "Federal Trial Possible," *Houston Post,* 7 October 1977, 1A, 19A.

157. Ibid., 131. "Testimony of Mary Sinderson," ibid., p. 135.

158. The grand jurors "no-billed" the officers, that is, they believed an indictment in the case would not be "a true bill"; when an indictment issues, it is designated "a true bill" by the foreman of the grand jury. The case lay dormant for nearly three years, but after the Torres incident the Southern District's Civil Rights Division reexamined the case. "Police Investigating 'Unresolved Question' in Death of Suspect," *Houston Post,* 7 April 1978, 1A; and "The Joyvies Case: Companion Not Aware Suspect Had Pistol in Car with Him," *Houston Post,* 8 April 1978, 1A, 27A.

159. "Officer Kills Man Following Chase," *Houston Post,* 9 February 1977, 14A. Mays, and two other officers, claimed that Webster emerged with a pistol in his hand, and the officers reported that they found an unloaded pistol near the body (it was later traced to a Globe Discount Store in Houston, where it had been shipped in 1964). The shooting incident was referred to a grand jury, and Mays was "no-billed." Tom Curtis, "The Throwdown," *Texas Monthly,* August 1979, p. 75.

160. Canales and Sinderson directed AUSA Lupe Salinas to investigate the Webster incident, to the exclusion of all other cases. Canales made this decision because, in his words, "[s]omething smelled awful in that case and it had to be resolved." "Testimony of J. A. Tony Canales," in *Hearings on Police Practices,* 134. After an aggressive investigation Salinas found conclusive evidence that the gun police had reported finding in Webster's possession was traceable to the HPD property room. Curtis, "The Throwdown," 165. Ultimately, Sinderson prosecuted the officer who killed Webster for violating the teenager's civil rights, then planting the gun to excuse the unjustified shooting. Decisions in the Webster case are reported at *United States v. Mays, et al.,* 460 F.Supp. 573 (1978); and, 470 F.Supp 642 (1979).

161. Pete Wittenberg, "Federal Jury Indicts 4 Former Officers: Fifth Ex-officer in Torres Case Pleads Guilty to Misdemeanor," *Houston Post,* 21 October 1977, 1A, 19A.

162. The first count alleged that the four officers conspired with Brinkmeyer to deprive Torres of his liberty without due process of law. The first count further alleged that the conspiracy resulted in death (violation of § 241). The second count charged that the same four officers—while acting under color of law—willfully deprived Torres of his constitutional right not to be deprived of liberty without due process of law (in violation of § 242). The third count alleged that Denson willfully assaulted Torres by pushing him into the Buffalo Bayou, thereby depriving him of his constitutional rights without due process of law. The third count further alleged that this act resulted in Torres's death (these acts, the indictment charged, were in violation of both § 241 and § 242).

163. Conspiring to withhold or interfere with testimony is a violation of 18 U.S.C. § 371, and actually withholding such testimony violated 18 U.S.C. § 1510. Only three of the four defendants were charged on all counts. Janish was not indicted on the final joint count relating to the alleged cover-up, because he had not encouraged Elliott to lie about the beating if interviewed by HPD superiors. See Indictment, Crim. No. H-77–107, *United States v. Denson*, NARA-SWA, RG 276, box 142, folder 78–2102. The indictment identified the victim as "Joe Luna Torres Jr. (also known as Joe Campos Torres)." Again, the alternative nomenclatures employ Torres's mother's name (Campos) and his father's (Luna).

164. Fred King, "Politicians Welcome Grand Jury's Action," *Houston Post*, 21 October 1977, 3A. The same day Canales released the indictments, the four defendants, former HPD officers Denson, Orlando, Janish, and Kinney, appeared before U.S. Magistrate Judge Norman W. Black. McDonald argued that Black should maintain the bonds at ten thousand dollars each. But Black granted the bond petition, set arraignment for 28 October, and released the defendants. As part of a plea agreement with the U.S. attorney's office, which he had signed on 1 July, Brinkmeyer had testified before the grand jury and agreed to testify for the government in a federal trial. In addition, the bargain required Brinkmeyer to admit before U.S. Magistrate Judge H. Lingo Platter that he had conspired with the other four officers to violate Torres's civil rights, and that he struck and assaulted a handcuffed prisoner. Therefore, Brinkmeyer pleaded guilty to a misdemeanor violation of the federal statute, which carried a maximum penalty of one year in prison and a one-thousand-dollar fine. He was released on his personal recognizance. Pete Wittenberg, "Federal Jury Indicts 4 Former Officers: Fifth Ex-officer in Torres Case Pleads Guilty to Misdemeanor," *Houston Post*, 21 October 1977, 1A, 19A.

165. Fred King, "Relief Expressed at Indictments," *Houston Post*, 21 October 1977, 3A. This prediction proved incorrect, but the group of protesters that did parade in Houston for the third consecutive weekend was the smallest crowd yet. Fewer than two dozen activists turned up in front of the federal building on Saturday, as compared with the hundreds appearing a week earlier on the steps of police headquarters. "Group Protests Joe Torres Case," *Houston Post*, 23 October 1977, 6D.

166. "Swift Indictments in Torres Case Could Aid Carter-Hispanic Relations," *Houston Post*, 23 October 1977, D4.

167. *United States v. Hayes*, 589 F.2d 811 (5th Cir., 1979); cert. denied, 444 U.S. 847 (1979); "Ex-marshal's Sentence May Change," *Houston Post*, 23 October 1977, 9A. Defense attorneys for the indicted HPD officers in the Torres case began to worry about potential negative effects from the Hayes case's notoriety after a reporter published a story that quoted a federal prosecutor discussing past civil rights convictions. According to AUSA James R. Gough, chief of the appellate and civil rights divisions in the Southern District, a prosecutor should go into a civil rights case knowing the odds are against conviction. Pete Wittenberg, "Convicting Police in Rights Charges Proves Difficult," *Houston Post*, 24 October 1977, 1A, 23A.

168. Judge Sterling instructed Ramsey to stop making speeches and ordered Andrews to return to his counsel table when he began aggressively cross-examining Officer Elliott from in front of the jury box. Pete Wittenberg, "Tension Eases in Trial of 4 Ex-police Officers," *Houston Post*, 29 January 1978, 1D.

169. Pete Wittenberg, "City Police Rookie Recounts Testimony in Torres Death," *Houston Post*, 27 January 1978, 3A.

170. On 31 January 1978, Sterling granted Kinney's motion for severance from the other three defendants. Docket, pp. 7–8, Crim. No. H-77–107 (S.D. Tex., 1977), *United States v. Denson*, NARA-SWA, case files of U.S.C.A., 5th Cir., RG 276, box 142, folder 78–2102.

171. Pete Wittenberg, "Elliott Recounts Chain of Events in Torres Death," *Houston Post*, 28 January 1978, 4A; Curtis, "Support Your Local Police," 82; and *United States v. Denson*, 588 F.2d 1112 (5th Cir., 1979).

172. Pete Wittenberg, "Court Hears of Pair's Statements: Torres Reported Pushed into Water," *Houston Post*, 29 January 1978, 1D.

173. Pete Wittenberg, "Police Chief Critical of Violence," *Houston Post*, 31 January 1978, 16A.

174. Docket, pp. 8–9, Crim. No. H-77-107 (S.D. Tex., 1977), *United States v. Denson*, NARA-SWA, case files of U.S.C.A., 5th Cir., RG 276, box 142, folder 78–2102.

175. Pete Wittenberg, "Jokes of Alleged Pushing of Torres 'Hero Worship,' Denson Maintains," *Houston Post*, 2 February 1978, 3A.

176. Pete Wittenberg, "Orlando Says Breaking of Rules Worried Him," *Houston Post*, 3 February 1978, 1B.

177. Pete Wittenberg, "Ex-officer Testifies Torres Swam Away," *Houston Post*, 4 February 1978, 28A.

178. The prosecution and defense traded several recalled or rebuttal witnesses on 5 February, and then made closing statements. Pete Wittenberg, "Janish Spoke of Having 'Fun' Harassing Mexicans, Witness Says," *Houston Post*, 6 February 1978, 3A. For a complete list of witnesses, see docket, pp. 8–9, Crim. No. H-77-107 (S.D. Tex., 1977), *United States v. Denson*, NARA-SWA, case files of U.S.C.A., 5th Cir., RG 276, box 142, folder 78–2102.

179. Pete Wittenberg, "Torres Case Goes to Jury: Panel Hears Final Arguments against Ex-officers," *Houston Post*, 7 February 1978, 3A.

180. "No Verdict Yet in Torres Case," *Houston Post*, 8 February 1978, 8A.

181. U.S.C. § 241.

182. That is, acting under color of law, the officers willfully struck Torres and deprived him of his constitutional right not to be deprived of liberty without due process of law. A misdemeanor, this carried a maximum sentence of one year in prison and a one-thousand-dollar fine. 18 U.S.C. § 242. Pete Wittenberg, "3 Former Officers Convicted of Violating Torres' Rights," *Houston Post*, 9 February 1978, 1A, 27A.

183. The felony provision of 18 U.S.C. § 242.

184. This charged that they conspired to discourage Elliott from telling the FBI about the incident. Conviction carried a five-year maximum sentence and a ten-thousand-dollar fine. Docket, p. 11, Crim. No. H-77-107 (S.D. Tex., 1977), *United States v. Denson*, NARA-SWA, case files of U.S.C.A., 5th Cir., RG 276, box 142, folder 78–2102.

185. Sinderson handled civil rights before Canales established the division, but this was her first experience trying a criminal defendant on a civil rights charge. Pete Wittenberg, "Three Former Officers Convicted of Violating Torres' Rights," *Houston Post*, 9 February 1978, 1A, 27A.

186. The bill referred to in the text was sponsored by Republicans Edward Brooke of Massachusetts and Charles Mathias of Maryland. Mark Goodin, "Texas Lawyer Asks Senate Panel to Halt 'Genocide' on Chicanos," *Houston Post*, 9 February 1978, 4A.

187. Ed Jahn, "Many Will Await Sentencing to See If Justice Served," *Houston Post*, 9 February 1978, 1A, 27A.

188. On the Saturday before the scheduled sentencing, each of more than five hundred supporters of the convicted former officers paid ten dollars to attend a fundraising barbecue with Denson, Orlando, and Janish in Bear Creek Park. The organizers donated the proceeds, less expenses, to help them defray the cost of their defense. Fred King, "Benefit Barbecue: $10-a-Paper-Plate Affair Raises Funds for Ex-officers," *Houston Post*, 26 March 1978, 7A. The

same week, Chief Caldwell announced he was adding two detectives, one woman and one man, to the IA Division, bringing the unit's roster to eight detectives, two lieutenants, and a captain. The stated reason for the expansion was that the current division could not handle the load, which was averaging some seventy-five new complaints per month. The division was able to clear only thirty-two of the seventy-eight complaints in February. "Caldwell to Expand Police Probe Squad," *Houston Post*, 25 March 1978, 19A.

189. Transcript, 28 March 1978, p. 19, Crim. No. H-77–107 (S.D. Tex., 1977), *United States v. Denson*, NARA-SWA, case files of U.S.C.A., 5th Cir., RG 276, box 142, folder 78–2102.

190. Ibid., p. 18.

191. Ibid., p. 20.

192. Ibid., p. 21.

193. Harris County District Attorney Vance announced that because Janish would receive no more punishment from state assault charges than he would get from the federal sentence, the state would dismiss its case. When the sentences were announced, Caldwell was unavailable for comment: he was in Washington, D.C., describing his experiences as HPD chief to the Justice Department's Community Relations Service. Pete Wittenberg, "Three Ex-officers Given One-Year Terms: Torres' Mother Unhappy," *Houston Post*, 29 March 1978, 1A, 23A. Joan Glantz, chair of the Houston chapter of the ACLU, criticized Sterling for declaring that lengthy prison time would have "little impact" and suggested that if that was true, then the individuals serving hard time in prison for killing police officers should be set free. Ed Jahn and George Flynn, "McConn Supports Protest," *Houston Post*, 30 March 1978, 1A, 23A.

194. Members of Houston's city council also went on record defending the HPD against Sterling's insinuation that it was the department and not the defendants at fault for the death of Torres. Houston's mayor Jim McConn said, "If he meant by that that all of the department is inclined to throw people into the bayou, then I disagree violently with that." Ed Jahn, "Many Critical of Punishment and Comments by the Judge," *Houston Post*, 29 March 1978, 1A, 23A.

195. Joe Torres's brother, Gilbert Torres, said, "I got more than that when I broke probation as a kid." Bill Curry, "Three Ex-Policemen Draw 1-Year Terms; Mexican-Americans Bitter over Sentences in Houston Death," *Washington Post*, 29 March 1978, 1A.

196. Jahn, "Many Critical of Punishment and Comments by the Judge."

197. Richard Vara, "Espejo: Violation of Trust the Central Issue of Joe Torres Case," *Houston Post*, 2 April 1978, 2D.

198. These state laws already existed but were not much used (or of much use) in prosecutions of the police. The then-current "public oppression" law set the maximum penalty at one year and a two-thousand-dollar fine. "Texas 'Justice': Civil Rights Laws Too Weak, Minorities Say," *Houston Post*, 2 April 1978, 9D.

199. "Sentences in Torres Case Disappointing, Hill Says," *Houston Post*, 7 April 1978, p. A13.

200. For a time after the sentencing, Sterling was guarded by the U.S. marshal because of reported threats on his life. See Associated Press, 4 October 1979.

201. Jahn and Flynn, "McConn Supports Protest."

202. Although pressuring or even punishing Sterling was the goal of many of the Mexican Americans' suggestions, PASSO's Reyes apparently did not mean his comment ironically. Wittenberg, "Who Is Ross Sterling?"

203. Further, a judge sponsored by conservative Republican Senator John Tower. Jahn, "Many Critical of Punishment and Comments by the Judge."

204. Mr. Hector Garcia of the coalition should not be confused with Dr. Hector Garcia, founder of AGIF.

205. Morales announced that his group intended to "push for justice" in the Randall Webster case. Jahn, "Many Critical of Punishment and Comments by the Judge."

206. The organizers invited the mayor and council members to participate. Mayor McConn said he supported the right to assemble peaceably and declared his sympathy with the Mexican American cause. But he announced that he could not march, since he was recovering from an operation. Jahn and Flynn, "McConn Supports Protest."

207. Bill Curry, "Hispanics Protest in Houston," *Washington Post*, 3 April 1978, 3A.

208. People United abandoned the larger rally but spent only twenty minutes at headquarters. Jim Asker, "Demonstrators Protest Torres Case Sentences," *Houston Post*, 3 April 1978, 1A. Public condemnation of Sterling and his decision was not universal. The officers' families announced that they considered the sentences to be fair. Ramsey and Bennett announced they would abandon the appeal of the state conviction but delayed announcing whether they planned to appeal the federal conviction. Wittenberg, "Three Ex-officers Given One-Year Terms: Torres' Mother Unhappy." Bill Curry, "Three Ex-Policemen Draw 1-Year Terms; Mexican Americans Bitter over Sentences in Houston Death," *Washington Post*, 29 March 1978, 7A.

209. Jahn and Flynn, "McConn Supports Protest."

210. Specifically, the motion said that Sterling exceeded his authority under 18 U.S.C. § 3651, which authorized federal courts to suspend imposition of execution of sentences only "[u]pon entering a judgment of conviction of any offense not punishable by death or life imprisonment." Motion to Correct Sentence, 5 April 1978, p. 1, Crim. No. H-77–107, NARA-SWA, case files of U.S.C.A., 5th Cir., RG 276, box 142, folder 78–2102.

211. The motion also argued that Sterling's assertion that the defendants would never be police officers again was speculative. Because exile from the force was not a condition of probation, the defendants could conceivably join a police department, although probably somewhere else. Motion to Correct Sentence, 5 April 1978, p. 4, Crim. No. H-77–107 (S.D. Tex., 1977), *United States v. Denson*, NARA-SWA, case files of U.S.C.A., 5th Cir., RG 276, box 142, folder 78–2102.

212. Ibid., p. 5.

213. Pete Wittenberg, "Torres Case Sentence Illegal, U.S. Claims; Correction Asked," *Houston Post*, 6 April 1978, 1A, 27A. Texas Attorney General Hill said he believed that the prosecution was justified in calling upon Sterling to reconsider. "Sentences in Torres Case Disappointing, Hill Says."

214. Emphasis added. The defense attorneys claimed Judge Sterling was aware of the prosecution's opinion on the matter at the time of sentencing but had decided it was appropriate to grant the former officers supervised probation. Defendants' Response to Government's Motion to Correct Sentence, 11 April 1978, p. 2, Case Crim. No. H-77–107 (S.D. Tex., 1977), *United States v. Denson*, NARA-SWA, case files of U.S.C.A., 5th Cir., RG 276, box 142, folder 78–2102. Meanwhile, the defense attorneys reported for their clients Denson and Orlando that they would not appeal the convictions. Wittenberg, "Torres Case Sentence Illegal, U.S. Claims; Correction Asked."

215. Memorandum and Order, 17 April 1978, pp. 2–3, Case Crim. No. H-77–107 (S.D. Tex., 1977), *United States v. Denson*, NARA-SWA, case files of U.S.C.A., 5th Cir., RG 276, box 142, folder 78–2102. The federal statutes in question are 18 U.S.C. § 1111 (second-degree murder), 18 U.S.C. § 2031 (rape), and 18 U.S.C. § 1201 (kidnapping).

216. Memorandum and Order, 17 April 1978, p. 1, Case Crim. No. H-77–107 (S.D. Tex., 1977), *United States v. Denson,* NARA-SWA, case files of U.S.C.A., 5th Cir., RG 276, box 142, folder 78–2102. Bruce Cory, "Judge Rejects U.S. Bid In Houston Police Case," *Washington Post,* 19 April 1978, 1A.

217. Jo Ann Zuniga, "Twenty Years Later, Houston Still Remembers Moody Park Riots," *Houston Chronicle,* 7 May 1998, 39A.

218. Notice of Appeal, 17 May 1978, Case Crim. No. H-77–107 (S.D. Tex., 1977), *United States v. Denson,* NARA-SWA, case files of U.S.C.A., 5th Cir., RG 276, box 142, folder 78–2102. Fifth Circuit Case No. 78–2102 relates to the appeal of the sentence. An additional file for the *Denson* case, the request for mandamus in Fifth Circuit Case No. 78–2508, is contained in RG 276, box 21, folder 78–2508. For most purposes, the two are logically treated as a single case.

219. The statute giving U.S. district courts this power is 28 U.S.C. § 1361. The *writ* of mandamus no longer exists in American law. Under the Federal Rules of Civil Procedure, "extraordinary" writs have been abolished in favor of a motion or complaint "in the nature of mandamus," which accomplishes the same legal object. Fed. R. Civ. P., Rule 81(b).

220. Memorandum and Order, 19 May 1978, p. 1, Case Crim. No. H-77–107 (S.D. Tex., 1977), *United States v. Denson,* NARA-SWA, case files of U.S.C.A., 5th Cir., RG 276, box 142, folder 78–2102.

221. Ibid., at p. 3.

222. Ibid., at p. 3.

223. Borges, "Tony Canales: Going against the Grain."

224. Petition for Writ of Mandamus, 14 July 1978, and defendant's Response to Petition for Writ of Mandamus, 21 August 1978. Both No. 78–2102, and Case No. 78–2508 (5th Cir., 1979), *United States v. Denson,* NARA-SWA, case files of U.S.C.A., 5th Cir., RG 276, box 142, folder 78–2102, and RG 276, box 21, folder 78–2508.

225. *United States v. Denson,* 588 F.2d 1112 (5th Cir., 1979), 1116. The federal statute relating to suspension of sentence and probation is 18 U.S.C. § 3651.

226. *United States v. Denson,* 588 F.2d 1112, 1117–19.

227. Ibid., 1124–25.

228. Furthermore, according to Judge Sterling's own order, he had "been assisted in this [sentence formulation] by thoughtful memoranda from counsel, from the professionals in the probation office, and letters from many interested citizens." Ibid., 1130–32.

229. Circuit Judge Irving L. Goldberg agreed with everything in the opinion, except the denial. In his dissenting opinion he noted that the majority convincingly argued that a sentence of probation was plainly illegal and that mandamus was a proper remedy. Goldberg wrote that "[h]aving gone that far I would not balk at issuing the writ." Ibid., 1133 (including notes).

230. "Torres Cases Sentences Stand despite Illegality, Court Says," *Houston Post,* 6 February 1979, 1A, 15A.

231. Pete Wittenberg and Barbara Canetti, "Two of 3 Officers Convicted in Webster Case," *Houston Post,* 5 April 1979, 1A, 27A.

232. Pete Wittenberg, "Two Ex-officers Receive Probated Sentences," *Houston Post,* 15 May 1979, 1A, 19A. Decisions in the Webster case are reported at *United States v. Mays et al.,* 460 F.Supp. 573 (1978); and 470 F.Supp 642 (1979).

233. Mark Carreau, "Webster Ruling Spurs Call for Better Screening of Jurists," *Houston Post,* 16 May 1979, 20A. In the Joyvies case the judge ordered former HPD officer Clarence

Burkett to testify under a grant of immunity. He told the jury that he fired a pistol provided by his partner, who then handed the gun to another officer to place in the teenager's car. He testified that the actions were necessary to make things "flow smoothly," since Joyvies "obviously dumped" a gun he fired at officers during the chase. Pete Wittenberg, "Judge Orders Acquittal of 2 Ex-police Officers," *Houston Post,* 26 July 1979, 1A, 23A.

234. Joan Glantz of the ACLU said that the jury apparently deliberated carefully, and although many may not agree with their verdict, it would be inappropriate to second-guess. However, she added: "I think some people are going to be angry and not believe what the jury obviously believes." "Some Accept Webster Case Verdict: Minority Activist Reactions Range from Cool to Heated," *Houston Post,* 5 April 1979, 16A. Two weeks later, Mayor McConn publicly defended the HPD record. "Houston Police the Best, Mayor Says," *Houston Post,* 17 May 1979, 14A. "State LULAC Chief's Outlook Gloomy," *Houston Post,* 18 May 1979, p. 4A.

235. Wittenberg, "Judge Orders Acquittal of 2 Ex-police Officers."

236. Ibid.

237. "Cops Cleared of Gun Plot after Slaying," *Charlotte Observer,* 26 July 1979, 6A.

238. Sinderson pointed to the "moral bankruptcy" displayed by one such witness, who bragged of deceitful and illegal conduct and said that "it was not wrong and [he] would do it again." Wittenberg, "Judge Orders Acquittal of 2 Ex-police Officers"; and Lynne Brock, "'Throw-down' Gun Case Pair Given Acquittal," *Houston Chronicle,* 25 July 1979, 1A, 4A. Sinderson also filed criminal civil-rights charges against the chief of the Jacinto City Police Department, for torturing a confession out of a murder suspect. On 30 June 1979, after a trial in the court of U.S. District Judge Carl. O. Bue Jr., jurors acquitted the then exchief and two of his former officers. "Acquittals Wind Up 2 Years of Probes, Trials," *Houston Post,* 26 July 1979, A22.

239. In July 1979 Carter nominated Benjamin Civiletti to succeed the retiring Griffin Bell as U.S. attorney general. During his confirmation hearings Civiletti told members of the Senate Judiciary Committee that the Justice Department was studying patterns of brutality, in anticipation of filing possible civil rights lawsuits against several city governments. Jim Craig, "Justice Dept. Ponders Police Misconduct Suits," *Houston Post,* 28 July 1979, 1A, 27A [emphasis added]. A change in state law thereafter allowed the Harris County district attorney's office to establish its own civil rights division, charged primarily with investigating allegations of police misconduct. Mary Flood, "Vance Names New Chief of Civil Rights Division," *Houston Post,* 11 July 1979, 6A.

240. *United States v. Denson,* 593 F.2d 3 (1979).

241. *United States v. Denson,* 603 F.2d 1143, 1147, 1145.

242. Ed Jahn, "New Torres Case Sentences Given: Terms Could Reduce Time Served; Mexican-Americans Upset," *Houston Post,* 31 October 1979, 1A.

243. Pete Wittenberg, "Hispanic Leaders Pleased with Ruling," *Houston Post,* 5 October 1979, 4A.

244. Ibid.

245. Gene Lyons, "Reporter," *Texas Monthly,* November 1980, p. 144 [emphasis in original].

246. Charles R. Babcock, "U.S. Prosecution Ruled Out in Slaying of Hispanic Boy," *Washington Post,* 15 July 1978, 3A. LULAC had also called for federal intervention in the case of Larry Ortega Lozano. On 22 January 1978 Larry Ortega Lozano died from wounds he received while in custody in Ector County. Sheriff Elton Faught claimed Lozano had injured

himself by ramming his head against a cell window, perhaps in an effort to commit suicide. A pathologist identified ninety-two separate bruises on Lozano's body and concluded that the evidence was "incompatible with suicide." "Texas 'Justice': Civil Rights Laws Too Weak, Minorities Say," *Houston Post*, 2 April 1978, 9D.

247. "Texas: Wetbacks Hit Back," *Economist*, 24 March 1979, p. 52.

248. Mark Carreau, "Webster Ruling Spurs Call for Better Screening of Jurists," *Houston Post*, 16 May 1979, 20A. They also called on the president to appoint more judges with Hispanic surnames. "Five Groups Demanding 2 Spanish-named Judges in West Texas District," *Houston Post*, 19 July 1979, 7A.

249. Unnamed, but quoted in "Texas: Wetbacks Hit Back."

250. Approximately 90 percent of Mexican Americans in Texas who voted in 1976 voted for President Carter, which gave him his thin margin of victory in the state. "Swift Indictments in Torres Case Could Aid Carter-Hispanic Relations," *Houston Post*, 23 October 1977, 4D.

251. U.S.C. § 133. The act also increased the number of federal appellate judges on the Fifth Circuit from fifteen to twenty-six. See also: "House OKs More Courts, 12 in Texas," *Houston Post*, 8 February 1978, 7A.

252. The Omnibus Judgeship Act of 1978. Pub. L. No. 95–486, 92 Stat. 1629, revising 28 U.S.C. § 133. For legislative history of this act, see *U.S. Code Congressional and Administrative News* (1978), 3569.

253. Christopher E. Smith, *Courts, Politics, and the Judicial Process* (Chicago: Nelson-Hall, 1993), 113–14. President Carter was a proponent of reform by other means, as well. He created nominating committees to vet judicial candidates. On 8 November 1978 he signed an executive order (Ex. Ord. No. 12097; 43 F.R. 52455), calling for the establishment of standards and guidelines for the merit selection of U.S. district judges.

254. Barbara Brooker, "Bell to Take Part in Judicial Post Nominee Selection," *Houston Post*, 20 February 1977, 5B.

255. "DeAnda," in *Judges of the United States*. Also, Student News Feature, "Judge James DeAnda: Graduate Blazed Trails in Texas Civil Rights," *Townes Hall Notes*, fall 2000, pp. 74–77.

256. For Title 7 of the 1964 CRA, see 42 U.S.C. § 2000e-5(k). W.H., "Judging Tadic," *American Lawyer*, September 1995, p. 62.

257. "McDonald," in *Judges of the United States*.

258. "Kazen," in *Judges of the United States*. Kazen was the nephew of U.S. Rep. Abraham Kazen (D-Texas). "Senate Confirms 5 Federal Judges for Southern District of Texas," *Houston Post*, 11 May 1979, A16.

259. "Black," in *Judges of the United States*.

260. "Cire," in *Judges of the United States*. See also "Proceedings of the Memorial for Hon. George E. Cire," 14 May 1986, included in 662 F.Supp. (1986), LXXI–LXXXIV.

261. Ironically, this was the same week Cowan handed down his decision in the Webster case. "Senate Confirms 5 Federal Judges for Southern District of Texas," *Houston Post*, 11 May 1979, A16.

262. Chief Judge Garza, to "My dear Judges and Judges-to-Be," 20 January 1979, clerk's files of Chief Judge Reynaldo G. Garza, folder 5. For Judge Cowan, see Lipartito and Pratt, *Baker & Botts*, 209.

263. Chief Judge Garza to "Dear Mr. Thomas," 29 March 1979, clerk's files of Chief Judge Reynaldo G. Garza, folder 5.

264. Chief Judge Garza, to "My dear Judges," 12 May 1979, clerk's files of Chief Judge Reynaldo G. Garza, folder 5.

265. Judge Ross N. Sterling to "Dear Chief Judge Garza," 29 June 1979, clerk's files of Chief Judge Reynaldo G. Garza, folder 4.

266. Chief Judge Garza to "My dear Judges," 12 May 1979, clerk's files of Chief Judge Reynaldo G. Garza, folder 5. See also "Equalization of Houston Civil Cases as of September 30, 1979," table, clerk's files of Chief Judge John V. Singleton, folder 1.

267. Chief Judge Garza, Revised Judicial Work Assignments, memorandum, 31 May 1979, clerk's files of Chief Judge Reynaldo G. Garza, folder 5.

268. "Gibson," in *Judges of the United States.*

269. Chief Judge Garza, to "My dear Judges," 12 May 1979, clerk's files of Chief Judge Reynaldo G. Garza, folder 5.

270. Fisch, *All Rise,* 142–45, 149–54, 162. By 1980 it was clear the increase to twenty-six judgeships in 1978, which had been necessary to match the growth in the number of cases appealed to the circuit, had also resulted in a sprawling, unwieldy administration. It also led to inconsistent, unpredictable decisions. In an unusual direct petition to Congress, the active judges of the Fifth Circuit unanimously requested that the circuit be split, citing this step as necessary to the delivery of "consistent, fair, and expeditious justice." Five months later, Congress passed a bill to effect the realignment. President Carter, in his public comments after signing the bill, commended the Congress for promptly acting in response to the needs of the federal courts. This executive, congressional, and judicial solidarity came after eighteen years of bitter political controversy. Barrow and Walker, *A Court Divided,* 1–2. On 15 October 1980 President Carter signed the congressional measure, which took effect on 1 October 1981. The law divided the old circuit into a reconstituted Fifth Circuit, containing the District of the Panama Canal Zone and the states of Texas, Louisiana, and Mississippi, and a newly constituted Eleventh Circuit, consisting of the states of Florida, Georgia, and Alabama. Fifth Circuit Court of Appeals Reorganization Act of 1980 (Pub. L. No. 96–452; revising 28 U.S.C. § 41 [enacted H.R. 7665; signed 15 October 1980]). See also, for a general treatment of the creation, development, and personnel of the Fifth Circuit, Couch, *History of the Fifth Circuit.*

271. "Gibson," in *Judges of the United States.* Mexican Americans had called on the president to appoint more judges with "Spanish" surnames. "Five Groups Demanding 2 Spanish-named Judges in West Texas District," *Houston Post,* 19 July 1979, A7.

272. "Jesse Clark, Longtime U.S. District Clerk, Dies," *The Houston Chronicle,* 25 April 1993, A31.

273. Under the 1979 amendment, for example, "section 3162 of this chapter shall become effective and apply to all cases commenced by arrest or summons, all informations or indictments filed, on or after July 1, 1980." The Speedy Trial Act Amendments Act, 18 U.S.C. §§ 3161–74 (ch. 208); as amended by Pub. L. No. 96–43, 93 Stat. 332 (2 August 1979).

274. Roland E. Dahlin II [federal public defender] to "Dear Judge Singleton, Re: Speedy Trial Act: Our Final Plan," 21 April 1980, clerk's files of Chief Judge John V. Singleton, folder 2.

CHAPTER 7. Adjuncts and the Oversight of Corporate Misconduct

1. Chief Judge Garza to "My dear Judges," 28 December 1978, clerk's files of Chief Judge Reynaldo G. Garza, folder 5.

2. Mark Obbie, "The Judges," *Houston Post,* 5 January 1986, 1D.

3. Fed. R. Civ. P., Rule 53.

4. Farrell, "Function and Legitimacy," 236. Also, Posner, *Federal Courts,* 9. For more on the contemporary use of special masters, see Farrell, "Special Masters," 575. The Federal Judicial Center is the research and educational "think tank" of the federal judiciary created by Congress in 1967 (see 28 U.S.C. §§ 620–29).

5. Calavita, Pontell, and Tillman, *Big Money Crime,* 151–57, and generally.

6. Pub. L. No. 95–598, of 6 November 1978, codified at 28 U.S.C. §§ 151–58. In the original 1978 version of the law, bankruptcy judges could hear cases related to bankruptcy proceedings, such as a civil suit involving a company which had filed under Title 11, as well as cases actually brought under Title 11. Bankruptcy judges were appointed by the circuit judges to serve fourteen-year terms; they could be removed by the judicial council in that circuit. Moreover, their salaries could be reduced by an act of Congress. In a four-person plurality decision, the Supreme Court upheld a Minnesota district judge's ruling that the original 1978 act was unconstitutional. The justices held that Congress had vested the bankruptcy judges with the "power and prestige" of Article III federal judges, without giving them the necessary independence. The court stayed its judgment until 4 October 1982, to enable lawmakers to amend the laws. *Northern Pipeline Construction v. Marathon Pipeline,* 102 S.Ct. 2858 (1982). It was a "badly fragmented" ruling, because the distinction between Article III "constitutional" courts and Article I "legislative" tribunals was and is controversial. Wright, *The Law of Federal Courts,* 50–52. In response to the court's ruling in *Marathon,* the Congress passed the Bankruptcy Amendments and Federal Judgeship Act of 1984 (Pub. L. No. 98–353, 10 July 1984, 98 Stat. 338), which clarified that bankruptcy judges served fixed terms and were paid fixed salaries (which were tied to the salaries of district judges). The Southern District of Texas was authorized to have six bankruptcy judges, which the appellate judges in the Fifth Circuit appoint for terms of fourteen years. 28 U.S.C. § 152. Bankruptcy judges are paid 92 percent of what life-tenured district judges are paid. 28 U.S.C. § 153.

7. Neely, *Judicial Jeopardy,* pp. 35–37. In addition to trial duties, bankruptcy judges may serve on bankruptcy appellate panels ("BAPS"), to review decisions by individual bankruptcy judges. 28 U.S.C. § 158. The response to the creation of these courts has not been overwhelmingly positive and is often ambivalent at best. See, generally, Seron, *Judicial Reorganization.* For a discussion of the rise of these specialized judges, see Resnik, "History, Jurisdiction, and the Federal Courts," 171, nn. 65–76, and accompanying text. For an exploration of the rationale for splitting jurisdictions among a proliferating variety of these less-independent non–Article III judges, see generally Baum, "Specializing the Federal Courts," 217–24.

8. Bankruptcy judges may issue final decisions in "core proceedings" in bankruptcy but not in other cases. 28 U.S.C. § 157(b) (1994). Their function is distinct, but their role is similar to that of U.S. magistrates. Formerly called U.S. magistrates, the title from their creation in 1968, these officials were raised to higher power, recognition via the current title, and arguably more prestige, by the Judicial Improvements Act of 1990. The U.S. district judges in each district appoint full-time magistrate judges for terms of eight years. 28 U.S.C. § 631(e) (1994). Magistrate judges hear some pretrial matters as designated by a district judge, make rulings with an opportunity for objection to the district judge, and preside at civil trials with the consent of the parties. 28 U.S.C. § 636(b)(c) (1994). Magistrate judges also are paid 92 percent of what life tenured district judges are paid. See 28 U.S.C. § 634 (1994). See Smith, "From U.S. Magistrates to U.S. Magistrate Judges," pp. 210–15.

9. The regulatory reforms enacted during the New Deal had long-lasting effects. Insti-

tutions continued to fail throughout the 1930s, but at a reduced pace, and by the end of Depression era, the number of bank failures was negligible. The failure rate increased in the 1970s but then reached an unprecedented level. Federal Deposit Insurance Corporation, *History of the Eighties,* 3, fig. 1.1.

10. Zelden, "From Rights to Resources," 484–89.

11. Resnik, "Managerial Judges," 436–37 n. 239.

12. For a study of the authority and activities of the Antitrust Division, see Weaver, *Decision to Prosecute.* Weaver promised to treat that government agency's "history, personality, and style." Ibid., vii. According to the Houston lawyer Stephen D. Susman, who was the lead plaintiffs' attorney in the ensuing civil lawsuit, the criminal probe may have been initiated after a tip-off from an industry insider. Susman could only speculate about this whistleblower, however; the civil plaintiffs did not actually know why the government opened the probe. Rob Meckel, "Jury Decides against Box Maker; Damages Could Exceed $1 Billion," *Houston Post,* 14 September 1980, 1A.

13. *In re Corrugated Container Antitrust Litigation,* 556 F.Supp. 1117 (S.D. Tex., 1982), 1157. This title consolidated the claims and appeals of dozens of parties to the overall multidistrict litigation. The parties to specific actions are separately named in various subtitles, but for the sake of clarity, equivalently titled cases will hereafter be abbreviated *In re* CCAL, with appropriate report citations; subtitles will not appear.

14. Hon. Hubert L. Will, "Judicial Responsibility for the Disposition of Litigation," 75 F.R.D. 117 (1976), 123–25. This article is from the *Proceedings of Seminar for Newly Appointed United States District Judges,* conducted by the Federal Judicial Center in Washington, D.C., 13–18 September 1976 (89–427).

15. *In re* CCAL, 556 F.Supp. 1117 (S.D. Tex., 1982), at 1157. For Fifth Circuit support of Judge Singleton's statement of this "judicial policy," see *In re* CCAL, 659 F.2d 1322 (5th Cir., 1981), 1325.

16. The explicit admission that settlement is essentially a method to "buy peace" is common in judicial opinion, and Singleton used the phrase early in the litigation. He rejected a motion because "[d]efendants have little incentive to buy peace from plaintiffs if they may be obliged to litigate the same claims against other defendants." The motion in question, brought by the defendants in the civil suit, would have allowed them to file cross-claims against the other defendants. *In re* CCAL, 84 F.R.D. 40 (S.D. Tex., 1979), 41.

17. *In re* CCAL, 620 F.2d. 1086 (5th Cir., 1980), at 1088. A federal district judge is authorized to grant "use" immunity upon a petition from the prosecution (18 U.S.C. §§ 6001–5). Under various state and federal statutes, a witness may be granted immunity from prosecution to obtain testimony. This grant of protection must be compatible with constitutional privileges against self-incrimination (U.S. Const., amend. V); however, it does not need to be any greater. Under "transactional" immunity, a person is entitled to protection from prosecution of the *specific* criminal offense being alleged by the government; the prosecutor is thereafter barred from using evidence based on or derived from his or her testimony, but that person is not constitutionally entitled to protection from *all* prosecutions arising from alleged criminal transactions (that is, evidence from other sources may be used to prosecute the witness under related charges). On the other hand, "use" immunity prohibits prosecutors from using *in any manner* the witness's immunized testimony in connection with *any* criminal prosecution of the witness. Some states grant one or the other, but the federal government adopted "use" over "transactional" immunity in 1970; see "Immunity," *Black's Law Dictionary,* abridged 6th ed. (St. Paul, Minn.: West Publishing, 1991). The Congress

enacted the change in the Organized Crime Control Act of 1970, which repealed a variety of immunity standards (including transactional) and established limited use and derivative use immunity provisions. For the legislative history, see *U.S. Code Congressional and Administrative News* (1970), 4007. The U.S. Supreme Court upheld these changes in *Kastigar v. United States,* 406 U.S. 441 (1972).

18. *In re* CCAL, 556 F.Supp. 1117 (S.D. Tex., 1982), at 1143–54.

19. The change, enacted in 1974 under the Antitrust Procedures and Penalties Act (Pub. L. No. 93–528), substituted felony penalties (a fine not exceeding $1 million for a corporation, a fine not exceeding $100,000 for a person, or imprisonment not exceeding three years), for the earlier misdemeanor penalties (a fine not exceeding $50,000 or imprisonment not exceeding one year), in the Sherman Act (15 U.S.C. ch. 1, §§ 1–7 [Commerce and Trade: Monopolies and Combinations in Restraint of Trade]).

20. In 1974, for example, the companies charged with felonies had total sales revenue of $1.4 billion. In the same year the companies charged with misdemeanors sold approximately $800,000 worth of product. Pete Wittenberg, "Box Manufacturers Charged with Antitrust Violations," *Houston Post,* 26 January 1978, 24C. The defendants were manufacturers of either finished corrugated cardboard containers or the specially treated, weather resistant, high-tensile-strength paper sheets used in box construction (referred to in the industry by the trade name "Kraft liner board"). Some produced both boxes and sheets. For general purposes, corrugated cardboard is made by gluing a single sheet of corrugated paper between two sheets of liner board. Boxes are then fabricated by cutting, folding, and gluing this board into the desired size and shape. For heavy-duty applications, more layers of corrugated paper and sheets of liner board, as many as three, are alternated. *In re* CCAL, M.D.L. No. 310; 447 F.Supp. 468 (J.P.M.L., 1978), at 469.

21. *In re* CCAL, 620 F.2d. 1086 (5th Cir., 1980), at 1088. In general, the plaintiffs each alleged that beginning in 1960 and continuing until at least 1975, manufacturers and coconspirators engaged in a nationwide conspiracy to fix, raise, maintain, and stabilize the prices of corrugated containers. *In re* CCAL, M.D.L. No. 310; 441 F.Supp. 921 (J.P.M.L., 1977), at 922. The section of the Sherman Antitrust Act that criminalized "combinations in restraint of trade" is currently codified at 15 U.S.C. § 1; some of the plaintiffs also sought damages under the Clayton Act, 15 U.S.C. § 15. By statute, plaintiffs could be awarded treble monetary damages. See *In re* CCAL, 643 F.2d. 195 (5th Cir., 1981), at 202.

22. In 1968 the Congress authorized the Judicial Panel on Multi-district Litigation (staffed by seven circuit and district judges, no two of whom could be from the same circuit, with all members to be designated by the chief justice of the U.S. Supreme Court) to transfer to a single court various actions that were pending in different federal districts but involved common questions of fact (this allowed coordination of pretrial proceedings or trial). The panel could initiate consolidation or grant a motion by plaintiffs, but the transferee district court must consent to the transfer (28 U.S.C. § 1407). The panel, under its chairman, Judge John Minor Wisdom of the U.S. Court of Appeals for the Fifth Circuit, was cognizant that the federal grand jury in Houston was already grappling with these issues and had gathered more than 1.5 million documents directly related to marketing structures in the corrugated container industry. Therefore, the panel quickly granted the plaintiffs' motion to consolidate the suits. On 29 November 1977, with Singleton's consent, the panel transferred the first of many cases to his court. *In re* CCAL, M.D.L. No. 310; 441 F.Supp. 921 (J.P.M.L., 1977), 924. For the notification of the Southern District judges, that they would have cases removed from their own dockets to be consolidated on Singleton's, see also Chief Judge Garza to "My

dear Judges, In re: Corrugated Container Antitrust Litigation," 15 November 1977, clerk's files of Chief Judge Reynaldo G. Garza, folder 3.

23. *In re* CCAL, 643 F.2d. 195 (5th Cir., 1981), 202. Authority to create a steering committee is granted under the multidistrict statute (28 U.S.C. § 1407), to streamline complex litigation.

24. *In re* CCAL, 643 F.2d 195 (5th Cir., 1981), at 209. For Susman, see Stuart Meiher, "Group of Antitrust Lawyers Riles Clients, Opponents by Seeking $50 Million in Fees," *Wall Street Journal*, 21 October 1982, 31B.

25. *In re* CCAL, 643 F.2d 195 (5th Cir., 1981), 203–4, 209.

26. Ibid., 205.

27. *In re* CCAL, 687 F.2d. 52 (5th Cir., 1980), 53.

28. Many investigative tools were ordinarily available through the civil discovery process. According to the Federal Rules of Civil Procedure, litigating parties may obtain pertinent information through discovery by one or more of the following methods: "depositions upon oral examination or written questions; written interrogatories; production of documents or things or permission to enter upon land or other property, for inspection or other purposes, physical and mental examinations; and requests for admission." (Fed. R. Civ. P., Rule 26[a]).

29. *In re* CCAL, 643 F.2d. 195 (5th Cir., 1981), at 203. In fact, the steering committee (established before the consolidation of the second group of cases with the first) was composed entirely of lawyers representing container purchasers rather than sheet plant purchasers.

30. He certified the class without formally ruling on the sheet purchaser's motion. *In re* CCAL, 80 F.R.D. 244 (S.D. Tex., 1978), mandamus denied, No. 78–3684 (5th Cir., 1978). The request for class certification required Singleton to examine the prerequisites for class action as set forth in the Federal Rules of Civil Procedure. In essence, certification required four things: (1) a sufficient number of parties such that joinder was impracticable; (2) questions of law and fact common to the proposed class; (3) claims or defenses typical of the class named; and (4) representatives which will protect the interests of the class as a whole. Moreover, the judge had to rule that the benefits of the class action form were superior to those inherent in numerous individual claims. (Fed. R. Civ. P., Rule 23). Eventually, forty-four out of fifty-five consolidated plaintiffs filed their lawsuits as class actions; the eleven nonclass plaintiffs are referred to as the "opt-out" plaintiffs. *In re* CCAL, 643 F.2d. 195 (5th Cir., 1981), 202.

31. *In re* CCAL, 643 F.2d. 195 (5th Cir., 1981), 203.

32. *In re* CCAL, 1979–1 Trade Reg. Rep. (CCH) par. 62,690 (S.D. Tex., 1979), 77,882.

33. *In re* CCAL, Pretrial Order No. 7 (26 December 1978).

34. *In re* CCAL, 1980–81 Trade Cas. par. 63,163 (S.D. Tex., 1979). This huge sum was not made public at the time. In order to protect the integrity of the process, because news of a large settlement might taint jury attitudes toward the defendants, Singleton sealed the settlement records until after the criminal trial ended. Pete Wittenberg, "Corrugated Box Lawsuits' Settlement Ordered Unsealed," *Houston Post*, 2 May 1979, 3A; also see Winston Williams, "Cardboard Makers to Pay $300 Million to End Pricing Suit," *New York Times*, 2 May 1979, pp. A1, D4.

35. *In re* CCAL, 643 F.2d. 195 (5th Cir., 1981), at 204–5. The first "hardship" case was settled when Consolidated Packaging, a felony indictee, paid $187,000 per point, and the second when Interstate Container paid $375,000 per point. *In re* CCAL, 556 F.Supp. 1117 (S.D. Tex., 1982), 1151–53.

36. *In re* CCAL, 643 F.2d. 195 (5th Cir., 1981), 208.

37. Ibid., 205.

38. The remaining defendant pleaded not guilty to a misdemeanor. Winston Williams, "Cardboard Makers to Pay $300 Million to End Pricing Suit," *New York Times*, 2 May 1979, A1, D4. Singleton set fines for the individuals substantially lower than the maximum allowed penalties, usually a few thousand dollars, gave them probation, and ordered them to perform community service. Even so, he assessed $2.5 million in fines on those defendants who pleaded guilty or no contest. Raul Reyes, "Corrugated Cardboard Boxes Involved: 2 Firms, 6 Men Cleared in Price-Fix Case," *Houston Chronicle*, 28 April 1979.

39. The rules of criminal procedure protect grand jury matters from public disclosure (Fed. R. Crim. P., Rule 6).

40. The government tried the felony charges under *United States v. International Paper Co. et al.* [Crim. No. H-78-11] (S.D. Tex., 1978). The misdemeanor charges came under *United States v. Boise Cascade Corp. et al.* [Crim. No. H-78-12] (S.D. Tex., 1978). See *United States v. International Paper Co. et al.*, 457 F.Supp. 571 (S.D. Tex., 1978) [memorandum opinion dated 14 July 1978], at 572 n. 1.

41. The last defendant, a vice president of the Hoerner Waldorf Company, was scheduled to be tried separately on the misdemeanor count. After the verdict an official in the Justice Department refused to say whether the government would drop the charge against him. Raul Reyes, "Corrugated Cardboard Boxes Involved—2 Firms, 6 Men Cleared in Price-Fix Case," *Houston Chronicle*, 28 April 1979.

42. *In re* CCAL, 1979–1 Trade Reg. Rep. (CCH) par. 62,690 (S.D. Tex., 1979), 77,881.

43. Preliminary findings are contained in Pretrial Order No. 31 (1 August 1979). According to the Federal Rules of Civil Procedure, the judge has the discretion either to dismiss class actions or approve settled compromises to class actions (Fed. R. Civ. P., Rule 23[e]).

44. The notice advised recipients they would have the option of participating in or opting out of the class, or of participating in the class action but objecting to the settlement. The majority of the plaintiffs elected to participate; several parties to the class action continued to oppose. A few opted out, but several remained in the class action but became "objectors." They variously claimed that the notice of the settlement was defective, because it omitted necessary details and because a separate notice should have been sent regarding the pending action as well as the proposed settlements. The complaints encompassed claims of inadequate representation, investigation, remuneration, and notification. One group, engaged in a state-law antitrust suit in from South Carolina, were also potential class members but objected to the settlements and the notice, on grounds similar to those listed in the text. Finally, several of the plaintiffs objected to the proposed release of state claims. *In re* CCAL, 643 F.2d. 195 (5th Cir., 1981), 205–6.

45. *In re* CCAL, 1980–81 Trade Cas. par. 63,163 (S.D. Tex., 1979).

46. Salop and White, "Private Antitrust Litigation," 23–26.

47. *In re* CCAL, 643 F.2d 195 (5th Cir., 1981), 212.

48. Ibid., 217 n. 32.

49. *In re* CCAL, 643 F.2d. 195 (5th Cir., 1981), 207.

50. Ibid., 206–7.

51. Ibid., 202.

52. Ibid., 212–13.

53. "Additional Findings of Fact and Conclusions of Law concerning Class Action Settlements," in *In re* CCAL, 1980–81 Trade Cas. par. 64,114 (S.D. Tex., 1981); especially see the appended notes, "Findings and Conclusions of General Relevance," 76,692–76,696.

54. *In re* CCAL, 659 F. 2d 1322 (U.S.C.A., 5th Cir., 1981).

55. *In re* CCAL, 556 F.Supp. 1117 (S.D. Tex., 1982), 1144–53.

56. Ibid., 1144–45.

57. Ibid., 1145.

58. Ibid., 1145–46.

59. Ibid. Other defendants presented similar difficulties, and Singleton approved settlements with them for similar reasons. The evidence against the unindicted firms, the Fibre Box Association (FBA), and the Crown Zellerbach Corporation (CZC), was also weak, circumstantial, or nonexistent. FBA paid nothing, but as part of settlement, it agreed to provide assistance in discovery. CZC agreed to settle for $1 million, from which it would immediately pay $62,500, to defray the plaintiffs' costs of litigation. Ibid., 1147–49.

60. Ibid., 1149–51.

61. Ibid.

62. Ibid., 1151–53.

63. The last settlement Singleton described, before moving on to the final act in the Mead drama, was relatively small. The Flintkote Company offered to pay $220,000, plus interest, in March 1980. By September 1982, when the plaintiffs agreed to settle, this had grown to $319,377. *In re* CCAL, 556 F.Supp. 1117 (S.D. Tex., 1982), 1153. The U.S. Supreme Court denied a petition for certiorari to review the prior settlements on 24 May 1982. See *CFS Continental, Inc. v. Adams Extract Co.*, 102 S. Ct. 2283 (1982), 73 L.Ed.2d 1294 (1982).

64. *In re* CCAL, 620 F.2d. 1086 (5th Cir., 1980), 1088–89.

65. *In re* CCAL, 620 F.2d. 1086 (5th Cir., 1980), 1088–89.

66. Singleton issued the second order after Hopkins also maintained his silence (Pretrial Orders, dated 25 January and 7 February); the rules of criminal procedure provide that disclosure "otherwise prohibited by this rule of matters occurring before the grand jury may also be made . . . when so directed by a court, preliminarily to or in connection with a judicial proceeding" (Fed. R. Crim. P., Rule 6(e)(3)(C)(i)). In this instance "transcripts" referred not only to complete or partial records of courtroom testimony, but also the records of interviews. *In re* CCAL, 687 F.2d. 52 (5th Cir., 1980), 53. The Fifth Circuit dismissed as moot an appeal of these orders, because it came before them after the civil trial concluded. *In re Corrugated Container Grand Jury*, 659 F.2d. 1330 (5th Cir., 1981), cert. denied, 102 S.Ct. 1994 (1982).

67. Recorded in Civ. No. H-80–1284 (S.D. Tex., 1980), vol. 1, 12–14. Judge Singleton is quoted in: *In re* CCAL, 620 F.2d. 1086 (5th Cir., 1980), 1089.

68. The contempt citation is Pretrial Order No. 40 (6 March 1980). The judge can find a witness in contempt for refusing to respond according to Fed. R. Civ. P., Rule 37(b); the penalties are assessed under authority of the recalcitrant witness statute (28 U.S.C. § 1826). But Singleton stayed the penalties while Franey appealed. *In re* CCAL, 620 F.2d. 1086 (5th Cir., 1980), 1089.

69. *In re* CCAL, 620 F.2d. 1086 (5th Cir., 1980), at 1089–90. Again, Singleton stayed the orders pending appeal. Fleischacker's contempt citation is recorded in Civ. No. H-80–1307 (S.D. Tex., 1980), vol. 2, at 71; Hopkins's in Civ. No. H-80–1338 (S.D. Tex., 1980), 24.

70. *In re* CCAL, 620 F.2d. 1086 (5th Cir., 1980), 1090. Singleton authorized himself to preside in Fleischacker's deposition under Pretrial Order No. 39 (6 March 1980), granting him the power to act as a "temporary" judge in the Southern District of New York.

71. *In re* CCAL, 620 F.2d. 1086 (5th Cir., 1980), 1091. The provision that states an order must be given by a district court where the deposition is being taken is in the same rule regarding a judge's power to find a witness in contempt for refusing to respond (Fed. R. Civ.

P., Rule 37). According to the rules, the witness can be deposed only in the county where subpoenaed, or within forty miles of the place where it was served (Fed. R. Civ. P., Rule 45). As noted, the rules are intended to limit the expense and inconvenience to witnesses, who should not be compelled to travel long distances to appeal decisions.

72. *In re* CCAL, 620 F.2d. 1086 (5th Cir., 1980), 1091. The multidistrict statute clearly authorized the judge in consolidated cases to act as a judge in another district (28 U.S.C. § 1407[b]), but the Fifth Circuit opinion noted that the legislative history of the statute showed that the statute was to be governed by the Federal Rules of Civil Procedure. For the relevant legislative history of the multidistrict statute, see *U.S. Code Congressional and Administrative News* (1968), 1898–1900.

73. The Second Circuit took up the question on 23 June, just four days after the Fifth Circuit announced its decision, which seems an astonishing turnaround in a judicial system perennially subject to case backlogs. Fleischacker had simultaneously filed appeals in the Fifth and Second Circuits: the Second dismissed it without prejudice, pending the Fifth's finding, and reinstated the case after the Fifth held it had no jurisdiction. *In re* CCAL, 644 F.2d. 70 (2d Cir., 1981), 73–74.

74. *In re* CCAL, 644 F.2d. 70 (2d Cir., 1981), 78–80.

75. This fact was significant because the state of Ohio had no statute of limitations for criminal antitrust violations; see Ohio Rev. Code Ann. § 1331.12.

76. *In re* CCAL, 620 F.2d. 1086 (5th Cir., 1980), 1095.

77. Ibid., at 1095. Circuit Judge Johnson dissented, arguing that Singleton was as qualified, and as authorized, as the circuit judges to determine whether something was or was not tainted. The Fifth Circuit denied a rehearing and rehearing en banc on 14 August 1980.

78. The class action cases had been settled, but the plaintiffs who had opted out of the class were still pursuing some cases. *In re* CCAL, 655 F.2d. 748 (7th Cir., 1981), 749–50. By this time Judge Singleton was handing out six months in prison for contempt. Ibid., 755.

79. *In re* CCAL, 655 F.2d. 748 (7th Cir., 1981), 754. Circuit Judge Sprecher dissented. Ibid., 755–66.

80. Judge Sprecher repeated many of his same arguments from his previous dissent. *In re* CCAL, 661 F.2d. 1145 (7th Cir., 1981), 1159. Chief Judge Cummings now dissented, reiterating Judge Swygert's earlier reasoning, Ibid., 1159. Around the time of Conboy's appeal, the U.S. Court of Appeals for the D.C. Circuit ruled on a similar case. The judges reached Sprecher's conclusions on the first hearing. On 28 August 1981 Circuit Judge Wald, for the court, held that Singleton could not compel John W. Culy, who had worked for both Weyerhaeuser and Corrugated Container Company, to testify over his Fifth Amendment invocation. The case was different from the others in that Culy received only a verbal promise from the investigators (an FBI agent and a law student, who told him they were empowered to act as agents of the grand jury) that he would not be prosecuted for his answers given in an interview session in October 1977. Culy was not sworn, immunized, or subpoenaed by the grand jury. The transcript of his interview, however, was given to the grand jury. In April 1981 Singleton ruled Culy in contempt by telephone. *In re* CCAL, 662 F.2d. 875 (D.C. Cir., 1980), 878–79. More so even than Sprecher in regarding Conboy, Wald doubted that Culy's testimony, which "did not receive anything remotely resembling statutory use immunity," was protected from future prosecution. Ibid., 888. These practices encouraged the objections, raised by the criminal defendants, as "grand jury abuse," supra, n. 9.

81. The results of the case, *Pillsbury v. Conboy* (459 U.S. 248 [1982]), will be discussed below.

82. *In re* CCAL, 667 F.2d. 4 (5th Cir., 1982). On remand Singleton "rebalanced" and decided that the need for additional discovery still "outweighed" the interest in secrecy. The Fifth Circuit affirmed his decision on 13 September 1982. *In re* CCAL, 687 F.2d. 52 (5th Cir., 1982).

83. *In re* CCAL, 687 F.2d. 52 (5th Cir., 1982).

84. *In re* CCAL, 620 F.2d. 1086 (5th Cir., 1980), 1088. Stuart Meiher, "Group of Antitrust Lawyers Riles Clients, Opponents by Seeking $50 Million in Fees," *Wall Street Journal*, 21 October 1982, 31B.

85. *In re* CCAL, 556 F.Supp. 1117 (S.D. Tex., 1982), 1144.

86. Rob Meckel, "Jury Decides against Box Maker; Damages Could Exceed $1 Billion," *Houston Post*, 14 September 1980, 1A.

87. Singleton would not let defendants sue one another based on responsibility for their contribution to shared liability. The judge rejected motions on these claims because he believed that to allow them would hopelessly complicate an already massive class action. Most important, cross-claims would render negotiated settlements impossible, because they would remove the incentive to "buy peace." See supra, n. 4; and *In re* CCAL, 84 F.R.D. 40 (S.D. Tex., 1979), 41. The Fifth Circuit affirmed Singleton's decision regarding contribution. *In re* CCAL, 606 F.2d 319 (5th Cir., 1979). The defendants opened the question again when they appealed the overall settlement of the case. *In re* CCAL, 643 F.2d 195 (5th Cir., 1979), 224–25. The defendants, on appeal, had cited a relevant case pending before the U.S. Supreme Court, but the Fifth Circuit noted that the issues were mooted when the Supreme Court in that case held that a federal antitrust defendant had no right to contributions from coconspirators. *In re* CCAL, 659 F.2d 1322 (5th Cir., 1981), 1329. The Supreme Court opinion appeared in *Texas Industries, Inc. v. Radcliff Materials, Inc.*, 101 S.Ct. 2061 (1981). Cross-claims are common in tort cases, especially those brought by insurance companies, where parties are apt to sue to recover costs of litigation arising from their own settlements or adverse judgments. These are distinguished from counterclaims, which are asserted against opposing parties; see "Cross-claim," *Black's Law Dictionary*. The district court's ruling on motions for cross- and counterclaims are governed by the rule that states, in part: "A pleading may state as a cross-claim any claim by one party against a co-party arising out of the transaction or occurrence that is the subject matter either of the original action or of a counterclaim therein . . . [these] may include a claim that the party against whom it is asserted is or may be liable to the cross-claimant for all or part of a claim asserted in the action against the cross-claimant" (Fed. R. Civ. P., Rule 13[g]).

88. Section 4 of the Clayton Act authorizes the recovery of treble damages in private antitrust litigation (15 U.S.C. § 15 [ch. 1, Commerce and Trade: Monopolies and Combinations in Restraint of Trade: Suits by persons injured]). The plaintiffs had charged Mead with "fraudulent concealment," that is, withholding a fact that it was legally or morally bound to disclose. Because the jury did not hold this to be true, the damage period was limited to 7 March 1973 to 31 December 1975, inclusive. *In re* CCAL, 556 F.Supp. 1117 (S.D. Tex., 1982), 1144.

89. Sullivan, *Handbook*, 769–74.

90. Chief Judge Singleton to "Dear Mr. Johnson," 21 October 1980, clerk's files of Chief Judge John V. Singleton, folder 3.

91. *In re* CCAL, Pretrial Order No. 62 (27 January 1981).

92. Section 1.46, *Manual for Complex Litigation* (Washington, D.C.: Federal Judicial Center, 1969). The second edition of the *Manual* appeared in 1985, the third in 1994.

93. *In re* CCAL, 556 F.Supp. 1117 (S.D. Tex., 1982), 1144.

94. Although at that time no judgment had been entered by the master, on 21 July 1982 Mead filed its motion for entry of judgment notwithstanding the verdict or, in the alternative, for new trial, or for a contested partial judgment. The judge deferred ruling on the motion until after the entry of a judgment. *In re* CCAL, 556 F.Supp. 1117 (S.D. Tex., 1982), 1144.

95. *In re* CCAL, 556 F.Supp. 1117 (S.D. Tex., 1982), 1154.

96. Ibid., 1144.

97. Ibid.

98. The nonclass actions were already concluded. Eighteen major purchasers of corrugated boxes, including Kraft and Wilson Foods, had opted out of the class action and filed their own separate lawsuits. Judge Singleton took the opt-out cases to trial in 1981. The opt-out trials lasted three and one-half months and followed lines similar to the class suit. Singleton ordered discovery and approved settlements, but his orders were often appealed. On appeal, 15 April 1981, Singleton ordered the release of certain grand jury statements (Pretrial Order No. 64). *In re* CCAL, 556 F.Supp. 1117 (S.D. Tex., 1982), 1118. On 14 January 1982 Fifth Circuit remanded this order and instructed Singleton to review the grand jury materials to determine whether, in light of all the information that had been uncovered and discovered since 1979, it was still necessary to violate the standing policy of maintaining confidentiality. *In re* CCAL, 687 F.2d. 52, and 667 F.2d 4 (5th Cir., 1982). On 17 May 1982 Singleton reviewed the motions and information revealed since his disclosure order. He decided that some transcripts were necessary, if only to "refresh" the memory of some witnesses who actually were trying to cooperate. By that time, the testimony might have been five or even six years old. *In re* CCAL, 556 F.Supp. 1117 (S.D. Tex., 1982), 1119.

99. *In re* CCAL, 556 F.Supp. 1117 (S.D. Tex., 1982), 1141–42.

100. Ibid., 1154–56. When Singleton issued his final opinion in the litigation, on 30 November, he refused to rule on another request from the plaintiffs to compel testimony from a previously immunized witness. He noted only that his earlier orders had resulted in conflicting decisions in the circuits, and the U.S. Supreme Court had agreed to consider the issue. *In re* CCAL, 556 F.Supp. 1117 (S.D. Tex., 1982), 1121. The Supreme Court did reverse Singleton on 11 January 1982, holding that compelling testimony over valid Fifth Amendment claims was impermissible. The use of a transcript and repeating verbatim or tracking prior immunized testimony during new interviews did not imply that the resultant interview testimony was immunized, unless it was given under a duly authorized assurance of immunity. *Pillsbury v. Conboy,* 459 U.S. 248 (1982), 252–64.

101. Singleton was thinking primarily of the proposed Antitrust Equal Enforcement Act (S. 995), introduced 10 April 1981. The legislation would provide that, with respect to defendants who have settled a particular case, the courts were authorized to reduce plaintiffs' claims against nonsettlers by an amount equal to treble the damages attributable to the settling company's sales. The judge discussed this and other bills; see *In re* CCAL, 556 F.Supp. 1117 (S.D. Tex., 1982), 1155.

102. Ibid., 1156.

103. Ibid., 1157.

104. Ibid., 1129–30.

105. Stuart Meiher, "Group of Antitrust Lawyers Riles Clients, Opponents by Seeking $50 Million in Fees," *Wall Street Journal,* 21 October 1982, 31B.

106. Ibid.

107. Ibid.

108. Ibid.

109. *In re* CCAL, 556 F.Supp. 1117 (S.D. Tex., 1982), 1128–30.

110. Diane Freeman, "Fifty-five Law Firms to Get $40.7 Million in Fees for Corrugated Box Antitrust Case," *Houston Post*, 3 September 1983, 1A.

111. Ibid. Thirty-three "objectors" to the ruling reserved the right to appeal, but their Dallas-based attorney, Morris Harrell, declined to comment because he had not had an opportunity to read the judge's order. Alan Bernstein, "U.S. Judge Awards $44 Million in Fees to Lawyers in Case," *Houston Chronicle*, 3 September 1983, 22A. The dollar number changes, based on the definition of "fee"; some estimates include reimbursements as well as hourly rates.

112. Diane Freeman, "Fifty-five Law Firms To Get $40.7 Million in Fees for Corrugated Box Antitrust Case," *Houston Post*, 3 September 1983, 1A.

113. Alan Bernstein, "U.S. Judge Awards $44 Million in Fees to Lawyers in Case," *Houston Chronicle*, 3 September 1983, 22A.

114. Ibid.

115. Ibid.

116. Ibid.

117. George T. Barrow, undated typescript, "A Tribute to Judge John V. Singleton," 3–4. From Judge Singleton's personal files, of a 1992 speech honoring his retirement from the federal bench. Barrow was one of Singleton's former law partners from private practice.

118. Judge Singleton could also be raucous in the courtroom. In the summer of 1971, he entered a swift judgment for a sailor's injury, after becoming "visibly annoyed" at the sailor's request for a full trial on the matter (an admiralty case does not require a jury). Singleton reportedly cut off the attorney's objection by stating: "No more arguments. As they say in the song, 'When you're hot you're hot. When you're not, you're not.' " See "Go, Judge Go," *Texas Observer*, 18 June 1971. Thinking that this anecdote presented the judge in an unflattering light (it also mistakenly referred to him as "Joe Singleton," a different individual who was then a Texas state judge), attorney Joseph D. Jamail came to Singleton's defense as "one of the finest judges" on the court; see Jamail's letter to the editor, "Scurrilous Attack" (replying to "Go, Judge Go"), in *Texas Observer*, 16 July 1971.

119. Fed. R. Civ. P., Rule 16. The movement toward settlement and ADR had its detractors. See Owen Fiss, "Against Settlement," *Yale Law Journal* 93 (1984): 1073–74.

120. Jesse E. Clark [clerk] to "Dear Ms. Simms," with various attached letters, 31 March 1983, clerk's files of Chief Judge John V. Singleton, folder 6. Also, Jesse E. Clark, letter of recommendation, 16 December 1982, clerk's files of Chief Judge John V. Singleton, folder 6; and Myron M. Sheinfeld to "Gentlemen, Re: Texas Bar Foundation Outstanding Jurist Award," 13 April 1988, clerk's files of Chief Judge John V. Singleton, folder 15.

121. Charlene Gaines [chief deputy clerk] to "Jim McCullough, Supervisor, criminal section–Houston," 3 June 1980, clerk's files of Chief Judge John V. Singleton, folder 2.

122. Chief Judge Singleton to "Dear Judge Butzner," 6 March 1980, clerk's files of Chief Judge John V. Singleton, folder 2. For the news and the personal and professional responses to Judge Cire's health problems, see Chief Judge Singleton to "Dear Mr. Thomas," 29 October 1979, and Chief Judge Singleton to "Dear Mr. Thomas," 26 November 1979, clerk's files of Chief Judge John V. Singleton, folder 1.

123. Jesse E. Clark to "Dear Judge Singleton, Re: Justification for Distribution of Work in the Southern Constellation within the Southern District of Texas," 19 December 1980, clerk's files of Chief Judge John V. Singleton, folder 1.

124. "Head," in *Judges of the United States.*

125. "Hinojosa," in *Judges of the United States.*

126. Oral history interview with Robert J. O'Conor Jr. by Steven H. Wilson, 2 January 1998.

127. Chief Judge Singleton to "My dear Judges," 2 April 1984, clerk's files of Chief Judge John V. Singleton, folder 8. Chief Judge Singleton to "Dear Mr. Clark," 14 December 1984, clerk's files of Chief Judge John V. Singleton, folder 9.

128. Chief Judge Singleton to "Dear Mr. Johnson," 27 September 1984, clerk's files of Chief Judge John V. Singleton, folder 8.

129. Chief Judge Singleton, Judicial Work Assignments, unsigned memorandum, December 1984, clerk's files of Chief Judge John V. Singleton, folder 9.

130. Chief Judge Singleton to "Dear Mr. Clark," 8 May 1985, to "Dear Jesse," 21 November 1984, to "Dear Judge Clark," 17 May 1985, clerk's files of Chief Judge John V. Singleton, folder 9. Jesse E. Clark to "Chief Judge John Singleton, Subject: Dockets of Judges Cire and O'Conor," 31 May 1985, Chief Judge Singleton to "My dear Judges," 4 June 1985, Chief Judge Singleton to "Dear Chief Judge Clark," 11 September 1985, clerk's files of Chief Judge John V. Singleton, folder 11.

131. "Hughes," in *Judges of the United States.* "Gramm's Record," *Texas Lawyer,* 8 April 1991, p. 14.

132. "Hittner," in *Judges of the United States.* Oral history interview with David Hittner by Steven H. Wilson, 7 June 2000.

133. Texans sought to overcome their troubles in the oldest investment, real estate, or the newest, high technology, but few of these schemes bore enough fruit to bring about general economic recovery. Still, in the face of adversity some Texans were ever-optimistic. Perryman, *Survive and Conquer,* 76–77.

134. Jesse E. Clark to "Dear Chief Judge Singleton," 26 March 1986, clerk's files of Chief Judge John V. Singleton, folder 12. The U.S. district courts have original jurisdiction, "exclusive of the courts of the states," in all matters of bankruptcy. 28 U.S.C. § 1334. This exclusive character of the federal statutes is founded on art. I, § 8 of the U.S. Constitution, which authorized the U.S. Congress to enact a "uniform" law of bankruptcy. The earliest comprehensive federal bankruptcy statute was the Bankruptcy Act of 1898, which is currently codified as Title 11 of the United States Code (11 U.S.C. § 1 et seq.), while federal laws concerning the subject "Banks and Banking" are contained in Title 12 (12 U.S.C.).

135. Some of this is Jesse H. Jones's personal legacy, no doubt. Even the first banking collapse in thirty-eight years, that of the Sharpstown State Bank in Houston in the early 1970s, took place amidst political scandal and a fraud investigation by the Securities and Exchange Commission, not during a panic. The Sharpstown scandal was the result of an eruption of public corruption. It led to loss of public confidence in politics, but no erosion of confidence in banks. See, generally, Kinch and Procter, *Texas under a Cloud.*

136. See Mason, *Transformation of Commercial Banking,* 68–69; and White, "Banking Industry in Trouble," 19–20.

137. The banks were also gambling that the oil industry would rebound. FDIC chairman Seidman referred to First City National Bank as "virtually the ministry of finance for the petroleum industry." Because FCNB was founded by Judge J. A. Elkins and was run by the judge's son, Seidman referred to Vinson and Elkins (V&E), one of Houston's largest law firms (also founded by Judge Elkins), as the industry's "attorney general." See Seidman, *Full Faith and Credit,* 143. Under Judge Elkins's guidance, FCNB and V&E were tied by finan-

cial interdependence as well as corporate kinship; Elkins invested law firm profits in the bank rather than distributing them to V&E partners, and the firm provided legal services to the bank at below market rates. Hyman, *Craftsmanship and Character*, 299. Given the geology of oil-rich Texas and the Port of Houston's place in its geography, V&E's long association with the oil business was natural. The firm's legal services included litigation but also energy-related regulatory lobbying (state and national). Some law firms with strong regional ties to the oil business suffered during the slack economy. Others grew during the boom and were able to consolidate gains during the bust, because lawsuits continued when other business ended. But even these fortunate few recognized the value of broadening their scope. Houston's largest law firms, like many institutions including the city of Houston and the state of Texas, were tempered by the ordeal of the 1980s, learned from the experience to diversify their economic bases, and worked to limit future dependence on the oil industry. V&E had diversified its business and adapted to new opportunities and changing markets for legal services ad hoc. Over several decades V&E added related patent, tax, insurance, and admiralty expertise as necessary, a random process that resulted in inefficiencies as the firm grew to include hundreds of attorneys. In 1979, before national economic recession but during a period of rapid growth and generational flux within, V&E's managing partners sponsored an internal "study group" charged with identifying opportunities for positive change in firm governance. Over the next few years, V&E implemented many of the recommendations for organizational reform. For example, an informal "oil group" became part of a larger designated "energy group" and the "banking law group" was redesignated as the "banking/business finance section." The results were more than cosmetic; the more formal bureaucratic structure clarified the firm's missions and strategies, while at the same time individuals retained the flexibility necessary to respond to volatility. The success of the reform is demonstrated by V&E's continued profits, which rose from some $28 million to $98 million annually between 1981 and 1988, when other firms suffered "red ink and drastic downsizings." Ibid., 441–47, 487–93, quoted at 489. The even older Houston law firm Baker and Botts (B&B), one of Vinson and Elkins's traditional rivals, is similarly identified with the energy industry, and B&B also weathered the 1980s by seizing new opportunities and through "controlled expansion." Lipartito and Pratt, *Baker & Botts*, 203–15, quoted at 212. In 1986 the "biographers" of another of Houston's major institutions, the Texas Commerce Banks, concluded that although sharp fluctuations in the oil-related sectors of the Texas economy had "not yet abated, it seems safe to assert that on balance this era [1971–86] brought much more good than harm to Texas Commerce." Buenger and Pratt, *But Also Good Business*, 335. However, the authors also note that when they wrote in February 1986, oil prices dropped "precipitously" in the first two months of the year; they chose "to avoid the role of seers into the future" and instead concentrated on summarizing the past. Ibid., 303 n.

138. The Depository Institutions Deregulation and Monetary Control Act of 1980. Pub. L. No. 96–221, 94 Stat. 132, codified as amended in various sections of 12 U.S.C.

139. The Depository Institutions Act of 1982 (usually known for its congressional sponsors as the Garn–St. Germain Act) expanded the ability of thrifts to invest in commercial loans and loans secured by nonresidential real estate loans. Pub. L. No. 97–320, 96 Stat. 1469, codified as amended in various sections of 12 U.S.C.

140. The highest rate of failures was nonetheless in Texas. Between 1980 and 1994, 599 banks failed in Texas, for a combined loss of $60.2 billion in assets. The next highest rate was in Oklahoma (also an oil-dependent state), which experienced 122 failures, for a loss

of $5.8 billion. Federal Deposit Insurance Corporation, *History of the Eighties,* 291, esp. n. 1. Regarding the Texas situation, see Fabritus and Borges, *Saving the Savings and Loan.* Also, to learn why Texas earned its reputation as a freewheeling environment for S&L insolvency see, generally, O'Shea, *The Daisy Chain.*

141. The literature warning of possible regulatory contradictions began to proliferate early in the decade, before the worst of the crisis. Usually, authors focused on the storm clouds forming over the thrift industry, but some were optimistic, if cautious, regarding the effects of deregulation. This was to be expected, as the thrifts had been experiencing the most changes in regard to federal regulation and supervision. One observer, Andrew S. Carron, for example, raised the alarm one year, then declared deregulation a possible success. See, generally, Carron, *Plight of the Thrift Institutions;* Carron, *Rescue of the Thrift Industry.* See, also generally, Woerheide, *Savings and Loan Industry;* Balderston, *Thrifts in Crisis;* and, Benston, *Savings and Loan Association Failures.*

142. The awesome public spectacle of the collapses spawned a genre of literature which chronicled the cautionary tale. See Rom, *Public Spirit;* and Pilzer with Deitz, *Other People's Money.* Even those authors who called the situation a mere "crisis" could regard it a "crime." See Calavita, Pontell, and Tillman, *Big Money Crime;* and Mayer, *Greatest-Ever Bank Robbery.*

143. The most scathingly critical literature often tied the disaster to political corruption. See Adams, *The Big Fix;* Waldman, *Who Robbed America?;* Day, *S&L Hell;* Seidman, *Full Faith and Credit;* Eichler, *The Thrift Debacle;* White, *The S&L Debacle;* Barth, *Great Savings and Loan Debacle;* Lowy, *High Rollers;* and Glasberg and Skidmore, *Corporate Welfare Policy.* For one who reads this flurry of accounts, with their differing perspectives and agendas, only one thing is absolutely clear about the affair: writing a book about the banking and especially the S&L collapse was a good way to get your name in print.

144. See Shelton et al., *Houston.*

145. Seidman, *Full Faith and Credit,* 160–67.

146. Pub. L. No. 101–73, 103 Stat. 183, codified at 12 U.S.C. §1437. The act abolished the Federal Savings and Loan Insurance Corporation (FSLIC) and the Federal Home Loan Bank Board (FHLBB). The insurance previously administered by the FSLIC was transferred to the FDIC, while the regulatory functions of the FHLBB were transferred to the new Office of Thrift Supervision (OTS). See "Transfer and Recodification of Regulations Pursuant to Financial Institutions Reform, Recovery and Enforcement Act," 54 Fed. Reg. 49411 (1989). The OTS was effectively a regulatory descendant of a New Deal agency, the Reconstruction Finance Corporation (RFC), because the stated purposes of the new organization were: (1) to provide affordable home mortgages; (2) to establish procedures to resolve failed thrifts; (3) to improve regulation and ensure a well-capitalized independent thrift insurance fund; (4) to establish stronger capital asset requirements for thrifts; and (5) to enhance enforcement powers of federal regulators to protect against "fraud, waste and insider abuse." 1989 *U.S. Code Cong. & Admin. News,* at pp. 103–4. After FIRREA, the FDIC administered two insurance funds: the Bank Insurance Fund (BIF) to insure commercial banks; and the Savings Association Insurance Fund (SAIF) to insure thrift institutions such as savings and loan associations. 12 U.S.C. §1821.

147. A group of three that included the First City Bancorporation and RepublicBank Corporation failures. The southwestern region (including Texas, Oklahoma, Louisiana, New Mexico, and Arkansas) suffered the worst failures. Federal Deposit Insurance Corporation,

History of the Eighties, 291. Early in 1987, the First City Bancorporation, the holding company for a family of banks which included Houston's First City National Bank (FCNB), sought FDIC protection. After an infusion of federal cash and a change of management, the company survived the early crisis, but failed and revived in 1991 and then failed for the last time in 1992. The RepublicBank Corporation merged with InterFirst Corporation in early 1986, to create the largest holding company in Texas, the First Republic Corporation. By early 1987 First Republic sought FDIC assistance. Regulators forced an even more radical restructuring, and sold the company to the North Carolina National Bank (NCNB), which eventually became the NationsBank system. See Seidman, *Full Faith and Credit,* 142–55.

148. *MCorp v. Board of Governors of the Federal Reserve System,* 101 Bankr. 483, at 486 (S.D. Tex., 1989), Houston Division, Case No. 89–02312-H3–11, Civil Action No. 89–1677, Adversary No. 89–0298. Banks cannot file for bankruptcy; instead, they must either reorganize or liquidate under the nation's banking laws. Bank holding companies, however, are not prohibited from entering bankruptcy. Also, although they are regulated by banking agencies, they cannot be reorganized or liquidated under the laws for banks. Congress amended both the banking and the bankruptcy laws several times but has not resolved this inconsistency.

149. *In re MCorp,* 160 Bankr. 941, at 964.

150. The antebellum history of American national banking is long and tortured. In brief, the first Bank of the United States was established by Alexander Hamilton, then lapsed after its charter expired. In 1819 Chief Justice John Marshall, for the U.S. Supreme Court, confirmed Hamilton's initial interpretations and held that the U.S. Congress had power to establish national banks under the Constitution, by way of the provision relating to borrowing and coining money (art. I, § 8). *McCulloch v. Maryland,* 4 Wheat. (17 U.S.) 316 (1819). After the 1836 lapse of the charter of the second Bank of the United States, no federal official could intervene effectively in the economy, a result that was the stated intent of President Andrew Jackson's veto of the charter's renewal in 1832. See "Veto of the Bank Renewal Bill," in Heffner, *A Documentary History,* 94. The ensuing "whirlwind" of financial speculation is chiefly credited for causing, or at least extending and deepening, the national depression of 1837–43, which clouded the administration of Jackson's successor, President Martin Van Buren. Meyers, *The Jacksonian Persuasion,* 108–10.

151. Act of June 3, 1864, ch. 106, § 52, 13 Stat. 115 (codified as 12 U.S.C. § 21). The decision to pass the 1864 National Banking Act is briefly described by Paludan, *Presidency of Abraham Lincoln,* 111–13.

152. The National Currency Act of 1864 established the comptroller of the currency within the Department of the Treasury. 12 U.S.C. §1.

153. Chernow, *The House of Morgan,* 128–30.

154. The Federal Reserve, or "Fed," is the so-called "lender of last resort" and lends funds to member banks at the short-term "prime rate" set by the governing board. The rise or fall of the prime rate influences the availability of credit to the buying, building, or investing public. Therefore, the Fed also affects the growth or contraction of the national, and often global, economy. See, generally, Greider, *Secrets of the Temple.*

155. Wicker, *Banking Panics,* xv. Roosevelt acted under the enabling provision of the "Trading-with-the-Enemy Act," which stated that "the President may investigate, regulate, or prohibit, under such rules and regulations as he may prescribe, by means of licenses or otherwise, any transactions in foreign exchange, and the export, hoarding, melting, or earmarking of gold or silver coin or bullion or currency." This was a dubious use of the

act, but one that officers at the Treasury Department had already considered and urged, unsuccessfully, upon outgoing President Herbert Hoover. Kennedy, *Banking Crisis of 1933*, 157–60.

156. Wicker, *Banking Panics*, 3.

157. Kennedy, *Banking Crisis of 1933*, 227. See also Wicker, *Banking Panics*, 148–49. Federal regulation of the thrift industry, separate but related to the banking industry, also began in earnest during the Great Depression. Faced with the failure of more than seventeen hundred thrifts, building and loan associations, mutual savings banks, and savings and loan associations, the Congress passed the Federal Home Loan Bank Act of 1932, at the request of President Herbert Hoover. This act created the RFC, which was authorized to provide emergency funding to thrifts. The RFC, initially chaired by Charles G. Dawes, replaced the short-lived NCC but fulfilled many of the same functions of facilitating credit. The RFC provided over $100 million in aid to thrifts in its fifteen years of existence. The act also authorized the creation of twelve district banks to loan money to financial institutions and created the Federal Home Loan Bank Board (FHLBB) to manage the district banks. The following year, Congress enacted the Home Owners' Loan Act (HOLA), which authorized the FHLBB to grant federal charters to S&L associations.

158. The holiday's success gained for Roosevelt critical early momentum and allowed his administration to consolidate Americans' resurgent confidence. Under what became the New Deal, Congress extended federal regulation of financial institutions. It enacted along with the additional oversight structural changes intended to prevent similar national crises of credit and currency. Leuchtenburg, *Roosevelt and the New Deal*, 158–61.

159. U.S.C. § 191. A legal or equitable proceeding, "receivership" is the status of being in the care of a "receiver" appointed by a court or agency to administer business, or protect assets, during a legal dispute. The receiver is responsible for preserving the assets and value of the property owned by the insolvent business, usually to enable sale of assets or property to recompense creditors.

160. Glass-Steagall was not part of the New Deal; it was the final act in a drama that had been playing since the October 1929 crash. Congressional reformers took aim at the speculators they blamed for the nation's crisis, including not only the bankers but especially the stock and securities dealers of Wall Street. For example, the act erected a wall between deposit banks and securities dealers, forcing Wall Street's venerable J. P. Morgan and Co. to separate its investment banking business, which arranged financing for speculative ventures (through stock and bond issues), from its commercial banking, which took in deposits and extended loans (for purchasing such issues). Chernow, *The House of Morgan*, 349–53, 374–77.

161. The FDIC currently insures the accounts of qualified depositors up to one hundred thousand dollars (12 U.S.C. §1821).

162. See, generally, Park, *Contagion of Bank Failures;* and Cottrell, Lawlor, and Wood, *Depository Institution Failures.*

163. Act of June 16, 1933, ch. 89, 8, 48 Stat. 168 (codified at 12 U.S.C. 1811). In 1934 Congress also attempted to increase the public confidence in the thrift industry. The National Housing Act created the Federal Savings and Loan Insurance Corporation (FSLIC, as a counterpart to the commercial banking sector's FDIC), to provide insurance to small thrift depositors. The act also created the Federal Housing Administration, which provided insurance to mortgage lenders.

164. Leuchtenburg, *Roosevelt and the New Deal*, 60. The New Deal became the training ground for a generation of "bright young men" eager to serve the cause of reform, but the

president also needed experienced men in his administration. Soon after taking office, Roosevelt appointed Houstonian Jesse H. Jones, a prominent banker and real estate developer, and already a member of the board of the RFC during the Hoover years, to be its chairman. Jones exhibited the vigorous qualities Roosevelt appreciated: in 1931 Jones orchestrated an unprecedented cooperative effort among politicians, lawyers, and businessmen that had been credited with preventing the collapse of Houston's banks, including Jones's own National Bank of Commerce. He remained chairman of the RFC until 1945, even as he served as Roosevelt's secretary of commerce during World War II. Commentators estimated that during his years of service, Jones exercised powers second only to the president. Buenger and Pratt, *But Also Good Business,* 1, 107, 77. Once the bank holiday stabilized the situation, Jones was among those in the president's inner circle who suggested that "restoration of public confidence in the banks" might be accomplished by federally sponsored deposit insurance. After so publicly placing the crisis of confidence, that is, "fear itself," high on the list of national maladies, the new president opposed deposit insurance. But after the idea proved its merit, Roosevelt cited it as among his administration's significant achievements. In his memoir Jones describes the president's initial reluctance to support deposit insurance. Jones with Angly, *Fifty Billion Dollars,* 45–46. Banking regulations have been updated and extended in the years since the New Deal. The Board of Governors of the Federal Reserve System has generally been the body entrusted with the greatest power. For example, the Financial Institutions Supervisory Act of 1966 (FISA; 12 U.S.C. §1818), the Bank Holding Company Act of 1956 (BHCA; 12 U.S.C. § 1841), and the International Lending Supervision Act of 1983 (ILSA; 12 U.S.C. § 3901) gave the Fed substantial additional regulatory authority over banks and bank holding companies. However, the laws also established judicial review of board actions.

165. MCorp was a Dallas-based bank holding company, although it was a Delaware-chartered corporation. *MCorp v. Clarke,* 755 F.Supp. 1402, at 1404 (N.D. Tex., 1991).

166. *In re MCorp,* 160 Bankr. 941, at 944–45 (S.D. Tex., 1993); Houston Division, Civil Action No. H-93–395.

167. The damages represent the total of the individual claims. The suit began as separate actions by several plaintiffs but was consolidated for all purposes on 30 August 1985. The claims followed news reports that the bank was near failure (the reports may have contributed to the troubles by sparking a run on assets). Around the same time, the former president and vice president of MBank Abilene (actually its predecessor, Abilene National Bank) were indicted for violating numerous banking statutes, including embezzlement, falsifying a loan application, and filing a false income tax return. See *United States v. Kington and Earney,* 801 F.2d 733 (5th Cir. 1986), cert. denied, 107 S.Ct. 1888 (1987). On 15 April 1988 the former bank president was convicted on thirty-seven counts and sentenced to twelve years in prison. See *MBank Abilene v. LeMaire,* 1989 Tex. App. LEXIS 801, at 806 n. 3 (Court of Appeals of Texas, 14th District, Houston; No. C14–86–00834-CV). Because of local publicity, MBank requested a change of venue for the civil suit, and the civil trial had been transferred to Fort Bend County. *LeMaire v. MBank Abilene* (240th District Court Fort Bend County, Tex., Trial Court Cause No. 52,567). MBank Abilene appealed, alleging 153 points of error. *MBank Abilene v. LeMaire,* 1989 Tex. App. LEXIS 801 (Court of Appeals of Texas, 14th District, Houston, No. C14–86–00834-CV).

168. *United States v. MBank Abilene,* 1986 U.S. Dist. LEXIS 18592 (N.D. Tex., 1986); Civ. A. No. 1–86–143K.

169. U.S.C. § 91. In its entirety, § 91 provides: "All transfers of the notes, bonds, bills

of exchange, or other evidences of debt owing to any national banking association, or of deposits to its credit; all assignments of mortgages, sureties on real estate, or of judgments or decrees in its favor; all deposits of money, bullion, or other valuable thing for its use, or for the use of any of its shareholders or creditors; and all payments of money to either, made after the commission of an act of insolvency, or in contemplation thereof, made with a view to prevent the application of its assets in the manner prescribed by this chapter, or with a view to the preference of one creditor to another, except in payment of its circulating notes, shall be utterly null and void; and no attachment, injunction, or execution, shall be issued against such association or its property before final judgment in any suit, action, or proceeding, in any State, county, or municipal court." (Revised Statutes of 1873–74, tit. LXII, ch. 4 § 5242). An 1873 amendment to the National Bank Act added the anti-injunction, etc., provision to the original § 5242, which previously dealt only with preferential transfers of funds. *United States v. MBank Abilene,* 1986 U.S. Dist. LEXIS 18,592, at 18,600 (N.D. Tex., 1986); Civ. A. No. 1–86–143-k.

170. In *Pacific National Bank v. Mixter,* 124 U.S. 721 (1887), the justices considered "whether an attachment can issue against a national bank before judgment in a suit begun in the Circuit Court of the United States" and concluded that none could issue before judgment in a state or federal suit (at 724–27). The next time the court studied 12 U.S.C. §91, in *Earle v. Pennsylvania,* 178 U.S. 449 (1900), garnishment of a depositor's property, not the bank's property, was at issue. In *Earle* the justices held that "an attachment sued out against the bank as garnishee is not an attachment against the bank or its property, nor a suit against it, within the meaning of that section" (at 454). Finally, in *Van Reed v. Peoples' National Bank,* 198 U.S. 554 (1905) the court affirmed the *Mixter* interpretation, applying 12 U.S.C. §91 "to all conditions of national banks, whether solvent or insolvent" (at 559).

171. *Third National Bank v. Impac Limited, Inc.,* 432 U.S. 312 (1977), at 324.

172. *United States v. MBank Abilene,* 1986 U.S. Dist. LEXIS 18592 (N.D. Tex., 1986); Civ. A. No. 1–86-143K.

173. The defendants responded with a motion to dismiss, on grounds of inappropriate venue and lack of court jurisdiction. On the venue issue, the court found sufficient cause to hear the case in the Northern District, because that was where the bank did the majority of its business. The defendants all resided in the Southern District of Texas, where the original state trial was held. Regarding jurisdiction, the defendants alleged that the court lacked both in personam and subject matter jurisdiction. A federal court must show that it has both subject matter and personal jurisdiction over defendants before it may issue a preliminary injunction. The judge decided that he did have both and denied their motion. In addition, the defendants argued that the United States lacked standing to pursue a claim on behalf of MBank; but the district court declared that according to the Supreme Court's decision in *In re Debs,* 158 U.S. 564 (1895), the United States had standing to sue in its own courts to prevent interference with its powers and functions. Finally, the judge noted that under 28 U.S.C. § 1345, a federal district court has jurisdiction over all cases in which the United States is a plaintiff, as it was in the MBank suit. *United States v. MBank Abilene,* 1986 U.S. Dist. LEXIS 18592, at 18593–95 (N.D. Tex., 1986); Civ. A. No. 1–86-143K.

174. *United States v. MBank Abilene,* 1986 U.S. Dist. LEXIS 18,592, at 18,593 (N.D. Tex., 1986); Civil Action No. 1–86-143K.

175. MBank Abilene not only held some $169 million in insured deposits, it also held the FDIC's own $50 million certificate of deposit (which, after deducting the $100,000 in-

sured by law, added $49.9 million to the losses). If no other financial institution assumed the bank's liabilities, the FDIC, the largest unsecured creditor, would be liable for the total $218.7 million. *United States v. MBank Abilene*, 1986 U.S. Dist. LEXIS 18592, at 18,609–11 (N.D. Tex., 1986); Civ. A. No. 1–86-143K.

176. *United States v. MBank Abilene*, 1986 U.S. Dist. LEXIS 18592, at 18,596–99 (N.D. Tex., 1986); Civ. A. No. 1–86-143K.

177. According to the judge, there had been only one case dealing with the "precise issue," and he was persuaded by the ruling in that case, *Loews' Incorporated v. Superior Court of the State of California*, 301 P.2d 64 (Cal. 1956). A state court interpreted "final judgment" to mean one "from which no appeal can be taken" (at 72). *United States v. MBank Abilene*, 1986 U.S. Dist. LEXIS 18,592, at 18,602, 18,605 (N.D. Tex., 1986); Civ. A. No. 1–86-143K.

178. The district court did remark that, although not construing the meaning of the language, the court noted in all three of the early versions that the precursor statute to § 91 was "deliberately placed at the end of the preferential transfer section" of the Banking Code. *Mixter* at 726–27; *Earle* at 453; *Impac* at 322–24. In *Mixter* the court took Congress's intent to be equality among creditors in the division of assets upon insolvency. Also, the court noted the fact that there was a depression in 1873, the year the original act was amended, in *Impac*. *Impac* at 317. See *United States v. MBank Abilene*, 1986 U.S. Dist. LEXIS 18592, at 18,603 (N.D. Tex., 1986); Civ. A. No. 1–86-143K.

179. Ibid., 18,604.

180. Ibid., 18,607.

181. Ibid.

182. Ibid., 18,608–9.

183. Ibid., 18,610.

184. Ibid., 18,613.

185. Ibid., 186,12–13. On 6 April 1989 the Texas Court of Appeals upheld the damages for two of the plaintiffs but overturned the remaining three, for a total final judgment against MBank Abilene of $18.5 million. *MBank Abilene v. LeMaire*, 1989 Tex. App. LEXIS 801, at 892 (Court of Appeals of Texas, 14th District, Houston, No. C14–86-00834-CV).

186. *FDIC v. Taylor*, 727 F.Supp. 326, at 327 (S.D. Tex., 1989); Houston Division, Civ. A. No. H-89–1463.

187. Under Texas law the recorded abstract of judgment created a lien on all real property of MBank located in Harris County. Tex. Prop. Code Ann. § 52.001 (Vernon 1984). See *United States v. Taylor*, 881 F.2d 207, at 208 (5th Cir., 1989).

188. *United States v. Taylor*, 881 F.2d 207, at 209 (5th Cir., 1989).

189. The defendants appealed on the decision regarding the federal government's standing, and the U.S. Court of Appeals for the Fifth Circuit agreed with the Northern District court that the interest stemming from the OCC's obligation to ensure the safety and soundness of the national banking system for the benefit of depositors and the general public provided sufficient standing for the United States to bring the action in federal courts. *United States v. LeMaire*, 826 F.2d 387 (5th Cir. 1987), esp. at 388 n. 1, 390; cert. denied, 485 U.S. 960 (1988). Although the federal district court signed the TRO, this did not occur until nine minutes after Taylor filed the abstract of her state judgment. *United States v. Taylor*, 881 F.2d 207, at 209 (5th Cir., 1989).

190. The Southern District order issued in *United States v. Taylor*, Civ. A. No. H-89–0672.

191. *United States v. Taylor*, 881 F.2d 207, at 209 (5th Cir., 1989).

192. Taylor did not argue that the judgment was "final," but the circuit invoked *LeMaire* (826 F.2d at 390), just to remind the parties that it was not. *United States v. Taylor,* 881 F.2d 207, at 209 (5th Cir., 1989).

193. FDIC *v. Taylor,* 727 F.Supp. 326, at 327 (S.D. Tex., 1989), Houston Division, Civ. A. No. H-89–1463.

194. Fed. Reg. 820 (1984); codified at 12 C.F.R. § 225.4(a)(1).

195. Policy Statement, 52 Fed. Reg. 15707, at 15,708 (1987). Therefore, "unsafe" or "unsound" practices are not only potential violations of the "source of strength" rule, but of 52 Fed. Reg. 15707–9, or both. The Fed had authority to issue the regulation and the subsequent policy statement through the broad language of the Bank Holding Company Act of 1956 (BHCA), 12 U.S.C. § 1841 et seq. (1988 ed. and Supp. II). The BHCA's § 1844(b), Section 5(b), stated, "The Board is authorized to issue such regulations and orders as may be necessary to enable it to administer and carry out the purposes of this chapter and prevent evasions thereof."

196. *MCorp v. Board of Governors of the Federal Reserve System,* 900 F.2d 852, at 860 (5th. Cir., 1990), No. 89–2816.

197. An example of "open-bank" aid is an infusion of cash to a still solvent but faltering bank in order to keep it open; "closed-bank" aid indicated closing the bank, declaring it insolvent, and rendering aid through the protection of bankruptcy receivership.

198. Bishop described MCorp's dealings with FDIC in his "Affidavit in Support of Plaintiffs' Motion for Partial Summary Judgment," sworn 21 December 1989. See *MCorp v. Clarke,* 755 F.Supp. 1402, at 1404 (N.D. Tex., 1991).

199. *MCorp v. Clarke,* 755 F.Supp. 1402, at 1405 (N.D. Tex., 1991), esp. n. 5.

200. Ibid. Another company filed suit against MCorp in Delaware seeking an injunction that would prohibit the holding company from downstreaming assets, charging that such a move would amount to a fraudulent conveyance under Texas law. This suit was stayed pending the outcome of the MCorp litigation before U.S. District Judge Hughes of the Southern District of Texas. *Charlifco and Charter National Life Insurance Co. v. MCorp,* Del. Chancery Court Civ. A. No. 10426, filed November 9, 1988.

201. Seidman, *Full Faith and Credit,* 155–58. Seidman was the head of the FDIC, until he was removed in February 1990. The book is both his memoir of the crisis and his defense against his many critics.

202. See *MCorp v. Clarke,* 755 F.Supp. 1402, at 1404 (N.D. Tex., 1991).

203. The minimum capital levels are established by statute (12 U.S.C. §3907). See *MCorp v. Clarke,* 755 F.Supp. 1402, at 1405 (N.D. Tex., 1991).

204. *MCorp v. Board of Governors of the Federal Reserve System,* 900 F.2d 852, at 853 (5th. Cir., 1990), No. 89–2816.

205. *Board of Governors of the Federal Reserve System v. MCorp,* 502 U.S. 32, at 35 (1991), esp. n. 5. The FISA authorized the Fed's board to institute the administrative proceedings, and empowered the Fed to issue cease-and-desist orders to banks and also to holding companies if "in the opinion of the appropriate Federal banking agency, any insured depository institution . . . is engaged or has engaged, or the agency has reasonable cause to believe that the depository institution . . . is about to engage, in an unsafe or unsound practice in conducting the business of such depository institution, or is violating or has violated, or the agency has reasonable cause to believe that the depository institution or any institution-affiliated party is about to violate, a law, rule, or regulation." 12 U.S.C. §§ 1818(b)(1) and (3) (1988 ed., Supp. II), amended by FIRREA, Pub. L. No. 101–73, §§ 901(d), 902(a)(1)(A).

206. *MCorp v. Clarke,* 755 F.Supp. 1402, at 1404 (N.D. Tex., 1991). MCorp could challenge the order under 12 U.S.C. § 1818(c)(2).

207. Ibid., 1405.

208. FDIC board minutes of 25 October 1988, at 021285, quoted in *MCorp v. Clarke,* at 1414.

209. Emphasis added. FDIC board minutes of 2 November 1988, reconvened 3 November, at 022234–5, quoted in *MCorp v. Clarke,* at 1414–15.

210. FDIC board minutes of 2 November 1988, reconvened 3 November, at 022236, quoted in *MCorp v. Clarke,* 1414–15.

211. Ibid., 1415.

212. FDIC board minutes of 2 November 1988, reconvened 3 November, at 022299, 022302, quoted in *MCorp v. Clarke,* 1415, esp. n. 27. In a preliminary ruling in another case, U.S. District Judge Fitzwater stated that the FDIC also "manufactured" the insolvency of First RepublicBank Delaware. *Senior Unsecured Creditors' Committee of First RepublicBank Corp. v. FDIC,* 749 F. Supp. 758 (N.D. Tex., 1990).

213. *MCorp v. Clarke,* 755 F.Supp. 1402, at 1416 (N.D. Tex., 1991).

214. The plaintiffs brought the initial suit under chapter 7. Ibid., 1405. On March 31 bankruptcy judge Cornelius Blackshear granted an MCorp motion to convert the chapter 7 proceeding to chapter 11, which would allow the company to continue to operate, protected from its creditors, while it reorganized. Five days later, Judge Blackshear authorized the transfer of the proceedings to the Houston bankruptcy court, where two MCorp subsidiaries had already filed chapter 11 petitions. Meanwhile, five MCorp creditors, including Shearson Lehman Hutton, formed an informal creditors' committee. Susan Beck, "Big Suits: South," *American Lawyer,* May 1989, p. 25.

215. *MCorp v. Clarke,* 755 F.Supp. 1402, at 1405 (N.D. Tex., 1991).

216. Ibid., 1406.

217. Ibid., 1406.

218. The twenty MBanks declared insolvent were MBank Abilene, MBank Alamo (San Antonio), MBank Austin, MBank Brenham, MBank Corsicana, MBank Dallas, MBank Denton County (Lewisville), MBank Fort Worth, MBank Greenville, MBank Houston, MBank Jefferson County (Port Arthur), MBank Longview, MBank Marshall, MBank Mid-Cities (Arlington), MBank Odessa, MBank Orange, MBank Round Rock, MBank Sherman, MBank Wichita Falls, and MBank The Woodlands. Ibid., 1406 n. 7.

219. Ibid., 1407.

220. Bank One and the FDIC subsequently disagreed over exactly which assets Bank One had purchased from the FDIC, but reached a settlement between themselves. But, according to Judge Hughes, in his opinion in a later case related to the MCorp matter, Bank One simply spent the next three years "on the sideline while the debtors, the FDIC, and a host of creditors, real and imagined . . . fought, regrouped, and refought in court." *United States v. Bank One,* 170 Bankr. 899, at 900 (S.D. Tex., 1994); Houston Division, Civil Action No. H-90–2929. In another proceeding, related to the DIBB's failure to continue administering a benefits plan for its new employees, Southern District Judge Samuel Kent noted that between 28 March 1989 and 5 May 1989, there was a "complete vacuum of authority," regarding a benefits plan. But Judge Kent commended one employee, Stephanie Burks, who "stepped up to the plate, in a remarkable fashion, bringing order to chaos, and ensuring, throughout the period of transition, as smooth and orderly a flow of benefits as possible to those in critical need." The judge remarked that "[t]his Court is genuinely honored to have observed, through her

testimony, her actions during this time. If ordinary citizens were entitled to the receipt of some sort of medal, for heroism in ordinary affairs, [Burks] would surely be a most worthy recipient." *Taylor v. Bank One,* 137 Bankr. 624, at 637 (S.D. Tex., 1992), Houston Division, Civ. A. No. H-90-3815.

221. *MCorp v. Board of Governors of the Federal Reserve System,* 101 Bankr. 483 at 485 (S.D. Tex., 1989); Houston Division, Civ. A. No. 89–1677.

222. *MCorp v. Board of Governors of the Federal Reserve System,* 900 F.2d 852, at 853–54 (5th. Cir., 1990); No. 89–2816. The actions were assigned the following case numbers: the involuntary petition filed in New York was No. 89–02848-H2–11; the voluntary petition filed in Texas by MCorp Management was No. 89–02324-H5–11; and the voluntary petition filed in Texas by MCorp Financial, Inc., was No. 89–02312-H3–11. *MCorp v. Board of Governors of the Federal Reserve System,* 101 Bankr. 483 at 485 (S.D. Tex., 1989), Houston Division, Civ. A. No. 89–1677.

223. Federal Reserve Act, 48 Stat. 183 (1933). Section 23 sets forth restrictions on member bank holding companies' corporate practices, including restrictions on "self-dealing," that is, transactions between subsidiary banks and nonbank affiliates. Section 23A prohibited a bank from extending credit to a nonbank affiliate unless the loan was secured by collateral having a market value of at least 100 percent of the loan. 12 U.S.C. §371(c). *Board of Governors of the Federal Reserve System v. MCorp,* 502 U.S. 32, at 34–34 (1991), esp. n. 2.

224. *MCorp v. Board of Governors of the Federal Reserve System,* 101 Bankr. 483 at 485 (S.D. Tex., 1989); Houston Division, Civ. A. No. 89–1677.

225. U.S.C. § 362(a).

226. *MCorp v. Board of Governors of the Federal Reserve System,* 900 F.2d 852, at 854 (5th. Cir., 1990), No. 89–2816.

227. *MCorp v. Board of Governors of the Federal Reserve System,* 101 Bankr. 483, at 484 (S.D. Tex., 1989); Houston Division, Case No. 89–02312-H3–11, Civ. A. No. 89–1677, Adversary No. 89–0298.

228. Ibid., 485.

229. The relevant portion of the bankruptcy code provides: "The district court in which a case under title 11 is commenced or is pending shall have exclusive jurisdiction of all of the property, wherever located, of the debtor as of the commencement of such case, and of property of the estate." 28 U.S.C. § 1334(d).

230. U.S.C. § 105.

231. U.S.C. § 1818(i).

232. *MCorp v. Board of Governors of the Federal Reserve System,* 101 Bankr. 483, at 485 (S.D. Tex., 1989), Houston Division, Case No. 89–02312-H3–11, Civ. A. No. 89–1677, Adversary No. 89–0298.

233. Ibid., 490.

234. Judge Hughes noted previous cases in which similar limitations had been "overridden through control of the debtor's estate having been entrusted to the authority of the bankruptcy court" and recalled other cases in which conflicts had been resolved in favor of the application of the bankruptcy code in matters affecting the court of claims and the tax court (which are administrative courts rather than judicial courts), both of which exercised jurisdictional grants parallel to the Fed's. Even in rem proceedings in admiralty, which were "particular liquidation actions," might yield to the bankruptcy code, although "maritime jurisdiction is directly a judicial power of international significance." *MCorp v. Board of*

Governors of the Federal Reserve System, 101 Bankr. 483, at 487 (S.D. Tex., 1989), Houston Division, Case No. 89–02312-H3–11, Civ. A. No. 89–1677, Adversary No. 89–0298.

235. Ibid., 486.

236. Ibid., 486.

237. With regard to weighing costs and benefits, Judge Hughes stated that "[n]either an interest of the public nor an interest of a group of nonparties will be harmed by this injunctive solution to the regulatory conflict." Ibid., 491.

238. However, the injunction did not apply to "parallel" agencies such as the OCC or the FDIC, which could still "independently pursue their regulatory mandates." Ibid., 491.

239. Ibid., 485.

240. Ibid., 489.

241. Ibid.

242. Ibid., 491.

243. On 30 April 1990 MCorp lost its claim in the first major proceeding in the bankruptcy. MCorp had moved to cancel a lease with the owner of its former offices, Tower Center, in order to avoid a past-due rent payment of $49 million. The owner naturally opposed, claiming the occupancy agreement was not subject to rejection. After considering the evidence, briefs, and arguments, Judge Clark concluded the Tower Center landlord was correct and found MCorp liable for the rent. *In re MCorp,* 122 Bankr. 49 (S.D. Tex., 1990), Bankruptcy Court, Houston Division, Case Nos. 89–02312-H3–11, 89–02324-H5–11, 89–02848-H2–11, 89–02312-H3–11.

244. *MCorp v. Clarke,* 755 F.Supp. 1402, at 1407 (N.D. Tex., 1991).

245. *MCorp v. Board of Governors of the Federal Reserve System,* 900 F.2d 852, at 854 (5th. Cir., 1990); No. 89–2816.

246. Beyond the bankruptcy proceedings, litigation arising from the government's seizure of the MBanks and related regulatory acts included *MCorp v. Clarke,* CA3–89–831-F; *MBank New Braunfels, N.A. v. FDIC,* CA3–89–1064-F; *MCorp v. United States of America,* H-92–959; *FDIC, as Receiver for MBank Abilene, N.A. v. The North River Ins. Co.,* CA3–89–2138-F; *SRE Real Estate Fund v. MCorp Properties,* 91–1599, 192d Judicial Dct., Dallas; *MCorp v. The Prentiss/Copley Investment Group,* H-91–1131; and *MCorp v. Board of Governors of the Federal Reserve System,* H-89–1677. Each of these cases gave rise to its own eddies in the courts, of course. See *In re MCorp,* 160 Bankr. 941, at 945 (S.D. Tex., 1993), Houston Division, Civ. A. No. H-93–395.

247. U.S.C. § 1818(h). *MCorp v. Board of Governors of the Federal Reserve System,* 900 F.2d 852, at 855 (5th. Cir., 1990); No. 89–2816.

248. According to the Fifth Circuit, the relevant portion of this code was the provision that stated: "Notwithstanding any Act of Congress that confers exclusive jurisdiction on a court or courts other than the district courts, the district courts shall have original but not exclusive jurisdiction of all civil proceedings arising under title 11, or arising in or related to cases under title 11." 28 U.S.C. § 1334(b). See *MCorp v. Board of Governors of the Federal Reserve System,* 900 F.2d 852, at 855 (5th. Cir., 1990); No. 89–2816.

249. Ibid., 855.

250. Again, the relevant statute provided: "The district court in which a case under title 11 is commenced or is pending shall have exclusive jurisdiction of all of the property, wherever located, of the debtor as of the commencement of such case, and of property of the estate." 28 U.S.C. § 1334(d).

251. Emphasis added. Again, this refers to § 23 of the Federal Reserve Act, which restricted transactions between subsidiary banks and affiliates. 12 U.S.C. § 371(c). *MCorp v. Board of Governors of the Federal Reserve System,* 900 F.2d 852, at 856, 858 (5th. Cir., 1990); No. 89–2816. See also Stan Soocher, "Court Decisions: 5th Circuit," *National Law Journal,* 16 July 1990, p. 29.

252. The panel acknowledged that Congress had not explicitly defined "unsafe or unsound," which left the regulatory agencies some discretion. But the judges also observed that lawmakers adopted an "authoritative definition" when they passed the act, which (quoting from 112 Cong. Rec. 26474 [1966]): "embrace[d] any action, or lack of action, which is contrary to generally accepted standards of prudent operation, the possible consequences of which, if continued, would be abnormal risk or loss or damage to an institution, its shareholders, or the agencies administering the insurance funds." *MCorp v. Board of Governors of the Federal Reserve System,* 900 F.2d 852, at 861–63 (5th. Cir., 1990); No. 89–2816.

253. Ibid., 864.

254. Again, this refers to § 23 of the Federal Reserve Act, which restricted transactions between subsidiary banks and affiliates. 12 U.S.C. § 371(c). See *MCorp v. Board of Governors of the Federal Reserve System,* 900 F.2d 852, at 853 (5th. Cir., 1990); No. 89–2816. See also Stan Soocher, "Court Decisions: 5th Circuit," *National Law Journal,* 16 July 1990, p. 29.

255. On 6 August 1990 the Fifth Circuit denied the government's request for a rehearing en banc. *MCorp v. Board of Governors of the Federal Reserve System,* 911 F.2d 730 (5th. Cir., 1990), No. 89–2816. The Supreme Court subsequently granted certiorari, 499 U.S. 904 (1991). Meanwhile, the related litigation continued. On 16 November 1990 Judge Hughes decided MBank Houston owed Robert Ontiveros money under a lease. The FDIC, as MBank's receiver, bore the liability of $125,000 plus interest. *Ontiveros v. MBank,* 751 F.Supp. 128 (S.D. Tex., 1990), Houston Division, Civ. A. No. H-89–1402.

256. Again, the FIRREA of 1989. Pub. L. No. 101–73, 103 Stat. 183 (1989). FIRREA is codified at 12 U.S.C. § 1437.

257. U.S.C. 1821(d)(12), as amended by FIRREA, § 212(a).

258. *United States v. Taylor,* 881 F.2d 207 (5th Cir., 1989).

259. *FDIC v. Taylor,* 727 F.Supp. 326, at 327 (S.D. Tex., 1989), Houston Division, Civ. A. No. H-89–1463. According to Judge Hittner, the legislative history of FIRREA indicated that the ninety-day stay provision was intended to give the FDIC "breathing room" immediately upon appointment but did not allow the FDIC to stay proceedings at any point, regardless of the length of its involvement. The judge noted that the House report on FIRREA said that "the appointment of a conservator or receiver can often change the character of litigation; the stay gives the FDIC a chance to analyze pending matters and decide how best to proceed." H.R. Rep. No. 54(I), 101st Cong., 1st sess. 331 (1989), reprinted in 1989 *U.S. Code Cong. & Admin. News* (103 Stat.) 86, 127.

260. U.S.C. 1821(d)(13)(B), as amended by FIRREA, § 212(a).

261. *FDIC v. Taylor,* 727 F.Supp. 326 at 328 (S.D. Tex., 1989), Houston Division, Civ. A. No. H-89–1463. Taylor made two additional arguments against the FDIC's authority to remove the case to federal court: first, that by removing a case in which a motion for new trial or a corrected state court judgment was pending, the federal district court was unlawfully vested with appellate jurisdiction (an alleged violation of 28 U.S.C. §§ 1330–66); second, that the Seventh Amendment of the U.S. Constitution prevented removal, because it subjected state jury findings to an unconstitutional reexamination by a federal district court. Judge Hittner

decided that FIRREA did not moot these issues, but he ruled against Taylor on other grounds (at 331).

262. Because FIRREA abolished the FSLIC and designated the FDIC as its inheritor, these questions became especially pertinent in similar litigation surrounding the savings and loan industry.

263. *MCorp v. Clarke,* 755 F.Supp. 1402 (N.D. Tex., 1991).

264. When the Fed seized the twenty MBanks on March 29 and 30, the combined closings constituted the third largest bank failure in U.S. history. Susan Beck, "Big Suits: South," *American Lawyer,* May 1989, p. 25. Or it might have been the second largest failure. "MCorp Plan Rejected," *National Law Journal,* 20 January 1992, p. 19. The dozen banks named were the Brenham, Corsicana, Denton County, Jefferson County, Longview, Marshall, Mid-Cities, Odessa, Orange, Sherman, Wichita Falls, and The Woodlands MBanks. *MCorp v. Clarke,* 755 F.Supp. 1402, at 1407 (N.D. Tex., 1991). In addition to the named defendant, Robert Clarke, who was the comptroller of the currency, the defendants included the FDIC and DIBB. Shahram Victory, "Big Suits: South," *American Lawyer,* April 1991, p. 31.

265. *MCorp v. Clarke,* 755 F.Supp. 1402, at 1407 (N.D. Tex., 1991).

266. FIRREA, § 212(a).

267. In a study it issued on 4 January 1989, the FDIC stated that when a holding company was involved, the FDIC was justified in withholding full payment to nondeposit creditors, even as it covers the entire loss for uninsured depositors. The authors wrote that "[t]he legal basis supporting this approach has not been codified . . . but arises from established common law" (quoted from the FDIC's "Deposit Insurance for the Nineties: Meeting the Challenge"). The judge believed the evidence indicated that, notwithstanding this report, the FDIC was "fully aware it was operating according to an untested—and shaky—legal theory." See *MCorp v. Clarke,* 755 F.Supp. 1402, at 1419 (N.D. Tex., 1991). These valuations of a recovery against the FDIC, whether discounted or not, would be in the form of receiver's certificates as a claim against the final net assets of a failed bank. *In re MCorp,* 160 Bankr. 941, at 951 (S.D. Tex., 1993), Houston Division, Civ. A. No. H-93–395.

268. National Bank Act, 12 U.S.C. §§ 91; made applicable to the FDIC by 12 U.S.C. § 1821(d). Since it had been "plainly construed" to mandate equal treatment for all creditors of a failed institution, Judge Porter agreed that the FDIC's policy of showing preferences violated the act's express provisions. *MCorp v. Clarke,* 755 F.Supp. 1402, at 1422 (N.D. Tex., 1991). These arguments, regarding the possibility of full compensation saving the MBanks, were highly speculative; after the FDIC declared the insolvency of the Dallas and Houston MBanks, the regulators immediately declared the creditor banks to be insolvent as well. *MCorp v. Clarke,* 755 F.Supp. 1402, at 1407–8 (N.D. Tex., 1991), esp. nn. 10, 11. The exception was MBank New Braunfels, which sued the FDIC in a separate action. See *MBank New Braunfels v. FDIC,* 721 F.Supp. 120 (N.D. Tex., 1989), and 772 F.Supp. 313 (N.D. Tex., 1991). In a similar recent case, the Northern District's Chief Judge Barefoot Sanders held that a bank holding company and ten of its subsidiary banks were entitled to be paid in full by the FDIC, as were other creditors, rather than the 67 percent of par the regulators offered. Judge Sanders ruled that the agency could not discriminate among claims under the bank act and said that this unequal treatment triggered the failure of twelve otherwise healthy TAB institutions, out of twenty-two TAB banks closed. *Texas American Bancshares, Inc. v. Clarke,* 740 F.Supp. 1243, at 1248 (N.D. Tex., 1990). Judge Porter took note of the precedent in making his own decision. See *MCorp v. Clarke,* 755 F.Supp. 1402, at 1412 (N.D. Tex., 1991).

269. U.S.C. §§ 1346(b), 2671, et seq. Under FTCA, MCorp would first have to present its claim to the proper administrative body and would not be allowed to maintain the suit until the federal agency it was suing (in this case, the Federal Reserve Board) had made a final disposition of the claim. But MCorp was suing for damages under alleged violations of the National Bank Act, which granted the district court's jurisdiction. 28 U.S.C. § 1348.

270. *MCorp v. Clarke,* 755 F.Supp. 1402, at 1407–8 (N.D. Tex., 1991), esp. nn. 10, 11.

271. Ibid., 1408.

272. FIRREA, § 212(j).

273. The judge ruled that "[f]undamental fairness demands that banks and their creditors be able to know what laws will be applied to them at the time insolvency is declared, so they can best plan for the future, rather than being surprised months later." *MCorp v. Clarke,* 755 F.Supp. 1402, at 1419 (N.D. Tex., 1991). In the face of all of the charges, the government had attempted to invoke the doctrine of sovereign immunity, that is, the understanding that the government was exempt from defending itself against a lawsuit, unless it consents to be sued. For reasons stated in the text, Judge Porter ruled the suit was authorized. Ibid., 1407–8. Also, Chief Judge Sanders defined the FDIC as a "quasi-private" governmental entity and ruled that "[t]he FDIC has . . . the same broad 'sue and be sued' language in its governing statute, [but] . . . is not entitled to claim sovereign immunity." *Texas American Bancshares, Inc. v. Clarke,* 740 F.Supp. 1243, at 1249 (N.D. Tex., 1990).

274. *MCorp v. Clarke,* 755 F.Supp. 1402, at 1413 (N.D. Tex., 1991).

275. Ibid., 1404. Under the Federal Rules of Civil Procedure, summary judgment is proper only where the judge finds "no genuine issue as to any material fact." Fed. R. Civ. P., Rule 56(c).

276. *MCorp v. Clarke,* 755 F.Supp. 1402, at 1414 (N.D. Tex., 1991).

277. Ibid., 1414. See also Shahram Victory, "Big Suits: South," *American Lawyer,* April 1991, p. 31.

278. *MCorp v. Clarke,* 755 F.Supp. 1402, at 1422 (N.D. Tex., 1991). Having reached his decision on other grounds, Judge Porter declined to address MCorp's constitutional claims, such as the company's contention that seizure of the MBanks had been in violation of the Fifth Amendment's due process and just compensation clauses. Ibid., 1423.

279. Judge Porter ordered MCorp to submit a brief and affidavits to justify the compensatory relief the company sought. Ibid., 1423. The judge gave MCorp thirty days to file the claim. On 4 March the company proposed three alternatives: (1) $70 million (the net worth of the solvent MBanks the FDIC forced into insolvency); (2) $122 million (the capital of the banks); or (3) returned control over the seized banks and $327 million (the sum of loans owed to them). Shahram Victory, "Big Suits: South," *American Lawyer,* April 1991, p. 31. The federal regulators filed a motion to reconsider on 15 February. Rich Reecer, Brenda Sapino, and Mary Hull, "*MCorp and MCorp Financial Inc. v. Robert Logan Clarke, Comptroller of the Currency, et al.,*" *Texas Lawyer,* 25 February 1991, p. 20. Unsurprisingly, the company opted for the third plan, the most expensive for its government antagonists, but Judge Porter died on 6 November, before he could rule on the damages. "FDIC Nearly Shut Out in MCorp Suit," *Texas Lawyer,* 18 November 1991, p. 38.

280. Richard Connelly, "FDIC on Losing Streak in MCorp Litigation; Rulings and Retreats Cut $700 Million from Original Claims," *Texas Lawyer,* 24, June 1991, p. 7.

281. See Judge Hughes's rulings in *In re MCorp Financial, Inc., et al.* (S.D. Tex., 1992) Civ. A. No. H-90–2929. Judge Hughes was addressing the "adverse domination" rule, but his

ruling apparently conflicted with U.S. District Judge Sim Lake's holding in *FDIC v. Howse*, 736 F.Supp. 1437 (S.D. Tex., 1990). The Howse case impacted the S&L crisis.

282. *In re MCorp,* 160 Bankr. 941, at 945 (S.D. Tex., 1993), Houston Division, Civ. A. No. H-93–395.

283. But Judge Hughes dismissed the FDIC's claims for its losses sustained in litigation involving the banks it controlled. Richard Connelly, "FDIC on Losing Streak in MCorp Litigation; Rulings and Retreats Cut $700 Million from Original Claims," *Texas Lawyer,* 24 June 1991, p. 7. See Judge Hughes's rulings in *In re MCorp Financial, Inc., et al.* (S.D. Tex., 1992) Civ. A. No. H-90–2929.

284. *In re MCorp,* 160 Bankr. 941, at 946 (S.D. Tex., 1993); Houston Division, Civil Action No. H-93–395.

285. See Judge Hughes's rulings in *In re MCorp Financial, Inc., et al.* (S.D. Tex., 1992) Civ. A. No. H-90–2929. Also, "FDIC Nearly Shut Out in MCorp Suit," *Texas Lawyer,* 18 November 1991, p. 38. MCorp reportedly expected to spend $50 million to settle disputed claims and expenses, which would leave the company some $370 million to settle its remaining debt. "FDIC Loses Round in MCorp Bankruptcy," *National Law Journal,* 25 November 1991, p. 6. On 6 May 1992 the Fifth Circuit dismissed an appeal of Judge Hughes's actions. *In re MCorp,* 963 F.2d 369 (5th Cir., 1992), No. 91–2831 (dismissal of S.D. Tex., Houston Division, Civ. A. No. H-90–2929).

286. These oral presentations before the Supreme Court included extensive briefs prepared and released by U.S. Solicitor General Kenneth Starr. *Board of Governors of the Federal Reserve System v. MCorp,* 502 U.S. 32 (1991). One legal commentator noted that in addressing the Fed's "source of strength" regulation, the court would have to decide "whether it prefers good policy or good law," because from the perspective of corporate finance, the rule made "eminent sense." But the commentator noted that there may be constitutional problems with "imposing liability after the fact on shareholders who had no reason to expect that they might be assessed at the time they purchased stock." See Geoffrey Miller, "Dealing Down: Whether the Fed Can Compel Banks to Be the 'Source of Strength' for Troubled Subsidiaries Is a Top Draw for the Supreme Court," *Recorder,* 9 October 1991, p. 8; Geoffrey Miller, "Source-of-Strength Doctrine a Source of Trouble; Policy Forces Holding Company to Throw Good Money after Bad," *Connecticut Law Tribune,* 30 September 1991, p. 18; and Geoffrey Miller, "Source of Strength; A Source of Trouble," *Legal Times,* 30 September 1991, p. 22.

287. All members joined the ruling except Justice Clarence Thomas, who did not participate. *Board of Governors of the Federal Reserve System v. MCorp,* 502 U.S. 32, at 37–45 (1991). See "*Board of Governors of the Federal Reserve System v. MCorp,* 90–913 and 90–914," *National Law Journal,* 16 December 1991, p. 49; David Nadvorney, "District Court Couldn't Enjoin Federal Reserve Proceeding," *National Law Journal,* 23 December 1991, p. 40.

288. *Board of Governors of the Federal Reserve System v. MCorp,* 502 U.S. 32, at 39 (1991).

289. U.S.C. § 362(b)(4) provided: "The filing of a petition . . . or of an application . . . does not operate as a stay . . . of the commencement or continuation of an action or proceeding by a governmental unit to enforce such governmental unit's police or regulatory power." *Board of Governors of the Federal Reserve System v. MCorp,* 502 U.S. 32, at 40 (1991), esp. n. 10.

290. *Board of Governors of the Federal Reserve System v. MCorp,* 502 U.S. 32, at 42–45 (1991).

291. *MCorp v. Board of Governors of the Federal Reserve System*, 958 F.2d 615 (5th. Cir., 1992); No. 89–2816.

292. In April 1991 the Fifth Circuit heard oral arguments in an appeal of Northern District Chief Judge Barefoot Sanders's *Texas American Bancshares* (or TAB) decision. On 27 February 1992 a Fifth Circuit panel reversed Chief Judge Sanders's ruling that FDIC violated the National Bank Act by paying less for the claims of subsidiary banks of the (TAB) holding company than it paid to outside creditors. See *Texas American Bancshares, Inc. v. Clarke*, 954 F.2d 329 (5th Cir., 1992), No. 90–1674. According to the appellate judges, although the law had been enacted five months after the TAB (and MCorp) banks closed, FIRREA nonetheless authorized FDIC to treat some of those banks' creditors more favorably than others, without violating (or, in Judge Porter's words, "flouting") the National Bank Act. Lawyers for MCorp, who were preparing similar claims against FDIC for an April trial before Judge Hughes, scrambled to distinguish their case from the appellate ruling. On 3 March, MCorp lawyers hand-delivered a five-page letter to Hughes, requesting postponement of a hearing regarding cross-motions for partial summary judgment. The TAB decision may have derailed MCorp's attempt to translate the Dallas triumph before Judge Porter into a victory at the upcoming Houston trial. In light of the TAB decision, moreover, FDIC moved for a reconsideration on Porter's ruling. The late Judge Porter's successor, Judge Jorge A. Solis, had been waiting for the Fifth Circuit's decision in TAB before he made a move on the damages issue. Finally, although the circuit judges reached their decision in TAB without "setting foot into the legal quagmire of whether FIRREA applies retroactively," they also recognized that the result would be the same under the 1989 statute. Karen Donovan, "Fifth Circuit Ruling Throws Major Fly in MCorp Ointment," *National Law Journal*, 16 March 1992, p. 21.

293. The MCorp debtors filed their original proposed plans on 11 March 1991, a second set on 7 June, and a third on 11 September 1991. The debtors revised the third plans on 30 September 1991, and these were the plans presented for Judge Clark's review. *In re MCorp*, 137 Bankr. 219, at 221–23 (S.D. Tex., 1992), Bankruptcy Court, Houston Division, Case Nos. 89–02312-H3–11, 89–02324-H5–11, 89–02848-H2–11 (jointly administered under Case No. 89–02312-H3–11).

294. *In re MCorp*, 137 Bankr. 219, at 221 (S.D. Tex., 1992), Bankruptcy Court, Houston Division, Case Nos. 89–02312-H3–11, 89–02324-H5–11, 89–02848-H2–11 (jointly administered under Case No. 89–02312-H3–11).

295. Judge Clark was authorized to rule on reorganization plans under 28 U.S.C. §§ 1334 and 157, as well as a standing order in the Southern District of Texas (dated 9 August 1984). *In re MCorp*, 137 Bankr. 219, at 236 (S.D. Tex., 1992), Bankruptcy Court, Houston Division, Case Nos. 89–02312-H3–11, 89–02324-H5–11, 89–02848-H2–11 (jointly administered under Case No. 89–02312-H3–11). The bankruptcy judge concluded that the debtors failed to establish that their plan was in the best interest of the creditors. Among the other grounds for her denial were: (a) the requisite classes, such as outside debtors, had not accepted the plan; (b) the debtors failed to prove the value of their assets; and (c) a number of the proposed provisions violated the bankruptcy code. See *In re MCorp*, 139 Bankr. 820, at 821–24 (S.D. Tex., 1992), Houston Division, Civ. A. No. H-92–199. The same day, Clark rejected the motion of one of MCorp's creditors to change his negative vote on the proposed recovery plan. This creditor had filed a $207,196 claim against the holding company on 5 September 1989 but had not reached a settlement agreement with the company by 15 October 1991, when he voted to reject the plan. Later, the creditor came to an agreement and wanted to vote to accept the plan. Judge Clark noted that the timing of the change was "highly suspect, and the

evidence does not overcome the possibility of improper motivation." Therefore, she denied the motion, pursuant to Bankruptcy Rule 3018(a). *In re MCorp,* 137 Bankr. 237, at 239 (S.D. Tex., 1992), Bankruptcy Court, Houston Division, Case Nos. 89–02312-H3–11, 89–02324-H5–11, 89–02848-H2–11 (jointly administered under Case No. 89–02312-H3–11).

296. "MCorp Plan Rejected," *National Law Journal,* 20 January 1992, p. 19.

297. A district court has jurisdiction to hear appeals from the "final judgments, orders, and decrees, and with the leave of the court, from interlocutory orders and decrees, of bankruptcy judges entered in cases and proceedings referred to the bankruptcy judges." 28 U.S.C. §158(a). See *In re MCorp,* 139 Bankr. 820, at 821 (S.D. Tex., 1992), Houston Division, Civ. A. No. H-92–199. The creditors included employees, senior bondholders (who had a claim of approximately $354 million), other seniors (claimants with senior status seeking under $1 million), junior bondholders (those with a claim of approximately $134 million, whose notes were issued earlier than the senior bonds), and insurers. *In re MCorp,* 160 Bankr. 941, at 946 (S.D. Tex., 1993), Houston Division, Civ. A. No. H-93–395.

298. *In re MCorp,* 139 Bankr. 820, at 821 (S.D. Tex., 1992), Houston Division, Civ. A. No. H-92–199. Principal Mutual (PM) was an Iowa insurance company that became a mortgage lender to MCorp's now defunct landlord. PM became the landlord of the Mercantile Center, the complex of buildings that served as MCorp's Dallas headquarters. PM asserted claims of some $53 million. Shearson Lehman Hutton (Shearson) was the largest holder of MCorp money market preferred shares, the most senior class of equity. Shearson was entitled to a distribution from the estates after the junior bonds were paid. Shearson's claim is for $117.5 million. *In re MCorp,* 160 Bankr. 941, at 946 (S.D. Tex., 1993), Houston Division, Civ. A. No. H-93–395.

299. See 28 U.S.C. § 1292(b).

300. *In re MCorp,* 139 Bankr. 820, at 824 (S.D. Tex., 1992); Houston Division, Civ. A. No. H-92–199. Judge Hughes continued to hear cases related to the MCorp insolvency, but occasionally cases came before Hughes in which MCorp was creditor rather than the debtor. For example, on 4 August 1993 Judge Hughes ruled that a debtor cannot later litigate a claim that it should have raised in bankruptcy proceedings. In May 1987 Westland Oil Developing Corporation, an exploration company, owed MBank Houston over $17 million on two promissory notes. After defaulting on the notes, Westland met with three MBank officers to try to restructure the debt. Westland contended that they reached an oral agreement on 2 October 1987 but that MBank officers changed the terms of the agreement on 6 October, repudiating the earlier agreement. On 6 October, Westland filed for bankruptcy under chapter 11. Westland then sued MCorp Management Solutions, Inc. (MSI), for fraud and breach of contract based on the alleged repudiation of the oral agreement. But because Westland had not adequately disclosed its claim as an asset in its bankruptcy, Hughes barred the claim. *Westland Oil Development v. MCorp,* 157 Bankr. 100, at 104 (S.D. Tex., 1993), Houston Division, Civ. A. No. H-91–1608.

301. "MCorp Plan OK'd," *National Law Journal,* 18 October 1993, p. 17.

302. *In re MCorp,* 160 Bankr. 941, at 948 (S.D. Tex., 1993), Houston Division, Civ. A. No. H-93–395.

303. Ibid., 944.

304. Ibid., 945.

305. Ibid., 951.

306. *In re MCorp,* 160 Bankr. 941, at 957 (S.D. Tex., 1993); Houston Division, Civil Action No. H-93–395.

307. Ibid., 964.

308. Ibid., 964. MCorp's wrangling with the Fed, unprecedented when originally filed and unique in several of its more complicated and conspiratorial characteristics, nevertheless became an exemplar for the troubled banking industry in Texas. This proved to be a boon to the legal profession, as "boutique" law firms specializing in bankruptcy litigation emerged to compete with established firms, and all attempted to ride the wave of insolvencies to prosperity. For example, when FDIC indicated in spring 1992 that it was contemplating legal action against the former outside directors of MBank Dallas, the directors devised a list of firms to consider for the defense work, many with FDIC defense experience. The "Big League" list of finalists included Dallas's Strasburger and Price, Houston's Vinson and Elkins, and the Dallas office of New York's 634-lawyer Weil, Gotshal, and Manges. The directors then held a "beauty contest" by inviting the finalists to pitch their services. McKool Smith, a 17-lawyer Dallas litigation boutique formed in August 1991, won the "hotly contested" event. Miriam Rozen, "MCorp Contest Win Sweet for McKool Smith," *Texas Lawyer*, 13 April 1992, p. 1. See also "Corrections," *Texas Lawyer*, 20 April 1992, p. 1; and Miriam Rozen, "MBank's Beauty Contest: Who Won?" *American Lawyer*, May 1992, p. 26. Despite the difficulty of winning management malpractice cases, the former directors' insurers paid in excess of $39 million to settle potential claims against MBank Dallas officials by FDIC. *In re MCorp*, 160 Bankr. 941, at 951 (S.D. Tex., 1993), Houston Division, Civ. A. No. H-93–395. Under terms of the agreement, three insurance companies paid FDIC a total of $39.92 million to extinguish any potential claims against the former officers and directors arising from the 1989 failure of MBank Dallas. The FDIC had maintained that the twenty-six former officers and directors were liable for damages suffered by MBank Dallas, although no suit had been filed against them. The former officials included former Dallas Cowboys quarterback Roger Staubach, who had been an outside director of MBank Dallas. The officers and directors admitted no liability or wrongdoing, and the settlement agreement states that they settled "to avoid the uncertainty, trouble and expense of litigation." The agreement also releases from liability all other present or former officers and directors of the nineteen other MBanks in Texas that were closed by federal regulators in March 1989. Rich Reecer, "MBank-Dallas/FDIC Settlement," *Texas Lawyer*, 16 August 1993, p. 20. The settlement was similar to the one FDIC reached with officials of the former First Republic Bank, which resulted in the payment of $23 million. "Executives of Former Bank Reach Settlement," *Legal Intelligencer*, 9 August 1993, p. 5.

CHAPTER 8. Masters, Magistrates, and Managerial Judges

1. Citizens' committees were important tools of judicial management of school integration in the 1970s. During the 1980s judges vested more oversight responsibility in school cases to lay committees. Their members consulted with school boards, monitored progress or lack of it toward the establishment of a unitary system, and reported to the judge regarding compliance with court orders. The fact-gathering functions could have been undertaken by the plaintiffs or government intervenors. Federal district judges delegated monitoring responsibilities to the lay panels instead, in part because judges learned that resolution of the school desegregation controversy ultimately depended on gaining community support for court orders. See "Desegregation Suit Settled in Houston," *Washington Post*, 28 November 1984, A12; and: "HISD Freed from Desegregation Suit," UPI, 31 August 1989.

2. Cooper, *Hard Judicial Choices,* 209–23. See also Yarborough, *Johnson and Human Rights,* chap. 12.

3. See Martin and Ekland-Olson, *Texas Prisons,* generally.

4. Advisory Commission on Intergovernmental Relations, *Jails,* 146–47. See Resnik, "Managerial Judges," 386–87, 411–12.

5. Zeese, "Drug War Forever?" 252. Also see, generally, Marion, *Federal Crime Control Initiatives;* Johns, *War on Drugs;* and Bertram et al., *Drug War Politics.*

6. Pub. L. No. 99–570, 100 Stat. 3207–2; codified at: 21 U.S.C. 841(b)(1).

7. See Stith and Cabranes, *Fear of Judging,* 1–5, and generally; Tonry, *Sentencing Matters,* chap. 6; and Wicharaya, *Simple Theory.* The Speedy Trial Act of 1974, Pub. L. No. 93–619, 88 Stat. 2076; codified at 18 U.S.C. §§ 3161–74.

8. Beale, "Federalizing Crime," 48–49.

9. Administrative Office of the United States Courts, *Federal Court Management Statistics.*

10. Robert J. Pellicoro [chief, Clerks Division, Administrative Office of the U.S. Courts] to "All Clerks of United States District Courts, Subject: Caseload Projections," 13 May 1976, clerk's files of Chief Judge Reynaldo G. Garza, folder 1.

11. Chief Judge Garza to "Dear Mr. Bates, Re: Budgetary Needs for Our Court As per Your Letter of April, 30, 1976," 29 May 1976, V. Bailey Thomas to "Dear Judge Garza," 28 May 1976, clerk's files of Chief Judge Reynaldo G. Garza, folder 1.

12. Fisch, *All Rise,* 119–20, 130.

13. Under 18 U.S.C. § 3401.

14. Sear, "Supporting Personnel," 250–52.

15. The same author concluded that, given that few prosecutions and light sentences are no deterrent, U.S. attorneys gave "apparent low priority" to these immigration violations. In fiscal year 1972, for example, the INS arrested 505,949 aliens, of whom 430,213 were Mexican, and detected 433,082 prosecutable violations. Of these cases, the government closed 402,618 by general waiver, that is, probably by encouraging or allowing "voluntary departure." Only 30,464 cases were ever presented to federal attorneys, who then prosecuted only 13,060 and won convictions for 12,189. Toney, *Control of Illegal Mexican Migration,* 53–57, 73.

16. Congress established the office of United States magistrate in the Federal Magistrates Act of 1968, Pub. L. No. 90–578, 82 Stat. 1107 (codified as amended at 18 U.S.C. §§ 3401–2). Magistrates replaced the U.S. commissioners. Under the 1968 act a federal district judge may designate a magistrate to preside over certain pretrial hearings, to conduct evidentiary hearings and submit recommendations for disposition, and to serve as a special master. 28 U.S.C. §§ 631–39 (1982). Full-time magistrates are appointed for eight-year terms, and part-time magistrates are appointed only for four-year terms. Unlike federal district judges, magistrates are appointed not by the president with the advice and consent of the Senate, but by the judges of the district in which the magistrate will operate. They may also be removed by the district court judges whom they serve. Downs, "Boundaries of Article III," 1033.

17. *Trop v. Dulles,* 356 U.S. 86 (1958), 101.

18. With regard to the "hands off" doctrine, Hirschkop and Millemann wrote that the "simple failure of the courts to review prison conditions blunt[ed] the success of important constitutional inquiries, impede[d] the flow of information and encourage[d] abuse." Hirschkop and Millemann, "Prison Life," 837.

19. Bell, "Prisoners' Rights," 162–63. For the "hands off" doctrine in the Fifth Circuit, see

Startti v. Beto, 405 F.2d 858 (5th Cir., 1969). Some observers find it surprising that the retreat from hands-off is a legacy of the Burger court, known as generally more conservative on federal intervention than its predecessor, the Warren court. See Advisory Commission on Intergovernmental Relations, *Jails,* 144–45. However, William Turner, an attorney who specialized in assisting prisoners in their efforts to reform prison conditions through litigating, noted that the rise in section 1983 prisoner cases would not have occurred without the Warren court's decisions, including *Monroe v. Pape,* 365 U.S. 167 (1961), and the various criminal procedural decisions, such as *Miranda v. Arizona,* 384 U.S. 436 (1966), *Mapp v. Ohio,* 367 U.S. 643 (1961), and *Fay v. Noia,* 372 U.S. 391 (1963). Turner, "When Prisoners Sue," 629 (§ 1983 refers to the CRA of 1871, 42 U.S.C. § 1983).

20. *Jackson v. Godwin,* 400 F.2d 529 (5th Cir., 1968). Judge Hooper concurring, 544.

21. Turner, "When Prisoners Sue," 611.

22. Bell, "Prisoners' Rights," 165–66.

23. *Brooks v. Texas,* 371 F.2d 619 (5th Cir., 1967). See also *Hollins v. Beto,* 373 F.Supp. 1246 (S.D. Tex., 1974).

24. *Johnson v. Avery,* 393 U.S. 483 (1969). See also *Novak v. Beto,* 453 F.2d 661 (5th Cir., 1971); rehearing denied, 456 F.2d 1303 (5th Cir., 1972). In 1968 the court required desegregation of a prison. However, the justices acknowledged that security needs might limit the extent of the desegregation order. *Lee v. Washington,* 390 U.S. 333 (1968).

25. *Lamar v. Kern,* 349 F.Supp. 222 (S.D. Tex., 1972); *Guajardo v. McAdams,* 349 F.Supp. 211 (S.D. Tex., 1972); and *Baker v. Beto,* 349 F.Supp. 1263 (S.D. Tex., 1972). Martin and Ekland-Olson, *Texas Prisons,* 56. See also "Note: Prison Mail Censorship," 87. In a 1974 case concerning Nebraska prisons, the U.S. Supreme Court affirmed the power of federal district courts to review all of these matters, that is, prisoner complaints of discipline, court access, and abridged speech through censored mail. *Wolff v. McDonnell,* 418 U.S. 539 (1974), 574–78.

26. Turner, "When Prisoners Sue," 658, see app. A.

27. *Dreyer v. Jalet,* 349 F.Supp. 452 (S.D. Tex., 1972), 488. Prisoners did not only file civil rights suits. Many sought habeas corpus review in the federal courts. But the majority of inmate-initiated lawsuits were civil rights complaints. Their complaints made up 18 percent of all new civil actions filed nationwide in fiscal year 1970, when approximately sixteen thousand individual prisoners petitioned for some form of relief. Ibid., 485, esp. n. 15.

28. *Alberti v. Sheriff of Harris County,* 406 F.Supp. 649 (S.D. Tex., 1975), 678.

29. Among the listeners were Southern District judges Seals and Singleton, and their future colleague, state judge George Cire. "Too Many Inmates in Texas Prisons, Beto Says," Houston Chronicle, 7 March 1971.

30. *Dreyer v. Jalet,* 349 F.Supp. 452 (S.D. Tex., 1972), 475–76.

31. *Ruiz v. Estelle,* 503 F.Supp. 1265 (S.D. Tex., 1980). By 1992 there were more than fifty thousand inmates in Texas prisons. Frank R. Kemerer, "The Truth about Ruiz," *Texas Lawyer,* 5 October 1992, p. 16. For Judge Justice, see Kemerer, *William Wayne Justice,* chap. 15. Also see Feeley and Rubin, *Judicial Policy Making,* 80–85. Finally, see, generally, DiIulio, *Courts, Corrections, and the Constitution.*

32. Such an appointment would have been in accordance with the magistrate's act, 28 U.S.C. § 636(b)(2), the Federal Rules of Civil Procedure, Fed. R. Civ. P., Rule 53.

33. *Alberti v. Sheriff of Harris County,* 406 F.Supp. 649 (S.D. Tex., 1975), 678.

34. *Ruiz v. Estelle,* 503 F.Supp. 1265 (S.D. Tex., 1980). For Nathan, see Kemerer, *William Wayne Justice: A Judicial Biography,* 380.

35. Fed. R. Civ. P., Rule 53. I choose in the text to refer to master and ombudsman inter-

changeably. A judge might appoint a master rather than a lay panel in desegregation cases as well, but the judge usually empowered the master to act far beyond the fact-finding tasks of committees in school cases. See Kirp and Babcock, "Judge and Company," 313. As Charles Zelden has noted, dependence on community observers in school cases was similar to the judiciary's long-standing reliance on trustees or receivers in cases of bankruptcy. Zelden, "From Rights to Resources," 499–502.

36. Nathan, "The Use of Masters," 421.

37. See *Ruiz v. Estelle,* 679 F.2d 1115 (5th Cir., 1981), 1129.

38. "Note: 'Mastering' Intervention," 1068, 1084–85; Ware, "Federal Intervention," 943. In the 1980s Fiss argued that the "bureaucratizing" courts should curb their use of special masters for monitoring and enforcing judicial decisions in institutional litigation. Fiss, "Bureaucratization of the Judiciary," 1461–63.

39. Farrell, "Function and Legitimacy," 237. See also Farrell, "Coping with Scientific Evidence," 927.

40. *Dreyer v. Jalet,* 349 F.Supp. 452 (S.D. Tex., 1972), 468–69.

41. For writ writers and "jailhouse lawyers," see Turner, "When Prisoners Sue," 635.

42. *Dreyer v. Jalet,* 349 F.Supp., 471, 473.

43. Ibid., 469.

44. Ibid., 470.

45. Ibid., 471.

46. Ibid., 471–72. For Jalet's struggle with Beto and the TDC, see Feeley and Rubin, *Judicial Policy Making and the Modern State,* 80.

47. *Dreyer v. Jalet,* 349 F.Supp., 471 n. 6.

48. *Cruz v. Beto,* 405 U.S. 319 (1972).

49. *Dreyer v. Jalet,* 349 F.Supp., 456–57.

50. Ibid., 472.

51. Ibid., 458–60.

52. Ibid., 474.

53. Ibid., 460, 491.

54. Ibid., 475.

55. Ibid., 487.

56. Ibid., 491.

57. Ibid., 489–90.

58. Ibid., 491. In a July 1973 per curiam opinion, the Fifth Circuit affirmed Judge Bue's ruling. *Dreyer v. Jalet,* 479 F.2d 1044 (5th Cir., 1973).

59. *Alberti v. Klevenhagen,* 790 F.2d 1220 (5th Cir., 1986), 1225–26.

60. *Alberti v. Heard,* 600 F.Supp. 443 (S.D. Tex., 1984), 457.

61. Ibid., 457.

62. *Alberti v. Sheriff of Harris County,* 406 F.Supp. 649 (S.D. Tex., 1975), 654; *Alberti v. Klevenhagen,* 790 F.2d 1220 (5th Cir., 1986), 1222.

63. *Alberti v. Sheriff of Harris County,* 406 F.Supp. 649 (S.D. Tex., 1975), 654.

64. *Alberti v. Sheriff of Harris County,* 937 F.2d 984 (5th Cir., 1991), 987.

65. *Alberti v. Sheriff of Harris County,* 406 F.Supp. 649 (S.D. Tex., 1975), 655.

66. Ibid., 656, 678.

67. Ibid., 678. Also see *Alberti v. Klevenhagen,* 790 F.2d 1220 (5th Cir., 1986), 1231.

68. *Alberti v. Klevenhagen,* 1229.

69. Ibid., 1222.

70. Judge Carl Bue to "Dear Judge Connally," 1 August 1974, clerk's files of Chief Judge Ben C. Connally, folder 4.

71. *Cruz v. Estelle*, S.D. Tex., Houston Division, Civ. A. No. 70-H-1098. See Chief Judge Reynaldo G. Garza to "Gentlemen," 17 January 1975, clerk's files of Chief Judge Ben C. Connally, folder 4.

72. Pub. L. No. 94–559 (19 October 1976), amending 42 U.S.C. § 1988.

73. The language of the statute tracks the language of fee provisions in other civil rights statutes, including Title 7. CRA of 1964, 42 U.S.C. § 2000e-5(k).

74. *Cruz v. Beto*, 453 F.Supp. 905 (1977), 906, Houston Division, Civ. A. No. 71-H-1371.

75. *Alberti v. Sheriff of Harris County*, 937 F.2d 984 (5th Cir., 1991), 987. *Alberti v. Klevenhagen*, 606 F.Supp. 478 (S.D. Tex., 1985); *Alberti v. Heard*, 600 F.Supp. 443 (S.D. Tex., 1984).

76. UPI, 22 May 1982.

77. UPI, 21 March 1985.

78. *Alberti v. Klevenhagen*, 790 F.2d 1220 (5th Cir., 1986), 1230.

79. Ibid.

80. Ibid., 1231.

81. See *Miller v. Carson*, 563 F.2d 741 (5th Cir., 1977), 753. *Alberti v. Klevenhagen*, 790 F.2d, 1232, incl. n. 3.

82. *Alberti v. Klevenhagen*, 790 F.2d 1220 (5th Cir., 1986), 1231.

83. Ibid.

84. Deborah Tedford and Joe Stinebaker, "Federal Control over 4 County Jails at End," Houston Chronicle, 10 August 1995, 1A.

85. *Alberti v. Klevenhagen*, 660 F. Supp. 605 (S.D. Tex.1987).

86. Jerry Urban, Clay Robison, and Lisa Teachey, "Judge Reaffirms Fines Against State over Jail Crowding," *Houston Chronicle*, 24 March 1993, 17A.

87. Deborah Tedford and Joe Stinebaker, "Federal Control over 4 County Jails at End," *Houston Chronicle*, 10 August 1995, 1A.

88. See Kemerer, *William Wayne Justice*, chap. 15.

89. Deborah Tedford and Joe Stinebaker, "Federal Control over 4 County Jails at End," Houston Chronicle, 10 August 1995, 1A.

90. Under 28 U.S.C. §§ 2254 and 2255.

91. The 1976 amendment is Pub. L. No. 94–577, 90 Stat. 2729. See Fed. R. Civ. P., Rule 73, which authorizes federal district judges to refer cases to magistrates in accordance with 28 U.S.C. § 636(c). According to Anthony Downs, once a case is delegated to a magistrate, only two elements distinguish the magistrate from the federal judge. First, the magistrate does not have the power to punish for civil or criminal contempt. Second, the case before the magistrate may be removed to the district court upon motion of the court or "under extraordinary circumstances shown by any party." See 28 U.S.C. § 636(c)(6)-(e).

92. The Federal Magistrate Act of 1979 is Pub. L. No. 96–82, 93 Stat. 643 (codified at 28 U.S.C. §§ 631–39). Although the magistrates exercised authority similar to that of federal judges, they did and do not have tenure or salary protections under the U.S. Constitution's Article III. Magistrates are appointed for limited terms by the federal district judges whom they serve. Full-time magistrates are appointed for eight-year terms; part-time magistrates only for four-year terms. A statute protects salaries from diminution during their terms, but no provision in the Constitution prevents Congress from eliminating this protection. Compare the description of magistrates in 28 U.S.C. §§ 631–34 with that of federal district

judges in 28 U.S.C. § 133. Downs, "Boundaries of Article III," 1032–33. Also, "Note: Article III Constraints," 1023.

93. Sear, "Supporting Personnel," 13–18 September 1976, Washington, D.C., 75 F.R.D. 89 (1977), at 237, 250–52. For example, when in October 1979 U.S. Attorney Tony Canales indicted four former Houston police officers for depriving Joe Torres of his civil rights by causing his death by drowning, the officers immediately went before Norman W. Black, one of the U.S. magistrate judges in the Southern District of Texas. Black scheduled their arraignment, set their bond at ten thousand dollars each, and released them. A fifth officer implicated in Torres's death had testified before the federal grand jury and had agreed to testify for the prosecution in the trial. As part of a plea bargain with the U.S. attorney's office, this defendant admitted that he had conspired with the other officers to violate Torres's civil rights. He went before U.S. Magistrate Judge H. Lingo Platter to plead guilty to a misdemeanor violation of the federal criminal civil rights statute. Platter released him on personal recognizance. Pete Wittenberg, "Federal Jury Indicts 4 Former Officers: Fifth Ex-officer in Torres Case Pleads Guilty to Misdemeanor," Houston Post, 21 October 1977, 1A.

94. The 1976 amendments to the magistrates' statutory authority was partly a response to the Supreme Court's decision in *Wingo v. Wedding*, 418 U.S. 461 (1974), which interpreted the statute to bar a magistrate from rendering decisions on habeas corpus petitions. In 1980 the Supreme Court upheld Congress's delegation to magistrates of some judicial authority under the 1976 Magistrates Act. *United States v. Raddatz*, 447 U.S. 667 (1980), 682–83. Since, federal courts of appeals have ruled that the delegation of final decision-making powers to magistrates is consistent with Article III. The Fifth Circuit upheld this delegation in *Puryear v. Ede's Ltd.*, 731 F.2d 1153 (5th Cir., 1984). Downs, "Boundaries of Article III," at 1033–34. See Smith, "Who Are the United States Magistrates?" 143; Seron, *The Roles of Magistrates;* and Smith, *Magistrates in the Federal Courts.*

95. Chief Judge Garza to "My Dear Carl," 10 September 1976, V. Bailey Thomas to "Dear Judge Garza," 10 September 1976, Chief Judge Garza to "Dear Magistrates," 8 November 1976, V. Bailey Thomas, "Processing of 1983 Prisoner Complaints," 11 November 1976, clerk's files of Chief Judge Reynaldo G. Garza, folder 2.

96. Under the court's general order and local rules, any party to the case could within ten days file a written objection to a magistrate's proposed findings, recommendations, or report. Chief Judge Singleton, "General Order No. 80–5: In the Matter of Jurisdiction and Procedures for United States Magistrates for the Southern District of Texas," 16 June 1980, clerk's files of Chief Judge John V. Singleton, folder 11.

97. Clerk Jesse E. Clark to "Dear Chief Judge Singleton, Re: General Order No. 80–5," 26 November 1985, clerk's files of Chief Judge John V. Singleton, folder 11.

98. Chief Judge Singleton to "My Dear Judges," 27 August 1981, clerk's files of Chief Judge John V. Singleton, folder 4.

99. Chief Judge Singleton, "General Order 82–4, Re: Assignment, Consolidation, and Transfer of Prisoner Litigation," 29 March 1982, clerk's files of Chief Judge John V. Singleton, folder 6.

100. Chief Judge Singleton to "Mesdames and Gentlemen," 19 November 1982, clerk's files of Chief Judge John V. Singleton, folder 6. See also Clerk Jesse E. Clark to "Dear Judge Singleton," 18 November 1982 clerk's files of Chief Judge John V. Singleton, folder 6.

101. H. Lingo Platter [U.S. magistrate] to "Dear Judge," 14 September 1983, clerk's files of Chief Judge James DeAnda, folder 1.

102. Chief Judge Singleton to "Dear Mr. Pellicoro," 27 September 1984, clerk's files of Chief Judge John V. Singleton, folder 8.

103. Chief Judge Singleton to "Dear Mr. Pellicoro," 27 September 1984, clerk's files of Chief Judge John V. Singleton, folder 8. See also Administrative Office of the United States Courts to "Chief Judge, United States Court of Appeals for the Fifth Circuit [and] Chief Judges, United States District Courts for the Southern Districts of Mississippi and Texas, Subject: Survey Reports on Magistrate Positions," 28 October 1985, and Jesse E. Clark [clerk] to "Dear Chief Judge Singleton," 7 November 1985, clerk's files of Chief Judge John V. Singleton, folder 11.

104. See Houston Magistrates to "Judge DeAnda, Subject: Prisoner 1983 Cases," 25 July 1986, clerk's files of Chief Judge James DeAnda, folder 2.

105. Judge DeAnda to "Dear John," 1 October 1986, clerk's files of Chief Judge James DeAnda, folder 2.

106. Judge DeAnda to "Dear John," 1 October 1986, clerk's files of Chief Judge James DeAnda, folder 2.

107. Judge DeAnda to "Dear John," 1 October 1986, clerk's files of Chief Judge James DeAnda, folder 2.

108. Chief Judge Singleton to "Dear Chief Judge Clark, Re: District Guidelines to Process Prisoner Litigation," 16 December 1986, clerk's files of Chief Judge John V. Singleton, folder 13.

109. Ibid.

110. Judge DeAnda to "Dear Judge Singleton," 28 April 1987, clerk's files of Chief Judge James DeAnda, folder 2. Also, Chief Judge Singleton to "Dear Fellow Judges," 25 February 1987, clerk's files of Chief Judge John V. Singleton, folder 14.

111. Judge DeAnda to "Dear John, Re: 1983 Prisoner Civil Rights Docket," 3 November 1987, clerk's files of Chief Judge James DeAnda, folder 2.

112. Chief Judge DeAnda to "Dear Wayne, Re: Assignment of Eastern District Magistrates," 16 June 1988, William Wayne Justice to "Dear Jim, Re: Eastern District of Texas Civil Rights Cases Filed by T.D.C. Inmate-Plaintiffs Confined in Southern District of Texas," 10 June 1988, clerk's files of Chief Judge James DeAnda, folder 2.

113. Lyles, *Gatekeepers,* 129–44. In February 1986 Reagan formally abolished the independent nominating committees that had been created by President Carter to vet judicial candidates. Executive Order No. 12553, 51 F.R. 7237.

114. U.S. Department of Justice, Office of Legal Policy, "Guidelines on Constitutional Litigation," 19 February 1988, pp. 10, 121, 118. For changes in Justice Department policy under Ronald Reagan, see also Baker, "Attorney General as a Legal Policy-maker," 45–48; and Baker, *Conflicting Loyalties,* 95–98. The Reagan administration's determination to restrain government "activism" frustrated would-be civil rights claimants. The Justice Department was the only federal agency empowered by the 1972 Equal Employment Opportunity Act to sue employers that are governments, governmental agencies, or political subdivisions (Pub. L. No. 92–261, § 4, 86 Stat. 103; codified at 42 U.S.C. § 2000). Days, "In Honor of *Brown v. Board of Education,*" 991–94.

115. Pete Yost, "Meese Says Drugs Crossing Southwest Border with Illegal Aliens," AP, 17 September 1986. Also see Merrill Hartson, "INS Posts Record Number of Border Interceptions," AP, 10 October 1985.

116. Barry, Browne, and Sims, *The Great Divide,* 42–46, 65–68; Behdad, "INS and Outs," 103–4; and Mary Thornton, "INS Being Thrust into Crime-Fighting Role; Internal Report

Says Illegal Activities by Aliens 'Appear to Be Escalating Dramatically,' " Washington Post, 28 January 1987, A4.

117. U.S.C. § 1385.

118. U.S.C. §§ 371–78. The Department of Defense has provided airplanes, helicopters, and other equipment to civilian agencies, and the navy has used sophisticated radar to patrol coastal areas. Brickey, "Criminal Mischief," 1151–52. These efforts culminated in the posses establishment in 1986 of the Joint Task Force Six (JTF-6) under Operation Alliance. Barry, Browne, and Sims, *The Great Divide*, 75–79.

119. Dunn, *Militarization of the U.S.-Mexico Border*, 80–83.

120. Act of 8 November 1984, 98 Stat. 3362.

121. Pub. L. No. 99–570, 100 Stat. 3207–2; codified at 21 U.S.C. § 841(b)(1).

122. Stith and Cabranes, *Fear of Judging*, 6–8.

123. Pub. L. No. 99–570, 100 Stat. 3207 (1986) (codified as amended at 21 U.S.C. §§ 801–971). Congress imposed, for example, mandatory minimum sentences for simple possession. See 21 U.S.C. 844(a).

124. U.S.C. 841(b)(1)(B). The maximum term for this offense is forty years.

125. (b)(1)(A). The maximum sentence for these offenses is life imprisonment. In both instances the mandatory minimum is raised to twenty years if death or bodily injury ensues. These mandatory penalties for first-time drug offenders were more severe than "sentences typically meted out to first-time robbers or rapists." Wisotsky, "Crackdown," 904.

126. U.S.C. 841(b)(1)(a).

127. *United States v. Victor Ayala-Gonzalez*, 1987 U.S. Dist. LEXIS 12787 (S.D. Tex., 1987), Crim. No. L-87–204.

128. *United States v. Victor Ayala-Gonzalez*, 1987 U.S. Dist. LEXIS 12787 (S.D. Tex., 1987); Crim. No. L-87–204.

129. Judge George P. Kazen to "Dear Jim," 7 December 1990, clerk's files of Chief Judge James DeAnda, folder 7.

130. Brickey, "Criminal Mischief," 1155. Mandatory minimums and especially the sentencing guidelines established by the 1984 Comprehensive Crime Control Act were never popular with judges. Some judges felt the guidelines forced them to make decisions on prison sentences without considering other solutions such as fines. W. John Moore, "Courting Disaster," *National Journal*, 3 March 1990, p. 502.

131. Brickey, "Criminal Mischief," 1153.

132. Ann Pelham, "Just Saying 'No' to Federal Drug War," *Legal Times*, 6 November 1989, p. 7.

133. Mark Ballard, "Oncken's Stormy Tenure Enters Final Chapter," *Texas Lawyer*, 2 April 1990, p. 1.

134. Robert Elder Jr., "Congress Catches Heat for Federal Court Woes; Texas Districts Want More Money, Less Meddling," *Texas Lawyer*, 27 January 1992, p. 4. Ann Pelham, "Just Saying 'No' To Federal Drug War," *Legal Times*, 6 November 1989, p. 7. Moore, "Courting Disaster." Ann Pelham and Richard Connelly, "U.S. Judges Oppose Federal Day Measure; Biden Proposes Shifting Drug Cases from State Courts," *Texas Lawyer*, 28 May 1990, p. 12. Mark Ballard, "Bill to Add U.S. Judges Shortchanges Texas by 6; Legislation Would Add 3 New Courts in Southern District, 1 in Western," *Texas Lawyer*, 18 June 1990, p. 4.

135. Mark Obbie, "Federal Judges Say Job No Picnic: Too Many Cases, Too Little Pay, So Much Scrutiny," *Houston Post*, 5 January 1986, 1A, 18A.

136. Ballard, "Oncken's Stormy Tenure Enters Final Chapter."

137. Jesse E. Clark [clerk] to "Hon. James DeAnda," 13 December 1988, clerk's files of Chief Judge James DeAnda, folder 3. See also Jesse E. Clark [clerk] to "Dear Senator Bentsen," 30 June 1989, and Chief Judge James DeAnda to "Dear Judge Clark," 29 November 1990, clerk's files of Chief Judge James DeAnda, folder 7. Ann Pelham, "Just Saying 'No' To Federal Drug War," *Legal Times*, 6 November 1989, p. 7. Moore, "Courting Disaster." Ann Pelham and Richard Connelly, "U.S. Judges Oppose Federal Day Measure; Biden Proposes Shifting Drug Cases from State Courts," *Texas Lawyer*, 28 May 1990, p. 12. Mark Ballard, "Bill to Add U.S. Judges Shortchanges Texas by 6; Legislation Would Add 3 New Courts in Southern District, 1 in Western," *Texas Lawyer*, 18 June 1990, p. 4.

138. Mark Ballard, "Secret Interviews Begin Search to Replace Oncken; Gramm Committee Examines Applicants' Management Styles," *Texas Lawyer*, 28 May 1990, p. 4.

139. Ibid.

140. Gary Taylor, "A Departure?" *National Law Journal*, 14 March 1988, p. 2. Judge McDonald later joined the international criminal court at the Hague. See also W.H., "Judging Tadic," *American Lawyer*, September 1995, 62.

141. "Hoyt," in *Judges of the United States*.

142. Chief Judge DeAnda to "Dear Mr. Clark," 17 June 1988, clerk's files of Chief Judge James DeAnda, folder 2. Jesse E. Clark to "Honorable Chief Judge James DeAnda, Subject: Meeting of Active Houston Judges, July 20, 1988, at 3:00 p.m.," 20 July 1988, Jesse E. Clark to "Dear Chief Judge DeAnda, Re: Procedures for the Management of the McDonald Docket," 13 July 1988, Jesse E. Clark to "Dear Chief Judge DeAnda," 20 August 1988, Chief Judge DeAnda to "Mr. Jesse Clark, Clerk," 10 August 1988, Jesse E. Clark to "Dear Chief Judge DeAnda, Re: Revised Distribution of Work Order," 20 August 1988, clerk's files of Chief Judge James DeAnda, folder 3.

143. "Lake," in *Judges of the United States*.

144. "Harmon," in *Judges of the United States*.

145. "Kent," in *Judges of the United States*.

146. "Rainey," in *Judges of the United States*.

147. Ballard, "Secret Interviews Begin Search to Replace Oncken."

148. Woods was appointed as the temporary replacement but was subsequently confirmed for a full term in the office. "Woods Now Temporary U.S. Attorney," *Texas Lawyer*, 26 November 1990, p. 6.

149. Even in that area, however, Woods was more selective than some U.S. attorney's offices. See Calavita, Pontell, and Tillman, *Big Money Crime*, 223–24 n. 17.

150. Hughes, "Don't Make a Federal Case Out of It," 156.

151. The other four HIDTAS were centered on large cities: Houston, New York City, Miami, and Los Angeles. Remarks of Senator Dennis DeConcini (D.-Ariz.), 30 July 1990, Phoenix, Arizona, hearing before the Subcommittee on Treasury, Postal Service, and General Government, Committee on Appropriations. U.S. Senate, Committee on Appropriations, 101st Congress, 2d Session, S. Hrg. 101–1109. The hearing proceedings were published as *Southwest Border High-Intensity Drug Trafficking Designation*.

152. See Jesse E. Clark [clerk] to "All U.S. District Judges," 16 November 1990, Clark to "Chief Judge James DeAnda, Re: Case Assignment," 15 April 1991, Clark to "Dear Chief Judge DeAnda," 13 June 1990, clerk's files of Chief Judge James DeAnda, folder 7.

153. Office of National Drug Control Policy, National Drug Control Strategy, app. A, 131–36. Dunn, *The Militarization of the U.S.-Mexico Border*, 52–61. Also see Mike Glenn, "Laredo

Patrol Welcomes Military, but Some Residents Say It's Too Much," Houston Chronicle, 3 September 2000, 1A, 20A.

154. See "Border Control—Revised Strategy Is Showing Some Positive Results," U.S. House of Representatives, Report to the Chairman, Subcommittee on Information, Justice, Transportation and Agriculture, Committee on Government Operations (December 1994).

155. "Prepared Statement of Mary Lee Warren, Deputy Assistant Attorney General, Criminal Division, Department of Justice, before the House Appropriations Committee, Subcommittee for Commerce, State, Justice, and the Judiciary," Federal News Service, 19 March 1997.

156. Statement of Gus de la Vina, 27 April 1999, p. 12, in hearing before the Subcommittee on Immigration, Committee on the Judiciary. U.S. Senate, Committee on the Judiciary, 106th Congress, 1st Session, S. Hrg. 106–441. The hearing proceedings were published as *The Need for Additional Border Patrol.*

157. See Brookings Institution, *Immigration in U.S.-Mexican Relations.*

158. P.L. 103–322, § 130006, 108 Stat. 1796, 2028 (1994), 2029.

159. Departments of Commerce, Justice, and State, the Judiciary, and Related Agencies 1995 Appropriations and 1994 Supplemental Appropriations Act, P.L. 103–317; H.R. 103–708, 103rd Cong., 2d sess. (1994). The 1995 Appropriations Act provided the INS $54.5 million to hire 700 new Border Patrol agents, to redirect 250 agents, and to fund 110 support staff for the agents. The act included $154.6 million for automation, communications, and other technologies to enable agents to spend less time on administrative activities, such as preparing arrest reports.

160. P.L. 104–208, § 107 (1996).

161. Andrea, "Escalation of U.S. Immigration Control," 593. Barry, Browne, and Sims, *The Great Divide,* 46–48, 69–71.

162. Richard Connelly, "Slow Motions," *Texas Lawyer,* 18 November 1996, p. 1. See also Sue Anne Pressley, "Cases Pile Up As Judgeships Remain Vacant; Drug Crackdown, Immigration Inundate U.S. Courts in Texas," *Washington Post,* 15 May 1997, p. A1.

163. Richard Connelly, "The Next Wave," *Texas Lawyer,* 18 November 1996, p. 1.

CONCLUSION: Just, Speedy, and Inexpensive Resolutions

1. The quoted passage referred to the circuit courts of appeals, but the point is also relevant to the business of federal district courts. Frankfurter and Landis, *Business of the Supreme Court,* 11.

2. Fiss, "Bureaucratization of the Judiciary," 1442.

3. Most studies note the increase during the twentieth century of the administrative complexity of the federal courts. On the specifics of administrative developments in the years since those studies, see the extended essay by Chandler, "Some Major Advances," and the abbreviated essay by Jones, "Future of the Federal Courts," 17–20, 44–45.

4. Cover, "Origins of Judicial Activism," 1314.

5. Federal judges continued to be involved in redistricting, insofar as they review voter districts for compliance with voting rights laws, but the courts maintain no continual oversight of the electoral process. See, generally, Davidson, "The Voting Rights Act," 34–35; and Scher, Mills, and Hotaling, *Voting Rights and Democracy,* 26–29.

6. Berger, *Government by Judiciary.*

7. *Alberti v. Klevenhagen,* 790 F.2d 1220 (5th Cir., 1986). Judge Brown concurring, 1231.

8. Rehnquist, quoted from his annual report on the federal judiciary (issued on 1 January 1990), in Moore, "Courting Disaster."

9. Little, "Principles of Federalization," 1037. Transcript, National Public Radio, *All Things Considered,* Robert Siegel, host, Nina Totenberg reporting, "Rehnquist against Making Crimes Federal," 4 February 1992.

10. Ann Pelham and Richard Connelly, "U.S. Judges Oppose Federal Day Measure; Biden Proposes Shifting Drug Cases from State Courts," *Texas Lawyer,* 28 May 1990, p. 12. Jesse E. Clark [clerk] to "Dear Judge DeAnda," 9 May 1991, clerk's files of Chief Judge James DeAnda, folder 8. See also Mark Ballard, "In Session: Fed's Big Fish Might Be Small-Time Dealers to State," *Texas Lawyer,* 8 July 8 1996, p. 2.

11. Jesse E. Clark [clerk] to "Dear Chief Judge DeAnda," 13 June 1990, clerk's files of Chief Judge James DeAnda, folder 7.

12. U.S.C. § 471 (1990).

13. Jim Zook, "Civil Case Study Aims at Backlog," *Houston Chronicle,* 14 November 1991, p. A31.

14. U.S.C. § 631. See Smith, "From U.S. Magistrates to U.S. Magistrate Judges," 210–15. But, also see Baum, "Specializing the Federal Courts," 217–24. For a review of cases regarding the limits of magistrates' role, see "A Constitutional Analysis of Magistrate Judge Authority," 150 F.R.D. 247 (1993).

15. Robert Elder Jr., "Congress Catches Heat for Federal Court Woes; Texas Districts Want More Money, Less Meddling," *Texas Lawyer,* 27 January 1992, p. 4.

16. Moore, "Courting Disaster."

17. Mary Pat Flaherty and Joan Biskupic, "Prosecutors Can Stack the Deck; Sentencing Powers Shift from Judges," *Washington Post,* 7 October 1996, p. A1.

18. Ibid.

19. Richard Connelly, "The Next Wave," *Texas Lawyer,* 18 November 1996, p. 1.

20. Hughes, "Don't Make a Federal Case Out of It," 161.

21. See Nagel, "Separation of Powers," 661; and Fletcher, "The Discretionary Constitution," 635. The irony was borne out by the increasing criticism of prosecutors. Mark Ballard, "In the Line of Fire: Federal Prosecutors Can No Longer Operate with Virtual Impunity. They Are Taking Hits from the Bench, Their Courthouse Opponents and the Justice Department," *Texas Lawyer,* 5 February 1996, p. 1.

22. Chief Judge DeAnda to "Dear Mr. Cook, Attention: Judgeship Survey," 7 October 1991, clerk's files of Chief Judge James DeAnda, folder 9.

23. Senator Joseph R. Biden Jr. to "Dear Chief Judge DeAnda," 22 June 1992, clerk's files of Chief Judge James DeAnda, folder 9. Chief Judge [Western District] Lucius D. Bunton to "Dear Judge DeAnda/Jim," 24 January 1992, clerk's files of Chief Judge James DeAnda, folder 9. Chief Judge DeAnda to "Dear Senator Biden," 19 March 1992, clerk's files of Chief Judge James DeAnda, folder 9. DeAnda to "Dear Ms. Comberrel," 21 February 1992, clerk's files of Chief Judge James DeAnda, folder 9.

24. Jerry Urban, "Bentsen to Play Role in 12 Judgeships," *Houston Chronicle,* 26 November 1992, A43.

25. Ibid.

Selected Bibliography

MANUSCRIPT COLLECTIONS

Bue, Carl O., Jr., U.S. District Judge. Papers. Houston Metropolitan Research Center.

Seals, Woodrow B., U.S. District Judge. Papers. Houston Metropolitan Research Center.

Singleton, John V., U.S. District Judge. Papers. Held by John V. Singleton.

U.S. District Court, Southern District of Texas. Case files. Record Group 21. National Archives and Records Administration–Southwest Regional Archives, Fort Worth, Tex.

———. Clerk's files of chief judges. Office of the Clerk of the Court, U.S. District Court, Southern District of Texas.

PUBLISHED SOURCES

Abraham, Henry J. *The Judicial Process: An Introductory Analysis of the Courts of the United States, England, and France.* 7th ed. New York: Oxford University Press, 1998.

Abrams, Norman. "Internal Policy: Guiding the Exercise of Prosecutorial Discretion." UCLA *Law Review* 19 (1971).

Ackerman, Bruce. "Law and the Modern Mind." *Daedalus* 103 (1974).

Adams, James Ring. *The Big Fix—Inside the S&L Scandal: How an Unholy Alliance of Politics and Money Destroyed America's Banking System.* New York: John Wiley and Sons, 1990.

Allen, Kevin J. "Investigation and Police Practices: Overview of the Fourth Amendment." *Georgetown Law Journal* 88 (May 2000).

Allsup, Carl. *The American GI Forum: Origins and Evolution.* Austin, Tex.: Center for Mexican American Studies, 1982.

Alschuler, Albert W. "The Defense Attorney's Role in Plea Bargaining." *Yale Law Journal* 84 (1975).

———. "The Prosecutor's Role in Plea Bargaining." *University of Chicago Law Review* 36 (1968).

———. "The Trial Judge's Role in Plea Bargaining, Part I." *Columbia Law Review* 76 (1976).

Amar, Akhil Reed. *The Constitution and Criminal Procedure: First Principles.* New Haven: Yale University Press, 1997.

Amsterdam, Anthony G. "Criminal Prosecutions Affecting Federally Guaranteed Civil Rights: Federal Removal and Habeas Corpus Jurisdiction to Abort State Court Trial." *University of Pennsylvania Law Review* 113 (1965).

Andreas, Peter. "The Escalation of U.S. Immigration Control in the Post-NAFTA Era." *Political Science Quarterly* 113 (1998–99).

Bailey, Richard. "The Starr County Strike." *Red River Valley Historical Review* 4 (1979).

Baird, Bryce M. "Federal Court Abstention in Civil Rights Cases: Chief Justice Rehnquist and the New Doctrine of Civil Rights Abstention." *Buffalo Law Review* 42 (1994).

Baird, Robert M., and Stuart E. Rosenbaum, eds. *Pornography: Private Right or Public Menace?* Buffalo: Prometheus Books, 1991.

Baker, Liva. *Miranda: Crime, Law, and Politics.* New York: Atheneum, 1983.

Baker, Nancy C. "The Attorney General as a Legal Policy-Maker: Conflicting Loyalties." In *Government Lawyers: The Federal Legal Bureaucracy and Presidential Politics,* edited by Cornell W. Clayton. Lawrence: University Press of Kansas, 1995.

———. *Conflicting Loyalties: Law and Politics in the Attorney General's Office, 1789–1990.* Lawrence: University Press of Kansas, 1992.

Balderston, Frederick E. *Thrifts in Crisis: Structural Transformation of the Savings and Loan Industry.* Cambridge, Mass.: Ballinger, 1985.

Barbaro, Fred. "Ethnic Resentment." In *Black/Brown/White Relations: Race Relations in the 1970s,* edited by Charles V. Willie. New Brunswick, N.J.: Transaction Books, 1977.

Barr, Alwyn. *Black Texans: A History of African Americans in Texas, 1528–1995.* 2d ed. Norman: University of Oklahoma Press, 1996.

Barrow, Deborah J., and Thomas G. Walker. *A Court Divided: The Fifth Circuit Court of Appeals and the Politics of Judicial Reform.* New Haven: Yale University Press, 1988.

Barry, Tom, Harry Browne, and Beth Sims. *The Great Divide: The Challenge of U.S.-Mexico Relations in the 1990s.* New York: Grove Press, 1994.

Barth, James R. *The Great Savings and Loan Debacle.* Washington, D.C.: AEI Press, 1991.

Bass, Jack. "Faces Turned to the Future." *Houston Law Review* 34 (1998).

———. *Unlikely Heroes: The Dramatic Story of the Southern Judges of the Fifth Circuit Who Translated the Supreme Court's "Brown" Decision into a Revolution for Equality.* New York: Simon and Schuster, 1981.

Bator, Paul, Daniel Meltzer, Paul Mishkin, and David Shapiro, eds. *Hart and Wechsler's "The Federal Courts and the Federal System."* 2d ed. Westbury, N.Y.: Foundation Press, 1973.

———. *Hart and Wechsler's "The Federal Courts and the Federal System."* 3d ed. Westbury, N.Y.: Foundation Press, 1988.

Baum, Lawrence. "Specializing the Federal Courts: Neutral Reforms or Efforts to Shape Judicial Policy?" *Judicature* 74 (December–January 1991).

Beale, Sara Sun. "Federalizing Crime: Assessing the Impact on the Federal Courts." In *The Federal Role in Criminal Law,* edited by James A. Strazzella. Thousand Oaks, Calif.: Sage, 1996.

Becker, Howard S. "History, Culture, and Subjective Experience: An Exploration of the Social Bases of Drug-Induced Experiences." *Journal of Health and Social Behavior* 8 (1967).

Beer, Peter. "Keeping Up with the Jones Act." *Tulane Law Review* 61 (1986).

Beeth, Howard, and Cary D. Wintz, eds. *Black Dixie: Afro-Texan History and Culture in Houston.* College Station: Texas A&M University Press, 1992.

Behdad, Ali. "INS and Outs: Producing Delinquency at the Border." *Aztlán* 23 (Spring 1998).

Belknap, Michal R. *Federal Law and Southern Order: Racial Violence and Constitutional Conflict in the Post-"Brown" South.* Athens: University of Georgia Press, 1995.

———. *To Improve the Administration of Justice: A History of the American Judicature Society.* Chicago: American Judicature Society, 1992.

Bell, Barry R. "Note: Prisoners' Rights, Institutional Needs, and the Burger Court." *Virginia Law Review* 72 (1986).

Bell, Derrick A., Jr. "*Brown v. Board of Education* and the Interest-Convergence Dilemma." *Harvard Law Review* 93 (1980).

Benston, George J. *An Analysis of the Causes of Savings and Loan Association Failures.* New York: Salomon Brothers Center for the Study of Financial Institutions, 1986.

Berger, Raoul. *Government by Judiciary: The Transformation of the Fourteenth Amendment.* 2d ed., with a foreword by Forrest McDonald. Indianapolis: Liberty Fund, 1997.

Berki, R. N. "Marcuse and the Crisis of the New Radicalism: From Politics to Religion." *Journal of Politics* 34 (1972).

Bermant, Gordon, and Russell R. Wheeler. "Federal Judges and the Judicial Branch: Their Independence and Accountability." *Mercer Law Review* 46 (1995).

Bernard, Richard M., and Bradley R. Rice, eds. *Sunbelt Cities: Politics and Growth since World War II.* Austin: University of Texas Press, 1983.

Bertram, Eva, Morris Blachman, Kenneth Sharpe, and Peter Andreas. *Drug War Politics: The Price of Denial.* Berkeley and Los Angeles: University of California Press, 1996.

Bickel, Alexander M. *The Least Dangerous Branch: The Supreme Court at the Bar of Politics.* Indianapolis: Bobbs-Merrill, 1962.

Birnberg, Gerald M. "Notes: *Brown v Board of Education* Applies to Mexican-American Students and Any Other Readily Identifiable Ethnic-Minority Group or Class." *Texas Law Review* 49 (1971).

Blackmun, Harry A. "Section 1983 and Federal Protection of Individual Rights—Will the Statute Remain Alive or Fade Away?" In *The Evolving Constitution: Essays on the Bill of Rights and the U.S. Supreme Court,* edited by Norman Dorsen. Middletown, Conn.: Wesleyan University Press, 1987.

Blasi, Vincent, ed. *The Burger Court: The Revolution That Wasn't.* New Haven: Yale University Press, 1983.

Blum, Karen M., and Kathryn R. Urbonya. *Section 1983 Litigation.* Washington, D.C.: Federal Judicial Center, 1998.

Blumberg, Rhoda Lois. *Civil Rights: The 1960s Freedom Struggle.* Rev. ed. Boston: Twayne, 1991.

Bodenhamer, David J., and James W. Ely Jr., eds. *Ambivalent Legacy: A Legal History of the South.* Jackson: University Press of Mississippi, 1984.

Bozell, L. Brent. *The Warren Revolution: Reflections on the Consensus Society.* New Rochelle, N.Y.: Arlington House, 1966.

Bradley, Craig M. *The Failure of the Criminal Procedure Revolution.* Philadelphia: University of Pennsylvania Press, 1993.

Brickey, Kathleen F. "Criminal Mischief: The Federalization of American Criminal Law." *Hastings Law Journal* 46 (1995).

Brofman, Bernard, and Chandler Davidson, eds. *Controversies in Minority Voting: The Voting Rights Act in Perspective.* Washington, D.C.: Brookings Institution, 1992.

Brookings Institution. *Immigration in U.S.-Mexican Relations: A Report of the U.S.-Mexican Relations Forum.* Washington, D.C.: Brookings Institution, 1998.

Brown, Jeffrey V. "Note: *Penrod Drilling Corp. v. Williams:* The Sinking of Another Maritime Anomaly." *Houston Law Review* 31 (1994).

Brown, John R. "Admiralty Judges: Flotsam on the Sea of Maritime Law?" *Journal of Maritime Law and Commerce* 24 (1993).

———. "Hail to the Chief: Hutcheson, the Judge." *Texas Law Review* 38 (December 1959).

Browning, Rufus P., Dale Rogers Marshall, and David H. Tabb. *Protest Is Not Enough: The Struggle of Blacks and Hispanics for Equality in Urban Politics.* Berkeley and Los Angeles: University of California Press, 1984.

Buckholz, Robert E., Jr., Daniel J. Cooper, Alan Gettner, Joan Guggenheimer, Edward S.

Rosenthal, and Mark B. Rotenberg. "Special Project: The Remedial Process in Institutional Reform Litigation." *Columbia Law Review* 78 (1978).

Bue, Carl O., Jr. "Admiralty Law in the Fifth Circuit—A Compendium For Practitioners: I." *Houston Law Review* 4 (1966).

Buenger, Walter L., and Joseph A. Pratt. *But Also Good Business: Texas Commerce Banks and the Financing of Houston and Texas, 1886–1986.* College Station: Texas A&M University Press, 1986.

Burger, Warren E. "The Courts on Trial." 22 F.R.D. 71 (1958).

Burma, John H., ed. *Mexican Americans in the United States: A Reader.* Cambridge: Schenkman, 1978.

Calavita, Kitty. *Inside the State: The Bracero Program, Immigration, and the INS.* Austin: University of Texas Press, 1999.

Calavita, Kitty, Henry N. Pontell, and Robert H. Tillman. *Big Money Crime: Fraud and Politics in the Savings and Loan Crisis.* Berkeley and Los Angeles: University of California Press, 1977.

Caram, Dorothy F., Anthony G. Dworkin, and Néstor Rodriguez, eds. *Hispanics in Houston and Harris County, 1519–1986.* Houston: Hispanic Forum, 1989.

Caro, Robert A. *The Years of Lyndon Johnson.* Vol. 1, *The Path to Power.* New York: Vintage Books, 1990.

———. *The Years of Lyndon Johnson.* Vol. 2, *The Means of Ascent.* New York: Vintage Books, 1991.

Carp, Robert A., and C. K. Rowland. *Policymaking and Politics in the Federal District Courts.* Knoxville: University of Tennessee Press, 1983.

Carp, Robert A., and Ronald Stidham. *The Federal Courts.* 3d ed. Washington, D.C.: Congressional Quarterly [CQ] Press, 1998.

———. *Judicial Process in America.* 2d ed. Washington, D.C.: Congressional Quarterly [CQ] Press, 1993.

———. *Judicial Process in America.* 4th ed. Washington, D.C.: Congressional Quarterly [CQ] Press, 1998.

Carron, Andrew S. *The Plight of the Thrift Institutions.* Washington, D.C.: Brookings Institution, 1982.

———. *The Rescue of the Thrift Industry.* Washington, D.C.: Brookings Institution, 1983.

Carson, Clayborne. *In Struggle: SNCC and the Black Awakening of the 1960s.* Cambridge: Harvard University Press, 1995.

Carter, Thomas P. *Mexican Americans in School: A History of Educational Neglect.* New York: College Entrance Examination Board, 1970.

Castillo, Leonel. "The Growth of Hispanic Political Power in the Houston Area." In *Hispanics in Houston and Harris County, 1519–1986,* edited by Dorothy F. Caram, Anthony G. Dworkin, and Néstor Rodriguez. Houston: Hispanic Forum, 1989.

Castro, William R. "The Origins of Federal Admiralty Jurisdiction in an Age of Privateers, Smugglers, and Pirates." *American Journal of Legal History* 37 (1993).

Chandler, Henry P. "The Problem of Congestion and Delay in the Federal Courts." *Annals* 328 (1960).

———. "Some Major Advances in the Federal Judicial System, 1922–1947." 31 F.R.D. 307 (1963).

Chase, Harold W. *Federal Judges: The Appointing Process.* Minneapolis: University of Minnesota Press, 1972.

Chayes, Abram. "The Role of the Judge in Public Law Litigation." *Harvard Law Review* 89 (1976).
———. "The Supreme Court, 1981 Term: Foreword: Public Law Litigation and the Burger Court." *Harvard Law Review* 96 (1982).
Chenoweth, Lawrence. "The Rhetoric of Hope and Despair: A Study of the Jimi Hendrix Experience and the Jefferson Airplane." *American Quarterly* 23 (1971).
Chepesiuk, Ron. *Sixties Radicals, Then and Now: Candid Conversations with Those Who Shaped the Era.* Jefferson, N.C.: McFarland, 1995.
Chernow, Ron. *The House of Morgan: An American Banking Dynasty and the Rise of Modern Finance.* New York: Simon and Schuster, 1990.
Chevigny, Paul. "Section 1983 Jurisdiction: A Reply." *Harvard Law Review* 83 (1970).
Clark, Charles E. "Objectives of Pre-trial Procedure." *Ohio State Law Journal* 17 (1956).
Clark, Christine Gail. "Comment: The Sky is Falling—The ALI's Efficient Response to Courts in Crisis?" *Brigham Young University Law Review,* 1995.
Clark, David S. "Adjudication to Administration: A Statistical Analysis of Federal District Courts in the Twentieth Century." *Southern California Law Review* 55 (1981).
Clayton, Cornell W., ed. *Government Lawyers: The Federal Legal Bureaucracy and Presidential Politics.* Lawrence: University Press of Kansas, 1995.
Cockcroft, James D. *Outlaws in the Promised Land: Mexican Immigrant Workers and America's Future.* New York: Grove Press, 1986.
Cole, George F. *Politics and the Administration of Justice.* Beverly Hills, Calif.: Sage, 1973.
Cole, Thomas R. *No Color Is My Kind: The Life of Eldrewey Stearns and the Integration of Houston.* Austin: University of Texas Press, 1997.
"Comment: Admiralty: Conflict of Law on the High Seas—The States and the Death on the High Seas Act." *Tulane Law Review* 59 (1985).
Complete Texas Statutes. Kansas City, Mo.: Vernon Law Book Co., 1920.
Compton, Nina H., and Garrett T. Newland. "The Functional Border Equivalent." *Journal of Borderlands Studies* 7 (fall 1992).
Compton, Nina H., and Del Wells. "The Constitutionality of Search and Seizure in the Extended Border Area by Border Patrol Officers." *Journal of Borderlands Studies* 3 (fall 1988).
"A Constitutional Analysis of Magistrate Judge Authority." 150 F.R.D. 247 (1993).
Cooper, Phillip J. *Hard Judicial Choices: Federal District Court Judges and State and Local Officials.* New York: Oxford University Press, 1988.
Corsi, Jerome R. *Judicial Politics: An Introduction.* Englewood Cliffs, N.J.: Prentice-Hall, 1984.
Cottrell, Allin F., Michael S. Lawlor, and John H. Wood, eds. *The Causes and Costs of Depository Institution Failures.* Boston: Kluwer, 1995.
Couch, Harvey C. *A History of the Fifth Circuit, 1891–1981.* Washington, D.C.: Bicentennial Committee of the Judicial Conference of the United States, 1984.
Cover, Robert M. "The Origins of Judicial Activism in the Protection of Minorities." *Yale Law Journal* 91 (1982).
Craig, Richard B. *The Bracero Program: Interest Groups and Foreign Policy.* Austin: University of Texas Press, 1971.
Currie, Brainerd. "Unification of the Civil and Admiralty Rules: Why and How." *Maine Law Journal* 17 (1965).
Currie, David P. "The Three-Judge District Court in Constitutional Litigation." *University of Chicago Law Review* 32 (1964).

Curtis, Dennis E. "The Effect of Federalization on the Defense Function." In *The Federal Role in Criminal Law,* edited by James A. Strazzella. Thousand Oaks, Calif.: Sage, 1996.

Curtis, Lynn A., ed. *American Violence and Public Policy: An Update of the National Commission on the Causes and Commission of Violence.* New Haven: Yale University Press, 1985.

Curtis, Thomas A. "Note, Recess Appointments to Article III Courts: The Use of Historical Practice in Constitutional Interpretation." *Columbia Law Review* 84 (1984).

Davidson, Chandler. *Biracial Politics: Conflict and Coalition in the Metropolitan South.* Baton Rouge: Louisiana State University Press, 1972.

———. "Negro Politics and the Rise of the Civil Rights Movement in Houston, Texas." Ph.D. diss., Princeton University, 1968.

———. *Race and Class in Texas Politics.* Princeton: Princeton University Press, 1990.

———. "The Voting Rights Act: A Brief History." In *Controversies in Minority Voting: The Voting Rights Act in Perspective,* edited by Bernard Brofman and Chandler Davidson. Washington, D.C.: Brookings Institution, 1992.

Davis, F. James. *Who Is Black? One Nation's Definition.* University Park: Pennsylvania State University Press, 1991.

Day, Kathleen. *S&L Hell: The People and the Politics Behind the $1 Trillion Savings and Loan Scandal.* New York: W. W. Norton, 1993.

Days, Drew S., III. "In Honor of *Brown v. Board of Education:* Vindicating Civil Rights in Changing Times." *Yale Law Journal* 93 (1984).

DeAnda, James. "Civil Rights—Need For Executive Branch to Take Positive Steps to Rectify Discrimination in Jury Selection, Voting Eligibility, and School Enrollment." In *The Mexican American: A New Focus on Opportunity,* by the Inter-Agency Committee on Mexican American Affairs. Washington, D.C.: U.S. Government Printing Office, 1967.

De Grazia, Edward. *Girls Lean Back Everywhere: The Law of Obscenity and the Assault on Genius.* New York: Random House, 1992.

De La Garza, Rodolfo O., Frank D. Bean, Charles M. Bonjean, Ricardo Romo, and Rodolfo Alvarez, eds. *The Mexican American Experience: An Interdisciplinary Anthology.* Austin: University of Texas Press, 1985.

De León, Arnoldo. *Ethnicity in the Sunbelt: A History of Mexican Americans in Houston.* Houston: Mexican American Studies–University of Houston, 1989.

Delgado, Richard. "Book Review: Rodrigo's Fifteenth Chronicle: Racial Mixture, Latino-Critical Scholarship, and the Black-White Binary." *Texas Law Review* 75 (1997).

Delgado, Richard, and Victoria Palacios. "Mexican-Americans as a Legally Cognizable Class under Rule 23 and the Equal Protection Clause." *Notre Dame Law Review* 50 (1975).

DiChiara, Albert, and John F. Galliher. "Dissonance and Contradiction in the Origins of Marihuana Decriminalization." *Law and Society Review* 28 (1994).

DiIulio, John J., Jr., ed. *Courts, Corrections, and the Constitution: The Impact of Judicial Intervention on Prisons and Jails.* New York: Oxford University Press, 1990.

Dinan, John J. *Keeping the People's Liberties: Legislators, Citizens, and Judges as Guardians of Rights.* Lawrence: University Press of Kansas, 1998.

Diver, Colin S. "The Judge as Political Powerbroker: Superintending Structural Change in Public Institutions." *Virginia Law Review* 65 (1979).

Dolezal, Charles, Ray Gross, and Ronald Howard. "The Use of Computers for Student Assignment in Desegregation." Appendix B in Texas Advisory Committee to the U.S. Commission on Civil Rights, *School Desegregation in Corpus Christi, Texas,* by the Texas Advisory Committee to the U.S. Commission on Civil Rights. Washington, D.C.: U.S. Government Printing Office, 1977.

Donato, Rubén. *The Other Struggle for Equal Schools: Mexican Americans in the Civil Rights Era.* Albany: State University of New York Press, 1997.

Dorsen, Norman, ed. *The Evolving Constitution: Essays on the Bill of Rights and the U.S. Supreme Court.* Middletown, Conn.: Wesleyan University Press, 1987.

Downs, J. Anthony. "The Boundaries of Article III: Delegation of Final Decisionmaking Authority to Magistrates." *University of Chicago Law Review* 52 (1985).

Du Bois, W. E. B. *The Souls of Black Folk.* Chicago: A. C. McClurg, 1903.

Dunn, Timothy J. *The Militarization of the U.S.-Mexico Border, 1978–1992: Low Intensity Conflict Doctrine Comes Home.* Austin, Tex.: Center for Mexican American Studies, 1995.

Duxbury, Neil. "Faith in Reason: The Process Tradition in American Jurisprudence." *Cardozo Law Review* 15 (1993).

Ehrlich, Paul R., Loy Bilderback, and Anne H. Ehrlich. *The Golden Door: International Migration, Mexico, and the United States.* New York: Ballantine Books, 1979.

Eichler, Ned. *The Thrift Debacle.* Berkeley and Los Angeles: University of California Press, 1989.

Eisenberg, Theodore, and Stephen C. Yeazell. "The Ordinary and the Extraordinary in Institutional Litigation." *Harvard Law Review* 93 (1980).

Eisenstein, James. *Counsel for the United States: U.S. Attorneys in the Political and Legal Systems.* Baltimore: Johns Hopkins University Press, 1978.

Elliott, E. Donald. "Managerial Judging and the Evolution of Procedure." *University of Chicago Law Review* 53 (1986).

Enker, Arnold. "Perspectives on Plea Bargaining." In *Task Force Report: The Courts,* by the President's Commission on Law Enforcement and Administration of Justice. Washington, D.C.: U.S. Government Printing Office, 1967.

Eskridge, William N., Jr., and Phillip P. Frickey, eds. "The Making of the Legal Process." *Harvard Law Review* 107 (1994).

Evans, Sara. *Personal Politics: The Roots of Women's Liberation in the Civil Rights Movement and the New Left.* New York: Alfred A. Knopf, 1979.

Fabritus, M. Manfred, and William Borges. *Saving the Savings and Loan: The U.S. Thrift Industry and the Texas Experience, 1950–1988.* New York: Praeger, 1989.

Fairbanks, Robert B., and Kathleen Underwood, eds. *Essays on Sunbelt Cities and Recent Urban America.* College Station: Texas A&M University Press, 1990.

Fallon, Richard H., Jr. "Reflections on the Hart and Wechsler Paradigm." *Vanderbilt Law Review* 47 (1994).

Farrand, Max, ed. *The Records of the Federal Convention of 1787.* 4 vols. New Haven: Yale University Press, 1937.

Farrell, Margaret. "Coping with Scientific Evidence: The Role of Special Masters." *Emory Law Journal* 43 (1994).

———. "The Function and Legitimacy of Special Masters." *Widener Law Symposium Journal* 2 (1997).

———. "Special Masters." In *Reference Manual on Scientific Evidence.* Washington, D.C.: Federal Judicial Center, 1994.

Faser, Ronald. *1968: A Student Generation in Revolt.* London: Chatto and Windus, 1988.

Feagin, Joe R. *Free Enterprise City: Houston in Political and Economic Perspective.* New Brunswick, N.J.: Rutgers University Press, 1988.

Federal Deposit Insurance Corporation. *History of the Eighties—Lessons for the Future: An Examination of the Banking Crises of the 1980s and Early 1990s.* Vol. 1. Washington, D.C.: FDIC, 1997.

Feeley, Malcolm M. "Perspectives on Plea Bargaining." *Law and Society Review* 13 (1979).

Feeley, Malcolm M., and Edward L. Rubin. *Judicial Policy Making and the Modern State: How the Courts Reformed America's Prisons.* Cambridge: Cambridge University Press, 1998.

Fehrenbach, T. R. *Lone Star: A History of Texas and the Texans.* New York: Macmillan, 1968.

Fernandez, Raul A. *The Mexican-American Border Region: Issues and Trends.* Notre Dame, Ind.: University of Notre Dame Press, 1989.

Fiddler, Charles N. "The Admiralty Practice in Montana and All That: A Critique of the Proposal to Abolish the General Admiralty Rules by Amendments to the Federal Rules of Civil Procedure, and a Counterproposal." *Maine Law Journal* 17 (1965).

Fisch, Louise Ann. *All Rise: Reynaldo G. Garza, the First Mexican American Federal Judge.* College Station: Texas A&M University Press, 1996.

Fish, Peter Graham. *The Politics of Federal Judicial Administration.* Princeton: Princeton University Press, 1973.

Fisher, Louis. "The Judge as Manager: Involvement of Judges in Public Welfare." *Public Manager* 25 (1996).

Fisher, Robert. "The Urban Sunbelt in Comparative Perspective: Houston in Context." In Robert B. Fairbanks and Kathleen Underwood, eds., *Essays on Sunbelt Cities and Recent Urban America,* edited by Robert B. Fairbanks and Kathleen Underwood. College Station: Texas A&M University Press, 1990.

Fiss, Owen M. "The Bureaucratization of the Judiciary." *Yale Law Journal* 92 (1983): 1461–63.

———. *The Civil Rights Injunction.* Bloomington: Indiana University Press, 1978.

———. "The Supreme Court 1978 Term. Foreword: The Forms of Justice." *Harvard Law Review* 93 (1979).

Fitzgerald, Keith. *Face of the Nation: Immigration, the State, and the National Identity.* Stanford: Stanford University Press, 1996.

Flemming, Roy B. "Contested Terrains and Regime Politics: Thinking about America's Trial Courts and Institutional Change." *Law and Social Inquiry* 23 (1998).

Fletcher, William A. "The Discretionary Constitution: Institutional Remedies and Judicial Legitimacy." *Yale Law Journal* 91 (1982).

Foley, Neil. *The White Scourge: Mexicans, Blacks, and Poor Whites in Texas Cotton Culture.* Berkeley and Los Angeles: University of California Press, 1997.

Frankfurter, Felix, and James M. Landis. *The Business of the Supreme Court: A Study in the Federal Judicial System.* New York: Macmillan, 1927.

Freedman, Warren. *The Constitutional Right to a Speedy and Fair Criminal Trial.* New York: Quorum Books, 1989.

Freyer, Tony A. *Forums of Order: The Federal Courts and Business in American History.* Greenwich, Conn.: JAI Press, 1979.

Freyer, Tony A., and Timothy Dixon. *Democracy and Judicial Independence: A History of the Federal Courts of Alabama, 1820–1994.* Brooklyn: Carlson, 1995.

Friedelbaum, Stanley H. "The Warren Court and American Federalism—A Preliminary Appraisal." *University of Chicago Law Review* 28 (1960).

Friedman, Lawrence M. *Crime and Punishment in American History.* New York: Basic Books, 1993.

———. *A History of American Law.* 2d ed. New York: Simon and Schuster, 1985.

———. "Opening the Time Capsule: A Progress Report on Studies of Courts over Time." *Law and Society Review* 24 (1990).

———. *Total Justice.* New ed. New York: Russell Sage Foundation, 1994.

Friendly, Henry J. *Federal Jurisdiction: A General View.* New York: Columbia University Press, 1973.

Fritz, Christian G. *Federal Justice in California: The Court of Ogden Hoffman, 1851–1891.* Lincoln: University of Nebraska Press, 1991.

Funston, Richard Y. *Constitutional Counterrevolution? The Warren Court and the Burger Court: Judicial Policy Making in Modern America.* Cambridge: Schenkman, 1977.

Galanter, Marc S. "Reading the Landscape of Disputes: What We Know and Don't Know (and Think We Know) about Our Allegedly Contentious and Litigious Society." *UCLA Law Review* 31 (1983).

Gammel, H. P. N., comp. *The Laws of Texas, 1822–1897.* Austin, Tex.: H. P. N. Gammel, 1898.

Garcia, F. Chris, ed. *La Causa Politica: A Chicano Politics Reader.* Notre Dame, Ind.: University of Notre Dame Press, 1974.

Garcia, Ignacio M. *Chicanismo: The Forging of a Militant Ethos among Mexican-Americans.* Tucson: University of Arizona Press, 1997.

———. *Viva Kennedy: Mexican Americans in Search of Camelot.* College Station: Texas A&M University Press, 2000.

Garcia, Juan Ramon. *Operation Wetback: The Mass Deportation of Mexican Undocumented Workers in 1954.* Westport, Conn.: Greenwood Press, 1980.

Garcia, Mario T. *Mexican Americans: Leadership, Ideology, and Identity, 1930–1960.* New Haven: Yale University Press, 1989.

Gibbons, John J. "The Legacy of the Burger Court." In *The Burger Court,* edited by Bernard Schwartz. New York: Oxford University Press, 1998.

Gilmore, Grant, and Charles L. Black Jr. *The Law of Admiralty.* Brooklyn: Foundation Press, 1957.

Ginsburg, Ruth Bader. "The Burger Court's Grappling with Sex Discrimination." In *The Burger Court: The Revolution that Wasn't,* edited by Vincent Blasi. New Haven: Yale University Press, 1983.

Gitlin, Todd. *The Sixties: Years of Hope, Days of Rage.* New York: Bantam Books, 1987.

Glasberg, Davita Silfen, and Dan Skidmore. *Corporate Welfare Policy and the Welfare State: Bank Deregulation and the Savings and Loan Bailout.* New York: Aldine de Gruyter, 1997.

Glazer, Nathan. "Should Courts Administer Social Services?" *Public Interest* 50 (1981).

Glenn, Charles L., with Esther J. de Jong. *Educating Immigrant Children: Schools and Language Minorities in Twelve Nations.* New York: Garland, 1996.

Glick, Ronald, and Joan Moore, eds. *Drugs in Hispanic Communities.* New Brunswick, N.J.: Rutgers University Press, 1990.

Goldman, Sheldon. *Picking Federal Judges: Lower Court Selection from Roosevelt through Reagan.* New Haven: Yale University Press, 1997.

Goldman, Sheldon, and Thomas P. Jahnige. *The Federal Courts as a Political System.* New York: Harper and Row, 1971.

Gonzàlez, Guadalupe, and Marta Tienda, eds. *The Drug Connection in U.S.-Mexican Relations.* San Diego: Center for U.S.-Mexican Studies/University of California, San Diego, 1989.

Gonzalez, Henry B. "An Attack on Chicano Militants." In *A Documentary History of the Mexican Americans,* edited by Wayne Moquin with Charles Van Doren. New York: Praeger, 1971.

Gonzalez, Manuel G. *Mexicanos: A History of Mexicans in the United States.* Bloomington: Indiana University Press, 1999.

Gordon, Alan R., and Norval Morris. "Presidential Commissions and the Law Enforcement Assistance Administration." In *American Violence and Public Policy: An Update of the National Commission on the Causes and Commission of Violence,* edited by Lynn A. Curtin. New Haven: Yale University Press, 1985.

Gozansky, Nathaniel E., Kenneth Gignilliat, and William Horwitz. "School Desegregation in the Fifth Circuit." *Houston Law Review* 5 (1968).

Gray, Autumn. "Note: Effects of the American Indian Religious Freedom Act Amendments on Criminal Law: Will Peyotism Eat Away at the Controlled Substances Act?" *American Journal of Criminal Law* 22 (1995).

Graham, Hugh Davis. *The Civil Rights Era: Origins and Development of National Policy, 1960–1972.* New York: Oxford University Press, 1990.

Green, Milton D. "The Situation in 1959." *Annals* 328 (1960).

Greenberg, Jack. *Crusaders in the Courts: How a Dedicated Band of Lawyers Fought for the Civil Rights Revolution.* New York: Basic Books, 1994.

Greenfield, Gary A., and Don B. Kates Jr. "Mexican Americans, Racial Discrimination, and the Civil Rights Act of 1866." *California Law Review* 63 (1975).

Greider, William. *Secrets of the Temple: How the Federal Reserve Runs the Country.* New York: Simon and Schuster, 1987.

Griffin, Richard W. "Drugs and Political Corruption in South Texas." *South Texas Studies* 2 (1991).

Grinspoon, Lester. *Marihuana Reconsidered.* 2d ed. Cambridge: Harvard University Press, 1977.

Gross, Ariela J. "Litigating Whiteness: Trials of Racial Determination in the Nineteenth-Century South." *Yale Law Journal* 108 (1998).

Grossman, Joel B., and Austin Sarat. "Litigation in the Federal Courts: A Comparative Perspective." *Law and Society,* winter 1975.

Gutiérrez, Armando, and Herbert Hirsch. "The Militant Challenge to the American Ethos: 'Chicanos' and 'Mexican Americans.'" In *La Causa Politica: A Chicano Politics Reader,* edited by F. Chris Garcia. Notre Dame, Ind.: University of Notre Dame Press, 1974.

Hall, Howard. *The Warren Court's Conceptions of Democracy: An Evaluation of the Supreme Court's Apportionment Opinions.* Rutherford, N.J.: Fairleigh Dickinson University Press, 1971.

Hall, Kermit L. *The Magic Mirror: Law in American History.* New York: Oxford University Press, 1989.

Hall, Kermit L., and James W. Ely Jr., eds. *An Uncertain Tradition: Constitutionalism and the History of the South.* Athens: University of Georgia Press, 1989.

Hall, Kermit L., and Eric W. Rise. *From Local Courts to National Tribunals: The Federal District Courts of Florida, 1821–1990.* Brooklyn: Carlson, 1991.

Halpern, Stephen C. *On the Limits of the Law: The Ironic Legacy of Title VI of the 1964 Civil Rights Act.* Baltimore: Johns Hopkins University Press, 1995.

Hamilton, Alexander, James Madison, and John Jay. *The Federalist.* Edited by Benjamin Fletcher Wright. Cambridge: Harvard University Press, Belknap Press, 1961.

Harris, Cheryl I. "Whiteness as Property." *Harvard Law Review* 106 (1993).

Harris, Joseph P. *The Advice and Consent of the Senate: A Study of the Confirmation of Appointments by the United States Senate.* New York: Greenwood Press, 1968.

Hart, Henry M., Jr., and Herbert Wechsler, eds. *The Federal Courts and the Federal System.* Westbury, N.Y.: Foundation Press, 1953.

Haskell, Paul G. "Judicial Review of School Discipline." *Case Western Reserve Law Review* 21 (1970).

Healy, George W., III. "Remedies for Maritime Personal Injury and Wrongful Death in American Law: Sources and Development." *Tulane Law Review* 68 (1994).

Heer, David M. *Immigration in America's Future: Social Science Findings and the Policy Debate.* Boulder, Colo.: Westview Press, 1996.

———. *Undocumented Mexicans in the United States.* Cambridge: Cambridge University Press, 1990.

Heffner, Richard D., ed. *A Documentary History of the United States.* 5th ed. New York: Penguin Books, 1991.

Heinz, Anne M., and Wayne A. Kerstetter. "Pretrial Settlement Conference: Evaluation of a Reform in Plea Bargaining." *Law and Society Review* 13 (1979).

Hellman, Arthur D., ed. *Restructuring Justice: The Innovations of the Ninth Circuit and the Future of the Federal Courts.* Ithaca: Cornell University Press, 1990.

Hero, Rodney E. *Latinos and the U.S. Political System: Two-Tiered Pluralism.* Philadelphia: Temple University Press, 1992.

Hess, Matthew V. "Comment: Good Cop–Bad Cop: Reassessing the Legal Remedies for Police Misconduct." *Utah Law Review,* 1993.

Heumann, Milton. "A Note on Plea Bargaining and Case Pressure." *Law and Society Review* 9 (1975).

Heydebrand, Wolf, and Carroll Seron. *Rationalizing Justice: The Political Economy of Federal District Courts.* Albany: State University of New York Press, 1990.

———. "The Rising Demand for Court Services: A Structural Explanation of the Caseload of the U.S. District Courts." *Justice System Journal* 11 (1986).

Himmelstein, Jerome L. *The Strange Career of Marihuana: Politics and Ideology of Drug Control in America.* Westport, Conn.: Greenwood Press, 1983.

Hirsch, Alan, and Diane Sheehey. *Awarding Attorney's Fees in and Managing Fee Litigation.* Washington, D.C.: Federal Judicial Center, 1994.

Hirschkop, Philip, and Michael Millemann. "The Unconstitutionality of Prison Life." *Virginia Law Review* 55 (1969).

Hoffer, Peter Charles. *The Law's Conscience: Equitable Constitutionalism in America.* Chapel Hill: University of North Carolina Press, 1990.

Hoffman, Walter E. "Purposes and Philosophy of Sentencing." In *Proceedings of Seminar for Newly Appointed United States District Judges,* 13–18 September 1976, Washington, D.C., 75 F.R.D. 89 (1977).

Horwitz, Morton J. *The Transformation of American Law, 1780–1860.* Cambridge: Harvard University Press, 1977.

Howard, A. E. Dick. "State Courts and Constitutional Rights in the Day of the Burger Court." *Virginia Law Review* 62 (1976).

Hufstedler, Shirley M. "Comity and the Constitution: The Changing Role of the Federal Judiciary." In *The Evolving Constitution: Essays on the Bill of Rights and the U.S. Supreme Court,* edited by Norman Dorsen. Middletown, Conn.: Wesleyan University Press, 1987.

Hughes, Lynn N. "Don't Make a Federal Case out of It: The Constitution and the Nationalization of Crime." *American Journal of Criminal Law* 25 (1997).

Hurst, James Willard. *Law and the Conditions of Freedom in the Nineteenth Century United States.* Madison: University of Wisconsin Press, 1956.

Hyman, Harold M. *Craftsmanship and Character: A History of the Vinson and Elkins Law Firm of Houston, 1917–1997*. Athens: University of Georgia Press, 1998.

———. *A More Perfect Union: The Impact of the Civil War and Reconstruction on the Constitution.* New York: Alfred A. Knopf, 1973.

Ittig, Judith B. "The Rites of Passage: Border Searches and the Fourth Amendment." *Tennessee Law Review* 40 (1973).

Jacob, Herbert. "Trial Courts in the United States: The Travails of Exploration." *Law and Society Review* 17 (1983).

Jaros, Dean. "Biochemical Desocialization: Depressants and Political Behavior." *Midwest Journal of Political Science* 16 (1972).

Jarvis, Robert M. "Rethinking the Meaning of the Phrase 'Surviving Widow' in the Jones Act: Has the Time Come for Admiralty Courts to Fashion a Federal Law of Domestic Relations?" *California Western Law Review* 21 (1985).

Jenkins, C. H. *The Revised Civil Statutes of Texas, 1925, Annotated.* Austin, Tex.: H. P. N. Gammel, 1925.

Jensen, F. Kenneth. "The Houston Sit-In Movement of 1960–61." In *Black Dixie: Afro-Texan History and Culture in Houston,* edited by Howard Beeth and Cary D. Wintz. College Station: Texas A&M University Press, 1992.

Johns, Christina Jacqueline. *Power, Ideology, and the War on Drugs: Nothing Succeeds like Failure.* New York: Praeger, 1992.

Johnsen, Roger A. "Judicial Manpower Problems." *Annals* 328 (1960).

Johnson, Bruce D., and Gopal S. Uppal. "Marihuana and Youth: A Generation Gone to Pot." In *Drugs and the Youth Culture,* edited by Frank R. Scarpitti and Susan K. Datesman. Beverly Hills, Calif.: Sage, 1980.

Johnson, Frank M. "Observation: The Constitution and the Federal District Judge." *Texas Law Review* 54 (1976).

Johnson, John W. *The Struggle for Student Rights: "Tinker v. Des Moines" and the 1960s.* Lawrence: University Press of Kansas, 1997.

Jones, Jesse H., with Edward Angly. *Fifty Billion Dollars: My Thirteen Years with the RFC (1932–1945).* New York: Macmillan, 1951.

Jones, Richard C. "Changing Patterns of Undocumented Mexican Migration to South Texas." In *The Mexican American Experience: An Interdisciplinary Anthology,* edited by Rodolfo O. De La Garza, Frank D. Bean, Charles M. Bonjean, Ricardo Romo, and Rodolfo Alvarez. Austin: University of Texas Press, 1985.

Jones, Robb M. "The Future of the Federal Courts: The Long-Range Plan by the Judicial Conference Advocates a Change in Legislative Perspective." *Judges Journal,* fall 1995.

Jonnes, Jill. *Hep-Cats, Narcs, and Pipe Dreams: A History of America's Romance with Illegal Drugs.* New York: Scribner, 1996.

Judges of the United States. 2d ed. Washington, D.C.: Bicentennial Committee of the Judicial Conference of the United States, 1983.

Justice, Blair. *Violence in the City.* Fort Worth, Tex.: Leo Potishman Fund, 1969.

Kalman, Laura. *The Strange Career of Legal Liberalism.* New Haven: Yale University Press, 1996.

Kalven, Harry, Jr. "The Bar, the Court, and the Delay." *Annals* 328 (1960).

Kaplan, Barry J. "Houston: The Golden Buckle of the Sunbelt." In *Sunbelt Cities: Politics and Growth Since World War II,* edited by Richard M. Bernard and Bradley R. Rice. Austin: University of Texas Press, 1983.

Kellar, William Henry. *Make Haste Slowly: Moderates, Conservatives, and School Desegregation in Houston.* College Station: Texas A&M University Press, 1999.

Kemerer, Frank R. *William Wayne Justice: A Judicial Biography.* Austin: University of Texas Press, 1991.

Kennedy, Susan Estabrook. *The Banking Crisis of 1933.* Lexington: University Press of Kentucky, 1973.

Kinch, Sam, and Ben Procter. *Texas under a Cloud.* Austin, Tex.: Jenkins, 1972.

Kinch, Sam, and Stuart Long. *Allan Shivers: The Pied Piper of Texas Politics.* Austin, Tex.: Shoal Creek, 1973.

Kinder, Douglas Clark, and William O. Walker III. "Stable Force in a Storm: Harry J. Anslinger and United States Narcotic Foreign Policy, 1930–1962." *Journal of American History* 72 (1986).

King, James Lawrence. "Management of Civil Case Flow from Filing to Disposition." 75 F.R.D. 15 (1977).

Kirp, David L. "Proceduralism and Bureaucracy: Due Process in the School Setting." *Stanford Law Review* 28 (1976).

Kirp, David L., and Gary Babcock. "Judge and Company: Court-Appointed Masters, School Desegregation, and Institutional Reform." *Alabama Law Review* 32 (1981).

Kirstein, Peter N. *Anglo over Bracero: A History of the Mexican Worker in the United States from Roosevelt to Nixon.* San Francisco: R&E Research Associates, 1977.

Kluger, Richard. *Simple Justice: The History of "Brown v. Board of Education" and Black America's Struggle for Equality.* New York: Vintage Books, 1975.

Kobylka, Joseph F. *The Politics of Obscenity: Group Litigation in a Time of Legal Change.* New York: Greenwood Press, 1991.

Krauss, Melvyn B., and Edward P. Lazear, eds. *Searching for Alternatives: Drug-Control Policy in the United States.* Stanford, Calif.: Hoover Institution, 1991.

Kurland, Philip B. "Enter the Burger Court: The Constitutional Business of the Supreme Court, O.T. [October Term] 1969." *Supreme Court Review,* 1970.

———. "1971 Term: The Year of the Stewart-White Court." *Supreme Court Review,* 1972.

———. *Politics, the Constitution, and the Warren Court.* Chicago: University of Chicago Press, 1970.

Kutler, Stanley I. *Privilege and Creative Destruction: The Charles River Bridge Case.* Baltimore: Johns Hopkins University Press, 1971.

Lacombe, Dany. *Blue Politics: Pornography and the Law in the Age of Feminism.* Toronto: University of Toronto Press, 1994.

Ladino, Robyn Duff. *Desegregating Texas Schools: Eisenhower, Shivers, and the Crisis at Mansfield High.* Austin: University of Texas Press, 1996.

"Lagging Justice." *Annals* 328 (1960) [special issue].

Landsberg, Brian K. *Enforcing Civil Rights: Race Discrimination and the Department of Justice.* Lawrence: University Press of Kansas, 1997.

Langbein, John H. "Understanding the Short History of Plea Bargaining." *Law and Society Review* 13 (1979).

Larsen, Lawrence H. *Federal Justice in Western Missouri: The Judges, the Cases, the Times.* Columbia: University of Missouri Press, 1994.

Lawrence, Regina G. *The Politics of Force: Media and the Construction of Police Brutality.* Berkeley and Los Angeles: University of California Press, 2000.

Leary, Timothy. *Changing My Mind, among Others: Lifetime Writings, Selected and Introduced by the Author.* Englewood Cliffs, N.J.: Prentice-Hall, 1982.

———. *Flashbacks: An Autobiography.* Los Angeles: J. P. Tarcher, 1983.

———. *High Priest.* New York: NAL-World, 1968.

———. "The Politics, Ethics, and Meaning of Marijuana." In *The Marihuana Papers,* edited by David Solomon. New York: Signet Books, 1968.

Leuchtenberg, William E. *Franklin D. Roosevelt and the New Deal, 1932–1940.* New York: Harper and Row, Torchbooks, 1963.

———. *The Supreme Court Reborn: The Constitutional Revolution in the Age of Roosevelt.* New York: Oxford University Press, 1995.

Levin, A. Leo, and Russell R. Wheeler, eds. *The American Judiciary: Critical Issues.* Beverly Hills, Calif.: Sage, 1982.

Levin, Betsy, and Philip Moise. "School Desegregation Litigation in the Seventies and the Use of Social Science Evidence: An Annotated Guide." *Law and Contemporary Problems* 39 (1975).

Levit, Nancy. "The Caseload Conundrum, Constitutional Restraint, and the Manipulation of Jurisdiction." *Notre Dame Law Review* 64 (1989).

Levy, Leonard W., ed. *The Supreme Court under Earl Warren.* New York: Quadrangle Books, 1972.

Liddy, G. Gordon. *Will: The Autobiography of G. Gordon Liddy.* New York: Dell, 1980.

Lipartito, Kenneth, and Joseph Pratt. *Baker and Botts in the Development of Modern Houston.* Austin: University of Texas Press, 1991.

Lipset, Seymour Martin. *Rebellion in the University.* Boston: Little, Brown, 1971.

Litman, Harry, and Mark D. Greenberg. "Dual Prosecutions: A Model for Concurrent Federal Jurisdiction." In *The Federal Role in Criminal Law,* edited by James A. Strazzella. Thousand Oaks, Calif.: Sage, 1996.

Little, Rory K. "Myths and Principles of Federalization." *Hastings Law Journal* 46 (1995).

"Longitudinal Studies of Trial Courts." *Law and Society Review* 24 (1990) [special issue].

Lopez, Gerald P. "Undocumented Mexican Migration: In Search of a Just Immigration Law and Policy." *UCLA Law Review* 28 (1981).

Lopez, Ian F. Haney. "Race, Ethnicity, Erasure: The Salience of Race to LatCrit Theory." *California Law Review* 85 (1997).

———. *White by Law: The Legal Construction of Race.* New York: New York University Press, 1996.

Lowy, Martin. *High Rollers: Inside the Savings and Loan Debacle.* New York: Praeger, 1991.

Lyles, Kevin L. *The Gatekeepers: Federal District Courts in the Political Process.* Westport, Conn.: Praeger, 1997.

Mabry, Cynthia R. "The Supreme Court Opens a Pandora's Box in the Law of Warrantless Automobile Searches and Seizures—*United States v. Ross.*" *Howard Law Journal* 26 (1983).

Machann, Clinton, and James W. Mendl Jr., trans. and eds. *Czech Voices: Stories from Texas in Amerikán Národní Kalendár.* College Station: Texas A&M University Press, 1991.

Mackey, Thomas Clyde. "Red Lights Out: A Legal History of Prostitution, Disorderly Houses, and Vice Districts, 1870–1917." Ph.D. diss., Rice University, 1984.

Madsen, William. *The Mexican-Americans of South Texas.* New York: Holt, Rinehart and Winston, 1964.

Majka, Theo J. *Farmers' and Farm Workers' Movements: Social Protest in American Agriculture.* New York: Twayne, 1995.

Maraist, Frank L. "Federal Injunctive Relief against State Court Proceedings: The Significance of *Dombrowski*." *Texas Law Review* 48 (1970).

Maril, Robert Lee. *Texas Shrimpers: Community, Capitalism, and the Sea*. College Station: Texas A&M University Press, 1983.

Marion, Nancy E. *A History of Federal Crime Control Initiatives, 1960–1993*. Westport, Conn.: Praeger, 1994.

Martin, Steve J., and Sheldon Ekland-Olson. *Texas Prisons: The Walls Came Tumbling Down*. Austin: Texas Monthly Press, 1987.

Martinez, George A. "Legal Indeterminacy, Judicial Discretion, and the Mexican-American Litigation Experience: 1930–1980." *University of California Davis Law Review* 27 (1994).

Mason, Alpheus T. *The Supreme Court: Palladium of Freedom*. Ann Arbor: University of Michigan Press, 1962.

Mason, James Eliot. *The Transformation of Commercial Banking in the United States, 1956–1991*. New York: Garland, 1997.

Matusow, Allen J. *The Unraveling of America: A History of Liberalism in the 1960s*. New York: Harper and Row, 1984.

Mayer, Martin. *The Greatest-Ever Bank Robbery: The Collapse of the Savings and Loan Industry*. New York: Charles Scribner's Sons, 1990.

McClymer, John F. "The Americanization Movement and the Education of the Foreign-Born Adult, 1914–1925." In *American Education and the European Immigrant, 1840–1940*, edited by Bernard J. Weiss. Urbana: University of Illinois Press, 1982.

McFeeley, Neil D. *Appointment of Judges: The Johnson Presidency*. Austin: University of Texas Press, 1987.

McKnight, H. Brent. "How Shall We Then Reason? The Historical Setting of Equity." *Mercer Law Review* 45 (1994).

Medina, Harold R. *The Anatomy of Freedom*. Edited by C. Walter Barrett. New York: Henry Holt, 1959.

Meier, Matt S., and Feliciano Ribera. *Mexican Americans/American Mexicans: From Conquistadors to Chicanos*. 1972 [as *The Chicanos*]. Reprint, New York: Hill and Wang, 1993.

Meltzer, Daniel J. "Deterring Constitutional Violations by Law Enforcement Officials: Plaintiffs and Defendants as Private Attorneys General." *Columbia Law Review* 88 (1988).

Meyers, Marvin. *The Jacksonian Persuasion: Politics and Belief*. Stanford: Stanford University Press, 1957.

Mezey, Susan Gluck. *In Pursuit of Equality: Women, Public Policy, and the Federal Courts*. New York: St. Martin's Press, 1992.

Miller, Arthur R. "Comment: Of Frankenstein Monsters and Shining Knights: Myth, Reality, and the 'Class Action Problem.'" *Harvard Law Review* 92 (1979).

Miller, Leonard G. *Double Jeopardy and the Federal System*. Chicago: University of Chicago Press, 1968.

Montejano, David. *Anglos and Mexicans in the Making of Texas, 1836–1986*. Austin: University of Texas Press, 1987.

Mooney, H. F. "Popular Music since the 1920s: The Significance of Shifting Taste." *American Quarterly* 20 (1968).

Mooney, Patrick H., and Theo J. Majka. *Farmers' and Farm Workers' Movements: Social Protest in American Agriculture*. New York: Twayne, 1995.

Moquin, Wayne, with Charles Van Doren, eds. *A Documentary History of the Mexican Americans*. New York: Praeger, 1971.

Moretti, Daniel S. *Obscenity and Pornography: The Law under the First Amendment.* New York: Oceana, 1984.
Morgan, Patricia A. "The Making of a Public Problem: Mexican Labor in California and the Marijuana Law of 1937." In *Drugs in Hispanic Communities,* edited by Ronald Glick and Joan Moore. New Brunswick, N.J.: Rutgers University Press, 1990.
Munoz, Carlos. *Youth, Identity, Power: The Chicano Movement.* New York: Verso, 1989.
Murchison, Kenneth M. *Federal Criminal Law Doctrines: The Forgotten Influence of National Prohibition.* Durham, N.C.: Duke University Press, 1994.
Murphy, Walter F., and C. Herman Pritchett, eds. *Courts, Judges, and Politics: An Introduction to the Judicial Process.* 3d ed. New York: Random House, 1979.
Murrah, Alfred P. "Pre-Trial Procedure: A Statement of Its Essentials." 14 F.R.D. 417 (1953).
Musto, David F. *The American Disease: Origins of Narcotic Control.* 3d ed. New York: Oxford University Press, 1999.
Nagel, Robert F. "Separation of Powers and the Scope of Federal Equitable Remedies." *Stanford Law Review* 30 (1978).
Nathan, Vincent. "The Use of Masters in Institutional Reform Litigation." *University of Toledo Law Review* 10 (1979).
Navarro, Armando. *The Cristal Experiment: A Chicano Struggle for Community Control.* Madison: University of Wisconsin Press, 1998.
———. *Mexican American Youth Organization: Avant-Garde of the Chicano Movement in Texas.* Austin: University of Texas Press, 1995.
Neely, Richard. *Judicial Jeopardy: When Business Collides with the Courts.* Reading, Pa.: Addison-Wesley, 1986.
Nelson, Dorothy W. *Cases and Materials on Judicial Administration and the Administration of Justice.* Saint Paul, Minn.: West, 1974.
Nelson, Eugene. "Who Is César Chávez?" In *The Mexican-Americans: An Awakening Minority,* edited by Manuel P. Servin. Beverly Hills, Calif.: Glencoe Press, 1971.
Nelson, William E. *The Fourteenth Amendment: From Political Principle to Judicial Doctrine.* Cambridge: Harvard University Press, 1988.
Nelson-Cisneros, Victor B. "UCAPAWA Organizing Activities in Texas, 1935–50." *Aztlán* 9 (1978).
"New Accent on Civil Rights: The Mexican American." *Civil Rights Journal* 2 (winter 1969).
Ngai, Mae M. "The Architecture of Race in American Immigration Law: A Reexamination of the Immigration Act of 1924." *Journal of American History* 86 (1999).
"Note: Article III Constraints and the Expanding Civil Jurisdiction of Federal Magistrates: A Dissenting View." *Yale Law Journal* 88 (1979).
"Note: Border Zone Search Law: The Search for a Definition of Functional Equivalents of the Border." *Texas International Law Journal* 16 (1981).
"Note: Developments in the Law: Section 1983 and Federalism." *Harvard Law Review* 90 (1977).
"Note: Double Prosecutions by State and Federal Governments: Another Exercise in Federalism." *Harvard Law Review* 80 (1967).
"Note: The Federal Anti-injunction Act and Declaratory Judgments in Constitutional Litigation." *Harvard Law Review* 83 (1970).
"Note: Implementation Problems in Institutional Reform Litigation." *Harvard Law Review* 91 (1977).

"Note: Limiting the Section 1983 Action in the Wake of *Monroe v. Pape.*" *Harvard Law Review* 82 (1969).

"Note: 'Mastering' Intervention in Prisons." *Yale Law Journal* 88 (1979).

"Note: Prison Mail Censorship and the First Amendment." *Yale Law Journal* 81 (1971).

"Note: Search and Seizure at the Border—The Border Search." *Rutgers Law Review* 21 (1967).

Novak, William J. *The People's Welfare: Law and Regulation in Nineteenth-Century America.* Chapel Hill: University of North Carolina Press, 1996.

Oakley, John B. "The Myth of Cost-Free Jurisdictional Reallocation." In *The Federal Role in Criminal Law,* edited by James A. Strazzella. Thousand Oaks, Calif.: Sage, 1996.

O'Connor, Karen. *Women's Organizations' Use of the Courts.* Lexington, Mass.: Lexington Books, 1980.

O'Connor, Karen, and Lee Epstein, "A Legal Voice for the Chicano Community: The Activities of the Mexican American Legal Defense and Education Fund, 1968–82." In *The Mexican American Experience: An Interdisciplinary Anthology,* edited by Rodolfo O. De La Garza, Frank D. Bean, Charles M. Bonjean, Ricardo Romo, and Rodolfo Alvarez. Austin: University of Texas Press, 1985.

O'Hara, James B. Introduction to *The Burger Court,* edited by Bernard Schwartz. New York: Oxford University Press, 1998.

Oppenheimer, Martin. *The Sit-In Movement of 1960.* Brooklyn: Carlson, 1989.

Oren, Laura. "Comment: The Legal Status of Undocumented Aliens: In Search of a Consistent Theory." *Houston Law Review* 16 (1979).

Orfield, Gary. "Congress, the President, and Anti-busing Legislation, 1966–1974." *Journal of Law-Education* 4 (1975).

O'Shea, James. *The Daisy Chain: How Borrowed Billions Sank a Texas S&L.* New York: Pocket Books, 1991.

Paludan, Phillip Shaw. *The Presidency of Abraham Lincoln.* Lawrence: University Press of Kansas, 1994.

Panetta, Leon A., and Peter Gall. *Bring Us Together: The Nixon Team and the Civil Rights Retreat.* Philadelphia: J. B. Lippincott, 1971.

Park, Sangkyun. *Contagion of Bank Failures: The Relation to Deposit Insurance and Information.* New York: Garland, 1992.

Patenaude, Lionel V. "Garner, Sumners, and Connally: The Defeat of the Roosevelt Court Bill in 1937." *Southwestern Historical Quarterly* 74 (July 1970).

Patterson, James T. *"Brown v. Board of Education": A Civil Rights Milestone and Its Troubled Legacy.* New York: Oxford University Press, 2001.

Peckham, Robert F. "The Federal Judge as a Case Manager: The New Role in Guiding a Case from Filing to Disposition." *California Law Review* 69 (1981).

Peltason, J. W. *Fifty-eight Lonely Men: Southern Federal Judges and School Desegregation.* 1961. Reprint, Urbana: University of Illinois Press, Illini Books, 1971.

Perryman, M. Ray. *Survive and Conquer—Texas in the 80's: Power—Money—Tragedy . . . Hope!* Dallas: Taylor, 1990.

Pike, Fredrick B. *FDR's Good Neighbor Policy: Sixty Years of Generally Gentle Chaos.* Austin: University of Texas Press, 1995.

Pilzer, Paul Zane, with Robert Deitz. *Other People's Money: The Inside Story of the S&L Mess.* New York: Simon and Schuster, 1989.

Pole, J. R. *The Pursuit of Equality in American History.* Rev. ed. Berkeley and Los Angeles: University of California Press, 1993.

Posner, Richard A. *The Federal Courts: Challenge and Reform.* Cambridge: Harvard University Press, 1996.

———. *The Federal Courts: Crisis and Reform.* Cambridge: Harvard University Press, 1985.

Powe, Lucas A., Jr. *The Warren Court and American Politics.* Cambridge: Harvard University Press, Belknap Press, 2000.

Pratt, Joseph A., and Christopher J. Castaneda. *Builders: Herman and George R. Brown.* College Station: Texas A&M University Press, 1999.

———, Tyler Priest, and Christopher J. Castaneda. *Offshore Pioneers: Brown and Root and the History of Offshore Oil and Gas.* Houston: Gulf, 1997.

Proceedings of Seminar for Newly Appointed United States District Judges. 13–18 September 1976, Washington, D.C. 75 F.R.D. 89 (1977).

Procter, Ben H. "The Modern Texas Rangers: A Law Enforcement Dilemma in the Rio Grande Valley." In *The Mexican-Americans: An Awakening Minority,* edited by Manuel P. Servin. Beverly Hills, Calif.: Glencoe Press, 1970.

Pulido, Laura. *Environmentalism and Economic Justice: Two Chicano Struggles in the Southwest.* Tucson: University of Arizona Press, 1996.

Purcell, Edward A., Jr. "Social Thought." *American Quarterly* 35 (1983).

Pycior, Julie Leininger. *LBJ and Mexican Americans: The Paradox of Power.* Austin: University of Texas Press, 1997.

Quezada, J. Gilberto. *Border Boss: Manuel B. Bravo and Zapata County.* College Station: Texas A&M University Press, 1999.

Quiñones, Juan Gómez. *Chicano Politics: Reality and Promise, 1940–1990.* Albuquerque: University of New Mexico Press, 1990.

Quiroz, Ann Dee. "Black, White, and Brown: The Houston Council on Human Relations and Tri-racial Relations in Houston." M.A. thesis, University of Houston, 1998.

Rabin, Robert L. "Agency Criminal Referrals in the Federal System: An Empirical Study of Prosecutorial Discretion." *Stanford Law Review* 24 (1972).

Rachal, Patricia. *Federal Narcotics Enforcement: Reorganization and Reform.* Boston: Auburn House, 1982.

Ramos, Henry A. J. *The American GI Forum: In Pursuit of the Dream, 1948–1983.* Houston: Arte Público Press, 1998.

Rangel, Jorge C., and Carlos M. Alcala. "Project Report: De Jure Segregation of Chicanos in Texas Schools." *Harvard Civil Rights–Civil Liberties Law Review* 7 (1972).

Read, Frank T., and Lucy S. McGough. *Let Them Be Judged: The Judicial Integration of the Deep South.* Metuchen, N.J.: Scarecrow Press, 1978.

Reference Manual on Scientific Evidence. Washington, D.C.: Federal Judicial Center, 1994.

Rendón, Armando B. *Chicano Manifesto: The History and Aspirations of the Second Largest Minority in America.* 1971; reprint ed., Berkeley, Calif.: Ollin and Associates, 1996.

———. "How Much Longer . . . The Long Road?" *Civil Rights Digest* (summer 1968).

The Report of the Commission on Obscenity and Pornography. New York: Random House, 1970.

Resnik, Judith. "From 'Cases' to 'Litigation.'" *Law and Contemporary Problems* 54 (summer 1991).

———. "History, Jurisdiction, and the Federal Courts: Changing Contexts, Selective Memories, and Limited Imagination." *West Virginia Law Review* 98 (fall 1995).

———. "Managerial Judges." *Harvard Law Review* 96 (1982).

Rhinehart, Marilyn D., and Thomas H. Kreneck. "The Minimum Wage March of 1966: A Case Study in Mexican-American Politics, Labor, and Identity." *Houston Review* 11 (1989).

Riches, William T. Martin. *The Civil Rights Movement: Struggle and Resistance.* Houndmills, U.K.: Macmillan Press, 1997.

Riggs, Burkeley N., and Tamera D. Westerberg. "Judicial Independence: An Historical Perspective." *Denver University Law Review* 74 (1997).

Roach, Kent. "The Limits of Corrective Justice and the Potential of Equity in Constitutional Remedies." *Arizona Law Review* 33 (1991).

Roediger, David R. *Toward the Abolition of Whiteness: Essays on Race, Politics, and Working Class History.* London: Verso, 1994.

Rom, Mark Carl. *Public Spirit in the Thrift Tragedy.* Pittsburgh: University of Pittsburgh Press, 1996.

Rosenberg, Gerald N. *The Hollow Hope: Can Courts Bring About Social Change?* Chicago: University of Chicago Press, 1991.

Rosenzweig, Paul S. "Functional Equivalents of the Border, Sovereignty, and the Fourth Amendment." *University of Chicago Law Review* 52 (fall 1985).

Rowan, Helen. "A Minority Nobody Knows." In *Mexican Americans in the United States: A Reader,* edited by John H. Burma. Cambridge: Schenkman, 1978.

Rowland, C. K., and Robert A. Carp. *Politics and Judgment in Federal District Courts.* Lawrence: University Press of Kansas, 1996.

Roybal, Edward R. "Mexican-American Casualties in Vietnam." In *A Documentary History of the Mexican Americans,* edited by Wayne Moquin with Charles Van Doren. New York: Praeger, 1971.

Ruiz-Cabañas, Miguel. "Mexico's Changing Illicit Drug Supply Role." In *The Drug Connection in U.S.-Mexican Relations,* edited by Guadalupe Gonzàlez and Marta Tienda. San Diego: Center for U.S.-Mexican Studies/University of California, San Diego, 1989.

Saari, David J. *American Court Management: Theories and Practices.* Westport, Conn.: Quorum Books, 1082.

Salinas, Guadalupe. "Comment: Mexican-Americans and the Desegregation of Schools in the Southwest." *Houston Law Review* 8 (1971).

Salinas, Guadalupe, and Isaias D. Torres. "The Undocumented Mexican Alien: A Legal, Social, and Economic Analysis." *Houston Law Review* 13 (1976).

Salop, Steven C., and Lawrence J. White. "Private Antitrust Litigation: An Introduction and Framework." In *Private Antitrust Litigation: New Evidence, New Learning,* edited by Lawrence J. White. Cambridge: Massachusetts Institute of Technology Press, 1988.

Saltzburg, Stephen A. "The Unnecessarily Expanding Role of the American Trial Judge." *Virginia Law Review* 64 (1978).

Samora, Julian, Joe Bernal, and Albert Peña. *Gunpowder Justice: A Reassessment of the Texas Rangers.* Notre Dame, Ind.: University of Notre Dame Press, 1979.

Samora, Julian, with Jorge Bustamante and Gilberto Cardenas. *Los Mojados: The Wetback Story.* Notre Dame, Ind.: University of Notre Dame Press, 1971.

San Miguel, Guadalupe, Jr. *Brown, Not White: School Integration and the Chicano Movement in Houston.* College Station: Texas A&M University Press/Center for Mexican American Studies at University of Houston, 2001.

———. " 'The Community is Beginning to Rumble': The Origins of Chicano Educational Protest in Houston, 1965–1970." *Houston Review* 13 (1991).

———. *"Let All of Them Take Heed": Mexican Americans and the Campaign for Educational Equality in Texas, 1910–1981.* Austin: University of Texas Press, 1987.

———. "Mexican American Organizations and the Changing Politics of School Desegregation in Texas, 1945–1980." *Social Science Quarterly* 63 (1982).

Sarat, Austin. "Understanding Trial Courts: A Critique of Social Science Approaches." *Judicature* 61 (1978).

Sayer John W., and Daniel L. Rotenberg. "Marijuana in the Houston High Schools—A First Report." *Houston Law Review* 6 (1969).

Scalia, Antonin. *A Matter of Interpretation: Federal Courts and the Law.* Princeton: Princeton University Press, 1997.

Scarpitti, Frank R., and Susan K. Datesman, eds. *Drugs and the Youth Culture.* Beverly Hills, Calif.: Sage, 1980.

Schauer, Frederick. "Fear, Risk, and the First Amendment: Unraveling the 'Chilling Effect.'" *Boston University Law Review* 58 (1978).

Scher, Richard K., Jon L. Mills, and John J. Hotaling. *Voting Rights and Democracy: The Law and Politics of Districting.* Chicago: Nelson-Hall, 1997.

Schill, Gus A., Jr. "Available Forums and Recoverable Damages in Offshore Personal Injury Litigation in the Fifth Circuit: A Review and Analysis." *Houston Law Review* 16 (1978).

———. "Moragne-Gaudet: Three If by Sea?" *Houston Law Review* 13 (1976).

———. "The Unsolvable Puzzle of Maritime Personal Injury Litigation: One False Move and You're Out." *Houston Law Review* 24 (1987).

Schuck, Peter H. *The Judiciary Committees: A Study of the House and Senate Judiciary Committees.* New York: Grossman, 1972.

Schwartz, Bernard, ed. *The Burger Court.* New York: Oxford University Press, 1998.

Sear, Morey L. "Supporting Personnel." In *Proceedings of Seminar for Newly Appointed United States District Judges,* 13–18 September 1976, Washington, D.C., 75 F.R.D. 89 (1977).

Seidman, L. William. *Full Faith and Credit: The Great S&L Debacle and Other Washington Sagas.* New York: Times Books, 1993.

Seron, Carroll. *Judicial Reorganization: The Politics of Reform in the Federal Bankruptcy Court.* Lexington, Mass.: Lexington Books, 1978.

———. *The Roles of Magistrates: Nine Case Studies.* Washington, D.C.: Federal Judicial Center, 1985.

Servín, Manuel P., ed. *The Mexican-Americans: An Awakening Minority.* Beverly Hills, Calif.: Glencoe Press, 1970.

———. "The Post–World War II Mexican-American, 1945–1965: A Non-achieving Minority." In *The Mexican-Americans: An Awakening Minority,* edited by Manuel P. Servín. Beverly Hills, Calif.: Glencoe Press, 1970.

Seymour, Whitney North, Jr. *United States Attorney: An Inside View of "Justice" in America under the Nixon Administration.* New York: William Morrow, 1975.

Sharp, Elaine B. *The Dilemma of Drug Policy in the United States.* New York: Harper Collins, 1994.

Shelton, Beth Anne, Nestor P. Rodriguez, Joe R. Feagin, Robert D. Bullard, and Robert D. Thomas. *Houston: Growth and Decline in a Sunbelt Boomtown.* Philadelphia: Temple University Press, 1989.

Shoemaker, Don, ed. *With All Deliberate Speed: Segregation-Desegregation in Southern Schools.* New York: Harper and Brothers, 1957.

Simon, James F. *In His Own Image: The Supreme Court in Richard Nixon's America.* New York: David McKay, 1973.

Sims, Harriet J. "Recent Developments." *Georgetown Law Journal* 65 (1977).

Sims, John W. "The American Law of Maritime Personal Injury and Death: An Historical Review." *Tulane Law Review* 55 (1981).

Sitkoff, Harvard. *The Struggle for Black Equality, 1954–1980*. New York: Hill and Wang, 1981.

Skolnick, Jerome H. *Above the Law: Police and the Excessive Use of Force*. New York: Free Press, 1993.

Smith, Christopher E. "From U.S. Magistrates to U.S. Magistrate Judges: Developments Affecting the Federal District Courts' Lower Tier of Judicial Officers." *Judicature* 75 (December–January 1992).

———. *United States Magistrates in the Federal Courts*. Westport, Conn.: Praeger, 1990.

———. "Who Are the United States Magistrates?" *Judicature* 71 (1987).

Smith, Walter Elwood, Jr. "Mexicano Resistance to Schooled Ethnicity: Ethnic Student Power in South Texas, 1930–1970." Ph.D. diss., University of Texas at Austin, 1978.

Soifer, Aviam, and H. C. Macgill. "The *Younger* Doctrine: Reconstructing Reconstruction." *Texas Law Review* 55 (1977).

Spivack, John M. *Race, Civil Rights, and the United States Court of Appeals for the Fifth Judicial Circuit*. New York: Garland, 1990.

Stith, Kate, and José A. Cabranes. *Fear of Judging: Sentencing Guidelines in the Federal Courts*. Chicago: University of Chicago Press, 1998.

Strazzella, James A., ed. *The Federal Role in Criminal Law*. Thousand Oaks, Calif.: Sage Publications, 1996.

Struve, Walter. *Germans and Texans: Commerce, Migration, and Culture in the Days of the Lone Star Republic*. Austin: University of Texas Press, 1996.

Suiter, James R. "Comment: Self-Incrimination and Registration Statutes: A Case against Constitutionality." *Houston Law Review* 4 (1966).

Sullivan, Lawrence Anthony. *Handbook of the Law of Antitrust*. Saint Paul, Minn.: West, 1977.

Tachau, Mary K. Bonsteel. *Federal Courts in the Early Republic: Kentucky, 1789–1816*. Princeton: Princeton University Press, 1978.

Terkel, Studs. *My American Century*. New York: New Press, 1997.

Thackston, Frank S., Jr. "Seamen's Remedies—An Analysis." *Mississippi Law Journal* 52 (1982).

Thomas, Robert D., and Richard W. Murray. *Progrowth Politics: Change and Governance in Houston*. Berkeley, Calif.: Institute of Governmental Studies Press, 1991.

Thompson, Thomas. *Blood and Money*. New York: Dell, 1976.

Tidwell, Patricia A. "James V. Allred of Texas: A Judicial Biography." M.A. thesis, Rice University, 1991.

Tirado, Miguel David. "Mexican American Community Political Organization: The Key to Chicano Political Power." In *La Causa Politica: A Chicano Politics Reader*, edited by F. Chris Garcia. Notre Dame, Ind.: University of Notre Dame Press, 1974.

Toney, William T. *A Descriptive Study of the Control of Illegal Mexican Migration in the Southwestern U.S.* San Francisco: R&E Research Associates, 1977.

Tonry, Michael. *Sentencing Matters*. New York: Oxford University Press, 1996.

Torgerson, Dial. "'Brown Power' Unity Seen behind School Disorders." In *Mexican Americans in the United States: A Reader*, edited by John H. Burma. Cambridge: Schenkman, 1978.

Tribe, Laurence. "The Puzzling Persistence of Process-Based Constitutional Theories." *Yale Law Journal* 89 (1980).

Trujillo, Armando L. *Chicano Empowerment and Bilingual Education: Movimiento Politics in Crystal City, Texas*. New York: Garland, 1998.

Turner, William Bennett. "When Prisoners Sue: A Study of Prisoner Section 1983 Suits in the Federal Courts." *Harvard Law Review* 92 (1979).

Vallance, Theodore R. *Prohibition's Second Failure: The Quest for a Rational and Humane Drug Policy.* Westport, Conn.: Praeger, 1993.

Vandiver, Frank. *The Southwest: South or West.* College Station: Texas A&M University Press, 1975.

Vines, Kenneth N. "The Role of Courts of Appeals in the Federal Judicial Process." In *Courts, Judges, and Politics: An Introduction to the Judicial Process,* 3d ed., edited by Walter F. Murphy and C. Herman Pritchett. New York: Random House, 1979.

Wald, Patricia M. "Bureaucracy and the Courts." *Yale Law Journal* 92 (1983).

Waldman, Michael. *Who Robbed America? A Citizen's Guide to the Savings and Loan Scandal.* New York: Random House, 1990.

Walker, Samuel. *In Defense of American Liberties: A History of the ACLU.* 2d ed. Carbondale: Southern Illinois University Press, 1999.

Walker, William O. *Drug Control in the Americas.* Albuquerque: University of New Mexico Press, 1981.

Waltman, Jerold. "How Liberal Was the Fifth Circuit Court of Appeals in the 1950s? A Look at Minimum Wage Litigation." *Southern Studies* 6 (1995).

Waples, Gregory L. "Note: From Bags to Body Cavities: The Law of Border Search." *Columbia Law Review* 74 (1974).

Ware, Michael. "Federal Intervention in State Prisons: The Modern Prison Conditions Case." *Houston Law Review* 19 (1982).

Warren, Earl. "Address." 35 F.R.D. 181 (1964), 182.

Wasby, Stephen L. *Continuity and Change: From the Warren Court to the Burger Court.* Pacific Palisades, Calif.: Goodyear, 1976.

———. *Race Relations in an Age of Complexity.* Charlottesville: University Press of Virginia, 1995.

Wasserstein, Bruce. "The Courts and the Campus." In *With Justice for Some: An Indictment of the Law by Young Advocates,* edited by Bruce Wasserstein and Mark J. Green. Boston: Beacon Press, 1970.

Wasserstein, Bruce, and Mark J. Green, eds. *With Justice for Some: An Indictment of the Law by Young Advocates.* Boston: Beacon Press, 1970.

Watson, Harold K. "Modern Practice Considerations in Maritime Personal Injury Litigation: Procedural Weapons for Venue Battles." *Tulane Law Review* 68 (1994).

Weaver, Robert C. "The Suburbanization of America." In *School Desegregation: The Courts and Suburban Migration; A Consultation Held in Washington, D.C., 8 December 1975,* edited by the U.S. Commission on Civil Rights. Washington, D.C.: U.S. Commission on Civil Rights, 1975.

Weaver, Suzanne. *Decision to Prosecute: Organization and Public Policy in the Antitrust Division.* Cambridge: Massachusetts Institute of Technology Press, 1977.

Webb, Walter Prescott. *The Texas Rangers: A Century of Frontier Defense.* 2d ed. With a foreword by Lyndon B. Johnson. Austin: University of Texas Press, 1965.

Weiss, Bernard J., ed. *American Education and the European Immigrant, 1840–1940.* Urbana: University of Illinois Press, 1982.

Weston, Paul B., and Kenneth M. Wells. *The Administration of Justice.* 3d ed. Englewood Cliffs, N.J.: Prentice-Hall, 1977.

Wheeler, Russell R. *Origins of the Elements of Federal Court Governance.* Washington, D.C.: Federal Judicial Center, 1992.

Wheeler, Russell R., and Howard R. Whitcomb, eds. *Judicial Administration: Text and Readings.* Englewood Cliffs, N.J.: Prentice-Hall, 1977.

White, G. Edward. *Tort Law in America: An Intellectual History.* New York: Oxford University Press, 1980.

White, Lawrence. *The S&L Debacle: Public Policy Lessons for Bank and Thrift Regulation.* New York: Oxford University Press, 1991.

———. "Why Is the U.S. Banking Industry in Trouble? Business Cycles, Loan Losses, and Deposit Insurance." In *The Crisis in American Banking,* edited by Lawrence White. New York: New York University Press, 1993.

———, ed. *Private Antitrust Litigation: New Evidence, New Learning.* Cambridge: Massachusetts Institute of Technology Press, 1988.

Whitmer, Peter O., with Bruce van Wyngarden. *Aquarius Revisited: Seven Who Created the Sixties Counterculture That Changed America.* New York: Macmillan, 1987.

Wicharaya, Tamasak. *Simple Theory, Hard Reality: The Impact of Sentencing Reforms on Courts, Prisons, and Crime.* Albany: State University of New York Press, 1995.

Wicker, Elmus. *The Banking Panics of the Great Depression.* New York: Cambridge University Press, 1996.

Wilkinson, J. Harvie, III. *From Brown to Bakke: The Supreme Court and School Integration: 1954–1978.* New York: Oxford University Press, 1979.

Willie, Charles V., ed. *Black/Brown/White Relations: Race Relations in the 1970s.* New Brunswick, N.J.: Transaction Books, 1977.

Willoughby, W. F. *Principles of Judicial Administration.* Cambridge: Harvard University Press, 1994.

Wisotsky, Steven. "Crackdown: The Emerging 'Drug Exception' to the Bill of Rights." *Hastings Law Journal* 38 (1987).

Woellner, Fredric P. "The Teaching of American History as a Factor in Americanization." *School and Society* 13 (May 1921).

Woerheide, Walter J. *The Savings and Loan Industry: Current Problems and Possible Solutions.* Westport, Conn.: Quorum Books, 1984.

Wolohojian, G. R. "Judicial Taxation in Desegregation Cases." *Columbia Law Review* 89 (1989).

Woods, L. A. "Official Communication from the State Superintendent of Public Instruction." In *With Texas Public Schools,* no. 1. Austin: Texas Department of Education, 1948.

Woodward, C. Vann. *The Strange Career of Jim Crow.* 2d rev. ed. New York: Oxford University Press, 1966.

Wright, Charles A. "The Constitution on the Campus." *Vanderbilt Law Review* 22 (1969).

———. *The Law of Federal Courts.* 4th ed. Saint Paul, Minn.: West, 1983.

Yale, Harris J. "Note: Beyond the Border of Reasonableness: Exports, Imports and the Border Search Exception." *Hofstra Law Review* 11 (1983).

Yankwich, Leon R. " 'Short Cuts' in Long Cases." 13 F.R.D. 41 (1953).

Yarborough, Tinsley E. *Judge Frank Johnson and Human Rights in Alabama.* University: University of Alabama Press, 1981.

Yatter, Douglas K., David E. DePianto, Marisa L. Megur, and Karin Scherner-Kim. "Investigation and Police Practices: Warrantless Searches and Seizures." *Georgetown Law Journal* 88 (May 2000).

Zagel, James, and Adam Winkler. "The Independence of Judges." *Mercer Law Review* 46 (1995).

Zagrans, Eric H. "'Under Color of' What Law: A Reconstructed Model of Section 1983 Liability." *Virginia Law Review* 71 (1985).
Zamora, Emilio. *The World of the Mexican Worker in Texas.* College Station: Texas A&M University Press, 1993.
Zeese, Kevin B. "Drug War Forever?" In *Searching for Alternatives: Drug-Control Policy in the United States,* edited by Melvyn Krauss and Edward P. Lazear. Stanford, Calif.: Hoover Institution, 1991.
Zeigler, Donald H. "An Accommodation of the *Younger* Doctrine and the Duty of the Federal Courts to Enforce Constitutional Safeguards in the State Criminal Process." *University of Pennsylvania Law Review* 125 (1976).
———. "A Reassessment of the *Younger* Doctrine in Light of the Legislative History of Reconstruction." *Duke Law Journal,* 1983.
Zelden, Charles L. "From Rights to Resources: The Southern Federal District Courts and the Transformation of Civil Rights in Education, 1968–1974." *Akron Law Review* 32 (1999).
———. *Justice Lies in the District: The U.S. District Court, Southern District of Texas, 1902–1960.* College Station: Texas A&M University Press, 1993.
Zimring, Franklin E., and Gordon Hawkins. "Towards a Principled Basis for Federal Criminal Legislation." In *The Federal Role in Criminal Law,* edited by James A. Strazzella. Thousand Oaks, Calif.: Sage, 1996.

GOVERNMENT DOCUMENTS

Administrative Office of the United States Courts. *Annual Report of the Director.* Washington, D.C.: U.S. Government Printing Office, 1938–.
———. *Federal Court Management Statistics.* Washington, D.C.: U.S. Government Printing Office, 1968–.
Advisory Commission on Intergovernmental Relations. *Jails: Intergovernmental Dimensions of a Local Problem.* Washington, D.C.: U.S. Government Printing Office, 1984.
Congressional Record. Washington, D.C.: U.S. Government Printing Office, 1873–.
Federal Bureau of Narcotics. *Report on the Traffic in Opium and Other Dangerous Drugs.* Washington, D.C.: U.S. Government Printing Office, 1966.
Inter-agency Committee on Mexican American Affairs. *The Mexican American: A New Focus on Opportunity.* Washington, D.C.: U.S. Government Printing Office, 1967.
President's Commission on Law Enforcement and Administration of Justice. *Task Force Report: The Courts.* Washington, D.C.: U.S. Government Printing Office, 1967.
President's Commission on Organized Crime. *America's Habit: Drug Abuse, Drug Trafficking and Organized Crime.* A report to the president and attorney general. Washington, D.C.: U.S. Government Printing Office, 1986.
Public Papers of the Presidents of the United States. Washington, D.C.: U.S. Government Printing Office, 1898–.
Texas Advisory Committee to the U.S. Commission on Civil Rights. *School Desegregation in Corpus Christi, Texas.* Washington, D.C.: U.S. Government Printing Office, 1977.
———. *Sin Papeles: The Undocumented in Texas.* Washington, D.C.: U.S. Government Printing Office, 1980.
U.S. Commission on Civil Rights. *The Federal Civil Rights Enforcement Effort—1974.* Vol. 7, *To Preserve, Protect, and Defend the Constitution.* Washington, D.C.: U.S. Government Printing Office, 1977.

———. *The Federal Role in the Administration of Justice.* Washington, D.C.: U.S. Government Printing Office, 1980.

———. *Fulfilling the Letter and Spirit of the Law: Desegregation of the Nation's Public Schools.* Washington, D.C.: U.S. Government Printing Office, 1976.

———. *Hearing Held in Corpus Christi, Texas, 17 August 1976.* Washington, D.C.: U.S. Government Printing Office, 1976.

———. *Hearing Held in San Antonio, Texas, 9–14 December 1968.* Washington, D.C.: U.S. Government Printing Office, 1968.

———. *Hearings on Police Practices—Houston, Texas—1979.* Washington, D.C.: U.S. Government Printing Office, 1979.

———. *Mexican-American Educational Study.* Report 1, *Ethnic Isolation of Mexican-Americans in the Public Schools of the Southwest.* Washington, D.C.: U.S. Government Printing Office, 1970.

———. *Mexican Americans and the Administration of Justice in the Southwest: Summary.* Washington, D.C.: U.S. Government Printing Office, 1970.

———. *Police Practices and Civil Rights: Hearings.* Washington, D.C.: U.S. Government Printing Office, 1981

———. *School Desegregation: The Courts and Suburban Migration, A Consultation Held in Washington, D.C., 8 December 1975.* Washington, D.C.: U.S. Government Printing Office, 1975.

———. *Who Is Guarding the Guardians? A Report on Police Practices.* Washington, D.C.: U.S. Government Printing Office, 1981.

U.S. Department of Justice. Drug Enforcement Administration. *Fact Sheet.* Washington, D.C.: Drug Enforcement Administration, 1978.

———. Immigration and Naturalization Service. *Annual Report.* Washington, D.C.: U.S. Government Printing Office, 1924–.

———. Office of Legal Policy. "Guidelines on Constitutional Litigation." 19 February 1988.

U.S. House Committee on Government Operations. Subcommittee on Information, Justice, Transportation and Agriculture. "Border Control—Revised Strategy Is Showing Some Positive Results." Report to the chairman of the subcommittee. 103d Cong., 2d sess., December 1994. Washington, D.C.: U.S. Government Printing Office, 1995.

U.S. Senate Committee on Appropriations. Subcommittee on Treasury, Postal Service, and General Government. *Southwest Border High-Intensity Drug Trafficking Designation.* 101st Congress, 2d sess., S. Hrg. 101–1109, 30 July 1990. Washington, D.C.: U.S. Government Printing Office, 1991.

U.S. Senate Committee on the Judiciary. *Hearings before the Subcommittee on Constitutional Rights.* Washington, D.C.: U.S. Government Printing Office, 1971.

———. *Reform of the Federal Criminal Laws.* Part 1, *Report of the National Commission on Reform of Federal Criminal Laws.* Washington, D.C.: U.S. Government Printing Office, 1971.

———. Subcommittee on Immigration. *The Need for Additional Border Patrol at the Northern and Southern Borders of the United States to Further Deter Illegal Immigration and Drug Smuggling.* 106th Cong., 1st sess., S. Hrg. 106–441, 27 April 1999. Washington, D.C.: U.S. Government Printing Office, 2000.

Index